DATE DUE

In the Tracks
of Tamerlane:

Central Asia's Path
to the 21st Century

In the Tracks of Tamerlane:

Central Asia's Path to the 21st Century

edited by Dan Burghart
Theresa Sabonis-Helf

NATIONAL DEFENSE UNIVERSITY

CENTER FOR TECHNOLOGY AND NATIONAL SECURITY POLICY

WASHINGTON, D.C.

2004

NDU
CTNSP

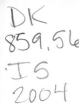
The opinions, conclusions, and recommendations expressed or implied within are those of the individual authors and do not represent the views of the other contributors, the Department of Defense or any other agency or department of the Federal Government. This publication is cleared for public release; distribution unlimited.

Portions of this work may be quoted or reprinted without further permission, with credit to the Center for Technology and National Security Policy. A courtesy copy of any reviews and tearsheets would be appreciated.

Library of Congress Cataloging-in Publication Data
      / edited by Dan Burghart and Theresa Sabonis-Helf.

   Includes bibliographical references.

      ISBN 1-57906-068-4
      1. Asia, Central — Social Conditions — 1991 –   2. Asia, Central — Politics and government — 1991 –   3. Asia, Central — Economic conditions.
      Daniel L. Burghart.   II. Title.

First Printing, July 2004

NDU CTNSP publications are sold by the U.S. Government Printing Office. For ordering information, call (202) 512-1800 or write to the Superintendant of Documents, U.S. Government Printing Office, Washington, D.C. 20402. For GPO publications on-line access their Web site at: http://www.access.gpo.gov/su_docs/sale.html.

For current publications of the Center for Technology and National Security Policy, consult Natioonal Defense University Web site at: http://www.ndu.edu/ctnsp/publications.html.

Contents

Part III—Security Issues

Preface

Daniel L. Burghart and Theresa Sabonis-Helf

When examining the ebb and flow of events in the region called Central Asia, one is struck by the magnitude of the impact that this area has had throughout history. Yet in spite of this record, very little is known about this part of the world today. Central Asia always has found itself wedged between Europe and Asia, and as such, has been at the crossroads of relations between the two. In physical terms, this can be seen graphically in the trade routes of the Great Silk Road. In philosophical terms, it is an area where Western beliefs met and mingled with Eastern ways, often resulting in unusual and unique hybrids of thought and culture. Nor has the area's significance been limited to that of providing a meeting place for other cultures. For over 100 years, between the thirteenth and fifteenth centuries, the armies of Genghis Khan and later Tamerlane spread from Central Asia to conquer and exert their influence over an area larger than the conquests of Alexander, Rome or Hitler. The repercussions of these conquests can still be seen today and serve as a reminder of the impact the region has had, and may again have, on world events.

Great though this influence may have been, history dictated that after Central Asia's zenith, there followed a period of decline. During this time, the region seemed to slip from the world stage, surpassed in importance by other areas, such as the newly discovered Americas. Though the reasons for this decline are many and varied, the end result was that the region seemed to fall from the attention of most scholars, political leaders and the public in general. That the region still held importance for its residents goes without saying; that it continues to be important to the major regional actors bordering the area will be shown. Still, little was known or written about Central Asia after the time of Tamerlane, other than that it was a far off and mysterious part of the world that few people traveled to or cared about. This remained the case throughout most of the twentieth century, until events following the breakup of the Soviet Union brought the region into new prominence and focus.

Many events can be pointed to as affecting the status of the region; however, three stand out beyond all others as having an impact both on the peoples of Central Asia and, in turn, their relations with the rest of world. The breakup of the Russian/Soviet Empire, just as with the fall of other great empires, sent shockwaves through the area and beyond. The opportunity for the region to rule itself, as opposed to being ruled by others, has meant significant changes in the politics, economy and social fabric found there. Yet as important as these changes have been, they would have little meaning or impact on the rest of the world were it not for the second major event associated with Central Asia: the discovery of potentially extensive reserves of gas and oil. Although the size of these stores is debated and in truth has yet to be determined, they are significant enough to warrant global attention and interest as an alternative fuel source in a world concerned with the dwindling stocks of hydrocarbons. These reserves hold the promise of economic development and prosperity, but as has been seen elsewhere in the world, this promise can be a two-edged sword with as many downsides as benefits. Finally, in the aftermath of September 11, the potential of terrorism both originating from and affecting the region need hardly be elaborated. For all these and other reasons, the world is showing renewed interest in Central Asia.

The genesis of this book is a response to that interest. While many works dealing with Central Asia appeared between 1991 and 1995, taking advantage of the fact that for the first time outside observers had relatively easy access to the region, far fewer texts have appeared since then. As often happens, general interest migrated to other parts of the world, leaving the area to be covered by a small community of specialists. Yet events continued to occur and changes continued to take place, so that ten years after independence, it seemed essential to "take stock" of what has transpired during this period, as well as to look at future prospects. To accomplish this, we have assembled a collection of scholars and regional specialists who are closely associated with Central Asia and whose works cover a broad range of problems facing the region. Rather than focus on a country-by-country analysis, each author was asked to write about a specific topic and how it played out in at least two of the countries of the region. They were further asked to project the potential significance of their observations for the region over the next 15 years and how the "lessons learned" to date might be applied in the future.

For the purposes of this book, the changes that have taken place in Central Asia have been grouped into three general categories, political, economic and security. The specific subjects included in each category reflect major problems or areas of concern. Although the list of these topics is in no way all-inclusive, it does reflect a general consensus of the specialists gathered here as to the key issues that must be addressed when discussing the region overall. Each of these topics has an impact that goes beyond individual country borders, and while some may affect certain countries more than others, all have consequences for the region as a whole. Because of this, the traditional approach which would look at each country individually has been eschewed in favor of an approach that focuses on problems that are regional in nature, and thus must be addressed in a regional context. In some cases, the authors compare how different countries have addressed the same problem; in others, the issues are transboundary in nature and the authors examine regional solutions. Although it is hoped that this work will appeal to a wide audience, three groups in particular may benefit from its approach: policy makers who need a general background on the issues associated with the region; regional specialists who are seeking information on specific issues that challenge the region; and technical specialists who wish to see how their areas of interest affect the region as a whole. Finally, the views of the authors reflected here represent a wide range of opinions that are often at odds with one another. No attempt has been made to resolve these differences, and they are presented to the reader for her or him to evaluate and make their own determination as to the weight they want to assign each. Out of a diversity of ideas and differences of opinion, better solutions to the problems the area faces hopefully can be found and better policies formulated to implement these solutions.

Contents

After an overview of the region by Daniel L. Burghart, Part I — Political Changes begins with a chapter on the international politics affecting the region. Written by Wayne Merry, a retired Foreign Service Officer with extensive experience in the former Soviet Union, the chapter provides a context for understanding the various external influences that can be seen in the region, as well as the reactions of the local political "apparat" to these influences. In the next chapter, Gregory Gleason looks in greater detail at the current domestic political situation in the region, and the prospects for meaningful political reform. In the chapter on legal reform, Roger D. Kangas summarizes the steps that already have been taken in this area, a necessary precondition for meaningful reform in the areas of politics and the economy. This is followed by a discussion of human rights by Michael Ochs, a Congressional staff member who has followed these issues for more than a decade. Human rights in Central Asia are arguably worse than anywhere else in the former Soviet Union, and must be improved if any of these states hope to be accepted into the community of nations. Sylvia W. Babus' chapter furthers the political track by discussing outside efforts at democracy building. With first hand experience in many of these programs, she provides a unique insight into "what works and what doesn't" on the ground. Finally, Tiffany Petros takes on the difficult task of assessing the role of Islam in defining the region and its future.

Part II — Economic Concerns begins with Theresa Sabonis-Helf's examination of the impact of hydrocarbon development on the economics and politics of the energy-rich countries of the region. Next, Daene C. McKinney, a noted hydrographic engineer, addresses the complex topic of water in Central Asia, detailing its economic, political, and security implications, as well as ongoing efforts to resolve disputes over the equitable distribution of water in a peaceful manner. Genevieve Grabman examines issues of public health, and using the example of Kyrgyzstan, postulates the role that reform of health care systems can play in improving the well-being of the region's most vital economic resource—its people. Kevin D. Jones does the same with regard to land privatization, probably one of the most difficult issues that all of the former Soviet Republics have had to face, given their socialist background and the state ownership of land associated with it. Economic development within the context of sustainable development is addressed by Alma Raissova and Aliya Sartbayeva-Peleo, two Central Asian scholars with extensive experience in this field. Although economic development has been a major goal of all of these states, these authors stress the need for such development to be moderated so as to achieve "sustainable development" goals. Closely related to these arguments, David S. McCauley enumerates the environmental challenges facing the region and also examines the efforts of international donors and the Central Asian states to meet these challenges. Finally, Kalkaman Suleimenov describes the steps being taken to rationalize the distribution of electricity in Kazakhstan and the surrounding area. As a regional government official, his piece is enlightening both in terms of the information it provides and as an example of how local officials are attempting to come to grips with the problems they have inherited from the old Soviet system.

In Part III — Security Issues, Emily E. Daughtry begins with a review of the Cooperative Threat Reduction (CTR) Program and its impact on Central Asia. CTR is often cited as the most effective program the U.S. Government has had with members of the former Soviet Union. She documents the program's efforts in the region and shows how its successes to date can be built in the future. Next, Jennifer D.P. Moroney examines existing security frameworks in Central Asia and the likelihood that these frameworks, and the organizations which comprise them, can provide the stability the region needs as a precondition for future development. Nancy Lubin examines what is characterized as the greatest threat to Central Asian security—drug trafficking and its impact on both the political and social spheres of society. Closely tied to this is the illicit trade in human beings. Here Saltanat Sulaimanova brings a regional perspective to this problem, as well as to the larger issue of migration to and from the area. Finally, three chapters are dedicated to Central Asian relations with the three major world powers that have active interests in the region—China, Russia and the United States. Matthew Oresman provides a detailed account of China's interests in Central Asia, as well as the response of the Central Asian states to Chinese initiatives. Captain Robert Brannon summarizes Russia's interests and concerns and also outlines U.S.-Russian relations with regard to area. Finally, Olga Oliker looks at U.S. concerns in Central Asia and postulates how these concerns might be addressed in the future.

With the new millennium a new cycle of history is beginning, one in which it seems clear that Central Asia will play an increasingly significant role on the world stage. Though its importance may have ebbed and flowed with time and the circumstances in which the region has found itself, Central Asia continues to exist at the crossroads of East and West. Wheras the technologies used to traverse these crossroads and the nature of the journey may have changed, the geography and the people who occupy it remain the same. Those from the region who follow in the tracks of Tamerlane, will face many of the same challenges their ancestors did. However, they have at their disposal a broad new range of resources to help them address these challenges, including many provided by foreign sources. Their success in using these resources effectively will, in turn, determine the course they take, as they advance into the twenty-first century.

Acknowledgments

The primary sponsor for this work has been the Pre-Conflict Management Project for Central Asia at the National Defense University (NDU). The goal of this project, done under the auspices of the Center for Technology and National Security Policy (CTNSP), is to lessen the likelihood of a crisis arising by addressing problem areas before they become crises and by being proactive with regard to their resolution. This book seeks to support achievement of this goal by bringing the problems endemic to the region to light. Also, as part of the preconditions for addressing these problems, the Project is developing a Central Asian Data Exchange, envisioned to be the largest single source of information on the region. It is hoped that with both knowledge of the problems that the region faces and sufficient information about these problems, solutions can be formulated and policies implemented that ultimately will assist in bringing about the peace and stability that the region so desperately needs.

In addition to the generous support of the Pre-Conflict Management Project and its Director, Joe Eash, several individuals and organizations have played key roles in bringing this project to completion. Thanks are particularly owed to the NDU Foundation and Frank Eversole, whose support early in the process allowed this work to be initiated. Hans Binnendijk and Michael Baranick of the CTNSP provided not only fiscal support, but also administrative assistance and most importantly, encouragement throughout the project. Kathleen Toomey Jabs and Leah Johnson performed above and beyond the call of duty in doing the technical edits for the work. Their efforts greatly improved the quality of the text and helped bring it to its final published form. Thanks are also due to the NDU Graphics Division, especially Rick Vaughn for his layout work and cover design and Holly Gannoe who brought the work to completion under the supervision of Alex Contreras, Chief of Graphics.

Gavin Helf provided equally valuable assistance by translating the chapters originally written in Russian into clear expository English. The staff of the NDU Library provided research assistance throughout the preparation of the text, and the NDU community overall, provided the supportive academic environment that helped to bring this work to its conclusion.

Finally, many thanks must be given to our contributors, whose work on this volume has gone beyond what might be expected for an academic work and passed into the realm of a labor of love. Not only have they been willing to share their hard earned expertise, but they have freely given that most precious commodity for any scholar, their time. Without their efforts there would be no book. By their efforts, they have helped to mark and define the path for those who follow in the tracks of Tamerlane, so all such travelers may find their way to a better future.

Dr. Daniel L. Burghart   Dr. Theresa Sabonis-Helf

In the Tracks of Tamerlane:

Central Asia's Path to the 21st Century

In the Tracks of Tamerlane: Central Asia's Path to the 21st Century[1]

Daniel L. Burghart

W hile there is hardly a corner of the world that has not been affected in one way or another by the events of September 11, the repercussions are especially evident in the region known as Soviet Central Asia.[2] The countries and people in this region were already in the process of adjusting to the major changes in their status brought about by the breakup of the Soviet Union a scant ten years before, when they were plunged into the international spotlight. Even though proximity to Afghanistan and the hiding place of Osama Bin Laden was the catalyst for this most recent round of attention, the fact that the region sits astride some of the largest known gas and oil reserves in the world already had brought the area a fair amount of notoriety.

Though interest in Central Asia appears to be a fairly recent phenomenon, this should hardly be the case. Throughout history, the area, bracketed roughly by the Caspian Sea and China, has served as the crossroads of Asia and Europe and been home to succeeding waves of migrating populations as well as the great Silk Road. Empires have risen and fallen, only to rise again in different forms; groups have been dominant and then been assimilated by succeeding dominant groups. Although history is filled with the names of these groups and their leaders, ranging from the armies of Alexander the Great to the Arabs and the Turks, the ones best known in the West are the Mongols and Tartars who, under Tamerlane, spread their influence to the gates of Europe in the late fourteenth century.[3] After the death of Tamerlane, the region fell under succeeding outside influences, most notably Russian and British, in what Kipling referred to as "The Great Game." Yet even as the object of the game rather than a player, Central Asia retained an importance to those around it.

Today finds the countries of Central Asia in a period of rebirth, not only in terms of outside interest, but also in their own self-awareness of their potential importance on the global scene. Almost no one would be willing to predict that any single country from the region, or even the region as a whole, is going to rise up and attempt the type of political dominance exerted by Tamerlane 600 years earlier. On the other hand, through their control of hydrocarbon resources, the countries of Central Asia stand poised to exert an influence far beyond what anyone might have expected as little as a dozen years ago. Following in the tracks of Tamerlane, the countries of the region are seeking to carve a path that will define the nature of their existence well into the twenty-first century and beyond, a path whose repercussions will be felt throughout the world. With this in mind, it seems appropriate to examine where the tracks of Tamerlane's successors may lead.

Picking up the Trail

Before one can successfully follow any trail, it is necessary to be familiar with the land on which it is located. Central Asia roughly can be considered bounded in the west by the Caspian Sea, which separates the region from the Caucasus. From west to east, the region stretches over 1500 miles, encountering few natural obstacles until the mountains of western China. These mountains, the Tien Shan, literally "the Roof of the World," run southwest into the Himalayas making up a large portion of present-day Kyrgyzstan and Tajikistan, before turning south into Afghanistan. The remainder of the southern border becomes desert in what is present day Turkmenistan. The bulk of the territory is arid grassland or steppe, which stretches from the desert and mountains in the south to the Siberian forest or "Taiga" of Russia that forms its northern boundary. Overall, the area comprises more than a million and a half square miles.[4]

The land contained in this region, for the most part, is a vast plain. The soil, while fertile, suffers from a continental climate that does not guarantee sufficient moisture for most crops; as a result, the people in this area traditionally have been nomads. Substantial runoff from the mountains is carried to the region by several rivers, primarily the Amu Dar'ya and Syr Dar'ya, which fill the Aral Sea in the east-central part of the plain. Those areas without sufficient water have reverted to desert, as found in Turkmenistan. The climate, without the benefit of the moderating influence of an ocean, tends to be harsh, with temperatures ranging from 120 degrees Fahrenheit in the summer to minus 40 and below in the winter. Although less than ideal for agriculture, the land possesses tremendous mineral wealth in addition to the already mentioned supplies of gas and oil. Almost every strategic metal can be found in Central Asia, especially in the mountains of the south, and new deposits continue to be discovered.

As might be expected, the geography of the region has influenced its history and development. With few natural borders to define or protect it, the region has been subject to the influences of wave after wave of tribes and peoples who have crisscrossed the landscape. Those who stayed to occupy the land for any time tended to be nomadic, grazing their herds on the abundant grasslands and then moving with the seasons, the weather, or at the prodding of their neighbors. While the original inhabitants have been all but lost in history, it can be determined that waves of Mongols from the east, Persians from the south, and Turkic peoples from the south and west all dominated portions of the region at one time or another, intermarrying with the local populations and making their contribution to the existing cultures. Arab invaders in the tenth and eleventh century brought with them the Islamic faith, which continues to be the dominant religious influence, though its practice tends to be far from the stringent form found in other parts of the world.

If there was one unifying influence at any time in the region's history, it would be the period of conquest and domination by Tamerlane, or Timur as he is known locally. Born outside of Samarkand in the fourteenth century, Tamerlane claimed to be descended from the great Mongol leader Genghis Kahn, though other evidence exists that he was, in fact, of Tartar origin.[5] After securing a local base of operations, he began a quarter of a century of conquest that has few rivals in history. He conquered Persia and the lands now comprising Iraq, Azerbaijan and Armenia. He then invaded Russia and moved west of the Ural River before being called back to put down a revolt in Persia. After conquering Mesopotamia and Georgia, he turned his attention to India, storming Delhi and advancing into the Himalayan foothills before withdrawing. He then turned west again, capturing Syria, defeating elements of the Ottoman Empire, and receiving tribute from both Byzantium and Egypt. Only his death en route to invading China in 1405 stopped the expansion of his empire to an area greater than that achieved under Genghis Khan.[6]

While successful on the battlefield, Tamerlane failed in creating a governing structure that could perpetuate his empire, and it soon broke up into a collection of tribes, *khanates*, and independent city-states after his death. This patchwork of entities exerted control over various portions of the territory, without any one being able to control the whole. However, starting with the rule of Peter the Great in Russia in the late seventeenth century, external influences began to make their presence felt. The Russians spread their influence from the northwest at the same time the British influence began spreading from India in the southeast. Central Asia was caught between these two great empires. Given the competition between Russia and Great Britain, Central Asia became the buffer, with each nation vying for the type of influence that would give it an advantage over the other. The consequences of this arrangement for the local population are brilliantly described in the works of Peter Hopkirk.[7] The collapse of Tsarist Russia did little to change this situation in the twentieth century, as the Bolsheviks were quick to establish themselves in the region, and continued to perform the same basic functions as the previous regime.

Although Russification meant that the local populations were, at best, second-class citizens with local rulers co-opted by, or at worst token figureheads for, Russian domination, there were benefits. Literacy was brought to the region, so that by the end of the Soviet rule better than 90 percent of the local populations could read and write. Health standards were improved, and while agriculture continued to be the primary source of revenue, fledgling industries were introduced. Though the area's mineral wealth was exploited, the necessity of introducing the infrastructure needed for this exploitation provided the region with essential communications and transportation facilities. In addition, security in the region was insured on two levels. Externally, the region's borders were secured by the Soviet military; internally, the organs of the Soviet State provided stability. While possibly not an ideal existence, it was one that the local populations, for the most part, seemed willing to embrace.

Independence – Old Wine in New Bottles?

It has often been commented, and not without justification, that the states of Central Asia did not seek independence in 1991, but instead had it thrust upon them.[8] Leaders such as Kazakhstan's Nursultan Nazarbaev argued strongly for the continuation of some sort of union, which among other things would ensure the continuation of the power and perks enjoyed by the ruling elite. This elite was a mixture of local ethnic and Russian nationals, who were all products of the Soviet system and were less than enthused to see it go. Still, these leaders had gotten to the positions that they occupied by being astute politicians in the sense of reading the prevailing trends and being ready to jump on the train (or caravan) wherever it might lead. While it is sometimes commented that local national leaders were merely figureheads who did their Russian masters' bidding, this is an oversimplification of an extremely complex working relationship.

Moscow, for the most part, had recognized the need for ethnic leaders as a way of ennsuring the complacency, if not the loyalty, of the local populations. Those times when this lesson was forgotten, as when Gorbachev tried to appoint an ethnic Russian as head of the Kazakh republic in 1996, resulted in massive unrest.[9] In truth, these local leaders were likely to be zealots in their allegiance to Moscow, since they owed their positions to "the center" and not to any local movements or activity. Having said that, local leaders already had developed their own local support structures, based among other things on family, tribal or clan affiliation. In this sense, the Soviet system actually had adapted and grafted itself onto the existing ruling patterns already in place in Central Asia.

With independence and without the need for vetting from Moscow, the local structures came into greater prominence, though it can be argued that this was more a matter of visibility than any great shift in the existing order. Russians who had been part of this structure either departed to return to Russia or were moved to less visible positions, allowing local ethnic populations to occupy a greater share of the leading roles. This did not occur overnight, as there were often not enough qualified locals to fill all these positions; however, there were sufficient numbers so that the predictions of social collapse due to removal of ethnic Russians from the existing order never materialized.[10]

The situations facing the newly independent states of Kazakhstan, Kyrgyzstan, Uzbekistan, Tajikistan, and Turkmenistan were strikingly similar in both number and nature. All of the countries shared a common geo-strategic location in the world, manifested among other things, by lack of access to the sea and general remoteness from established world trade routes. All of the republics were controlled by a small elite that had been molded by years in the communist party and a socialist (or what passed as socialist) system. As a legacy of that system, all of the republics had high rates of literacy and a body of trained workers, especially in comparison with other developing areas of the world, though the quality of that education and the skills possessed by those workers may have left something to be desired. Each country also inherited a crumbling infrastructure, in terms of industry, transportation and services, yet what was there did provide the rudiments required for a civilized society to function. A dependency on raw materials, both natural resources and agricultural products, was the basis for the economies in all of the new states and provided the majority of their income. One major aspect of these economies, closely related to the dependence on natural resources, was a legacy of environmental problems stemming from the exploitation of these resources under the Soviet regime.

Despite the similar situations faced at the outset, Kazakhstan, Kyrgyzstan, Uzbekistan, Tajikistan, and Turkmenistan each have struck out on their own path since independence, leading each to come up with different approaches to deal with the problems they collectively faced. That such differences exist should hardly be surprising, since in spite of their similarities, each country has elements that make it different from the others, ranging from geographic and cultural peculiarities to those relating to the personalities of their leaders and composition of their elites. Parts of these differences are tied to their relations with each other, for each is unique in terms of the neighbors with whom they must deal. In Soviet times these differences were present, but had less significance under the overarching template put in place by Moscow. Now, with decision-making effectively decentralized to the respective regional capitals, the perspective has changed from the one that Moscow provided. Thus, to gain an appreciation for these differences in perspective, it is necessary to look at each of these countries in turn before returning to examine the region as a whole.

Kazakhstan

As the largest of the five former republics in terms of landmass, Kazakhstan's location as the northernmost country in Central Asia gives it the distinction of being the only former republic in the region with a shared land border with Russia. In truth, it can be argued that Kazakhstan, on at least its northern portion, should not be equated to the rest of the area. Commentators during Soviet times would use the phrase Central Asia and Kazakhstan, indicating that the two were somehow different. During the 1930s, when the borders of the republics were drawn, it has been said that Stalin specifically included a large portion of what had traditionally been considered Russian lands, so as to ensure the loyalty of the region. Whether true or not, the result was that at the time of independence only 40 percent of the population were ethnic Kazakhs, with another 40 percent Russian, and the remainder comprised mostly of other Slavic ethnic groups. This led to an early concern that the northern, ethnically Russian portion of the country would move to break away from the new state and attempt to reintegrate with Russia. While there have been scattered incidents caused by Russian nationalist groups, the majority of the Russian population seems resigned, if not content, with their current situation. This can be attributed to the fact that stories coming back from Russia indicated that conditions there were worse then those in Kazakhstan.[11] In addition to other mineral resources, Kazakhstan possesses the largest oil reserves in Central Asia, with some estimates indicating that these reserves may make the country the new Saudi Arabia.[12] Thus, the country's future is inexplicably tied to the development of these reserves.

Externally, Kazakhstan's security concerns were perhaps best described by the country's Defense Minister, who on several occasions has commented that with Russia to the north, China to the east, Islamic fundamentalism to the south and disputes over the Caspian to their west, Kazakhstan finds itself in a tough neighborhood.[13] Still, with an external border of approximately 6,000 miles, only the portion with China is guarded, representing the concerns of the Kazakhs themselves.[14] In the south, Kazakhstan shares borders (and border disputes) with three of the other Central Asian States, Kyrgyzstan, Uzbekistan and Turkmenistan. Of these, relations with the Kyrgyz are the most cordial, most strained with the Uzbeks, and fall somewhere in-between these two with the Turkmen. Kazakhs and Kyrgyz are extremely close ethnically, and the marriage of the daughter of Kazakh President Nazarbaev to a son of Kyrgyz President Askar Akaev led to speculation that the two would eventfully merge into one.[15] This situation is reversed with Uzbekistan, which is viewed as a rival in terms of being the dominant power in the region. The border with Turkmenistan is composed largely of desert and is of little concern.[16] What is of concern is the eventual division of sovereignty over portions of the Caspian Sea and the tremendous energy deposits there. Indeed, the division of the Caspian Sea and the oil wealth associated with it may be one of the thorniest security issues the country faces in the future.

Though less openly discussed by the Kazakhs themselves, there exist several equally telling concerns that may affect the long-term security of the country. In addition to the normal problems associated with a weak economy, the inability to generate sufficient jobs, especially outside of the large cities such as Almaty, has led to staggering levels of unemployment. In cities such as Termez, the only real option for young people to obtain money is to enter into the illicit drug trade, a growing concern throughout the region. Not only does this represent yet another level of illegal activity in a society known for corruption, but drug use among young people has skyrocketed as availability has increased.[17] Also related to the weak economy is the inability of the government to address effectively the myriad of environmental problems left from Soviet times. The diversion of waters from the Aral Sea for irrigation use and contamination left at sites associated with the Soviet nuclear program are but two examples of large-scale problems that impact both the economy and health of the population, and add further burdens to a system unable to cope with either the scope or the costs of correcting such problems. Finally, the ruling establishment, beginning with President Nazerbaev, actively has taken measures to stifle dissent and ensure the continuity of their rule. While effective in the short term, by allowing no outlet for the frustrations arising from internal problems such as those described, this may create a situation in the long term where dissent turns violent and the fragile social structure of the country is torn apart.

Kyrgyzstan

In contrast to Kazakhstan, Kyrgyzstan is the second smallest country in Central Asia in land size and population, and some would argue the least significant. Roughly 80 percent of its territory is taken up by the Tien Shan Mountains, limiting the amount of land available for agriculture. It also lacks the energy reserves of its sister states, and while the country does possess some mineral wealth, it is extremely difficult to extract at a profit. The one resource that it does possess, water flowing from runoff in the mountains, is a two-edged sword. Although the potential exits to harness this water for the production of badly needed energy, any interruption of the flow also has the potential of bringing the country into conflict with its downstream neighbors, especially Uzbekistan, which depends on this water for irrigation. In addition to Uzbekistan in the west, Kyrgyzstan shares borders with Kazakhstan to the north, China to the east, and Tajikistan to the west and southwest. There are border disputes with all of these countries, the most contentious of which center on the Ferghana region in the southwestern part of the country.

The Ferghana Valley is an extremely fertile area shared with Uzbekistan and Tajikistan. Besides containing some of the richest, and therefore most desirable land in the region, it is home to the most fervent brand of Islam found in Central Asia. While this in itself might not be a concern to the Kyrgyz, the area has served as a base of support for movements such as the Islamic Movement of Uzbekistan (IMU) and has been tied with outside radical groups, such as the Taliban. In 1999, IMU forces moved through Kyrgyz territory and engaged Kyrgyz security forces during an attempt to escape attack from Uzbekistan. This, in turn, sounded alarm bells in Bishkek, and President Akaev was quick to join in the chorus of other Central Asian leaders decrying the threat fundamentalists posed to stability in the region, not to mention their own positions of power.

Domestically, Kyrgyzstan suffers the same problems as the other Central Asian countries, though the way these problems combine is unique to the Kyrgyz situation. Ethnic Kyrgyz constitute a little more than 50 percent of the population, with Russians the next largest group at 22 percent. Uzbeks constitute 12 percent of the population, making them the largest Central Asian ethnic minority outside of their home territory and a concern for the Kyrgyz government, which has several disputed border areas with their far larger and more powerful Uzbek neighbor. Although the country suffered a severe economic downturn tied with the collapse of the ruble in 1998, the fact that a large number of people still owe their existence to subsistence agriculture meant they did not starve. In terms of domestic politics, President Akaev is the only Central Asian ruler who was not a party apparatchik at the time of independence. A university professor and physicist, not only was he popularly elected, but his early rule was marked by hopeful signs of genuine political and economic reform. Unfortunately, time and pressure from his neighbors have made him more politically repressive. This, in turn, has begun to radicalize the opposition, a trend the does not bode well for future stability, something that the country desperately needs.

Uzbekistan

Though Kazakhstan is the largest of the Central Asian states in terms of landmass, the largest in population and arguably the most dynamic is Uzbekistan. Geo-strategically located in the center of the region, it is the only country that shares a border with each of the other states. This allows it to claim concerns with regard to the affairs of all the others since they have the potential of affecting its own interests. Sitting astride internal lines of communication and commerce also places Uzbekistan in a position to exert influence to see that its concerns are addressed. At the same time, with the exception of a small border area with Afghanistan, Uzbekistan does not share a border with any of the external regional actors, specifically Russia, China or Iran, and thus is insulated from the sort of pressures that can be mounted on its neighbors. While not possessing the quantities of oil and gas that Kazakhstan and Turkmenistan do respectively, Uzbekistan does have sufficient energy reserves to be independent of outside sources, unlike Kyrgyzstan. If there is an external dependency, it is on water from Kyrgyzstan, which is used for the irrigation of cotton, the country's primary cash crop.

This favorable turn of geography has allowed Uzbekistan a fair amount of leeway in its relations with its neighbors, as well as with other states in the region. Uzbekistan has been the most fervent of the five in asserting its existence as an entity separate from Russia. With no shared border and only eight percent of its population ethnic Russians, the political leadership has felt free to institute a number of measures to separate itself from its former "big brother," ranging from refusing to participate in Commonwealth of Independent States (CIS) functions to eliminating the use of the Cyrillic alphabet.[18] Likewise, Uzbekistan is far enough away from China to not feel particularly threatened. Within the region, Uzbeks believe themselves to be superior and often adopt an arrogant attitude in their relations with other states and people.[19] This is particularly irksome to the Kazakhs, who openly resent their treatment as "country cousins." Not surprisingly, Uzbekistan has border disputes with all of its neighbors. Although to date the Uzbeks have not resorted to the use of force to resolve these disputes, their size and economic potential, combined with their attitude, has led the other states to believe that the Uzbeks might resort to force if they felt it in their best interests. The Uzbeks themselves believe that they should be the dominant power in the region and give the impression that they are willing to take issue with anyone who does not share this belief.

While Uzbekistan seems to have been dealt a favorable hand in terms of its external security, this has not been the case with regard to its internal affairs. President Islam Karimov has established a regime that is one of the most repressive in the region. In an effort to insure no opposition to his rule, Karimov not only has silenced what little legitimate opposition there was to his regime, but gone on to suppress potential opposition in the form of new Islamic groups. Though nominally claiming to be a Muslim, Karimov views the more conservative variants of the faith who refuse to bend to his every whim and decree as representing a threat to his rule. His response has been to ruthlessly crack down on what he calls the threat of "fundamentalism" and arrest more than 7,000 dissenters. This, in turn, has only served to act as a catalyst for an actual Islamic opposition to form, the IMU. This movement has been blamed for the 1999 bombing of government offices in the capital of Tashkent and is responsible for an armed insurgency in the southern part of the state centered in the Ferghana region. Although Karimov has been quick to try to tie this movement with al Qaeda and the Taliban, it appears to be a domestic opposition movement that only has grown with efforts to repress it. Parallels have been drawn between this process and what took place in Iran under the Shah, where increasingly harsh efforts to suppress conservative Islamic leaders led to public discontent and the eventual overthrow of royal rule. Whether the same outcome will come to pass in Uzbekistan is yet to be determined; however, in spite of warnings of the possible consequences, Karimov has shown little or no inclination to change his policies.

Tajikistan

Of all the countries in the former Soviet portion of Central Asia, Tajikistan comes the closest to claiming the title for being the first "failed state." Though sharing borders with two other Central Asian states, Kyrgyzstan and Uzbekistan, as well as with China and Afghanistan, the country's primary security concerns have been domestic rather than external. Part of this can be explained in the territory it occupies; the terrain is extremely mountainous with more than 50 percent of the country above 10,000 feet altitude.[20] While occupying a crossroads of sorts, the country is also extremely inaccessible to the outside world and difficult to travel even internally. The arable land is composed mostly of valleys running between the various mountains, which, with runoff from mountain snows, possess sufficient water for agriculture. The Tajik people themselves are descended from Iranian speaking people, making them the only republic in Central Asia not sharing a Turkic heritage. The Tajiks comprise 62 percent of the population of roughly 6.2 million, with Uzbeks in the northern part of the country making up the next largest group, 23 percent, and Russians filling in approximately seven percent.

Historically, based on their Persian background, the Tajiks occupied a type of elite status within the region. Yet always subject to the influence of regional actors, the area of Tajikistan was at one time controlled by the Emirate of Bukhara in Uzbekistan, the Afghanistan government, and eventually the Russian Empire, though control is used in the loosest sense, since both the terrain and the independent nature of Tajik mountain tribes were less than hospitable to outsiders. This became particularly apparent when Soviet forces tried to reestablish control of the region after the Bolshevik revolution, leading to the Basmachi revolt that was put down in 1924. With Kyrgyzstan to the north, China to the east, Afghanistan to the south, and Uzbekistan to the west, Tajikistan has long found itself in a far from enviable situation with regard to geo-strategic location. Only the ruggedness of the terrain, as well as its isolation, has served to preserve its sovereignty.

Neither of these, however, have been enough to ensure domestic stability. Falling prey to clan politics and animosities, Tajikistan rapidly degenerated into a protracted civil war between various domestic factions after independence, and the Russian military forces remaining in the country were left to try and preserve some semblance of order. This conflict, while originally not centered on religious differences, became more so as the losing side sought support from Islamic factions outside their borders, in particular from Afghanistan. This turn of events worried both Tajikistan's Central Asian neighbors and Russia, which maintains the 201st Motorized Rifle Division in the country in an attempt to stem the influx of fundamentalist forces from the south. A ceasefire and power sharing agreement reached in 1997 brought an uneasy truce to the fighting, which continues to flare up now and again. As a result, President Imomali Rakhmonov, who first came to power in elections in 1994, continues to preside over an assembly of factions and clans whose sole unifying tenant would seem to be that everyone is exhausted from the continual fighting that has marked the country since the breakup of the Soviet Union.

Turkmenistan

Of all the former Central Asian republics, Turkmenistan is the one that, paraphrasing Lenin, has taken "two steps back" since independence, but has yet to take a step forward, and in fact may be continuing its backward path. A large but sparsely populated nation (4.5 million in an area equal to California plus half of Oregon), most of the country is occupied by the Kara Kum or black sand desert. Turkmen were originally nomads who drove their herds in search of forage; only with the coming of Russian rule and irrigation projects during the Soviet period did agriculture develop in importance, and this mostly tied with the cultivation of cotton. While hardly the type of environment that would at first be cause for optimism, the country sits astride some of the largest natural gas reserves in the world and early prospects for development fueled by the profits from gas sales seemed bright. Instead, Turkmenistan has found itself a prisoner, both of its geography and of a political regime that has been described as mirror imaging all of the worst aspects of Stalin's cult of personality.

Externally, Turkmenistan's problem is with finding a secure route to send its gas to world markets. Bordered in the north by Kazakhstan and Uzbekistan, in the east by Afghanistan, in the south by Iran, and in the west by the Caspian Sea, the primary existing pipelines used for Turkmen gas flow through Russia, which controls both the amount of this flow and its destination.[21] To avoid this Russian chokehold, Turkmenistan has attempted to negotiate routes to the south and west. The former, involving Iran, has been frowned on by the United States, without whose support financing is all but impossible. The other alternative, some sort of trans-Caspian route exemplified by the long heralded Baku-Cheyhan line, has yet to get far beyond the drawing board. The gas that does make it to market via Russia is often routed to countries such as Ukraine, which are renowned for not paying for their energy supplies. Complicating this situation, in the early 1990s Turkmenistan borrowed heavily in international finance markets against profits from future gas production. Now these debts are beginning to fall due, and with still no reliable way to get their gas to market, Turkmenistan is increasingly finding itself in a cash-flow crunch.

Further compounding these problems is the nature of the Turkmen regime itself. Headed by Saparmurat Niyazov, Turkmenistan's Communist Party head at the time of the breakup of the Soviet Union, the government has evolved into an autocracy that bends to the every whim of the ruler. As just one example of the control exerted by Niyazov, a referendum held in 1994 on whether to extend his term in office to 2002 was passed by a margin of 1,959,408 for, to 212 against.[22] Since that time, Niyazov has declared himself President for Life and has taken on the moniker of Turkmenbashi, roughly translated as father of the Turkmen people. Along with autocratic rule at home, he has adopted a policy of positive neutrality in his foreign relations. This policy can best be summarized as the forswearing of all foreign alliances and connections, resulting in an almost isolationist stance that has not helped attempts to gain outside assistance for development in Turkmenistan. Recently, this policy has been modified somewhat. While initially shunning contacts with Russia and other former Soviet republics, the fear of Islamic fundamentalism has brought Turkmenistan into regional security consultations with its neighbors. Likewise, in the aftermath of September 11, some agreements have been reached with the United States to allow the use of Turkmen facilities in the war against terrorism. Still, these negotiations have done little to soften the harsh nature of the Niyazov regime, whose sole concern appears to be its own self-perpetuation.

The Security Situation Post-September 11

Although much has been said and written about the effects of September 11, September 14 may well prove to be a more important date for Central Asia. On that day, the first mention was made in the open press about the stationing of American forces in the region as part of the Global War on Terrorism. Along these lines, three of the five former Soviet Central Asian states, Uzbekistan, Kyrgyzstan and Tajikistan, were approached about using their territory to support U.S. military operations. Uzbekistan, in particular, was of interest because of the shared common border with

Afghanistan and the presence of Termez, the former Soviet military base that had been a primary logistics staging area during the Soviet-Afghan war. While Tajikistan also shared a border with Afghanistan, the condition of facilities there required substantial work before they could be used. Kyrgyzstan, which did not share a border, did have a relatively modern airport and soon became the home to more than 3,000 U.S. Air Force personnel supporting air operations into Afghanistan. Kazakhstan, located further from the fray, also offered support to the Americans, while Turkmenistan, with the longest border with Afghanistan, continued its policy of positive neutrality, though making several pro "anti-terrorist coalition" statements and quietly allowing the transit of humanitarian assistance.

Though the speed with which this coordination was orchestrated was surprising to some observers, the groundwork for this effort actually had been laid throughout the 1990s. Shortly after the breakup of the Soviet Union, the United States established diplomatic relations with all of the former republics in Central Asia and opened embassies in each as soon as it was possible. Included in the embassy staffing were military officers, designated either as Military Representatives or fully accredited Defense Attachés. Their job throughout the 1990s was to establish ties with the host nation militaries, coordinate material assistance and military education programs, escort host countries officers on official visits to the United States, and perform an entire range of activities that fell under the Clinton Administration general policy of engagement. Central among these programs were: foreign military sales and assistance, International Military Education and Training (IMET), Partnership for Peace (PfP), courses offered at the Marshall Center in Germany, and the creation of a Central Asian Peacekeeping Battalion (CENTRAZBAT). While all these programs, as well as others, had specific goals in mind, the cumulative effect was to establish relationships and procedures for working with these counties, as well as to create a cadre of military within each of the countries involved who had experience in working with U.S. forces. Though difficult to quantify, there can be no doubt that these efforts facilitated establishing a U.S. military presence in Central Asia, once it was decided that this was necessary in the battle against terrorism.

Perhaps more surprising than the speed of this deployment, or even that it should have taken place at all, was the response of the Russian government to Americans operating in what had been traditionally a Russian sphere of influence. Though protests rapidly appeared from military leaders and opposition politicians in the Russian press, these were just as quickly countered by none other than Russian President Vladimir Putin, who welcomed the American move as part of his overall support for the war on terrorism. While the changing nature of the U.S.-Russian relationship in the aftermath of September 11 is still being evaluated, it is enough to note that President Putin did much to stifle domestic criticism of U.S. deployments. Russians themselves seemed to be torn between the image of America as a former sworn enemy now conducting military operations on their very doorstep and the realization that American efforts would, in the long run, help Russia and the other countries of Central Asia counter what all now viewed as one of their greatest concerns—the spread of Islamic fundamentalism. For their part, U.S. officials, such as General Tommy Franks, the U.S. Central Command (CENTCOM) commander, emphasized that although the United States did not know how long forces would remain, it was not America's intent to maintain these forces and installations in the region on a permanent basis.

From the standpoint of the regional actors, the events of September 11 may have served as a catalyst in a number of respects. While the threat of Islamic fundamentalism spreading from the south long had been pointed to as a significant security concern, other problems and regional disputes, combined with a lack of outside recognition for these concerns, had resulted in few concrete steps being taken to address this threat. Prior to September 11, the formation in 1998 of the "Shanghai Five" (Russia, China, Kazakhstan, Kyrgyzstan and Tajikistan, and more recently the addition of Uzbekistan, to make "5 plus 1") was the most notable attempt to form a regional security coordinating body.[23] Since September 11, there has been a flurry of meetings, visits and continuing contacts designed not only to coordinate efforts in the war against terrorism, but also to take steps toward insuring regional security in the future. The most obvious result has been an increase in security assistance to the region, primarily from the United States, but from other nations as well. Though much of this effort is directly tied to the ongoing conflict, the attention focused on the region has brought about other assistance, such as the recent agreement signed between the United States and Uzbekistan to clean up the former Soviet biological testing site at Vozrazhdeniya (Rebirth) Island. However, assistance alone will not provide security. The greater significance in the long term may be that with a common cause uniting both the Central Asian States and the major external actors with interests in the region, a climate now exists where achieving a true cooperative security environment may be possible.

Some Thoughts for the Future

While outlining a comprehensive strategy for Central Asia is beyond the scope of this compendium, it might be worthwhile to point out the elements that must be considered as a starting point. It first should be noted that, in spite of the problem areas noted above, all of the states, to a greater or lesser degree, have achieved an element of success in orchestrating their affairs. All five continue to exist as sovereign states ten years after the breakup of the Soviet Union. At the time of the breakup, their viability as nations, and even their capability of continuing to exist, was highly questioned. With the exception of Tajikistan, all have managed to avoid major domestic conflicts, and while the form and policies of the governments that exist today may not be to our liking, the fact that they have been able to constitute and maintain themselves as sovereign states must be acknowledged. That the states did this with limited resources, little or no experience in governance, and in a geo-strategic environment that was less than ideal at best, speaks even more to the likelihood that with proper aid and nurturing the countries in this region can continue to exist and develop in the future.

To move forward will require several things. First, the states must possess sufficient means to ensure the continued integrity of their territory. All of the states inherited portions of the Soviet forces stationed on their territory, including a large number of armored vehicles and a force structure built along the Soviet model. Unfortunately, this has proven to be as much of a liability as a blessing. The forces they possess are not necessarily the ones they need. The money to maintain these existing forces uses up limited funding that would be better spent on meaningful military reform. All of the countries involved have plans for military reform that call for downsizing and modernization, with the goal of achieving small, high tech, and highly mobile force structures to act as deterrents to any outside threats.[24] Unfortunately, limited resources, opposition from the existing military (which feels it might lose its perks and privileges if such reforms were carried out), and bureaucratic inertia all stand in the way of such changes. Cooperative programs with foreign militaries, such as PfP with NATO, have made some progress, and the more members of the regional militaries are exposed to Western ideas and ways, the easier reform will be. Training programs for other institutions normally associated with state security, such as interior troops and customs officials, also will help. The ultimate goal in all of these efforts is to achieve a balance, so that each country believes it has the capability to defend its own territory against the threats it perceives, without creating a force that is perceived as a threat by its neighbors.

Once stability and security can be guaranteed, the stage will be set for economic development. The long-term stability of the states in the region is not dependent on military capability as such, but on economic viability that ensures the well-being of the nation. One of the reasons often cited for the failure to attract the outside investment so desperately needed is the fear by such outside sources that regional instability will put their investments at risk. This is particularly true in the energy sector where large investments in infrastructure, such as pipelines and refineries, must be made up front. These types of facilities are extremely vulnerable to attack, both from external and domestic threats. Consequently, investors are reluctant to make long term commitments where they fear even a slight risk of regional conflict. If regional stability can be achieved, the area's wealth in minerals and energy will bring the capital that can serve as the engine for other forms of development, thereby increasing the well being of the populations and heading off domestic sources of discontent by offering the prospect of a better future.

With economic development must come political change and the issue of political reform. One of the debates that continues, not only with regard to the countries of the former Soviet Union but also with almost all developing states, is whether economic reform, designed to create a market economy, can be carried out at the same time as political reform, designed to achieve some type of representational democracy. While certainly the ideal, there are numerous examples, beginning with Russia, that would seem to indicate that trying to accomplish both at the same time is just "too hard." Focusing on political reform, while possibly more manageable, means that the creation of the economic basis to answer the needs of the people must be postponed. Any government pursuing such a policy places itself at risk no matter how democratically inclined and well intentioned. However, focusing on economics first brings its own set of problems, as seen in the number of dictatorships that have claimed to be ruling in the name of the people and stability, but ended up enriching their own pockets while doing whatever was necessary to maintain power for themselves. At best, advocates of the latter strategy point to examples, such as South Korea, where authoritarian governments were tolerated, but continually nudged toward democracy as economic conditions at home improved. At worst, the example of Iran under the Shah looms large, where toleration and support of an authoritarian regime was justified as a strategic necessity, but ultimately resulted in catastrophic consequences for the United States.

All of these concerns lead to the question of how the West in general, and the United States in particular, should approach Central Asia, so as to protect both its own interests and those of the people in the region. While there is probably no set answer to such a question, some general guidelines would seem apparent. First, the key to stability in the region depends on creating an environment where development of the area's resources proceeds relatively unhindered and where profits from that can be put back into development of the region as a whole. To do this requires that the countries in the area themselves understand that there is more to be gained by regional cooperation than with traditional animosities. That the leadership of these countries can work together when faced by a common threat has been proven by recent events and the combined efforts to combat the threat perceived from Islamic fundamentalism. If this cooperation can be expanded to other spheres, a large step in the right direction will have been taken. Next, some sort of agreement must be made between the outside influences vying to achieve access and influence in the region, primarily among the "great powers." The acceptance by President Putin of an American military presence in what has traditionally been Russia's "home turf" is again an example that can be built on, where the players involved accept that there is more to be gained by all from a stable and prosperous Central Asia, than one that is not. Finally, the regional leaders must realize that their legacy will be measured by the condition in which they leave their countries, as opposed to their own individual wealth and power. While Tamerlane created a mighty empire, it quickly disintegrated after his death because he failed to establish any viable structure for ensuring its continuation once he was gone. If this lesson is lost on those who would follow in the tracks of Tamerlane, they must constantly be reminded of it, lest history repeat itself and the region, once again, fail to take the place in the world order it is capable of achieving.

Notes

[1] An earlier version of this chapter was published in *European Security*, http://www.tandf. co.uk,Vol. 11, no. 3, Winter 2002.

[2] Though specialists disagree on exactly what comprises "Central Asia," this paper examines the five former Soviet Republics of Kazakhstan, Kyrgyzstan, Uzbekistan, Turkmenistan and Tajikistan.

[3] For a concise summary of Tamerlane's accomplishments, see R. Ernest Dupuy and Trevor N. Dupuy, *Harper's Encyclopedia of Military History* (New York: HarperCollins Publishers, Inc. 1993), 424-425.

[4] A complete listing of areas and distances cited here can be found in M. Wesley Shoemaker's, *Russian and the Commonwealth of Independent States 2002*, (Harpers Ferry, Stryker-Post Publications, 2002).

[5] Dupuy and Dupuy, 424.

[6] Ibid., 424-425.

[7] Hopkirk's trilogy, which includes *The Great Game, Like Hidden Fire*, and *Setting the East Ablaze* (New York: Kodansha America, Inc. 1994, 1994 and 1995 respectively) combine to give the definitive history of the region from ancient times to the beginning of the twentieth century.

[8] Shoemaker, 74.

[9] Ibid., 182.

[10] For detailed breakdowns of the percentages of various ethnic groups, see individual country listings in Shoemaker, *Russia and the Commonwealth of Independent States 2002*.

[11] In a conversation with the author, a member of the Kazakh Foreign Ministry noted that, while everyone pointed to the fact that two million ethnic Russians left Kazakhstan to return to Russia in the period from 1991-1994, very few noted that some 600,000 returned between 1995 and 1999. While his figures cannot be confirmed, a return of ethnic Russians to Kazakhstan has been noted by several sources.

[12] Martha Brill Olcott, *Kazakhstan—Unfulfilled Promise* (Washington: Carnegie Endowment for International Peace, 2002), 3.

[13] The author was present when the Kazakh Defense Minister M. Altinbayev made this comment to Secretary of Defense Cohen during an official visit to Washington D.C. in 1998.

[14] While formally maintaining that their goal was to have good relations with all of their neighbors, members of the Kazakh military, on multiple occasions, told the author that their greatest security concern relating to their neighbors was with China.

[15] Though much speculation has surrounded this pairing, it appears that the two, who met while both were attending school in the United States, were genuinely in love. Unfortunately, as of this writing, the two have separated.

[16] There have been discussions about closing this border, not because of any threat posed by Turkmen, but because Turkmenistan has no visa requirements on Iranians crossing their border, and several Iranians have been found to have entered Kazakhstan without documentation, in spite of Kazakhstan requiring such visas.

[17] In a discussion with the author, one local official indicated that he believed up to 40 percent of the youth in his region were drug users. He further went on to say that, because unemployment in the area was 60 percent, the only work youth could get was in the drug trade, where they were paid with a portion of the drugs they were trafficking.

[18] This made traveling in cities such as Tashkent extremely interesting in the early years after independence, when the Cyrillic street signs had been removed, but nothing was put up to take their place.

[19] This type of attitude has been observed by the author on numerous occasions and is repeatedly noted by other Central Asian ethnic groups when describing Uzbek behavior.

[20] Ibid., 186.

[21] It has been a longstanding Russian policy that Turkmen gas is routed for CIS consumption, while Russian gas is sent to hard currency customers. This leaves Turkmenistan in the awkward position of trying to collect from countries like Ukraine that have a habit of not paying for the gas they use.

[22] Shoemaker, 194.

[23] C. Fairbanks, S. Frederick Starr, C. Richard Nelson and Kenneth Weisbrode, *Strategic Assessment of Central Asia* (Washington, DC: Central Asia-Caucasus Institute, 2001), 36.

[24] Recognizing the near impossibility of maintaining a force capable of defending the long borders involved, each country envisions the type of force that could be kept in the central part of their country and then be rapidly deployed to repel any outside threat.

Part I

Political Changes

Chapter 2

The Politics of Central Asia: National in Form, Soviet in Content

E. Wayne Merry

The politics of Central Asia—limited in this discussion to the five states of former Soviet Central Asia—are neither as obscure nor as complex as is sometimes thought. Certainly, the region and each of its component societies are rich in indigenous traditions and culture and they did not merit the Western neglect, which was their lot during their incorporation in the Russian and Soviet empires. Nonetheless, the contemporary political institutions and prospects of the five states—Kazakhstan, Kyrgyzstan, Tajikistan, Turkmenistan, and Uzbekistan—reflect little of the millennial history of the region, other than for purposes of propaganda, but are instead overwhelmingly the products of their recent Soviet past. Future Central Asian generations may draw on pre-Soviet traditions to deal with modern issues, whether for good or ill, but today's ruling elites remain wedded to the Soviet way of doing things, which is how they came to power in the first place.

Alone among the nearly 30 successor states of the former "socialist camp," ranging from Albania to Mongolia, Central Asia has experienced no regime change. The bosses and ruling elites today are those of the late Gorbachev era with some purging, especially of Slavs. Regime change elsewhere has not always been positive, for example, in Belarus, but every other socialist successor state has at least experienced a political or a generational transformation of top leadership, or both. However, in the five Central Asian states, the rulers that came to power within the Communist Party of the Soviet Union (CPSU), with all that implies about methods and mentality, have stayed. They have remained in power by applying Soviet techniques to independent statehood. While some Communist parties have produced remarkably progressive figures, a few even validated by genuine popular elections, this has not been true in Central Asia, where old-style CPSU politicians retain power indefinitely with periodic sham ballots of affirmation.

Thus, a key starting point in understanding the region is the recognition that these countries cannot be compared properly with the Slavic or Caucasian successor states of the Soviet Union, and still less with the Baltic or East European countries. Rather, the Central Asian regimes are in the same category of governance as those of Cuba and North Korea, with whom they have much in common. They are a combination of post-colonial nationalism and neo-Sovietism, and can be characterized as "national Soviet" in form.

The decade since the Soviet collapse and the emergence of the Central Asian republics as independent states (albeit, initially, reluctant ones) is a short period in political development, although other successor states experienced rapid changes in the same time. These are regimes of the first post-colonial generation, comparable to many African and Asian countries three or four decades ago. Present conditions in these states are neither stable nor reliable indicators of what they will be like in the second and third post-colonial generations. In common with other post-colonial experience, including that of North America, Central Asia will almost certainly undergo dramatic changes in the coming decades. Political and economic systems will alter, and borders may move. This analysis will not speculate about what Central Asia will look like in mid-century, other than to note that straight-line extrapolations of that future from the present will certainly be wrong. We can, however, reasonably look at the region's prospects in the next decade, based on an examination of the twin identities which define its politics today—post-colonial and neo-Soviet—and its potential to respond successfully to the challenges it faces.

The Imperial Legacy in the Heart of Eurasia

Properly speaking, "Central Asia" is much larger than the five states under consideration, encompassing significant parts of the Russian Federation and the People's Republic of China, plus much of Iran, Afghanistan, and Pakistan. In terms of culture, and especially of religious culture, much of Central Asia remains occupied by alien political systems based in Moscow and Beijing. The region sometimes known as "Turkestan" (to reflect the Turkic ancestry of many of its inhabitants) was divided into western and eastern areas of domination under Russian and Chinese rule in the nineteenth century. The famous "Great Game" rivalry between Imperial Russia and Imperial Britain in the same century drew lines defining the southern frontier of Western Turkestan, an identity reinforced by the violent imposition of Soviet rule in Central Asia in the twentieth century.

Soviet nationality policy, under the motto "National in Form, Socialist in Content," was in reality little more than the age-old imperial device of divide-and-rule. Stalin deliberately drew republic borders in Central Asia to separate large and potentially unruly ethnic groups—in particular, the Uzbeks and Tajiks—into ethnically-mixed areas for political administration and to create majority-minority tensions to facilitate Soviet rule. The states which emerged from the failure of Soviet power in late 1991 had external borders which no rational ethnographer would have drawn for titularly-ethnic "nation states" and reflect little more than Joseph Stalin's nationality policies. These states should be seen first and foremost as political systems, rather than as reflecting national identities.[1]

Challenges of Post-Colonialism

Irrational borders spawning ethnic conflicts are common in the Third World as legacies of European imperialism. While one always should be cautious in applying general principles of political development to diverse societies, what European powers wrought on the African continent is, in broad outline, very similar to the imperial handiwork of the Soviet Union in Central Asia. This point, while seemingly obvious, is important because Western analysis of Central Asia sometimes treats the region's problems as entirely *sui generis* and ignores relevant experience of other parts of the Third World.

To simplify, if one wants to project in broad outline where Central Asia is likely to go, it is instructive to look at where Central Africa has been. The objective circumstances of the post-colonial experience of the two regions are sufficiently similar, despite obvious differences, to make the comparison useful. The parallels are particularly acute in the realm of politics, with the Central Asian regimes even less likely to adopt political pluralism or genuine rule of law than the bosses of Central Africa have been, because neo-Soviet regimes possess better instruments of domestic repression combined with the habits of an ideological monopoly of power. Central African rulers also have positive models in their former European overlords, while those of Central Asia are surrounded by the dubious examples of Russia, Iran, Pakistan and China. Central Asian elites dislike comparisons with other Third World regions and proclaim, and perhaps even believe, themselves to be exceptional. However, the assertion of national exceptionalism is well-nigh universal and is generally a poor excuse for rigid or reactionary policies. An objective observer cannot help but notice how after ten years of independence the Central Asian states are traveling down a well-trodden Third World path.

To be fair, the region's problems are the poisoned legacy of imperial exploitation and would pose huge challenges even to progressive leaders. As with most imperialism in Africa and Asia, Russia conquered Central Asia for purposes of domination and exploitation, rather than for mass colonization. While Slavic people did enter and settle in the region, they did so slowly and without demographically displacing indigenous populations. The only major Slavic settlement region in Central Asia (analogous to South Africa) is the heavily-Russified northern part of Kazakhstan, which, at some point, could either attempt secession to join Russia or demand effective self-rule. Elsewhere, the Slavic inhabitants of Central Asia were not rural *pieds noirs* as in French Algeria or British Kenya, but urban dwellers and members of the administrative and technical elite. This set the stage for "white flight" after independence and a rapid loss of many skilled Slavic cadres who left the region for personal security or from loss of status and employment. In parallel, Soviet military formations in Central Asia were largely composed of local conscripts, led by both Slavic and native officers, thus allowing the new states to inherit established armed forces, though with a loss of many Russian officers.

The Enduring Mentality of Empire

In common with imperial practice elsewhere, the Soviet Union maintained its rule in Central Asia by developing and training local elites in ways that deliberately alienated them from the broad mass of the native population. These cadres were living extensions of the power of Moscow and often became more Soviet in mentality than the Russians themselves. They enjoyed great status and affluence, all dependent on their position in the Soviet *nomenklatura* with its shared attitudes, practices and imperial vernacular. While spoken Russian became common throughout Central Asia, though weak in rural areas, local elites employed the imperial language in preference to their mother tongues for purposes of prestige, education, communication within the broader Soviet elite, and for acceptance by their Slavic overlords. Higher education often took aspiring members of native *nomenklaturas* to Moscow (as Africans went to Paris or London) to acquire the habits, manners and lifestyles of the imperial "center." Such persons often had little contact or empathy with the poor and semi-educated masses at home, who were a constant reminder of the privileges and comforts they obtained by serving the empire and potentially could lose in the post-colonial environment. In the Central Asian case there was the additional factor of ideology, which, however much cynicism may have attached to the ideals of communism, did reinforce the arrogance of elites in their possession of scientific socialism, making them even less inclined to accept political pluralism or accountability after independence.

While use of Russian is fading on the streets in Central Asia, it is likely to remain the elite *lingua franca*. The only regional substitute would be Uzbek, an unwelcome option for other nationalities. Although English as the world language has spread very quickly among younger and educated people in the region, this will not obviate the need for a regional language to communicate with other successor states, which can only be Russian. By way of comparison, English has not displaced French or Portuguese in much of Africa but occupies a place alongside. In Central Asia, the utility of maintaining Russian is obvious, from its use in technical manuals to ease of dealing with the region's leading trading partners. However, as in other parts of the Third World, the persistence of the imperial language sustains imperial attitudes and behavior, especially in officialdom.

Manmade Economic Nightmares

Central Asia also has parallels with Africa and South Asia in the inherited burden of misdevelopment and unbalanced economies. In the Soviet plan, Central Asian economies were structured around commodity exploitation, with consequent massive ecological damage. While Soviet planners did not employ the terminology of plantation colonies, they were even more single-minded than their capitalist counterparts in fostering commodity mono-cultures, especially of cotton in Central Asia. The depletion of water supplies, degradation of soil, and destruction of the existing nomadic and farming environment are well-documented, in some places attaining ecocide, as in the overuse and near evaporation of the Aral Sea. The focus of the Soviet central plan on the extraction of minerals and hydrocarbons, combined with the use of Central Asia for testing nuclear, chemical and other weapons, produced a legacy of economic imbalance at least as severe as the coffee, hemp or cocoa-based economies of sub-Saharan Africa or of "banana republics."

In addition, Central Asia is challenged by the results of the most benign of imperial policies, the spread of public health services and sanitation, which, in turn, have led to rapid demographic growth. In common with much of the Third World, these states face population increases far beyond their ability to generate new employment, especially given the deterioration of Soviet-era infrastructure and the limited job-producing capacities of high-capitalization commodity-extractive industries such as oil and gas. The loss after 1991 of investment funds and subsidies from the Soviet central plan robbed the newly-independent states both of the wherewithal to maintain existing industry and agriculture and of the means to establish productive enterprises independent of the Russian market (even assuming that local political interference and corruption would have allowed such enterprise). A by-product of population growth is distortion of education, as schools established in the colonial period churn out graduates in excess of available jobs equivalent to their training, which in Central Asia is often oriented to Soviet-era standards. While public education is an area where Central Asia is ahead of some Third World regions, the advantage is eroding in many skills, especially in high technology where Indian and Chinese training models are more competitive.

Politics Following the Worst Models

It is in the political realm, however, that the post-colonial experience of the Third World is most relevant to Central Asia, in the replication there of what in Africa is called the "Big Man" regime type. Such regimes tend to be dominated by members of single ethnic groups or clans and by the enshrinement in power of a single individual or, more commonly, a Great Leader and his family (leading to the *sotto voce* witticism in several post-Soviet states that Stalin's quest to build "socialism in one state" has been replaced by the goal of "socialism in one family"). Such regimes do not distinguish public from private wealth, transforming corruption from a form of social deviance into effective state policy. These regimes maintain political control by strictly limiting participation in the political process; by extending state authority over a wide range of civil institutions, including business, labor unions, organized religion, and the media (or, as playwright Tom Stoppard once put it, by establishing a "relatively free press" in the form of a press run by one of the ruler's relatives);[2] and by lecturing Western critics that the local populations are "not ready" for democracy which "takes time." Finally, such regimes almost invariably encounter a crisis when attempting a generational transfer of power within the ruling family or clan, as the authority and legitimacy of the first post-colonial "Big Man" creates shoes too large for a successor to fill.

The Central Asian regimes, with individual variations, fulfill all the "Big Man" criteria. This is not only because of their former Soviet experience, but also due to policy choices by the new regimes. Among socialist successor states there have been cases of political maturation mostly in Eastern Europe and the Baltics; violent transfers of power as in Azerbaijan, Armenia and Georgia; democratic transitions which made things no better or worse as in Belarus, Ukraine and Moldova; and shifts of public opinion to either left or right, or, as in Bulgaria recently, in both directions at the same time. Alone among socialist successor states, the Central Asian regimes still are of the first post-colonial generation, while all the rulers, perhaps with the exception of Kyrgyzstan, intend to remain in personal control indefinitely. These are classic "Big Man" regimes of the type Africa has experienced to its continuing cost. In common with their African counterparts, these states will experience systemic crisis when they finally transfer power, especially difficult where there are dynastic aspirations as in Kazakhstan.

A Genuine, if Grim, Exceptionalism

As the Central Asia regimes replicate the experience of "Big Man" states, they are also different and exceptional, although not in a positive sense. In contrast to other parts of the Third World, these five states remain strongly Soviet in institutions and practices. While the Communist Party is gone in a formal sense, its personnel and methods remain in revamped ruling parties under national banners. The leaders, to a man, are all former Soviet Communist Party bosses, who changed their Communist lapel pins for nationalist ones while retaining a purely Soviet approach to political power. While many of the Soviet successor states have regressed badly in recent years, only in Central Asia have the bosses of the Soviet era avoided competitive politics or the challenge of a legitimate ballot box.

In sharp contrast to Third World leaders who took part in anti-colonial movements or at least aspired to independence, Central Asia's rulers were propelled into independence by happenstance. These states entirely lack the genuine nationalist credentials of the Baltic States, Caucasian republics or Ukraine—let alone those of Eastern Europe. With the exception of Kyrgyz leader Askar Akaev, the rulers opposed Gorbachev's efforts to reform the sclerotic Soviet system and welcomed the reactionary coup attempt of August 1991. At the time of the Soviet collapse, they hoped to remain within some kind of renewed Soviet system, with Moscow providing subsidies and support for their rule.[3] As cosmetic nationalists, the party bosses who chanced to be in power when their republics became independent could not inspire an "end of empire" boost in public morale common when Third World liberation movements come to power. For most inhabitants, very little changed politically other than the removal of the top tier of Moscow-based party icons and the suitable enlargement of portraits of the former republic CPSU First Secretary as new national president. In other respects, daily life for average people became even harder and more repressive than under Gorbachev.

The single factor that most sharply distinguishes the Central Asian states from most post-colonial countries is their possession of the fully-formed mechanisms of a modern authoritarian police state. While other imperial powers developed security agencies in their colonies and in some cases bequeathed them to the new governments, none bear comparison with the Soviet KGB which passed almost intact into the hands of the new Central Asian rulers. This advantage assured a high level of domestic control by the new regimes, except in Tajikistan, which quickly descended into civil conflict, and in the Ferghana Valley, an area of serious unrest during much of the Soviet period. The comparative social peace enjoyed by the Uzbek, Kazakh, Turkmen and, until recently, Kyrgyz regimes is in large measure due to the coercive Soviet institutions they have employed with greater vigor than had been true under Gorbachev. In particular, the repression of peaceful manifestations of independent religious activity is more severe in post-Soviet Central Asia than had been the case under late Soviet rule.[4]

In addition, these countries inherited the former Soviet armed forces deployed on their territories. These were not first-line units like those stationed in Germany or along the Chinese border; most were reserve or mobilization formations of limited operational capability. Nonetheless, they constituted substantial military establishments for newly-minted Third World states. In the Kazakh case the presence of parts of the former Soviet strategic nuclear arsenal engaged the United States directly in Central Asia for the first time, which brought substantial financial and technical benefits to Kazakhstan and provided some limited improvements to their conventional armed forces. At independence, Uzbekistan by accident possessed one of the world's largest inventories of conventional heavy weaponry due to the Soviet practice of using the dry Uzbek interior as a parking lot for treaty-limited equipment (especially battle tanks, artillery and armored personnel carriers) withdrawn from west of the Urals under the provisions of the Treaty on Conventional Armed Forces in Europe (CFE). While this weaponry greatly exceeded Uzbek defensive requirements, it fed Tashkent's pretensions to regional hegemony. Uzbekistan also possessed the best officer corps in the region, significant training facilities, and a more balanced overall force structure than its neighbors. Turkmenistan and Kyrgyzstan inherited armed forces of greatly inferior quality and operational capabilities, and the prolonged civil conflict in Tajikistan not only dissipated its limited military strength but soon required intervention by Russian and regional troops.[5]

In sum, although some Western critics have perceived in Central Asia a reversion to a kind of pre-Soviet "Asiatic despotism," the reality may be even worse. A form of medieval rule could not long succeed in the contemporary world, but a modern police state—with sufficient political will at the top—can be quite robust. Across the region, the will power has not yet faltered. Indeed, the regimes become more rather than less repressive with each manifestation of domestic unrest or attempts at political pluralism. Therefore, sadly, Central Asia is not so much moving in the tracks of Tamerlane, but regressing into those of the CPSU and KGB.

Geography and Geology as Destiny

Central Asia's potential to meet its challenges is limited by objective circumstances in addition to its political makeup. First, it is the most land-locked region on the globe and suffered a long enforced separation from the outside world by the Soviet prohibition on interaction with historic neighbors, especially Iran and China. While most colonies are incorporated into an imperial trading system, they nonetheless retain some contact with the broader world. In contrast, Soviet policy insulated the Central Asian peoples from their ethnic and spiritual hinterlands, while all legal economic activity was oriented northward toward Russia despite natural trading routes to the east and south.

The opening of the region's external frontiers in 1991 introduced external influences, which the regimes perceived as challenges rather than as opportunities. To the west, Turkey initially saw itself as the natural leader of Turkic peoples of the former Soviet Union. However, as Turkey made efforts to exercise a benign hegemony in Central Asia, its leaders quickly encountered cultural tensions and conflicting agendas. The regional leaders rejected Turkish pretensions and disliked the Kemalist political model. To the southwest, Iran and some other Islamic states sponsored construction of mosques and training of religious personnel and introduced a radical tinge into the traditionally moderate Central Asian practice of Islam. Islamic proselytizers alarmed the elites of the region who exhibited their Soviet-trained incomprehension of religion and fear of any challenge to the state monopoly of belief. To the south, the Tajik-Afghan frontier had been fairly porous during much of the Soviet decline and ceased to be an effective barrier after 1991, contributing to the complex domestic conflicts in Tajikistan and greatly expanding the narcotics trade. More worrisome was the importation of Taliban and al Qaeda-inspired extremism into some of the poorest parts of Central Asia, such as the Ferghana Valley. Finally, to the east, the immense and growing Chinese economy quickly established a major trading presence in Central Asia, while Beijing exhibited concern about separatist tendencies in its own slice of "Turkestan," Xinjiang. Under the umbrella of the Shanghai Cooperation Organization, China is expanding its influence in Central Asia to include even military ties, probably with a long-term view to replacing Russia as regional hegemon.[6]

Of all post-colonial regions of the world, Central Asia is the most distant from any ocean and the most cut off from direct interaction with the global economy, and hence from the positive influences of globalization. The problem of transit through neighboring states, most with ambitions in Central Asia, limits regional economic prospects and potential for political reform. The countries of Central Asia remain critically tied to Moscow despite Russia's own status as a semi-failed economy. The Central Asian states want to diversify their external trade, but have little to offer to the more balanced economies of Eurasia. At the same time, investment from First World economies is concentrated in commodity exploitation, mainly oil and gas. Western business engagement in the region in other than extractive investments actually has declined in recent years, due to disappointed expectations, corruption and regime interference. One business survey assessed Western investment potential in Central Asia beyond the hydrocarbon sector as negligible.[7] The only important external economy now expanding in a broad range of commerce in the region is the Chinese, which is certainly freighted with political influence.

A Future Built on Oil, Gas, Water, and Drugs

In the early 1990s, the Western vision of vast oil and gas wealth in Central Asia obscured the seriousness of the region's economic plight, but even the substantial recent discoveries in the Northern Caspian basin can no longer conceal that these states are not Persian Gulf emirates in the making. Most of the region has little or no hydrocarbons. Only Kazakhstan has major proven oil reserves on a scale to become significant on world markets. Turkmenistan's vast holdings of natural gas are an asset largely devoid of a market. Turkey was the logical customer, but Ankara already has contracted to purchase more gas from other sources than it may be able to use in the years ahead. The proposed trans-Afghanistan pipeline for Turkmen gas faces many obstacles, not the least of which is that India (the largest potential customer) does not want to depend on a pipeline crossing Pakistan for energy supplies. In addition, the global hydrocarbon market is much more diversified than it used to be, with the higher transport and transit costs of Central Asian energy creating a price disadvantage. Finally, as in other hydrocarbon-rich countries, oil investments tend to distort broader economic development, discourage enterprise, warp labor markets, and spawn corruption. In this regard, Central Asia is following the examples of Nigeria and Indonesia rather than that of Norway.

For the region as a whole, two other commodities are likely to be as or more important than hydrocarbons. The first of these is water, due to the inherent aridity of most of Central Asia and to the depredations of Soviet development policies, which drained the Aral Sea, over-exploited the few rivers and depleted water tables. The water-rich areas of Kyrgyzstan and Tajikistan might seem natural complements to the energy-rich but water-poor areas to the west and north, but the deal is not so simple. Water is a shortage item for most inhabited parts of Central Asia. The mountainous states are unable to satisfy the needs of their northern neighbors and face the dilemma that supplying water for summer use in the lowlands prevents hydroelectric generation in the winter. The Uzbek and Kazakh authorities prefer to sell their oil and gas on world markets for hard currency than swap it for Kyrgyz water, while Tashkent prefers saber-rattling toward Bishkek rather than commercial compensation. The regime in Ashgabat is fostering vast new irrigation schemes and a "Lake of the Golden Turkmen" which, if realized, would require the entire flow of the major regional rivers. Thus, rather than serve as a regional unifying factor, water is a cause of tension and rivalry.[8]

The other commodity likely to dominate Central Asia in the years ahead is narcotics, as the region is the main transit route toward growing European markets for the output of Afghanistan, today the largest raw opium producer in the world. As elsewhere, the vast illegal profits involved in the narcotics trade easily can overwhelm weak political institutions and dominate fragile economies. If comparatively mature republics like Colombia can be enervated by this commerce, how likely are the Central Asian states—much poorer than in Soviet days and already famous for corruption—likely to withstand the pressure? The fatal double impact of this burgeoning illegal trade is that it appeals to the dispossessed of society excluded from other economic opportunities while suborning law enforcement and politics. The narcotics traffic is also likely to fund extremist Islamist elements of the region, especially in places like the Ferghana Valley that combine population growth, poverty, religious ferment and political repression.[9]

What Lies Ahead?

The probability is high that all five Central Asian regimes will suffer systemic failure. Failure in this context can mean one or both of two things. First, they can fail to achieve viability in the tasks of modernization and in reversing their decline ever deeper into the Third World. Second, they can fail as structures of political control. By the first definition, the Central Asian states already are failures, having all moved in the wrong direction on almost every relevant index, with little likelihood of more than cosmetic reforms in the years ahead. By the second definition, the regimes are currently successful, but in unsustainable ways.

The basis of regime failure in Central Asia is their Janus-like combination of post-colonial and neo-Soviet forms of governance. "Big Man" regimes throughout the Third World have demonstrated a very high failure rate in modernization and development. There are instances of limited success, for example, Tunisia and Malaysia, but they combine fairly moderate authoritarian rule with avenues for political pluralism, free speech and non-violent change. The Third World regimes most similar to those of Central Asia are case studies of lost opportunities for economic progress and eroding living standards since the end of colonial rule. Central Asian officials respond to such comparisons by saying their future will be better due to their stronger Soviet-style institutions. This is curious logic, as the Soviet model suffered systemic failure over a broader geographic area and in more varied conditions than any other form of governance in modern times. Even fascism did not collapse so completely, and often only under external pressure. Why should Soviet-style institutions and policies which failed in the Baltics and Balkans, in Albania and Ethiopia, in the Slavic states and the Caucasus, from Eastern Germany to East Asia, now prove viable in Central Asia to meet the demands of the post-Cold War world? Nothing is less probable. Indeed, the amalgam of "Big Man" and neo-Soviet ruling modes is almost a certain guarantor of systemic failure of the first type: failure to meet the needs of developing societies.

What are the prospects of failure of the second type? Cannot the addition of neo-Soviet police-state methods to Third World authoritarianism preserve regimes in power for long periods regardless of their substantive failings? Perhaps. This is the core political issue for Central Asia. Will these neo-Soviet regimes collapse more quickly than would a typical Third World dictatorship or can they prolong the process of decay behind a facade of nationalism for years to come? Will the internal contradictions of these systems (contradictions of a truly Marxian character) cause them to implode relatively quickly or will the rulers demonstrate that they learned well their lesson from Gorbachev's experiment, the lesson not to ease up the strong hand of dictatorship? In short, are these regimes rigid and brittle or rigid and strong? The region's rulers believe the latter, that the Soviet Union would have endured indefinitely under a forceful leader. They clearly credit themselves with the strength necessary to deny reforms at home and to defy pressure for reforms from abroad, especially after the 2001 terror attacks on the United States.[10]

However, in the long term, the Central Asian states can avoid systemic failure only by true modernization, especially fostering development of active civil societies. Civil society refers to activity taking place between the institutions of the family and the state. In advanced countries, even those with very large state sectors, civil society encompasses most business activity, labor unions, organized religion, media, political parties, science and culture, and other organized human endeavors. In authoritarian regimes, the state seeks control if not outright monopolization of these roles. The importance of a vibrant civil society is that most creative human enterprise takes place there, as does essential pluralism and accountability of state institutions. The health of a country's civil society bears a close correlation to its success in responding to political and economic challenges. By this standard, the Central Asian states rank extraordinarily low. All five regimes seek monopolies of civil institutions and treat independent organized activity as threatening to their control, which, indeed, it is. While Kazakhstan and Kyrgyzstan were initially somewhat amenable to civil society development, they reversed course to the comfortable Soviet norm. Barring regime changes, prospects throughout the region for expansion of civil society are very poor.

Diversity Within the Regional Pattern of Failure

A case-by-case examination of the five current regimes indicates they are likely to experience different fates, at least in terms of the timing of their ultimate failure as power systems. Turkmenistan and Kyrgyzstan, the worst and least-repressive regimes, respectively, are the most likely to experience regime change or at least significant political turmoil in the near term. Kazakhstan and Uzbekistan have the wherewithal and authoritarianism to hold on considerably longer.

The megalomaniac ruler of Turkmenistan, Saparmurat Niyazov, emulates some of the world's worst dictators in his cult of personality; Romania's Nicolae Ceaucescu and Jean-Bedel Bokassa of the short-lived Central African Empire are legitimate comparisons. In addition to his assumed name of Turkmenbashi or Father of the Turkmen, Niyazov has been anointed by his stooge parliament as president for life, a field marshal, and "The Great," among many other honorifics. However, for all his vainglory, Niyazov does not exercise the kind of bloodthirsty tyranny needed to maintain his rule for the long haul. While life in Turkmenistan certainly is marked by pervasive repression, it lacks the anxiety psychosis of a true Stalinist state. This weakness, combined with fatuous incompetence in running the economy (with fantasy statistics, such as the allegation of 21 percent growth in 2001), make Turkmenistan a good candidate for regime change by disgruntled domestic forces. The supposed coup attempt in late 2002, the facts of which are still unclear, may indicate the potential for an end to Niyazov. More recently, Niyazov has challenged Moscow in ways that inspired condemnation even by the Russian State Duma and is also verging on open conflict with Uzbekistan. How and when the transition will come is unclear (who could have said in advance what would expose Ceaucescu's feet of clay?), but it is difficult to believe the sixty-two year old Niyazov will remain in power as long as his regional neighbors.[11]

Kyrgyzstan President Askar Akaev is a great disappointment to many in the West who naively saw him as a Jeffersonian democrat in the heart of Asia. Sadly, a better parallel is Zimbabwe's Robert Mugabe, who also won many admirers in his early years before his agenda narrowed to maintaining personal power. The two men betrayed supporters at home and abroad as they presided over corrupt regimes (the rot starting in their own households), moved to imprison former close political collaborators, became increasingly intolerant of criticism, suspicious of all domestic opposition, and unresponsive to Western pressures. Akaev has, so far, been less heavy-handed in his repression than Mugabe or his Central Asian counterparts. The mass popular unrest in Djalalabad province during 2002 demonstrated genuine grassroots opposition, which could be difficult to control over time. Akaev has at least held out the public prospect of leaving office voluntarily at the end of his current term in 2005, but the common regional practice is to extend terms at will.[12] Akaev's blatant manipulation of a series of constitutional changes to shore up his hold on power in early 2003 does not bode well for a peaceful transition. Indeed, Akaev's very moderation, by regional standards, may prove his undoing, as his poor stewardship of the economy gives little basis to appeal for public support of his continued rule.[13]

Tajikistan is something of a special case, due to the extended and complex civil violence of much of the post-Soviet period, which dominated domestic politics. So far, the 1997 arrangements that brought most of the fighting to an end have held up. Nonetheless, Tajikistan remains in many ways the most fragile of the Central Asian states and the one most dependent on external economic and military support to retain cohesion. The regime of Imomali Rakhmonov is little more than a Russian protectorate and resembles some of the weak states of Francophone Africa, which are sustained through French beneficence and occasional intervention. As a semi-failed state for most of its independent history, Tajikistan is a poor prospect for serious reforms or even basic steps toward modernization. In many respects, Tajikistan resembles Angola, where the enervating impact of prolonged civil strife deprives domestic political and economic life of normal incentives, replacing these with the distortions of a war society and its potential for corruption, official malfeasance, and deterioration of what remains of civil society. In such conditions, political reform faces huge hurdles.[14]

If Kazakhstan maintains its current political order, it will be because the regime of Nursultan Nazarbaev has petroleum revenues adequate to buy and bribe his continuation in power. While in different hands the oil wealth might create real development, it is clear from the past decade that Kazakhstan has the same kind of "kleptocratic" ruling system that dissipated the riches of Nigeria and Indonesia.[15] These examples of oil-rich but probity-poor states demonstrate that money flow can prolong a "Big Man" in power for years, but the regime ultimately will fail due to the corrosion of social peace and the inability of the ruling clique to keep a firm grip on political realities. There is little prospect of a voluntary regime change in Kazakhstan, as Nazarbaev had his term prolonged in 1995, extended in 1998, and has openly spoken of a new term in 2007.[16] In such circumstances, opposition elements have few alternatives but to encourage domestic unrest, hoping the security forces will abandon the rulers in the face of massive popular protests (as did occur in Indonesia and Nigeria). Thus far, Nazarbaev and his clan have met every manifestation of opposition with harsher and more repressive measures, including arresting moderate politicians and journalists despite Western protests. In severe circumstances the regime could experience a loss of will or an inability to have its orders obeyed, but for the time being Nazarbaev's rule looks likely to continue for a considerable time, with the waste of the country's petroleum earnings lasting for at least as long.[17]

Finally, Uzbekistan is likely to retain authoritarian rule for an extended period. Among the Central Asian regimes, the Uzbek is truest to its Soviet roots. Islam Karimov certainly does not lack will in using his security services to repress any manifestation of a genuine civil society, including even moderate religious practice. However, as ever more moderate Moslem practitioners are imprisoned, tortured or killed, the trend in underground Islamic teaching moves in increasingly extreme directions. This trend can only go from bad to worse. How bad things already are is shown by the fact Tashkent treats statistics on use of the death penalty as a state secret. Although Uzbekistan began the 1990s with the best regional prospects for balanced economic development combined with moderate petroleum wealth, these opportunities have been wasted in an unreformed structure of state controls and disincentives for enterprise or investment.[18]

Karimov combines relative youth and a focused political intelligence with a boundless ambition in his control of Central Asia's largest population. His aspirations for regional hegemony and his still-active dreams of a restored "Turkestan" centered on Tashkent (and himself) not only obviate effective regional cooperation but shift state priorities onto external ambitions at the expense of pressing domestic needs. Like the ill-fated Shah of Iran, it is difficult for such a self-absorbed ruler to accommodate change at home while lusting for regional great power status, especially as Karimov sees nothing really wrong with a Soviet-style centrally-directed economy and monopolization of civil society. The weakness of Karimov's outlook is illustrated by the analysis of a courageous Uzbek human rights activist who noted that Karimov initially had considered following the Turkish Kemalist model of development, but ruled it out because it involved a free press and genuine political opposition; he then toyed with the post-Mao Chinese model, but thought it allowed far too much economic freedom; he then examined the South Korean model, but again judged its openness and vibrant civil society as intolerable for Uzbekistan; finally, Karimov settled on a model he could feel entirely comfortable with, that of North Korea.[19] Therein lies Karimov's near-term strength and long-term fallibility: He knows how to dominate but not how to adapt to changing circumstances. Such a regime—whether in Pyongyang or in Tashkent—may last a long time, but ultimately has painted itself into a corner with no exit.

What Is To Be Done?

Although prospects for the five Central Asian regimes vary, the countries all need the same things. First, regime change. The neo-Soviet "Big Man" leadership in every Central Asian state has demonstrated inability and unwillingness to adapt to the conditions of the modern world. New leadership is required, although one cannot have high expectations for what may come in the initial transition. Second, political pluralism.

This need not mean participatory democracy in the Western sense, but at least the involvement of all ethnic, geographic and economic groups in governance and in accountability for policies. Third, expansion of the civil society. The state effort to control activities not related to the necessary roles of government effectively prohibits creativity and development. The challenges of modernization can only be met outside the stultifying embrace of a pervasive bureaucracy, while an active civil society is also the best antidote to state-sponsored corruption.

Obviously, such a program of political change in Central Asia is not currently in the cards, nor will change be easy or perhaps, even peaceful when it comes. The region's periphery does not supply good role models, as Russia, Iran, Pakistan and China are themselves examples of regimes in need of reform. Even the more positive experience of Turkey and India show how slow, difficult and uneven progress can be, while also proving that current conditions in Central Asia are far worse than they need be. One thing is certain: "Stability" is no answer to the problems of Central Asia; indeed, a focus on stability is the heart of the problem. Central Asia needs profound political and economic transformations to escape its neo-Soviet morass—changes comparable to those of Eastern Europe—and the sooner the better.

Notes

[1] Zamira Eshanova, "Central Asia Border Issues: An Eighty-Year-Old Headache for Region," Radio Free Europe/Radio Liberty (RFE/RL), Prague, October 18, 2002.

[2] Tom Stoppard, *Night and Day* (Faber,1978).

[3] Author's diplomatic reporting from United States Embassy, Moscow, 1991-94.

[4] Briefing on Religious Liberty Issues in Central Asia, United States Commission on Security and Cooperation in Europe, Washington, March 7, 2002; "Central Asia: Islam and the State," International Crisis Group (ICG), Osh/Brussels, July 10, 2003.

[5] Author's experience as Regional Director for Russia, Ukraine, and Eurasia in the Office of the Secretary of Defense, Washington, 1995-97.

[6] Discussed in the author's "Russia and China in Asia: Changing Great Power Roles," American Foreign Policy Council, Washington, 2002, 41-47; "Central Asia Fears Over China's Power," *RFE/RL Newsline,* Prague, June 17, 2003.

[7] Robert Cottrell, "Asian Entanglement," *Financial Times*, April 17, 2002.

[8] Michael Wines, "Grand Soviet Scheme for Sharing Water in Central Asia is Foundering," *New York Times*, December 9, 2002, 14; "Turkmen Lake Project Marks Third Birthday," *RFE/RL Newsline,* Prague, May 7, 2003.

[9] Justin L. Miller, "The Narco-Insurgent Nexus in Central Asia and Afghanistan," *In the National Interest*, 2, no. 18 (May 7, 2003); "The Globalization of Narcotics," RFE/RL Organized Crime and Terrorism Watch, Vol. 3, no. 19 (June 5, 2003).

[10] "Central Asia: Fault Lines in the New Security Map," (Osh/Brussels: ICG, July 4, 2001); Hooman Peimani, "Abusing the 'War on Terrorism' in Central Asia," *Central Asia-Caucasus Analyst* (August 14, 2002); "Central Asian Perspectives on 11 September and the Afghan Crisis," (Osh/Brus-

sels: ICG, September 28, 2001); "Central Asia: Last Chance for Change," (Osh/Brussels: ICG, April 29, 2003).

[11] "Turkmen Leader Renames Months After Himself, His Mother At Grand Council," *BBC Monitoring International Reports*, August 9, 2002; RFE/RL Central Asia Report, 2, no. 31 (August 15, 2002); Claudia Rosett, "The Real World," *Wall Street Journal*, August 28, 2002; Sergei Blagov, "Turkmenistan and Its Leadership Cult," *Turkistan Newsletter*, September 7, 2002; "Cracks in the Marble: Turkmenistan's Failing Dictatorship," (Osh/Brussels: ICG, January 17, 2003); RFE/RL Central Asian Report, 3, no. 22, (June 26, 2003).

[12] *RFE/RL Central Asia Report*, 3, no. 9, (February 27, 2003).

[13] "Kyrgystan at Ten: Trouble in the 'Island of Democracy,'" (Osh/Brussels: ICG, August 28, 2002); "Kyrgyzstan's Political Crisis: An Exit Strategy," (Osh/Brussels: ICG, August 20, 2002); *RFE/RL Central Asia Report*, 2, no. 32, (August 22, 2002); *RFE/RL Central Asia Report*, 2, no. 34, (September 5, 2002); *RFE/RL Central Asia Report*, 3, no. 6, (February 6, 2003); *RFE/RL Central Asia Report*, 3, no. 29, (August 29, 2003).

[14] Konstantin Parshin, "Of Tajik War and Peace," *Transitions Online* (August 22, 2002); "Tajikistan: A Roadmap for Development," (Osh/Brussels: ICG, April 24, 2003).

[15] Jeff Gerth, "Bribery Inquiry Involves Kazakh Chief, and He's Unhappy," *New York Times*, December 11, 2002, 16; Seymour Hersh, "The Price of Oil," *The New Yorker*, July 9, 2002; *RFE/RL Organized Crime and Terrorism Watch*, 3, no. 17, May 15, 2003.

[16] "Kazakhstan's President Says He Might Run For Another Term," *RFE/RL Newsline*, September 23, 2002.

[17] Robert G. Kaiser, "Kazakh's Season of Repression," *The Washington Post*, July 22, 2002; *RFE/RL Central Asia Report*, 2, no. 24, September 5, 2002; *RFE/RL Central Asia Report*, 3, no. 48, January 2, 2003.

[18] "Uzbekistan at Ten: Repression and Instability," (Osh/Brussels: ICG, August 21, 2001); *RFE/RL Central Asia Report*, 2, no. 33, August 29, 2002; "Uzbekistan: U.S. Rubber Stamps Human Rights," Human Rights Watch, New York, September 9, 2002; "Uzbekistan's Reform Program: Illusion or Reality?," (Osh/Brussels: ICG, February 18, 2003); "Uzbekistan: Religious Freedom Survey," Forum 18 News Service, Oslo, July 16, 2003.

[19] Briefing at RFE/RL's Washington office, March 28, 2002.

Chapter 3

Reform Strategies in Central Asia: Early Starters, Late Starters, and Non-Starters

Gregory Gleason

For nearly a decade prior to independence, Central Asian governments had discussed reform in the context of economic "acceleration" and governmental "restructuring" (*perestroika*). Soon after independence in 1991, all five Central Asian states developed new strategies to meet the immense challenges of post-communist transformation and "de-statification." Today, after more than 12 years of reform efforts, it is clear that none of these Central Asian states have been successful in attaining their goals for political and economic development. To date, no country has announced that reform has been brought to its conclusion. To the citizens of Central Asia, reform has become a permanent condition of governance and more of an explanation for why things do not work than for why they do. In order to change that perception, significant work remains to be done and many challenges must be faced.

On the whole, the governments of the Central Asia states have been more enthusiastic about economic than political reform. The reasons for giving priority to economic reform are straightforward and to a large extent understandable. First, existing political leaders and government officials sought to increase their states' economic potential without limiting their own ability to benefit from their positions as public officials.[1] They were inclined toward economic reforms that offered the promise of greater economic rewards, but shied away from political reforms that might give advantage to competing individuals or groups. Second, the leading analytical approaches to development stressed that economic reform should be ordered logically prior to political reform.[2] According to many analysts, countries that suffer from poverty, insufficient investment in human capital, underdeveloped infrastructure, antagonistic or exploitative trading relationships, excessive bureaucracy and government over-regulation, cannot be expected to implement political reforms successfully. However, once economic reforms begin to create new opportunities, the theories maintain, new constituencies will form and political reform will follow. A third reason why economic reform has been more forthcoming than political is that the international community has provided more moral, technical and material assistance in this area. The level of external support offered by international donor institutions is a matter of academic debate. Some analysts view the post-communist support offered by the donor community as insufficient, misguided and generally irrelevant to the domestic circumstances of the countries. Whatever the real effects of international aid, international donors have, in fact, played a crucial role in communicating the expectations of the international community for political and economic practices.

While the Central Asian countries have made headway in economic reform, they face the criticism that economic reform alone cannot engender the long-term social and cultural changes that also are needed. For people to demand integrity, accountability, fair play, openness, and effective administration from their governments, they must be prepared to provide public support in the form of taxes and public participation in shared self-government. For democratic development to be truly sustainable, cardinal changes must take place in the relationship between the individual and the state. Moreover, some analysts argue that the long-term viability of economic change hinges upon the character of governance. Poor governance quickly cancels the benefits of economic transformation and growth.

What strategies for reform have been adopted by the Central Asian states? What is the relationship between economic reform strategies and political reform strategies? How successful have these strategies been? This chapter surveys the relationship between economic and political reform in Central Asia, arguing that the assumptions, methods, conduct, and results of political reform strategies have varied significantly by country. The chapter concludes with extrapolations of reform trends for future Central Asian political development.

Economic Reform and Political Reform

The principal development challenge to emerge from communism is one of transforming previously authoritarian, centrally planned societies into market-led democracies, with vibrant economies and open political systems. The rationale for these changes is not primarily cultural, but functional. Globalization clearly tends to reward those countries that succeed in such practices and punish those who do not. In order to succeed in globalized commercial and information markets, governments find themselves under pressure to conform to accepted international standards of policy and practice.

Prevailing international standards tend to be those practiced and promulgated by the upper-income countries of the West. As a consequence, "best practice" in political and economic organization tends to be identified with practices that are prevalent in Europe and North America. Although political organization in the developed world exhibits a variety of institutional forms and procedures, a small number of principles are common to all economically advanced, stable democracies. The political organization of advanced countries tends to stress individual rights, voluntary contractual relationships, popular political participation, limited government, public accountability and financial transparency.

These features are common, but not necessarily self-initiating and self-regulating. They do not emerge from good intentions alone, but depend upon a finely tuned and continually evolving framework of public processes. Most often, public organizations are used to ensure that rules, standards, norms and procedures of openness are enforced. For example, although markets are elemental forms of human exchange and have been in existence as long as people have been free to enter into relationships and transactions on a voluntary basis, market relationships are not self-establishing and self-regulating in all cases. They require that governments or some alternative organizations solve collective action problems by discouraging free riding, opportunism and rent-seeking behavior.

Over the years, the world's international financial institutions, led by the World Bank and the International Monetary Fund (IMF), have developed a consensus on policy prescriptions to help their member countries solve problems of economic development. Informally, this set of policy prescriptions has come to be known as the "Washington consensus." An externally motivated structural adjustment package usually involves policy correctives in a number of areas including: fiscal responsibility; disinflationary policies; price liberalization; trade liberalization; currency stabilization; and foreign investment attraction. A policy package may, for instance, seek to tighten fiscal discipline through reducing government budget deficits and subsidies to private sector, helping to privatize public enterprises that might work more efficiently in the private sector, and bringing interest rates into line with market forces. Another type of package may also seek to aid in opening national economies to foreign imports and establishing conditions to support foreign exports on the basis of comparative advantage. The policies of the "Washington consensus" have been criticized for differentially serving commercial interests represented primarily in developing countries. Critics claim that the Washington consensus tends to encourage underdeveloped countries to rely on importing industrial goods made in the advanced countries while exporting primary commodities and raw materials for markets in the developed countries. Prices for industrial goods tend to be less sensitive to changes in market cycles. Primary commodity prices, in contrast, tend to fluctuate widely, creating destabilizing cycles of boom and bust in the underdeveloped countries. These cycles are reflected in the instabilities and uncertainties that characterize political processes in developing countries. As the Central Asian states emerged from the Soviet period to become independent countries, they quickly became subject to the pressures of the international marketplace.

At the time of independence in Central Asia, all the governments and important political leaders of the region endorsed the ideas of democratic politics and market-oriented economics. Yet the countries adopted very different national strategies for achieving their goals.[3] After more than a decade of independence, it is apparent that the differing development strategies adopted by the five new governments of Central Asia in the first years of independence have led to significantly different policy outcomes.

In assessing how the contrasting strategies of these states affected their progress toward economic liberalization and democratization, it must be acknowledged that progress toward democracy in all the Central Asian states has been limited. Four of the five Central Asian states are governed by former leaders of the Communist Party, and each of the Central Asian republics are largely administratively run by former communist party officials. By the end of the first decade of independence, all the governments of Central Asia had "presidents,"[4] but in all cases, these were officials from the Soviet *apparat* or high rungs of the Soviet establishment. Moreover, all the countries established "presidential" systems, giving the presidents the power to rule by decree.

Although all of the countries have conducted elections, none of the governments can be said to have conformed to international standards for free and fair elections. Three of the governments have former communist leaders who have extended their mandates in extra-constitutional ways. None of the governments has what could be described as an independent judiciary. None of the governments has established a functioning legislature with true powers of the purse. Even in the most open and liberal of the countries—Kazakhstan and Kyrgyzstan—the parliaments have been routed by presidential decree. Judging by the benchmark criteria for measuring democratic progress used by Freedom House,[5] in the years since independence the Central Asian societies have failed to realize their potential for democratic change.[6]

Although the Central Asian states may have made limited progress toward establishing sustainable systems of democratic governance, important relative differences do exist among them. The status of democratic reform is quite different in each of the states. To some extent, these differences are the product of Fortuna—some of the Central Asian countries have significant natural resource endowments, some have advantages of position, some have simply been fortunate. But much of the variation can be attributed to the substantive policies pursued by the states in the a wide variety of areas, including governance, rule of law, adjudication of disputes, human and civil rights, treatment of dissidents and opposition, treatment of non-nationals, and tolerance for religious, ethnic, and territorial differences.

While the international community has urged the countries of Central Asia to adopt policies that would encourage democratization, by far the most important impetus for change—both in terms of donor resources and in steps taken by the countries themselves—has come in the form of international efforts to support relatively non-political "governance" reforms or "structural reform." Structural reform of governance standards, policies, and practices generally is regarded as a way of inducing changes that will help bring countries into line with international standards—without compromising the countries' national sovereignty and right to non-interference in domestic affairs.[7] Structural reform is seen as a non-political process of improving the technical capacity of governments to carry out public policy. To the extent that this is accurate, structural reform does not entail "modernization" or "westernization," rather, it implies conformance with standards, policies and practices of the international community.

Structural reform, in the broadest sense, is anything that happens within a country that allows the country to participate more effectively in the global economy. Structural reform entails a process by which a country's institutions, policies and practices are brought into line with prevailing international standards. The purpose of structural reform is to create a favorable policy environment for accountable, transparent policy, with well-defined public and private sectors working in ..... reinforcing ways to promote prosperity and sustainable development. Countries undertake structural reform programs because they realize that participation in the global economy requires policy conformance with international standards. Some structural reform measures are narrowly economic in their purpose; others are more broadly oriented and aim to improve the policy environment that facilitates economic activity. Policy changes alter the status quo, producing winners and losers. As a consequence, all policy changes influence the balance of constituencies in a society. Moreover, economically oriented structural changes and politically oriented structural changes are linked in terms of reciprocal effects.

However the relationship between structural economic reform and democratization is, at best, a probabilistic one. While free markets in the long run may lead to free minds, the effects of long run processes often are beyond the time horizons of most political systems. Political leaders rarely rely upon economic change to bring about desired political change. For this reason, political leaders often adopt conscious strategies of political reform to further their goals. All political leaders, even the most cynical, have some concept of the public interest.

There are typically two basic thrusts of political reform strategies, one formal and the other informal. The first method is to use political institutions to shape future political change. The formal political institutions offer ways of engaging elected officials, representatives and the public in the process of change. The other method relies upon political exchange. This method consists primarily of using economic reform to support favorable constituencies. All economic changes, even the most non-political, necessarily produce winners and losers. Political leaders recognize that no matter how strong or deep their support, they are surrounded by challenges and sometimes even by threats. Using the changes introduced by economic reform to reward friends and punish enemies is one of the most fundamental forms of political strategy, and far more important in most developing countries than using the formal political institutions themselves.

The formal institutions of democratic governance require an accountable executive branch, a deliberative legislature, an honest and fair judiciary, and the governance standards of probity, transparency, and efficiency necessary to carry out the public mandate. Promoting change through the use of the formal political institutions requires reliance upon civil procedure, elections, public participation, recognition of the professional independence of the judiciary, and the vetting processes of operational independence of auditors and review commissions. None of these strike insecure political leaders as efficient mechanisms of rule.

Reliance on political exchange to reward supporters and punish those who dissent or oppose the government appears to many political leaders to be a more direct, and thus more efficient, means of achieving objectives. Even when political leaders are not so cynical as to see the political process as consisting primarily of quid pro quo exchanges, they nonetheless tend to interpret the public interest in terms of their own desire to garner support and avoid opposition.

The pages to follow survey the main features of structural reform in the countries of Central Asia. Extensive data and information are available regarding the results of economic structural reform. Much less is available regarding the results of political reform. What has not yet emerged is whether each country has arrived at its current state as a result of specific economic or political factors.

Kazakhstan: Outlines of a Petrocracy

Many areas of Kazakhstan's macro-economic reform have been successful and some provide a model for other post-communist countries.[8] Soon after independence, the Kazakh government established a legal foundation and regulatory system for a private economy.[9] The government introduced a convertible national currency, the *tenge*. It moved quickly to establish sound monetary and fiscal policies, including modern civil and tax codes as well as banking and investment laws in accordance with international standards. The government also carried out macroeconomic reforms including price liberalization and freeing markets from government controls. It turned major enterprises over to the private sector, including a majority of the power generation facilities and coalmines. Seeking to encourage international trade and foreign investment, the government passed environmentally sound oil and gas legislation that met international standards.[10]

In contrast with these economic policy successes, Kazakhstan has made less headway in other areas. On the whole, the economic benefits of Kazakhstan's rapid economic growth have been available to only a small portion of the population. With an average per capita annual income of $1,300 in 2000, most Kazakhstan citizens still had not benefited fully from the transition to market based economics. Structural reform means that changes must take place in the country's economic structure. These changes will benefit some, but will be detrimental to others. The costs of structural reform, that is the unemployment created by closing out-of-date enterprises, the loss of value of tangible assets, and the psychological uncertainty introduced by the reforms, are rarely borne by the rich. The costs of structural reform usually are imposed upon the poor or the less well politically connected. In the wake of structural reform, Kazakhstan continued to rely upon oil sector revenues, fiscal redistribution and foreign donor assistance to finance the costs of structural adjustment. Unless exceptional steps are taken, further development of Kazakhstan's oil and mineral sectors cannot be expected to lead to a wide redistribution of income. The situation is also grim in the agricultural sector where adequate investment in infrastructure, such as roads, processing equipment and farm inputs is lacking. Moreover, the banking reforms virtually ignored agriculture, failing to provide much needed credits for farm expansion. Although Kazakhstan has adopted a private pension system, moving ahead of other former communist countries, the social safety net has worn thin in many areas.

Given Kazakhstan's decade of experience with structural reform, one of the critical issues for Kazakhstan's future is how economic and political reforms will be linked in terms of policy cycles. Economic development strategies that emphasize a dominant economic sector under close government control run substantial risks. Too heavy a reliance on primary commodity exports could lead to the so-called "Dutch disease"—a situation in which oil-rich countries draw in large amounts of foreign capital for needed oil development, but find that the resulting strong exchange rates hinder their ability to competitively price other goods and services. While the government may be able to count on future revenue from rents on oil and gas extraction rather than from broadly based and relatively unpopular forms of taxation such as personal income tax or excise taxes, the political consequences of government dependence on such an easily monopolized sector as oil and gas can present real challenges to other aspects of liberalization. Government control of the natural resource sectors has led to policies that conceal incomes, compromise fiscal transparency and benefit insiders far more than the general public. The long-term success of Kazakhstan's structural reform is likely to rest upon policies that serve to diversify the economy on a sector and regional basis.

The political reform strategy of Kazakh political leaders has put little emphasis on the formal political institutions, or, for that matter, reform. When the first post-Soviet legislature proved to be recalcitrant from the point of view of the executive, it was dissolved summarily in December 1993 by the order of the president. The new parliament elected in March 1994 proved not much more effective and also was dissolved. Since then, the president has succeeded in winning overwhelming voter approval for a new constitution which greatly expanded his powers. In addition, Kazakh leadership has used adroitly the results of economic reform to politically enfranchise its supporters.

Privatization created a stratum of "new Kazakhs" who gained influence in government and society because of their wealth, which largely was acquired as a result of government supplied credits and special benefits. Back door privatization through "management contracts" and other stratagems allowed close supporters of the political leadership to profit in the early post-communist reform. The government's emphasis on the development of an export-led economy, particularly energy and minerals, helped promote the expansion of a stratum of close supporters who had everything to gain from continuing their support and everything to lose by arguing in favor of new directions.

Kyrgyzstan: Winning Friends and Losing Ground

Kyrgyzstan's enthusiasm for reform early on earned it a reputation as the "democratic showcase of the former Soviet Union." Soon after independence, the Kyrgyz government embraced the international financial institutions' policy prescriptions known as the "Washington consensus."[11] Following the standard policy prescription, the Kyrgyz leadership sought to liberalize prices, scale back the size and scope of government, introduce competition, and encourage foreign trade. Kyrgyzstan attempted to implement these prescriptions in good faith, but at the same time, faced substantial obstacles to successful economic reform. While the economic reform measures did result in rapid and significant advances in state capacity, they did not lead to expected economic growth, improvements in social welfare, or do much to improve the government's capacity to protect civil rights. Furthermore, these economic policy changes had negligible effects and in some instances even negative effects on the processes of political liberalization.

Kyrgyzstan's particular path is closely related to its unusual background and circumstances. Prior to independence, Kyrgyzstan occupied a highly specialized niche in the communist economic system, serving primarily as a provider of commodities for industries located in the European parts of the Soviet Union. When cut off from Soviet-era suppliers and customers, Kyrgyzstan's small and uncompetitive industrial enterprises quickly became insolvent. The agricultural sector was blocked from access to farm inputs such as tractors and advanced agricultural technology. Unable to import expensive farm equipment and technology, the country quickly began slipping toward low-technology subsistence farming. The transition to an open trading economy also proved difficult. Between 1991 and 1994 farm and industrial output fell, trade dropped, inflation soared, and the government ran a large fiscal deficit. The Kyrgyzstan economy reached a nadir in 1994, at about the time that foreign development assistance began to arrive. The International Monetary Fund (IMF), the World Bank, the Asian Development Bank, the European Bank for Reconstruction and Development, and the other major international financial institutions began pumping money into the Kyrgyzstan economy to make an example of this small, rugged country that was willing to risk the unknowns of entering quickly into the world economy.

Not until 1996 did the Kyrgyzstan economy begin to rebound from the post-Soviet Union collapse contraction. During the period 1995 through 1997, inflation was reduced, the budget deficit as a proportion of GDP was cut in half, and with international donor assistance, the Kyrgyzstan government made good headway in establishing the legal and regulatory foundation for a market economy. Kyrgyzstan carried out privatization of small enterprises and overhauled the country's banking and financial systems. In 1998, the Kyrgyzstan constitution was amended to allow for private land ownership and Kyrgyzstan became the first post-Soviet country to join the World Trade Organization. The Kyrgyzstan government eliminated export registration in 1998 and export duties in 1999.

Kyrgyzstan's population has been growing modestly since independence. The estimated population was five million people in mid 2001.[12] Prior to independence, Kyrgyzstan's workforce was spread evenly among agriculture, industry and services. Yet in the past decade, industrial employment dropped to less than half of its 1991 level and industrial production saw steep declines, especially in the early years after independence. With the exception of a few mining sectors, the industries have not rebounded. Coal production in 2000 was less than a quarter of its 1991 level, although hydroelectric production did increase. During the same time, agricultural employment grew by 50 percent. Agricultural output, which dropped initially after independence, increased overall by the end of the decade. Russia, historically Kyrgyzstan's largest destination for exports, was overtaken by Germany for first place among Kyrgyzstan's export partners after the 1998 Russian financial crisis. Russia continued to be the largest source of imports for Kyrgyzstan, followed by imports from neighboring Uzbekistan and Kazakhstan.

While the numbers and trends are discouraging in many sectors, Kyrgyzstan, in absolute terms, has made the most visible progress of the Central Asian states toward becoming a democratic institution. Even though Kyrgyzstan retained a "presidential" form of government, the parliament has grown relatively independent and challenges presidential authority on key issues. Opposition political figures are often subject to harassment and intimidation, but the very fact that such figures do speak out indicates a domestic political context where competing views and constituencies have some room to maneuver. Non-governmental civic organizations are becoming more widespread and influential. In 2000, heads of local administrations were elected for the first time rather than appointed. While Kyrgyzstan's human rights record receives criticism from international organizations, more open discussions and fewer instances of direct coercion and intimidation of human rights activists occur there than in other Central Asian states.[13]

Despite these promising signs, freedom of the press has suffered, aided in part by a growing government concern with terrorism and insurgency. The political reform strategy of Kyrgyz political leaders, like that of Kazakh leaders, places only minor emphasis on formal political institutions. In 2001, the World Bank Institute of governance indicators ranked Kyrygzstan as below the fortieth percentile in all six key governance categories.[14] Electoral process, judicial independence, and human rights practices in Kyrgyzstan have been criticized by leading international human rights organizations, such as Human Rights Watch and the Organization for Security and Cooperation in Europe.

In Kyrgyzstan, just as in Kazakhstan, when the first post-Soviet legislature proved to be recalcitrant, it was summarily dissolved by the order of the president. A new parliament that favored pro-government candidates was elected in a voting process managed by a central electoral commission. The Kyrgyz government has found that the informal processes of reform offer more easily manipulated mechanisms for influencing supporters and opponents. Kyrgyz officials also have found that their influence over government credits may be used to their advantage and many have profited from their connections. Conversely, some high ranking government officials who fell out of favor have been prosecuted for corruption.

Tajikistan: The Struggle for Reconciliation and Development

Physically remote and economically isolated from its neighbors by the specter of political instability, Tajikistan's social and economic indicators cascaded downward in the first five years of independence. Between 1992 and 1996, the Tajik economy contracted by nearly 40 percent.[15] As much as 40 percent of the country's population was directly affected by the civil strife; as many as 50,000 people lost their lives; 600,000 were displaced; and 60,000 fled to neighboring countries.[16] Thousands of women were widowed and tens of thousands of children were orphaned. The wartime damage was compounded by a series of natural calamities that beset the country, including torrential rains, floods and earthquakes. By the beginning of 1997, the year of the Tajik peace accord, Tajikistan ranked 115 out of 174 in the United Nation Development Programme (UNDP) Human Development Index.[17]

In 1996 the Tajik government embarked on the first comprehensive effort at structural reform and the adoption of international standards of fiscal and monetary management. The economic program targeted reducing inflation, regularizing relations with external creditors, increasing foreign exchange reserves, liberalizing external trade and payments, and improving the social safety net. The government liberalized bread and grain prices, replacing bread subsidies with targeted price compensation payments. Trade restrictions were almost completely eliminated, as export and import licenses and duties were lifted. The state grain fund was terminated while liberalization of cotton marketing was begun. Shortly after these initial steps toward structural reform were taken, the continuing costs of the civil conflict, in addition to weak commodity prices, drove the government to abandon some aspects of its reform program and policy targets. Faced with a widening budget deficit, the government resorted to administrative measures late in 1996 to raise new revenue and imposed export and excise taxes and import duties, as well as halted foreign exchange auctions in favor of directed lending of foreign exchange by the National Bank of Tajikistan (NTB). Following a United Nations brokered peace agreement that was signed in June 1997, the Tajik economy began to turn around.[18] In 1997, the country registered the first post-independence economic growth, as GDP grew by 1.7 percent, with most of the gain in the last quarter of the year. Since then real GDP has been growing in Tajikistan on an annual basis. Inflation, which had reached 164 percent in early 1997, declined to 2.7 percent in 1998 as the GDP grew by more than five percent.[19]

Significant changes still must take place for Tajikistan's structural reforms to spur political liberalization. Tajikistan, like all of the countries of Central Asia, claims to support the principle of free trade. However, unsatisfactory arrangements regarding government subsidies, currency controls, banking, customs and taxation, infrastructural development, and control over access to markets, continue to hamper trade and development in the country. At the urging of international financial institutions, the Tajik government undertook a comprehensive program of structural economic reform. The government's program was established in the form of a policy matrix with timetable benchmarks. The priorities for the structural reform agenda were: improved governance, privatization, bank restructuring, land reform and energy sector reform. Governance measures included reform of the treasury system and establishment of a single independent auditing agency. The goal of privatization was to raise productivity and support growth targets, as well as assist in achieving fiscal goals, by bolstering revenues and lowering direct or indirect subsidies. In structural reform, particular emphasis was placed on measures that would lead to a greater use of monetarized commercial transactions and a reduction in inefficient and non-transparent barter relations.

Much of the legal and regulatory framework for reform was already in place. As early as March 1992, the Tajikistan Supreme Soviet, their parliament, had approved land reform legislation giving citizens the right to own, lease and inherit land. Both the Tajik constitution and the laws on privatization guaranteed property rights, including intellectual property, real estate and business property. Agricultural land remained under state ownership, but could be leased. Under the land code, lease rights are inheritable and may be sold. The initial privatization process in Tajikistan moved slowly, stalled by the civil conflict and a weak banking sector. With the assistance of the World Bank and the IMF, the "Law of the Republic of Tajikistan on Privatization of State Property in the Republic of Tajikistan" was passed on May 16, 1997. This law established the framework for privatization, including a legal framework, title registry, and procedural guarantees. New privatization legislation changed the process from a top-down to a competitive bottom-up program, with more rapid wholesale transfer of assets into the private sector.

Banking reform followed a similar course. In 1994 a new law, "On Banks and Banking Activities," established procedures for forming statutory capital and specified the processes for: starting and terminating commercial bank activities, issuing and recalling licenses for bank audits, filing bankruptcies, and operating non-banking financial organizations. A new tax code took effect in January 1999, while a reform in the value-added-tax (VAT) took effect in July. These improvements in tax policy and administration contributed to an improvement in government revenue in 1999. However, the practice of tax offsets remained a hindrance to full monetization of the economy.[20] To enhance the role of the domestic currency, the Ministry of Finance started collecting all taxes in Tajik rubles in September 2000.

The Tajik government has made major efforts in its foreign trade sector through improvements in the public infrastructure for transport, communication and banking services. As these efforts succeed, they can be expected to exacerbate the trends in the region regarding organized crime and drug trafficking. Traffickers use legitimate transportation infrastructure and banking operations in order to move their wares and to conceal the funds derived from trade in handguns, weapons materials, drugs, drug precursors and drug production materials.

Mirroring the economic reform strategy, Tajikistan's political reform strategy is extraordinarily complex. The growth of the Tajik economy has not created a class of "new Tajiks" in the way that Kazakhstan's economic development has. Moreover, most of the political competition in Tajikistan takes place in the context of civil war. While the civil war seemed to center on ideology, in fact, the most significant dimensions of the dispute were regional, reflecting Tajik traditions of long-standing. The winners in the early years of reconciliation were the battlefield commanders who had sided with the Rahkmonov government. Gradually, members of this coalition broke up as the leader of the Hujand faction fell from favor. More recently, the country's political leadership has distanced itself from this group as the political situation has grown more stable. What is not clearly understood is the degree to which the government has benefited directly or indirectly from the region's drug trade revenues. Journalists have speculated on relations between government officials and the drug traffickers, but these accusations have proven to be ephemeral, in part, because Tajikistan for a time is one of the most dangerous countries in the world to be a journalist.[21]

Turkmenistan: The New Sultanate

Among the countries of Central Asia Turkmenistan has been the most resistant to the adoption of genuine structural reform. Those changes that have taken place have been, for the most part, directed at increasing the capacity of the state and in particular at enhancing the glory and authority of the country's authoritarian president, Saparmurat Niyazov. Bordered by Iran and Afghanistan to the south, Kazakhstan to the north, Uzbekistan to the north and east, and the Caspian Sea to the west, Turkmenistan's deserts dominate the country's physical terrain. Turkmenistan is a country with great potential for economic development but is constrained by physical circumstances and poor governance.

In mid 2001, Turkmenistan had an estimated population of 5.5 million people, growing at an annual rate of 1.3 percent.[22] Turkmenistan's workforce historically had been predominantly agricultural and service oriented. However, since independence, the service workforce has diminished in size and the agricultural workforce and industrial labor sectors have each grown by about 25 percent. Official statistical materials on economic activity, supplied by the Turkmenistan government, are viewed with skepticism by outside observers. According to the statistical data provided by the state, agricultural production is reported to have increased substantially in the years since independence, especially the production of food and forage crop. Cotton production also is reported to have increased sharply.

While agriculture is the largest employer in Turkmenistan, the country's energy sector is the largest revenue earner. Because gas and oil sectors revenues are so closely related to Turkmenistan government revenues (with allegations that gas revenues have enriched individuals responsible for public decision making) and because those revenues are critical to Turkmenistan's official credit rating, statistical reporting on the energy sector is an item of great sensitivity for the Turkmen government. The government began concealing production figures for natural gas in 1997, and some suggest actual output levels for gas and other forms of industrial production in the latter 1990s are considerably below 1991 pre-independence levels. Turkmenistan's foreign trade figures are similarly unreliable. Thus, it is difficult to develop a clear picture of Turkmenistan's balance of payments. There are indications that the 1998 financial crisis in Russia impacted heavily on Turkmenistan's balance of payments, by leading to the cancellation of Russian gas orders along with delays in outstanding payments. Some evidence also shows that Turkmenistan ran a significant balance of payments deficit in recent years. Despite Turkmenistan's great potential energy wealth, problems of administration and governance have prevented the country from fully benefiting from its natural resource base.

Turkmenistan's first and only president, Saparmurat Niyazov, was the former first secretary of Turkmenistan's communist party during the Soviet period. Until the Soviet collapse, Niyazov appeared to be a staunch communist, ideologically committed to the Soviet Union. However, as the Soviet Union began unraveling, Niyazov changed his ideological colors, assuming the position of a Turkmen nationalist. Like other Central Asian communist party leaders who suddenly became presidents of independent states, Niyazov was a public proponent of building a democratic, market-oriented state. Since independence, however, Turkmenistan's progress in democratization has been negligible. Political authority is concentrated in the office of the president, with little legislative or judicial autonomy. Non-governmental civic initiative is routinely curtailed, and political opposition figures are isolated and excluded from the political process. Human rights abuses are frequent and severe. While Turkmenistan was ranked in the top fiftieth percentile in terms of political stability in 2001 by the World Bank Institute governance indicators, the country scored in the bottom tenth percentile in the categories of regulatory quality, voice and accountability, and government effectiveness.[23]

Turkmenistan's political reform strategy does not warrant the dignity of being called a reform strategy. The political leaders have done little more than to pay off friends and eliminate enemies. Any idea of reform ended with the assassination attempt on Niyazov's life in late 2002.[24] In the wake of this event, the country's human rights situation has deteriorated markedly as the sole criterion for advancement in the society has become unquestioned loyalty to the country's leader.

Uzbekistan: National Consolidation and Social Consensus

Uzbekistan, with an estimated population of 25.1 million people in mid 2001, has the highest rate of population growth among the Central Asian countries.[25] Traditionally, Uzbekistan's workforce has been oriented toward the largest sector of the economy, agriculture. However, over the past decade, while the agricultural workforce has continued to increase, the largest employment growth has occurred in light industry, food processing, and the service sector. Cotton remains the mainstay of Uzbekistan's agriculture, but crop diversification has occurred as Uzbek agricultural officials, in response to the demand for more foodstuffs, have placed greater emphasis on the production of cereals and grains. Industrial diversification, reflecting market forces, also has taken place. Coal production has fallen substantially, while oil, natural gas and electricity production have increased. Although Russia traditionally has been Uzbekistan's primary trading partner, the Uzbek government has sought to diversify its trade patterns. Uzbek foreign trade began to develop in the early 1990s, but the import of manufactured goods and luxury items led to trade deficits in 1996. To restrain the growth of this deficit, promote domestic production, and curb capital flight, the Uzbek government introduced import substitution measures in 1996. Between 1996 and 2001, Uzbekistan's self-reliance measures profoundly impacted both its domestic and foreign markets.

Under the stern leadership of President Islam Karimov, the country's first and only president and a former communist party chief, Uzbekistan has become a highly authoritarian state. The executive branch dominates the administration, the legislature and the judiciary. The activities of non-governmental civic organizations as well as the media are tightly monitored and controlled by the government. Fundamental freedoms of speech, association and political expression are similarly limited by the government. However, strident political opposition, fueled by insurgency movements originating during the Afghanistan war and in the Tajik civil conflict, has grown increasingly active over the past decade, breaking into violence in the late 1990s. In response to the growth of political opposition, the Uzbek government mounted significant counter-insurgency efforts, which have had the effect of stifling civil and human rights. The 2001 World Bank Institute governance indicators ranked Uzbekistan in the bottom third percentile in all six key governance measures.[26]

Still, Uzbekistan's political reform strategy has been the most successful in Central Asia in terms of supporting the political stability of the leadership. It remains to be seen though, if this strategy has succeeded in consolidating political support within the country. Critics of the Karimov regime claim that the government's stress on the "Uzbek path" with its go-slow approach to macroeconomic structural reforms has undercut the expected benefits of true market liberalization. Uzbekistan's strategy emphasizes: self-sufficiency in energy and food grains; the export of primary commodities, particularly cotton and gold; and the creation of an internally oriented services market. Fundamental reforms in agriculture, state enterprises, state procurement, and the financial sector, (including foreign exchange) have been postponed. The reforms that have been enacted primarily have benefited middle-level government officials who tend to support the Karimov regime. It is quite possible that the economic rationale of these policies was much less important than the political considerations.

In the mid-1990s, a significant political opposition emerged within Uzbekistan, fueled by popular dissatisfaction with stagnating incomes, government intervention in the economy, and a dearth of opportunities for meaningful participation in public affairs. As the Uzbek government consolidated political control during the mid-1990s with heavy-handed methods, some government opponents were drawn to Islam as a natural counterforce to the new regime. Seeing this development as a threat, the Uzbek government identified Islam with the political opposition and began a series of campaigns aimed at isolating and neutralizing opponents of the regime by branding them as criminals, Islamic political fanatics and terrorists. The counterinsurgency campaign cast a wide net, ensnaring both the regime's legitimate and illegitimate opponents alike.

The situation in Uzbekistan changed dramatically following the September 11 terrorist attacks on the United States. The American response led to the formation of an international coalition to remove the Taliban from power. The realignment of strategic purpose in the region brought Uzbekistan's foreign policy closely into sync with the strategic policies of the United States in the region. This new coalition fundamentally altered Uzbekistan's role in international affairs. Central Asia, with Uzbekistan at its center, once again became a hotly contested area, a "Great Game" for influence in Asia. The country's prominent role in the U.S. formed international coalition brought Uzbekistan considerable international goodwill within the global diplomatic community. In March 2002, President Karimov met with President George W. Bush in Washington, D.C. and reaffirmed Uzbekistan's commitment to accountable, democratic government, an open economy, and the observance of international standards of civil rights. The year 2002 also witnessed a series of visits to Uzbekistan by high-level diplomatic and military delegations from a number of countries and international organizations, culminating with the visit to Uzbekistan by United Nations Secretary General Kofi Annan in October. Uzbekistan's political reform strategy clearly had acquired an international dimension to complement the domestic. The Uzbek government's increasing emphasis on the importance of conforming to international standards of practice created rising expectations for substantive change.

Conclusions

This survey of the structural reform policies pursued by the Central Asia republics since independence leads to a few general conclusions about the process of reform, and the role of deliberate government strategies in promoting it. The success in economic reforms has not been uniform, but it has been notable and in some countries, particularly Kazakhstan, significant. Economic reform strategies are never purely economic in the sense that they always entail some political consequences. Every reform strategy has a political aspect.

Reform is not free of risk. One of the most significant consequences of the disintegration of communism was the steep decline in government revenues. Since independence the new leaders of the post-communist states have faced rising public expectations and declining financial resources. Even those reform-oriented leaders who sought to conduct real reforms found financing reform to be more challenging than expected. Financing reform, in fact, may be the single most difficult task confronting the political leader in any country undertaking post-communist transition. To support the changes they favor, political leaders must somehow mobilize resources, and this usually entails winning supporters and neutralizing opponents. The experience of the Central Asian states illustrates the myriad compromises involved in carrying out economic and political reforms.

Notes

[1] See Beverly Crawford, ed., *Markets, States, and Democracy: The Political Economy of Post-Communist Transformation* (Boulder: Westview Press, 1995); Richard Pomfret, *The Economies of Central Asia* (Princeton: Princeton University Press, 1995 NJ); and Roald Z. Sagdeev and Susan Eisenhower, eds., *Central Asia: Conflict, Resolution and Change* (Chevy Chase: CPSS Press, 1995).

[2] Janos Kornai, *The Socialist State: The Political Economy of Communism* (Princeton: Princeton University Press, 1992).

[3] Strategy is defined here as way in which ends are brought into line with means.

[4] Nursultan Nazarbaev, now president of Kazakhstan, is the former first secretary of the Kazakh republic communist party organization. Islam Karimov, now president of Uzbekistan, is the former first secretary of the Uzbek republic communist party organization. Saparmurat Niyazov, now president of Turkmenistan, is the former first secretary of the Turkmen republic communist party organization. Imomali Rakhmonov, now president of Tajikistan, is a former Kuliab region communist party official. His predecessor as president, Rakhmon Nabiev (who died under mysterious circumstances in May 1993), was the former first secretary of the Tajik republic communist party organization. Among the Central Asian leaders, only the president of Kyrgyzstan, Askar Akaev, did not belong to the former party *nomenklatura,* although in some respects even Akaev, a physicist who was trained in Leningrad, can be considered a member of the Soviet intellectual elite.

[5] Freedom House is an international philanthropic research organization established in 1937 by Eleanor Roosevelt. It has grown to become one of the world's most respected research organizations on subjects of human rights and governance standards.

[6] The Freedom House Annual Surveys measure progress toward democratic ideals on a seven-point scale for political rights and for civil liberties (with 1 representing the most free and 7 the least free). Changes in countries' scores from year to year are monitored via annual surveys. The political rights measurement addresses the degree of free and fair elections, competitive political parties, opposition with an important role and power, freedom from domination by a powerful group (e.g. military, foreign power, totalitarian parties), and participation by minority groups. The civil liberties measurement addresses the degree to which there is a free and independent media; freedom of discussion, assembly and demonstration; freedom of political organization; equality under the law; protection from political terror, unjustified imprisonment and torture; free trade unions, professional and private organizations; freedom of religion; personal social freedoms; equality of opportunity; and freedom from extreme government corruption.

[7] The basic axioms of the Westphalian international system, following Grotius (1583-1645), assert that all states enjoy national sovereignty, sovereign equality, territorial integrity, and the right of non-interference in domestic affairs.

[8] Nursultaqn Nazarbaev, *Kazakhstan-2030: Prosperity, Security and Ever Growing Welfare of all the Kazakhstanis* (Almaty: Ylim, 1997).

[9] The expression "Kazakhstan government," as opposed to "Kazakh government," is sometimes used to avoid the implication of ethnicity. While ethnic Kazakhs make up more than a majority of the country's population, other ethnic groups, including Russians, Ukrainians, Koreans, and many others, also make up the country's citizenry. To use the term Kazakh government, some observers contend, implies a "government of Kazakhs." One convention that has been adopted to avoid this problem is to refer to the "Kazakhstani government." This expression does seem to imply generality and thus refers to the "government of Kazakhstan citizens." However, the Kazakh language is a Turkic language, and the "ani" suffix is Persian in origin, not Turkic. Persian is not spoken in Kazakhstan. The expression, therefore, does not represent an indigenous form. In this chapter, for the sake of simplicity, I simply refer to the governments by the national names. I intend no ethnic exclusiveness with this convention.

[10] Sally N. Cummings, *Kazakhstan: Centre-Periphery Relations* (London: The Royal Institute of International Affairs, 2000).

[11] One celebrated critique appears in the work of the former Chief Economist of the World Bank who came to see the international financial institutions' policies as counterproductive. See Joseph Stiglitz, *Globalization and its Discontents* (New York: W. W. Norton, 2002).

[12] Population Reference Bureau 2001 World Population Data Sheet. Available on-line at www. prb.org.

[13] Assessment materials on civil and human rights are drawn from the annual and periodic reports produced by Amnesty International, Freedom House, Human Rights Watch, and from the annual Country Reports on Human Rights Practices issued by the U.S. Department of State. See in particular the annual compilation on human and civil rights in post-communist countries, *Nations in Transit*. *Nations in Transit* appears annually under the editorship of Alexander J. Motyl, Arch Puddington, and Amanda Schnetzer and is published by Longman Publishers.

[14] See the Governance Research Indicators Dataset maintained by the Governance Group at the World Bank Institute. These indicators are available on the internet at the World Bank's site (www. worldbank.org).

[15] International Monetary Fund, "Republic of Tajikistan: Recent Economic Developments," *IMF Staff Country Report* no. 00/27 (March 2000), 50.

[16] "UNHCR Report on Tajikistan," "January 1993-March 1996"; United Nations High Commissioner on Refugees, May 1996, 4. Also *see* "Return to Tajikistan, Continued Regional and Ethnic Tensions," *Human Rights Watch/Helsinki* (HRW/H), 7, no. 9, (May 1995), 4-7.

[17] The ranking in the Human Development Index of the *UN Human Development Report* in 1997 was 115; in 1998 it was 118. Tajikistan rose in the 1999 HDI rank to 108. The 2000 HDI ranking was 110.

[18] IMF, "Republic of Tajikistan—Recent Economic Developments," IMF Staff Country Reports no. 96/55 (July 8, 1996).

[19] IMF, "Republic of Tajikistan—Recent Economic Developments," IMF Staff Country Reports no. 98/16 (February 11, 1998).

[20] Tax offsets occur when enterprises that supply the government with goods and services are not paid in cash but in compensating reductions of tax payments. Non-monetized transactions are more likely to lack transparency than cash transactions.

[21] See *Attacks on the Press in 1999* (New York: The Committee to Protect Journalists (CPJ), 2000).

[22] Population Reference Bureau, "2001 World Population Data Sheet." Available on-line at www.prb.org.

[23] Governance Research Indicators Dataset maintained by the Governance Group at the World Bank Institute (<www.worldbank.org>).

[24] Although official accounts are contradictory, the Turkmenistan government has claimed that four former government ministers organized an armed attack on the Turkmen president on November 25, 2002. A group of gunmen were said to have fired shots at the President's motorcade after a truck blocked the path of the president's car. The following day, the Turkmenistan government claimed to have arrested 16 people in connection with the assassination attempt. On December 2, the General Prosecutor, Gurbanbibi Atajanova, announced that 23 people had been arrested for involvement in the coup attempt. According to Atajanova, the government discovered proof that former Foreign Minister Boris Shikhmuradov masterminded the assassination plot from Russia in order to take political power himself. On December 18, Atajanova provided a public report on Turkmenistan national television in which she detailed a sequence of events and claimed that Boris Shikhmuradov directed the assassination attempt from inside Turkmenistan. She further claimed he had entered the country November 23, from Uzbekistan, with the help of the Uzbek Ambassador to Turkmenistan, Abdurashid Kadyrov. The report claimed that Shikhmuradov, together with other conspirators, remained in hiding in the Uzbek Embassy until December 7. On December 24, a website under the direction of Shikhmuradov issued a statement which claimed that Shikhmuradov had been in Turkmenistan since September 2002. On December 25, Turkmen President Niyazov announced that Boris Shikhmuradov had been captured. Four days later, Turkmen national television aired footage of Shikhmuradov in a purported confession admitting to masterminding the assassination attempt. A chilling account of these events is available in Emmanuel Decaux, "OSCE Rapporteur's Report on Turkmenistan," OSCE Office for Democratic Institutions and Human Rights (March 12, 2003).

[25] Population Reference Bureau, "2001 World Population Data Sheet." Available on-line at www.prb.org.

[26] See the Governance Research Indicators Dataset maintained by the Governance Group at the World Bank Institute. These indicators are available on the internet at the World Bank site (<www.worldbank.org>).

Chapter 4

Legal Reform in Central Asia: Battling the Influence of History

Roger D. Kangas

For much of the past decade, discussions of legal reform in Central Asia have been couched in terms of "Soviet-era versus Western approaches" with respect to how laws are codified and how improvements might be made. More fundamental to the current debates and the problems facing the Central Asian states in the twenty-first century is the influence of pre-Soviet tradition on the contemporary legal environment.[1] Specifically, the region must resolve the contradiction inherent in the impersonal nature of codified law, and the fluid, personal aspect of the current power relationships that reflect long-held traditions in the region.

Lack of true reform in countries such as Turkmenistan and Kazakhstan has created relatively high levels of mistrust, doubt, and concern among the respective populations, thus weakening the ability of states to carry out their constitutional and legal duties. This was a problem that faced great unifiers of the past, such as Tamerlane.[2] The notion of creating a strong state structure and a concurrent legal environment was of utmost importance to this medieval leader of Central Asia. His contemporary counterparts face similar problems. Adherence to the law, as such, is tainted by mistrust among the general population and capricious violations by those supposedly charged with enforcing it.

This chapter is an effort to assess the developmental level of legal regimes in the five Central Asian states. When discussing such broad notions as legal reform, one must be mindful of defining terms. In this instance, the focus will be on the notion of rule of law, which can be defined as the ability to abide by an external, abstract set of norms that allow members of a society to co-exist. When there are disputes, the parties involved seek solutions through a mechanism framed by these very norms. The empirical evaluation of constitutions, legal and criminal codes, and the ability of law enforcement agencies to abide by such measures are fundamental.[3] In evaluating the legal aspect of the Central Asian states, the basic developments of these concepts in Central Asian society will be outlined. With independence, the Central Asian governments had to quickly create their own structures, the products of which were largely follow-on measures from the previous era. However, in the past decade some changes of note have occurred, providing a modest base for comparison of the respective developmental paths of the five Central Asian states. Finally, the current challenges to true legal reform in the region will be assessed and the efforts of foreign assistance measures designed to address these concerns outlined. While the governments of Central Asia have been self-congratulatory in their own assessments of legal reform at home, the reality appears to be different.

Legal Antecedents

Central Asia has had a long history of legalism and legal studies. Documents and books showing early efforts at creating rule of law are often on display in national museums in Central Asia.[4] Unfortunately, intertwined with the tradition of legal scholarship in the region are the results of despotism that prevailed for the past half-millennium. It was often the case that rather complex legal codes repeatedly were flaunted by ruling houses or dynasties at various times. This tension between "rule of law" and the absolute authority of the ruler is key to understanding legal traditions in Central Asia.

Given the rich history of the region, it is no surprise to find many layers of legal structures, political entities, and the interpretative framework for them. These influences have been both positive and negative, and reflect the tension between the need to standardize law and the ability of leaders to assert their own authority. While this tension parallels events in Europe throughout the past two millennia, unique aspects of the Central Asian environment ensured that the outcome would be different. Moreover, these differences themselves are often difficult for outsiders to fully understand, as they reflect cultural patterns specific to the region. These developments have been visible in both the pre-Russian and Russian/ Soviet eras, which have provided their own lasting legacies to Central Asian legal thought.

The Pre-Russian Legacy

It is impossible to assess thoroughly the pre-Russian legal tradition in Central Asia in a few pages. However, several key points can be stressed, as noted by past works on this subject.[5] One can point to four specific waves of influence in the pre-Russian era: Islamic, Mongol, Timurid and Emirate/Khanate. Each of these periods created potential frameworks for legal discourse and action, but at the same time gave significant latitude to the ruling elite and, ultimately, the leader.

Islamic

First of all, in accounts of pre-Soviet Central Asia, a strong emphasis on the role of Islam is present in the creation of political and societal relationships. The adherence to the Muslim faith was, and remains, the cornerstone of interpersonal interaction. Law, as a system of governance, was rooted in the Islamic tradition introduced to the region as early as the late-600s A.D., but really took root when the region was consolidated a century later. Unlike past invaders, the Muslim forces of the eighth and ninth centuries sought to do more than simply conquer territory. As an example, when Alexander the Great traveled through Central Asia in the third century B.C. and subdued regional potentates, his goal was to pacify the region for territorial and financial gain, before proceeding to the next target of opportunity. He did not consider instilling new legal codes or frameworks within the region.[6] In contrast, the Islamic invasion of the eighth century A.D. involved the actual conversion of communities and the total restructuring of belief and fealty systems. As happened in other territories conquered by Muslim armies, there was a fundamental understanding that Islam as a way of life would dominate, replacing what existed prior to its arrival.[7]

From a legal perspective, the central element of Islamic tradition in the region was Shari'at law. Based upon a mix of sources, such as the Qu'ran, hadith and subsequent documents, Shari'at law was, and remains, an evolving concept.[8] Indeed, over the centuries, differences of interpretation within the Muslim community have arisen. Such law was critical in the settled regions of Bukhara, Khiva and other oases communities, as these were more regulated than nomadic regions. Bukhara and Samarkand, in particular, became centers of Islamic jurisprudence and learning for the entire Muslim world in the tenth and eleventh centuries. What was created in these cities eventually was applied to the surrounding region. However, as time passed, these cities represented a much more conservative and unreformed interpretation of Islam, especially as Central Asia was cut off from most of the Sunni Muslim world by the sixteenth century.[9]

The above sequence of events was particularly important to the settled regions of Central Asia. In contrast, the nomadic communities in Central Asia, while incorporating some aspects of Islamic law into their legal codes, also relied heavily on existing traditional measures. Called by different names, such practices often were honed to reflect the specific needs and communal priorities of a given group. The most common term used was Adat, which is often called customary law. Adat was regulated through precedent and past practices.[10] Moreover, it took into account differences between tribal and clan grouping, with the variations found among Kazakh, Uighur, Kyrgyz and Turkmen clans. Power of arbitration often rested in the hands of a particular individual (the bey among the Kazakhs, for example).

Overall, the Islamic influence created a framework for Central Asia within which legal issues could be evaluated and discussed. It also linked the region to the broader, outside world and afforded legitimacy to the ruling elite. After all, if this elite could structure its authority under the auspices of Islam, the population could not legitimately seek an alternative form of government. The significance of Islam was thus profound: It offered both a way in which people could interact within society and also provided justifications for the form of government that dominated the region.

Mongol

The thirteenth century saw the introduction of the Mongolian public administrative system, the longer-lasting influence of the invasion and conquest by the armies of Genghis Khan.[11] The great Khan introduced to the region a form of public administration that permitted a rather thin layer of Mongolian, Turkic and Chinese bureaucrats to rule over vast swaths of territory. For the next two centuries, the Mongol empire gradually broke up into a number of sub-regions, with Central Asia falling under the authority of Genghis Khan's son Chaghatai. The Chaghatai dynasty ruled Central Asia until the beginning of the fifteenth century.[12]

During this period, the basic concepts of Islamic jurisprudence survived, but were subsumed under Mongol law. The reality of having such a far-reaching empire meant that at local levels, autonomy was allowed. As long as the subjects in the region paid their taxes and supported the larger empire at specific times, they were left alone. The Mongols were the first major empire in the region where the center of power was a significant distance away from Central Asia, and thus required the employment of indigenous bureaucrats and lawgivers. Ultimately, this proved to be the undoing of Mongol control over Central Asia.

Timurid

The collapse of the Mongol empire's hold over Central Asia in the fifteenth century was due primarily to the rise of Tamerlane also known as Timur the Lame.[13] The historic significance of this period is less a case of how the legal framework changed, as to how its legitimacy was articulated. For the most part, the Timurids adopted the same structure as their predecessors. The successive reigns of Shah Rukh and Ulugh Beg saw a greater emphasis on reinforcing Islamic precepts into the legal framework.

Perhaps more important was that legal authority was indigenous and not dependent upon an outside power. For the first time in almost 700 years, the seat of power and the cultural roots of authority were from Central Asia itself. Interestingly, the Timurid dynasty exemplified the same caprice and omnipotent power that previous leaders had.[14] This was because there remained the strong belief that the ruler was above the law, and that the personal qualities of Central Asian leadership were paramount. However, even today's scholars note that this shift of legal authority from an outside source to a local one was a critical step forward for legal developments in the region. Though the Timurid period is often cast as one mired in violence and expansion, the very survival of the state depended on a cohesive legal regime.

Khanate/Emirate

Barely 100 years later, the unified, Timurid political system came crashing down. The armies of Shaybani Khan sacked the key cities of Samarkand and Bukhara and drove the Timurid dynasty out of the region. Babur, who was the ruler at the time, eventually re-established his authority in the South Asian subcontinent, founding what was to become the Moghul dynasty. Within Central Asia, Shaybani Khan was unable to solidify his authority over the entire region, and competing political entities soon emerged. Thus began an era of fragmented Khanates and Emirates in Central Asia.[15]

With the demise of any unifying force, rule of law also was fragmented. Dynastic leaders ruled the key political entities in Central Asia. Writers and poets of the succeeding centuries noted, often with despair, the lawlessness that prevailed across the region.[16] Indeed, intellectuals from Bukhara found reason to criticize the form of government in the state, hoping to reform the system to reflect a more legally sound system. This was particularly true in the late-nineteenth century, when the rulers of the Emirate of Bukhara were Muzaffar al-Din and Abd al-Ahad.[17] In short, while a written and precedent-based tradition of rule of law in Central Asia existed prior to the Russian conquest, it remained at odds with the political reality of the time. Ultimately, law became a mere shell for despotic rule.

The Jadidist movement exemplified the pressure for political and legal reform in Bukhara and Khiva. Much has been written on the competing reform agendas of the Jadids.[18] Even the more conservative members of this movement advocated a change in the current legal regime in the protectorates. Whether it was a return to traditional Shari'a law or the introduction of Western (Russian) law, the consensus view was that the very nature of political power in the region was an impediment to order and progress. Because of the absolute authority of the Emir of Bukhara and Khan of Khiva, such reform efforts ultimately failed. Consequently, up through the Russian Revolutions of 1917, the legal reformers of Central Asia often remained in exile.

Russian and Soviet-era Law

For the present-day regimes in Central Asia, the Russian and Soviet eras hold special significance. The existing legal structures in the region are products of what transpired during this period, as is the current generation of political officials and legal experts. The institutional arrangements that developed were at odds with the traditional notions of law cited earlier, but in numerous instances, one finds a merger of such concepts and an accommodation of traditional forms of authority within the new Russian, and then Soviet, legal regime.

Imperial Russia

The territories fully incorporated in the Russian Empire saw a more forceful introduction of Russian law. The protectorates of Bukhara and Khiva, on the other hand, were able to rely on their own traditions. From the Russian perspective, the feeling was that Russian law was superior to local custom and law; however, the general policy allowed local law to exist in certain cases.[19] As Russian political structures were established in the region—particularly in the area of today's Kazakhstan, Kyrgyz Republic, and parts of northern Uzbekistan—the Russian overlords had to decide the extent to which local law would prevail. These regions, designated

Turkestan and Transcaspia, saw the development of Russian law not only for Russian subjects, but also for the indigenous population.

The application of law was always a challenge, as noted by evaluations coming from St. Petersburg. In the 1880s and again in the early 1900s, commissions were sent from St. Petersburg to evaluate the colonial rule in the region. For example, the Giers Commission of 1882 focused on how effective public administration could develop where there was a dearth of qualified officials and a lack of proper funding.[20] Most critically assessed was the notion that bureaucrats resorted to relying on traditional, and often corrupt, forms of governance.

Bukhara and Khiva, the two remaining protectorates, remained stagnant in their own personality-based systems.[21] The frustration experienced by reform-minded individuals in these territories prompted some to find common cause with various revolutionary and reformist groups in Russia itself, including the radical Bolshevik faction of the Russian Social Democratic and Labor Party—the precursor to the Communist Party of the Soviet Union (CPSU).[22] Thus, ironically, the Jadidist reformers came to the conclusion that external assistance would most likely be required to enact change in their countries—and they sought assistance from groups that would eventually result in their downfall.[23] Naturally, there were critical debates within the reformist community and a significant number did not side with the Bolsheviks, either joining the local insurgencies[24] against the Red Army or simply emigrating.

The Soviet Period

The Soviet era actually began with a nod towards local custom. It was not until the mid-1920s that various diktats were announced which folded local courts and juridical proceedings into the Soviet experience.[25] By the 1930s, the Central Asia region was under Soviet control, although this continued to be a struggle for Soviet officials in the ensuing decades. The tension between trying to enforce objective legal codes and the reality of personal rule continued through this period, often with tragic results. Soviet publications and contemporary studies are replete with accounts of how the Soviet government tried to quickly institute their own legal norms in the region. From the initial "unveiling" campaign in the 1920s, which advocated that women should remove their traditional veils as a sign of modernity, to the legal restrictions placed on Islamic organizations, the Soviet leaders sought to radically transform the concept of law in Central Asia.[26]

In the beginning, the Soviet leaders were keen to introduce law as a form of social engineering and development. As noted by Peter Solomon in his work on Soviet law, the ramifications were legion. Law played several key roles: it was an explanation of socialist legality, it possessed an educational function, and it legitimized the new economic system that was being put in place. It was imperative to ensure that the population understood how and why the centrally planned economic system was necessary. Indeed, economic crimes were often considered more severe than crimes of violence, with a greater share of capital punishment decisions made for embezzlement, forgery and bribery.[27]

While varying in practical importance, "socialist law and order" (*sotsialisticheskaya zakonnost' i pravoporiadok*) was the defining framework during most of the Soviet period. During the 1920s and 1930s, Stalin flaunted these laws and the notion that a legal structure was in place seemed dubious at best. The arbitrary nature of the Great Purge has been well documented, and it was the object of Soviet legal reform in the 1950s and 1960s, when there was an attempt to return to "Soviet law." Central Asia experienced all of these shifts within the Soviet system. In reaction to the Stalinist era, the emphases on institutions and frameworks were critical to the Soviet leaders. For example, in 1987, the CPSU Central Committee adopted a resolution entitled "On Measures to Increase the Role of the Prosecutor's Oversight in Strengthening Socialist Legality and Law and Order." Such cumbersome measures were designed to specify how the Procuracy, for example, could carry out its duties.[28]

Because of its subservient place in the Soviet Union, Central Asia did not become a source of reform or opposition. For the most part it was a passive participant in these discussions—with one important exception. During the Brezhnev era, there was a return to the sort of administrative policies that existed during the Mongol and Imperial Russian periods— one of demanding fealty and loyalty from the region while simultaneously leaving the internal workings of the region to the devices of the local leaders.[29] Up through the Gorbachev reforms of the 1980s, there were varying interpretations of the extent to which this *de facto* autonomy existed.

Contrast of Traditional and Soviet Structures

It was the emphasis on institutions and structures within the Soviet system that created problems for the Central Asians. Ultimately, the role of personalities remained important in Central Asia, in spite of measures adopted during the Soviet period. Highlighting the problems on Soviet law in the region was the "Cotton Scandal" of the 1980s, often referred to as the "Uzbek Affairs." In it, Soviet investigators uncovered a widespread corruption network in the Central Asian republic of Uzbekistan that involved government officials fabricating cotton production figures. By recording higher-than-actual numbers for cotton harvests, extra income was provided to local officials. Scores of top officials in the Uzbek S.S.R. were indicted, tried and punished for a range of economic crimes centering around the misrepresentation of data on annual cotton harvests. Indeed, First Secretary of the Uzbek Communist Party, Sharaf Rashidov, was suspected of being the key figure in this scandal, but his death in November 1983 pre-empted any trial or serious investigation.[30] However, the long-term damage of this event was that it pitted the Russian perception of local adherence to law (or the lack thereof) with the Uzbek feeling that law was really a tool of the Russians to repress the local community.[31]

The Gorbachev reform agenda further exacerbated tensions in the region vis-à-vis Moscow. Not only did Gorbachev replace key leaders in the republics, but he also stressed the need to combat lawlessness and corruption in Central Asia. Indeed, the stereotype within the Soviet Union of Central Asians as being lazy and corrupt had fallen to a new low. The legacy of the cotton scandal and Russian view of the archaic clan relations that permeated the systems in the region only worsened the situation.[32] Limited attempts were made in 1989 and 1990 to reform the entire Soviet legal framework, divorcing it from communist ideology. However, any lasting impact was cut short as a result of the dissolution of the Soviet Union in 1991.

At the time of independence, the Central Asian states found themselves in difficult situations with respect to the legal regimes in the newly created countries. Previously, legislation had been dictated from the central government, with such efforts not being trusted. Now, the burden was on the new national governments to establish order. But serious questions faced these states: Should there be a return to past legal frameworks? Did this require a reconsideration of Islamic law? How did one factor in traditional custom, or even the historic legacies of individuals such as Tamerlane? These questions became the subject of discussion and debate within the region and among Western scholars, shaping the understanding of legal reform in Central Asia. As will be seen, each state approached these questions with great trepidation and concern, mainly as there was a sense that too much reform could lead to political and social instability.

Respective Frameworks of Legal Regimes in Central Asia

Common to all five Central Asian states was the suddenness of in-dependence. Initial legal structures were often replications of the existing Soviet models. When reforms along Western lines were introduced, one saw slight divergence from the foundations of socialist legalism. However, the extent to which these new legal norms were adopted varied, often with a gap between what was on paper and what took place in practice. In the past decade, all five countries of Central Asia have introduced distinct structures, such as constitutions, legal codes and procedures for law en-forcement agencies. At the same time, there are difficult challenges, includ-ing the forms of leadership, corruption and an inability or lack of desire by officials to actually enforce these very codes. Not surprisingly, the extent to which a given country has been able to develop legal reforms depends upon a number of internal dynamics.

Kazakhstan

Communist Party of Kazakhstan First Secretary Nursultan Naz-arbaev assumed the position of "President of the Kazakh S.S.R." in the waning months of the Soviet Union and has remained in office ever since. An erstwhile supporter of Gorbachev's reform agenda in the 1980s, Nazarbaev took on the public persona of a reformer himself.[33] As a result, there was a flurry of legislation in the early-1990s that suggested a real ef-fort to transition from an authoritarian communist party system to one based on rule of law.[34] He presented an initial constitution in 1993 and electoral laws in 1994 that supported a more vibrant notion of political pluralism. These provided a template for diversifying power and author-ity within the Kazakhstani political and legal system. Indeed, the electoral laws may have been too successful, for the legislature began to challenge Nazarbaev's reform measures and sought to introduce their own.

By 1995, it was clear that the country was not developing into a de-mocracy. The constitution had been re-written and extensive legislative re-form was enacted in that year under the auspices of correcting potentially corruptive rules and regulations. In addition, the constitutional reform was carried out in order to minimize the importance of the legislature, which could have developed as a base of opposition to the president.[35] To his critics, it was obvious that Nazarbaev passed criminal codes directed against his opponents and created legal support for maintaining his tenure in office.

Eventually, attention was directed at a broader range of legal issues. The 1997 criminal code currently sets the framework for legal actions in the country.[36] For the most part, it remains a hybrid document, including some of the Soviet-era rights and responsibilities, as well as new concepts introduced from Western advisors and programs. These include the rights of citizens, criminal procedures, the rights of the detained, and other basic measures. Questions continue to arise as to how these are to be enforced. Either the wording is sufficiently vague, or the responsibilities of law enforcement agencies are simply not spelled out. Perhaps most troubling from a structural perspective is that the legal system is exclusively an executive branch prerogative. The Interior Ministry, which houses the police and security forces, is responsible for upholding the law. On occasion, these forces are unaware of legislative changes and ignore acts by the legislature. Law enforcement officials continually stress that they do not have the resources sufficient to fight real corruption and crime. When one sees police officials signaling cars for inspection at major intersections in Almaty in order to extort money from the motorists, it is clear that corruption hits at all levels of the law enforcement community.[37]

In addition to these structural challenges, other problems remain. While a legal regime exists in the country, the personal rule of President Nazarbaev remains paramount, and he has repeatedly used the legal system to undermine his political opposition. The apogee of these attacks came in 2001, when former Prime Minister Akezhan Kazhegeldin was tried in absentia for crimes ranging from corruption to abuse of power. Another individual who was targeted in recent years is the former Akim (Governor) of Pavlodar Oblast, Galymzhan Jakianov. Charged and convicted on corruption charges in 2002, Jakianov had reportedly challenged Nazarbaev on a number of procedural issues, specifically that Akims should be directly elected and not appointed by the President.[38]

In sum, legal reform in Kazakhstan is at a crossroads. After an initial flurry of activity and a de-Sovietization of the legal language, it is still difficult to conclude that the country has a strong sense of rule of law. Arbitrary enforcement, irregular funding of police and a leadership system that encourages the outright flaunting of the law by top officials underscore the range of problems that still confront Kazakhstan. That these issues are at least being discussed in the country is an indicator that reform is possible; however, recent signs are less than hopeful.

The Kyrgyz Republic

Perhaps the most intriguing case of legal reform in the 1990s was the Kyrgyz Republic. Once cast as a showcase success story for the region, the government of President Askar Akaev received extensive support from international aid organizations and foreign governments to create an island of democracy in Central Asia. For much of the 1990s, foreign analysts continued to support this belief.[39] However, electoral missteps in the late-1990s and a series of attacks on opponents to the president soured this belief.

Compared to the other states in the region, the Kyrgyz Republic does have a more developed sense of rule of law. The Kyrgyz legislature adopted its first post-Soviet constitution in 1993, a document praised by numerous outside organizations and governments as being the most progressive in Central Asia.[40] Citizenship is not restricted by language competency or ethnicity, and basic rights of speech, assembly, religion, movement and even ownership of private property are all noted. It took another five years, but a completely new criminal code has been introduced in the country. Up to that point, a hybrid of Soviet-era and new measures were in place. In the new code, particular attention is paid to what the courts, procurators and law enforcement agencies can and cannot do. For the latter, detailed restrictions on search and seizure, detentions and arrests, and even evidence handling are provided.[41] The new code represents certain innovations that have taken place in the areas of law enforcement and prosecution. The court system that was established is based on a prosecutorial model more in line with European countries than the former Soviet Union.

Similar to the situation in Kazakhstan, the reality is somewhat less encouraging. Ethnic minorities, especially the Uighurs, claim that they are purposefully targeted in police actions. In addition, they complain of unfair practices in employment and advancement in the government sector and in state-owned business. The sense of being second class citizens permeates such groups. Some, such as the Russians, Ukrainians and Germans, have left for their home countries. The government has made gestures to these groups by creating societies that can channel interests in cultural events and educational institutions, but these are often underfunded and poorly supported.[42] Religious groups, in particular, feel pressure directed at them as part of the global war on terrorism. As a result of the actions in Afghanistan following the September 11 attacks in the United States, Kyrgyz officials have stepped up their own measures against suspected terrorist supporters in the country. Not surprisingly, this approach has targeted ethnic minorities and religious-based organizations.

Another noticeable shortcoming in the country's rule of law is that key opposition figures remain subject to harassment. Daniyar Usenov and Feliks Kulov are undoubtedly the most celebrated cases, but other activists are targeted as well. These individuals have voiced their opposition to President Akaev's administration and have questioned the reform measures enacted in the past decade. These figures were not allowed to run in the 2000 presidential election on dubious, technical grounds, thus Akaev avoided a situation where he might not actually continue in office.[43] In fact, President Akaev repeatedly has used the legal system to target opponents and have them declared ineligible to stand for office. In addition, Zamira Eschanova, the editor of *Res Publica*, periodically spends time in jail for her articles criticizing the president, proving the fact that the media has limits, as well.

This emphasis on protecting the reputation of the president underscores an emerging trend in the country: the elevation of the status of Askar Akaev to that of supreme leader. While his authority is perhaps less secure than that of his neighbor, Nazarbaev, it is apparent that Akaev is not above obviating the rule of law to strengthen his position. As he maneuvers through restrictions on running for an additional term in office in 2004, it is likely that he will be declared immune from all prosecution if, or when, he eventually steps down as president.

Uzbekistan

Unlike the governments of Kazakhstan and the Kyrgyz Republic, Uzbekistan was reticent to accept Western assistance in attempting legal reform. Indeed, when the Uzbek constitution was under review for ratification by the *Oliy Majlis* (legislature), an external panel of the American Bar Association was given barely a week to assess, evaluate and make recommendations on the document. The constitution was accepted in December 1992, without including any of their cursory comments. As with the other Central Asian states, the Uzbek constitution lists a range of freedoms: speech, religion, assembly, property ownership, and the like. In an effort to stress the multi-ethnic nature of Uzbek society, the right to express one's national heritage is also enshrined in the constitution.[44]

The current criminal code was enacted in 1994, with several amendments and additions taking place since that time. In 1998, the code was overhauled and the death penalty restricted for certain types of crimes. Further reforms took place in late-2001 and punishments were reduced for many non-violent crimes. Given troubles with the Islamic Movement for Uzbekistan (IMU), Hizb ut-Tahrir and the conflict in Afghanistan, crimes related to acts of terrorism were given high priority, and are currently the only ones permitting capital punishment.[45] In the years after the Afghan campaign, the government has expressed a sense of being under siege.

Structurally, the Uzbek judicial system is quite comprehensive. A Constitutional Court oversees the legality of parliamentary laws and executive decrees, a Supreme Court is the highest court for criminal and civil cases, and a Supreme Economic Court oversees matters such as privatization law, foreign investment and monetary disputes. The court system exists at multiple levels, with local level courts and appellate equivalents at regional and *wiloyat* (state) levels. Ostensibly, one can appeal cases to higher levels, much along the lines of the U.S. court system.[46]

Since independence, Uzbekistan has followed a path of solidifying the power of the executive, creating a rather feeble legislature, and establishing a legal code that is impressive on paper, but has enough loopholes to allow the government to do as it wishes. For example, the president is now above reproach with respect to prosecution, and those who criticize him are subject to investigation and trial. More important, with respect to the rule of law, the president has the ability to override *Oliy Majlis* decisions and circumvent normal legislative procedures if he deems it necessary. Rule by decree has been the norm for much of the past decade.

Perhaps the most common criticisms leveled against the Uzbek notion of rule of law is that it is arbitrary and that law enforcement agencies enact it with varying levels of excess. The government arrested thousands of individuals following the February 1999 bombings in Tashkent, often holding them for weeks and months before pressing charges. Human Rights Watch, a non-governmental organization that focuses on human rights conditions worldwide, has been particularly vocal on Uzbekistan's record. Years after the February bombings, some individuals still remain in custody and have yet to be officially charged. Once an individual is charged, trials have become difficult to monitor and it appears that irregular standards are being used time and again.[47]

The Interior Ministry, which is responsible for the prison system in Uzbekistan, has been accused of being responsible for numerous deaths of prisoners under suspicious circumstances. These prisoners range from individuals suspected of being Islamic extremists to secular political opponents, most of whom find themselves in the Jaslyk prison, located in the far western reaches of the country. More recently, Human Rights Watch reported additional cases of mistreatment and persecution of secular opposition figures.[48]

The problem of Uzbek human rights abuses has been the topic of several protests by foreign Ambassadors to the country, most notably the Ambassadors from the United Kingdom and the United States. Of particular concern has been that Uzbekistan is of strategic importance to the United States. Human rights groups have often said that Uzbekistan is now using this connection to shield its own abusive policies. On the other hand, several amnesties of prisoners have taken place in recent years and it seems that the Uzbek government is being more receptive to the criticisms levied against it by the international community.[49]

As with the Kyrgyz Republic and Kazakhstan, the presidential system of Uzbekistan dominates the country's political process, ultimately affecting the notion of rule of law. As in the other two states, Uzbek leaders tend to act as if personal connections and influence are much more important than impersonal laws. The fact that Uzbekistan was never considered to be a bastion of reform actually might help it in the near future, for unlike in Kazakhstan and the Kyrgyz Republic, the international community still has some interest in seeing if reforms can take place. Indeed, the U.S. government expressed this argument in the early-2000s.

Turkmenistan

Without question, the most dubious legal regime in Central Asia belongs to Turkmenistan. As with the other countries, a constitution and basic legal code were adopted in the first few years. Much of this was a direct regurgitation of the Soviet-era documents, replete with the same flowery verbiage. The reality remains much the same—rule of law is arbitrarily honored and the government itself does not abide by these documents.

The current constitution was ratified in May 1992. Not surprisingly, it harkens to the 1977 Soviet constitution with its emphasis on citizen responsibilities, as opposed to rights. There is the usual listing of rights, such as speech, assembly, religion and press. However, these are limited by Article 19, which notes that they cannot harm the social order and national security. The constitution is also silent on the issue of enforcement of rights. The criminal code finally was modified in June 1997. Like those of its neighbors, Turkmenistan's code notes punishments, procedures and rights.

The court system of Turkmenistan is structurally balanced: Local and regional courts hear criminal and civil cases. Decisions can be appealed to the higher levels, if that level deems the case important enough.

At the highest level is a Supreme Court, which ostensibly only will hear cases of national importance. The president appoints all judges and chairs the Supreme Court. The court system to date has not challenged the constitutionality of any presidential decree or law, nor has it established a strong legacy of legality. Making things more difficult, no independent lawyers currently practice, and the notion of fair legal representation is still wanting.[50]

The Interior Ministry is responsible for enforcing the criminal code. International human rights organizations repeatedly have criticized the means by which police and security forces uphold the law.[51] Human rights violations are legion and the conditions of prisons are considered to be some of the worst in the former Soviet Union. Minority groups and religious organizations, in particular, have experienced the difficult legal environment. For example, the Law on Religious Organizations restricts the way in which faiths can be registered in the country. Given the number of signatures needed, only the Sunni Muslim and Eastern Orthodox faiths are technically legal.[52]

The personalistic rule of President Saparmurat Niyazov means that, ultimately, the caprice of a leader sets the tone for politics and society in Turkmenistan. Individuals who run afoul of the president often are convicted on trumped-up charges. President Niyazov has declared that a fundamental feature of Turkmen law is the adherence to the *Ruhnama*, or "holy book" that he supposedly wrote.[53] It is a collection of sayings and narratives that suggest specific ways in which Turkmen must live. This book, representative of Niyazov's leadership style, discards any form of structure and objectivity.

In short, Turkmenistan represents perhaps the widest gap between rhetoric and practice. However, it is also important to note that international organizations seldom are able to conduct interviews or collect data in the country independent of official Turkmen sources. Thus, it is difficult to gauge the extent to which rule of law issues are actually being addressed within the country's judicial and political systems. At best, anecdotes from exiles or observations from foreigners working in the country are the most reliable information.[54]

Tajikistan

A possible exception to these rather pessimistic case studies is Tajikistan. Mired in a civil war for most of its first six years after independence, Tajikistan has been viewed as a country in perpetual crisis and lawlessness. A number of volumes have been published outlining the course of events that dominated the country between the years of 1992, when the fighting began, and 1997, when a peace accord was signed.[55] To an extent, the government was never able to extend a rule of law to the entire country. Indeed, today pockets of Tajikistan remain effectively outside of the central government's control.[56]

However, an important legal reform development in Tajikistan is the founding document of the National Reconciliation Committee that set the terms of the 1997 peace agreement. In it, the warring sides agreed to abide by certain rules, based on an equitable sharing of political offices in the government. The Constitution of 1994 remains the primary legal document of the country. Again, on paper, the constitution lists a range of individual freedoms and responsibilities. Yet the period of the civil war witnessed countless violations of constitutional authority. A reversal of this trend was, and remains, a key element of the post-war agreement. The criminal code has yet to be significantly reformed and the current structure resembles that of the Soviet period. In short, the notion of "guilty until proven innocent" prevails, and harsh penalties still apply to most levels of crime, including economic crimes, which were often deemed the most severe in the Soviet Union.

Tajik law does prohibit discrimination for ethnic, religious and gender reasons, although this is not always enforced. Uzbek minorities, for example, consistently complain of being left out of the political process. In addition, religious minorities have difficulties in Tajikistan. Jews, Baha'is and Zoroastrians are often relegated to fringe status in the country. Sunni Islam remains paramount in the country with the small Russian minority practicing Eastern Orthodox. In addition to the common problems of arbitrary enforcement and government caprice, regional and local warlords periodically use their own form of frontier justice. Every year, rival clans murder scores of officials and businessmen. This form of frontier justice is particularly problematic in the outlying regions, especially the Badakhshon region.[57]

Following the example of the other four presidents, Imomali Rakhmonov also has created conditions where ultimately he will be immune to any future prosecution if he steps down from office. Still, the focus on the leader does not exist as strongly in Tajikistan as it does in, say, Turkmenistan. However, it is clear that individual personalities and familiar relationships dominate the political process in Tajikistan. Moreover, the groups excluded from this inner circle, such as the Uzbeks of Sogd wiloyat, find themselves unprotected in the legal system.

Basic Dilemmas and Reform Efforts

To varying degrees, all five Central Asian states face the conundrum of trying to establish viable legal systems. At the same time, the respective presidents are reluctant to give up their power and actually abide by "rule of law" principles. These challenges have been the focus on international assistance programs, the success of which is dependent upon how diligently the countries accept and implement reform.

Challenges

Corruption

Without question, corruption is deemed critical in Kazakhstan and the Kyrgyz Republic, according to public opinion polls. One would suspect that such views are held in the other three states of the region, although full, clear surveys on the situation are not forthcoming. As opposed to notions of episodic corruption in the respective states, corruption in Central Asia is seen as being systemic.[58] While much of what is known about corruption in Central Asia is based on a few studies and anecdotal evidence, they shed light on the general problem throughout the region.[59]

Not surprisingly, the effect of corruption on the legal system is profound. To ensure judgment, payments must be made. Judges are poorly and irregularly paid, and often are swayed by much-needed financial gain in their decision-making. Likewise, defense attorneys require fees beyond their salary, and even investigative police require some form of bribery. Studies by Transparency International and Freedom House indicate that such corruption exists in all five Central Asian states.[60] However, because of access problems, it is not surprising that the only detailed studies have taken place in Kazakhstan and the Kyrgyz Republic.[61]

Ultimately, this type of corruption erodes the moral foundation of the legal system and precludes citizens from truly respecting the judicial process. This lack of confidence means that citizens often go to alternative sources of justice, including tribal and clan leaders or even the mafia and other criminal elements. The former only reinforces traditional modes of authority while the latter perpetuates a lack of adherence to the law.

Retribution

The legal system in each of the countries has been used to punish political opposition, often on spurious charges. In Kazakhstan, political opponents of Nazarbaev, such as Akezhan Kazhegeldin, have been brought up on charges of corruption. The same can be said for Abdy Kuliev in Turkmenistan, Feliks Kulov in the Kyrgyz Republic, and Shukhrullo

Mirsaidov in Uzbekistan. In Uzbekistan, such charges also befall regional hakims and other subordinates of Karimov, when they're deemed to be getting too powerful. The Cabinet of Ministers today is a collection of survivors of these periodic, but not fatal, purges. In Kazakhstan, even a family figure has been recently charged with corruption: The previously mentioned Zhakianov, who was the Hakim of Pavlodar Oblast, is a relative of Nazarbaev's wife.

Nowhere is the legal system used with such caprice as in Turkmenistan. For many years, President Niyazov has used the legal system to charge his opponents and subordinates who are acquiring too much power with various crimes to remove them from possible opposition. It is rare for top officials to remain in the same office for more than a year, and in the past three years, the president has completely re-staffed his cabinet on several occasions. The November 2002 assassination attempt was yet another pretext for reshuffling individuals in the power ministries.[62] It is interesting to note that these charges, particularly the ones that deal with abuse of office or corruption, are probably grounded in reality. However, the arbitrary nature of filing charges against some corrupt *hakims* while letting another equally corrupt official go free is what many find disturbing. Indeed, all of the problems previously noted are accentuated when retribution against actual forms of corruption are unevenly applied.

Retribution is not only directed against political figures. In addition to the case of Zamira Eschanova in the Kyrgyz Republic, the political leaders have targeted other journalists. In October 2002, Sergei Duvanov, a journalist from Kazakhstan, was charged with sexual crimes. That he was about to embark on a speaking tour of the United States and Europe to discuss the state of the media in Kazakhstan was most likely more than a coincidence; previously, he had written negative articles about the Nazarbaev family.[63] In general, due to such potential threats, journalists in the region tend to censor themselves and avoid such confrontations.

Transparency

Another factor is transparency, which is defined for this context as the ability to clearly see and evaluate the decision-making process in the legal system. In short, a transparent process is one in which there is an openly-understood logic, devoid of back-room deals and capriciousness. According to the non-governmental organization Transparency International, the states of Central Asia fare poorly in this respect. In recent reports where the states have been mentioned, their rankings are abysmal and charges of systemic corruption are rife. Besides these external evaluations, anecdotal evidence from citizens and officials in the region indicate that this is a key concern for domestic stability and ultimately, regional security. Uncertainty plays a large part in the legal system and corrodes any confidence that citizens of the Central Asian countries have in a reform agenda.

This situation parallels that of the Khanate period in Central Asian history, as well as the Soviet era. The difference today is that foreign investment was not a factor during those times. Indeed, besides eroding the public confidence in the legal code, the impact on foreign investment must be noted. According to a number of impartial reports, the business climate in all five Central Asian states is abysmal, at best, for potential investors—unless they are the major corporations in the energy sector. The basic rule of thumb is that all discussions that are looked on favorably at the presidential level are most likely going to succeed.[64] However, those that have to deal with the ministries and bureaucracies of the region more often than not fail. In the long run, the reality of an unstable business environment may be the most harmful effect of the lack of effective legal systems in Central Asia.[65]

Efforts at Reform

The question that remains, in light of this rather pessimistic appraisal, is what can be done? Indeed, legal professionals have been working for over a decade to rectify the current situation and infuse a more rigorous adherence to law. Surprisingly, there have been internal efforts as well, although these tend to be adversely affected by financial constraints. In Kazakhstan and the Kyrgyz Republic, independent lawyers have established their own associations. In Uzbekistan, a similar effort is underway for defense attorneys. Because the legal professions in each of these states had been state-run for much of the past century, the level of independence remains rather low. In addition, human rights organizations within the countries have attempted to register in order to open up offices within the respective countries, with a recent success being the legalization of the Human Rights Society of Uzbekistan in 2002. It is hoped that if such offices do open—whether for international or country-based groups—they will provide the impetus for governments to be more transparent in the legal reform process.

The key obstacles for reform efforts, as noted, are financial and structural. In both areas, international organizations have played key roles. Initially, groups such as the American Bar Association provided expert advice on the drafting of legal codes and constitutions. However, the problem has been that with each re-write of constitutions, power becomes more centralized and obstacles for opposition groups greater. Indeed, advice offered by outside observers has largely been ignored.

In other areas, success has been greater. The American Bar Association continues to support one of the earliest efforts to aid the legal system in Central Asia: the Central and East European Law Initiative (CEELI) Project. Working with lawyers in the region, CEELI lawyers and staff members conduct analyses of draft laws and civil codes, as well as train the newly-emerging cadre of lawyers within these countries. Initiated in all states, CEELI remains active in Kazakhstan, Uzbekistan and the Kyrgyz republic.[66] Other non-governmental organizations are also engaged in the region, offering their services to governments and non-governmental associations alike.

Because the obstacles noted above adversely affect the economic and business climate in Central Asia, the World Bank has remained engaged in the reform process. This international financial institution is devoting resources to stabilizing the legal regimes in the countries, so as to promote a more active investment climate. In addition, transparency is a central theme in recent Bank reports, which note the trend towards limited improvements in Kazakhstan and the Kyrgyz Republic, with more serious shortcomings in Uzbekistan.[67] As one example, the World Bank is initiating a legal reform project in Kazakhstan that has a budget of up to $18.5 million.

This compliments an initiative by the European Bank of Reconstruction and Development (EBRD) on court reform that is being offered to all five Central Asian countries. According to EBRD officials, this effort follows on legal reform measures that have included reform programs on transaction security, bankruptcy law, telecommunications, leasing, arbitration, and taxation. Finally, the European Union (EU) has focused its attention on strengthening the legal regime in Central Asia. Through its Technical Assistance to the Commonwealth of Independent States (TACIS) Program, the EU has offered training programs for procurators and other legal experts. Perhaps more ambitious is the effort by the EU to create a common legal regime in the Central Asian and South Caucasus regions, paralleling the efforts to do the same within Europe. Such goals are long-term, but it is clear that support is available.

With each of these efforts, there are shortfalls and obstacles. The United States Agency for International Development (USAID), which contributes millions of dollars in assistance to the region each year, must balance out programs for legal reform with those devoted to economic, environmental, educational and health reform, to name a few. Moreover, as security assistance continues to be a high priority for the countries in the region, the receptivity of the governments for extensive legal aid is questionable.

Conclusion

In each of the Central Asian states, efforts have been made to resuscitate legal systems that many considered to be moribund. Both internal and external organizations have initiated reform measures, although it is too early to tell how effective they will be. More broadly speaking, several observations can be made regarding the status of legal reform in Central Asia. First of all, all of the countries have made efforts to use the discourse of Western legalism in their respective frameworks. Second, this has both been a product of, but also a reason for, substantial international assistance in reconstructing constitutions, legal codes, and procedures for law enforcement agencies. Third, in spite of this aid, much remains to be done. It is clear that many of the pre-Soviet and Soviet-era traditions and methods are still applicable to the current states, and a true transition to a rule of law society has yet to take place.

In all five states, while there is evidence that legal reforms are taking place, much work is still required. Indeed, it appears as if the initial flurry of activity involved in creating actual codes and constitutions was deemed sufficient and the actual enforcement of the laws has yet to be fully implemented. That said, it is also clear the respective states are attempting to reshape the legal discourse from the Socialist legalism framework of the twentieth century to a more Western-oriented legal code that focuses on rights and responsibilities of the individual, as opposed to groups. However, even this latest layer of legal discourse has yet to tackle what remain key dilemmas and challenges to the respective systems.

Admittedly, it has been just over a decade and to expect a complete transformation in such a short period of time is asking too much. Since a transition in logic, theory and belief is required, it is no surprise that common citizens and those who find themselves in the legal system are more than cynical. Fundamental to the problem of legal reform in Central Asia is the notion of trust. Do the respective populations actually believe in the authority of law in their countries, versus the notion of a powerful leader? Are those surrounding the leaders viewed as mere kleptocrats who are pillaging the system in manners little different than their Soviet-era predecessors? To date, the status is mixed. While the situation varies in the respective countries, the problems are still apparent in all.

The problem of trust is a significant legacy from the Soviet era. Because justice and law were deemed arbitrary, a general lack of trust and respect for the concept of law developed. Previous, indigenous forms of law were banned, leading some to insist that return to such practices would enhance the respect for law. That said, it is evident that even pre-Soviet/pre-Russian law was not always seen as just and fair. When given the option of having a case heard in a Russian or a Shari'at court, the parties involved often opted for the Russian court, where renumeration was in monetary terms, not in disfigurement or death. In the Soviet era, the legal system was seen as competent at the lower level for minor offenses. However, for politically designated crimes, it was seen as a tool of the Communist Party. Today, it seems, this mentality has not changed. Ultimately, for the political systems of Central Asia to survive past the current generation of autocrats, a sound and credible legal system must be firmly entrenched. The written and rhetorical foundations exist—now it is incumbent upon the five states to put meaning into these words.

Notes

[1] For the purposes of this chapter, Central Asia is defined as the states of Kazakhstan, the Kyrgyz Republic, Tajikistan, Turkmenistan, and Uzbekistan. Clearly, references to pre-1924 Central Asia will include names of states and empires that existed within the geographic setting of these five states.

[2] Harold Lamb, *The Earth Shakers* (Garden City, NY: Doubleday, 1949); Rene Grousset, *The Empire of the Steppes: A History of Central Asia*, translated by Naomi Walford (New Brunswick, NJ: Rutgers University Press, 1970), 409-469.

[3] The challenge remains trying to assess what is in writing and what is actually enforced. Throughout much of the Soviet period, laws were quite extensive and often appeared to be rather fair and judicious. The actual implementation of these laws, on the other hand, revealed a system that was often capricious and unbalanced. Often legal codes were used for political reasons and to maintain a certain power relationship.

[4] Many of these are designed to prove the origin of certain civilizations in the region, predating those outside Central Asia. Perhaps as a Soviet legacy, they are also presented as relics ("perezhitki") of oppressive, pre-capitalist societies. This is particularly evident in the national museum in Bukhara, Uzbekistan.

[5] For an assessment of these periods, see Grousset, *op cit*. The strengths of these traditions are discussed in Edward A. Allworth, *The Modern Uzbeks: From the Fourteenth Century to the Present, a cultural history* (Stanford, CA: Hoover Institution Press, 1990), and Vasiliy V. Barthold, *Four Studies on the History of Central Asia*, translated by V. Minorsky and T. Minorsky (Leiden: NL: E.J. Brill, 1958).

[6] Peter Green, *Alexander of Macedon 356-323 B.C.: A Historical Biography* (Berkeley, CA: The University of California Press, 1992). This is also assessed in Russian scholarship. See I.S. Shiffman, *Aleksandr makadonskii* (Leningrad: "Nauka," 1988).

[7] A basic precept of the growing Muslim world was to establish a broad framework within which various societies and cultures could live. These developments were evolutionary and reflected a maturation of Islamic thought over the first several centuries of the faith's existence. See Wilfred Cantwell Smith, *Islam in Modern History* (Princeton, NJ: Princeton University Press, 1957), and Svat Soucek, *A History of Inner Asia* (Cambridge, UK: Cambridge University Press, 2000).

[8] Shafi'is Risala, *Islamic Jurisprudence*, translated by Majid Khadduri (Baltimore, MD: The Johns Hopkins Press, 1961).

[9] The "decline" of these Central Asian centers of learning was the result of geographic isolation, the struggles of the Islamic world vis-à-vis the European Christian world, and even the opening up of trade routes to the orient that bypassed the "great silk road." Consequently, Central Asian Islam did not experience the reform movements that took place in the Arab world in the eighteenth and nineteenth centuries.

[10] For a concise discussion of Adat, see Anuar Galiev, *"Traditional Institutions in Modern Kazakhstan"* (1997), electronically published by the Slavic Research Center in Hokudai, Japan, <http://src-h.slav.hokudai.ac.jp/sympo/97summer/galiev.html>.

[11] Depending upon the source material and transliteration method, Genghis Khan is also referred to as Chinggis Khan or Ghenghis Khan, among others. See Leo de Hartog, *Genghis Khan: Conqueror of the World* (London: I.B. Tauris, 1989), and Robert Marshall, *Storm from the East: From Genghis Khan to Khublai Khan* (Berkeley, CA: The University of California Press, 1993).

[12] Grousset, op cit., 326-346.

[13] Of the Barlas tribe, Tamerlane (1336-1405) was a local political and military figure who quickly consolidated his authority by forging alliances or defeating opponents in swift attacks. At the time of his death, Tamerlane had conquered most of Central Asia and territories stretching into modern-day Iran, Afghanistan, Pakistan, and China.

[14] Soucek, *op cit.*

[15] Seymour Becker, *Russia's Protectorates in Central Asia: Bukhara and Khiva, 1865-1924* (Cambridge, MA: Harvard University Press, 1968). See also Helene Carrere d'Encausse, *Islam and the Russian Empire: Reform and Revolution in Central Asia* (London: I.B. Tauris, 1988).

[16] Adeeb Khalid, *The Politics of Muslim Cultural Reform: Jadidism in Central Asia.* (Berkeley, CA: The University of California Press, 1998), and Faizulla Khodzhaev, *Kistorii revoliutsii v Bukhare* (Tashkent: Uzbekskoe gosizdat, 1926).

[17] In Central Asian history, these two Emirs were notorious for their corrupt regimes and opulent lifestyles at a time when the "forces of modernization" were slowly enveloping the Emirate. Critics from within the country wrote of the regime's shortcoming, and Russian officials in Central Asia parlayed this into a dependency relationship by creating a "protectorate system" for Bukhara and the neighboring Khanate of Khiva. See Seymour Becker, *op cit.*

[18] See Khalid and Carrere d'Encausse as two excellent studies of Jadidism at this time. "Jadidism" itself means "new school," or "new method" and represented a reformist movement that existed in the Muslim regions of the Russian empire and the neighboring protectorates in the late-nineteenth and early-twentieth centuries. Modeled after the reformist movements that emerged in nineteenth-century Egypt and the twentieth-century Ottoman Empire, this reform movement had a number of sub-groupings. Some advocated political reform; others sought a return to a "more pure" form of Islam; and still others emphasized a greater unity of the various Turkic peoples. The Jadidist movement was eventually overtaken by events in the Russian empire, particularly the Bolshevik Revolution and the creation of the Soviet Union, at which time many either emigrated or were victims of the Stalinist purges for being "nationalists."

[19] Helene Carrere d'Encausse, "Organizing and Colonizing the Conquered Territories," in *Central Asia: 120 Years of Russian Rule*, edited by Edward Allworth (Durham, NC: Duke University Press, 1989), 151-171. For a range of interpretations of this policy, see *Russia's Orient: Imperial Borderlands*

and Peoples, 1700-1917, edited by Daniel R. Brower and Edward J. Lazzerini (Bloomington, IN: Indiana University Press, 1997).

[20] Carrere d' Encausse, 155.

[21] Khalid, *op cit.*

[22] Tragically, the Jadidists believed that the Bolsheviks would ultimately leave the region alone, supported by Lenin's concept of "national self-determination." However, by the mid-1920s, J.V. Stalin had compromised the parameters of national self-determination so much that it was impossible for the minority regions to gain their independence. The respective leaders of the various ethnic regions were subsequently targeted in the purges of the 1930s. See Richard Pipes, *The Formation of the Soviet Union: Communism and Nationalism, 1917-1923* (New York: Atheneum, 1980).

[23] This was the dilemma faced by regional elite such as Faizulla Khojaev. A member of the Young Bukharans, Khojaev agreed to work with the new Soviet government and was instrumental in bringing Bukhara into the Soviet Union as a central component of the newly-formed Uzbek Soviet Socialist Republic. He remained active in Uzbek politics until 1937, when he was arrested for a range of anti-state crimes. He was executed the following year. The bulk of this "First Generation" of Central Asian leaders met similar fates. See Alexandre Bennigsen and S. Enders Wimbush, *Muslim National Communism in the Soviet Union* (Chicago, IL: The University of Chicago Press, 1979).

[24] The most prominent insurgency was the "Basmachi" movement, which lasted from 1919-1923 as a full-fledged force and until the early 1930s as a less-effective guerilla force. See Glenda Fraser, "Basmachi (parts I and II)," *Central Asian Survey* (1987) 6, no. 1, 1-73, and 6, no.2, 7-42.

[25] Gordon B. Smith, "The Legal System: Toward a Civil Society," in *Soviet Politics: Struggling with Change* (New York: St. Martin's Press, 1992), 202-232.

[26] For a discussion of restrictions on Central Asian culture, see Shoshana Keller, *To Moscow, Not Mecca: The Soviet Campaign Against Islam in Central Asia, 1917-1941* (New York: Praeger, 1991).

[27] See Peter Solomon, *Soviet Criminal Justice Under Stalin* (Cambridge, UK: Cambridge University Press, 1996).

[28] For an assessment of the legal reforms that took place in the 1980s, see works by Eugene Huskey, including "Soviet Justice in the Age of Perestroika," *Christian Science Monitor,* August 22, 1989, 18 and "The Soviet Criminal Process: Expanding the Right to Counsel in Pre-Trial Proceedings," *American Journal of Comparative Law,* 34, no. 1 (1986).

[29] Gregory Gleason, "Fealty and Loyalty: Informal Authority Structures in Soviet Asia," *Soviet Studies,* 43, no. 4 (1991).

[30] Even today, there is controversy surrounding Rashidov's death. Russian journalists claim that he committed suicide, while those sympathetic to him suggest a more sinister demise. Most likely, his death was through natural causes (officially, a heart attack). Through much of the 1980s, his reputation was tarnished in the Soviet Union. It was not until the 1990s that President Islam Karimov officially "rehabilitated" Rashidov. For an assessment of the "Cotton Scandal," see Gregory Gleason, "Nationalism or Organized Crime? The Case of the 'Cotton Scandal' in the USSR," *Corruption and Reform,* 5, no. 2 (1990), 87-108.

[31] James Critchlow, *Nationalism in Uzbekistan: A Soviet Republic's Road to Sovereignty* (Boulder, CO: Westview Press, 1991).

[32] James Critchlow, "Prelude to 'Independence': How the Uzbek Party Apparatus Broke Moscow's Grip on Elite Recruitment," in *Soviet Central Asia: The Failed Transformation,* edited by William Fierman (Boulder, CO: Westview Press, 1991), 131-158.

[33] Nursultan Nazarbaev, *My Life, My Times, and the Future* (London: Pilkington Press, 1998).

[34] Martha Brill Olcott, "Nursultan Nazarbaev and the Balancing Act of State Building in Kazakstan," in *Patterns in Post-Soviet Leadership,* edited by Timothy J. Colton and Robert C. Tucker (Boulder, CO: Westview Press, 1995), 169-190.

[35] The drama of this intra-Kazakh power struggle is well noted in Martha Brill Olcott, *Kazakhstan: Unfulfilled Promises* (Washington, DC: CEIP, 2002).

[36] "Kazakhstan," *Nations in Transit, 2002 Report* (New York: Freedom House, 2003), 217-220.

[37] A common practice is for *militsia* (police) to occasionally flag motorists down and cite a violation. However, a modest "fee" will generally satisfy the arresting officer, and the motorist is allowed to proceed. While motorists dislike this occurrence, some do see it as the only way in which street police actually get paid (wage arrears are major problems in government departments).

[38] Ironically, Jakianov was viewed as a "protégé" of Nazarbaev, distantly related to the president via Nazarbaev's wife.

[39] For writings that assess these conflicting reputations, see Bruce Pannier, "The Kyrgyz Republic: The Early Dawn of a Bright Day?," *Transition OnLine* <www.tol.cz>, January 16, 1998 and John Anderson, *Kyrgyzstan: Central Asia's Island of Democracy* (New York: Harwood Academic Publishers, 1999).

[40] Eugene Huskey, "Kyrgyzstan: The Fate of Political Liberalization," in *Conflict, Cleavage, and Change in Central Asia and the Caucasus*, edited by Karen Dawisha and Bruce Parrott (Cambridge, UK: Cambridge University Press, 1997), 242-276.

[41] "Kyrgyz Republic," *Nations in Transit, 2002 Report* (New York: Freedom House, 2003), 233-235.

[42] In the mid-1990s, the Kyrgyz government established the "Slavonic University" in Bishkek, which would be an institute designed to cater to Russian-speaking citizens of the country. Because of the relatively high number of non-Kyrgyz speakers, there is a greater effort to establish such entities.

[43] Most likely, President Akaev would have received the plurality of votes in a potential second round and would have continued his term in office. However, the fear of receiving anything less than an overwhelming majority is perceived to be a weakness in the region—perhaps a holdover from the Soviet-era elections where 95 percent+ "voter approvals" were common.

[44] Roger Kangas, "State Building and Civil Society in Central Asia," in *Political Culture and Civil Society in Russia and the New States of Eurasia*, edited by Vladimir Tismaneanu (Armonk, NY: M.E. Sharpe, 1995), 275-277.

[45] One can see a parallel with the Soviet death penalties for economic crimes. Terrorist groups today challenge the legitimacy of the current regime, much in the way that "speculators" and "capitalists" were seen as challengers to the legitimacy of the centrally-planned economy of the Soviet Union.

[46] "Uzbekistan," *Nations in Transit, 2002 Report* (New York: Freedom House, 2003), 423-425.

[47] In mid-February 1999, a series of bombs exploded in Tashkent, killing and injuring scores of Uzbekistani citizens. While no group claimed responsibility, the government has concluded that it was the work of Islamic terrorists, specifically the IMU. Over 2000 individuals were arrested in the ensuing months, with over 100 receiving significant prison terms or the death penalty. The government explanation of these events can be found in the sensationalist book by Oleg Yakubov, *The Pack of Wolves: The Blood Trail of Terror* (Moscow: Veche Publishers, 2000).

[48] *Persecution of Human Rights Defenders in Uzbekistan* (New York: Human Rights Watch, May 1, 2003) is a recent example of these reports. Also see *Uzbekistan at Ten: Repression and Instability*, Asia Report N.21 (Osh/Brussels: International Crisis Group, August 21, 2001).

[49] Critics of the United States' global war on terrorism use the "geopolitical argument" in explaining why it maintains ties with Uzbekistan. The U.S. Congress has had several hearings on this issue since October 2001.

[50] "Turkmenistan," *Nations in Transit, 2002 Report* (New York: Freedom House, 2003), 395-398.

[51] *Cracks in the Marble: Turkmenistan's Failing Dictatorship*, Asia Report no.44 (Osh/Brussels: International Crisis Group, January 17, 2003).

[52] "Unrecognized" faiths include Baha'is, various Evangelical Christian groups, and Hare Krishnas, among others. Churches with strong missionary components find it particularly difficult to work in Turkmenistan.

[53] Saparmurat Niyazov, *Ruhnama* (Ashgabat, TK: TurkGosIzdatel'stvo, 2002). The book is published in Turkmen, Russian, and English and is currently being translated into other languages as well.

[54] For example, when the International Foundation for Election Systems conducted public opinion surveys in Central Asia on issues of politics, economics, and social welfare, four of the five countries permitted the surveys to take place, even allowing the U.S.-based Non-Governmental Organization to partner with local organizations. Turkmenistan refused to permit the survey to take place.

[55] See Shirin Akiner, *Tajikistan: Disintegration or Reconciliation?* (London: Royal Institute of International Affairs, 2002) and Muriel Atkin, *The Subtlest Battle: Islam in Soviet Tajikistan* (Philadelphia, PA: The Foreign Policy Research Institute, 1989).

[56] Tajikistan is over 90 percent mountainous, with the eastern part of the country including some of the most remote villages in the region. Outside of Dushanbe, the government's control is sometimes challenged, although any violence is considered low-intensity as compared to the period of the civil war.

[57] *Central Asia: The Politics of Police Reform,* 14-20.

[58] Simply put, "episodic" corruption suggests that cases of corruption are isolated and are based on specific personalities and situations. They do not reflect on the legal or political system as a whole. "Systemic" corruption, on the other hand, is just that: corruption is required to function in the society, and the very nature of corruption permeates all levels of society—from politics to economy to healthcare and education.

[59] Nancy Lubin, *Central Asians Take Stock: Reform, Corruption, and Identity* (Washington, DC: USIP, 1995).

[60] While Transparency International has not conducted an in-depth study of Central Asia, they have included specific cases in the region for their annual reports. See <www.transparency.org> for further information, as well as the country reports in Freedom House's *Nation in Transit, 2002 Report, op. cit.*

[61] These "rates" refer to illegal fees that one must pay for items ranging from licenses for restaurants, building permits, entrance fees for schools, opportunities for certain jobs, etc., See Roger Kangas and Craig Olson, *Anticorruption Assessment: Pavlodar Oblast, Kazakhstan* (Bethesda, MD: Development Alternatives Incorporated, November 1998).

[62] On November 25, 2002, shots were allegedly fired at President Niyazov's car as he drove to office in Ashgabat. Almost immediately, key opposition figures such as Boris Shikhmuradov, Hudaiberdy Orazov and Nurmuhammed Hanamov were implicated. In addition, Niyazov went so far as to suggest the Uzbek and American ambassadors were somehow linked to the "criminal organization" that was out to assassinate him. Roger Kangas, "Memories of the Past: Politics in Turkmenistan," *Analysis of Current Events*, Vol.14, no.4 (December 2002),16-19.

[63] The investigation and trial have been covered extensively by the publication Eurasianet (<www.eurasianet.org>).

[64] This is a theme addressed by a number of recent articles, including Charles William Maynes, "America Discovers Central Asia," *Foreign Affairs*, Vol. 82, no. 2 (Mar/Apr 2002), 120-132; Martha Brill Olcott, "Pipelines and Pipe Dreams: Energy Development and Caspian Society," *Journal of International Affairs*, Vol. 53, no. 1 (Fall 1999), 305-323; and most recently Mark Berniker, "Despite Corruption Concerns, Kazakhstan Continues to Lure Investors," <www.eurasianet.org> (April 28, 2003).

[65] This view was most recently expressed in a report by the International Crisis Group at the time of the annual conference of the European Bank of Reconstruction and Development (EBRD), which was held in Tashkent, Uzbekistan in May 2003. See *Central Asia: A Last Chance for Change* (Osh/Brussels: International Crisis Group, April 29, 2003).

[66] For a variety of reasons, Uzbekistan remains a difficult country for the ABA to work. However, when addressing less political issues, such as property law, progress has been made. For example, see *Analysis of the Draft Civil Code Section on Property Rights for the Republic of Uzbekistan* (Washington, DC: CEELI, January 19, 1996).

[67] *Anticorruption in Europe and Central Asia* (Washington, DC: World Bank, May 2003).

Chapter 5

Human Rights in Central Asia [1]

Michael Ochs

The defining trend of political development in Central Asia has been the emergence of presidents far more powerful than the legislative and judicial branches of government. Central Asian constitutions generally sanction this imbalance by according the head of state extremely broad prerogatives. But the actual practice of presidential rule has transcended constitutional provisions, which also formally enshrine separation of powers. Only in Kyrgyzstan, for example, has parliament occasionally managed to frustrate the executive. Kazakhstan's few opposition-minded legislators at best can try to embarrass their president. Elsewhere in the region, parliaments are rubber stamp institutions, while courts everywhere reliably rule in political cases as instructed by the powers that be. Official justifications for the phenomenon of "super" presidents in Central Asia emphasize the need for a strong hand to consolidate independence, ram through reforms and maintain stability during a difficult transition period. More cynical views point to still strong "eastern" and/or Russian-Communist traditions of exercising authority.

The most extreme case of authoritarianism is Turkmenistan, where Saparmurat Niyazov sponsors a full-scale cult of personality while overseeing the most repressive regime in the former Soviet Union. In Tajikistan, by contrast, President Imomali Rakhmonov has had to make concessions: a military stalemate in the 1992-1997 civil war forced him to come to terms with Islamic and democratic opposition groups and agree to a formal coalition government.

Rounding out the spectrum are Uzbekistan's Islam Karimov, Kyrgyzstan's Askar Akaev, and Kazakhstan's Nursultan Nazarbaev. Karimov, after permitting some political opposition, in mid-1992 banned all dissidence. Akaev and Nazarbaev tolerate opposition parties but curtail their influence—Nazarbaev much more effectively than Akaev.

Central Asian publics for the most part have accepted strongman rule, though not without grumbling, when possible. This is not surprising, considering the regimes' control of security organs, law enforcement, and prosecutorial agencies; the region's lack of democratic traditions; and the natural human focus on surviving severe economic decline. Moreover, after seeing the bloodshed in Tajikistan (or Azerbaijan or Georgia), many people are grateful for "stability."

At the same time, a series of unfair elections has deepened popular disillusionment with "democracy." Most people believe that presidents and lower level officials derive significant economic gain from their positions and will not willingly leave office. Consequently, relatively few protests have been lodged against the development of executive privilege. Only in 2002, in the most liberal Central Asian country—Kyrgyzstan—has this pattern begun to change.

When the Central Asian countries joined the Organization for Security and Cooperation in Europe (OSCE)[2] in 1992, their leaders pledged to implement all past and future commitments of the Helsinki process. In fact, however, they want no part of democracy. The best evidence for this proposition is their miserable record of elections. It is unclear what the region's presidents fear more—losing or not winning by an astronomical figure—but it is certain they rig elections and strive to eliminate all risk from electoral exercises.[3]

Apologists often point to Central Asian traditions and argue that democracy must be built slowly. But while an undemocratic history, real or alleged Islamic fundamentalism, the Soviet legacy, and poverty are all important, leaders determined to remain in office require repressive political systems. Implementing commitments on democracy, the rule of law and human rights would create a level playing field for challengers and let the media expose presidential misdeeds.

Another key factor in Central Asia's poor human rights record is high-level corruption. Presidents wishing to continue enriching their families and friends (or "clans") cannot allow a free press or an independent judiciary. Nowhere is the nexus between corruption and intimidation of the press clearer than in Kazakhstan, where journalists who write about foreign investigations into President Nazarbaev's finances risk physical retribution or legal action.

Nor is normal politics possible. Fear of the consequences if an outsider should come to power and uncover the scale of abuse induces leaders to ensure that no serious rivals emerge and that elections are carefully controlled—when they take place at all. The result has been the emergence of an entire region in the OSCE space where fundamental freedoms are ignored. Along with large-scale conflicts like Kosovo or Bosnia, unresolved low-level conflicts such as Nagorno-Karabakh and Abkhazia, and the trafficking in human beings, the systemic flouting of commitments on democratization and human rights in Central Asia is the single greatest problem facing the OSCE.

Consequently, human rights observance in these states has tended to reflect not the leaders' commitment to reform, but rather goading from abroad. Such pressure, however, has had—and can have—only limited effect. While the United States had urged progress in democratization even before September 11, Central Asian leaders apparently had concluded that Washington is more focused on strategic and economic interests and the threat of Islamic fundamentalism. U.S. disapproval of lagging democratization never kept American businessmen from seeking to exploit Central Asia's natural resources or restrained Washington from encouraging them. Nor did flagrant human rights abuses cause the United States to cut significantly programs such as Partnership for Peace, cease foreign aid, or otherwise slow the development of bilateral relations.

After September 11, the U.S. government moved to consolidate its relationships with Central Asian states, seeking cooperation in the war on terrorism. But Washington also made plain its expectations of some type of political reform, warning that without such reform, Islamic radicalism would threaten stability in Central Asia and the entire Western world.

Kyrgyzstan's Akaev and Uzbekistan's Karimov faced incursions by the Islamic Movement of Uzbekistan (IMU) in 1999 and 2000. They and other regional leaders quickly pledged support in the campaign against terrorism and seem happy to build closer ties with the United States. But loosening their grip on power is as unpalatable to them as ever. And if they saw little reason to fear sanctions or abandonment by Washington before September 11, they apparently feel even less concern now, with U.S. troops deployed in Uzbekistan and Kyrgyzstan, and military and intelligence cooperation developing apace. By the end of 2002, all Central Asian presidents, except Turkmenistan's Niyazov had been to the White House to meet President Bush.

Bush Administration officials deny that the U.S. human rights agenda has taken a back seat to military and anti-terrorism collaboration. They claim that working together on security facilitates the raising of human rights issues, more often and with greater success.[4] As evidence, they point to incremental victories, such as Uzbekistan's registration of an independent human rights organization and the sentencing to jail terms of policemen who had tortured detainees.

Still, regional leaders have not shown any sign that they are ready for fundamental, systemic changes. On the other hand, indications of growing ferment abound. Since September 11, opposition and human rights activists have complained that growing U.S. closeness with Central Asian governments has emboldened these governments to indulge their repressive instincts with a greater conviction of impunity. Perhaps despairing of reliable American pressure for reform, opposition groups apparently have begun to count more on their own endeavors to create societies which respect human rights. These efforts have had mixed results so far, and the prospects for reform from below seem bleak.

Kazakhstan

In the early 1990s, Kazakhstan seemed to be building a democratic state with societal input into decision-making and relative freedom of speech. Today, President Nursultan Nazarbaev gives every indication of intending to remain in office for life. He has kept the legislative and judicial branches well in hand while not permitting any alternative sources of power to emerge, and turned energy- and resource-rich Kazakhstan into a virtual family enterprise. Meanwhile, the possibilities for opposition political activity or speaking one's mind have narrowed and become increasingly dangerous.[5]

With normal politics impossible inside Kazakhstan, an important locus of opposition activity has gone abroad. Former Prime Minister Akezhan Kazhegeldin, whom Nazarbaev has accused of corruption and who cannot safely return home, has led a campaign of international lobbying, providing information about Nazarbaev's regime to Western governments and anyone willing to listen. These efforts have helped publicize alleged corruption, which Nazarbaev has sought to stifle inside Kazakhstan through control of the media.

In late 2001, Nazarbaev faced several new threats, including an open rupture with his powerful son-in-law and an attempt to mount an intra-elite opposition movement. Nazarbaev responded with a crackdown, in spite of U.S. government calls for political liberalization in Central Asia. He quashed all challenges and intensified assaults on the opposition media, indicating both his concern and his sense of impunity.

Nazarbaev, elected president in 1990 by Kazakhstan's Supreme Soviet, confirmed his position in a non-contested election in 1991. In 1995, he inaugurated a period of presidential rule and convened an Assembly of the People, which extended his tenure until 2000. Official results gave Nazarbaev 81.7 percent of the vote in the first nominally contested, pre-term presidential election in January 1999. Because of the exclusion of would-be candidates, intimidation of voters, and attacks on independent media, the OSCE's Office of Democratic Institutions and Human Rights (ODIHR) refused to send observers. A small reporting mission concluded that the "election process fell *far* short" of OSCE standards.

In October 1999, Kazakhstan held elections for parliament's lower chamber, in which political parties, for the first time, could submit party lists for 10 of the 77 seats. *Otan* (Fatherland), Nazarbaev's party, came in first, followed by the opposition Communist Party, the pro-presidential Civic Party, and the Agrarian Party. In the first round, ODIHR observers saw some improvements in the legislative framework and lauded the in-troduction of party list voting, but criticized the second round. Citing fla-grantly falsified protocols and continued interference by officials, ODIHR judged that the election fell short of OSCE commitments.

Freedom of association is restricted in Kazakhstan. Opposition parties, such as the Communist Party and the Republican People's Party (RPPK) have been registered and allowed to function, and some of them have parliamentary representation. But it was only after long delays that the RPPK registered, as a result of strong OSCE pressure before the Octo-ber 1999 parliamentary election.

Recent attempts to create new opposition parties, especially the Democratic Choice of Kazakhstan (DCK), have been crudely suppressed. Two DCK leaders are in jail: Mukhtar Ablyazov, former Minister of Power, Industry, and Trade, and Galymzhan Zhakiyanov, former Governor of Pavlodar. In July 2002, Ablyazov was sentenced to six years in jail; in Au-gust of the same year Zhakiyanov received a seven-year term. Nazarbaev clearly wanted to make an example of them for any other would-be op-position activists among Kazakhstan's officials.

On June 25, 2002, Kazakhstan's parliament raised from 3,000 to 50,000 the number of members needed for party registration and re-quired parties to have a branch office and at least 7,000 members in each of Kazakhstan's regions. The new law likely will lead to the de-registration of most of the 19 parties currently represented in parliament. The OSCE Center in Almaty strongly criticized the law for threatening political plu-ralism, but to little visible effect. Indeed, in recent months the number of parties has since shrunk to nine and the RPPK is no longer registered.

Freedom of assembly is restricted in Kazakhstan. A March 17, 1995 presidential decree, issued while parliament was disbanded, remains in force and limits the ability of citizens to participate in unsanctioned demonstrations. Gaining permission for such gatherings is difficult, and authorities have detained or jailed violators. For example, on April 25, 2002, police in Almaty detained 12 members of the RPPK and other opposition groups to prevent them from picketing a hotel where a government-sponsored media conference was taking place. The demonstrators hoped to publicize the government's systematic violations of human rights and media freedoms. They were held for seven hours before being charged and then put on trial.[6]

Freedom of speech is highly restricted in Kazakhstan. Dariga Nazarbaeva, the president's daughter, runs Khabar, the main TV station. Newspapers and TV can report on intra-government discord and low-level corruption. But stories about Nazarbaev, his family or allegations of their corruption are likely to result in harassment or worse. In 1996 and 1997, the government began closing down independent TV and radio stations by manipulating tenders for broadcasting permits. In 1998, the publisher of *Karavan* was forced to sell the country's most popular newspaper, which is now widely believed to belong to the president's relatives. Cruder methods were employed in September 1998, when the offices of the opposition newspaper *21st Century* were firebombed.

As a result of these policies, the opposition press largely has been silenced. In May 2000, the New York-based Committee to Protect Journalists (CPJ) placed Nazarbaev on its annual list of "Ten Worst Enemies of the Press." The head of the OSCE office in Kazakhstan said in June 2002 that independent and opposition media in Kazakhstan face increasing legal and economic pressures, while national media are concentrated in the hands of persons close to Nazarbaev.[7]

In May and June 2002, after official revelations about a secret Swiss bank account with $1 billion under Nazarbaev's name, the assault on independent media intensified. Irina Petrushova, the editor of an opposition newspaper, found a decapitated dog hung by its paws outside her office. On a screwdriver driven into its torso was a warning: "There won't be a next time." The Almaty TV station TAN was forced off the air when its cable was sliced in the middle of the night.[8]

On August 28, 2002, independent journalist Sergei Duvanov was severely beaten by three men. He already had been charged with "insulting the honor and dignity of the president" after writing an internet article about the international investigation into alleged corruption by Nazarbaev. On October 27, Duvanov was arrested on charges of raping a teenage girl. He maintains his innocence and many human rights groups in Kazakhstan and abroad view the charge as politically motivated. If convicted, Duvanov could face a 10-year jail term. In January 2003, Duvanov—whose case attracted substantial international attention—was sentenced to three and a half years in jail. Another journalist who published an article on alleged corruption, Lira Baseitova, suffered the worst of tragedies: her daughter died in mysterious circumstances while in police custody on June 21, 2002.

Kazakhstan initially permitted fairly unrestricted religious freedom, but in the mid-1990s the government increasingly sought control over new religious groups. In 1998, the national security apparatus (KNB), concerned about Islamic extremism, became more active in the surveillance and deportation of Muslim missionaries. KNB leaders openly stated that prohibiting the spread of Islamic and Christian "religious extremism" was a top priority.

Religious groups must register to rent or purchase property, employ workers, or obtain visas for foreign co-religionists. A new article in the Administrative Code, introduced in 2001, imposes criminal sanctions on leaders of groups refusing to register, and local authorities have detained and beaten leaders of groups which do not. In addition, parliament introduced a new religion law broadening the government's ability to control and monitor religious groups. However, the Constitutional Council deemed the draft law unconstitutional in April 2002, and President Nazarbaev chose not to appeal. While officially the law may not be on the books, the number of fines and court orders closing down churches of Baptists who refuse to register steadily has increased.

Kyrgyzstan

Under President Askar Akaev, Kyrgyzstan was long the most democratic country in Central Asia. Parliament enjoyed some independence, and while several newspapers which covered high-level corruption were forced to close, criticism of the government and even of Akaev was possible. In this relatively liberal atmosphere, civil society blossomed. In the second half of the 1990s, however, the honeymoon ended. In 1999, when several politicians announced their intention to run for president, Akaev's regime turned toward open repression. Since then, various opposition leaders have been arrested, co-opted or otherwise removed from politics, while independent media have come under severe pressure. Both Kyrgyzstan's reputation as an oasis of freedom in Central Asia and Akaev's democratic image have dissipated.

In early 2002, pent-up popular discontent erupted after the arrest in January of a southern legislator, Azimbek Beknazarov, who opposed a border deal that would cede territory to China. On March 17, police fired on demonstrators denouncing his imprisonment and six people died. In the ensuing crisis, thousands of people protested all over the country; Akaev was forced to dismiss his government in May and agree, in principle, to a coalition government.

On August 26, Akaev decreed the formation of a Constitutional Council to redistribute powers among the president, government and parliament. Kyrgyzstan's plan to hand over presidential prerogatives to other branches of government was unique in Central Asia and, if all sides had acted in good faith, could have served as an important precedent for neighboring countries. Yet well into 2003, tensions remain as high and some opposition groups—including several parliamentarians—are determined to bring down Akaev. To date, Kyrgyzstan remains the only country in Central Asia where civil society is powerful enough to pose a possible threat to the president.

In a snap presidential election held in December 1995, two would-be candidates were disqualified shortly before the vote. By the late 1990s, Akaev faced more serious challengers, especially from Felix Kulov, leader of the *Ar-Namys* (Honor) party, who had been Vice President, Minister of National Security, Governor of Chu oblast and Mayor of Bishkek. Another contender was entrepreneur and independent parliamentarian Danyar Usenov, who headed the *El Bei Bechara* or Party of Poor People.

In the February-March 2000 parliamentary election, the authorities barred three of four opposition parties. They excluded Usenov from running in the second round and ensured Kulov's defeat; the ODIHR explicitly concluded that he had been robbed of victory. On March 22, 2000, the Ministry of National Security arrested Kulov for alleged abuse of power while he was Minister of National Security. He has since been sentenced to a 10-year jail term and is considered a political prisoner by Amnesty International and other human rights groups.

With his leading rivals jailed or out of the race, Akaev won easy re-election in the October 2000 election. Despite rumors that he would hold a referendum to extend his tenure from five years to seven, in August 2001 Akaev denied any such intentions and has not done so.

In May 2002, the CPJ listed Kyrgyzstan among the world's 10 worst places to be a journalist. Newspapers critical of the government have been crippled by slander lawsuits. Such publications include *Asaba*, which has resumed publication with a new editor. After the editorial offices of *Vecherniy (Evening) Bishkek* were occupied by the militia in 1999 and the chief editor forced out; it reportedly now is run by Akaev's relatives.

In 1995, chief editor Zamira Sydykova of the opposition newspaper *Res Publica* received a suspended sentence for libel and was banned for 18 months from working as a journalist. She was jailed again in 1997 for libel and Amnesty International condemned her sentence. *Res Publica* most recently had to pay $2,700 in fines for allegedly having offended a claimant's "honour and dignity." The paper was not published from January to May 2002, until it paid the fine.

Freedom of assembly has been restricted in Kyrgyzstan. Hina Jilani, the Special Representative of the U.N. Secretary General on Human Rights Defenders, said in summer 2001 that "the right to denounce and protest human rights violations has been repressed . . . and that freedom of assembly and freedom of association, though guaranteed by the Constitution, are frequently violated in practice." In 2002, however, large crowds demonstrated throughout the country, particularly in the south. The January arrest of parliamentarian Azimbek Beknazarov mobilized thousands of protesters who blocked the country's main highway. They demanded the release of Beknazarov (which was done on May 19); the resignation of Akaev; the rescinding of the border accord with China; and the punishment of officials responsible for the March 17 shootings.

In September 2002, the opposition again organized a large protest movement which aimed to descend on Bishkek and force Akaev out. Another bloody confrontation seemed likely, with unpredictable consequences. On September 12, however, both sides blinked: the marchers dispersed after the authorities promised to punish those responsible for the Aksy shootings by November 15. Afterwards, the authorities became more adept at managing demonstrations, which for the most part have ceased.

More than 30 political parties now are registered in Kyrgyzstan. Four opposition political parties—*Ar-Namys*, *Ata-Meken*, *El* and the *People* parties—have united to form the Peoples Congress. The imprisoned Felix Kulov was elected chairman of the movement.

Kyrgyz authorities have targeted non-government organizations (NGOs) critical of the government, especially the Kyrgyz Human Rights Committee, headed by Ramazan Dyryldaev. The Committee was de-registered in 1995 and 1998 and its members have regularly experienced harassment; about fifteen have been arrested at various times. In July 2000, the authorities occupied the Committee's offices, which they sealed, effectively shutting down the NGO. Dyryldaev, in Vienna at the time, remained there, fearful of arrest. He returned to Kyrgyzstan only in May 2002, accompanying Gerard Stoudmann, Director of the ODIHR, and continues his political activity. Still, several of Dyryldaev's associates have been beaten by police. With large-scale demonstrations almost a daily occurrence in 2002, NGO leaders, especially those with oppositionist leanings, have been singled out for criticism in the government-controlled media.

Kyrgyzstan has enjoyed a degree of religious freedom since independence, although recent government actions are troubling. The State Commission on Religious Affairs, created in 1996, oversees registration of religious groups and is charged with protecting freedom of conscience. However, under a 1997 presidential decree, all religious communities now must register with the Ministry of Justice. While many Muslim and Christian religious communities have registered successfully, the government repeatedly has turned down the Catholic Church, whose members are mainly ethnic Kyrgyz.[9] In addition, the registration of new churches has slowed, as the government fears creating religious-based conflicts in rural areas.

Due to security concerns about Islamic extremists, the government has intensified its surveillance of mosques throughout the country. In 2002, the government also issued a decree tightening publishing regulations for religious groups and called for an "audit," which would affect Muslim and Christian groups equally.[10] Work is underway on a new religion law. Input from an OSCE/ODIHR Panel of Experts on Freedom of Religion or Belief is expected to try to safeguard religious rights.[11]

Tajikistan

Tajikistan is the only country in Central Asia that has endured a civil war. After the September 1991 declaration of independence, the United Tajik Opposition (UTO), a cluster of nationalist and Islamic groups, took up arms against the Russian-backed Popular Front led by Imomali Rahkmonov and elites from the southern Kulyab province. The conflict turned into a struggle between secularists and Islamists, leading to the death of at least 50,000 people, the displacement of some 800,000 and widespread economic devastation.

War weariness and military stalemate brought about the June 1997 accord ending the hostilities. In return for disarming which occurred by 1999, the opposition was to receive 30 percent of government posts until parliamentary elections in 2000 and, in fact, UTO members have been given government posts at national and local levels. Thus, Tajikistan is the only Central Asian country where the government has formally reached an agreement with the opposition about nominal power sharing, and where a legal Islamic political party may function openly.

While Rahkmonov largely has consolidated power and controls the countryside, former guerillas still hold sway in some areas, undermining overall stability. Several high-ranking officials have been assassinated, including a deputy interior minister, a former UTO political representative, a peace accords negotiator, a presidential foreign policy advisor, and a Minister of Culture. Democratic institutions and rule of law remain weak; most of the population is impoverished and the rebuilding of dysfunctional institutions has been slow. Drug use has risen sharply, and the country is a major transit points for narcotics. Moreover, the return of Islamist fighters from Afghanistan has raised concern about religious extremism. Tajikistan's prospects hinge on whether, in this unpromising environment, the government can build democratic institutions, combat rampant corruption and develop the economy.

Tajikistan's record on elections is poor. Rahkmonov became president in November 1994, subsequently extending his five-year term to seven. The OSCE declined to monitor the 1995 parliamentary elections, which the UTO refused to recognize while continuing its armed rebellion. In the November 1999 presidential elections, Rahkmonov ran alone: two candidates were excluded a month before the election, while Two others withdrew in protest. An Islamic Renaissance Party (IRP) candidate was registered just before election day. On election eve, Rahkmonov and Abdullah Nuri, former UTO leader and now head of the IRP, agreed to hold fair, multiparty elections the following year to make up for the flawed presidential race.

But the February-March 2000 elections were preceded by violence, including bomb blasts in Dushanbe. A joint OSCE-UN mission cited many irregularities, concluding the election fell far short of OSCE standards. Still, six parties fielded candidates, giving voters some choice. The balloting itself was peaceful; all parties received free air-time on state media, and all candidates were permitted to hold rallies. Official tallies gave the ruling PDP about 65 percent, the Communist Party 23 percent, and the IRP 7 percent. By breaking the 5 percent threshold, the opposition was given two seats in parliament.

Though conditions for journalists have improved markedly since the civil war, the state controls many of the publishing and media outlets. The government offers "friendly advice" to reporters about content, and the State Committee on Television and Radio controls the issuing of licenses—which are expensive and require long waits. As a result, journalists often exercise self-censorship. The government also maintains financial control by subsidizing nearly all publications and electronic facilities, as well as the country's only publishing house. Still, the IRP maintains its own independent printing press.

Asia-Plus, an independent Tajik news agency, began broadcasting in September 2002, making it the capital's first non-governmental source of information. *Asia-Plus* originally sought a license in 1998; its application was rejected in July 2002. President Rahkmonov, under international pressure, had to intervene to reverse the decision. Dushanbe remains without an independent television station, although independent stations do operate in other cities, particularly in the relatively liberal northern region of Soghd. In August 2002, TV Servis was granted a license to rebroadcast 12 foreign television channels in Dushanbe.

Journalists who offend the government or powerful individuals risk arrests, beatings or worse. In May 2000, Saifullo Rahimov, the director of the state radio and television, was murdered. Saifadin Dostiev, correspondent of the Tajik-language service of Radio Free Europe/Radio Liberty (RFE/RL), was badly beaten the same month. However, *Internews* reported no beatings of journalists in 2002, and in July of the same year, charges were dropped against Dodojon Atovulloyev, exiled editor of *Charoghi Ruz*, which often had been critical of the government.

Freedom of assembly is limited in Tajikistan. NGOs and political groups must obtain permits from local authorities to demonstrate; demonstrations are rare and participants normally do not face reprisal. Permits for political rallies, however, are more difficult to obtain than those for NGO-related events. In May 2001, local Kulyab authorities obstructed an IRP meeting and briefly detained two members. The authorities strictly-controlled political demonstrations prior to the 1999 presidential elections.

Five political parties are registered in Tajikistan. Rahkmonov's People's Democratic Party is dominant; the leading opposition party is the IRP, which no longer calls for an Islamic state but rather a society in which "Muslims would be accorded a fitting place." The IRP was registered in September 1999 following the reversal of a law prohibiting parties based on religious affiliation. Some IRP members occupy senior government posts (including Minister of Emergency Situations, Deputy Prime Minister, and most other deputy ministerial posts), and its members hold local positions as well.

Registration of political parties can be an arduous process. In several cases, applications were denied on technicalities, such as "insufficient membership," or for unknown reasons. Six parties were banned in 1999 alone, as was the *Adolatkhoh* (Justice) Party last year in two oblasts. Moreover, the government has "made politically motivated arrests, and there were credible allegations of cases of illegal government detention of rival political factions."[12]

The NGO community is fairly active in Tajikistan; officials estimate some 2000 are operating. *Freedom House* (2002) reports that the government generally does not interfere in their operations, and that "groups that do not officially register are not necessarily illegal." Advocacy by Tajik NGOs yielded Resolution 132, which slashed registration fees for community organizations and national-level NGOs. The number of registered NGOs dramatically increased in 2001: 320 NGOs were registered that year alone, a 35 percent increase from the previous year.

Though the Islamic party is legal and its representatives are in government, mosques and religious schools must be approved by the religious authorities (muftiate). Tajik authorities required all mosques to re-register two years ago, resulting in the closure of smaller and more radical ones, and religious schools had to submit their curricula to authorities. In an unpopular move, Tajik authorities also outlawed the use of loudspeakers for call to prayer in large cities. Although members of *Hizb ut-Tahrir,* whose explicit goal is the non-violent restoration of the Caliphate, have been arrested in Tajikistan, the number of arrests is much smaller than in neighboring Uzbekistan, and trials appear to be more open.

Christian groups that do not comply with registration procedures have faced petty harassment, and others have had their applications turned down. In late 2001, three Christian churches were bombed. In one of these cases, Islamic extremists reportedly were involved; in the other two, three persons were accused and one escaped. Baha'i and Hare Krishna groups have experienced some instances of discrimination; in 1999, Abdullah Mugharebi, a prominent Baha'i leader, was murdered.

Turkmenistan

President Saparmurat Niyazov has created a near-totalitarian political system and one of the world's most repressive regimes. He has not allowed alternative leaders, political parties, or movements to emerge and has maintained Soviet-style controls on a fearful populace. A defining feature of Niyazov's political system is his cult of personality. He renamed himself Turkmenbashi "father of the Turkmen" and calls himself "The Great." In 2002, Niyazov released the *Rukhnama*, a book of his teachings that citizens must study, and he appears intent on displacing other sources of historical information and spirituality.[13] In August 2002, he renamed the months of the year, reserving two for himself and his deceased mother.

In November 2001, former Foreign Minister Boris Shikmuradov resigned from the government, fled the country, and declared his opposition to Niyazov. His move sparked other defections and marked the first time that a group of former high-ranking officials publicly declared their intention to topple Niyazov and formed a movement in exile to do so. Niyazov responded by purging the security apparatus—hitherto seen as his staunchest prop—and the military.

On November 25, 2002, official Turkmen sources reported an assassination attempt on Niyazov. Opposition representatives disclaimed any involvement and accused Niyazov of staging an attack to justify the mass arrests which followed. According to opposition and independent sources, scores of people, especially relatives of opposition leaders, have been jailed and tortured. Some, including Boris Shikmuradov, who was either captured or turned himself in at the end of December, have already confessed on television. At least two of those sentenced reportedly have died in prison.

Saparmurat Niyazov has never demonstrated the slightest inclination to loosen his control of Turkmen society, to rethink his views or to regard seriously his OSCE human rights commitments. There is no reason to expect any liberalization in Turkmenistan while he is in power or to believe that he will leave office voluntarily.

All elections in Turkmenistan have been farces. Races were uncontested in the December 1994 parliamentary election, and official figures claimed 99.8 percent turnout. Though seats were nominally contested in the December 1999 parliamentary elections, the ODIHR declined to send observers, concluding that the pre-election process "does not meet minimal OSCE commitments for democratic elections."

Saparmurat Niyazov was the first Central Asian leader to cancel elections. In January 1994, he organized a referendum to extend his tenure in office until 2002; according to official results, 99.9 percent of the electorate cast ballots, and 99.99 percent of voters approved the initiative. In December 1999, the *Halq Maslakhaty* (People's Council), ostensibly the country's highest representative body but actually a rubber stamp for Niyazov, gave him the right to remain in office permanently. His virtual coronation as "president for life" flagrantly flouts OSCE commitments, which call for regular and competitive elections. Niyazov has since announced that he will remain in office until 2010, when contested presidential elections will be held.

There is no freedom of speech in Turkmenistan. All media are rigorously censored and glorify Niyazov. In May 2002, Freimut Duve, the OSCE's Representative on the Media, offered the following assessment to the OSCE's Permanent Council: "Turkmenistan . . . is the only member of the OSCE where currently media freedom . . . is non-existent . . . the notion of freedom of the media has not undergone any real changes since the days of the Soviet regime." On December 12, Duve said, "In this 'declared democracy' the media are currently being used to humiliate and terrorise anybody who is even remotely contemplating the legitimacy of the current state of affairs. Some of the television programmes I have been informed about remind me of the show trials on Soviet radio and in the newspapers during the thirties."

Freedom of association is forbidden in Turkmenistan, the only remaining one-party state in the former Soviet bloc. The Democratic Party is the sole registered party. No opposition groups were ever registered and none are allowed to function today. In May 2002, Niyazov said, "Turkmenistan will get a multiparty system and an opposition in time, but it has had more important things to do since independence, such as ensuring that the people's living standards don't plummet." In fact, living standards have plummeted for the great majority of the population.

According to independent sources, there are about 500 NGOs in Turkmenistan, of which 60 are registered. However, no new NGOs have been registered since 1995, nor can NGOs engage in any activity that even hints of political opposition. In June 2002, representatives of various Turkmen parties and NGOs convened in Vienna. Turkmenistan's opposition-in-exile formed a coordinating-consultative body, called the "Roundtable of the Turkmen democratic opposition." Members include "Agzibirlik," the Russian community of Turkmenistan, the Communist Party, the Social-Democratic Party of Turkmenistan, the Board of Veterans of the Turkmen international warriors, the Turkmen diaspora in Afghanistan and Iran, the National Patriotic Movement of Turkmenistan, the National Democratic Movement of Turkmenistan, and the popular social movement "Mertebe." To date, this body has held meetings and issued statements condemning ongoing human rights abuses but has not visibly been able to undermine Niyazov's position.

There is no freedom of assembly in Turkmenistan. The atmosphere has been so repressive that one rarely even hears of attempts to organize demonstrations. Nevertheless, RFE/RL reported in April 2002 that protesters gathered outside the building of the Committee for National Security (KNB) in Ashgabat for the second day to complain about misdeeds by the security organs and to demand the punishment of KNB members who violated the law.[14] In August 2002, opponents of Niyazov's regime reportedly distributed anti-government leaflets in the main bazaar in Ashgabat.

The most publicized demonstration in Turkmenistan took place in July 1995, when about 1,000 people marched in Ashgabat and called for new presidential and parliamentary elections. Subsequently, law enforcement officials described the marchers as "drug addicts" on television, and several participants remained in jails for years afterwards. They were released before Niyazov's 1998 visit to Washington.

Turkmenistan allows no freedom of religion. The 1991 Law on Freedom of Conscience and Religious Organizations, amended in 1995 and 1996, requires religious groups to have 500 adherents in each locality wishing to register. Unregistered communities may not hold any religious meeting or proselytize. Individuals caught participating in such meetings risk monetary fines and criminal sanctions.[15]

Accordingly, approved religious communities are limited to government approved Sunni mosques and Russian Orthodox Churches. Government raids against unregistered religious groups are common, often followed by arrests and seizures of property. The government even bulldozed an unregistered Adventist Church in 1999, seized the property, and now is turning the site into a public park.[16] While longtime Baptist prisoner Shalgeldi Atakov was released in January 2002, several Jehovah's Witnesses remain jailed for refusing to swear an oath of loyalty to President Niyazov. Recently, Turkmen authorities forced a group of Protestants from a small eastern village to renounce their faith and swear an oath on Niyazov's *Ruhnama*.[17]

Uzbekistan

Under President Islam Karimov, Uzbekistan is a repressive police state, where opposition is banned, media are censored, and civil society has been crippled. Karimov apparently means to remain in power indefinitely and has manipulated elections for that purpose. None of the five parties in Uzbekistan's parliament can even be remotely considered oppositionist. The courts are tightly controlled, sentencing those accused of political or religious crimes to long prison terms.

The most populous country of Central Asia, Uzbekistan is also the state where political Islam has emerged as a threat, particularly in the form of the Islamic Movement of Uzbekistan (IMU), which the U.S. Government has classified as a terrorist organization. For the last five years, Karimov's regime has been engaged in a virtual war against religious Muslims who want to worship outside state-controlled mosques. Uzbek and international human rights groups estimate that thousands of people have been jailed; planting of evidence is common, as is torture in prison. Karimov has ignored advice from many sources, including Washington, which warns that his crackdown only strengthens the radical Islamic dangers he claims to be combating.

Since the post-September 11 rapprochement with Washington, Karimov has made some gestures: He permitted the registration of an independent human rights organization, amnestied prisoners, and most recently, has claimed that pre-publication censorship has been lifted. In 2002, two cases were reported of policemen who had tortured detainees receiving jail terms. On August 29, 2002, Karimov urged "radical" democratic changes, telling parliament that the country is ready for freedom of the media, political activity, independent courts, and economic liberalism.[18] Based on past practice, however, there is no reason to expect more than tactical concessions or to look forward to genuine political reform.

In the December 1991 presidential election, Karimov allowed Mohammad Solih, poet, writer, and leader of the opposition *Erk* party, to run. Abdurrahim Polat, leader of the opposition *Birlik* movement, was not allowed to register as a candidate. Official figures gave Solih about 12 percent of the vote, in Uzbekistan's last election with any suspense.

The OSCE refused to send observers to the 1999 parliamentary elections, in which five pro-government parties participated. In the January 2000 presidential elections, which OSCE also did not monitor, the person permitted to run against Karimov said he would vote for the incumbent. Still, Karimov was not content with another five-year term. In January 2002, Uzbekistan held a referendum which extended his tenure in office from five years to seven.

There is no freedom of assembly in Uzbekistan. Attempts to organize demonstrations are rare and participants are usually jailed. Still, on April 23, 2002, more than 20 women protesting the torture of their relatives in prison gathered on a Tashkent street. They were quickly surrounded by militia and KGB and dragged into waiting buses. This was the second such attempted demonstration in recent months.[19]

On August 27, 2002, Uzbek authorities detained Elena Urlaeva and another woman who were protesting government abuses outside the Ministry of Justice. The next day, the two were transferred to a psychiatric hospital for compulsory treatment, including forced administration of drugs.[20]

Freedom of association is not permitted in Uzbekistan. Karimov created several pro-government parties, perhaps to check the power of the National Democratic Party (successor to the Communist Party) and to create a semblance of pluralism. These parties include *Adolat* (Justice); *Milliy Tiklanish* (National Rebirth), and *Fidokorlar*, apparently Karimov's favorite. However, since 1992, the opposition parties *Erk* and *Birlik* have not been able to participate in elections or distribute literature. *Erk* spokesmen claim party members are in jail for their political activity and are tortured; *Erk* activists not in jail are closely monitored by police. A September 21, 2002 appeal by the Human Rights Society of Uzbekistan listed eight of its members behind bars.

On April 4, 2002, Karimov said he would meet with opposition members in exile who return to Uzbekistan, particularly if they could promote economic reforms. His invitation extended only to those not involved in terrorist activities, especially the February 1999 explosions in Tashkent, and those who do not seek to reestablish the Caliphate, i.e., *Hizb-ut-Tahrir*. But there is no reason to expect sanctioned opposition parties soon.

After September 11, Karimov yielded to American pressure on behalf of independent human rights groups. Before Karimov's visit to Washington in March 2002, the Ministry of Justice registered the Independent Human Rights Organization of Uzbekistan, a breakthrough by Uzbek standards. Other independent human rights groups remain unregistered, although they do function. The best known is the Human Rights Society of Uzbekistan. Recently, several more have emerged, including *Ezgulik* (Good Deed) and *Mazlum* (The Oppressed). On May 21, 2002, *Ezgulik*'s application for registration was rejected by the Ministry of Justice.

There is no freedom of speech in Uzbekistan. While stories about low-level corruption may appear, Karimov and his policies are off-limits. Those who try to print or distribute unsanctioned newspapers or bulletins, such as those associated with *Erk* or *Birlik*, risk criminal penalties. Karimov has himself criticized Uzbekistan's media, skirting the issue of how media can develop in such a tightly run political system. On May 10, 2002, he raised the issue on national TV, acknowledging that, "Despite what is in our laws . . . we are still far from international standards. The media today is not the fourth estate that it is in all developed countries."

Shortly thereafter, Uzbekistan's chief censor lost his job and on May 13, for the first time, Uzbek newspapers were published without censorship. Nevertheless, the Committee to Protect Journalists declared in Tashkent on June 10 that little has changed, as the authorities "routinely encourage self-censorship by threatening critical journalists with imprisonment." The CPJ called for the release from prison of journalists Mukhammad Bekjonov, Yusuf Rozimurodov, and Majit Abdurahimov.[21] Karimov's commitment to media freedom remains to be demonstrated and pending the publication of articles critical of government policy should not be taken seriously.

Uzbekistan's government claims that Islam has regained its revered place after 70 years of Soviet atheism and indeed, many new mosques have been opened. But Karimov has always feared politicized Islam and sought to control religion. He has some reason to worry, especially about two organizations that openly challenge the state's avowedly secular stance—the IMU and *Hizb-ut-Tahrir* (Party of Freedom). The IMU, which is linked to al Qaeda, has pledged to overthrow Karimov, and in 1999 and 2000 staged incursions into Kyrgyzstan with the aim of establishing bases in Uzbekistan. *Hizb-ut-Tahrir*, though professedly non-violent, is openly anti-Semitic and anti-Western.

Accordingly, the Uzbek Government decides who may become an Imam and what can be preached in mosques.[22] Moreover, Imams require periodic re-approval from the Muftiate, the State's Committee on Religion and the National Security Committee. A 1998 law on religion restricts religious freedom to groups deemed a threat to national security, bans proselytizing and private religious instruction, and only permits government approved clerics to wear religious dress.[23] Under 1999 amendments to the criminal code, individuals attending an unregistered group risk three to five years in jail for belonging to an "illegal" group. Individuals caught attending meetings of "banned" religious groups face up to 20 years imprisonment.[24]

Since the February 1999 explosions in Tashkent, which Karimov called an assassination attempt and blamed on radical Muslims, thousands have been jailed for practicing Islam outside of government-regulated religious institutions, and for their affiliation with unregistered Islamic organizations. Human Rights Watch has documented more than 800 such cases since 1999; detainees are held in secret, tortured, and denied access to counsel. At trial, judges ignore allegations of torture—used to extract confessions—and sentence defendants to as many as twenty years in prison for possessing or distributing unsanctioned religious literature, belonging to unofficial religious organizations, or adherence to religious ideals viewed as hostile to the state.

Christian communities exist in relative peace as long as they do not attempt to proselytize to indigenous groups not traditionally Christian.

Still, a Baptist church in a Tashkent suburb has been ordered closed, and Jehovah's Witnesses have been fined and harassed.

Conclusion

In many aspects, citizens of Central Asian states enjoy less freedom than they did a decade ago. At that time, opposition movements could operate, even in Turkmenistan and Uzbekistan. The press was freer in the early 1990s in Kazakhstan and Kyrgyzstan than in 2002, and political pluralism had far better prospects. Tajikistan's unhappy experience would seem to indicate that only violence can bring the region's governments and opposition to terms.

Unfortunately, one cannot project with any confidence the development of democratic societies in Central Asia from today's trends. More likely outcomes are variations of "strongman" regimes, where leaders-for-life control their country's economic assets, while they and lower-level officials keep the press from informing the public about their misdeeds.

But the absence of even the possibility of normal politics leads to abnormal politics. The refusal of Central Asian leaders to allow turnover at the top or permit newcomers to enter the game means that outsiders have no stake in the political process and can imagine coming to power, or merely sharing in the wealth, only by extra-constitutional methods. Kyrgyzstan's protest movement in 2002 is one form of the phenomenon; the recent reported assassination attempt on Turkmenistan's Saparmurat Niyazov is another.

Only Kyrgyzstan offers some cause for cautious optimism. Akaev has pledged not to run for a third term in 2005. His stepping down would be unprecedented for the region, as would be a sincere, successful transfer of some of his presidential powers to other branches of government. The Kyrgyz model would not necessarily apply to neighboring states, whose leaders disdain Akaev as weak, but a redistribution of powers is a guide-post for reform. Perhaps more important, the 2002 demonstrations in Kyrgyzstan were the first large protests in Central Asia in years, indicating the depth of popular resentment and the capacity for public galvanization. They also showed Kyrgystan's leaders, opposition and public, as well as the entire region, that "street politics" is effective, whereas no other vehicle of registering popular discontent and influencing government policy works. The lesson will not soon be forgotten.

Notes

[1] This article is adapted from *Ten Years After,* a forthcoming report on the state of democratization and human rights in the twelve states of the Commonwealth of Independent States by the Commission on Security and Cooperation in Europe, U.S. Congress.

[2] The organization was called the Conference on Security and Cooperation in Europe (CSCE) until January 1995.

[3] The interested or skeptical reader can test this contention by looking up the reports of the OSCE's Office for Democratic Institutions and Human Rights (ODIHR), which has monitored elections in Central Asia for years—except when ODIHR declined because the conditions were too poor to justify an observation mission.

[4] See, for example, the testimony of Assistant Secretaries of State Elizabeth Jones and Lorne Craner at a Helsinki Commission hearing "U.S. Policy Towards the OSCE," October 10, 2002.

[5] For the best and most recent account, see Martha Olcott, "Kazakhstan: Unfulfilled Promise," Carnegie Endowment for International Peace, Washington 2002.

[6] *RFE/RL Newsline,* April 26, 2002.

[7] *RFE/RL Newsline,* June 14, 2002.

[8] Peter Baker, "New Repression in Kazakhstan: Journalists Targeted After President Implicated in Scandal," *The Washington Post*, June 10, 2002.

[9] International Religious Freedom Report-Kyrgyz Republic, Bureau of Democracy, Human Rights, and Labor, Department of State, 2001.

[10] Igor Rotar, "Kyrgyzstan: New Decree Set to Tighten Religious Controls," Keston News Service, February 8, 2002.

[11] Advisory Panel of Experts on Freedom of Religion and Belief of the OSCE/ODIHR, Analysis of the Draft Law of the Kyrgyz Republic "On Freedom of Religion and Religious Organizations," March 30, 2001.

[12] U.S. State Dept. Country Report on Human Rights, March 2002.

[13] In August 2002, he renamed the months of the year, reserving two for himself and his deceased mother. Claudia Rosett, "The Real World: Turkmenistan's Dictator Is No Joke to Those He Rules," *The Wall Street Journal Europe*, August 28, 2002.

[14] An RFE/RL correspondent on the scene estimated the group to number 300 the first day, about 50 the next. Niyazov, in sacking high-ranking members of the KNB, complained the service had been selling drugs, as well as torturing suspects and raping young women.

[15] International Religious Freedom Report-Turkmenistan, Bureau of Democracy, Human Rights, and Labor, Department of State, 2001.

[16] Ibid.

[17] Felix Corley, "Turkmenistan: Protestants Forced to Renounce Their Faith," Keston News Service, May 17, 2002.

[18] *The Washington Post*, August 30, 2002

[19] Human Rights Society of Uzbekistan, April 25, 2002.

[20] Human Rights Watch, "Uzbek Rights Defender in Psychiatric Detention," August 30, 2002.

[21] Khabar Television, Almaty, June 11, 2002. RFE/RL Newsline, June 12, 2002.

[22] Country Report on Human Rights Practices for 1993-Uzbekistan, Bureau of Democracy, Human Rights, and Labor, Department of State, (1994). Igor Rotar, "Special Report - Uzbekistan: Muslim Clergy Under State Control," Keston News Service, April 23, 2002.

[23] International Religious Freedom Report-Uzbekistan, Bureau of Democracy, Human Rights, and Labor, Department of State, 2001.

[24] Ibid.

Chapter 6

Democracy-Building in Central Asia Post-September 11

Sylvia W. Babus

C entral Asia is back on the map of U.S. foreign policy. After the September 11, 2001 terrorist attacks on the United States, the five "stans" of Central Asia became "frontline states" in the global war on terrorism, with important roles to play as strategic partners in military operations in Afghanistan and Iraq. Budgets for assistance funds soared. The bulk of the new funds paid for military equipment, training, and various forms of counter-terrorism programs. However, the heightened U.S. interest in closer strategic relationships with these states also was matched by renewed enthusiasm—and more money—for promoting democratic political development. In fact, the Bush administration's new conceptual framework for national security strategy and foreign aid offered strong reasons to build democracy in Central Asia.

This chapter will examine the scope and character of the democracy-promoting re-engagement in Central Asia. How much are we spending on such assistance, and what part does it play in our relationships with these states now? What kind of democracy promotion do we support, and how has our assistance changed over time? How does democracy promotion in Central Asia fit into the Bush administration's plans for national security and foreign aid? Specifically, how has our assistance changed since September 11? Is our assistance worthwhile? Despite the persistence of obstacles in the Central Asian environment, and despite some fundamental contradictions and tensions in the U.S. policy formulations, optimism persists about the value and long-term promise of such assistance.

Foreign assistance practitioners are cheering America's renewed interest in Central Asia and are eagerly expanding established democracy-building assistance activities — or designing new ones. Some of these initiatives are exciting, and all of them promise to enlarge the political space for political reform. However, all parties recognize that the room to maneuver is still extremely limited. None of the sitting governments appear ready to warm up to democracy just because the United States believes that repressive regimes produce discontent and potential terrorist recruits.

While some have charged that strategic-level alliances with today's undemocratic strongmen in Central Asia ruin the chances for meaningful democracy promotion, this charge seems overdone. The path toward democracy in Central Asia was rough and steep well before September 11, and the follow-on U.S. rush to embrace these governments as partners in the war on terror. Most of those who are implementing America's democracy-promoting assistance projects in Central Asia are both realistic and sophisticated about what can be accomplished. There is no reason to reject their faith that a prominent U.S. presence, coupled with greater visibility for Central Asia and attention to its societies, can enhance the possibilities for successful small steps forward in the coming years.

The Assistance Surprise: Suddenly, Close Ties with Central Asia

The Central Asian states did not take long to decide to support the U.S. war on terrorism, or the U.S. military action against the Taliban in Afghanistan.[1] By the end of September 2001, Russia had offered its support for a U.S. military presence in Central Asia, and all five states had offered use of their airspace, airports, roads, or bases in return for various forms of assistance. Agreements, memoranda, and joint declarations conveying these understandings were the subject of a number of high-level visits to and from the region in 2001 and 2002. In the case of Uzbekistan, a "nonspecific security guarantee" took the form of an American pledge to regard any external threat to Uzbekistani security "with grave concern."[2]

Congress quickly granted President Bush's request for more money to pay for expanded cooperation with the Central Asian (and other) frontline states, through supplemental appropriations in December 2001 and March 2002 that designated nearly $150 million in additional funding.[3] The effect was to quadruple total assistance funds for Uzbekistan, nearly double funding for the Kyrgyz Republic and Tajikistan, while sizably increasing funds for Kazakhstan and Turkmenistan. Some of the extra money did supplement assistance activities to support democratic and economic reform; however, the bulk of the funds were for security-related purposes. Much of this covered provision of equipment to support enhanced border security capabilities by ground or airborne forces, communications equipment for interoperability with U.S. forces, as well as improved counter-narcotics capacity.[4] The data for budgeted funds over the last four years is presented in Table 6–1. The trend in total obligated assistance funds appears also in Figure 6–1.

Table 6–1. **Budgeted Assistance to the Central Asian States, 1999 – 2002 (Millions)**

	1999	2000	2001	2002
Kazakhstan	74.49	71.04	74.92	86.25
Kyrgyzstan	64.19	50.11	41.60	93.53
Tajikistan	37.63	38.85	72.04	133.41
Turkmenistan	17.78	11.24	12.88	18.86
Uzbekistan	49.34	40.20	58.68	219.35

Data from the summary tables in "U.S. Government Assistance to and Cooperative Activities with Eurasia, Fiscal Year 2002." These figures represent total FSA and agency transfers budgeted, excluding the estimated value for donated commodity humanitarian assistance.

Figure 6–1. **USAID Funds for Central Asia, 1996 - 2002**

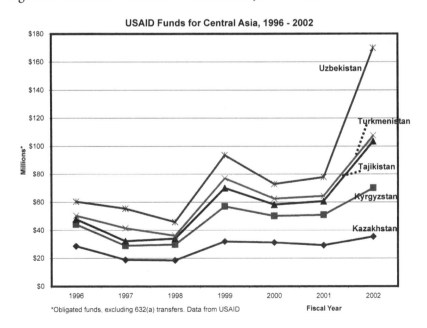

Figure 6–2. **Democracy Promotion as Part of USAID Assistance to the NIS, 1996-2002***

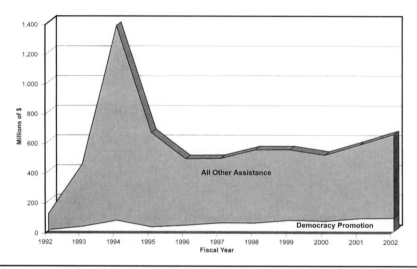

*NIS refers to the 12 former Soviet republics (excludes the Baltic states); Obligated funds from Agency transfers. Data from USAID and the Annual Reports of the Office of the Coordinator of US Assistance to Europe and Eurasia.

Just how much more money has been made available to promote democracy? Figure 6–2 gives a closer look at the trend in the proportion of U.S. Agency for International Development (USAID) funds obligated for democracy and governance activities. These funds are not large when compared with the millions made available for security, military, and law enforcement, but they still represent an overall increase.[6] Moreover, these funds were shared among a great many kinds of programs, ranging from activities to promote nuclear safety to medical advice about HIV/AIDS, to budget training, to student exchanges.[7] On the other hand, most democracy promotion activities have been relatively inexpensive. Where other kinds of assistance provided materials or equipment, democracy promotion generally has emphasized training as well as conferences, seminars and materials and small grants for citizen groups.

Promoting Democracy While Fighting Terrorism

What is the role of democracy promotion assistance in the post-September 11 environment? Has the global war on terrorism swept aside the old dream of democratic transformation in the former Soviet republics?

Strategic partnerships with the decidedly undemocratic governments of Kazakhstan, Kyrgyzstan, Tajikistan, Uzbekistan, and Turkmenistan certainly pose risks. Human rights groups quickly questioned the wisdom of closer ties to these states.[8] Despite widespread agreement that the United States would need the broadest possible set of cooperative partners to exterminate the kind of terrorism that had so brutally attacked the U.S. homeland, the five Central Asian states were not attractive partners. In the words of one observer:

> Courting these ex-Soviet republics has obliged the administration to cozy up to unsavory autocrats hitherto known chiefly for economic mismanagement, a contempt for democracy and human rights, and a single-minded determination to retain their hold on power by whatever means necessary . . . Freedom of religion does not exist, but then neither do most other freedoms, as the State Department's own annual report on human rights demonstrates.[9]

Another critic pointed out that these states could try to exploit the partnership to avoid political and economic reform:

> Clearly, these governments will wish to use the U.S. need for access to their territory to slacken pressure on them with regard to political and economic reform. Worse, aid money provided to autocratic governments may exacerbate corruption making better governance more difficult instead of less. They will also try to leverage their relationship with the United States in their regional rivalries with each other. And of course, the United States risks being associated with unpopular regimes in the eyes of the peoples of these countries, and suffering when those regimes eventually fall.[10]

From the outset, however, the Bush administration voiced their position that any partnership with these Central Asian governments would require the states to declare their commitment to democracy and market economies. Congress, too, wanted to ensure that the new security relationships would not eclipse U.S. support for democratic values. Proposed amendments to the legislation authorizing extra funding to the "frontline states" linked the new money to satisfactory human rights performance. There were no illusions: Everyone recognized that the Central Asian regimes were politically unsavory, and that it would be unwise—not to mention politically unacceptable—to neglect concerns about democracy and human rights when dealing with countries like the "Stans."

In every instance, agreements with the Central Asian states included provisions that renewed or confirmed their pledges to advance the reform agenda, both politically and economically. The U.S. side also affirmed its plans to continue efforts to promote democracy through foreign assistance to Central Asia, right along with heavy funding to re-equip and train military and security forces. While the increases in funding for democracy promotion are dwarfed by those for military and security assistance, more money for democracy really has been made available.

Fallow Ground: The Record of Democracy Promotion Prior to September 11

Initial efforts in the 1990s to promote democratic development in Central Asia did build contacts with reformers, exposed thousands to Western ideas, and helped local people experience the power of organized citizenry. However, the overall impact of the efforts by the United States and others was limited, given the authoritarian styles of the region's firmly entrenched leaders. While not identical, all the Central Asian regimes to some extent restricted speech, limited citizen action, avoided competitive elections, stifled dissent, and suppressed or harassed potential opposition. Uzbekistan and Turkmenistan also resisted the emergence of markets and entrepreneurs, perhaps fearing the political consequences of a restructured economy they could not control. This restrictive environment retarded the emergence of local reformers, and limited the possibilities for democracy promotion by outsiders.

The bleak outlook for democracy promotion in Central Asia prompted a reorientation of assistance strategy. A five-year assistance strategy for Central Asia prepared by USAID in 2000 lamented the "overall lack of reform across the region."[11] Noting that the Eastern European model of a "rapid, structural transition to open market democracy is not appropriate for the Asian republics," this new strategy called for a shift to a longer-term approach that would build pressure for change by expanding opportunities for citizen participation. That is, USAID would "concentrate assistance on selected organizations, enterprise and people at local levels to grow dialogue, pluralism, the non-governmental sector, and partnership to build common good and mutual interest in stable change."[12] In other words, USAID adopted a "democracy from below" approach, emphasizing indirect efforts to support a "more open, democratic culture, with emphasis on nongovernmental organizations, independent information and electronic media, and progressive parliamentarians."[13]

What had gone wrong? Primarily, it was anti-democratic behavior by governments. Each of the five Central Asian states provided some reason for disappointment. The bad news included Kyrgyzstan,[14] which had seemed to be a success story for democracy promotion in Central Asia because of its "progressive leadership, vocal commitment to democracy and a market-based economy."[15] However, President Askar Akaev's moves in 2001 to harass citizen groups and restrict independent media changed this assessment.[16]

Despite its initial pledges to join the world economy and create a democratic, secular system that would protect citizen rights, Uzbekistan proved resistant to both political and economic reform. USAID's 2000 report to Congress complained about the Uzbekistani government's reluctance to introduce broad-based market reforms, and the "serious debilitating effect" of its restrictions on convertibility and access to foreign currency. "Citizen participation in economic and political life [in Uzbekistan] is limited and ill-informed. Political opposition to the regime is not tolerated, and the upcoming elections are not expected to meet international standards."[17] A more recent report charged that Uzbekistan's leadership "remains entrenched in a closed and stagnant political and economic system . . . Citizens remain poorly informed and their participation in economic and political life restricted. Political opposition is not tolerated and interference with the independent media persists."[18]

Kazakhstan, often praised for its economic reforms, began to draw criticism for its political shortcomings. Unfair presidential elections, crackdowns on the media, and restrictions of freedom of assembly provoked a complaint in USAID's FY 2000 Congressional budget presentation that despite some "great strides" in civil society, "hoped-for changes have not occurred at the national level."[19]

Very little serious democracy promotion could occur in Tajikistan until the civil war had ended and recovery was underway. A political settlement in 1997 eventually brought the opposition into the national political process and created important openings for U.S. assistance directed at democracy building. However, this was a late start, and the subsequent American assistance program was quite small.

Turkmenistan, with a government uninterested in change, was clearly the most difficult case. As USAID's FY 2001 program summary noted, "the Government of Turkmenistan has not yet made a demonstrable commitment to democratic and economic reform. Turkmenistan remains a resolute one-party state with power vested in a communist-turned-nationalist leadership."[20]

These developments clearly showed that democracy promotion in Central Asia would be working, in practice, against governments. This seemed to make any real progress toward democracy building in this region part of a fundamentally political equation: Would the United States (and other democracy-promoting governments) be ready to pressure the governments of this region to tolerate and accept such programs? And how receptive would the Central Asian governments be to such pressures? Would further progress depend on unlikely political shifts within these states?

Just two months before the September 11 attacks, Michael Parmly of the State Department's Bureau of Democracy, Human Rights and Labor outlined a rather depressing state of affairs in testimony on Central Asia before hearings on the Hill. While he indicated the United States would not give up its efforts to support the emergence of democracy in this region, his statement left little room for hope so long as the current Central Asian governments remained in power. Parmly's statement on July 28, 2001 is worth quoting at length:

> The overarching goal of U.S. policy in Central Asia is to see these states develop into stable, free-market democracies, both as a goal in itself and as a bulwark against regional instability and conflict. This broader goal serves three core strategic interests: regional security, political/economic reform and energy development. While our security and energy interests are important, in the long run none of these goals can be achieved until these governments undertake comprehensive reforms to enfranchise their people both economically and politically. . . .
>
> We have therefore encouraged, both through across-the-board political engagement and a variety of assistance programs, the formation of democratic civil societies and the development of free-market economies . . . In some countries, there has been progress on economic reform. However, despite such efforts, progress towards democracy has been uneven at best, while in places like Turkmenistan, it is almost non-existent. Even more disturbing, however, has been the varying degrees of backsliding in countries like Kazakhstan and Kyrgyzstan . . . Political accountability, particularly as embodied by national elections, is the most obvious and well-monitored aspect of democracy. In this area, the Central Asian republics have performed abysmally . . . .

Unfortunately, our efforts to promote democracy and respect for human rights in Central Asia have not been enough. Indeed, these governments seem to be giving up on the reality of democracy (though they cling to the rhetoric). As a result, we have altered our approach. Democracy and human rights issues take up more of the agenda in our bilateral discussion . . . In addition we have reoriented our assistance programs to these states, shifting our democracy, economic and humanitarian assistance more toward direct grants to local communities or via local NGOs [non-governmental organizations], and rely less on government to government aid.[21]

Ambassador William Taylor, then serving as the U.S. Coordinator for U.S. Assistance to the New Independent States,[22] also appeared at these hearings. He raised the practical problem associated with the factors Parmly had described: "What can the United States do to help the people of Central Asia create democratic societies, given the fact that their governments are standing in the way of reform?"[23] This constraint, he said, explained why our democracy programs in Central Asia are "targeted almost exclusively at the non-governmental sector, with the exception of a few programs that work with reform-oriented local governments." He also noted the importance of support for local independent media outlets and praised the popular academic and professional exchanges that were exposing so many of Central Asia's young generation to the West.

Based on testimony by Ambassador Taylor and other regional experts, U.S. assistance providers had lowered their expectations for democratic change in Central Asia well before September 11, and shifted gears to longer-range strategies. This might be described as "democracy promotion from below," but how bold would such a strategy be? Whatever assumptions one makes about U.S. capabilities and resources, no foreign government can force change on an unwilling society. Even where groups and individuals in a foreign state are receptive or even eager for democratic change, official U.S. assistance programs to support them can only operate by agreement with the host government. Such governments may resist, inhibit, or forbid efforts to enhance civil society and empower citizens at the grass roots.[24] How far would the U.S. government be willing to go, and how successful would its attempts to carry out democracy building be?

Long-time democracy assistance providers have reacted differently to the range of options available. Some of them have objected strenuously to any suggestion that the United States "give up" by limiting support for pro-democracy forces in undemocratic countries. Everyone seems to support educational exchanges that may prepare more pro-democratic future generations, and sing the praises of support for the emergence of civil society in former socialist states.[25] But for those impatient to see progress, educational exchanges and efforts to promote cultural change are not enough. The poor prospects for indigenous democratic reform in Central Asia brought new attention to the foreign policy priorities that would be set by the new U.S. administration under President George W. Bush.

The Bush Administration Reframes Assistance Policies

The conceptual framework behind the Bush administration's new National Security Strategy, and a fresh approach to foreign assistance, give democratic values a prominent place. However, the new concepts have produced some still-unresolved tensions between national security and democracy promotion activities in Central Asia.

USAID, under its new Administrator Andrew Natsios, had already begun to redefine foreign assistance in ways that would emphasize performance, accountability, and cost-effectiveness. Essentially, this new approach stressed that assistance designed to support democratic development and market reforms would be wasted if it were given to governments unable or unwilling to pursue reforms. Early in 2002, USAID released a commissioned study[26] that buttressed these ideas by examining the accumulated experience of development assistance. This work attributed some of the failures of development assistance to faults of the recipient states themselves, noting that those performing most poorly had failed to achieve either democracy or good governance. Accordingly, the report offered five suggestions for promoting—and rewarding—political will to reform:

- Levels of foreign assistance must be more clearly tied to development performance, and to demonstrations of political will for reform and good governance.
- Good performers must be tangibly rewarded.
- If there is no political commitment to democratic and governance reforms, the United States should suspend government assistance and work only with nongovernmental actors.
- The United States should use its voice, vote and full influence within the World Bank and other multilateral development banks to terminate development assistance to bad governments and to focus on countries with reasonably good governance.
- The United States must work closer with other bilateral doors to coordinate pressure on bad, recalcitrant governments.[27]

This analysis also reflected impatience with undemocratic, nonreforming governments:

> Only if governance becomes more democratic and accountable will development occur in the poorly performing countries. And only with a comprehensive, consistent, 'tough love' approach from the international community is political will for governance reform likely to emerge and to be sustained . . . Political leaders must learn that they will pay a heavy international price for bad governance, forfeiting material resources and becoming more isolated diplomatically . . . Strategies for promoting democracy and good governance must focus relentlessly on generating and sustaining political will for systemic reform, with diplomacy and aid working hand in hand.[28]

President Bush incorporated the key elements of this incentive- and performance-based concept of foreign assistance in his proposal for a Millenium Challenge Account (MCA), announced in March 2002. His plan proposed a $5 billion annual increase in assistance to developing countries with the funds intended to support development projects by poor countries that have enacted sound policies and achieved some measurable progress. A key element of the MCA is the plan to fund projects proposed by developing countries themselves.[29] Congress has accepted this program, but at much lower levels of initial funding. Considerable controversy remains over how to identify qualifying countries and administer the assistance. Despite tough talk about the need to promote political will for democratic development, the overall approach of the MCA makes it inapplicable to the Central Asian states. Instead, the MCA is directed at reducing poverty more efficiently by working with reform governments in very poor states.[30]

But while a shift toward a "tougher" development assistance strategy seemed at odds with the new funding commitment to the Central Asian states, the Bush administration's strategy for dealing with terrorist threats appeared consistent with it. The National Security Strategy issued in September 2002 noted, "poverty, weak institutions, and corruption can make weak states vulnerable to terrorist networks and drug cartels."[31] Repression also makes states vulnerable to terrorists. Hence, democratic reform—and efforts by foreign allies and supporters to promote democratic reform—offer an antidote to the growth of terrorism. Democratic reforms are expected to promote good governance and improve prospects for prosperity, while also defusing unrest by assuring all citizens a voice and improving the prospects for justice. Deputy Assistant Secretary of State Lynn Pascoe in testimony to Congress on U.S. policy toward Central Asia made a practical link to assistance policy:

> Authoritarian governments and largely unreformed economies, we believe, create the conditions of repression and poverty that could well become the breeding grounds for further terrorism . . . Thus, not only do we believe it is strongly in our national interest to engage fully with these governments to urge the political and economic reforms that we judge are essential to alleviate the conditions that breed terrorism, but we also firmly believe it is in these countries' own national interests. When citizens, and especially youth, feel that they have a voice in how they are governed, when they believe that they have an economic stake in the future, then they are less likely to be attracted to a radicalized path cloaked in Islam that offers a utopian solution to their discontent. *It is extremely difficult to convince Central Asian leaders that long-term economic and democratic reforms are necessary to eliminate the roots of terrorism if we are not willing to help them counter terrorism in the short term and prove that we will be engaged for the long term.* (Italics supplied)[32]

How Does the United States Promote Democracy in Central Asia?

Dozens of programs, activities, and projects by many different U.S. government agencies and departments reflect the great variety of U.S. interests involved in our relationships with these countries. Most offer some form of technical assistance (advice and training), although a few provide equipment, and some give commodities, such as medicine, or surplus agricultural products that can be sold to support a designated purpose. Not all programs address development: U.S. assistance programs range from arms control efforts that involve dismantling and destroying weapons and support for safeguards to prevent the theft of nuclear materials, to training for public health and law enforcement officials. In contrast to the scale and costs of many of those programs, democracy-building activities generally involve relatively low-cost in-country training, advisors, and small-grants. USAID is the main administrator of such assistance, planning and monitoring activities it funds primarily through U.S. NGOs or companies under contracts, grants, and cooperative agreements.[33] USAID Missions abroad oversee implementation of the assistance, and play a critical role in ensuring that this aid is designed and assessed for results and impact.

Since American assistance began in the wake of the collapse of the Soviet Union, USAID has modified its strategies, specific assistance objectives, and methods incrementally and often. While it is true that almost any U.S.-sponsored assistance can be considered to contribute to democratic development, at least indirectly, USAID has identified several categories of democracy-promoting assistance that apply in most countries. This is a long list that can be sorted in various ways. By purpose these activities promote the rule of law, including fair legal procedures, civil and human rights, free speech, and independent courts; citizen participation in public life; democratic political processes, including competent legislatures, competitive elections, political parties; independent media; responsible local government; independent trade unions; civic education; and civil society.

The activities funded in the Central Asian states present similar packages, with variations that have reflected the opportunities and constraints in each society, political and economic circumstances, as well as overall socio-political conditions as they have evolved. The mix of assistance activities also has responded to emerging problems, and shifted focus as experience closed off or opened new areas of concern—or as funding levels rose or fell. This process of adaptation and adjustment is supported by regular program reviews and reports, as well as by assessments and evaluations contracted in particular activity sectors for specific countries.

Democracy-Promotion Packages Before and After September 11

The five Central Asian states present different needs and problems. A closer look at the democracy promotion packages before and after September 11 shows both the similarities and the variations. Turkmenistan, led by Saparmurat Niyazov, opted for a foreign policy of "positive neutrality," and remained uninterested in committing to Western-style reform. Tajikistan suffered civil war and faced recovery, political restructuring, and the need for reform, all at the same time. Desperately poor Kyrgyzstan embraced economic, fiscal and trade policy reform, and at first welcomed assistance that helped strengthen an emerging civil society. Kazakhstan, with key nuclear and space installations, quickly built solid security relationships with the West and set out to establish a market economy as well; however, democratic forms were shoved aside in the rigged elections of 1999. Uzbekistan was blessed with many natural resources, but limited its economic development options by turning away from Western-sponsored economic reforms. The Uzbekistani government says it is threatened by radical Islam, and uses this threat to justify harsh suppression of political and religious dissent.

In general, the political environment in all five Central Asian states has left little room for outsiders to encourage citizen empowerment or democratic laws and practices. All five governments have been unreceptive or actively hostile to some forms of democracy-building assistance activities, and all these governments stand accused of serious human rights abuses. According to the Organization for Security and Cooperation in Europe (OSCE), none of the elections in the region have met international standards for fair practices.[34] It is not surprising that the array of democracy-promoting assistance activities in each of the Central Asian states are somewhat similar, reflecting comparable circumstances and limitations as well as some common social features. The array of activities also reflects USAID's choices of programs appropriate to the agency's overall strategy for promoting democracy in the region. USAID's shift toward the non-governmental sector, work with citizens at the grass roots, and long-range programs, such as student exchanges, affected portfolios in all five countries.[35] By 2001, so little money was being spent on democracy promotion that even modest funding increases after September 11 meant doubling the resources for some existing activities, and unexpected funding for some new initiatives. USAID programming accounted for some of these increases, but grants issued by the State Department Bureau for Democracy, Human Rights and Labor (DRL) funded the most innovative steps. The DRL grants, made through the Human Rights and Democracy Fund, have emphasized political party building, training for human and civil rights advocacy, and support for free and independent media.[36]

In Uzbekistan, increasing citizen participation in non-governmental organizations was the chief emphasis through training, small grant programs, and civil society support centers. Counterpart International, the Initiative for Social Action and Renewal in Eurasia (ISAR) and Winrock International implemented these activities. Specialized advice on NGO legislation to help Uzbekistanis secure a better legal climate for citizen groups was provided by the International Center for Not for Profit Law (ICNL). USAID also funded Internews, an organization specializing in media development, to provide support to some independent local television stations, and to train journalists, including training on media law and legal rights. The American Bar Association's Central and East European Law Initiative (ABA/CEELI) provided modest programs of training and technical assistance to support legal professionals and help advance important reform legislation, as well as women's legal literacy. In view of

Uzbekistan's persistent failure to follow international standards for free and fair elections, the International Foundation for Electoral Systems (IFES) had bypassed technical elections assistance in favor of a civic education program for high school students, but this had ended before September 11.

How did this set of activities change after September 11? The activities underway or in the planning stages today represent a slightly different mix of old and new.[37] In Uzbekistan, the established programs already underway received additional funding which enabled them to expand their work to reach more people. Counterpart started a new civic advocacy program for NGOs, and ABA/CEELI opened the first free human rights legal clinic at Tashkent's main law school—to be followed by another in Namangan. Freedom House began a program to train and support human rights defenders and opened three resource centers for human rights NGOs that offer internet access, reference materials, and meeting space.[38] Both the National Democratic Institute (NDI)and the International Republican Institute (IRI) received funding to support political party building through training and seminars. Complementing an extension of an internet access program to Uzbekistani schools, USAID established a new program to support basic educational reform. The new money also funded two information initiatives: one on anti-trafficking, and the other, a new civic education project for high schools that may start in 2004. The Community Connections program began taking Uzbekistani professionals and entrepreneurs to the United States for short-term internships and training. Another new idea is a Central Asia regional project called the Community Action Investment Program (CAIP). CAIP works to defuse potential ethnic conflict by stimulating multi-ethnic community problem solving. This project initially targeted communities in the Ferghana valley, a troubled border region between Kyrgyzstan, Uzbekistan, and Tajikistan; but also parts of southern Uzbekistan, Lebap in Turkmenistan, and Shymkent and Turkestan in Kazakhstan.

In Kazakhstan, democracy promotion included a broad program of support for civic participation, as well as a set of activities to promote more effective and accountable local governments. Counterpart International provided training and grants to NGOs, supported civil society resource centers, and worked with ICNL and other donors to promote NGO-friendly legislation. ISAR promoted advocacy and community education by environmental citizen groups. Internews supported independent media and trained professional journalists. ABA/CEELI helped build professional associations of lawyers and judges, encouraged reforms in legal education, and assisted those working for an independent judiciary. IFES introduced and supported a civic education program for high schoolers that spread widely. The International Research and Exchanges Board (IREX) provided public access internet sites and training. The International City/County Managers Association implemented activities directed at local government officials designed to improve their management skills, their commitment to citizens, and their willingness to include citizen input.

After September 11, all democracy-promoting activities in Kazakhstan expanded somewhat. NDI received additional funding to support a full-time trainer, and thus increased its capacity for training political parties and democratic activists. NDI also expanded its civic advocacy work. The IRI established a presence and resumed its party-building work. More money has been allocated to support independent media through help for the National Association of Broadcasters and a production fund administered by Internews. Freedom House will be starting a new program of support for human rights defenders. Assistance to support judicial training is up, and the new CAIP began its work in ethnically mixed cities near the border with Uzbekistan. The National Endowment for Democracy received more money for grants to support public discussion on political issues.

Kyrgyzstan's set of democracy promoting assistance activities included elements similar to those in Uzbekistan and Kazakhstan. However, greater progress in the development of civil society, citizen advocacy, legal reform, and elected local governments enabled these assistance programs to have more advanced objectives. Civic organizations had begun to form social partnerships at the local level, and had demonstrated skill in forming coalitions to advocate for or against proposed legislation on a national basis. ABA/CEELI's rule of law program established legal information centers, and assisted Parliament with the development of a manual on legislative drafting. The NDI worked closely with a non-partisan national civic organization, the Coalition for Democracy and Civil Society, hosted seminars for political parties, and also conducted programs to support professional development of the members of Parliament.

New elements in Kyrgyzstan's democracy promoting assistance activities after September 11 included funding for an independent printing press; a new program in basic education; training and grants through the National Endowment for Democracy for human rights NGOs; support for NGO advocacy campaigns; and the region-wide CAIP, designed to reduce the potential for conflict in ethnically mixed areas. Freedom House has begun a program to support human rights defenders. Additional funds meant expanded efforts by existing activities—such as ABA/CEELI's work with lawyers and law students, and ARD/Checchi's commercial law training, and programs that support independent media. Both the NDI and the IRI received funding from the State Department's Human Rights and Democracy Fund (HRDF) to support work in Kyrgyzstan.[39] NDI and IRI programs work to promote the growth of democratically oriented political parties and parliamentary factions, foster the development of civil society, and encourage constructive dialogue between government and opposition groups. NDI has received additional support for its civic advocacy work, and its assistance to a dozen civil society resource and information centers. The Urban Institute's local government program was reoriented slightly to stress work with local governments to cultivate a more democratic civic culture—including support for public hearings.

Funding for Turkmenistan's democracy promotion assistance was tiny, even when compared with the budgets for the other Central Asian states. Assistance designed to promote democratic culture focused on Counterpart's program to help build non-political, non-governmental organizations and develop citizen advocacy. ABA/CEELI and others provided a smattering of training, seminars, and technical assistance to law students, legal professionals, and journalists. After September 11, the increase in funding for Central Asia meant that the existing NGO-support activities could expand, and gave them more money for community development grants and for the kind of civil society resource centers that had proved so helpful in other countries. The regional CAIP would be active in Turkmenistan as well, but has been slow getting started because of host government reluctance. USAID decided to use some of the new funds to introduce a basic education project that would help retrain teachers and introduce a modern curriculum into Turkmen schools—a long-term method for promoting democratic culture.

In Tajikistan, democracy promotion began modestly after the end of the civil war. Support for NGOs that promoted reconciliation and encouraged citizen participation in elections were key aspects of the initial efforts. USAID also funded training for political parties and legislators, voter education, civic education, and development work with legal professionals, journalists, and teachers. Small grants to NGOs supported advocacy campaigns that pressed for citizen access to Parliament and helped secure laws friendly to citizen groups and independent media. After September 11, the programs already underway received some additional funding. New initiatives included a civic advocacy center; a civic education program; anti-trafficking activities; a training program for journalists; more training for judges, lawyers, and law students; and a local government activity that offers training to city officials. With support from the Educational and Cultural Affairs Bureau at the State Department, IREX started a small grants program to train local media on anti-trafficking. The increased funds also supported new efforts in basic education, legal literacy campaigns, and a set of conflict prevention programs—including Tajikistan's substantial share of the CAIP.

Renewed Democracy Promotion: Is It Worthwhile?

An in-depth assessment of the impact of U.S. democracy promotion in Central Asia is clearly beyond the scope of this brief account. Practitioners who implement the small but vigorous activities in Central Asia are enthusiastic, and believe much more useful work could be done there. From their perspective, democratic development and the outlook for those who seek democratic change benefits when the United States takes a stand in its favor. This may be especially true for those who speak against human rights abuses. They—and their foreign supporters—are convinced that U.S. interest in their fate helps keep them alive and active.[40] Others are less hopeful about the merits of the re-engagement and more skeptical about the U.S. government's commitment to promote democracy while pursuing strategic partnerships against terrorism, despite many official statements confirming that both goals are central ones.[41]

Many recent assessments are gloomy. Martha Brill Olcott claims "developments are not moving in directions that the United States would want them to go. Central Asian leaders have made many promises that they would support democratic reform, but most of them are proving to be quite hollow." Acknowledging that U.S. assistance efforts "remain limited in scope and by necessity take the long-term view of the problem," she nonetheless concluded that overall, "the past year has been a dismal one for anyone who supports the goal of democratic transition in Central Asia."[42] Fiona Hill of the Brookings Institution has said that the new spotlight on Central Asia "has had little positive impact on domestic developments . . . Indeed, in the case of Central Asia, the war on terrorism has empowered governments to continue aggressive campaigns against their opponents and given an added impetus to repression."[43]

Lorne Craner, head of the State Department Bureau for Democracy, Human Rights, and Labor, has visited the region many times, and has spoken eloquently and often about the importance the U.S. places on the promises that our Central Asian partners have made to respect human rights.[44] However, human rights organizations have objected to his bureau's report on human rights support efforts as unrealistically optimistic.[45] The acting Assistance Coordinator, Tom Adams, recently provided an overall assessment that was upbeat, but offered frank appraisals of the "less than rosy" picture on democratic reform, where "noticeable backsliding" had occurred. Taking a historical view, he noted that "the Soviet successor states have faced more difficult transitions than initially anticipated – both due to their long tenure under Soviet rule and their lack of historical experience with democratic and market systems."[46] A similar tone of realistic, resigned, and unhappy appraisal appeared in USAID's most recent budget presentation to Congress:

> While economic growth for [Eurasia] has been positive, social conditions are dismal and trends in democratic freedoms are unfavorable . . . Lackluster reform in several countries has increased their economic and political isolation. With widespread corruption and an incomplete reform process, public trust in government and private institutions continues to deteriorate . . . Funding increases in Central Asia pose a different challenge. There, USAID is managing a greater magnitude of assistance resources with limited staff who manage activities in five countries. The program challenge is to continue pressing for progress in democracy and human rights within the context of high budget levels resulting from their cooperation in the war on terror.[47]

The Future: Keep On Keeping On

Clearly, the United States will continue its efforts to support democratic development in Central Asia. Whether or not the level of funding and energy applied to this task will survive the inevitable fall-off in intensity of our strategic cooperation with these states in the war on terrorism remains to be seen.[48]

Our approach to the newly independent states of Central Asia began with contradictions, and remains constrained by competing goals, assumptions and needs. In time, we learned that democracy building in these former socialist states will be a long process, and can become irreversible only if the next generation internalizes the norms, habits, and discipline of daily democratic practice. Experience has shown many ways that outsiders can help the process along, but also has taught respect for the complexity of the transformation task. To ensure success, each of these countries also must nurture its own democracy advocates who can and will lead the transformation, and forge a new civic culture to support and sustain the new system.

Foreign assistance in support of fundamental political transformation is a tricky business. Realists recognized that a true restructuring of the political system in the former Soviet republics would be a mammoth challenge. And despite pro-democracy declarations by the new leaders, the lack of democratic experience and the strength of statist approaches and attitudes presaged a long and difficult road. It did not take long to learn that pro-democracy assistance programs were a hard sell in Central Asia. Across the region, assistance programs accordingly adopted a longer time frame for thinking about democracy building, and shifted toward programs that were less overtly political or threatening to the sitting regimes.[49]

The mix of U.S. interests in the region has lent an interesting dynamic to relationships with these states, with some interesting effects on our democracy building activities. Security interests and larger foreign policy concerns in the region appeared at first to complement the efforts to help these states transform their economic and political systems. For example, the United States established a large presence very early in Kazakhstan, in order to support the removal of this large state's many nuclear weapons, employ its weapons scientists, and improve safety and security at its nuclear research institutions. This cooperative effort laid a solid foundation for security cooperation and good working relationships with its new government. Kazakhstan, along with Uzbekistan and Kyrgyzstan, also proved quite receptive to the various military training and exchange opportunities provided through NATO's nonthreatening Partnership for Peace.[50] All three states also helped build the Central Asian Peacekeeping Battalion, and participated in associated training. A steady traffic of military delegations to and from the United States paralleled a similar movement of administrators, educators, economists, and health officials invited to the United States for training. Promotion of trade and commerce in the region also seemed to have a reinforcing effect on our interest in economic transformation and serious movement toward world trade standards and free markets.

The Global War on Terrorism drove an American re-engagement in Central Asia—one that has included a re-energizing of our support for democracy there. This has brought a re-examination of lessons already learned about post-socialist transformations, and a search for a more effective mix of techniques and approaches that can achieve real progress without alienating the current regimes that ultimately may be affected by such changes.

The prospects seem mixed: The United States now has additional handicaps to overcome in convincing Islamic populations of its good intentions. Should the main currents of political reform in Central Asia takes an Islamic form, U.S. democracy promotion must remain appropriate to these cultural settings, while offering realistic and achievable alternatives to the region's entrenched autocracies. The political space is small, and the tolerance of these governments to outside meddling is likely to be low. However, even if America and its allies cannot find ways to leverage their new strategic role into greater local tolerance for democracy promotion efforts, the renewed engagement in support of democracy in Central Asia will still nurture constituencies for future change.

Notes

[1] See chapter 21 in this volume on U.S. security relations with Central Asia.

[2] For details about the reactions of Central Asian states to the September 11 attacks, and the first steps toward security cooperation with the U.S. against terrorism and the Taliban, see Jim Nichol, "Central Asia's New States: Political Developments and Implications for U.S. Interests," CRS Issue Brief IB93108, Updated April 1, 2003, 2-4 and 11-12. Previous versions of this IB were issued in August, October, and November 2002. The U.S.-Uzbekistan Declaration on their strategic partnership of March 2002 is available at <www.state.gov/p/eur/rls/or/2002/11711pf.htm>.

[3] Details regarding assistance in FY2002 may be found in Nichol, IB93108 as updated for August 30, 2002, 1415. The supplemental funds came through existing instruments (the Freedom Support Act, which authorizes assistance to the former Soviet Union), as well as through the new Emergency Response Fund.

[4] Details are available in the country assessments, in "U.S. Government Assistance to and Cooperative Activities with Eurasia, Fiscal Year 2002," the Annual Report of the Coordinator of U.S. Assistance to Europe and Eurasia, at <http://www.state.gov/p/eur/rls/rpt/c10250.htm>. Another source for information about U.S. assistance programs by country and region is the annual USAID Budget Presentation to Congress, available at <http://www.usaid.gov/policy/budget/>. USAID's Washington headquarters houses specialists in development and democracy assistance, supports strategic planning, compiles lessons learned, and oversees adjustments to assistance strategy and implementation. As a results-oriented organization, USAID routinely re-examines its assumptions about development, and the models and expectations that underlie the goals and objectives of its assistance programs. Such models and strategies are not just academic exercises, as they build on accumulated experience in many countries and incorporate awareness of the tools and methods appropriate and acceptable to their foreign hosts. While USAID is not directly involved in designing assistance sponsored by other government agencies, its staff and specialists often indirectly contribute to such plans. Some of these other-Agency assistance programs contribute to the promotion of democracy directly or indirectly. The most important such pro-democracy programs are lodged in the State Department. These include educational exchanges run by the Education and Cultural Affairs Bureau, visitors and educational assistance programs run by the Public Affairs Bureau, and grant funding to support human rights and democracy from the Bureau for Democracy, Human Rights and Labor. The office for coordination of U.S. assistance to Europe and Eurasia (housed in the State Department) holds responsibility for overall coordination and tracking and covers all sources of U.S. assistance in its annual reports.

[5] It should be noted that identifying which assistance funds support "democracy" can be tricky, and practices vary somewhat. Some accounts do not include educational exchange programs.

[6] The diversity of these assistance categories and activities can be reviewed in the annual reports of the Coordinator of U.S. Assistance to Europe and Eurasia, available on the internet at <http://

www.state.gov/p/eur/rls/rpt/c10250.htm>. An excerpt from the table of contents of the FY2001 report (Appendix A) provides a handy list of all the agencies that provide assistance.

⁷ See, for example, Bonnie Docherty, *Dangerous Dealings: Changes to U.S. Military Assistance Since September 11* (Human Rights Watch, 14:1, February 2002) available at www.hrw.org and Jennifer Windsor, Executive Director of Freedom House, Testimony before the House Committee on International Relations, July 9, 2003 on the State Department's report on "Supporting Human Rights and Democracy." (The testimony is available at <www.freedomhouse.org>.) Note that Freedom House (*Nations in Transit 2002*) rates all five Central Asian states as either "autocracies" or "consolidated autocracies."

⁸ Andrew J. Bacevich, "Steppes to Empire," *The National Interest* (Summer 2002), 44.

⁹ Charles Fairbanks, "Being There," *The National Interest* (Summer 2002), 40. Among the many others who raised such questions are: Pauline Jones Luong and Erika Weinthal, "New Friends, New Fears in Central Asia," *Foreign Affairs* (Mar-Apr 2002), 61-70; Elizabeth Wishnick, *Growing U.S. Security Interests in Central Asia* (Carlisle, PA: Strategic Studies Institute, October 2002); Jessical T. Mathews, "September 11, One Year Later: A World of Change," *Carnegie Endowment for International Peace Policy Brief* 18, August 2002 [available at <www.ceip.org>]; Thomas Carothers, "Promoting Democracy and Fighting Terror," *Foreign Affairs* (Jan-Feb 2003), 84-93; and the pair of articles on America in Central Asia by Charles Fairbanks and Andrew J. Bacevich in *The National Interest* (Summer 2002), 39–53.

¹⁰ *USAID's Assistance Strategy for Central Asia 2001-2005*, USAID Regional Mission for Central Asia, July, 2000. Available at <www.usaid.gov/regions/Europe_ eurasia/car/PDABS400.pdf> (accessed in November 2002) Hereafter: *USAID Central Asia Strategy*

¹¹ *USAID Central Asia Strategy.*

¹³ While the state is commonly called "Kyrgyzstan," the Constitution of 1993 refers to the government as the "Kyrgyz Republic."

¹⁴ From USAID's FY2001 Budget Justification program summary for Kyrgyzstan, available at <http://www.usaid.gov/pubs/bj2001/ee/kg/>.

¹⁵ The statement of Michael Parmly, Principal Deputy Assistant Secretary for the Bureau of Democracy, Human Rights and Labor, before the Subcommittees on International Operations and Human Rights, and Middle East and South Asia of the House Committee on International Relations, July 18, 2001, is available at <www.Eurasianet.org/departments/rights/articles/eav072701a.html> (Acessed June 2, 2003).

¹⁶ From the USAID Congressional Presentation for FY 2000, section on Uzbekistan, available at <www.usaid.gov/pubs/cp2000/eni/uzbekist.html> (accessed in June 2003).

¹⁷ From the program summary for Uzbekistan in USAID's FY2003 Congressional Budget Justification, available at <http://www.usaid.gov/pubs/cbj2003/ee/uz/> (accessed September 15, 2003).

¹⁸ From the program summary for Kazakhstan in USAID's FY2000 Congressional Presentation, available at <http://www.usaid.gov/pubs/cp2000/eni/kazak.html>.

¹⁹ From the Turkmenistan overview in the USAID FY2001 budget justification, available at <http://www.usaid.gov/pubs/bj2001/ee/tm/>.

²⁰ The statement by Michael Parmly, in Congressional testimony on July 18, 2001, is available at <www.Eurasianet.org/departments/rights/articles/eav072701a.shtml>.

²¹ This State Department position, established by the Freedom Support Act, has now been renamed the "Coordinator of U.S. Assistance to Europe and Eurasia."

²² William Taylor's remarks and prepared statement are available through the site in Note 21, or at <http://usinfo.state.gov/topical/econ/group8/summit01/wwwh01071805.html> (accessed 6/2/03).

²³ Ukraine's government, for example, has chafed under U.S. criticism of its elections, its treatment of journalists, and its business practices. The activities of U.S. organizations that work with Ukrainian political parties and democratic activists (some of which oppose the current President, Leonid Kuchma), have clearly been an irritant. The Ukrainian authorities withheld registration from both the National Democratic Institute and the International Republican Institute for more than two

years (2001– September 2003), yielding only after considerable pressure from the U.S. made it clear the bilateral relationship would suffer otherwise. (Ukrainian law requires foreign organizations to re-register when funding instrumentalities change, as they did for both NDI and IRI in 2001.)

[24] See, for example, Charles William Maynes, "A New Strategy for Old Foes and New Friends," *World Policy Journal* (Summer 2000, 17:2), 68-76. Maynes is President of the Eurasia Foundation, an organization that funds many civil society activities in former socialist states.

[25] *Foreign Aid In the National Interest: Promoting Freedom, Security, and Opportunity* (USAID, 2002) is available at <www.usaid.gov>.

Ibid., 10-11.

Ibid., 50-52.

[28] See the articles by Lael Brainard, "Compassionate Conservatism Confronts Global Poverty," and Steve Radelet, "Will the Millennium Challenge Account be Different?" *Washington Quarterly* (Spring 2004, 26:2), 149-87. Recent Congressional action is discussed in Susan B.Epstein, "Foreign Relations Authorization, FY 2004 and FY 2005: State Department, The Millennium Challenge Account, and Foreign Assistance," CRS Report RL 21986, Updated September 2, 2003.

[29] See the analysis by Steven Radelet, "Bush and Foreign Aid," *Foreign Affairs* (September-October 2003, 82:5), 104-117.

[30] The National Security Strategy is available at www.whitehouse.gov.

[31] B. Lynn Pascoe, Deputy Assistant Secretary for European and Eurasian Affairs, "The U.S. Role in Central Asia," Testimony before the Senate Foreign Relations Committee, Subcommittee on Central Asia and the South Caucasus, June 27, 2002. Available through www.state.gov.

[32] A helpful short overview of the instruments of U.S. assistance to the former Soviet republics is included in Curt Tarnoff, "The Former Soviet Union and U.S. Foreign Assistance," CRS Issue Brief IB95077 (Updated July 24, 2003), and previous versions. Tarnoff noted that USAID transfers some of the funds obligated to it for these states to other agencies (such as the Commerce, Justice, and Labor Departments). These transfers have grown from about one fourth to over 40 percent of the total—an indication that other agencies are more involved in designing and overseeing assistance to the region. This Issue Brief points out that very little cash is involved (except for equity investments and loans to the private sector), that close to three-fourths of our assistance goes to the private or non-governmental sector, and that roughly 78% of funds used for programs run by USAID are spent on U.S. goods and services.

[33] Reports of the OSCE's Office for Democratic Institutions and Human Rights may be located through the organization's website, <http://www.osce.org/>.

[34] Details about all assistance activities from all agencies and funders is available in the Coordinators Reports, available through the Department of State website. As sited above, the Report for 2002 is available at <http://www.state.gov/p/eur/rls/rpt/c10250.htm>.

[35] The State Department's Bureau for Democracy, Human Rights and Labor (<http://www.state.gov/g/drl/>) has taken on a more important direct role in democracy promotion through its administration of the Human Rights and Democracy Fund (HRDF). The Fund has grown from $9 million in 2000 to over $31 million in 2003. The Fund was intended to permit highly responsive support for unique or especially timely short-term human rights or democracy promotion projects. In 2003, $4.5 million was committed for projects in the non-Middle East Muslim world (including Central Asia), with the following priorities: 1) Empowerment of Muslim women, including projects that promote capacity building and/or networks of women or women's organizations, especially as they relate to human-rights; 2) Addressing the problem of disenfranchised youth and the need to reach out to this group to prevent growth of extremism; 3) Political reform programs that would entail support for conducting free and fair elections, issues of good governance and corruption; 4) Independent media and access to a diversity of sources of information; 5) Judicial systems, especially in the context of Shari'a; 6) Promotion of the compatibility of democracy with Islam; and (7) Civil society and increasing political participation.

[36] See Appendix B for a summary of USAID activities prepared by the USAID Central Asian Regional mission in Almaty. Again, the Coordinator's Report for 2002 is the best source for detail on the activities of all funders. See <http://www.state.gov/p/eur/rls/rpt/c10250.htm>.

[37] Two of the Freedom House centers were open as of November 2003 in Tashkent and Namangan; a third is planned, probably to open in 2004.

[38] IRI is currently in the process of re-establishing a resident office to support its work in Kyrgyzstan.

[39] The author interviewed representatives and officers of Counterpart International, ABA/CEELI, Freedom House, the National Democratic Institute, the International Republican Institute, and IREX, and is grateful for their assistance in preparing this chapter.

[40] In testimony before the subcommittee on the Middle East and Central Asia of the House International Relations Committee, October 29, 2003, Beth Jones, Assistant Secretary of State for European and Eurasian Affairs, reaffirmed that democracy promotion is a key pillar of U.S. policy in Central Asia. The testimony is available through the State Department website, <http://www.state.gov/p/eur/rls/rm/2003/25798pf.htm>.

[41] Martha Olcott, "Taking Stock of Central Asia," *Journal of International Affairs* (Spring 2003), 3-17.

[42] Fiona Hill, "Central Asia and the Caucasus: The Impact of the War on Terrorism," in *Nations in Transit* 2003 (Rowman and Littlefield: Freedom House, 2003), 39-49.

[43] See, for example, his remarks at a media roundtable in Tashkent, Uzbekistan, on June 7, 2002 at <www.state.gov/g/drl>.

[44] Jennifer Windsor, Executive Director of Freedom House, Testimony before the House Committee on International Relations, July 9, 2003 on the State Department's report on "Supporting Human Rights and Democracy." (The testimony is available at <www.freedomhouse.org>.)

[45] Thomas C. Adams, Acting Coordinator of U.S. assistance to Europe and Eurasia, "U.S. Assistance Programs in Europe: An Assessment," Statement to the House International Relations Committee, Subcommittee on Europe, March 27, 2003 (<www.state.gov/p/eur/rls/rm/2003/19203pf.ht>, accessed 6/2/2003).

[46] Europe and Eurasia, USAID Congressional Budget Justification, FY2004. (<www.usaid.gov/policy/budget/cbj2004/europe_eurasia/>, accessed June 2003).

[47] Budget levels for U.S. assistance to the former Soviet republics are coming down. While the largest drops are for Russia and Ukraine, this trend will affect Central Asia too. President Bush's FY 2003 budget cut the total outlay by four percent; his request for FY 2004 represented a cut of 24 percent from 2003. See Curt Tarnoff, "The Former Soviet Union and U.S. Foreign Assistance," (Updated July 24, 2003), 1, 4.

[48] I disagree with the analysis of Thomas Carothers, author of many works analyzing U.S. democracy assistance, who has suggested that the "transition paradigm" has died. See the debate in *Journal of Democracy* on this issue, beginning with the Carothers article, "The End of the Transition Paradigm" in the January 2002 issue, and continuing two issues later with essays by Guillermo O'Donnell, Kenneth Wollack, Ghia Nodia, and Gerald Hyman.

[49] All the Central Asian states but Tajikistan joined the PFP in 1994. Tajikistan joined after September 11, in 2002.

Chapter 7

Islam in Central Asia: The Emergence and Growth of Radicalism in the Post-Communist Era [1]

Tiffany Petros

T he breakup of the Soviet Union in 1991 allowed for the revival of Islam in the Central Asian states of Kazakhstan, Kyrgyzstan, Tajikistan, Turkmenistan, and Uzbekistan after seventy years of religious repression. Despite long-standing efforts by the Soviet regime to eliminate religious identity across the empire, the Central Asian populations maintained Islamic beliefs and traditions that had been handed down over centuries. The collapse of Communism and opening of state borders not only offered Central Asian Muslims new opportunities to practice their faith, but also allowed for the importation and development of radical forms of Islam.[2] Although the majority of Central Asian Muslims do not support radical Islam, radical Islamic movements have attracted followers among a growing minority of the population. Increased support for radical Islam in Central Asia over the past decade has been attributed to foreign influences, coupled with a rise in government corruption and oppression, and deteriorating economic conditions. Radical Islamic groups active in Central Asia have capitalized on public discontent and provided a voice of opposition to the secular authoritarian governments. Regional rulers have responded by outlawing all non-government sanctioned Islamic activity and have cracked down aggressively against both Islamic organizations and their followers.

Radical Islam in Central Asia also has attracted U.S. attention, particularly in the aftermath of the September 11 terrorist attacks. In 2001, the Central Asian states found themselves on the front lines of the global war on terrorism, as a U.S.-led coalition entered neighboring Afghanistan

139

to topple the hard-line Islamic Taliban regime. The Taliban was a known sponsor of al Qaeda—the network held responsible for the attacks on U.S. targets—and maintained ties to radical Islamic elements active in Central Asia. Central Asian leaders offered varying degrees of assistance to the U.S.-led Operation *Enduring Freedom* in an effort to enhance ties with the United States and further their fight against "Islamic terrorists" whom they blamed for anti-government activities at home. Uzbekistan and Kyrgyzstan were particularly active in this effort, offering the U.S. military basing rights in support of the operation. Although U.S.-led action in Afghanistan ultimately disrupted Taliban sponsorship of radical Islamic activity in Central Asia, Islamic radicalism continues to draw support from Central Asian populations.

This chapter will examine the roots of Islam in Central Asia and provide a brief historical overview of the changing relationship between Islam and the Central Asian peoples. This background is essential for understanding the emergence and growth of radical Islam in Central Asia since the early 1990s. The chapter will also examine the three Islamic elements that have had the greatest impact on Central Asia in recent years, the Islamic Movement of Uzbekistan (IMU), Hizb-ut-Tahrir (HT), and the Islamic Renaissance Party (IRP). Finally, it will seek to answer two questions: Why is radical Islam being embraced by a growing segment of Central Asian populations today? Does support for radical Islam in Central Asia pose a threat to regional regimes and/or U.S. interests in the region?

A Brief History of Islam in Central Asia

Early History

The radical Islamic elements that have gained support in Central Asia over the past decade differ greatly from strains of Islam indigenous to the region. Since Central Asian Islam traditionally has diverged from Islam found in other parts of the world, including the Middle East, Asia, and Africa, the recent drive toward radicalism in the region must be viewed in the context of the global Islamic movement.[3] However, before examining the factors that have given rise to radical Islam in Central Asia in the 1990s, one must briefly consider the history of Islam in the region. This history demonstrates that Islam has served and continues to serve as an important part of Central Asian identity. Although the populations of Central Asia have long embraced Islam, the identity has played a limited role as a vehicle for political mobilization. Given this history, the question arises as to whether or not radical Islam will serve as a mobilizing factor in Central Asia in the twenty-first century.

The path of Islam in Central Asia has been one of continuity and change. Islamic traditions have been passed down for centuries, despite periods of repression of the faith. The religion was first introduced to Central Asia in the seventh century by Arab invaders arriving from the Middle East. It was not until the ninth century, however, that Islam was adopted by local rulers and became the predominant religion in the region. During this period, Islam was promoted from the top down, rather than forced upon the Central Asian populations by foreign conquerors.[4] Central Asian rulers viewed their endorsement of Islam and its acceptance among the people as one means of creating and maintaining their bases of power. Support for Islam continued to grow in the tenth century, with the cities of Samarkand and Bukhara in present-day Uzbekistan becoming great centers of Islamic learning and culture.[6]

The majority of Central Asian Muslims embraced Sunni Islam, although Shia Muslims also can be found throughout the region. Shia minorities exist primarily in Tajikistan, but also have a presence in the cities of Bukhara and Samarkand.[6] Sunni Islam was first embraced by the settled populations of today's Tajikistan and Uzbekistan, while the nomadic peoples of Kazakhstan, Kyrgyzstan, and Turkmenistan maintained stronger ties to their pre-Islamic culture and beliefs. Sunni Islam eventually spread to Central Asia's nomadic populations by incorporating local traditions and aspects of Sufism—an indigenous form of Islamic mysticism.[7] Sufism appealed to the nomadic peoples by emphasizing a direct experience with God, as well as preaching tolerance and respect for other forms of worship.[9] Early differences in how Islam was embraced in Central Asia continue to be reflected in local practices in the region. In the twenty-first century, identification with Islam remains stronger in Tajikistan and Uzbekistan than in Kazakhstan, Kyrgyzstan, and Turkmenistan.[9]

Islam under Soviet Rule

Islam was an important aspect of Central Asian culture up to and including the period of Russian colonization of the region in the nineteenth century. Central Asian Muslims did not begin to experience repression at the hands of the Russians until after the Bolsheviks came to power at the end of World War I. In the 1920s, the Soviet state launched an attack on Islamic beliefs, traditions, and institutions as it initiated the process of replacing religion with a new form of "scientific atheism."[10] The crack down on Islamic identity coincided with Soviet leader Josef Stalin's creation of the five Central Asian republics between 1924 and 1936. The republics, including Uzbekistan (1924), Turkmenistan (1924), Tajikistan (1929), Kazakhstan (1936), and Kyrgyzstan (1936), had not existed previously as separate entities and had no historical basis for division. According to Martha Brill Olcott, Senior Associate at the Carnegie Endowment for International Peace, "Stalin drew the map of Soviet Central Asia not with an eye to consolidating natural regions, but rather for the purpose of reducing the prospects for regional unity."[11] Upon division, the five republics contained multiple ethnic groups, which had not yet come to view themselves as independent nationalities. As part of a larger effort to eliminate loyalty to the Islamic identity and replace it with loyalties to the newly formed republics, purges of the Muslim leadership also took place throughout the 1920s and 1930s.[12]

Official hostility toward Islam in the Soviet Union lifted slightly following World War II. The Soviet policy of suppression, which had marked the earlier period, turned to one of religious co-optation. Soviet authorities attempted to regulate Islam by creating an "official" authorized version of the religion. A Muslim Religious Board was formed and charged with overseeing "Official Islam" in the Central Asian republics. This body was one of four religious boards established in the Soviet Union. Despite these efforts to suppress and then co-opt Islam, the religion continued to serve as an important marker of identity for the Central Asian populations. Central Asian Muslims also continued to practice their own unofficial or "parallel Islam" underground.[13]

The Soviet invasion of Afghanistan in 1979 marked another significant turning point for Islam in Central Asia. The mobilization of thousands of Central Asian men to fight in the Soviet army against the Afghan *Mujahedeen* put many Soviet Muslims in contact with foreign Muslims for the first time. The Central Asian Muslims were impressed by the commitment the Afghan people had for Islam. They also recognized shared ethnic and linguistic ties with the people they were fighting. This reminded them of how the Soviet Union had incorporated their lands and deprived them of their true identity and national pride.[14] Contacts that were made between Central Asians and Muslims from Afghanistan, Pakistan, and Saudi Arabia during this period later would weigh heavily on the resurgence of Islam in Central Asia, following the breakup of the Soviet Union.

The relationship between Islam and Central Asia again entered a new phase with President Mikhail Gorbachev's rise to power in the Soviet Union in the mid-1980s. Along with the introduction of Gorbachev's policies of *glasnost* (openness) and *perestroika* (restructuring) came greater religious freedom. Gorbachev's reforms led to a religious revival in which many Central Asian Muslims were allowed to make a pilgrimage to the holy city of Mecca, Saudi Arabia for the first time. The reforms also allowed outside Islamic influences to begin filtering into Central Asia. Foreign Islamic governments, organizations, and individuals began sending money to Central Asia to fund the construction of new mosques and reinvigorate Islamic practices.[15] These influences would come to play an important role in the development of radical Islam in Central Asia in the 1990s.

The Rise of Radical Islam in Central Asia Post-Independence

Enternal Factors

The renewed interest in Islam that developed in Central Asia in the 1980s gained momentum following the collapse of the Soviet Union in 1991. Although the Soviet state actively tried to destroy the multiple loyalties of clan, family, republic, and religion, Islam remained an important source of identity for many Central Asians. Communism had promoted the idea that religion was incompatible with the Soviet ideology. Now that the ideology was discredited by the collapse of the Soviet empire, a new opportunity emerged for Central Asians to embrace their Islamic past.[16]

Once the Central Asian republics' borders were open to the world, among the first visitors were Islamic missionaries from Afghanistan, Pakistan, and Saudi Arabia. Pakistan and Afghanistan played a particularly significant role in influencing the revival and radicalization of Islam in Central Asia.[17] In addition to providing funding and religious training to support mosques and *madrassas* (religious schools), these sources distributed free copies of the Koran, which had been translated into Russian and other Central Asian languages.[18]

Sources in Saudi Arabia also contributed to the rise of Islam in Central Asia. In early 1990, these sources funded the development of *Adolat* (Justice)[19]—an Islamic movement that arose in the Uzbek part of the Ferghana Valley.[20] The movement worked not only to introduce Islam, but also to expose corruption and social injustice among the ruling regime. *Adolat* quickly gained support and began to spread across the Ferghana Valley in 1991. However, by March 1992, following the break up of the Soviet Union, the movement was banned by independent Uzbek authorities.[21] Leaders of this movement then fled to Tajikistan where they helped prepare for the Tajik civil war.

In addition to developing schools, mosques, and movements inside Central Asia, foreign actors also provided opportunities for future members of the radical IMU and HT to receive religious training abroad.[22] Through their activities, supporters of the Taliban in Afghanistan, militants in Pakistan, and followers of the Wahhabi movement (an extreme Sunni Islamic doctrine) found in Saudi Arabia, brought new strains of Islam to the region. These strains differed greatly from the form of Islam that had long-standing roots in Central Asia.

Internal Factors

Although external factors played a significant role in the emergence of radical Islam in Central Asia, they have not been alone in affecting the changing nature of Islam in the region. If there were not fertile ground for the radicalization of Islam in Central Asia, foreign radical elements would have been unable to attract support among the local populations. Support for radical Islam in Central Asia developed in large part as a form of opposition to authoritarian governments in the region. As government corruption and oppression increased and economic conditions deteriorated throughout the 1990s, segments of the Central Asian population viewed radical Islam as an alternative to the status quo. Not surprisingly, the rise of radical groups has been most pronounced in Uzbekistan where government repression has been most severe. There also has been a strong show of support for radical Islamic movements in northern Tajikistan and southern Kyrgyzstan, particularly among ethnic Uzbeks who have experienced discrimination based on their ethnicity.[23]

Immediately following the collapse of communism, Central Asian leaders initiated the restoration of mosques and other symbols of Islam as a means of distinguishing themselves from the Soviet system and increasing their legitimacy among the local populations. As evidence of their use of Islam to gain support, Central Asian leaders, including Uzbek President Islam Karimov, made the pilgrimage to Mecca and were sworn into office on the Koran.[24] Although Central Asian leadership made an effort to reembrace Islam, the regimes kept a watchful eye on religious activity. This was particularly true in southern parts of Central Asia where Islam had developed deeper ties, such as in Uzbekistan, Tajikistan, and the Ferghana Valley region of Kyrgyzstan.[25]

As it became clear that Islam was growing in importance and providing Central Asians a link with their past, regional rulers increasingly came to view Islam as a threat rather than an avenue for harnessing support for their leadership. The ruling elites wanted to ensure that Islam would not develop into a base of political opposition and, therefore, began to repress

Islam, as had been the tradition under the Soviet system. This reaction, in turn, pushed some moderate Muslims to embrace more radical views.[26]

The failure of Central Asian leaders to introduce democratic and/or economic reforms, coupled with the repression of Islam, increased support for radical Islamic elements.[27] Participating in radical activities also has provided many Central Asian youth with a sense of purpose and accomplishment not available elsewhere, given the lack of jobs and educational opportunities. The Central Asian governments must address these systemic issues, if the trend toward radicalism is to be halted.

Central Asian Government Responses to Radical Islam

The Central Asian regimes have been deeply concerned by the rise in radical Islam, which they attribute to meddling from Islamic movements abroad. Despite their shared concerns, the leaders of the Central Asian republics have responded differently to the emergence and growth of radical Islam in the region. Uzbek President Islam Karimov introduced a swift and severe crackdown on Islamic activity beginning in the early 1990s. In 1992, Islamic supporters gathered in Namangan, Uzbekistan to directly challenge President Karimov's policies and demand the legalization of Islamic structures. In response to this pressure, Karimov outlawed *Adolat* and began to suppress the Islamic opposition.[28] Repression against Islam became even more severe following an alleged attempt on the President's life in February 1999. Although Karimov was not killed in a series of six car bombings that ripped through the capital city of Tashkent, 13 others were left dead and several more injured.[29] Karimov and other Central Asian leaders used this incident, as well as the previous outbreak of civil war in Tajikistan, to justify outlawing political opposition. Mass arrests were instituted in Uzbekistan followed by the subsequent torture of Islamic opponents. Karimov's response to Islam throughout the 1990s forced many Uzbek Muslims to flee to neighboring Tajikistan and Afghanistan, where they helped to form and strengthen the radical IMU—an ally of Afghanistan's Taliban.[30]

As of 2003, President Karimov continues to keep a tight reign on Islamic activity in Uzbekistan. At present, an estimated 6,500 people are jailed in Uzbekistan due to their religious or political beliefs. Approximately half of those held have been accused of belonging to the radical Islamic movement HT, while the majority of the rest have been branded Wahhabis.[31] Not only has Karimov jailed a large number of Muslims, but the Uzbek government—like the Soviet government before it—monitors the Spiritual Board of Muslims in Tashkent. In addition to monitoring the

Board, the state frequently dictates to official clergy what they may or may not say in their religious sermons.

The other states of Central Asia have introduced similar policies, though they vary in degree of severity. In Turkmenistan, laws on religion are very restrictive. Although Islam does not have strong roots as an organized religion in Turkmenistan, President Saparmurat Niyazov "has combined widespread repression of any independent religious activity with attempts to create a pseudo-Islamic spiritual creed centered on his own personality."[32] Turkmenistan has seen the number of mosques operating in the country rise from four during Soviet times to 318 in 2003. The spending of millions of dollars on mosque construction, however, has primarily been aimed at Niyazov's "own glorification, rather than the religious needs of the people."[33]

Official response to radical Islam has been less in Kyrgyzstan and Kazakhstan, since these countries have not seen significant opposition from extremist groups. Unlike in Uzbekistan, religious communities have been tolerated in Kyrgyzstan and Kazakhstan, and laws on religion have remained more liberal. There have been arrests, however, particularly among individuals found distributing banned HT literature. In November 2002, Kyrgyz officials also introduced legislation restricting the licensing system for religious publications.[34]

Tajikistan has taken a different approach to dealing with the rise of Islam than have the other countries in Central Asia. It is the only country in the region that did not outlaw the emergence of an Islamic political party. Shortly after Tajikistan gained independence, a civil war broke out between members of the Communist elite and the opposition, which had Islamic backing. Although this conflict led to the other Central Asian states banning opposition parties in their own countries, in the case of Tajikistan, the IRP ultimately was able to gain seats in the government as a result of the negotiated ceasefire.

While Tajikistan may appear to have taken a more moderate stance on Islamic participation than the other republics, it should be noted that many view the Islamic party in Tajikistan as having been co-opted by the government, and therefore not a true voice of opposition. Others argue that despite Tajikistan's slightly more liberal laws on religion, compared to the other Central Asian republics, in reality the practice of respecting such laws has been undermined.[35] For example, the Tajik government requires the collection of 15,000 signatures for the building of a Mosque, whereas only 10 to 15 signatures are required to build a Christian church.[36] Tajik authorities also have cracked down on the expression of Islam in Soghd, the Tajik-controlled territory of the Ferghana Valley.

Although the Central Asian governments have taken different approaches to the rise of radical Islam in their respective countries, each is cautious about what public support for radicalism might mean for their leadership. This concern has led to the arrest of thousands of ordinary practicing Muslims along with the militants. Not only have prisoners been subjected to long jail terms, but they also have been tortured at the hands of the regimes.[37] In an attempt to gain tacit support for their repressive practices, the Central Asian governments have argued that their domestic fight against Islamic radicalism is but a small part of the global war on terrorism. By violating human rights in the name of cracking down on "radical Islamists" and "terrorists," however, regional rulers have strengthened support for the very opposition they have attempted to eliminate. The Central Asian leaders have tried to convince the United States that their secular, albeit authoritarian leadership, is the only alternative to the acceptance of radical Islam in the region.[38] This puts the United States in the position of choosing between two unwelcome options, and in the process legitimizing the actions of the current regimes.

Islamic Opposition in Central Asia

In order to translate support for radical Islam and opposition to regional governments into action, several organizations have been formed in Central Asia in support of radical ideals. These organizations differ in their tactics (violent vs. non-violent) as well as their goals (overthrow of existing government vs. becoming a viable opposition party). The three most significant organizations to emerge are the previously mentioned IMU, HT and IRP.

Islamic Movement of Uzbekistan

Among Islamic groups active in Central Asia, the IMU has received perhaps the most attention. Prior to the U.S.-led Operation *Enduring Freedom*, the IMU was considered the most radical Islamic organization operating in the region. The IMU was known to have close ties with the Taliban and had set up training bases in the north of Afghanistan. The IMU also reportedly was receiving financial backing from Osama bin Laden and his al Qaeda network, as well as from Saudi Arabia. Given the IMU's cooperation with known terrorists and involvement in violent attacks against regional regimes in Uzbekistan and Kyrgyzstan, the U.S. State

Department designated the group as a foreign terrorist organization in September 2000.[39]

The IMU began forming in 1992-1993, when future IMU members fled Uzbekistan in response to President Karimov's crackdown on Islamic activities. Some of these members, including future IMU military leader Juma Namangani, fled to Tajikistan and joined the Islamic Tajik opposition (later United Tajik Opposition) in its fight against the Communist government of Tajikistan from 1992 to 1997.[40] During the course of the Tajik civil war, Uzbek fighters met up with Afghan groups and began forging relationships with members of both the Taliban and the Northern Alliance. This led to the initial military training of Uzbek fighters in Afghanistan.

The IMU was founded officially in 1998 by ethnic Uzbeks dissatisfied with the more moderate stances of the IRP in Tajikistan. The initial goal of the IMU was to topple the Uzbek leadership. The organization's mandate was later enlarged to include overthrowing all of the region's secular governments and replacing them with regimes based on *Shari'a* (Islamic law). The IMU promised to form a state in the Ferghana Valley—a center of Islamic traditionalism for centuries.[41] In order to achieve their goal of removing Uzbek President Karimov from power, the IMU launched terrorist attacks against the Uzbek government in 1999, 2000, and 2001 from bases in neighboring Afghanistan and Tajikistan.[42] Although the IMU mainly operated out of Afghanistan, the movement also had set up bases in Tajikistan prior to 2001 and the beginning of the U.S.-led Operation *Enduring Freedom*.[43]

As of September 11, 2001, between 3,000 and 5,000 members of the IMU were believed to be operating in Central Asia. It was reported in early 2001 that the IMU had formed an umbrella organization called *Hezb-e Islami Turkestan* (Islamic Party of Turkestan) with the intention of expanding its areas of operation to include Kazakhstan, Kyrgyzstan, Tajikistan, and China's Xinjiang region.[44] IMU activities were significantly curtailed by U.S. involvement in Afghanistan. In November 2001, the IMU's military commander, Juma Namangani, was killed in a U.S. attack, and its political leader went underground. Most observers argue that the IMU no longer poses a significant threat in Central Asia, having lost its bases in Afghanistan, as well as its Taliban and al Qaeda sponsors.[45] Although the IMU is no longer active in Afghanistan, it continues to maintain ties to the IRP, which remains active in Tajikistan.[46]

Hizb-ut-Tahrir

HT, the Party of Islamic Liberation, is a second well-known Islamic movement that has taken hold in Central Asia and is steadily increasing its influence. It draws a large base of support among ethnic Uzbeks, as well as recruits among Kazakhs, Kyrgyz, and Tajiks. HT shares with the IMU the desire to overthrow the secular governments of Central Asia. In their place, HT proposes to introduce an Islamic Caliphate across present state borders in Central Asia similar to that established in seventh century Arabia following the death of the Prophet Mohammed. Like the IMU, HT does not offer a specific social, economic, or political agenda for governing the Caliphate. An important difference between HT and the IMU is that HT rejects violence as a means of bringing about political change. This has allowed the group to gain a broader base of followers than the IMU, which was in part discredited as a result of its support for violence.

The HT movement, headquartered in London, was first founded between 1952 and 1953 in the Middle East, and has since grown to operate in approximately fourty countries worldwide. The movement was originally established by Palestinian activist Taqiuddin an-Nabhani Filastyni, who served as a judge in the Jerusalem appeals court. Filastyni's successor, Abd al-Kadim Zallum, oversaw the introduction of HT to Central Asia in 1995 when the party opened its headquarters in Uzbekistan. HT activities quickly spread to the Ferghana Valley between 1995 and 1996, where it has been particularly successful in attracting support. By 2000, HT activities had branched out further to include parts of northern Tajikistan and southern Kyrgyzstan. As of 2003, the organization claimed to have 80,000 members from across Central Asia.[47]

HT originally drew its support from educated urban youth, mainly in Uzbekistan, who then helped to spread the HT message among poorer segments of the population living in rural areas.[48] HT has successfully drawn upon networks of family and clans in Central Asia, particularly in Uzbekistan and Kyrgyzstan, to recruit new members and increase participation in group activities. HT has relied on traditional social networks to distribute leaflets on HT goals. It also has developed a Web site to circulate information on the organization and its activities.[49] Although HT has increased its membership in recent years, there is little evidence that Central Asian Muslims support the introduction of *Shari'a*, or other strict Islamic practices as the organization advocates.[50] Instead, HT has gained support in Central Asia by serving as a voice of opposition in otherwise repressive political environments.

In response to growing popular support, the governments in Central Asia have cracked down on HT activities, and the organization has been banned across the region. In 2001, hundreds, if not thousands, of alleged HT members were arrested in Uzbekistan, Kyrgyzstan, and Tajikistan. Despite the arrests, HT continues to attract followers, especially in Uzbekistan and Kyrgyzstan. In southern Kyrgyzstan, 10 percent of the population is believed to be involved in HT activities.[51] The success of HT in Central Asia has been attributed in part to its ability to target its message to post-Soviet grievances. Unlike HT activities in London and elsewhere in the West, where the organization distributes leaflets and holds meetings denouncing the United States and Israel, in Central Asia the organization criticizes local governments for their inability to fight corruption, poverty, drug use, HIV/AIDS, and other social and economic ills. Since the outbreak of war with Iraq in 2003; however, there has been an increase of anti-Western/anti-U.S. sentiment expressed in HT literature being distributed in Central Asia.

HT has not been as broadly successful in Kazakhstan as it has been in other Central Asian countries, since Islam is not as widely embraced there as in the other former Soviet republics. Further, Kazakhstan's oil-economy has not left it in the dire conditions shared by other Central Asian states. Although HT is not likely to make significant inroads into Kazakhstan by capitalizing on poor economic conditions or anti-U.S./Western sentiment, support may be gained as popular disillusionment with Kazakh President Nursultan Nazarbaev increases. There is evidence that HT has made some headway in Kazakhstan, where HT literature has become more aggressive since the recent war in Iraq. In April 2003, two members of HT were detained by Kazakh authorities in the South of the country for distributing leaflets with statements against the United States and its British ally.[52]

Unlike the IMU, the United States has not designated HT to be a foreign terrorist organization, since it has not used violence to achieve its political goals. Although the United States distinguishes between the IMU and HT with respect to the "terrorist" label, the U.S. government continues to closely monitor HT activities.[53] There is concern that since the start of Operation *Enduring Freedom* and the global war on terrorism, the HT message has become increasingly militant. The fliers distributed by the group throughout Central Asia have begun to denounce the presence of coalition forces in Central Asia and have praised suicide attacks in Israel. Although HT has not been directly linked to involvement in violent activities, it is believed to incite violence, and could become a stepping-stone for disenfranchised youth who could be recruited into more violent Islamic groups. Some also fear more radical members of HT could break away from the organization and promote the use of violence to increase the pace of reforms in Central Asia.

Islamic Renaissance Party

The IRP was established in 1991 as an outgrowth of Gorbachev's reforms for the purpose of protecting the Islamic identity of the Muslims in the former Soviet Union. Given its objective, the party was able to gain publicity not only in the Soviet Union, but also among academics and strategists in the West.[54] IRP sought to increase awareness and understanding of Muslims in the Soviet Union, while representing their voice within the Communist framework.[55] However, the party remained fragmented with regional branches introduced throughout the Soviet Union.

The IRP gained increased attention during the civil war in Tajikistan from 1992 to 1997. The party, which claimed to support a moderate, nationalist version of Islam, was part of a larger anti-government coalition active during the Tajik civil war.[56] Although many labeled the party "fundamentalist," the IRP sought to unite clans during the civil war, and did not use the party to push for establishment of an Islamic state in Tajikistan.[57] The IRP is the only legally recognized religious party in Central Asia and entered the Tajik government as a result of a peace agreement ending the conflict.[58] Since becoming part of the government, the IRP has kept its commitment to work within the constitutional framework of Tajikistan. IRP Deputy Chairman Muhiddin Kabiri has emerged as the face of the party. He says that the IRP supports the existence of a secular democratic Tajikistan, but notes that the party approves of increasing religious traditions and values in state political life. According to Kabiri, Turkey is an example of a state that has been able to incorporate these values and could serve as a model to other states in the region.[59]

Although IRP has entered the Tajik government, its position as a voice of opposition has been weakened. Tajik President Imomali Rakhmonov has increasingly consolidated power in his own hands. While the ruling elite continues to view the IRP as "too Islamic for the government," radical Islamic forces have accused the party of selling-out to the state's interests. According to Kabiri, this view could serve to benefit radical Islamic elements, which can attract support from a population that continues to view itself as having little to no voice in general.[60]

Some observers have argued that the success of the IRP in working within the Tajik coalition government must not go unnoticed. Referring to IRP's participation in Tajikistan's governance, President of the Eurasia Foundation Charles Maynes said, "Unfortunately, the world largely ignored this experiment, the success of which could have had profound implications for the way that the Western world reacts to resurgent political Islam elsewhere . . . The Tajik example could well inform political developments in the region and elsewhere—and should help define Western perceptions of Islam."[61] Although Tajikistan continues to face multiple political and economic challenges, there is evidence that it remains one of the more open countries in Central Asia.

U.S. Interest in Central Asia and the Future

No single factor can fully explain the emergence and rise of radical Islam in Central Asia. The states of Kazakhstan, Kyrgyzstan, Tajikistan, Turkmenistan, and Uzbekistan have faced multiple and varied internal and external pressures since gaining independence, which have contributed to differing levels of support for Islamic radicalism. These pressures include: increasing government corruption and repression, declining economic conditions, and growing influence from foreign Islamic elements. The rise in popular support for radical Islamic groups in Central Asia can be viewed as a sign of discontent with the status quo, rather than a voice in support of Islamic government and radical views. The majority of Central Asian Muslims do not support the end of the secular state and many perceive radical Islamic groups as a threat to state and regional stability.

Scholars and practitioners continue to debate the nature of the threat posed by radical Islamic elements in Central Asia to regional regimes and/or U.S. interests. The majority of the Central Asian regimes have labeled all non-government sanctioned Islamic activity as "radical" and banned Islamic groups as "terrorist" organizations. The United States should guard against this hardline approach and consider that not all forms of Islam are dangerous or antithetical to U.S. interests. This is especially true in Central Asia, where Islam has long been respected as a tolerant religion and an important source of identity. In order to combat the spread of radical Islam in the region, the U.S. government and the Central Asian regimes should work to promote and incorporate moderate strains of Islam in a way that does not allow it to destroy the current order.[62] By banning all unauthorized Islamic activity, the regional regimes have effectively eliminated independent, moderate voices of Islam, which could be used to attract people away from radical groups and activities.[63]

In order to neutralize the influence of radical Islamic elements in Central Asia, significant political and economic changes also are needed. The introduction of reforms leading to political change and economic growth could lessen the appeal of radical Islamic organizations as a voice of opposition in Central Asia. However, if the current regimes disregard the worsening political and economic conditions, membership in organizations such as HT will grow and could have an increasingly destabilizing effect. Another danger is that HT or other radical Islamic groups could resort to violence in order to ensure that their message is heard.[64]

The United States is likely to maintain a long-term interest in Central Asia, given the region's strategic location, natural resources, and contributions to the global war on terrorism. While the United States seeks to maintain stability in Central Asia, it must not be perceived as blindly backing authoritarian secular governments without recognizing the need for opposition and reform. Recent global events have clearly demonstrated the importance of encouraging voices of moderation, while simultaneously promoting state stability. The United States does not want to see a situation in Central Asia where the only alternative to authoritarian regimes is radical Islam.

Notes

[1] The views expressed in this chapter are those of the author and do not necessarily represent those of DFI Government Services or the U.S. government. The author would like to thank Daniel Burghart, Sylvia Babus, Daniel Chiu, and Erin Craycraft for their comments on this chapter.

[2] In this chapter, the term "radical" refers to anti-Western forms of Islam that espouse the overthrow of secular regimes and introduction of *Shari'a* (Islamic law). It is recognized that the majority of Central Asian Muslims do not support this radical strain of Islam, though there is concern that support may rise and, in turn, threaten regional regimes and U.S. interests.

[3] Radical Islamic movements are not entirely new to Central Asia. For example, during WWI, Islamic militants forcefully opposed Russian government attempts to deploy Muslims to work near the front. Again in the 1920s, Muslim partisans in the so-called *Basmachi* movement opposed the takeover and advance of Soviet power into Central Asia. See Fiona Hill, "Central Asia: Terrorism, Religious Extremism, and Regional Stability," *Testimony before the House Committee on International Relations Subcommittee on the Middle East and Central Asia* (July 23, 2003), 2.

[4] Nazif Shahrani, *The Islamization of Central Asia: Politics, Economics and Society*, Woodrow Wilson Conference Participant June 11, 2003.

[5] The cities of Samarkand and Bukhara grew in wealth and prestige as a result of their location along the Silk Road, the trade route between the West and East. See Edward W. Walker, "Roots of Rage: Militant Islam in Central Asia," *Panel presentation at the University of California, Berkeley* (October 29, 2001), 1-9. Available at <http://socrates.berkeley.edu/~iseees/>, accessed July 2003.

[6] Ahmed Rashid, *Jihad: The Rise of Militant Islam in Central Asia* (New Haven: Yale University Press, 2002), 26.

[7] Walker, 3.

[8] Rashid, *Jihad*, 27.

[9] Walker, 3.

[10] Shahrani

[11] "A History of Islam in Central Asia, Part II," July 25, 2002. Available at <http:www.muslim-uzbekistan.com/eng/ennews/2002/07/ennews25072002.html>, accessed July 6, 2003.

[12] Walker, 3.

[13] Walker, 4.

[14] Rashid, *Jihad*, 6.

[15] Walker, 4.

[16] Rashid, *Jihad*, 5.

[17] Rashid, "Islam in Central Asia: Afghanistan and Pakistan," 213.

[18] Rashid, *Jihad*, 5.

[19] Michael Fredholm, *Uzbekistan & the Threat From Islamic Extremism*, Conflict Studies Research Centre (England: Defense Academy of the United Kingdom), 3.

[20] The Ferghana Valley encompasses bordering areas of Kyrgyzstan, Tajikistan, and Uzbekistan and claims a population of more than 10 million.

[21] Fredholm, 3.

[22] Rashid, *Jihad*, 10.

[23] Hill, 1.

[24] Shireen Hunter, *The Islamization of Central Asia: Politics, Economics and Society*, Woodrow Wilson Conference Participant, June 11, 2003.

[25] Svante E. Cornell and Regine A. Spector, "Central Asia: More than Islamic Extremists," *The Washington Quarterly* (Winter 2002), 194.

[26] Rashid, *Jihad*, 11.

[28] *Central Asia: Islam and the State*, (Osh/Brussels: International Crisis Group, July 10, 2003), 4.

[29] Walker, 7.

[30] *Central Asia: Islam and the State*, i.

[32] "Islam in Central Asia: Contrasts between Uzbekistan and Tajikistan," *The Economist* (May 15, 2003). Available at <http://www.uzland.uz/2003/may/16/11.htm>, accessed July 6, 2003.

[33] *Central Asia: Islam and the State*, i.

[34] Mike Redman, "Hizb-ut-Tahrir: Making Inroads into Kazakhstan?," *Central Asia-Caucasus Analyst* (June 4, 2003). Available at <http://www.cacianalyst.org/view_article.php?articleid=1460>, accessed July 6, 2003.

[35] *Central Asia: Islam and the State*, i.

[36] Hunter.

[37] Rashid, *Jihad*, 8.

[38] Rajan Menon, "The New Great Game in Central Asia," *Survival* 45(2003), 191.

[39] "Frequently Asked Questions about U.S. Policy in Central Asia," *U.S. Department of State Fact Sheet: Bureau of European and Eurasian Affairs* (November 27, 2002). Available at <http://www.state.gov/p/eur/rls/fs/15562.htm>, accessed July 6, 2003.

[40] Cornell and Spector, 196.

[41] Fredholm, 2.

[42] Rashid, *Jihad*, 8.

[43] "Frequently Asked Questions about U.S. Policy in Central Asia"

[44] Fredholm, 10.

[45] "Islam in Central Asia: Contrasts between Uzbekistan and Tajikistan"

[46] Cornell and Spector, 196.

[47] Fredholm, 13.

[48] "Frequently Asked Questions about U.S. Policy in Central Asia"

[49] For more information on Hizb-ut-tahrir see www.hizb-ut-tahrir.org

[50] David Lewis, ICG. Guest speaker at the Brookings Institution on July 11, 2003.

[51] Cornell and Spector, 200.

[52] Redman.

[53] "Frequently Asked Questions about U.S. Policy in Central Asia"

[54] "A History of Islam in Central Asia, Part III," July 27, 2002. Available at <http:www.muslim-uzbekistan.com/eng/ennews/2002/07/ennews27072002.html> accessed July 6, 2003.

[55] "A History of Islam in Central Asia, Part III"

[56] "Islam in Central Asia: Contrasts between Uzbekistan and Tajikistan"

[57] "A History of Islam in Central Asia, Part III"

[58] Neighboring Uzbekistan was disturbed by this development.

[59] "Islam in Central Asia: Contrasts between Uzbekistan and Tajikistan"

[61] Charles William Maynes, "America Discovers Central Asia," *Foreign Affairs,* 82 (2003), 120-132.

[62] Cornell and Spector, 203.

[63] Azizulla, ICG. Presenter at the Brookings Institution on July 11, 2003.

[64] Cornell and Spector, 203.

Part II

Economic Concerns

Chapter 8

The Rise of the Post-Soviet Petro-States: Energy Exports and Domestic Governance in Turkmenistan and Kazakhstan

Theresa Sabonis-Helf

T he future prospects for Kazakhstan and Turkmenistan are presumed to be better than the prospects for most post-Soviet states, since they are fortunate to have two of the most desirable commodities in the world: oil and gas. Oil is the most important internationally traded commodity—both in terms of value and volume. It would seem to follow, then, that possessing oil offers hope to a state that it also will have wealth and power. Hydrocarbons have indeed captured the lion's share of foreign and domestic investment in Turkmenistan and Kazakhstan, and both investment—and the returns that will follow—are expected to increase in the coming years. But even as Turkmenistan and Kazakhstan are beginning to enjoy signs of success in the international oil arena, their domestic economies and political structures are already beginning to show some of the classic negative side effects of becoming "petro-states," nations which are defined and to an increasing extent structured by their role as oil/gas exporters.

In spite of the perception that oil is a source of wealth for nations and can be an engine for development, the actual history of political and economic development in petro-states has not been one of success. In the words of one analyst, OPEC "is never far from disaster . . . partly because it's a cartel of mostly undemocratic, mostly impoverished nations that can balance their budgets only if oil prices stay above $25 a barrel."[1] In spite of the original goal of the OPEC states to "sow the oil wealth" and encourage

159

development that would last after their oil monies ran out, OPEC members on the whole now suffer double-digit inflation, cost overruns on vast public projects, insolvent banking sectors, and a collapse of agricultural and manufacturing sectors in those states that have them.[2] Most experts in the political economy of energy agree that being an oil exporting state is associated with certain pathological development tendencies, including lack of transparency, lack of separation of powers within the government, a conspicuous lack of equitable distribution of wealth and power, high levels of state debt, and a "permanent tendency toward rent seeking by state officials."[3]

Kazakhstan and Turkmenistan both already exhibit some "petro-state" tendencies. Are the classic political and economic instabilities of petro-states unavoidable? What are the larger global security ramifications if Turkmenistan and Kazakhstan continue to fail locally, while succeeding—or at least capturing market share—in global energy markets? This chapter begins with an overview of the classic problems of the petro-state. It will review the political and economic trends in Kazakhstan and Turkmenistan associated with their increasing reliance on energy exports, and conclude with the potential security implications of these developments.

The Problem of the Petro-State

One commonly known impact of oil booms in countries that have other, non-oil industries is Dutch Disease, so-called because of the unexpected impact the discovery of North Sea gas had on the Dutch economy. The discovery of gas caused the relative strength of the guilder to increase dramatically. This, in turn, made Dutch-manufactured products noncompetitive, causing unemployment and inflation within the country. The nation found itself unexpectedly impoverished by its riches in natural gas. The Dutch experience has been replicated in many other countries. In sum, newfound success in oil or gas tends to take a toll on all other industrial sectors within a country. Persistent Dutch Disease can cause domestic resources to shift away from traded commodities, such as manufactured goods and agriculture, toward non-traded goods, such as services and transportation.[4] This is not inevitable, but aggressive state policies are needed to protect against such effects.

Kazakhstan has been studying the problem of Dutch Disease since the early 1990s, and has made an effort to learn from Norway's successes in particular. However, Kazakhstan may have chosen to focus on the wrong petro-state pathology: a single economic effect rather than the political-economic interactive effects. Evidence from Turkmenistan and

Kazakhstan suggests that if Dutch Disease is a factor, it is but one of many pathologies and perhaps one of the lesser challenges these states are likely to face as they increasingly embrace energy exporting.

In 1979,[5] (during the second oil crisis of the 1970s) one of OPEC's two founders, Juan Pablo Perez Alfonzo, said about the oil in his native Venezuela: "It is the devil's excrement. We are drowning in the devil's excrement."[6] Within a few years the oil boom had caused dramatic, unanticipated economic and political problems in Venezuela, nearly destroying the government and the economy. In her book, *The Paradox of Plenty: Oil Booms and Petro-States*, Terry Lynn Karl examines Venezuela as a classic example of a state that found oil booms holding it captive to a particular path of underdevelopment, rather than providing the hoped-for resources that would serve as an engine for wider development.

Karl notes that the capital-deficient oil exporting states of Algeria, Indonesia, Iran, Nigeria, and Venezuela—although otherwise very dissimilar—evolved along the same lines following the oil booms of the 1970s. She demonstrates that these states followed a common trajectory in which the policy environment first became "petrolized," serving the interests of the oil industry, but not the larger state. Vested private interests, once entrenched, reinforced the further petrolization of the state. Increasingly, the state relied on "the progressive substitution of public spending for statecraft," and state capacity became even weaker. In the final, weakest stage, oil booms actually had "pernicious effects," leading to the economic decline and destabilization of the regimes.[7] This grim picture suggests that oil is a hidden curse, rather than a blessing, for a developing state. Why does oil appear to have the effect of weakening the state that relies upon it?

First of all, Karl makes the point that all her case states are "late developing" states, ones that were on the periphery of an already established global trading system. Boundaries were given them by colonialism, rather than established through conflict or negotiation by the states themselves. As a result, these states experienced oil booms before they had strong national identities or administrative structures. More important, these states depended on revenues from export rather than revenues from taxation. In states that tax a commodity, such as oil, instead of taxing their people, the state fails to develop a basic accountability link: government spending tends not to become an issue for public consideration.[8] The net result of reliance on export revenues is that the state is largely free to build a "no taxation, no representation" system of governance.[9] The state tends not to develop a coherent budgeting system, and since revenues are closely tied to

fluctuations in the price of energy exports, annual revenues are highly unpredictable. Instead of building a coherent public bureaucracy (the origins
of most government bureaucracies are in taxation), the petro-states tend
to engage in uncontrolled public spending. In years when oil revenues
are less than expected, the promise of oil enables them to borrow. During
times of high revenues, the public perception that oil booms should mean
new benefits for all often leads the state to extend subsidies and take on
expensive projects which cannot be abandoned when oil prices fall. Further complicating the problem of fiscal governance, oil booms can throw
the entire petro-state economy into hyperinflation, causing the state to go
further into debt even when revenues are at their highest.[10]

The limited capacity of a fledgling or weak state makes it more easily
captured by the strongest interests within the state—the energy interests.
Absent transparent democratic institutions, oil interests become the only
actors invited by the government to develop business policies, and hence
become the only non-state (or parastatal) voice that the government hears.
This means that the government increasingly tends to favor the energy
industry over time, and that politicization of the industry is inevitable.[11]
Limited state capacity also makes it impossible for the state to put in place
policies to protect against the economic effects of Dutch Disease. In the
absence of strong policy measures to diversify the economy, oil tends to
crowd out other sources of national productivity and state revenue, pushing the oil exporting state further along the trajectory Karl describes.

The Post-Soviet Petro-State?

If we apply Karl's definition of the "petro-state," four post-Soviet
states qualify: Azerbaijan, Russia, Kazakhstan, and Turkmenistan. In each
case, the oil and/or oil and gas sector is at the center of the state's economy,
accounting for a high share of total exports and a high share of gross domestic product (GDP).[12] For Kazakhstan, oil and oil products constituted
52.8 percent of exports in 2002.[13] For Turkmenistan, gas constituted 57
percent of exports in 2002 with oil accounting for an additional 26 percent.[14] Karl divides the oil exporting countries into "capital deficient oil exporters" and "capital surplus oil exporters." Her analysis focuses on capital
deficient oil exporters, which have larger populations, smaller reserves, and
lower per capita incomes than the capital surplus oil exporting states. She
asserts that capital deficient oil-exporting states feel their oil dependency
more acutely because "their opportunities are so clearly bounded."[15]

At present, Kazakhstan and Turkmenistan are capital deficient oil
exporters by this definition,[16] possessing skilled labor forces and relatively

diversified economies. They have been net importers of capital and appear to be capable, in the mid term, of absorbing all the revenues from energy market booms. In terms of reserves to population ratios and gross national product (GNP) per capita levels, (measures Karl uses in dividing capital surplus and capital deficit oil exporting states), they are also comparable to Algeria, Indonesia, Iran, Nigeria, and Venezuela, all capital-deficient case states according to Karl.[17] Table 8–1 shows these states in comparison with key OPEC members.

Table 8–1. Examples of Oil/Gas Exporting States[18]

State Type: (Capital Surplus or Capital Deficient)	Oil Reserves (billion bbls)	Nat Gas Reserves (trillion cubic feet)	Population (millions)	Oil Reserves per capita (billion bbl per million persons)	GNI per Capita (US$)
Capital Deficient					
Russia	60.000	1680.00	144.8	0.4140	1,750
Kazakhstan	9.000	65.00	14.9	0.6040	1,350
Azerbaijan	7.000	30.00	8.1	0.8642	650
Turkmenistan	0.546	71.00	5.4	0.1011	950
Iran	89.700	812.30	64.7	1.3860	1,680
Venezuela	77.800	148.00	24.6	3.1626	4,760
Capital Surplus					
Saudi Arabia	261.800	224.700	21.4	12.2336	8,460
Iraq	112.500	109.80	23.8	4.7269	--
Kuwait	96.500	52.70	2.0	48.2500	18,270
Libya	29.500	46.400	5.4	5.4629	--

All reserves estimates from Energy Information Administration, World Crude Oil and Natural Gas Reserves, Most Recent Estimates," from
PennWell Corporation, Oil & Gas Journal, Vol. 100 No. 52 (Dec 23, 2002), can be accessed at: http://www.eia.doe.gov/emeu/international/
reserves.html
   World Development Indicators 2003, World Bank
   Gross National Income per capita, World Development Indicators 2003, World Bank

Turkmenistan and Kazakhstan both reject the suggestion that they are developing economies, preferring the World Bank term "economies in transition." They do have some characteristics that differentiate them from typical developing countries: high literacy, full electrification, and an industrial infrastructure (albeit decaying in many places). Yet although the distinction between transition economy and developing economy can be analytically useful, Turkmenistan and Kazakhstan also share important characteristics with developing states that are relevant in examining oil export dependency: lack of transparent democratic institutions, a post-colonial legacy of limited state capacity (in the Soviet era, all critical decisions were made in Moscow), bloated public bureaucracies, and incompetent budgeting systems.

Both Turkmenistan and Kazakhstan have made fundamentally different choices about the ownership of their oil resources and the appropriate role of the state. In a sense, they are the most-different cases of post-Soviet petro-states. Is the petro-state model useful given the considerable differences? What, if anything, can be learned from the experiences of the OPEC states that might be applicable to both Kazakhstan and Turkmenistan? Sovietologists may be troubled to see the pathologies of Turkmenistan and Kazakhstan explained in oil terms, since non-oil exporting post-Soviet states share some of the most significant pathologies of corruption and imploding state capacity. The question of interest here is how, if at all, these states have managed to use their new-found oil wealth to offset the difficulties of transition from Soviet rule to independence, and how the exploitation of hydrocarbons is likely to shape their futures.

The OPEC states, like Kazakhstan and Turkmenistan, had to overcome social capital deficits to achieve independence and international economic power in their post-colonial era. In some important respects, OPEC states have failed to establish strong governments with internal and external legitimacy. Might there be a resource-driven model for post-Soviet transition that can draw usefully from their experience? This chapter will examine elements of similarity and difference in Turkmenistan and Kazakhstan, with an eye towards highlighting what a petro-state based analysis can contribute to understanding the evolution of post-Soviet governance.

The Case of Turkmenistan

Turkmenistan is the post-Soviet state most nearly resembling an OPEC-style petro-state. One also could observe that it is, perhaps, the post-Soviet state most nearly resembling the pre-perestroika Soviet Union. The "Sedar" (Great Leader) and "Turkmenbashi" (Father of the Turkmen), President-for-Life Saparmurat Niyazov, was a Communist Party boss in the 1980s, and had significant differences with Gorbachev over the desirability of reforming the Soviet system. After the collapse of the Soviet Union, Niyazov took his own Republic, renamed the Communist Party the Democratic Party (now the only legal party in Turkmenistan), and set out to preserve a Soviet-style authoritarian welfare state in a post-Soviet world. Mixing Soviet experience with classic OPEC enthusiasm for state ownership, state welfare, and state interventionism, Turkmenistan appears to have moved further along Karl's petro-state trajectory than the other Caspian states.

Political Factors in Turkmenistan

Politically, Turkmenistan is a highly authoritarian state. The Kalkh Maslakhaty (The People's Council) and the Mejles (Parliament) are not permanent legislative bodies; instead they are convened annually or at the pleasure of the President. There is virtually no free press. In 2002, the Special Representative of the Organization for Security and Cooperation in Europe (OSCE) summarized the situation in Turkmenistan by saying there existed an "absolute lack of any freedom of expression . . . unseen in the OSCE region since the establishment of the organization."[19] Turkmenistan has been described as a "sultanistic regime," a category of regimes first named by Max Weber, and characterized by personal rule, large-scale corruption, and manipulation of fear and rewards.[20] The key political aspects of Turkmenistan today include nation-building (that is, establishing a strong Turkmen identity among citizens), demographics, and Turkmenistan's international relations.

Nation-Building

The project of nation-building in a post-colonial state is a critical task for preserving identity and security. In Turkmenistan, nation-building has been helped somewhat by the fact that Turkmen constitute 78.5 percent of the population.[21] This population is divided among five key tribal/clan groups, which comprise the five welayats (oblasts) of Turkmenistan. Some scholars believe that divisions among these groups are possibly important faultlines.[22] In an effort to build a collective national identity, Niyazov has incorporated the symbols of each of the five key clans in the flag. His symbol for the nation, the five-headed eagle, also emphasizes this unity in diversity.

Russians were previously the largest ethnic minority in the country, but are currently second with an estimated 5.2 percent.[23] Turkmenistan's recent unilateral abrogation of the dual-citizenship pact with Russia means that Turkmenistan no longer recognizes dual citizenship and this has forced citizens to choose (and has raised significant protest in Russia). However, it also has had the desired effect of limiting the ability of expatriate Turkmen to mount opposition movements from abroad. Currently, the largest ethnic minority is Uzbek, at 9.8 percent.[24] The ethnic Uzbeks are a matter of some concern, as they are geographically concentrated near Bukhara, and have more cultural and geographic ties to Uzbekistan than to their own distant capital of Ashgabad.

Niyazov has made some aggressive efforts toward building a common national identity. As of 2000, Turkmen is the only state language and Cyrillic letters have been eliminated systematically from public view. The state is attempting forced assimilation through actions such as requiring Turkmen national dress in all schools even for non-Turkmen students.[25] The entire nation has adopted the president's book, *Ruhname*, for use in schools at all levels. First published in October 2001, this book is part history, part religion, and part mythology, placing the Turkmenbashi at the center of development of the Turkmen state, and Turkmenistan at the center of the history of mankind. In spite of the sometimes-absurd elements of the President's cult of personality, discernable popular discontent remains low.[26] In OPEC states and elsewhere, large-scale prestige projects are almost always justified in terms of nation-building, and increasing the pride of citizens in their government. In Turkmenistan, prestige projects abound. Niyazov has overseen the construction of a new monument every year since independence, the most recent being a statue in honor of his book.

Population

Although popular discontent remains low, and services relatively high, the number of citizens to supply is growing. Population explosion is a pattern typical of the OPEC states and markedly untypical of the post-Soviet states. Population explosion, coupled with rising expectations of that population, could make sustaining the level of state subsidies increasingly difficult over time, as has been the case in OPEC states. Curiously, in spite of the fact that the population is clearly growing rapidly, it appears that Turkmenistan is over-reporting its growth.

The Turkmen government claims a population of 5.73 million, an estimate that the United States has modified to 4.6 million.[27] Beneath the dubious state statistics, there is evidence that the state is having trouble providing its citizens with full services. Although Turkmenistan's absolute poverty level is lower than other Central Asian states—approximately 7 percent in 1998—mortality indicators are worse. At the same time, some state services have been reduced, most significantly in education. Compulsory schooling is now nine years, down from eleven, and free university education has been abolished. Evening classes also have been eliminated at the university level.[28]

International Relations

Key characteristics of the evolution of Turkmenistan in its first decade of independence include state weakness in international relations and extreme concentration of wealth and power in the hands of the President-for-Life. Turkmenistan espouses "positive neutrality towards all states," an official state policy registered with the United Nations. In practice, positive neutrality has been a means for Turkmenistan to avoid alliances and remain isolationist in all matters, except those dealing with the export of gas. This isolation is seen as necessary for the success of the socialist experiment at home.

Turkmenistan's geographic situation as a landlocked, gas exporting state, poses some persistent challenges. The pipelines built in the Soviet era all run through Russia, giving the Russians a near-monopoly on transit. Although Turkmen gas mixes in the pipes with Russian gas, Russia has ordered that all Turkmen gas be sold to the "near abroad," which means the states of the former Soviet Union. This policy, in place since 1994, forces Turkmenistan to collect from states with high payment arrears, such as Ukraine. It also affords Russia the luxury of being able to say to successor states that it is unable to trade gas debt for political favors. The only existing non-Russian line to which Turkmenistan has access is the Korpeje-Kord Kuy pipeline, a small gas line which runs from Turkmenistan to Iran. This line was opened in 1997 during a period when Turkmenistan had halted gas exports to Russia, due to Russia's lack of payment deliveries.[29]

However, other export routes are possible. The prospective future pipeline which holds the most attraction for Turkmenistan is the Trans-Afghan pipeline, a line which would originate in Turkmenistan and then extend across Afghanistan (avoiding Iran), continue to Pakistan, and possibly end in India. The Asian Development Bank currently is conducting a feasibility study on this project, based on a similar project that had been designed before the Taliban came to power in Afghanistan. Turkmenistan's enthusiastic pursuit of this pipeline has been an irritant to Russia, as has Turkmenistan's decision not to join a "Eurasian Alliance of Gas Producers," which Russia attempted to form in 2002. At that time, Turkmenistan noted that it preferred to engage in bilateral trade.[30] Since then, Turkmenistan has been securing long-term contracts with former Soviet republics, most notably Ukraine. Turkmenistan also has secured a favorable rate for its gas from Russia, although Russia persists in paying nearly half the amount in barter.[31]

In spite of the need to access as many markets as possible and the fact that Turkmenistan's share of offshore resources in the Caspian Sea is considerable under any agreement, Turkmenistan has contributed significantly to the stalling of development in the Caspian Sea.[32] Turkmenistan's position in the Caspian Sea dispute has been inconsistent. Its current position is that it "favors division of the seabed and water surface with a condition to keep 20 miles zones (sic) for free navigation."[33] Yet at times, Turkmenistan has supported Iran's position—that the sea should be managed as a lake, or divided evenly among the states. Under the median line approach to the Caspian, Turkmenistan would receive 18 percent, rather than the 20 percent it would be entitled to under an even division.

The key issue for Turkmenistan is a set of disputes with Azerbaijan over a field they both claim in the Caspian, called Kyapaz or Serder. The case has been referred to the International Court of Justice (ICJ), and some expect their decision to resolve the dispute.[34] Until this issue is resolved, the extent of Turkmenistan's reserves is difficult to determine—which accounts, in part, for the wide disparity of estimates among sources. However, the disagreement is also said to be connected to the personal rivalry between Niyazov and Azeri former President Heydar Aliyev.[35] It may be the case that a resolution will be possible, now that Aliyev has passed the presidency to his son. Only a negotiated solution is possible; no scientific precedent has been set on how to objectively determine if a body of water is a lake or a sea. The decision of which body of law applies must be made by the states themselves.

Economic Factors in Turkmenistan

Turkmenistan has a statist, highly indebted economy. Its currency remains unconvertible, and hence the legal and black-market exchange rates have a great discrepancy. By Turkmen reporting, real GDP has exceeded 1989 levels since 2001; if true, Uzbekistan and Turkmenistan are the only former republics with this level of success.[36]

Structure of the Economy

During the era of OPEC's rise to power, optimism concerning state-led development was high. It was believed that the state would "allocate oil windfalls . . . in such a way as to optimize popular satisfaction."[37] In OPEC states, state ownership of a majority of the oil industry continues to be a necessary component of membership. Turkmenistan resembles OPEC states in its economic structure, in that the state owns an overwhelming majority of the oil and gas industry. However, state ownership in Turkmenistan is even more extensive than in most OPEC states, since the government owns and manages all land and industrial structures. In fact, the state has used its gas wealth to prevent transition away from Soviet-style welfare authoritarianism.

Turkmenistan is proud that it is the one former Soviet republic that has not attempted to follow an International Monetary Fund (IMF) program for economic restructuring.[38] Rather than succumb to the "Washington consensus" as to the appropriate sequencing of economic transition, Niyazov has instead pursued an older (and largely discredited) development strategy—import substituting industrialization (ISI), and is financing this ISI strategy with natural gas exports. Turkmenistan has continued to invest in infrastructure, including non-oil infrastructure. In addition to the natural gas supply mentioned earlier, railways and motorways also are under construction, and a rail link was opened with Iran in 1996.[39]

The price of Niyazov's "socialism in one country" has been an increasing reliance on gas and oil for state revenues. The statistics in Table 8–2 end with 2001, the last year for which full data is available, but indicators suggest that Turkmenistan's reliance on hydrocarbon exports is continuing to increase. This means that the state is increasingly bound to hydrocarbon revenues, hence, increasingly hostage to fluctuations in price and increasingly likely to be responsive to the needs of only one industrial sector: oil and gas.

Table 8–2. **Energy as a Percentage of Exports**

	1998	1999	2000	2001
Turkmenistan	54.7	63.7	79.8	82.9
Kazakhstan	34.9	38.0	50.2	58.1
Russia	36.7	38.9	62.9	61.0

IV Energy data are aggregated somewhat differently for Russia. Estimated from tables in (EIU Russia), including mineral products and
chemicals. Data from EIU Turkmenistan, and The Economist Intelligence Unit, Kazakhstan Country Profile 2003, and Russia Country Profice 2003, The Economist Intelligence Unit Limited, (Henceforth EIU Kazakhstan, EIU Russia), London: 2003

As is common among petro-states, Turkmenistan has suffered from persistent problems with taxation; personal income tax accounts for only seven percent of revenues. Of this amount, approximately 68 percent of revenues collected are in money, with the remainder paid in barter of goods and services.[41] Most tax revenues are from value added taxes (VAT) and profit tax. The central bank, which had some limited autonomy from 1997 to 1999, now has none. Since the dismissal of its pro-reform director in May 1999, the Bank's role is confined to printing money to cover budget deficits and extending credit to state owned companies.[42] Even strong advocates of State Oil Funds for Azerbaijan and Kazakhstan concede that, in a state as strongly presidential and non-transparent as Turkmenistan, a fund would be unable to have any positive impact.[43]

Investment Climate

Turkmenistan has sought to attract foreign investment, but the perception that the business environment is unfavorable and the legal and regulatory systems non-transparent have caused investors to forgo most opportunities. The size of the shadow economy in Turkmenistan is estimated as 60 percent of the official GDP, which is in the upper half of Central Asian economies.[44] As is typical in petro-states, political power is closely intertwined with the hydrocarbons sector. President Niyazov is said to approve all contract awards personally.[45] Another indicator of the flow of energy and power is that the President's son, Murad Niyazov, is an owner of an offshore firm, registered in Cyprus, which is responsible for receiving payments for gas consumed by Ukraine.[46] The government has a reputation for shifting policies and demanding changes in already existing contracts, at the whim of the President. Consequently, Turkmenistan has one of the lowest private sector-to-GDP ratios in the region, estimated by the European Bank for Reconstruction and Development (EBRD) to be 25 percent.[47] Of an original list of 4,300 small enterprises and 280 medium-sized enterprises supposedly available for privatization, only 200 of the smaller and six of the medium had been sold by June 2000.[48] Even the oil and gas enterprises have trouble attracting investment.[49]

A key barrier to investment remains the lack of transparency of all government statistics. Uncertainty about the population of Turkmenistan already has been mentioned. There is also uncertainty about as basic an issue as whether Turkmenistan possesses the eleventh largest proven gas reserves in the world[50] or the fifth largest.[51] With such information being self-reported,[52] Turkmenistan's statistics in all sectors continue to be regarded as highly suspect. GDP is similarly difficult to estimate. EBRD, using a weighted average of official and unofficial exchange rates, arrives at the figure of $538, while the Economist Intelligence Unit, by estimating purchasing power parity, proposes $2574 as a more accurate reflection.[53]

Corruption, a standard feature of petro-states, is a definite problem. In spite of the high level of authoritarianism, corruption is widespread and borders are notoriously porous. In addition, Turkmenistan has a reputation for being a significant transit point for trafficking in narcotics and arms.[54]

Debt

Hydrocarbon industries dominate the economy, while the second largest industrial sector—construction—is financed largely by Niyazov's enthusiasm for prestige projects. As a result of large-scale subsidies, prestige projects, and state mismanagement of the economy, Turkmenistan already qualifies as a highly indebted country under World Bank classifications.[55] In contrast to the Russian experience (where windfalls in oil were immediately used in part for debt reduction), Turkmenistan appears to be continuing along a path of increasing indebtedness.

Table 8–3. **Debt as a Percentage of GDP**

	1997	1998	1999	2000
Turkmenistan	50.6	64.6	NA	NA
Kazakhstan	19.2	27.3	36.2	36.4
Russia	31.5	65.6	89.0	61.7

Data from (EIU Turkmenistan), (EIU Kazakhstan), (EIU Russia), Reference Tables from the appendices

Part of the debt can be accounted for by problems in 1997, when Turkmenistan ceased exporting gas during disputes with Russia about non-payment. But this does not fully account for the sheer magnitude of debt as shown in Table 8–3. High spending on domestic subsidies is typical of petro-states. It is estimated by a former Iranian Finance Minister that subsidies in the Persian Gulf ran as high as 10 to 20 percent in some years of the 1970s and 1980s.[57] Turkmenistan follows in this tradition. Domestic energy consumption is highly subsidized. Every citizen has a free natural gas quota, and far more households are connected to gas now than were 10 years ago. By 1999, fully 92 percent of households were connected, up from 40 percent in 1990.[58] This demonstrates a significant state commitment to expanding subsidies. In Turkmenistan a driver pays 400 manat (two cents) for a liter of gasoline, which is less than half the 1000 manat (four cents) he would pay for a liter of bottled water.[59]

The World Bank estimates that currently in Turkmenistan, 21 percent of GDP is spent on subsidies for oil and gas alone.[60] One side effect of this high level of energy subsidies is that consumption of energy per unit of GDP is estimated to be 13 times the U.S. level, making Turkmenistan the least efficient in a region of relatively inefficient countries.[61] Although energy is the most significant sector in terms of government subsidies, water is also heavily subsidized, which has important implications for the viability of agriculture in Turkmenistan.

Threats and Patterns of Governance

The governance strategy in Turkmenistan is one familiar to many OPEC states: following the "no taxation, no representation" model, the state is failing to establish competence in taxing or budgeting. A complete lack of transparency has made even the most basic statistics suspect, yet—based on the promise of hydrocarbons—the international community remains willing to lend money where it is unwilling to invest. President Niyazov has relied on hydrocarbon revenues to support a high level of uncontrolled public spending. In years of low gas export revenues, he has been willing to assume vast national debt in an effort to keep his people from experiencing a decline in their Soviet-era living standard. In effect, President Niyazov has implemented—for the time being—the system that Brezhnev attempted to apply to the whole Soviet Union: use of energy export revenues as a substitute for economic reform.

The key threats to Turkmenistan appear to be continued high debt levels and the complete absence of an apparent line of succession. The debt will be inherited by any subsequent government, even one that decides to make less of a commitment to state subsidies. The lack of an apparent successor (Ministers who attain too high a level of visibility are sacked, and the Parliament is generally regarded as being laughably weak) almost ensures that chaos will follow in the wake of the "Great Leader's" passing. Due to Russian and Iranian interests in the stability of the gas fields in Turkmenistan, a period of chaos in Turkmenistan could leave both Russia and Iran tempted to intervene.

The Case of Kazakhstan

Key characteristics of the evolution of Kazakhstan in its first decade of independence include continuing state weakness and limited state capacity, as well as increasing concentration of wealth and power in the hands of a few. Like Turkmenistan, it can be classified as a "sultanistic regime,"[62] a state that runs on highly personalized leadership, corruption, fear, and systematic rewards. In three significant areas—ownership, geography, and demography—Kazakhstan differs from the typical petro-state. Kazakhstan's approach to ownership reflected the post-Soviet pessimism about state-led development. Instead of considering oil revenues as belonging to "the nation as a whole," as do all the OPEC member states,[63] Kazakhstan has chosen to allow privatization and an unusually high level of direct international investment in extraction and development of the oil sector. In March 2002, in recognition of the openness of its market, Kazakhstan became the first CIS country to be granted a "market economy country" status by the United States.[64]

Political Factors in Kazakhstan

Kazakhstan is nominally democratic, but in reality it is a highly presidential, authoritarian state, though much more open and pluralist than Turkmenistan. The Senate (upper house) and the Majilis (lower house) are permanent legislative bodies, although they typically rely on leadership from the Ministries and Presidential apparat. Key opposition leaders are in exile, and political parties other than those supportive of the President do not tend to endure. Members of President Nursultan Nazarbaev's extended family own substantial stakes in promising private and parastatal industries. Key political aspects of Kazakhstan include the task of nation-building (that is, establishing a strong Kazakh identity among citizens), demographic information, and Kazakhstan's international relations.

Nation Building

Nation-building in a post-colonial state is a critical task for preservation of identity and security. Like many late-developing states, Kazakhstan faces significant challenges in its efforts towards nation-building. With the collapse of the Soviet Union, it inherited boundaries that do not reflect a polity with strong national loyalties or identity. In fact, Kazakhs, who constitute 53.4 percent of the population,[65] only achieved the status of an absolute majority in Kazakhstan following independence. Russians make up the largest minority ethnic group, with 30 percent of the population. Ukrainians and Uzbeks make up the next largest minorities with 3.7 and 2.5 percent, respectively.[66] The state was not unified by a struggle for independence. Rather, independence was thrust upon it when the Kazakh President and Communist Party Chief Nursultan Nazarbaev failed in his long-standing efforts to negotiate a compromise between Gorbachev and Yeltsin to prevent the Soviet Union from collapsing. With the onset of independence, Nazarbaev became the leader of a state with limited capacity to govern. Under the Soviet empire, all bureaucracy in the Soviet-era capital of Almaty was designed to require direction from Moscow.

In OPEC states and elsewhere, large-scale prestige projects are almost always justified in terms of nation-building, and some do increase the pride of citizens in their government. In Kazakhstan, the key prestige project has been construction of the new capitol city, Astana. Although the reason for moving the capitol is oft-debated, it probably was done for a mix of reasons, including an effort to better integrate the northern portion of the country, a desire to bring the center of power closer to Russia, and a desire of President Nazarbaev to create a new post-Soviet city to his own specifications, in the region of his own clan.

Population

Kazakhstan's demography and declining population appear to pose something of an opportunity to the state. In contrast to most OPEC states, which experienced dramatic population growth with their prosperity, the Kazakh government is more concerned about stemming population decline. The 2000 census delivered the unwelcome news that the population since independence had declined from 16.1 million in 1989 to 14.8 million. Much of the decrease can be attributed to emigration. A disproportionate share of emigrants have been ethnic Russians, which has caused a "brain-drain" of some key skills. At the same time, however, this has enabled ethnic Kazakhs to become a majority in their own territory for the first time since the 1920s.[67] Declining population eventually may lead to a shortage of manpower and other challenges, but it does spare Kazakhstan the classic developing petro-state challenge of meeting the rising expectations of a burgeoning population.

International Relations

Kazakhstan's geographic situation poses some persistent challenges for the country. As a landlocked, oil-exporting nation, distant from all its prospective consumers,[68] Kazakhstan is faced with the strategically critical choice of how to bring its oil to market. As in the case of Turkmenistan, this geographic factor forces the government to commit to long-term export strategies. The pipelines built in the Soviet era all run through Russia, giving the Russians a monopoly on transit of Kazakh oil. Russia has allocated irregular space in its pipelines to Kazakhstan since independence, consistently favoring Russian oil. In an effort to create a pipeline just for Kazakhstan, the Caspian Pipeline Consortium (CPC) was founded in 1993 and the pipeline opened in the summer of 2001. This pipeline also runs across Russian territory, but is owned by a mixture of state and private actors. However, problems with Russia over transit fees and privileges have persisted. In just one example, Russia is seeking to extend access to the pipeline to non-shareholders at shareholder rates.[69] Until an alternate route is constructed that does not cross Russia, Kazakhstan will remain reliant on Russian goodwill to get its oil to market.

Non-Russian possibilities for the future export of Kazakh oil do exist. China, for one, has expressed interest in an eastbound pipeline. Yet Russian-Kazakh trade relations remain fairly positive due to the power asymmetry between the states. Since September 11, the United States has encouraged Russia to make good-faith agreements with Kazakhstan to discourage the Kazakhs from moving more towards OPEC's sphere of influence. Kazakhstan and Russia, together with Belarus, Kyrgyzstan, and Tajikistan, are striving for a "harmonization of legislation" as a component of an eventual free trade zone. This movement towards harmonization gives Kazakhstan the opportunity to avoid capacity building. It also means that Kazakhstani legislation, in many sectors, is based very closely on existing Russian laws. Critics claim that the harmonization amounts to "legislation by white-out." It also ensures that weaknesses in Russian laws will most likely be passed on to the other four states.

One aspect of Russian-Kazakhstan cooperation has been on the Caspian Sea issue.[70] Kazakhstan consistently has supported the Russian position. When the positions of the other littoral parties remained unchanged after several years of negotiations, Russia and Kazakhstan were the first to sign a bilateral agreement in 1998, which marked borders on the seabed in keeping with the "Median Line" solution.[71] One cost to Kazakhstan of the Caspian Sea dispute that remains unresolved is that several pipeline options cannot be pursued without a resolution. The United States has expressed interest in Kazakhstan joining the Baku-Tbilisi-Ceyhan pipeline currently under construction. While the government of Kazakhstan expresses interest in each new option, at present no non-Russian routes are under construction.[72]

Economic Factors in Kazakhstan

Kazakhstan has an open economy. The currency is fully convertible and has been relatively stable since 1998. Real GDP has yet to exceed 1989 levels, but Kazakhstan is the only Central Asian state to have attained a GNP of over $1,000 per capita.[73] Kazakhstan also has a relatively small shadow economy, estimated at only 39 percent of its official GDP.[74] Wealth is very unevenly distributed, however, with 26 percent of the population below the poverty line.[75] Due, in part, to the high level of foreign investment, the UN Human Development Index ranks quality of life in Kazakhstan as the highest in Central Asia and the Caucasus.[76]

Structure of Economy

Kazakhstan, like most post-Soviet states, came to independence with a profound skepticism about the state's role in all sectors of social and economic development. Turkmenistan, in which the state retained control of most sectors, was the exception rather than the rule. In Kazakhstan, the state made little effort to cushion its population from the economic impacts of the Soviet Union's collapse. Instead, in the early years of independence, the population (like that in many other post-Soviet states) had their expectations dramatically reduced, even as oil production was beginning to provide windfalls to the state and elites.

Kazakhstan received enthusiastic support from international financial institutions and from the oil interests for its early decision to privatize most of the economy, including the oil sector. This privatization had the positive effect of preventing the state from sharply expanding, as happened in OPEC states during oil booms. Instead, Kazakhstan's oil industry rapidly became dependent on foreign investment; in the first quarter of 2002, foreign investors underwrote 80 percent of oil production.[77] Foreign investment was attractive initially because it had the short-term effect of providing emergency revenue in the wake of the Soviet collapse. Privatization was used to fill the budgetary gap, particularly during the time period of 1996 to 1998.[78]

Because of the dramatic opening of its industry to foreign investment as well as the simultaneous privatization of the domestic energy sector, by 1998 Kazakhstan was the largest per capita recipient of direct foreign investment in the Commonwealth of Independent States (CIS).[79] Yet in retrospect, the rush to privatize is sometimes regretted. As the state enjoys more success in oil exports, the government on several occasions has expressed a desire to renegotiate its contracts with foreign investors, many of which it now feels were not designed sufficiently in its favor.

Although the government is reluctant to improve its capacity in terms of its ability to tax or provide services, it has not been immune to the temptation of "prestige" projects. Such projects are a hallmark of petro-states and the new capital of Astana is a classic example. A richer and more established state, Germany, opted in recent years to move its capital slowly to Berlin, in order to reduce the cost. By contrast, government ministries in Kazakhstan were ordered to relocate to Astana within a year of the presidential announcement designating the new capital. Converting a small, provincial town in the Virgin Lands of the steppe into the nation's capital has been an expensive project, and a top investment priority for the government. Construction in Astana is estimated to have cost at least $500 million by 1999, not including the power and water infrastructure that was sorely needed.[80] In addition to direct government projects, oil companies, both foreign and domestic, also were expected to contribute to the President's new city. Luong estimates that Kazakh oil alone has spent $25 to 30 million in improvements in Astana.[81]

The Kazakh state also has failed to address the issue of taxation. State revenues declined to 20 percent of GDP by 1995, and dropped by an additional six percent in 1996. By 1997, the government acknowledged that it had been failing to collect taxes effectively, and created a new State Revenues Ministry. This Ministry was tasked with responsibility for fiscal policy, tax regulation, and customs. Tax revenues, as a percentage of GDP, continued their decline in 1998.[82] This lack of success is best explained by the government's conviction that it can rely primarily on oil and gas revenues; in 1998, it borrowed money rather than improving tax collection methods. The lack of success in raising tax revenues for the federal budget also may be explained by the simple fact that the State Revenues Ministry, like most lucrative Ministries, is headed by a relative of the President and has the power to determine the type and level of taxes applicable to each new oil contract. These contracts must be made directly with the government, each is unique and each is reviewed by President Nazarbaev.[83]

With the failure of other forms of taxation, increasing reliance on oil for state revenues has been inevitable. Energy exports constitute an increasing share of all exports in Kazakhstan, rising to the current level of 58.1 percent of total exports (see Table 8–2). Although energy as a percentage of exports remains lower in Kazakhstan than in Turkmenistan, the rates of increase are similar; Kazakhstan's reliance increased 23.2 percent from 1998 to 2001, only slightly less than Turkmenistan's increase of 28.2 percent during the same time period. Again, increased reliance means the Kazakh state is increasingly hostage to fluctuations in price and export levels, and the state is therefore increasingly likely to be responsive to the needs of the oil sector alone. One very good sign in Kazakhstan is the establishment of a new State Oil Fund, designed to provide consistent funding to the social sector. This is an oft-recommended strategy for improving the fiscal competence of petro-states.[84] Its success, however, depends on it being run in a transparent manner.

Investment Climate

Although privatization may have limited expansion of the state, it has not begun separating money from power. The presidential family remains vital to all oil deals, and the President himself is the principal partner of a number of major energy companies operating in Kazakhstan. The link between economic and political outcomes is both typical of petro-states and reminiscent of the former socialist systems.[85] It also leads inevitably to corrupt practices on the part of the foreign oil companies attempting to do business in Kazakhstan, as evidenced by the investigation of Exxon Mobil, said to be the largest U.S. investigation of alleged bribery abroad under the Foreign Corrupt Practices Act.[86] The level of corruption at the highest levels is widely recognized: in June 2000, a bill in parliament assured the President and his family lifetime immunity from charges of corruption.[87]

Kazakhstan has managed to put a spin on privatization that is a curious inverse of the tendency of the petro-state to expand. Instead, multinational corporations operating in Kazakhstan were asked, in the early crisis years, to assume certain social costs—in lieu of paying taxes. Hence, companies took on tasks such as paying back wages, building roads, and funding schools. Such participation had the short-term effect of making the regions more welcoming to foreign investment, but the long-term effect has been to deprive the federal government of revenues (tax exemptions were offered in exchange for these services at the local level). This practice also has served to trap the foreign companies into running Soviet-style "company towns," rather than devolving the management of such towns to local, elected authorities. The predictable consequence of such schemes, as Luong notes, has been "to place both the responsibility and the blame for local socioeconomic conditions on foreign investors rather than on government officials."[88]

A similar strategy was pursued when the insolvent electricity sector was sold to foreign investors; the government was able to direct the inevitable citizen hostility about higher tariffs towards the foreign investors and away from the state. The Belgian electricity company, Tractebel, is under investigation in Belgium for allegedly paying $55 million in bribes to its Kazakh business partners. Apparently, the money bought Tractebel very little, since regulators refused to raise the electricity rates, the life of the chief Tractebel representative has been threatened, and Tractebel ended up selling its holdings to a state company for $100 million—about half the amount it had invested.[89]

Debt

With the inability to tax or provide social services, coupled with presidential fondness for the new capital city, it is not surprising that Kazakhstan's external debt is rising. Although Kazakhstan's debt as percentage of GDP (36.4 percent in 2000—see Table 8–3) seems low compared to Turkmenistan (64.6 percent in 1998 and rising), in absolute terms Kazakhstan, by 1997, had accumulated the third largest debt among former Soviet republics, following Russia and Ukraine. As early as 1996, the state was spending almost 10 percent of its budget on debt service, while cutting back on domestic social programs.[90] A local journalist estimates that public expenditures by 1998 were running a half to a third of pre-independence levels.[91]

Threats and Patterns of Governance

Although a much weaker—and less ambitious—state than Turkmenistan, Kazakhstan also appears to follow the "no taxation, no representation" model familiar to OPEC states. Kazakhstan has failed to establish competence in taxation or budgeting. Transparency and high levels of corruption remain problematic. Rapid privatization was a short-term solution to offset the costs of collapse of the Soviet Union, but the one-time influx of revenues did not solve the deeper problems. In an effort to protect the weak state, without making efforts to strengthen its competence, Kazakhstan apparently has relied on a strategy of privatizing and using that privatization to shuttle blame for government deficiencies to foreign investors.

Kazakhstan does have some characteristics that may enable its development to depart from the classic petro-state pattern. Privatization is an encouraging sign, offering the potential of some market controls on government behavior. The State Oil Fund, if properly managed, may provide some fiscal discipline. The demographic decline of Kazakhstan suggests it will not be subject to the kind of social pressures caused by dramatic population increases in OPEC and other states such as Iran, Nigeria, and Indonesia.

However, if we match the evidence from Kazakhstan with Karl's trajectory, it appears that Kazakhstan has more in common with the "petrolization" trajectory than not. "Petrolization," that is, "a process by which states become dependent on oil exports and their polities develop an addiction to petrodollars,"[92] does appear to be under way. The state has not yet moved to dramatic public spending, but neither has it improved its state capacity or bureaucratic competence. Instead, the state appears to be capturing oil rents without accepting obligations to its people. This may be the first of the anticipated "pernicious effects," which will lead to economic decline and destabilization of the regime, but it is too early to say. For the moment, Kazakhstan watchers are more concerned that, as Luong notes:

> if current trends continue, Kazakhstan will emerge as a quasi-state – that is, one with international legitimacy but without the domestic capacity to generate sufficient revenue, address basic social problems, and promote even minimum levels of economic growth.[93]

As Kazakhstan continues to increase reliance on oil exports, and continues to fail to develop bureaucratic competence, one troubling trend is that, as a state with significant oil reserves, it can continue to borrow money in the international community. It thereby avoids structural changes and ensures that future generations will inherit substantial debt, as well as incoherent political and bureaucratic structures. Another troubling trend is that economic success in oil has not motivated the state to increase its provision of social goods, in spite of having acquired the resources necessary to do so. Public expectations for state support remain low. Instead of taking an OPEC-style approach toward "sowing the oil wealth," elites, and particularly the presidential family, have treated their own state as a colony to be exploited. This, in the end, will constitute the greatest threat to stability.

Petro-State Pathologies

An analysis that fails to take petro-state behavior into account may simply conclude that the problem in Turkmenistan is too much state, whereas the problem in Kazakhstan is not enough. A petro-state based analysis, on the other hand, offers some insight into the similarities of these states and their problems. Given the trajectory of oil-led development in other states, we cannot assume that the problems of either state will recede as they develop. Instead, we should expect that the transition to truly strong states will simply not occur here. Karl notes:

> That the petro-state depends on revenues generated by a depletable commodity, that this commodity produces extraordinary rents, and that these rents are funneled through weak institutions virtually ensure that the public sector will lack the authority and corporate cohesiveness necessary to exercise effective capacity.[94]

Kazakhstan and Turkmenistan are best understood as states tempted by the "no taxation, no representation" model characteristic of OPEC states. Because there is wealth to be had, and because all decisions are political, rent seeking by state officials promises to be a permanent tendency.[95] The states have not developed coherent budgeting systems or public bureaucracies—and wealth from hydrocarbon revenues means that they may indefinitely delay in these tasks. The two have different spending patterns, but both have been free to borrow against the future, since the international community has faith in the value of the energy resources, even if not in the wisdom of the states managing it. Early evidence suggests that the energy interests within the states are already capturing the state, and that these interests do not serve the cause of expanding democracy. In both states, although evidence of Dutch Disease is difficult to separate from the problems inherent in moving away from Soviet economies, there is evidence that other sectors continue to be pushed out by the oil sector, and that the state is falling further into disrepair in spite of increased wealth.

A petro-state based analysis offers a useful framework for outlining what is likely to happen to these states, and what trends should be most closely monitored. It is also useful in explaining how the future of the energy-rich post-Soviet states (including Russia and Azerbaijan as well as Turkmenistan and Kazakhstan) is likely to differ politically, as well as economically, from other post-Soviet states.

Global Security Implications

The centrality of hydrocarbons to the economies of Turkmenistan and Kazakhstan should not be confused with their significance to international energy markets. The resources of Central Asia represent incremental not large additions to the potential world supply. They may be significant at the margins, but the proven reserves suggest that these resources will be more important to the region and for would-be importing states such as Turkey and Pakistan, than to world markets overall. What these resources do represent are new avenues that could support diversity of supply, the possibility of new oil and gas supply routes to regions currently facing energy deficits, and new opportunities for investment for hydrocarbon companies long locked out of Middle East development.

There is little doubt that, in spite of important gains in efficiency, rising standards of living necessitate rising energy needs in the developing world. Hence, world demand for energy will continue to increase. The International Energy Agency predicts that world oil demand alone by 2010 will be 90 million bbl/day, which is 17 percent greater than present.[96] The age of oil is not yet past, nor is the boom and bust cycle that has characterized oil markets. The age of gas has barely begun, as European states establish policies that make gas an attractive source of energy. Turkmenistan and Kazakhstan offer the promise of an alternative to OPEC. The risks, however, are evident.

In the case of Turkmenistan, its resemblance to OPEC states is already striking. The high debt levels, over-extension of the state, absence of a line of succession, as well as the strategic sensitivity of its location, all make it difficult to argue that reliance on Turkmenistan for resources is in any way more sound than reliance on the OPEC states. In the case of Kazakhstan, one cannot be too sanguine about the ability of privatization to offset the pathologies associated with petro-states. Even if assets are nominally privatized, Kazakhstan remains a state politicized in the manner of other petro-states. Western states and investors should not be so enamored as to forget that:

> private sectors are just as rent-seeking as political authorities in oil-exporting countries, and systematically pressure these authorities to funnel oil money in their direction to finance inefficient and unproductive activities.[97]

A climate in which a wealthy state remains weak, accepting little obligation to provide social benefits for its population, is not superior to an over-extended state with limited capacity, and no more secure.

The possible regional and global implications of petrolization of either Kazakhstan or Turkmenistan need to be examined in a security context—especially if oil booms in an era of increasing scarcity actually have the "pernicious effects" of economic decline and regime destabilization. If diversification from OPEC sources leads to expanding the number of states with OPEC-like instabilities, the problem of avoiding petrolization should receive the active attention of both the oil importing, as well as exporting states.

Notes

[1] Justin Fox, "OPEC Has a Brand-New Groove," *Fortune*, October 14, 2002, 115.

[2] Terry Lynn Karl, "Crude Calculations: OPEC Lessons for the Caspian Region," Chapter 3 in *Energy and Conflict in Central Asia and the Caucasus,* Robert Ebel and Rajan Menon, eds. (Maryland: Rowman & Littlefield Publishers, 2000), 35.

[3] Terry Lynn Karl, *The Paradox of Plenty: Oil Booms and Petro-States* (Berkeley and Los Angeles: University of California Press, 1997), 63.

[4] See Jahangir Amuzegar, *Managing the Oil Wealth: OPEC's Windfalls and Pitfalls* (London and New York: I.B. Tauris & Co, 2001), 19-21, for a fuller discussion. Amuzegar is more skeptical of the economics of Dutch Disease than most analysts. He asserts that the Dutch Disease effect does not necessarily hold in countries with high unemployment.

[5] During this crisis, the price of oil jumped from $13 to $34 per bbl.

[6] Qtd. in Karl, *Petro-States*, 4.

[7] Karl, *Petro-States*, Chapter 1.

[8] See Karl, *Petro-States*, Chapter 3 for a full discussion of the importance of a citizen tax base.

[9] The application of "no taxation, no representation" to oil states is frequent in the literature. Its origins are unclear.

[10] The OPEC states have seen debt increase with each oil boom. See tables in Karl, *Petro-States*, appendix.

[11] See Karl, *Caspian*, 39.

[12] The World Bank uses 10 percent of GDP and 40 percent of total merchandise exports to classify a mineral economy. Karl applies the same formula to classify an oil economy. See Karl, *Petro-States*, Chapter 1. At the present time, Azerbaijan is the most reliant of the four on oil exports, at 90 percent of exports in 2002.

[13] *CIA World Factbook*, section on Kazakhstan.

[14] Ibid., section on Turkmenistan.

[15] Karl, *Petro-States*, 18.

[16] Karl has postulated that Kazakhstan may become a capital surplus state in the future, since it is more sparsely populated, and additional reserves are likely to be discovered (see Karl, *Caspian*, 29). However, Kazakhstan's population is large by capital surplus state standards: Iraq, with its 1973 population of 10.41 million, is the most populous of the capital-surplus states. In spite of its limited oil reserves, Turkmenistan is presumed to have the fifth largest gas reserves in the world. Given its sparse population, it may become a capital surplus state. At the moment, however, its export routes and options are sufficiently constrained that it is not functioning as a capital surplus state.

[17] Karl, *Petro-States*, Chapter 2.

[18] For a similar chart of non-FSU countries, see Karl, *Petro-States*, 18.

[19] Quoted in *Turkmenistan Country Profile 2003* (London: The Economist Intelligence Unit Limited, (Henceforth EIU Turkmenistan), 2003), 16.

[20] See Tanya Charlick-Paley, with Phil Williams and Olga Oliker, "The Political Evolution of Central Asia and South Caucasus: Implications for Regional Security," Chapter 2 in *Faultlines of Conflict in Central Asia and the South Caucasus: Implications for the US Army*, Olga Oliker and Thomas S. Szayna, eds., RAND Document Number MR-1598-A, 2003, 13-14.

[21] Thomas Szayna, "Potential for Ethnic Conflict in the Caspian Region," Chapter 6 in *Faultlines of Conflict in Central Asia and the South Caucasus*, Olga Oliker and Thomas S. Szayna, eds. (California and Washington DC: RAND, 2003), Table 6.8.

[22] See Nancy Lubin, "Turkmenistan's Energy: A Source of Wealth or Instability?" Chapter 6 in *Energy and Conflict in Central Asia and the Caucasus*, Robert Ebel and Rajan Menon, eds. (Maryland: Rowman & Littlefield Publishers, 2000).

[23] Szayna, Table 6.8.

[24] Ibid., Table 6.8.

[25] EIU Turkmenistan.

[26] Ibid.

[27] Ibid., 12.

[28] Ibid., 13 and 20.

[29] Lubin, 108.

[30] "Turkmenistan Undecided on Whether to Join Eurasian 'Gas OPEC'" Interfax News Agency, Petroleum Report, July 24, 2002.

[31] The current price, $44, is actually more than Turkmenistan would be likely to get from Western users, but Russia is currently paying half the amount in barter. Industry experts, personal interviews, Sept. 2003.

[32] In a condominium agreement, all littoral states would have an equal share in the lake's resources, regardless of the extent of their coastline, and would confer with each other on activities taken in the lake. Under a sea agreement, the littoral states would have exclusive economic zones and

free passage under the Law of the Sea. For a detailed discussion of the Caspian Sea issue, see Gawdat Bahgat, "Splitting Water: The Geopolitics of Water Resources in the Caspian Sea," *SAIS Review*, Vol. XXII, no. 2 (Summer-Fall 2002).

[33] "Caspian Legal Regime," summarized by the International Center for Caspian Studies, <http://caspiancenter.org/info_sp.shtml>.

[34] *CIA World Factbook*, Turkmenistan.

[35] See Martha Brill Olcott, "Regional Cooperation in Central Asia and the South Caucasus," Chapter 7 in *Energy and Conflict in Central Asia and the Caucasus*, Robert Ebel and Rajan Menon, eds., (Maryland: Rowman & Littlefield Publishers, 2000).

[36] EIU Turkmenistan, 25.

[37] Amuzegar, 14.

[38] EIU, Turkmenistan, 21.

[39] Ibid., 16.

[40] Data from EIU Turkmenistan, and The Economist Intelligence Unit, *Kazakhstan Country Profile 2003*, and *Russia Country Profile 2003* (London: The Economist Intelligence Unit Limited, (Henceforth EIU Kazakhstan, EIU Russia), 2003).

[41] EIU Turkmenistan, 22.

[42] Ibid., 8.

[43] Svetlana Tsalik, "The Hazards of Petroleum Wealth," Chapter 1 in *Caspian Oil Windfalls: Who Will Benefit?*, Svetlana Tsalik and Robert Ebel, eds. (Washington, DC: Central Eurasia Project, 2003), 12.

[44] Phil Williams, "Criminalization and Stability in Central Asia and South Caucasus," Chapter 4 in *Faultlines of Conflict in Central Asia and the South Caucasus*, Olga Oliker and Thomas S. Szayna, eds. (Washington, DC: RAND, 2003), Table 4-1.

[45] Lubin, 114.

[46] Centrasia, Daily Report 29 November, Russian-language Central Asian news site, at: <www.centrasia.ru>.

[47] EIU Turkmenistan, 18 and 22.

[48] Ibid., 22.

[49] Dragon Oil from UAE and Monument from the UK are involved in exploration--a small list, compared to activity in other post-Soviet, energy-rich states.

[50] EIU, Turkmenistan.

[51] CIA *World Factbook*, Turkmenistan.

[52] This is also because Turkmenistan prefers to count reserves that are in a Caspian Sea area where their ownership is disputed by Azerbaijan.

[53] EIU Turkmenistan, 20.

[54] See Lubin. Also see Williams.

[55] EIU Turkmenistan, 36.

[56] Data from EIU Turkmenistan, EIU Kazakhstan, EIU Russia; Reference Tables from the appendices.

[57] Iranian Finance Minister Jahangir Amuzegar, cited by Karl in *Caspian*, 36.

[58] EIU Turkmenistan, 16.

[59] Interviews, taxi drivers in Ashgabad, October 2003.

[60] EIU Turkmenistan, 16.

[61] Ibid., 16.

[62] See Charlick-Paley.

[63] See Amuzegar, Chapter 1.

[64] Embassy of the Republic of Kazakhstan, "Kazakhstan in Brief," June 2002.

[65] Szayna, Table 6.5.

[66] Ibid., Table 6.5.

[67] EIU Kazakhstan, 15.

[68] As Karl notes in *Caspian*, 33, Kazakhstan, Turkmenistan and Azerbaijan are the only oil exporting states without sea access.

[69] EIU Kazakhstan, 21.

[70] Russia has long supported the notion of free passage, with clear allocation of seabed rights. (This is usually known as the Median line solution). For a full discussion, *see* Bahgat SAIS.

[71] A median line solution would divide the Caspian Sea in accordance with the Law of the Sea treaty. See earlier section on Turkmenistan's international relations issues for an explanation of the median line debate.

[72] As noted, the Baku-Tbilisi-Ceyhan route is a non-Russian route, but for Kazakhstan to connect with it will require construction of undersea lines in the Caspian.

[73] Abraham S. Becker, "Some Economic Dimensions of Security in Central Asia and South Caucasus," Chapter 3 *Faultlines of Conflict in Central Asia and the South Caucasus: Implications for the US Army,* eds. Olga Oliker and Thomas S. Szayna, RAND Document Number MR-1598-A, 2003.

[74] Williams, Table 4-1.

[75] *CIA World Factbook*, Kazakhstan.

[76] Williams, 74.

[77] EIU Kazakhstan.

[78] Pauline Jones Luong, "Kazakhstan: The Long-Term Costs of Short-Term Gains," Chapter 5 in *Energy and Conflict in Central Asia and the Caucasus,* Robert Ebel and Rajan Menon, eds. (Maryland: Rowman & Littlefield Publishers, 2000), 80.

[79] Luong, 88.

[80] Ibid., 84.

[81] Ibid., as of 1999.

[82] Ibid., 85.

[83] Karl, *Caspian*, 46.

[84] See Tsalik for details

[85] Karl, *Caspian*, 40

[86] Steve LeVine, "US Bribery Probe Looks at Mobil-Firm's Role in Payments to High Kazakh Officials is Under Investigation," *Wall Street Journal,* April 23, 2003, A2.

[87] Charlick-Paley, 18.

[88] Luong, 90.

[89] Douglas Frantz, "Generating Much Heat but no Kazakh Profits," *The New York Times,* May 13, 2001, start page 3.8.

[90] Luong.

[91] Cited in Luong, 87.

[92] Karl, *Caspian*, 37.

[93] Luong, 80.

[94] Karl, *Petro-States*, 58.

[95] Ibid., 63.

[96] International Energy Association, International Energy Agency, *World Energy Outlook 2000,* The International Energy Agency, Paris: 2000. See website: www.iea.org/

[97] Karl, *Caspian*, 37.

Chapter 9

Cooperative Management of Transboundary Water Resources in Central Asia

Daene C. McKinney

S ince independence a little more than a decade ago, the Central Asian republics have been striving to develop fair and rational bases for sharing and using their water and energy resources. Inheriting a legacy of unsustainable economic development and environmental mismanagement, these former Soviet countries have faced extreme economic inefficiencies and ecological damage in their attempts to transition to market economies. The Central Asian republics depend on the rivers of the Aral Sea Basin for drinking water, irrigation, and hydroelectric power. In the upstream countries of the Basin, Kyrgyzstan and Tajikistan, the rivers are used for hydroelectric power, especially during winter months, while downstream, in Turkmenistan, Kazakhstan, and Uzbekistan, they are used for agricultural purposes in the summertime. The post-independence upstream shift in water use away from irrigation has created disputes between the upstream and downstream countries over how the region's transboundary waters should be managed. Successful cooperative sharing of water and other natural resources is essential for the long-term prosperity and security of the region.

Agriculture is the largest water consumer in the region and a major employer of the region's workforce, producing a large percentage of each country's gross domestic product (GDP). Yet water diversions for irrigation have resulted in severe problems in the downstream areas of the Syr Darya and Amu Darya Basins near the Aral Sea. Improving water quality and increasing water quantity to meet basic human needs in these environmentally damaged and economically depressed areas is an urgent need. However, providing this water through reduced agricultural water use may impose great economic damage on the basin countries. How does one choose? The ongoing questions of water management in Central Asia center on such paradoxical and too often restrictive choices. Finding solutions will not be easy because the problems are inherently complicated.

The main infrastructure systems of Central Asia were developed when the countries were part of one centrally administered area, in which natural and economic resources were shared and costs were subsidized. This is no longer the case, and the countries of Central Asia have each developed their own national approaches to resource use and economic development. The past decade has brought greater national self-sufficiency and governance but, at the same time, has contributed to a decline in economic integration and personal living standards among the republics.

Given the great dependence of the Central Asian economies on irrigated agriculture, the issue of water allocation, involving both quantity of water and timing of allocations, has emerged as a major factor in the republics' development. Agreements on the use of the region's shared water resources are evolving. How the use of water resources is finally settled will have substantial consequences for the long-term prosperity of these nations. In addition, the ongoing process of regional cooperation in the arena of natural resources management is a major factor in the long-term security of the region.

The Central Asian states have made great progress during the past 10 years in cooperative management of shared water resources. However, many issues remain unresolved and need continued development, including:

- Harmonizing, or at least coordinating, water management strategies and water codes among the nations of the region;

- Enhancing and strengthening the roles of regional water management bodies;

- Improving the 1998 Agreement on water and energy use in the Syr Darya Basin, which is due to renew itself for an additional five years in 2003;

- Improving water allocation in the Basin to account for the developing agricultural and hydropower sectors in the upstream countries, and the use of the water in downstream countries; and

- Proper financing of water infrastructure of interstate significance.

Central Asia is a region perpetually dependent on its water resources for existence and prosperity. Recent political changes in the region have created a situation in which a resource once managed by a single, centralized authority must now be jointly developed and managed by five sovereign nations. Many past decisions must be dealt with by the new governments, such as the tragedy of the Aral Sea decline and the legacy of over-developed irrigation systems. While new relations between the fledgling countries have been established in the area of water resources, much remains to be done to achieve secure and productive use of this resource. This chapter will examine the history of the region in terms of water issues, examine the ongoing strategies to deal with water management and finally discuss conclusions and challenges which remain within the region.

Figure 9–1. **Aral Sea Basin.**

The Aral Sea Basin

The Aral Sea Basin, the dominant geographic feature of the region in terms of water, comprises parts of Afghanistan and Kazakhstan, and most of the Kyrgyz Republic, Tajikistan, Turkmenistan, and Uzbekistan. Figure 9–1 shows the size of the Basin in relation to the region. The Aral Sea Basin occupies 1.51 million square kilometers (km²) of the total four million km² area of these countries. Topographically, the Aral Sea Basin ranges from the vast Turanian plains in the west to the tremendous mountain ranges of the Pamirs and Tien Shan in the east.

The climate in the northern part of the Basin is continental, whereas the southern part is subtropical. The high mountain areas are humid and account for the high volume of runoff in the Amu and Syr Darya rivers which run from the mountains through the desert to the Aral Sea. Water resources are mainly surface waters formed in the Tien Shan and Pamir mountain ranges. Melt water from extensive permanent snowfields and glaciers (more than 18,000 km² of ice cover) feeds the major rivers of the Aral Sea Basin, the Syr Darya, and Amu Darya, mostly during the spring and early summer thaw.

The Amu Darya Basin covers a broad area, about 1.33 million km², and the river—the largest river in Central Asia—has a length of 2574 km from the headwaters of the Pyanj River on the Afghan–Tajik border to the Aral Sea.[1] The Syr Darya Basin occupies about 484,000 km² and the river stretches some 2,337 km from the Naryn River headwaters in Kyrgyzstan through the Ferghana Valley, the Hunger Steppe, the Kyzyl Kum desert, before finally reaching the Aral Sea.[2] These two rivers account for about 90 percent of the region's annual river flow and provide roughly 75 percent (by area) of the water to Central Asia's irrigated agriculture. The Amu Darya has an average annual flow of 79.3 billion cubic meters (bcm), and the Syr Darya has a flow of 37.2 bcm.

Figure 9–2 and Table 9–1 show that Tajikistan and Kyrgyzstan together produce about 77 percent of the water in the Aral Sea Basin. Afghanistan contributes about 10 percent of the inflow to the Basin, but it has not been a party to the recent Aral Sea Basin management because of its political instability. However, this is likely to change in the future as agricultural development proceeds in Afghanistan. Afghanistan's participation in Amu Darya management notwithstanding, eventually its water needs will have to be considered along with the other Central Asian states. Historically, demand for water in Central Asia has been dominated by the needs of agriculture, which accounts for more than 90 percent of total water use. The downstream countries use about 85 percent of the Aral Sea Basin waters, while the upstream countries use the rest. Most of the countries have increased their demands for water in the last few years and there is little likelihood this situation will change any time soon.

Central Asia's agricultural expansion and population growth over the past three decades have placed a great strain on the water resources of the region. In 1960, the Aral Sea occupied an area of 66,000 km² and had a volume of 1060 bcm. Since 1960 the population in the Basin has grown from 13 million to more than 40 million people, water diversions have increased from 60 to 105 bcm, and irrigated lands have risen from 4.5 million hectares (ha) to just over eight million. As a result, the Aral Sea has lost half of its surface area and two-thirds of its volume and become an environmentally challenged area. Figure 9–3 charts the increase in irrigated lane and the corresponding diminished flow. In addition to the dwindling flow, inefficient irrigation systems and mismanagement of irrigation water diversions have resulted in elevated water and soil salinity levels, widespread environmental degradation, and diminished agricultural productivity.

Figure 9–2. **Aral Sea Basin Selected Characteristics: Population; Surface Water Flow Formation; ICWC Water Allocation; and Irrigated Lands.**

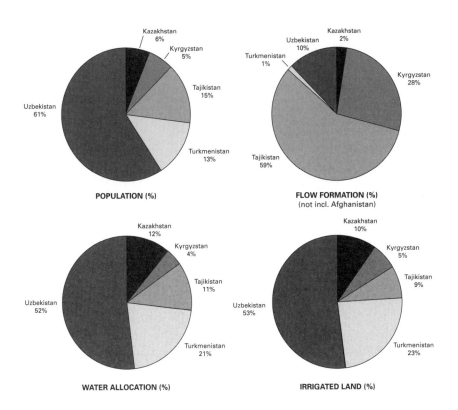

Figure 9–3. **Decline of the Aral Sea with Increased Irrigated Area in Central Asia**

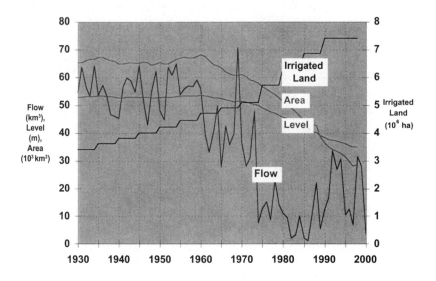

The Aral Sea Tragedy

Increased diversion of water from the Aral Sea Basin rivers over the past several decades allowed the development of a massive agricultural complex in Central Asia, while at the same time degrading the ecosystem and environment of the region. The Aral Sea level has decreased by more than 20 meters since 1950, causing the sea to separate into two water bodies, the Southern and Northern Aral Seas, each fed by the Amu Darya and Syr Darya, respectively. More recently, the Large Sea has split into western and eastern portions.

The desiccation of the Aral Sea has had major consequences for the population of the region in terms of employment and health. In some villages the majority of the population get their drinking water from irrigation canals and the Amu Darya. In dry years, the population considers the water too saline for drinking, tap water is limited or unavailable, and groundwater and surface water is saline and polluted by bacteria.[3] In Karakalpakstan and the lower delta of the Syr Darya, the incidence of common diseases associated with poor drinking water quality (typhoid, paratyphoid, dysentery, and viral hepatitis) is much higher than in the

Table 9–1. **Aral Sea Basin Characteristics**

		Kazakhstan*	Kyrgyzstan	Tajikistan	Turkmenistan	Uzbekistan	Afghan.	Total
Population	Mln	2.6	2.2	6.1	5.4	24.3	-	40.6
	% Ag	23	55	50	44	44	-	44.2
GDP	$	1,228	265	177	916	312	-	-
	% Ag	10	39	20	25	28	-	-
Flow Formation (bcm)	AD**	0	1.6	59.9	1.5	4.7	11.6	79.4
	SD	2.4	27.6	1	0	6.2	0	37.2
	Total	2.4	29.2	60.9	1.5	10.9	11.6	116.6
Water Allocation (bcm)	AD	-	0.24	9.08	22.02	33.9	-	65.24
	AD	12.29	4.03	2.46	-	19.69	-	38.47
	Total	12.29	4.27	11.54	22.02	53.59	-	103.71
Water Use	bcm	8.24	3.29	12.52	18.08	62.83	-	104.96
Irrigated Area ('000 ha)	AD	-	15	449	1.86	2.39	-	4.714
	SD	786	400	269	-	1.869	-	3.324
	Total	786	415	718	1.86	4.259	-	8.038

Source: Global Environmental Facility, Water and Environmental Management Project, Component A.1 Joint
Report 2 and Regional Report 2, 2002.
    *Aral Sea Basin oblasts of Kazakhstan only, South Kazakhstan and Kyzl Orda oblasts.
    **AD = Amu Darya Basin, and SD = Ayr Darya Basin.

rest of the Aral Sea basin. The salt content of Aral Sea now exceeds 60 parts per hundred and has killed the sea's ecosystems, eliminating the once commercially-valuable fishery and causing salt laden windstorms that are detrimental to the population's health. Most of the fish species that once flourished in the Aral Sea have perished as the salinity of the sea has increased over the past decades.[4] The Aral Sea has completely lost all of its commercial and most of its ecological importance as a fishery.

Karakalpakstan, an autonomous republic located in the delta of the Amu Darya within Uzbekistan, has suffered more than any other region in Central Asia from the cumulative effects of the Aral Sea crisis. Due to decades of agricultural development that paid more attention to centrally-planned quotas than the state of the environment, nearly the whole of Karakalpakstan is either salinized or waterlogged. Key factors in this disaster are the discharge of highly mineralized, pesticide-rich return flows into rivers; the use of unlined irrigation canals leading to waste and seepage of salts into groundwater; waterlogged fields leading to salty groundwater and salt runoff; and the lack of drainage facilities to remove unwanted water and chemicals from the fields.

The Aral Sea cannot be returned to its prior grandeur without totally disrupting the economies of the Basin states. In fact, there is little hope for even stabilizing the large, Southern Sea at its present level. Efforts are underway to stabilize or reverse the shrinkage of the Northern Sea, including a World Bank funded program of rehabilitation and reconstruction of hydraulic structures in the lower Syr Darya Basin; however, the area still ranks as one of the world's largest manmade ecological disasters and the outlook for future improvement is grim.

Regional Water Management in Central Asia

Pre-Independence

Soviet Water Management

Spurred by major directives for land reclamation and increased agricultural production beginning in the 1950s, Soviet planners developed comprehensive plans for the utilization of Central Asia's river basins. During this period, central planning organizations and ministries in Moscow directed water management in Central Asia. Each republic developed five-year plans that were coordinated by the state planning agencies and funded through the republican or central budgets of the Soviet Union. For transboundary basins, such as those in Central Asia, basin plans were developed by regional design institutes and included inter-republic and multisectoral aspects, as well as allocation of water for various uses. For the Syr Darya Basin, the last plan of the Soviet period was approved in 1982; for the Amu Darya Basin, in 1987. These plans included limits for water allocation between republics and targets for the development of irrigated lands within these limits.

During the drought years in the late 1970s, local authorities interfered in water allocation among the Aral Sea Basin republics. In the Syr Darya Basin, the situation became so tense that Moscow had to send authorities to ensure that water from the upper and middle areas of the Basin reached lower areas. In order to ensure compliance with inter-republican water allocations, region-wide Basin Water Organizations (BVOs) were established in 1986 in the Amu Darya and Syr Darya Basins. The BVOs were charged with managing water resources of the Basins according to the plans approved by the Soviet Ministry of Water Management. The BVOs had barely begun to function when the Soviet Union began its decline in 1988 and finally collapsed in 1991. As discussed below, these institutions were some of the only regional Soviet institutions to survive into the post-Soviet era.

Post-Independence

Interstate Coordination Water Commission (ICWC)

Given the heavy dependence of the Central Asian republics economies on irrigated agriculture, it was necessary to stabilize interstate water relations immediately after independence. In October 1991, the heads of the Republican water sectors developed a regional water resources management mechanism to replace the centralized system of the Soviet period. The newly independent countries signed an agreement "On Cooperation in the Field of Joint Management and Conservation of Interstate Water Resources."[5] This agreement established the ICWC for control, rational use, and protection of interstate water resources. The agreement acknowledged the equal rights of member states to use, and their responsibility to protect, the interstate water resources of Central Asia. The agreement affirmed the continuation of existing Soviet structures and principles of interstate water allocation, and was approved by the presidents of the Central Asian Republics.[6] The presidents later signed a declaration confirming the validity of previously signed agreements on water resources in the Aral Sea Basin.[7]

The ICWC is the highest level of transboundary water resources management in Central Asia. It is responsible for water management in both the Amu Darya and Syr Darya Basins. The ICWC makes decisions related to water allocation, monitoring, and management. It is comprised of the most senior water sector officials of the member countries, and it meets quarterly to determine water allocations to member counties. Decisions of the ICWC are by consensus, with each State having an equal vote in decisions. Scientific and information support to the ICWC is provided by the Scientific Information Center (SIC). The two Basin water management organisations, BVO Syr Darya and BVO Amu Darya (holdovers from the Soviet days), the SIC, and the ICWC Secretariat are the executing bodies of the ICWC.

Basin Water Management Organizations (BVOs)

Created at the end of the Soviet era, and operating as the executive organs of the ICWC, the BVOs Amu Darya and Syr Darya are responsible for the day-to-day operation of the main water supply facilities in the two Basins. The BVOs' duties include the following:

- Development of plans for water allocation to users in the Amu Darya and Syr Darya Basins, water diversions, and reservoir operation modes;

- Water supply to users, including those in deltas and the Aral Sea, according to approved limits for water diversion from transboundary water sources;

- Operation of all major hydraulic structures on both rivers, including reservoirs;

- Measurement of water flow through the main water intakes and across national borders;

- Design, construction, rehabilitation and operation of hydraulic structures, head water intakes, and inter-republic canals; and

- Maintenance of water quality in the rivers.

Using forecasts from the Central Asian Hydrometeorology Services, the BVOs prepare water allocation plans for ICWC approval at critical times during the year. These plans set the water releases from reservoirs and delivery to each water management region. The water allocation to each republic is established in accordance with previously mentioned schemes devised during Soviet times. Water delivery to the Aral Sea and its coastal zone is based primarily on the principle of "whatever is remaining." Even though the BVOs have the responsibility to monitor water quality, they do not fulfill these obligations. In addition, they are not responsible for water use in each country. As such, their role is mainly regional flow monitoring organizations. This provides some information that is useful in water management, but operational control and management is largely out of the hands of the BVOs and rests with the national water management agencies, resulting in a conflicting and contradictory role for them, since they were originally established as regional water management institutions and their current status (mainly monitoring water flow with staff and facilities exclusively on Uzbek territory) does not allow them to execute this role effectively.

International Fund for the Aral Sea (IFAS)

The Central Asian presidents created the IFAS to attract outside resources to coordinate and finance regional programs to overcome the problems associated with the desiccation of the Aral Sea.[8] Later the same year, the presidents established the Interstate Council for the Aral Sea (ICAS)[9] to manage regional programs.[10] The following year, the Central Asian presidents approved a "Program of Concrete Actions" on improving the situation in the Aral Sea Basin.[11] The program called for the development of a general strategy for: water sharing among the countries; rational water use; conservation of water resources in the Basin; and interstate legal acts on the use and protection of water resources from pollution. In 1997, ICAS and IFAS were merged and streamlined as a new IFAS under the rotating chairmanship of the president of one of the five member states.[12] The new IFAS' primary activities include:

- Raising funds for joint measures to conserve the air, water, and land resources of the Aral Sea Basin, as well as the flora and fauna;

- Financing

  - Interstate ecological research, programs, and projects aimed at saving the Aral Sea and improving the ecological situation in the region surrounding the Sea as well as resolving general social and ecological problems of the region;

  - Joint studies and scientific-technical efforts to rehabilitate the ecological balance, establish efficient use of natural resources, and manage transboundary waters;

- Establishing a regional environmental monitoring system in the Aral Sea Basin;

- Participating in implementing international programs on saving the Aral Sea and improving the ecology of the Basin.

An IFAS Management Board, consisting of Deputy Prime Ministers from each member country, also was formed. The Board develops priority measures for alleviation of the Aral Sea problems and organizes and coordinates the implementation of all regional programs associated with the problems of sustainable development in the Aral Sea Basin countries.

These main regional water and energy institutions have very limited capacity and function according to sometimes contradictory principles. The operation modes of hydrosystems in the Aral Sea Basin are determined and approved by ICWC without participation of the energy sector.

The operation plans are implemented by the energy sector without participation of the water sector. All of the executive bodies of the BVOs are located in Uzbekistan, and their staffs are formed entirely of Uzbeks. These organizations have, in principle, the status of interstate organizations, yet, due to the predominant influence of Uzbekistan, they do not rotate management staff or hire specialists from other republics. Until this system is remedied, the increased coordination necessary to ensure equitable water allocation and control is unlikely.

Framework Agreement on Water and Energy Use

Syr Darya Basin Agreements

Toktogul Reservoir in Kyrgyzstan is the largest in the Syr Darya Basin and the only one with multiyear storage capacity (14 bcm active storage volume). The reservoir was designed to operate in an irrigation mode with non-growing season (October through March) releases providing minimum electricity generation. Commissioned in 1974, the reservoir did not operate according to design until 1990, after the high water winter of 1988 filled the reservoir to capacity for the first time. The irrigation release regime follows natural cycles, but the reservoir's large storage can be used to continue these releases in periods of drought.

Before 1991, surplus power generated by irrigation releases in the growing season (April to September) from the Toktogul system was transmitted to neighboring regions of the Soviet Union. In return, these regions sent electric power and fuels (natural gas, coal and fuel oil) for Kyrgyzstan's two thermal power plants for winter heating needs.

This situation changed drastically in 1991 when independent states were established in Central Asia. Because of complications in intergovernmental relations and account settlements, the introduction of national currencies, and the increasing prices of oil, coal, natural gas and transportation, the supply of fuel and electricity sent to Kyrgyzstan from the other republics was reduced. This radically affected the structure of the Kyrgyz fuel-and-energy balance. Because of decreased fuel production in Kyrgyzstan, the output and distribution of heat from thermal power plants decreased by half and organic fuel consumption fell, resulting in a marked increase in the demand for electric power by the population for heating, cooking, and hot water supply. The Kyrgyz government responded to this demand by increasing wintertime hydroelectric generation from the Toktogul system.

Intensive use of water resources for power generation, along with changes in the Toktogul operating regime from summertime irrigation releases to wintertime energy releases, created serious problems in the Syr Darya Basin in the winter. Downstream reservoirs were not able to store the increased releases, and, in order to prevent flooding of the lower reaches of the Syr Darya Basin, discharges into the Arnasai depression in Uzbekistan were required. With no means to store the water, the discharges in Uzbekistan, more than one cubic kilometer per year, were, essentially, wasted for agricultural use.

Beginning in 1995, to alleviate these problems and reduce the waste, Kazakhstan, Kyrgyzstan, and Uzbekistan signed interstate protocols and agreements on the use of water and energy resources in the Syr Darya Basin. These specified the amount of compensatory deliveries of fuel and energy resources and releases from Toktogul reservoir. Based on these agreements, Uzbekistan and Kazakhstan receive excess energy from Kyrgyzstan generated by Toktogul reservoir in the summer, and in winter, they provide Kyrgyzstan with energy, respectively, by deliveries of natural gas and coal. To monitor this delicate arrangement, the Heads of State of the countries involved turned to their regional integration and development organization, the Executive Committee of the Interstate Council of the Central Asian Economic Community (EC CAEC). In 1996, the EC CAEC formed a Water and Energy Uses Round Table to develop a framework agreement addressing the Syr Darya Basin riparian republics competing uses for water. The work of the Round Table resulted in an agreement that created a framework addressing trade-offs between the competing uses of water for energy and agricultural production in the Basin.[13] Compensation is associated with a water release schedule that takes into account both upstream winter energy needs and downstream summer irrigation water demand. To date, the system has remained stable without major conflict and the agreement has entered the second five-year implementation period without major revision.[14]

Regional Cooperation Organizations

Over the past decade, the Central Asian states have sought to promote their separate national interests while also acting to enhance their common goals.[15] However, in many areas the losses from interstate competition exceed the gains from cooperation. The presidents of these countries have acknowledged the need to create a regional concert of interests. Several Central Asian organizations have been formed or joined over the past decade, many concerned with regional cooperation, security, and economic development. Some of the organizations, the most important being the CAEC and IFAS, have had a mandate to consider problems of the water, environment, and energy sectors.

As previously mentioned, IFAS was formed in 1993 as the leading institution for raising and administering funds to address the Aral Sea crisis. Constraints on IFAS, its credibility as a neutral broker, and its lack of a clear mandate to deal with multi-sectoral issues have, so far, kept it from successfully developing regional water management strategies or negotiating regional water and energy sharing agreements. This is why, in 1996, the CAEC stepped in to mediate the annual agreements on water and energy management for the Syr Darya Basin. IFAS recently has moved its Presidency and Secretariat to Dushanbe, Tajikistan and initiated a series of activities to revitalize this dormant and discredited organization. In late August 2002, the fist IFAS Board meeting in three years was held in order to assess the past activities and propose a new agenda. These ideas were confirmed and approved by the IFAS Heads of State in an early October 2002 meeting. In November 2002, the international donor community was asked to support the development of a new phase of IFAS activities. It remains to be seen if the new IFAS management can overcome the poor performance of the past and attract support for new activities.

The CAEC was formed to promote regional integration through economic cooperation in Central Asia. It had a broad mandate to promote regional economic cooperation and to organize and broker negotiations, such as those leading to the 1998 Syr Darya Agreement. Since the CAEC did not have direct competence in water or energy technical matters, it wisely relied on the national water and energy ministries, as well as the ICWC, the BVO Syr Darya, and the United Energy Dispatch Center (UDC Energia) to support negotiations.

The Central Asian Cooperation Organization (CACO) was established in 2002 by the Presidents of Kazakhstan, Kyrgyzstan, Tajikistan, and Uzbekistan under the leadership of the President of Uzbekistan. Turkmenistan has strong reasons for maintaining good relations with Uzbekistan due to the division of the Amu Darya River. However, Turkmenistan puts less emphasis on Central Asian regional cooperation and more emphasis on relations with the Caucasus, the Middle East, Iran, and Caspian egress routes.[16] This is evidenced by Turkmenistan's observer status in most regional cooperation organizations and refusal to participate in most regional water management activities. The four participating Central Asian states have yet to establish a CACO secretariat, although one is planned. There is some speculation that CACO was created to be the successor organization to the CAEC; however, no decision has yet been made on how CACO will work. Communiqués from recent meetings of the organization have indicated that it will take up the issues of water and energy.[17]

Summary of Post-Independence Experience

The experience of the Central Asian countries in addressing transboundary water management issues reveal several lessons:[18]

■ It is essential that the body organizing interstate discussions be considered sufficiently neutral in order to gain the trust of all parties. External support from similarly neutral third parties can play a crucial role in helping participants gain access to international expertise and add credibility to the process, but the riparians must work out the final details themselves.

■ Given sufficient high-level commitment to regional cooperation, the primary focus of regional organizations' discussions should be on technical issues, with legal and political matters held for later in negotiations. Without a firm sense that technical issues can be solved, no political progress can be made. However, regional cooperation is unlikely to be achieved through technical activities and projects alone; political will is the key.

■ It is important to take on a manageable set of issues rather than attempting to solve the full range of problems. The Central Asian Water and Energy Round Table group achieved positive results by focusing attention on the Syr Darya Basin, rather than taking on the full menu of issues in the Aral Sea Basin.

Country-Specific Issues[19]

Afghanistan

Though not part of Soviet Central Asia, Afghanistan borders three other Aral Sea Basin countries: Tajikistan, Uzbekistan, and Turkmenistan. About 8 percent of the flow of the Amu Darya is formed in Afghanistan. The Afghan portions of the Amu Darya Basin include the territory rimmed by the Panj and Amu Darya Rivers on the north, by spurs of the Bandi-Torkestan and the Hindukush Ridges on the south, the Kowkchen River valley in the east, and the Shirintagao River valley on the west.[20] Irrigable lands in this area exceed 1.5 million ha. About two-thirds of Afghanistan's GDP is derived from the agricultural sector, and although the country has large tracts of irrigable lands, only a small portion is used due to the past instabilities and low level of development.

Even though the Afghan lands in the Amu Darya Basin were the least developed in the past, many expect this will change in the future, placing even greater stress on the Aral Sea Basin countries downstream. Some estimate that Afghanistan may divert as much as 10 bcm from the Amu Darya in the future (compared to about 2 bcm today) if development plans are realized.[21] In October 2002 the Ministry of Irrigation, Water Resources, and Environment issued a list of short-term priorities which include rehabilitating irrigation canals and existing systems. Longer-term priorities include the Khushtapa, or "Good Hill" Project, which would pump water from the Amu Darya River into a canal to be transported to Mazar-I-Sharif to irrigate a large area there.

Tajikistan

Tajikistan, a small, mountainous country covering 139,800 km^2, is made up of a number of distinct and relatively isolated regions, separated by high mountain ranges. The Vaksh and Pyanj Rivers, the main tributaries of the Amu Darya, rise in the mountains of Tajikistan and Afghanistan. The flow formation within Tajikistan's portion of the Aral Sea Basin is 60.9 bcm and the interstate allocation of water to Tajikistan is 11.5 bcm. In 2000, 718,000 ha were irrigated in the Tajik portion of the Aral Sea Basin, requiring the diversion of 12.5 bcm of water to irrigation systems. Irrigated agriculture, using about 85 percent of the water, is the largest water consumer in the country. Still, the great elevation differences and large volumes of flow in the rivers of Tajikistan give the country important hydropower potential. Even now, Tajikistan is one of the world's largest producers of hydroelectric power. Whether this potential is tapped will depend upon future water negotiations and the ability of the Central Asian countries to achieve a sound policy.

In the past decade, the economy of Tajikistan experienced a sharp decline as industrial and economic relations with Russia were broken and civil war inflicted much damage on the country's infrastructure and human resources. Approximately 70 percent of Tajikistan's six million people live in rural areas, with about 50 percent of the population working in the agricultural sector, making Tajikistan the most rural of the former Soviet Republics. Tajikistan's main agricultural production areas lie in the irrigated valleys of the Amu Darya and Syr Darya tributaries. Cotton is the major cash crop accounting for about two-thirds of the gross production value of the agriculture sector.

Tajik water law, typical of all the countries of Central Asia, claims water to be the property of the national government. Water management in Tajikistan is transforming from the old command administrative system to newer market based incentives. In November 2000, a new Water Code was adopted that allowed transfer of irrigation systems management to the private sector with collective farms as the base for development of privatization and support of irrigation system operation. In an effort to provide the population with a secure food supply, the Tajik government intends to increase irrigated lands by 350,000 ha by the year 2010. Most of the water required for this agricultural expansion is predicted to come from water saved through increased irrigation efficiency. Efforts are in place to improve irrigation efficiency through the introduction of water charges and the improvement of infrastructure with the proceeds, as well as the introduction and development of cooperative water user associations. The new water code also establishes principles for Tajik cooperation in international water relations based on international water law principles.

Tajikistan is experiencing rapid population growth, a major factor affecting its economic development and water management policy. Achieving food security is an objective for the country, which will require improved agricultural productivity through increased irrigation efficiency and expansion of irrigated lands. During the Soviet period, the development of irrigated lands in Tajikistan was limited. The Soviets favored developments in downstream areas of the Basin. Hence, Tajikistan has inherited the consequences of this legacy and the allocation of the Amu Darya and Syr Darya waters according to the old Soviet scheme which favors downstream cotton production at the expense of expanded hydropower and agricultural development upstream. Tajikistan supports the creation of a new system of water allocation among the countries of the Basins that recognizes conjunctive use of water for agriculture and hydropower generation, prevention of pollution of transboundary waters, and elimination of adverse effects, but does not view this as a pressing issue at this time. However, Tajikistan is a strong supporter of the concept that the institutional structure of Central Asian water management should be improved through integration of the water and energy sectors at the regional level.

Kyrgyzstan

The Kyrgyz Republic is a mountainous country with an average height above sea level of 2,750 meters and a maximum height of 7,439 meters. This wide range of elevations, complex relief, protracted geologic development, and other factors result in a variety of natural conditions and a richness of natural resources. The Naryn River rises in the mountains of Kyrgyzstan, and, along with the Karadarya and Chirchik Rivers, is one of the main tributaries of the Syr Darya. The main watercourses of the Kyrgyz part of Aral Sea Basin are the Naryn, Karadarya, Sokh, and Chatkal rivers (Syr Darya Basin) and the Kyzyl Suu River (Amu Darya Basin). The flow formation within the Kyrgyzstan portion of the Aral Sea Basin is 29.2 bcm, and the interstate allocation of water to Kazakhstan from the Syr Darya is 4.27 bcm. The population of Kyrgyzstan in the Aral Sea Basin is about 2.2 million. Approximately 39 percent of Kyrgyzstan's GDP is derived from a severely disorganized and undercapitalized agricultural sector where about 55 percent of the total population works. In 2000, 415,000 ha were irrigated in the Kyrgyz portion of the Aral Sea Basin, requiring 3.3 bcm of water.

Like Tajikistan, Kyrgyzstan finds its agricultural development constrained by the Soviet-era water allocation scheme for the Syr Darya, which the Central Asian countries have agreed to honor until a new scheme can be developed and approved. In the meantime, Kyrgyzstan would like to expand its agricultural sector and needs additional water to do so. No transboundary water enters Kyrgyzstan from any source and about 44 bcm of runoff are formed within the country each year. These are transboundary waters since they feed the Syr Darya and, ultimately, the Aral Sea.

The presidential decree "On foreign policy of the Kyrgyz Republic in the sphere of water resources generated in Kyrgyzstan and flowing into neighboring countries" (June 1997) mandates the solution of interstate water problems, water allocation, and the use of economic instruments for promoting water conservation and efficient use of water and energy resources. The law "On interstate use of water objects, water resources and water facilities of the Kyrgyz Republic" (July 2001) confirmed the principles of cooperation of Kyrgyzstan with other countries in the field of water resources. However, the law states that all the waters in the territory of the country belong to the State and demands that the downstream countries pay for water emanating from Kyrgyzstan. This has caused a certain amount of conflict with Kazakhstan and Uzbekistan, both of which demand that Kyrgyzstan continue providing water free of charge, which would be available without regulation by reservoirs.

Regional water use agreements may be of little help to Kyrgyzstan. The 1998 Syr Darya Water and Energy Use Agreement regulates water use in the Syr Darya Basin. This agreement is based on the concept of compensation to upstream countries for lost energy production following a release. Yet this regime favors irrigated agriculture in downstream countries. Although Kyrgyzstan receives energy resources (electricity, coal, gas, and oil) in exchange for its water, these resources must be transported and transformed into electric power or heat at Kyrgyzstan's expense. As a result of this compensation arrangement, Kazakhstan and Uzbekistan receive water at very low cost.

The Kyrgyz energy sector depends on power generation from the Naryn cascade to satisfy a major portion of the domestic demand, which existing thermal generating facilities cannot handle. The continued use of the Toktogul reservoir in an energy generation mode, i.e. with increased water releases in the fall-winter period, seems inevitable without new generating facilities and capacity at thermal power stations. As recent experience has shown, providing the required energy generation and irrigation releases results in large fluctuations of accumulated storage in the Toktogul reservoir. Several proposals for the solution of this problem are being explored, such as energy conservation and demand management, and construction of new hydroelectric generating capacity. For now, Kyrgystan must continue to rely on the 1998 water-energy trade agreement with its downstream neighbors to obtain needed wintertime fuels.

Kazakhstan

Kazakhstan contains vast regions of steppe and most of the downstream portion of the Syr Darya Basin. The population of Kazakhstan in the Aral Sea Basin (South Kazakhstan and Kyzl Orda oblasts) is about 2.6 million. Approximately 10 percent of Kazakhstan's GDP is derived from agriculture, with about 23 percent of the population working in that sector.

Water availability in the Kazakh portion of the Aral Sea Basin depends on the water policy of upstream states, Uzbekistan, Tajikistan, and Kyrgyzstan. The Syr Darya flows 1,650 km through Kazakhstan from the border with Uzbekistan at the Chardara reservoir to the Aral Sea. The river's flow formed within Kazakhstan is 2.4 bcm and the interstate allocation of water to Kazakhstan from the Syr Darya is 12.3 bcm. Since 1990, Kazakhstan has reduced its irrigated area in the Syr Darya Basin because many unproductive farms have been taken out of production. Kazakhstan irrigated about 786,000 ha in 2000, requiring about 8.2 bcm of water. In recent years, productivity has declined due to low irrigation efficiency, lack of technical inputs (fertilizer and machinery), and lack of funds for proper technical and operational measures.

The most recent agreement on management and operation of the Naryn-Syr Darya cascade of reservoirs (March 1998) places certain obligations on Kazakhstan in order to receive irrigation water under the agreement. In particular, surplus summer electricity is delivered to Kazakhstan and, in return, Kazakh coal must be supplied to Kyrgyzstan in the wintertime. For Kazakhstan to accept large amounts (1.1 billion kWh) of Kyrgyz electricity in the summertime when demand is low requires restructuring the Kazakh national power distribution system and shutting down some thermal power stations in South Kazakhstan.[22] This has been very disruptive to the Kazakh power grid resulting in the need to sell expensive power to Kazakh customers reluctant to pay the combined price of power and water. If the Kazakh agricultural sector compensated the power sector for the increased price of the summertime electricity, the situation might improve.

The Water Code of the Republic of Kazakhstan was approved in 1993 and constitutes the legal basis for water policy in the country. Water use in the country is still determined by centrally controlled economic interests, with little regard for social and environmental consequences. There are eight Basins in the republic, each with its own BVO. The Kazakh portion of the Aral Sea Basin water management is carried out by the BVO Aral-Syr Darya. The BVOs manage water resources in the Basins, including water distribution between users, development of water supply plans, water use limits, and reservoir operation modes. Water Users Associations have been created in some areas, but so far they are insufficient to support many activities, particularly drainage and water supply works.

Since it receives most of its water resources from external sources, Kazakhstan recognizes transboundary rivers as a security problem and is motivated to seek international agreements on shared waters. Kazakhstan has a large agricultural sector dependent on an adequate supply of irrigation water. At times, the delivery of this water is complicated by upstream water use tradeoffs between energy and irrigation. This results in water shortages during growing seasons and flooding of lowland areas in winter seasons. Being a downstream country, Kazakhstan experiences difficult water quality problems, resulting from agricultural return flows discharged by mid-stream irrigation water use. Poor water quality (high salinity, fertilizer, and pesticide levels) impacts the health of populations in the downstream areas that must use this water for drinking as well as for agricultural production.

Believing that common positions and mutual interests can provide regional stability, Kazakh officials have suggested that a new regional water strategy for Central Asian be developed. This new framework would be based on standards of international water law; utilize an ecosystem ap-

proach; minimize limitations on riparian countries; and be based on common interests in water resources development, use, and protection within
each country.[23] Common principles of the water strategy would include
considering water needs in the lower reaches of Central Asian rivers, balancing water use between irrigation and energy production, and recycling
return flows from agriculture. The main international water law principles
that the new strategy would be based on include the following:[24]

- Transboundary water resources are the common property of Basin
  states;

- Basin interests take priority over those of individual states;

- Water supply is guaranteed to highest priority uses;

- States' obligation to observe the "equitable and reasonable use"[25]
  and to follow the "no harm"[26] principles;

- States' obligation to consult with other Basin states on development
  plans; and

- States' obligation to participate in joint monitoring of water quantity and quality.

Uzbekistan

Uzbekistan, with a population of over 24 million and 447,400 km²
of territory in the Aral Sea Basin, is at the center of Central Asia. About 60
percent of Uzbekistan's land area is desert steppe broken by irrigated, fertile oases along the Amu Darya and Syr Darya. Approximately 25 percent
of Uzbekistan's GDP is derived from agriculture with about 44 percent
of the population working in that sector. In western Uzbekistan lie the
ecologically damaged Amu Darya delta and the autonomous Republic of
Karakalpakistan. Overuse of the Amu Darya has reduced the sea to two-
thirds its former size and salinization of the area around the sea threatens
the environmental and economic viability of a region in which more than
one million people live.

Being dominated by desert and only partially mountainous, Uzbekistan contributes a modest amount of the flow to the Aral Sea Basin, 10.9
bcm, while the interstate allocation of water to Uzbekistan is 53.6 bcm. In
2000, 4.259 million ha were irrigated in the Uzbek portion of the Aral Sea
Basin requiring 62.8 bcm of water. The large amounts of water needed by
Uzbekistan to sustain the agricultural sector of its economy require that
it negotiate with its upstream neighbors on an almost continual basis. By
and large, the relations between Uzbekistan, Turkmenistan, and Tajikistan

in the Amu Darya Basin are good. However, the same is not true between Uzbekistan and its upstream neighbor, Kyrgyzstan, in the Syr Darya Basin. As previously discussed, there continue to be difficulties over the delivery of natural gas from Uzbekistan in return for delivered irrigation water. A major difficulty in efficient implementation of the 1998 water-energy agreement stems from Uzbekistan's need for, and Kyrgyzstan's lack of, hard currency. Monetizing the exchanges under the agreement would go a long way toward normalizing these trade relations.

Transboundary sources make up the bulk of the water resources available to Uzbekistan. Uzbekistan is therefore very concerned about transboundary water management. The main concerns of Uzbekistan regarding this issue include: further development of regional cooperation between Aral Sea Basin countries in management and use of transboundary water sources; availability and compliance with international agreements between the riparian countries of the Basins; the operating regime of transboundary reservoirs in the Basins, primarily, Toktogul, Kayrakum, and Nurek reservoirs; and the environment and effectiveness of the ICWC.[27] In addition, Uzbek officials call for improvement of information systems for water management and expansion of these systems to consider water quality, especially for transboundary sources.[28]

Turkmenistan

Turkmenistan covers an area of 488,100 km², but 80 percent of this area is desert. The desert is bounded by a series of oases watered by the Amu Darya in the north and by rivers (the Murgap, Tejen, Atrek) descending from the Kopetdag, Gershi, and other mountains in the south. The central and western regions have no significant natural waterways, but the Kara Kum Canal (more than 1300 km in length) brings water from the Amu Darya west to the Mary Oasis and onward past Ashgabat. Approximately 25 percent of Turkmenistan's GDP is derived from agriculture with about 44 percent of the population working in that sector.

The amount of river flow generated within Turkmenistan is extremely small, 1.5 bcm, whereas the interstate allocation of water to Turkmenistan is 22 bcm. In 2000, 1.86 million ha were irrigated in the Turkmen portion of the Aral Sea Basin requiring 18.1 bcm of water. The government expects irrigated lands to reach 2.2 million ha by 2010. The source of water to implement this expansion is somewhat of a mystery; however, it may come from reclaimed agricultural drainage water. The Kara Kum Canal is perhaps the most important water facility in Turkmenistan, supplying water to irrigate more than one million ha of farmlands. An average of 11.5

bcm is diverted into the canal each year from the Amu Darya. More than half of Turkmenistan's total agricultural products are grown in the Canal Zone. Today, the Canal is in a precarious condition with most of its control structures inoperative. Water flows according to hydraulic conditions, not management decisions. This situation may prove to be unsustainable in the future as the system continues to deteriorate.

Agricultural runoff is a major transboundary problem for Turkmenistan, causing downstream pollution affecting population health and reducing agricultural productivity in the Basin. Turkmenistan receives transboundary flows at several locations, including source water from the Amu Darya and agricultural drainage water from the Khorezm region of Uzbekistan. There is great concern about the quality of these waters, especially the return water, since it is a large volume and heavily polluted. Currently, Turkmenistan assumes responsibility for the disposal of this drainage water to the Sary-Kamush Lake, which has become polluted with salts and chemicals. In addition, the passage of this water through unlined canals creates drinking water pollution problems by contaminating groundwater sources. At present, no agreements exist on transboundary water quality in Central Asia. In order to prevent increased environmental damage from transboundary irrigation drainage water, Turkmenistan has proposed to the Uzbeks the development of a Transboundary Water Quality Agreement for the Amu Darya Basin, but there is no progress on this yet.

Regional Water Management Issues

The following are issues that must be addressed by the Central Asian republics if true progress is to be made on water issues at the regional level.

Financial Obligations of Regional Institution Members

The current provisions for financing the Executive Committee of the Intestate Fund for Saving the Aral Sea (EC IFAS) require that the host member country must cover the costs (salary and living expenses) of two representatives from each member country. The host country rotates between the members every two years. This has created an undue burden on the poorer countries of Central Asia, like Tajikistan, the current host country, which do not have the resources to cover many of these expenses. In the case of some host countries, this may be feasible, but in the case of others, it is impossible. This has resulted in an inability of EC IFAS to function properly.

The March 18, 1992 ICWC agreement does not reflect current conditions characterized by a severe lack of financing for water infrastructure and the varying rate at which the countries are making the transition to market economies. The member countries have not shared equitably in the financial obligations of joint water management and development under ICWC. Although the ICWC budget is confirmed each year, only Turkmenistan and Uzbekistan have met their obligations for operation and maintenance works. Only Uzbekistan has met the obligation for research, with a small contribution from the other states. The result is that the BVOs, as the operational arms of the ICWC, are desperately short on resources with which to carry out their work.

BVO Functions

According to the foundation documents of the BVOs, all main structures for controlling transboundary waters on the Syr Darya and Amu Darya rivers should be transferred to the temporary (but long-term) control of the BVOs. However, the only structures currently under BVO control are the main interstate canal structures in Uzbekistan. This situation creates uncertainty as to the role of the BVOs in managing regional water resources because the BVOs presently are not operational organizations controlling the critical structures in the Basins. If the ICWC member countries truly intend for the BVOs to be operational management organizations, then the main structures outside of Uzbekistan should be transferred to BVO control. On the other hand, if BVOs are intended as planning organizations to monitor system functioning and prepare operational plans, then the structures currently under BVO control in Uzbekistan should be transferred to Uzbek Ministry of Agriculture and Water Management (MAWR) control.

Water Quality Monitoring and Control

Water quality problems in Central Asia have yet to be addressed in any comprehensive way. One major problem is the disposal of agricultural return flows. The agricultural return flows with transboundary impacts are not strictly controlled. Adequate and up-to-date equipment for acquisition and processing of water data (both quantity and quality) in the main river Basins is still lacking. Agreement on appropriate interstate water quality standards have yet to be established and alternative mechanisms to achieve different water quality standards have yet to be explored. If these issues continue to be ignored there will be a continual degradation of drinking water quality in the lower reaches of the rivers.

Citizen Participation

Citizens are essential participants in forming national and local water and environmental policy. Informing citizens of opportunities to participate in such a system is often an important role of non-governmental organizations (NGOs). NGOs take on various roles in this regard, including education campaigns, assistance to government ministries in forming policy, legislation and regulations, independent assessment of conditions, and preparing legal actions when there is evidence of a threat to human health or to the environment. The participation of NGOs in the formation of policy requires access to accurate and timely information. The public should have the right to know what the standards are for potable, industrial, and irrigation water and for the concentration of certain elements at particular times. When the information is available to citizens about the real state of the environment, then citizens can formulate educated opinions about and demand environmental protection.

Syr Darya Agreement

The 1998 Syr Darya Agreement has achieved modest success in relieving tensions over water and energy use in the Basin. The signing of this Agreement by the four Prime Ministers demonstrated a show of support for cooperative management of the Basin's resources. This has provided an impetus for the parties to conduct difficult and serious negotiations each year since 1998.

Nevertheless, implementation of the agreement is difficult. A mechanism by which dry and wet year hydrologic conditions can be reflected in compensation needs to be established. In addition, Kyrgyzstan in particular suffers from a lack of longer-term assurance that compensation will, in fact, be made by downstream countries. The 1998 agreement specifies that surplus electricity from growing season releases is to be transferred to Kazakhstan and Uzbekistan, and compensation for irrigation storage in the reservoirs is to be made in amounts of fuel equivalent to this surplus energy. In recent wet years, the downstream countries have called for below average releases during the growing season. This has resulted in reduced surplus electricity deliveries to downstream countries, accompanied by reduced deliveries of fuel to Kyrgyzstan the following winter season. On the other hand, in dry years, downstream countries have called for above average releases in the growing season, resulting in additional surplus electricity delivered to downstream countries accompanied, in theory, by increased deliveries of fuels to Kyrgyzstan in the winter season. If the system is to be run fairly, Kyrgyzstan should receive credit for additional dry year electricity deliveries and be able to make "withdrawals" in fuels on dry year credit during wet years when there is a fuel deficit. Currently, this is not the case. Further negotiation and compromise will be needed to ensure an equitable method of compensation for water storage services during wet periods with attendant water releases during drought periods.

Amu Darya Agreements

The Amu Darya Basin is shared by Afghanistan, Tajikistan, Turkmenistan, and Uzbekistan. Afghanistan has not been an active partner in managing the water in the Basin. During the 1940s to 1970s, several agreements were reached between the Soviet Union and Afghanistan regarding the waters of the Amu Darya, including an allocation of nine bcm to Afghanistan. Despite these agreements, no more than two bcm per year has been diverted to Afghan use.

In the accounting and allocation of the Amu Darya waters to Basin states by the ICWC, neither 9 nor 2 bcm of water is considered. Turkmenistan and Uzbekistan signed a bilateral agreement in 1996 agreeing to split the waters of the Amu Darya below the river gauge at Kerki. Uzbekistan and Turkmenistan also have an informal, technical level agreement in operation and maintenance of the transboundary drainage water collectors which originate in Uzbekistan (Khorezm region) and terminate in Turkmenistan. These agreements should, but currently do not, take into account Afghanistan's water needs. Further amendments likely will be required to meet the increasing demands of all parties in the Amu Darya basin.

Conclusions

While not as effective as it could be, the capacity for shared water management exists in Central Asia. High level political will is needed to achieve such cooperative management of water resources, and that will seems to be lacking in Central Asia. Government officials from Turkmenistan and Uzbekistan often exhibit a desire to handle water management and other regional issues through the development of strictly bilateral arrangements and agreements. Yet consensus is needed among high level advisors to the Central Asian presidents that regional cooperation can lead to increased benefits, stability, and security for each individual country. Regional development assistance could demonstrate the mutual economic benefits to be derived from a multi-sectoral approach to regional cooperation in water resources management.

Multi-sectoral Paradigm for Regional Water Cooperation

Energy and agriculture sector policies have a large impact on water management in Central Asia. Currently, no mechanism is in place to coordinate or manage this inter-sectoral problem within most of the countries, let alone at the regional level. A new paradigm for regional water cooperation in Central Asia is needed. Water sector managers cannot solve the problems of regional cooperation alone. The Central Asian Heads of State need to motivate this approach or the various concerned sectors will not participate.

No new agreements on water or energy have reached the Heads of State for signature since 1998, and none are presently under development. Since it is a uni-sectoral, technical body, the ICWC is not the right forum to achieve this sort of government-to-government interaction. Interaction must occur at a higher level and it must be multi-sectoral. International donor agencies should try to promote consensus at the Prime Ministerial or Presidential level on principles of regional cooperation. In the Syr Darya Basin, Kazakhstan, Kyrgyzstan, and Tajikistan already understand this, only Uzbekistan remains to be convinced. In the Amu Darya Basin, increased downstream water stress in Turkmenistan and Uzbekistan, due to upstream Afghan water diversions, may convince the countries to contend with this serious problem.

Upstream-Downstream Priorities

Previous water management rules, based on the priority of irrigated agriculture, do not conform to current power generation needs of the upstream countries, Kyrgyzstan and Tajikistan. Attempts to resolve this issue on the basis of interstate energy barter have been moderately successful, but implementation of annual barter agreements has been complicated by difficulties in negotiating timely annual agreements. Renewed efforts are needed to: prepare annual agreements in a timely manner; develop multiyear schedules for compensation; include compensation for storage services as well as flow regulation; and move away from the barter system to a monetized exchange between the countries.

The present method of water allocation, based on Soviet era rules, does not take into account the emerging priorities of the now independent republics. Kyrgyzstan and Tajikistan often claim that the old water allocation rules limit the development of irrigation on their lands, and that they need to reassess their future water allocation. Downstream countries complain that poor water quality in the middle and lower reaches of the Basins is reducing agricultural production and damaging public health, and that remediation of this problem must be undertaken. In addition, growing water demands of Afghanistan may cause new stress on the system of water allocation.

Kambarata I and II Dams

Kyrgyz domestic energy demand has increased above the equivalent of the surplus summer electricity resulting from Toktogul irrigation releases. Negotiating higher winter fuel deliveries in exchange for the irrigation releases seems out of the question, and new energy generation capacity may be needed that can supply energy to Kyrgyz customers in the winter. Several organizations, such as the World Bank and U.S. Agency for International Development (USAID), are considering the economic feasibility of two dams designed in Soviet times, Kambarata I and II, which would be located upstream of Toktogul reservoir in Kyrgyzstan. Given the expected cost of the projects (about one billion U.S. dollars), Kyrgyzstan, Kazakhstan, and Uzbekistan are considering the formation of a consortium to jointly develop the projects. The projects would result in cheap summertime electricity which the consortium partners would try to market to third parties.

Non-governmental Stakeholder Participation

Non-governmental stakeholders are not active participants in Central Asian water management at the present time. The way that NGOs might participate is through public awareness and information exchange activities. In addition, NGOs can link local community opinion to the national debate on water policy.

The Central Asian water management officials have, for the most part, a negative reaction to the participation of NGOs in this sphere. Officials recognize that many NGOs take a very proactive approach and promote ideas of rapid change that are threatening to the water management structures of Central Asia. It will take time and patience on the part of both the NGOs and the water management officials to develop a complimentary, rather than antagonistic, relationship. There are now some NGOs not engaged in highly controversial activities who are accepted by the water management officials as participants in some activities. NGOs could function more effectively if they identified key water management stakeholders both geographically (upstream versus downstream) and topically. Such stakeholders would include water user associations or at least key collectives along the entire system of rivers; those involved with fisheries like Arnasai, reservoirs, and deltas; those providing river-based transport; those living in the areas subject to flooding based on alternative management regimes including new dam construction; industrial water users; municipal water users; and environmental groups working on aquatic ecosystems conservation, river pollution, and other issues.

Promotion of Regional Cooperation

Regional cooperation is unlikely to be achieved solely through technical activities and projects. On the national level, plenty of these are ongoing, and more are in the design stages. Regional cooperation will come by illustrating the benefits of participation in the development of joint, coordinated projects and the adoption of policies that bring benefits or reduce damages to multiple participants. These activities are not going to arise in a single sector, but they will span two or three sectors. Sustainable regional cooperation will most likely be achieved by creating a basis for assessing the national and regional benefits from technical investments, but these must be complemented by supportive national policy and institutional reforms, coupled with empowerment and capacity building for regional institutions.

Improved or appropriate technology is important in achieving increased water use efficiency and agricultural production. However, this does not address or promote regional cooperation. By and large, a drop saved by an Aral Sea Basin nation is viewed as another drop for expanding the nation's agricultural production, not for the Aral Sea. Improvements in irrigation efficiency in upstream areas will not necessarily result in more water flowing to the Aral Sea, rather the saved water will be diverted to new irrigated areas. In many cases, improvements in efficiency can significantly improve the economic benefits from national participation through regional approaches to water resources management.

The Central Asian states of Kazakhstan, Kyrgyzstan, and Tajikistan have expressed a strong desire to develop new agreements that satisfy these international concepts. However, there is still reluctance on the part of the major water using countries, in particular, Turkmenistan and Uzbekistan, to enter into discussions on this issue. One of the major hurdles in achieving regional cooperation in shared water resources in Central Asia is the focusing of the Republics' attention on international water law. Another issue is the lack of coordination in national water policies and legislation across the region. While the principle of national sovereignty must be upheld, there is no reason why the benefits from synchronization cannot be achieved.

Financing Regional Water Management Projects

A few projects have been proposed that might be considered for joint financing by the governments of Central Asia in the area of regional water management. Most prominent of these are the development of the Kambarata I and II dams in Kyrgyzstan. However, Kyrgyzstan is not in a position to finance this project alone and the proposal has been made for an international consortium of Central Asian countries for the joint financing of the project. Kazakhstan has expressed interest in participating in this consortium—if the conditions are favorable. By joining the consortium, Kazakhstan would change its water management position from being the most downstream country in the Basin to assuming a position in the uppermost part of the Basin and being able to exert some control over the water management decisions in that part of the Basin. Kyrgyzstan and Kazakhstan are both interested in attracting Uzbekistan into the Kambarata consortium. However, the direct benefit to Uzbekistan of joining the consortium is not as clear as that of Kazakhstan and, to date, Uzbekistan has not expressed much interest in joining such a consortium. However, Uzbekistan would be very concerned to see its neighbors working with each other and gaining additional control over the Basin's waters without a place reserved for its own interests in these matters.

Any decisions regarding major water management investments affecting the overall regional water management regime should be made with the full participation of all countries affected; otherwise this will undermine trust and the basis for regional cooperation in this sphere. The future management regime adopted for both the Syr Darya and the Amu Darya should be based on a comprehensive evaluation of options including new physical infrastructure, upgrading of existing physical infrastructure, and improved water management by user groups throughout the Basin. Such analysis, which must include Afghanistan for the Amu Darya, should amply demonstrate the benefits to be derived from regional cooperation as compared to unilateral or even bilateral decision-making and actions.

Coordination of Donors' Activities.

Coordination among donors is desperately needed in Central Asian regional water management activities. Lack of coordination in the past has been noted as a cause of duplication of efforts, reduced effectiveness of programs, inefficient use of funds, and lack of recognition of achieved results. Most of the major donor agencies active in the region are in a transition period at the moment. The Asian Development Bank (ADB) is entering the area; the World Bank is considering options for new initiatives; USAID is receiving expanded resources; the Swiss Development Commission is developing a new long-term assistance plan; and the Canadian International Development Agency (CIDA) is also considering new initiatives.

A uniform set of principles and objectives for the donors would serve to focus the efforts more effectively to achieve results. Although donor coordination cannot occur in the absence of government representatives, there is a need for a donor-led mechanism for information exchange and coordination. In the past, the World Bank and the United Nations Development Programme (UNDP) helped to organize periodic meetings.

Areas Not Yet Addressed

The technical issues of water use and management in Central Asia are well developed and sufficient studies have been carried out that provide a sound technical base for future work on water saving, efficiency increases, information and decision system support, and capacity building for regional institutions. Other areas not related to water use and management currently demand attention. These areas include the following:

- Water quality, including pollution from point and nonpoint sources and especially transboundary effects. This issue requires a mandate from a high government level before efforts can be undertaken to mitigate the effects of water pollution.

- Information and data exchange.

- Past experience in Central Asia has made the governments and donor agencies wary of the creation of regional water management databases, due to efforts to limit access to or use of these databases. What is needed is a new concept, where the raw data stays in the initiating country and reports are sent periodically to the other countries. The five national hydrometeorological services have been working on the development of regional cooperation and data sharing in their area for the past year or so, and the lessons learned from their efforts could be applied on a broader scale.

- Agricultural policy and its effect on national economies, water use, and environmental effects. Some of the food security measures implemented by some of the Central Asian states have had large economic impacts that have not been studied. Food security is primarily a national issue, but it does have regional environmental impacts.

■ Water allocation.

Water allocation has been identified by several of the Central Asian countries as an important issue, but Uzbekistan and Turkmenistan are reluctant to discuss this issue for fear of disrupting existing patterns of water use in their agricultural sectors. High-level governmental cooperation is required to tackle this issue.

As has been seen in this chapter, water management in Central Asia is a complex and critical issue affecting the security of all the nations of the region. Cooperative management of this vital resource could lead to great benefits in the future, while ignoring the opportunities for cooperation will lead to roadblocks in the development pathways of the countries. Many issues must be addressed to achieve regional management, but a firm foundation exists from which progress can be made.

Notes

[1] Y. Khudaiberganov, "About BWO Role in Amudarya Basin Water Resources Management Issues," ADB Regional Consultation Workshop, Cooperation in Shared Water Resources in Central Asia: Past Experience and Future Challenges, Almaty, September 26-28 2002.

[2] M. Khamidov, "Syr Darya River Water Resources Management and Environmental Effects Caused by Changing Natural River Flow Regime," ADB Regional Consultation Workshop, Cooperation in Shared Water Resources in Central Asia: Past Experience and Future Challenges, Almaty, September 26-28 2002.

[3] O. Atanyazova, "Health and Ecological Consequences of the Aral Sea Crisis," paper presented at the Third World Water Forum, Kyoto, March 18, 2003.

[4] United Nations Environment Programme (UNEP), "State of Environment of the Aral Sea Basin Regional Report of the Central Asian States 2000," <http://www.grida.no/aral/aralsea/english/fish/fish.html>.

[5] Almaty, February 18, 1992.

[6] Kyzyl Orda, March 26, 1993.

[7] Nukus, September 20, 1995.

[8] Tashkent, January 4, 1993.

[9] ICAS had as executive bodies: an Executive Committee (EC ICAS); the International Sustainable Development Commission (ISDC), and the ICWC (including the BVOs and SIC ICWC).

[10] Kyzl Orda, 23 March 1993.

[11] Nukus, January 11, 1994.

[12] Almaty, February 27, 1997; Tashkent March 20, 1997; and Tashkent May 30, 1997.

[13] Agreement on the Use of Water and Energy Resources of the Syr Darya Basin, Bishkek, March 17, 1998.

[14] Under the framework agreement, during 1998-2001, Kyrgyzstan met, on average, 86.5 percent of the planned irrigation water releases and 77.8 percent of the planned surplus electricity transmission. During the same period, Uzbekistan and Kazakhstan supplied to the Kyrgyz energy system 87.8 percent of the planned natural gas and 60.5 percent of the planned coal (A.K. Kenshimov, "Interstate Water Allocation in the Aral Sea Basin," Royal Haskoning, Tashkent, Uzbekistan, 2002).

[15] G. Gleason, "Inter-State Cooperation in Central Asia from the CIS to the Shanghai Forum", *Europe – Asia Studies*, Vol. 53, no. 7, 1077–1095, 2001.

[16] Ibid., 1084.

[17] RFEL, "Four Central Asian Presidents Meet in Dushanbe," <www.rferl.org/news-line/2002/10/2>.

[18] D. McCauley, "Establishing a Framework for Transboundary Water Management in the Syr Darya Basin of Central Asia," Issue Paper, U.S. Agency for International Development, Washington D.C., 2002; E. Weinthal, "State Making and Environmental Cooperation: Linking Domestic and International Politics in Central Asia," (Cambridge: MIT Press, 2002).

[19] The data and statistics used to characterize the countries of the region come mostly from the reports of the Global Environmental Facility, Water and Environmental Management Project, Component A.1 Joint Report 2 and Regional Report 2, 2002.

[20] I.S. Zonn, "Water Resources of Northern Afghanistan and Their Future Use," presented at Informal Planning Meeting: Water, Climate, and Development Issues in the Amudarya Basin, Philadelphia, June 18-19, 2002.

[21] Ibid., 9.

[22] In 2000, the Kyrgyz hydroelectricity production cost was 0.006 USD per kWh, and the export price was 0.01 USD per kWh. This price for the Kyrgyz electricity exceeds the cost of generation at the Kazakh thermal plants (about 0.006 USD per kWh). At these prices and without consideration of the value of the delivered water (0.004 USD per kWh or 0.0034 USD per cubic m), the Kyrgyz electricity is not competitive in the Kazakhstan power market.

[23] A.D. Ryabtsev, "Country Perspectives on Regional Cooperation in Shared Water Resources: Water Resources of Kazakhstan," in *Cooperation in Shared Water Resources in Central Asia: Past Experience and Future Challenges*; D. C. McKinney, ed., Proceedings of the Regional Consultation Workshop on Cooperation in Shared Water Resources in Central Asia: Past Experience and Future Challenges, Asian Development Bank, Manila, 2003, 168.

[24] UN Economic Commission for Europe (UNECE), "Convention on the Protection and Use of Transboundary Water Courses and International Lakes", Helsinki, 1992, and the UN "Convention on the Law of Non-navigational Uses of International Watercourses", 1997.

[25] The obligation of a country to utilize a watercourse in an equitable and reasonable manner and to cooperate in its protection and development. This principle affects economic policy of each Basin country.

[26] The obligation of a country to prevent, control, and reduce pollution of waters causing or likely to cause transboundary impact. This principle affects economic and environmental policies of the region and each nation in the basin.

[27] A.A.Jalalov, "Water Resources Management in Uzbekistan: Legal aspects and Directions of Improvement," in *Cooperation in Shared Water Resources in Central Asia: Past Experience and Future Challenges*; D. C. McKinney, ed., Proceedings of the Regional Consultation Workshop on Cooperation in Shared Water Resources in Central Asia: Past Experience and Future Challenges, Asian Development Bank, Manila, 2003, 168.

[28] Ibid., 47.

Chapter 10

Central Asian Public Health: Transition and Transformation

Genevieve Grabman

Adramatic demographic and epidemiological transition has occurred in Central Asia during the past decade, concurrent with the region's political and economic transition. This chapter attempts to explain the changing public health status in Central Asia by depicting the historical and social context in which public health is evolving. Kyrgyzstan, Kazakhstan, Uzbekistan, Tajikistan and Turkmenistan inherited their public health systems from the Soviet Union, and the demise of that empire has greatly impacted Central Asian public health. The collapse of centrally-controlled health care finance and planning precipitated an increased risk of sickness and death for the public. The newly independent Central Asian states began in the late 1990s to reform their national health systems in order to make public health care fiscally sustainable and responsive to health challenges. Still, Central Asia faces some critical health needs in the new millennium. Reflecting the region's transitional status, both chronic and infectious health conditions urgently require intervention from each nation's public health system.

Data and Statistics

Any study of Central Asian heath requires a caveat on the data it presents: data collection in all Central Asian countries is notoriously difficult, statistical analysis may be poor, and reported figures are often skewed for political purposes. The infant mortality rate is only one of many government-reported statistics that may have little resemblance to a real figure. Doctors' use of Soviet death criteria results in a systemic mislabeling of infant deaths as stillborns, thus the true number of babies who die after birth is higher than the reported infant mortality rate indicates.[1] Regional governments' human immunodeficiency virus (HIV) and acquired immunodeficiency virus (AIDS) statistics also may significantly underestimate infection rates, as legally-required residency permit systems discourage many groups particularly vulnerable to HIV infection from registering with authorities.[2] In Turkmenistan and Uzbekistan, official statistics are particularly suspect, given the autocratic nature of these governments.

A less distorted picture of public health in the region can be obtained by focusing on data from the Kyrgyz Republic, or Kyrgyzstan. Although data verification remains problematic, recent government-provided health data is relatively reliable. Kyrgyzstan's Ministry of Health has received extensive technical assistance from the World Health Organization in reporting health statistics. Kyrgyzstan was also the site of an extensive United States-led Demographic and Health Survey (DHS) in 1997, permitting comparison of official statistics with independently collected information.

Kyrgyzstan: A Proxy for Central Asia

In its population's longevity, morbidity, and mortality, Kyrgyzstan represents the mean of Central Asian public health.[3] Tajikistan and Turkmenistan, poorer countries than Kyrgyzstan, have higher mortality rates. Uzbekistan, a richer country than Kyrgyzstan, has lesser infant and under-five mortality rates and longer life expectancies. Until 1999, Kazakhstan's relative wealth also contributed to lower child mortality and higher life expectancy than in Kyrgyzstan.[4]

All of Central Asia is also mirrored in Kyrgyzstan's internal public health variations.[5] Kyrgyzstan's poorest *oblasts* or states, Talas, Naryn, and Batken, have the country's highest rates of infant and maternal mortality. In cold, dry Talas and Naryn, with climates similar to Kazakhstan, acute respiratory infections and tuberculosis are more problematic than in the rest of Kyrgyzstan. In the southern oblasts of Jalal-Abad, Osh, and Batken, as in Tajikistan and southern Uzbekistan, diarrheal diseases are the major cause of morbidity and mortality in children. In these Kyrgyzstani states, fertility rates are also much higher than in other oblasts, due to the cultural and religious beliefs of the southern Kyrgyzstan's Uzbek and Tajik populations. Further, during the late 1990s and until 2001, the southern portion of Kyrgyzstan suffered invasions by Taliban-backed militants. This armed insurrection undoubtedly crippled the health care system and caused higher death rates in the affected areas, a result similar to that seen in war-torn Tajikistan.

Northern oblasts Chuy and Issyk-Kol have the most favorable health indicators in Kyrgyzstan. Similar to all Central Asian capitals, wealth is concentrated around the capital city in Chuy oblast, and the population here has better access to higher quality health care than do people in other oblasts. Bishkek residents, like the inhabitants of all Central Asia's capital cities, enjoy the country's best health outcomes. Chuy and Issyk-Kol also have a high proportion of Russians living in them, similar to the demographics of Kazakhstan and many Central Asian capitals. Russians tend to have lower fertility rates and better mortality and morbidity outcomes than do native Central Asian peoples.

Finally, like the other Central Asian countries, Kyrgyzstan is reforming its Soviet-inherited health care system. Kyrgyzstan's health reform is the most advanced and widespread in Central Asia, having begun in the north of Kyrgyzstan, expanded to the south, and recently spread to Naryn and Talas. This health reform is expected to improve health outcomes throughout Kyrgyzstan.[6]

The Soviet Health System

The Soviet Union's Constitution was the first in the world to guarantee the right to health, stating, "Citizens of the U.S.S.R. have the right to health protection."[7] The Soviet health care system therefore was designed to provide all citizens—and especially rural populations—with access to a basic level of care. At the expense of preventative care, provider choice, and efficiency, Soviet socialized medicine achieved impressive public health accomplishments. The ratio of doctors and nurses to population was among the highest in the world. Many diseases once endemic, including diphtheria, smallpox, cholera, polio, whooping cough, and typhus, were virtually eradicated. On average and indicative of results seen in the Central Asian Soviet republics, USSR. life expectancies doubled between the 1917 October revolution and 1970.[8]

The Soviet health system was a single-payer scheme, where the government provided all health care free of charge, according to norms formulated by the Ministry of Health in Moscow and resource distribution determined by the Semashko All Union Research Institute in Moscow.[9] Republic-level health ministries were responsible for implementing Moscow's policies through oblast-level health departments. In turn, the oblast health departments directed health care through rayon (county) and at the city health administrations. In each republic and oblast, a sanitary epidemiological service (Sanepid or SES) oversaw the control of communicable diseases and acted as a "check" on the health departments' work.[10]

To provide universal health care coverage, the Soviet system automatically assigned each citizen to a polyclinic that assumed responsibility for the person's health and served as the portal of entrance to the medical care system.[11] The patient could not choose his or her physician; the patient's residence in a micro-district usually determined her polyclinic assignment. However, high ranking members of the Communist Party and employees in some collective enterprises, such as factories and farms, were assigned to clinics and hospitals reserved for their use. The one polyclinic per micro-district, staffed by an internist for men, a pediatrician for children, an obstetrician for women, a dentist, and a nurse, provided routine outpatient care to the micro-district's approximately 4000 people. In rural areas with long distances between polyclinics called *selskaya vrachebnaya ambulatorya,* or SVAs, people could receive basic care from first aid specialists and midwives at health posts *feldsher accousherski punkt* or FAPs.

If referred by their polyclinic or if self-referred, Soviet citizens could seek more advanced health care at the rayon's central town hospital and specialty polyclinics. In rural areas, limited medical care was available at small hospitals *selskaya uchaskovaya bolnitsia,* or SUBs. Still more specialized and better equipped hospitals for specific diseases and conditions— cancer, tuberculosis, sexually transmitted infections—could be found in the main city of each oblast and in republic's capital city.

Kyrgyzstan was a beneficiary of the Soviet health care system in many ways. Although costly and hospital-heavy, the Kyrgyzstan's Soviet health care system successfully decreased infant and child deaths and increased life expectancy. The Soviet system also provided all children and expectant mothers with free health care.[12] As a result, Kyrgyzstan's official infant mortality rate dropped from 111 in 1970 to 52 in 2001, and the under-five mortality rate decreased from 146 in 1970 to 61 in 2001.[13]

While it sounded like a positive situation for all involved, the Soviet model of health care had many drawbacks.[14] The system relied on vast numbers of specialists and multiple, redundant specialist facilities.[15] In turn, the system produced few community-level health professionals skilled in preventive care, such as generalists and nurse practitioners.[16] Many doctors were trained only to address the needs of a specific sex or age group suffering from a specific disease, while nurses had limited skills and undertook only basic tasks. As an example of the extreme overspecialization of Soviet health care, Kyrgyz obstetricians neither owned nor knew how to use stethoscopes. Clinical management required lengthy hospital stays for many conditions, such as tuberculosis and influenza, which could have been treated in outpatient facilities.[17] The system's financing structure encouraged this tertiary care focus by funding hospitals according to their bed quantity, rather than their number of patients. Such treatment and financing regimes required a large number of hospital beds, which led to low occupancy levels. Finally, the Soviet system failed to encourage a sense of health responsibility among the citizenry or innovation amongst the providers.[18] Government subsidies supported health care and the population grew to expect free healthcare services. No private health care or health insurance was necessary or permitted.

Soviet Collapse

With the disintegration of the Soviet Union in 1991, the disruption caused by a forced transition from a collectivist system to a market economy brought about a near collapse of the health care system in the newly independent states.[19] Like the other Central Asian nations, Kyrgyzstan was left utterly without money to support its social sector, including its public health systems.[20] The share of the government budget going to health care fell by about a third between 1991 and 1992.[21] At the same time, the percentage of the gross domestic product spent on health care fell from just over four to two percent.[22] The country's poor economic situation led to health services deterioration as equipment became antiquated, drug stocks dwindled, and buildings decayed.[23] Salaries for doctors and nurses, if paid at all, fell from 79 percent of the average salary in 1995 to just 59 percent in 1998.[24]

The resource requirements of Kyrgyzstan's socialized public health system became untenable in the 1990s. Hospitals swallowed 73 percent of the healthcare funds, while the primary healthcare system received only 16 percent of the already diminished health budget.[25] Focus on tertiary care resulted in resources being spread too thin, and in under-financing of local level services. In turn, this led to mandatory informal payments to healthcare providers, a practice particularly detrimental to the poor. The World Bank bluntly states, "Resources wasted on half-empty facilities, poorly insulated buildings, or medical technologies that do not function rob the system of resources that could be put to effective use" on the primary health care level.[26] A well-functioning health care system is the single most important element in reaching the poor with prevention and treatment.[27]

Central Asians' health status declined due to the effects of poverty and lack of health care access. In Kyrgyzstan and particularly in the country's rural areas, the poverty rate increased from 40 percent to 63 percent between 1993 and 1996.[28] Lack of funding for the state health care system barred large segments of the population from basic medical services,[29] as the need to pay for health care prevented or delayed some poor families from seeking care.[30] Lack of adequate health care and poor nutritional status played pivotal roles in the significant growth in Kyrgyzstan's infant and child mortality rate.[31] Life expectancy also dropped by several years, as Kyrgyzstanis struggled to obtain food and health care in the mid-1990s.[32]

Further indicating the dire state of Central Asia's post-Soviet public health, Kyrgyzstani tuberculosis (TB) incidence rates increased 100 percent from 1991 to 2000. While the upsurge followed trends expected for the Central Asian region,[33] Kyrgyzstan's TB incidence grew faster than any other former Soviet state.[34] New TB infections in Kyrgyzstan may soon approach Tajikistan's very high TB incidence of 250 cases per 100,000 people.[35]

Tuberculosis is a disease of poverty, easily spread in crowded conditions and infecting the sick and malnourished.[36] Through coughing, talking, or spitting, each person with active, untreated TB will infect on average between 10 and 15 people every year.[37] In infected people, the TB bacilli can lie dormant for several years; when an infected person's immune system is weakened, his or her chances of falling ill with active TB increase. Populations lacking food or adequate living space, alcoholics, and people living with HIV/AIDS are at particular risk of becoming infected with TB and in developing the active disease. As it spreads, TB further strains the already under-funded Central Asian public health systems by requiring them to provide needed treatment to the sick. Tuberculosis also greatly increases the burden on the poor, as the disease spreads through families and as its debilitating effects limit the ability of the poor to work and better their situations.

Post-Soviet Reforms

The Soviet health care system was wasteful and, as the system's 1990s collapse showed, unsustainable.[38] In response to the region's unabated economic crisis, Central Asia's health care systems have been forced to undergo a comprehensive reform to rationalize their financing and to emphasize primary care.[39] The type and pace of change differs in each of the countries, and Kyrgyzstan's reforms are the most complete and institutionalized.[40]

The national health reform program began in the north of Kyrgyzstan in 1996 and more recently expanded to the south and to Talas and Naryn oblasts. Kyrgyzstan's health reform fosters lower-cost primary care through the creation of family medicine practice groups (FGPs), rationalization of the health system's excess physical capacity, and development of a tax-supported healthcare financing system.[41] Supported by a World Bank structural assistance loan and U. S. Agency for International Development

(USAID) technical assistance, the Kyrgyz government determines the reform's objectives and implements and monitors its performance.

Radically departing from the prior system of assigning patients to doctors, the reformed health system permits families to choose their FGP from among those in the district. Each FGP is composed of a pediatrician, an internist, a gynecologist, and at least two nurses, all retrained in modern family medicine protocols. The FGP structure allows family members to receive their health care at one location, and FGPs act as gatekeepers to higher levels of care.

The architects of the health reform hoped that, if Kyrgyzstanis took personal responsibility for their own health and used FGPs' preventative and primary care services, the cost of Kyrgyzstan's system would decrease, and the health status of the population would improve. Consistent with these goals, a national Ministry of Health marketing team informs the Kyrgyz population about the ongoing reforms and conducts health promotional campaigns. Systemic reform cannot depend on health education efforts alone, however. "Financial investment in family group practices and outpatient drugs is necessary to give patients access to medicine at the primary healthcare level and to allow FGPs to function and to expand their scope of services."[42]

As a method of freeing funding for health reform, poorly utilized or redundant hospitals or specialized polyclinics are to be closed. Most of the facilities slated for closure are SUBs in rural areas or city hospitals. Despite being located close to remote population enclaves, these facilities have little or no supplies and offer very limited services when compared with hospitals and polyclinics in the rayon center cities. Staffing and heating excess buildings drains oblast health budgets, taking funds sorely needed for basic drugs, food, supplies, and salaries. Although individual doctors oppose closing health facilities, which provide them informal payment opportunities, the oblast health departments are committed to rationalizing the health sector's resources.[43] Money saved from closing high cost, underutilized hospitals creates pools of funds for FGP capital investments, provider salaries, and oblast drug supplies.[44]

Even with this rationalization of the systems' capacity, the revenues of Central Asian governments are insufficient to support national public health systems. In Kyrgyzstan, a mandatory health insurance fund (MHIF) provides additional resources for the health reform. The MHIF receives funds from earmarked payroll taxes and pools this money. Using innovative payment methods and based on information collected through new health information systems, the MHIF then allocates the funds to oblast health departments for essential drugs. For hospital services, patients must pay formalized, government-approved co-payments, although the MHIF covers the costs of medication.

The MHIF mechanism has given impetus to the health reform's implementation.[45] The availability of outpatient drugs provides an incentive to reduce hospital admissions and to expand primary healthcare services.[46] A government decree to include all children as MHIF beneficiaries in 2000 expanded the fund's role to include coverage of health services.[47] Further, formal patient co-payments have significantly reduced informal payments to health providers and corruption in the health system.[48] Providers now have a legitimate means of increasing their salaries, and patients are given prior notice of the charges for their health care.

Currently, among the Central Asian Republics, only Kyrgyzstan has a functioning MHIF. The other Central Asian republics are reluctant to replicate this off-budget financing system. Uzbekistan, Tajikistan, and Turkmenistan have not developed a health insurance fund, and Kazakhstan's MHIF lasted three years before it was eliminated due to political wrangling and because of the lack of legal and regulatory systems necessary for the MHIF's support.[49]

Kyrgyzstan's willingness to implement health sector reform has served as a catalyst for attracting and coordinating international health aid in Kyrgyzstan. A variety of governments and organizations, including the World Health Organization (WHO), World Bank, the European Bank of Reconstruction and Development, and the Asian Development Bank, have provided training and support for doctors, nurses, and midwives throughout the country. Other donors, such as the United Nations Children's Fund (UNICEF) and USAID, have provided immunizations and nutritional supplements and have conducted breastfeeding training classes.[50] Initial studies demonstrate that the reformed, rationalized, retrained, and refunded health care system also provides better quality services.[51] Improved public health and infant and child survival are expected from these efforts.[52]

Demographic and Epidemiological Transitions

The transitional state of Central Asia's public health system has precipitated changes in the area's patterns of population and disease growth. Immediately before and after the Soviet collapse, Central Asia's health indicators resembled those of a developing country with high birthrates but high infant and maternal death rates. The leading causes of death were infectious diseases. More recently, the causes of Central Asians' deaths are changing; chronic conditions more often found in developed countries, such as heart disease, are increasingly producing a greater percentage of deaths. At the same time, infant and under-five mortality rates appear to be improving throughout the region. Maternal mortality, preventable deaths due to pregnancy, childbirth, and abortion complications, is also decreasing. In 1990, 110 Central Asian mothers died for every 100,000 women having a live birth.[53] By 2002, the average maternal mortality ratio had dropped to 65 women per 100,000 having a live birth.[54]

Demographic Transition

Like the rest of Central Asia, Kyrgyzstan is undergoing a transition from high fertility and mortality rates to low fertility and mortality rates. Kyrgyzstan's total fertility rate is officially 2.5, which is relatively low.[55] Yet a high prevalence of abortion in Kyrgyzstan, as in all former Soviet countries, may obscure a much higher actual total fertility rate, suggesting that the country still is in the middle of a demographic transition.[56]

Central Asia's children face a moderate risk of death during their first five years of life. In 2001, for every 1,000 babies born alive in Kyrgyzstan, 52 died before their first birthday.[57] Of children under five years of age, 61 died for every 1,000 children.[58] Again, these official rates may understate the true number of deaths of Kyrgyz children. Others estimate that 76.5 infants die for every 1000 born alive.[59]

Most of Central Asia's population is slow-growing due to the effects of migration. In Kyrgyzstan, the crude birth rate is estimated at 26.06 births per 1,000 population; the crude death rate is expected to be 9.10 deaths per 1,000 population.[60] Rapid population growth is expected where a country's crude birth rate exceeds its crude death rate; yet Kyrgyzstan's population grew only by an estimated 1.46 percent in 2003.[61] This lower population growth resulted from 2.37 per 1,000 people migrating from Kyrgyzstan.[62]

Uzbekistan is an exception to Central Asia's demographic trend of lower birth and death rates. With 40 percent of its citizens younger than 16 years old, Uzbekistan's population is expected to double in 50 years to 50 million people.[63] Such rapid population growth clearly will exacerbate the deteriorating post-Soviet health system. To merely maintain its current level of health care, Tashkent will need to more than double the amount of resources dedicated to health services.[64]

Epidemiological Transition

Central Asia represents a pre- and post-epidemiological transition mix, where new health concerns, especially alcoholism and smoking, compound the effects of diseases spread due to poverty and the collapsing healthcare system. Throughout the region, the top causes of adult morbidity and mortality are both chronic and infectious conditions found in developing (pre-transitional) and developed (post-transitional) countries. Most adult deaths in Kyrgyzstan, for example, are attributed to respiratory infections, chronic cardiovascular conditions, and accidents or injuries.[65]

High mortality due to chronic, preventable conditions is characteristic of post-transitional countries. Cardiovascular disease is the largest contributor to the gap in mortality between Central Asia and industrialized countries, with rates about five times higher than in Western Europe.[66] The high prevalence of smoking, especially among Central Asian men, is the cause of much cardiovascular mortality.[67] Alcoholism is also contributing to a rising rate of mortality and morbidity due to cardiovascular disease deaths[68] and to injury, including injuries caused by alcohol-fueled domestic and gender-based violence.[69]

Rising rates of deaths from non-communicable diseases notwithstanding, sickness caused by infectious diseases indicates that Central Asian countries remain, in many ways, "developing countries." In Central Asia, infectious respiratory and diarrheal diseases kill many infants and young children.[70] Sexually transmitted infections are also spreading rapidly among Central Asian youth and adults.[71] Further, the region faces growing rates of tuberculosis and drug resistant tuberculosis infection.[72] For the Central Asian region, more years of life are lost to disability from communicable diseases, maternal and perinatal conditions, and nutritional deficiencies than from all non-communicable conditions combined.[73]

The effects of Central Asia's demographic and epidemiological transition can be summarized through a description of Kyrgyzstan's population. If they survive their early childhood, Kyrgyzstan's ethnically diverse 4.6 million people can expect to live, on average, for 68 years before succumbing to either a disease typical of a developing country or a lifestyle-related sickness common to a developed country. Given Kyrgyzstan's mortality rates due to respiratory disease, which are the highest in the former Soviet Union, Kyrgyz's risk of dying due to tuberculosis is particularly acute.[74]

Pressing Health Challenges

Central Asia in transition exhibits some of the worst features of both developed and developing countries, with high rates of heart disease and childhood infections.[75] This pattern indicates the importance of strengthening health education and addressing malnutrition and other infectious, chronic, and injury-caused health threats.

Health Promotion/Education

The lack of basic health education and health awareness promotion in Central Asia is perhaps the most important problem facing the region's health sector.[76] The region's top causes of mortality and morbidity—both infectious and chronic—could be addressed through education programs targeting both adults and children and focusing on behavior change. For example, if parents and children were taught the importance of handwashing after defecation and before food preparation, this would help prevent the incidence of diarrhea. Similarly, educating people about the risks of smoking and of non-monogamous, casual sexual behavior might cause people to avoid these behaviors. Given Central Asia's many childhood deaths from diarrhea, and the region's rising rates of mortality from smoking and morbidity from sexually transmitted diseases, health education is essential.

With decreasing health budgets, the Central Asian states' crumbling public health systems have scarce resources to develop and implement health promotion programs. The region's ongoing health reform gives the international community opportunities to assist Ministries of Health in the creation of health education projects. Consistent with the goals of health reform, preventative, community-level health initiatives are less expensive than the Soviet curative health system, and involve people in the health decisions that affect them.

In Kyrgyzstan, USAID formatted a health promotion pilot project in Chuy oblast. Through this project, FGPs give health talks in schools and businesses, set up information centers in communities to distribute health educational materials, and show video spots on prevention of various diseases, including sexually transmitted infections (STIs).[77] In Uzbekistan, this program trained Ferghana Oblast schoolteachers to develop plans for primary school health lessons. Lessons covered topics such as bodily and oral hygiene, nutrition and anemia, acute respiratory infections, diarrhea, "bad habits" (including smoking, alcohol, and drugs), and reproductive health focused on puberty.[78]

Health promotion work requires improving the communications skills of front-line, community health workers.[79] Increasing the skills of nurses is of particular importance in Central Asia, where 70 percent of the population is rural-based with little access to doctors.[80] In many cases, nurses and midwives at rural FAPs are the first and only health care providers available to the population. As part of the health reform in Kyrgyzstan, FGP nurse retraining programs in management of childhood illness and reproductive health are active in six of the country's seven oblasts.[81]

Nutrition

Malnutrition is one of the primary causes of under-five child mortality in Central Asia.[82] However, the effects of micronutrient deficiency reach far beyond mere mortality; both goiter and anemia are extremely prevalent in the region's women and children. In the Ferghana Valley, between 60 and 80 percent of women and young children suffer from anemia caused by an iron-poor diet.[83] Throughout the Central Asia republics, only non-iodized salt is commonly available, resulting in a steep rise in iodine deficiency disorders over the past five years,[84] and disabling up to 90 percent of young children in some areas of Kyrgyzstan.[85] Since a mother's iron or iodine deficiency may impair the cognitive and physical development of her children, the health of future Central Asians depends on addressing malnutrition now. To call attention to the problem of malnutrition in Uzbekistan, international donors created a three-part television series entitled "Simple Truth" that promotes the consumption of meat and other iron-rich foods.[86]

Another nutritional intervention, exclusive breastfeeding, could play an important role in reducing Central Asian infant and child mortality from causes other than malnutrition. Diarrhea and acute respiratory infection are responsible for much of the region's infant and child mortality and morbidity. Breastfeeding helps to prevent and reduce the incidence of diarrheal and respiratory disease in infants. Despite this beneficial effect of breastfeeding, many Central Asian mothers wean their infants or give their babies tea and other liquids.[87] Thus, increasing the number of mothers who exclusively breastfeed their children up to six months of age could reduce the infant and child mortality rate.

Infectious Disease

AIDS

In 1999, Central Asia had the world's steepest increase in HIV infection;[88] yet the true extent of AIDS—caused by HIV—in Central Asia is unknown, due to the lack of accurate reporting.[89] Kazakhstan's government reported the highest HIV/AIDS prevalence rates in Central Asia, with 1,122 HIV positive cases and 31 AIDS cases, but only 92 HIV infection cases are confirmed across the border in Kyrgyzstan.[90] Broader regional data may be a harbinger of an imminent AIDS epidemic, much worse than official figures indicate. From 1995 to 2000, the estimated number of HIV infections in Eastern Europe and Central Asia increased by more than twenty-fold, from less than 30,000 to more than 700,000.[91] The infection incidence similarly continues to grow exponentially in the region, with 250,000 new infections in 2000 alone. In Kyrgyzstan, the majority of new HIV cases are among injecting drug users (IDUs) living in Osh and the Ferghana Valley. In Osh and Bishkek, over 5 percent of IDUs are likely HIV infected.[92]

The AIDS epidemic will soon spread from IDUs to their sexual partners and to the general heterosexual population, indicated by a rapid rise in other STIs in the region. Central Asia syphilis prevalence rates exploded in the 1990s, jumping almost 150 percent in Kyrgyzstan from 1990 to 1996 and a staggering 225 percent in Kazakhstan during the same period.[93] In 1999, one in every 90 Kyrgyzstani men had syphilis.[94] Syphilis and HIV are both transmitted through unprotected sexual intercourse, so groups at risk for syphilis also are at risk for HIV. In addition, STI infection increases the likelihood of HIV transmission during unprotected sex.[95]

Central Asian adolescents are a particularly high-risk group for sexually transmitted infections, including syphilis and HIV. In Kyrgyzstan, the 1998 incidence of STIs in urban youth was 170 per 100,000, an infection rate considerably higher than the average urban population (100 infections per 100,000 people).[96] The causes of the disproportionate STI youth infection rate are likely due to adolescents' hazardous sexual activity and lack of disease prevention ability or knowledge. Indeed, 40 percent of sexually active urban adolescent Kyrgyz girls reported receiving remuneration for sexual intercourse.[97] This information about risk taking behavior portends a serious challenge to Central Asian public health.

Tuberculosis

Despite recent efforts to diagnose and control TB, the disease is spreading unabated in Central Asia. Kyrgyzstan is combating the most serious new epidemic of TB in the former Soviet Union. Of the country's 4.6 million people, 126.9 out of every 100,000, approximately 5837 people, are currently infected;[98] and the new infection rate may soon reach 250 per 100,000.[99]

The development of multi-drug resistant tuberculosis (MDR-TB) makes addressing tuberculosis infection a public health priority for all of Central Asia. MDR-TB is rising at alarming rates in the former Soviet Union and threatens global TB control efforts.[100] MDR-TB is virulent because the disease cannot be controlled by isoniazid and rifampicin, the two most powerful, and least expensive, anti-TB drugs.[101]

Drug-resistant TB is caused by inconsistent or partial chemotherapy—when TB patients do not take all their drugs regularly for the required period.[102] Central Asians often treat themselves for TB, purchasing antibiotics from street vendors and discontinuing treatment once they feel better, but before the TB bacilli are killed.[103] Health workers also may prescribe the wrong treatment regimens for a patient's TB. These TB drug treatments are individualized and do not follow WHO recommendations, resulting in low cure rates, cases of chronic infections, and drug-resistance.[104] Further, the TB drug supply is unreliable and treatment may be interrupted when delivery of medication is delayed.[105] Whereas during the Soviet period patients were treated with at least three anti-TB drugs, health personnel now often have to rely on only two drugs, isoniazid and rifampin. Given the high likelihood in the region of pre-existing resistance to one of these agents, this situation will lead to the generation and transmission of multidrug-resistant strains.[106]

TB infection is particularly rife in Central Asia's prisons. Prison inmates are more susceptible to the disease because TB spreads in the overcrowded, poorly ventilated cells, and because the prisoners themselves are often sick and malnourished.[107] Due to lack of treatment and medication, many prisoners develop MDR-TB.[108] Statistics from Kazakhstan show that the TB morbidity rate among prisoners is more than 20 times higher than among the general population.[109] In Kyrgyzstan, more than 10 percent of all inmates are likely infected with TB—close to 2,000 people in 40 prisons.[110] Of these, roughly 30 percent are likely to be infected with MDR-TB.[111] When prisoners are released and return home, they spread their MDR-TB to their communities.[112] In an effort to reduce prison costs and overcrowding, Kyrgyzstan offered amnesty to individuals convicted of petty crimes—nearly 50 percent of the prisoners in the country. Among the first groups scheduled to receive amnesty were prisoners with tuberculosis.[113]

Tuberculosis control in Central Asia is needed immediately before the disease spreads from Central Asia to other countries. The WHO is attempting to assist Central Asian governments in implementing a rapid TB detection and treatment strategy called Directly Observed Treatment,

Short Course (DOTS).[114] DOTS has been effective in controlling traditional TB, producing cure rates of up to 95 percent even in the poorest countries. DOTS also prevents the development of MDR-TB by ensuring the full course of treatment is followed. The World Bank has ranked the DOTS strategy as one of the "most cost-effective of all health interventions."[115]

Kyrgyzstan's government has prioritized TB eradication.[116] With WHO help, DOTS protocols are being taught to primary care practitioners at the community-level.[117] Generalists' wide coverage places them in a position to reach a much larger segment of the population than that attended by the Soviet vertical TB control system.[118] Yet the under-financed primary healthcare system in Kyrgyzstan is limited in the care it can provide. A six-month supply of drugs for DOTS costs eleven U.S. dollars per patient,[119] thus $50,000 is needed to treat those currently infected in Kyrgyzstan. A comprehensive TB control program also requires funds to support home visits to the most seriously ill in their communities, to ensure that the sick follow their treatment regimes.

Lack of funding in the health care system prevents countries from providing the expensive medicines needed to fight MDR-TB. Although international donors provide some TB medication, Central Asian Ministries of Health have no available funds to extend TB-control services to underserved populations, such as those in prison. While the WHO and others have vigorously promoted the DOTS program in Kyrgyzstan, little can be accomplished without targeted monetary support for the new TB protocols.

Gender-Based Violence

Central Asian women are suffering a growing incidence of domestic and other gender-based violence. Post-Soviet economic hardships, changing social roles of men and women, and men's alcohol consumption all contribute to a greater incidence of spousal beatings, and the revival of "traditional" practices harmful to women.[120] In particular, bride stealing, that is, the kidnapping, rape, and subsequent forced marriage of a young woman, has increased in Kyrgyzstan, Kazakhstan, and in some regions of Uzbekistan.[121] Ethnographers attribute the recent increase in bride stealing to young men's newfound ability to abuse women with impunity[122] and men's desire to avoid the "inconveniences" of courtship and a wedding.[123] In Karakalpakstan, Uzbekistan, bride stealing is related to the revived practice of "qalym," or bride price. Prospective grooms who wish to avoid paying a sizable qalym often resort to stealing their intended spouse without her consent.[124]

Only scant data is available describing the incidence of bride stealing, the prevalence of stolen brides, or the characteristics of the victim. A late 1990s study of women in a region in southern Kazakhstan found that 80 percent of these women were stolen as brides.[125] In 1996, *The Economist* estimated that one in five marriages of Kyrgyz (approximately 240,000 women) were a result of bride stealing.[126] Only one sociological survey has sought to depict both the practice and the characteristics of men and women involved in Kyrgyz bride stealings. A convenience sample of over 300 bride stealings found that the abducted brides ranged in age from 16 to 28 years old (average 19.4 years), while abductors ranged from 17 to 45 (average age 23.5 years).[127]

Bride stealing apparently occurs at such a rate that its harm to women constitutes a public health problem.[128] The tradition affects women's physiology and psychology. A woman may suffer physical trauma at the time of abduction. Many stealings involve the use of blunt force to "capture" the bride.[129] Following capture, the woman may be raped,[130] resulting in severe damage to her external and internal reproductive organs.[131] The bride stealing practice also may put women at risk for sexually transmitted infections. The stolen bride is not able to negotiate her sexual initiation with her new husband, and it is very unlikely that she will be able to insist on condom use during intercourse.[132] Similarly, bride stealing renders a woman completely vulnerable to her abductor and his family. This power imbalance puts the bride at risk of future domestic violence at the hands of her new husband.[133] For adolescents, bride stealing may result in a greater risk from maternal mortality due to obstructed labor, a problem in women whose physical development is not complete at the time of pregnancy.[134]

Bride stealing also harms women's psychological health.[135] A woman kidnapped and raped by a stranger is subject to severe mental trauma[136] and lingering post-traumatic stress disorder.[137] Even if a bride is able to reject her abduction and return to her home, she may suffer rejection from her peers and family.

Central Asian governments' prevention of bride stealing and other forms of gender-based violence is demanded by domestic and international law. The Kyrgyz Criminal Code, for example, imposes a two-year prison sentence on those who "steal" a person for the purposes of marriage.[138] In addition, Kyrgyzstan is party to human rights treaties that demand countries protect and promote women and girl's rights.[139] Despite these obligations to protect women, however, out of hundreds of thousands of women stolen, only two bride stealing cases were litigated in Kyrgyzstan from 1985 to 1996.[140] By failing to address violence against women, the Central Asian states also fail to protect the public's health.

Conclusion

With their transition from dependent Soviet states to independent countries, Kyrgyzstan, Kazakhstan, Uzbekistan, Tajikistan, and Turkmenistan have undergone massive economic, social, and political upheaval. These rapid changes have resulted in the Central Asian states' inability to maintain their Soviet-inherited health system. The Soviet Union obtained its public health successes through extensive financing of regional medical and epidemiological departments that operated according to centrally established goals. The system relied on a massive infrastructure of tertiary care facilities and required lengthy patient management by medical specialists. These public health protocols and systems were not financially or medically effective for independent, but bankrupt, Central Asia. The Central Asian governments' failure to provide preventative health care programs, coupled with the population's increasing poverty, created favorable conditions for the spread of infectious disease and the expansion of chronic, lifestyle-related health conditions.

Driven by their legal obligations to address the causes of sickness and death, and their desire to maintain their citizens' health, Central Asian republics began in 1992 to reform their public health systems. At least in Kyrgyzstan, these reformed health care systems focus on preventative care provided by better-trained generalists, and are supported by innovative financing schemes. The health reforms offer a mechanism for the Central Asian republics to increase the population's involvement in and understanding of health care decision making, thus decreasing the population's need for costly curative care. However, Central Asia's nascent public health systems already face challenges from the health problems of the region's epidemiological and demographic transition. In some areas, the majority of women and children suffer the effects of malnutrition. Simultaneously, HIV/AIDS and other sexually-transmitted infections, TB infection, and gender-based violence are increasingly prevalent.

Failure to take rapid action to meet these health challenges will have grim results for the whole of Central Asia. Governments and public officials who blindly ignore some public health threats, such as those affecting women or other marginalized groups, will contribute to the weakening of norms and laws that could lessen vulnerability and that could serve as tools for improving health status. In addition, lack of response to one health challenge can lead to the spread of incurable diseases throughout the region, even to areas yet untouched. The region's most pressing health conditions interact with one another, each rendering the population vulnerable to the others. As discussed in this chapter, abused women are likely to be infected with STIs; people infected with an STI like syphilis are more likely to contract HIV; and malnutrition weakens the population's resistance to TB, as does HIV infection.

Although it may have increased the health risks to the public, Central Asia's demographic, epidemiological, and political flux also offers the region unique opportunities for improving individuals' health knowledge, raising standards of care, and empowering women. It has been only a little more than a decade since the Central Asian republics' independence, and the countries are still searching for the most effective and efficient ways to structure their public health systems. In each nation, ongoing discussions about the potential for health care reform and engagement with international donor organizations indicate a willingness to exchange new ideas for old responses. The form such reforms take may differ in each Central Asian country, according to that country's needs and context, yet no more can the region afford curing its sick population primarily with hospitals and specialists. Central Asia's pressing health problems of malnutrition, sexually transmitted diseases, tuberculosis, and gender-based violence can be prevented only through increasing awareness about and by giving communities the resources (vitamins, condoms, DOTS medications, trained police, respectively) to address these conditions. Of paramount importance is for Kyrgyzstan, Kazakhstan, Tajikistan, Turkmenistan, and Uzbekistan to reaffirm a focus on community-based health promotion and education and a commitment to allocate funding to such programs.

Notes

[1] W. Ward Kingkade and Eduado E. Arriaga, "Mortality in the Newly Independent States: Patterns and Impacts," in *Premature Death in the New Independent States*, eds. J.L. Bobadilla et al., eds. (Washington, DC: National Academy Press, 1997), 157.

[2] Renata Rutman, "Antiquated Residency Rules Pose Public Health Threat in Central Asia," *Eurasia Insight* (December 29, 2001).

[3] United Nations Childrens Fund (UNICEF), "Basic Indicators" Statistical Table 1, State of the World's Children (2003) (reporting statistics from 2001), available at <http://www.unicef.org/sowc03/tables/table1.html>.

[4] Kazakhstan's reported infant and under-five child mortality has risen dramatically in the past two years; during the same time, life expectancy in the country has decreased. Compare UNICEF,

supra note 3 with UNICEF, State of the World's Children, "Basic Indicators" Statistical Table 1 (2001) (reporting statistics from 1999), available at <http://www.unicef.org/sowc01/tables/table1.html>.

[5] See generally, United Nations Development Program (UNDP), Kyrgyzstan: Common Country Assessment (Bishkek: UNDP 2001), 99-100 (noting regional variations in Kyrgyzstan).

[6] See generally, Republican Medical Information Center, Characteristics of the Health Care Delivery Network (Bishkek: Ministry of Health of the Kyrgyz Republic, 1999).

[7] Constitution of the Union of Soviet Socialist Republics, Article 42 (1977).

[8] Anita Parlow, "The Central Asia Health Care Collapse," *Eurasia Insight* (December 21, 2001).

[9] Martin McKee et al., eds., *Health Care Systems in the Central Asian Republics* (*European Observatory on Health Care Systems* (Buckingham: Open University Press, 2002), 7.

[10] N.N. Brimkulov and S.M. Kuchuleev, "Primary Health Care in Kyrgyzstan" (Rotems Foundation, 2001). Online, available at http://www.rotem.ro/engl/pages/kyrgyzstan.html, retrieved Aug. 31, 2003.

[11] McKee et al., supra note 9, 71.

[12] World Bank, *Making Transition Work for Everyone: Poverty and Inequality in Europe and Central Asia* (Washington, DC: World Bank Group, 2000), 258.

[13] UNDP, "Kyrgyzstan," Human Development Report 2003 (Oxford: Oxford University Press 2003), available at <http://www.undp.org/hdr2003/indicator/cty_f_KGZ.html>.

[14] McKee et al., supra note 9, 7.

[15] United States Agency for International Development (USAID), "Quality Primary Health Care," USAID Central Asian Republics Briefs (2003), available at <http://www.usaid.gov/regions/europe_eurasia/car/briefers/primary_health.html>.

[16] Julie DaVanzo and Clifford Grammich, "Dire Demographics: Population Trends in the Russian Federation" (Washington, DC: RAND, 2001), 50, available at http://www.rand.org/publications/MR/MR1273/.

[17] USAID, supra note 15.

[18] McKee et al., supra note 9.

[19] Alexander Casella, "Health Care Systems Under the Weather," *Asia Times Online* (January 18, 2001). Reprinted by Asia Human Rights Commission, online, at <http://www.ahrchk.net/news/mainfile.php/ahrnews_200201/2292/>, retrieved September 30, 2002.

[20] Cf. N. Almagambetova, "Overhauling the Health-care System in Kazakhstan," Lancet 354 (9175) (1999): 313 (discussing the financial crisis in Kazakhstan's social sector). Also cf. S. Keshavjee and M.C. Bacerra, "Disintegrating Health Services and Resurgent Tuberculosis in Post-Soviet Tajikistan: An Example of Structural Violence," *JAMA* 283(9) (2000):1201 (discussing the results of the financial crisis in Tajikistan's health sector).

[21] McKee et al., supra note 9, 38.

[22] Ibid.

[23] Ibid., 7.

[24] Ibid., 29.

[25] European Observatory on Health Care Systems, Health Care Systems in Transition: Kyrgyzstan (Copenhagen: European Observatory on Health Care Systems, 1996), 16.

[26] World Bank, supra note 12.

[27] Ibid.

[28] Peace Corps of the United States, Kyrgyz Republic: Country and Culture (2000). Online, available at <http://www.peacecorps.gov/countries/kyrgyzrep/culture.htm> retrieved Sept. 30, 2002.

[29] Casella, supra note 19.

[30] McKee et al., supra note 9, 103.

[31] World Bank, World Development Indicators Database, July 2002. Online, available at <http://www.devdata.worldbank.org/data-query, retrieved Sept. 30, 2002>.

[32] World Bank, supra note 12, 260; USAID, supra note 15.

[33] Kabar News Agency, "U.N.: 55 Percent of Kyrgyz Population Below Poverty Line," BBC Worldwide Monitoring (January 20, 2000).

[34] UNDP, supra note 13.

[35] Keshavjee and Becerra, supra note 20. At 88 cases per 100,000 people, tuberculosis prevelance in Kyrgyzstan already exceeds that in Tajikistan (83 cases/100.000 people), see UNDP, supra note 13.

[36] WHO, "Tuberculosis," Information Fact Sheet No. 104 (2000).

[37] Ibid.

[38] USAID, "Kyrgyzstan," FY 1998 Congressional Presentation (June 1998), available at <http://www.usaid.gov/pubs/cp98/eni/countries/kg.html>.

[39] Ibid.

[40] McKee et al., supra note 9, 7.

[41] Brimkulov and Kuchuleev, supra note 10.

[42] Personal communication with Sheila O'Dougherty, Regional Director, ZdravPlus, USAID/World Bank Central Asian Health Reform Project, Bishkek, Kyrgyzstan (October 10, 2000).

[43] Personal communication with Mary Murphy, Kyrgyzstan Program Manager, Zdrav Plus, USAID/World Bank Central Asian Reform Project, Washington, DC (August 25, 2002).

[44] See generally, ZdravPlus, Six Month Report, January - June, 2002, (Almaty, Kazakhstan: Abt Associates 2002), 44. This report states, "Under the old health financing system, the MOH or providers were unable to reinvest any savings they created, as they [the savings] would revert to the [Ministry of Finance]... Pooling funds allows reinvestment of savings as all the money is in one pool, not in budget line items. Provider payment systems allow providers the autonomy to create and reinvest savings."

[45] Michael Borowitz et al., "Conceptual Foundations for Central Asian Republic Health Reform Model," Technical Report of the ZdravReform Program (Almaty, Kazakhstan: Abt Associates, 1999).

[46] ZdravPlus, supra note 44, 45.

[47] McKee et al., supra note 9, 104.

[48] ZdravPlus, supra note 44, 46-47.

[49] Ibid., 4-5, 18. See also McKee et al., supra note 9, 104.

[50] USAID, supra note 38.

[51] ZdravPlus, "Quality Improvement System Improves Reproductive Health Services, Enhances Client Satisfaction, and Empowers Health Workers in Kyrgyzstan," Road to Results (Almaty: Abt Associates, 2001).

[52] Republican Medical Information Center, Characteristics of the Health Care Delivery Network (Bishkek, Kyrgyzstan: Ministry of Health of the Kyrgyz Republic, 1999).

[53] World Health Organization (WHO), "Annex Table 1: Basic Indicators," World Health Report 1999 (Geneva: WHO, 1999), available at <http://www.who.int/whr/2002/en/whr2002_annex1.pdf>.

[54] UNICEF, supra note 4 at "Women," Statistical Table 7.

[55] United States Central Intelligence Agency (CIA), "Kyrgyzstan," *CIA World Factbook* 2003 (Washington, DC: CIA, 2003), available at <http://www.cia.gov/cia/publications/factbook/geos/kg.html>.

[56] Population Resource Center, The Replacement on Abortion by Contraception in Three Central Asian Republics (Washington, DC: The Center, 1998).

[57] UNICEF, supra note 3.

[58] Ibid.

[59] B.A. Anderson and B.D. Silver, "Issues of Data Quality in Assessing Mortality Trends and Levels in the New Independent States" in Bobadilla et al., supra note 1.

[60] CIA, supra note 55.

[61] Ibid.

[62] Ibid.

[63] Antoine Blua and Bruce Pannier, "Central Asia; Uzbekistan Races to Reverse Health Trends as Population Booms (Part 3)," Radio Free Europe/Radio Liberty (RFE/RL) (March 22, 2002), available at <http://www.rferl.org/nca/features/2002/03/22032002125509.asp> .

[64] Ibid.

[65] C.M. Davis, "Health Care Crisis: The Former Soviet Union," RFE/RL Research Report (October 8. 1993).

[66] McKee et al., supra note 9, 61.

[67] Centers for Disease Control and Prevention (CDC), "Kyrgyzstan," Tobacco of Health: A Global Status Report (2000), available at <http://www.cdc.gov/tobacco/who/kyrgyzst.htm>.

[68] Alexandra Poolos, "East:Taking the Pulse of Post-Soviet Health Care (Part 1)," RFE/RL (March 22, 2002), available at <http://www.rferl.org/nca/features/2002/03/22032002125429.asp>.

[69] Expert Center for Social Research (Uzbekistan), "Consultations with the Poor: Participatory Poverty Assessment in Uzbekistan for the World Bank World Development Report 2000/01," National Synthesis Report (1999), 22.

[70] WHO, supra note 53, Annex Table 3. See also UNICEF, supra note 3 (showing that Kyrgyzstan's infant mortality rates and under-five mortality rates rates are similar to other Central Asian countries).

[71] World Bank Group, "Improving Health Status and Reforming Health Systems in Europe and Central Asia," ECA Sector Brief - Health (September 2000).

[72] Ibid.

[73] WHO, supra note 53, Annex Table 4.

[74] World Bank Group, supra note 71.

[75] McKee et al., supra note 9, 7.

[76] Cf. DaVanzo and Grammich, supra note 16.

[77] ZdravPlus, supra note 44, 33.

[78] Ibid., 55.

[79] Ibid., 30.

[80] See generally, "Tajikistan: Urgent Need for Health Education," Integrated Regional Informational Networks of the U.N. Office for the Coordination of Humanitarian Affairs (IRIN) - Kofarnihon (July 25, 2002).

[81] ZdravPlus, supra note 44, 36.

[82] WHO, "Annex Table 3," World Health Report 2000 (Geneva: WHO 2000).

[83] Blua and Pannier, supra note 63.

[84] "Kazakhstan: Boosting Nutrition with a Pinch of Salt," IRIN - Almaty (August 8, 2002).

[85] Personal communication with Rudy Rodrigues, Resident Project Officer, UNICEF-Kyrgyzstan, Bishkek, Kyrgyzstan (1998). See also, World Bank, supra note 12, 261.

[86] ZdravPlus, supra note 44, 36.

[87] Personal communication with Dr. Damira Tursunbekova, Technical Advisor, BASICS, USAID Child Survival Project, Bishkek, Kyrgyzstan (1998). See also, World Bank, supra note 12, 260.

[88] USAID, "Health Issues," USAID Central Asian Republics Briefs (2003), available at <http://www.usaid.gov/regions/europe_eurasia/car/briefers/health_issues.html>.

[89] Renata Rutman, "Antiquated Residency Rules Pose Public Health Threat in Central Asia," *Eurasia Insight* (December 29, 2001) (noting that the dearth of HIV data is related to Central Asia's continuing reliance on the residency registration system which hinders unregistered residents, such as refugees and internally displaced people, from seeking government-provided HIV counseling and treatment).

[90] WHO and UNAIDS, "Kyrgyzstan, 2001 Update," Epidemiological Fact Sheet (Geneva:UNAIDS/WHO, 2001).

[91] Doris S. Mugrditchian, UNAIDS, UNICEF, and USAID, Report from Conference on the Prevention of HIV/AIDS and Sexually Transmitted Infections in Central Asia, Almaty, Kazakhstan, May 16-19, 2001, 4.

[92] Ibid.

[93] WHO, "Syphilis Prevalence Rates in the Former Soviet Union Countries, 1990-1996," Global Prevalence and Incidence of Selected Curable Sexually Transmitted Infections (2001), 23. The incidence of syphilis has decreased from its 1997 apex to 73.5 per 100,000 population, see WHO and UNAIDS, "Kyrgyzstan, 2002 Update," Epidemiological Fact Sheet (Geneva:UNAIDS/WHO, 2002).

[94] Personal communication with Dr. Ainagul Isakova, Family Practice Group Director, Ministry of Health of the Kyrgyz Republic, Bishkek, Kyrgyzstan (1999). See also, UNDP, supra note 5, 100.

[95] UNAIDS, "Questions and Answers about AIDS: Prevention and Care" (2003), available at <http://www.unaids.org/Unaids/EN/Resources/Questions_Answers/Q_A+III_Selected+issues_prevention+and+care/Section+VIII_Sexually+Transmitted+Infections+(STIs).asp>, stating, "The prevention and treatment of STIs are key strategies in the fight against HIV/AIDS because the presence of STIs magnifies the risk of HIV transmission during unprotected sex tenfold."

[96] Mugrditchian, supra note 91 11.

[97] Ibid.

[98] UNDP, Kyrgyzstan 2000 program website. Online, available at <http://www.undp.kg/english/country.html>, retrieved September 30, 2002. Website notes an increase of TB over data reported in UNDP, supra note 5.

[99] Keshavjee and Becerra, supra note 20, 1201.

[100] Ibid.

[101] Ibid.

[102] Ibid.

[103] K. Lally, "As the Aral Sea Retreats, Dust and Disease Flourish," *The Sun* (Baltimore, MD) February 14, 1999, 1A.

[104] World Bank, supra note 12.

[105] WHO, supra note 25.

[106] Keshavjee and Becerra, supra note 20.

[107] International Helsinki Federation for Human Rights, "Kyrgyzstan," Annual Report (1999), available at <http://wwww.ihf-hr.org/reprots/ar99/ar99kyr.html>.

[108] Project Hope, News website (2000). Online, available at <http://www.projecthope.org/news/prisons.html>, retrieved September 30, 2002.

[109] Ibid.

[110] Roy Walmsley, UK Home Office Research, Development and Statistics Directorate, "Research Findings," World Prison Population List (1999), 88. See also, International Helsinki Federation for Human Rights, supra note 107.

[111] International Helsinki Federation for Human Rights, supra note 107.

[112] Cynthia Long and Doug Rekenthaler, Jr., "Phoenix-Like, Tuberculosis Rises Again to Threaten World Health," Disaster Relief website (March 26, 1999). Online, available at <http://www.disasterrelief.org/disasters/990319tuberculosis/>, retrieved September 30, 2002.

[113] "Kyrgyz Mull Amnesty for Half of Prison Population," Reuters (December 26, 2000).

[114] M.C. Raviglione et al., "Assessment of Worldwide Tuberculosis Control," 350(9078) Lancet (1997) 624-29.

[115] Ibid.

[116] Kabar News Agency, supra note 33.

[117] ZdravPlus, supra note 44, 43 (noting that the Kyrgyz MOH announced that it is developing an order making FGP doctors responsible for the continuation phase treatment of tuberculosis).

[118] A. Pio and K. Western, "Tuberculosis Control in the Americas, Current Approaches," 10 Bulletin Pan-American Health Org. 3 (1976).

[119] WHO, Treatment of Tuberculosis: Guidelines for National Programs (Geneva: WHO, 2nd ed., 1997).

[120] Expert Center for Social Research (Uzbekistan), supra note 69.

[121] Sue Lloyd-Roberts, "Plight of Kyrgyzstan Brides Who Are Kidnapped, Raped and Abandoned," Independent, March 6, 1999, 18 (arguing economic reasons for the revival of bride stealing). See also, Lori Handrahan, "Political Participation and Human Rights in Kyrgyzstan: Civil Society, Women, and a Democratic Future," 1 Women: Personal is Political, Local is Global (1997) (arguing that the renewal of bride stealing is a form of "political or national expression").

[122] U. Babakulov, "Kyrgyz Women Suffer in Silence," *ISAR* (April 10, 2001). Online, available at <http://www.isar.org>, retrieved September 30, 2002.

[123] Personal communication with Gulnara A. Aipaeva, Kyrgyz Ethnology Dept., American University in Kyrgyzstan, Bishkek, Kyrgyzstan (March 30, 2001).

[124] Expert Center for Social Research (Uzbekistan), supra note 69.

[125] Cynthia Werner, "Marriage, Markets, and Merchants: Changes in Wedding Feasts and Household Consumption Patterns in Rural Kazakhstan," 19 (1/2) *Culture & Agriculture* 6.

[126] "The Stolen Brides of Kyrgyzstan," 341 *The Economist* 40 (1996).

[127] Russ L. Kleinbach, *Kyrgyz Bride Kidnapping: Third Edition* (2001), available at <http://faculty.philau.edu/kleinbachr/new>.

[128] Compare with tuberculosis, which afflicts about 0.5 percent of Kyrgyzstan's population and is considered an epidemic warranting immediate action; see UNDP, Kyrgyzstan: Country Report (2000), available at <http://www.undp.kg/english/country.html>.

[129] Kleinbach, supra note 126, 12-14.

[130] Ibid.

[131] S.A. Baker & B. Beadnell, "The Role of Domestic Violence in Heterosexual Women's Sexual Safety," Nat'l. Conf. Women HIV 122 (1997) (abstract no. 122.3).

[132] Ibid.

[133] CDC, Family and Intimate Violence Prevention Team, Power and Control (September 12, 1998). Online, available at <http://www.cdc.gov/ncipc/dvp/fivpt/spotlite/power.html>, retrieved September 30, 2002.

[134] WHO, Division of Reproductive Health, World Health Day 1998: Maternal Mortality (1998). Online, available at <http://www.who.int/archives/whday/en/pages1998/whd98_01.html>, retrieved September 30, 2002.

[135] Monee Project, UNICEF, Innocenti Center, "Chapter 5," Regional Monitoring Report, 77 (6th report 1999).

[136] See generally, L. Miriam Dickinson et al., "Health-Related Quality of Life and Symptom Profiles of Female Survivors of Sexual Abuse," 8 Arch. Fam. Med. 35 (1999).

[137] American Psychiatric Association, *Diagnostic and Statistical Manual of Mental Disorders: DSM-IV* 4th ed. (Washington, DC: American Psychiatric Association, 1994).

[138] Criminal Code of the Kyrgyz Republic, Normative Acts §155 (1994).

[139] Convention on the Rights of the Child, G.A. Res. 25, U.N. GAOR, 44th Sess., Annex, Agenda Item 108, at 12-13, U.N. Doc. A/Res/44/25 (1989). Signed by Kyrgyzstan on July 7, 1990; ratified on October 21, 1991. International Covenant on Civil and Political Rights, G.A. Res. 2200, U.N. GAOR, 21st Sess., Supp. No. 16, at 53-54, U.N. Doc. A/6316 (1966); acceded to by Kyrgyzstan on October 7, 1994. International Covenant on Economic, Social, and Cultural Rights, G.A. Res. 2200, U.N. GAOR, 21st Sess., Supp. No. 16, at 51, U.N. Doc. A/6316 (1966); acceded to by Kyrgyzstan on October 7, 1994. Treaty for the Elimination of All Forms of Discrimination Against Women, G.A. Res. 34/180, U.N. GAOR, 34th Sess., Supp. No. 46, at 80, U.N. Doc. A/34/46 (1980); acceded to by Kyrgyzstan on February 10, 1997.

[140] "The Stolen Brides of Kyrgyzstan," supra note 125.

Chapter 11

From Rio to Johannesburg: Comparing Sustainable Development in Kazakhstan, Uzbekistan, and The Kyrgyz Republic

Alma Raissova and Aliya Sartbayeva-Peleo

The 1992 "Earth Summit" in Rio de Janeiro led to a conceptual breakthrough in the theory of sustainable development. By agreeing on "Agenda XXI," participating countries laid the groundwork for a new, long-term global partnership. Increased economic growth, social and political stability, and the rational exploitation and protection of natural resources were identified as inter-related and mutually reinforcing components of sustainable development.

One of the reasons the Central Asian states of Kazakhstan, Uzbekistan and Kyrgyzstan participated in the Rio conference was their eagerness for recognition by the international community as newly established, independent governments. They hoped to make themselves known by taking on the obligations of sustainable development formulated at this historic summit. The theory was that the implementation of these commitments would allow the countries of Central Asia to integrate into the international system, and collaborate on economic, environmental and social issues. Unfortunately, this has not happened—or at least not at the pace previously hoped. A decade later in Johannesburg, the World Summit attempted to speed up the process of attaining sustainable development. The result was another set of measures inadequate for the rapidly changing economic, environmental and political situations on the planet. The developed countries did not move far enough on implementing Rio's commitments to fighting poverty and promoting political stability in the world. The remaining countries, unfortunately, also could not live up to their lofty goals. Interethnic and religious conflicts in the Commonwealth of Independent States (CIS) countries speak to the failings of economic and sociopolitical development in these states and highlight the difficulties which lie ahead.

Sustainable development means different things to different people, but the most frequently quoted definition is from the UN report *Our Common Future* (also known as the Brundtland Report), which states, "Sustainable development is development that meets the needs of the present without compromising the ability of future generations to meet their own needs."[1] According to this definition, sustainable development, as well as a commitment to the environment, must include a social and humanitarian context. Hence, sustainable development focuses on improving the quality of life for all of the earth's citizens, without increasing the use of natural resources beyond the capacity of the environment to supply them.

The notion of "sustainable development" in the countries of Central Asia, particularly in Kazakhstan, Uzbekistan and Kyrgyzstan, is usually interpreted from the narrow perspective of environmental protection. The economic, social, and political aspects of sustainable development are given a secondary priority at best. In reality, sustainable development includes three independent elements of equal value and importance: economic, environmental and social:

> Sustainable development . . . assumes that all three of these areas are in balance, harmoniously interacting among each other to create the conditions for a blossoming of the human potential and self-actualization. Failure in one of the areas may lead to an unbalanced society and crisis, and ultimately to an implosion of society.[2]

Figure 11–1. **Components of Sustainable Development.**

Figure 11–1 presents a simplified schematic of sustainable development and its components. It is important to point out that undervaluing one component inevitably will lead to imbalance in the entire system. For example, unemployment caused by differing levels of economic development across the states of Central Asia inevitably leads to poverty, interethnic tension, a decrease in the effectiveness of the economy and disregard for environmental security. Some states, especially recently independent ones, are unable to address simultaneously problems in each area of sustainable development. Clear examples of this are the efforts of Kazakhstan, Kyrgyzstan and Uzbekistan to address the issues raised in "Agenda XXI." In the recent progress review of Agenda XXI implementation in Central Asia, there was a proposal to establish the institutional partnership through a regional agreement for effective management improvement in the areas of sustainable development and security in Central Asian countries. This proposal was supported by the statement of the Interstate Commission on Sustainable Development at the World Summit on Sustainable Development, which proposed "to put in place an economic mechanism and the signing of a subregional agreement" for strengthening the efforts of sustainable development in the region.[3] However, the introduction of economic mechanisms for reaching overall sustainable development goals presupposes the stable development of a market economy and the established institutional framework for using market techniques to reach social and environmental goals in an efficient way. The outlook for how well these countries will transition from the market-economy system perspective toward overall socioeconomic sustainability is uncertain and many policy-makers and theorists are skeptical.

Analyzing social and economic development in Central Asia over the past decade, it is possible to note certain tendencies toward reform in the region. The periods of reform may be divided into two stages. Table 11–1 shows that during the period 1991-1994, the new countries set almost identical tasks for themselves, and consequently achieved very similar results. During this initial stage, the countries attempted to prevent a sharp decline in the gross domestic product (GDP), which averaged about 10 percent annually, fight inflation, stabilize recently introduced national currencies, and control social and political tensions in the region. Reforms were aimed at stabilizing the principal macroeconomic indicators, particularly inflation. As an example, Kazakhstan's annual rate of inflation was brought from triple digits to 60 percent in 1995.

Beginning in 1995, the countries of Central Asia adopted different approaches to social and economic reform, which consequently led to differing results. A summary of these differences is shown in Table 11–1.

Table 11–1. **Stages of Social and Economic Development in Central Asia, 1991-2001 (Kazakhstan, Uzbekistan, and Kyrgyzstan)**

First Stage (1991 - 1994.)	Second Stage (1995 - 2001.)
■ Transition from Moscow-led (Soviet) system of economic management to republican level of management; ■ Introduction of national currency; ■ Establishment of two-level banking system; ■ Price liberalization; ■ Privatization of state-owned property	■ Pension reform (Kazakhstan); ■ Educational reform (Kazakhstan, Kyrgyzstan); ■ Health system reform (Kazakhstan, Kyrgyzstan); ■ Trade policy reform (Kazakhstan, Kyrgyzstan, Uzbekistan); ■ Tax reform (Kazakhstan, Uzbekistan); ■ Discussions on land reform (from state-owned to private property) (Kyrgyzstan, Kazakhstan).

After the financial shocks of the 1997 and 1998 global economic crisis, stabilization of world financial markets and favorable consumer prices led to a global economic revival in the year 2000. Global economic growth in 2000, when compared to the previous year, was up by 4.1 percent. Financial indicators for the majority of CIS countries were relatively stable, owing to improvements in principal macroeconomic indicators, and sound fiscal and monetary policies.

The countries of Central Asia were included in these macroeconomic improvements. Economic indicators of the International Monetary Fund (IMF), the World Bank, and the Asian Development Bank (ADB), all show positive tendencies in recent years in the principal macroeconomic growth indicators. According to the Fitch IBCA[4] investment rating, one of the main reasons for macroeconomic improvements in the region is an increase in national income from the extraction and export of natural resources. While the increase is good news for the CIS countries, it also has a downside. The states' increasing dependence on natural resources, such as oil, natural gas, coal and metals, causes more economic sensitivity to sharp price fluctuations in the world markets and presents budgetary challenges because of the uncertainty. However, it is possible to limit the negative consequences of these fluctuations through both direct government action (establishment of state funds, banks, and development of legislation) and through market-based regulation (tax, budget and monetary policies.).

One regulatory example is the National Oil Fund and Development Bank in Kazakhstan. The National Oil Fund can be used to counteract fluctuations in public finance resulting from changes in world market prices for oil exports. The Fund is modeled on the Norwegian oil fund experience, and managed by the National Bank of Kazakhstan.[5] The goals of the Development Bank of Kazakhstan are to:

- increase the effectiveness and efficiency of public investment activity,
- develop the production infrastructure and manufacturing industry, and
- promote the attraction of domestic and foreign investments into the national economy.[6]

To better understand the differences in approaches to stabilizing sharp fluctuations in the economic development and to establishing a market-based policy system in decision-making processes, it is necessary to examine each of the Central Asian countries in turn.

Kazakhstan

Kazakhstan has adopted a number of measures aimed at moving toward sustainable development. The country actively participates in the "Environment for Europe" and "Environment and Sustainable Development for Asia" processes as well as the preparation of the regional Central Asia Environmental Protection Plan. Active support is also given to the preparation of the Central Asian Sustainable Development Strategy (Subregional Agenda XXI for Asia).

In comparison with other CIS countries, Kazakhstan appears to have done well. There is relative social and political stability, the economy is on the upswing, and considerable attention is being paid to the rational use of natural resources and environmental protection.

Figures 11–2 and 11–3 show that in Kazakhstan, per capita GDP in 2002 was $1,645.80 compared with $382.61 in Uzbekistan, and $321.24 in Kyrgyzstan.[7] However, in spite of the marked difference in the GDP of Kazakhstan from other countries, this does not reflect the level of true sustainable development. As mentioned above, sustainable development should be measured in terms of interrelated indicators, which include social, economic and environmental variables.

Kazakhstan's critical social policy problem is the imbalance between the low level of public funding of the social sector, and the high level of state-mandated entitlements to the population. This is because of the contrast between promised social reforms announced by the government and those actually provided. During the economic crisis of 1998, these discrepancies caused a sharp deterioration in social welfare. Public funding for education decreased to 3.3 percent of GDP; for healthcare to 2.5 percent; and for poverty reduction to a mere one percent. The de-funding of social programs has led to a sharp decline in the condition of the physical plants as well as personnel safety in the education and healthcare sectors. As medical and educational services have deteriorated, skilled personnel have fled to other sectors of the economy and the costs for preschool and daycare, public utilities and other services have increased precipitously. Similarly, cuts in public expenditures for health care have caused a radical drop in the quality and quantity of medical services provided to the population.

Hasty reform of the educational system caused a near collapse of the preschool, elementary and secondary systems as well as professional and technical post-secondary education. The 1999 Education Law, in contrast to the draft 1996 Law, does not include state guarantees for preschool education, nor does it provide mechanisms to guarantee technical, professional and post-secondary education for low-income groups. There are also no provisions for providing student loans, without which, non-subsidized education is much less viable.

Unemployment remains the most serious problem in Kazakhstan. According to best estimates, the unemployment rate in the country may be as high as 30 percent. As a result, living standards have declined sharply. Real income in 1999 was a mere 10 percent of its 1991 level. By way of comparison, in Moldavia, Ukraine and Azerbaijan this figure is 25 percent, while in Russia it is about 50 percent.[8] A large portion of Kazakhstan's employed population has fallen below the poverty line. This, in turn, has caused a substantial reduction in average basic food consumption per capita. In 1999, consumption of meat and meat products, together with milk and milk products was only half of the 1991 level.[9]

One of the more pressing problems in the social sphere remains the "war on poverty," which is one of the main goals of the Earth Summit's Agenda XXI introduced at the Rio de Janeiro meeting in 1992. The poverty index in Kazakhstan shows that 28.1 percent of the population can be categorized as poor, that is, below the established poverty line. The main causes of poverty are involuntary unemployment and the low aggregate income of the population. Anti-poverty initiatives have taken the form of a number of efforts to develop and support small business and open access to capital through micro-credit programs.[10] At present, a new anti-poverty program is being developed with the assistance of international finance organizations and outside donors.

In accordance with the *Program on Privatization and Restructuring of State Property in Kazakhstan,* the vast majority of institutions in the social sphere (health care facilities, educational, cultural and arts facilities) were quickly privatized between 1996 and 1998. The process was completely undifferentiated: The simple sale of all assets took place with no provision for post-privatization financial support, state regulation or quality control. There was also a lack of enabling legislation to codify new relationships in the social sphere. By 1997, for example, more than 70 percent of pre-schools simply were closed.

In accordance with the Social Security Law of the Republic of Kazakhstan passed on June 20, 1997, a reform of the pension system was to have begun. The new pension system proposes a transition from collective entitlement to a more progressive system of individualized retirement savings. However, the transition to a new system has not been well thought out, and the main emphasis on speed rather than equality raises questions as to the viability of the new system. During the first decade of independence, Kazakhstan succeeded in creating a stable and peaceful country and putting in place much of the institutional infrastructure needed for the functioning of a market economy. However, the sustainability challenges of the socio-economic development have been more addressed at the central national level with institutional establishments and regulations, rather than through implementation of the centrally-approved policies/agendas and participation at the lower levels of local administration and district communities. All in all, the challenges which must be faced are daunting and sustainable development remains, at this point, a distant goal.

Uzbekistan

According to official Uzbek statistics, almost all of the main macro-economic indicators are on the upswing. However, foreign observers are of the opinion that the most important economic indicators are inflated by the Uzbek authorities. According to *Frankfurter Allgemeine Zeitung,* GDP growth in 1998 was not the 4.4 percent attested to by the Uzbek government, but a mere 2.5 percent. Individual successes in financial policy, particularly the reduction of the budget deficit to 3 percent of the GDP, were negated by the non-convertibility of the national currency.[11]

Furthermore, curtailment of the free market has led to a decline in direct foreign investment.

On paper, Uzbekistan enjoys the lowest level of "official" unemployment in Central Asia. During 1995-1997, this indicator was 0.3 percent; in 1998-1999, 0.4 percent; in 2000-2002, 0.5 percent. However, most experts reject the official data. The low level of unemployment in the country is explained by the fact that most of the unemployed are not registered with employment centers, and thus are not included in official estimates.

Privatization throughout Uzbekistan is proceeding exceptionally slowly. Implemented for the most part in name only, in the majority of cases, it has not saved the economy from overwhelming government influence, especially in the agricultural sector. Official numbers on privatization are also questionable. IMF data suggests that less than 30 percent of Uzbek enterprises were even partly privatized in 1998. Yet, according to official government information, 45.3 percent of enterprises during that period were in non-state hands.

In a majority of cases in Uzbekistan, privatization of small and medium state-owned enterprises has been completed. However, of those enterprises which have attempted to privatize, most have encountered serious problems. The registration process is exceptionally complicated. Many companies do not have access to foreign currency accounts and pressure from tax authorities remains strong. Moreover, the tax officers have direct access to the bank accounts of any enterprise. As the availability of capital in the country is limited, businesses are forced, in turn, to limit their activities or close shop altogether.

According to official data, privatization of agriculture also is nearly complete. Nonetheless, agricultural labor remains under the dominating influence of the government, just as in Soviet times. Agricultural enterprises and *dehkane*[12] cannot independently select which crops to grow. Seeds and agricultural equipment remain under state control, the harvest is sold to the government at fixed wholesale prices and private ownership of the land is forbidden.

The primary cause behind weak direct foreign investment in Uzbekistan, despite the adoption of new legislation, is the unfavorable investment climate. Foreign investors complain of the numerous bureaucratic hurdles they must overcome to do business and the few guarantees they receive that their investment will be protected from the sometimes arbitrary nature of official decision making. According to Western sources, official statistics issued by the Uzbek Ministry of Macroeconomics and Statistics do not reflect the true economic situation in the country. The data has a tendentious character and is the object of direct state manipulation. Independent observers point to evidence of a deterioration of the social and economic situation in Uzbekistan. In Uzbekistan, until recently, there were two official state-controlled exchange rates: a commercial rate for business transactions and a special rate for individuals. The official rate in 2002 was, on the average, 750 sums to one U.S. dollar; the commercial rate was 990 sums per U.S. dollar. However, on any given day, the black market rate might raise the rate to 1,150 sums for one U.S. dollar.[13] In addition, the government placed a restriction on the purchase of foreign currency for businesses operating in Uzbekistan. All of this represented serious obstacles for foreign investment, trade and business development in the country.

A recent IMF mission to Uzbekistan in fall 2003 brought some positive results. The mission pointed to monetary and fiscal policy dialogues and progress in implementing the Action Plan to Achieve Current Account Convertibility of the National Currency. One of the achievements of the government and Central Bank of Uzbekistan was the successful elimination of all multiple currency practices and exchange restrictions that were previously in place.[14]

Recently, tight monetary and fiscal policies have had some positive effects on the economy, including a decline in the inflation rate and the unification of the exchange rate. The introduction of convertibility provides a solid foundation for further liberalization of the economy, including free trade, agricultural reforms, privatization, banking sector improvement, and mitigation of investment climate.

Uzbekistan has very low levels of import and export activity. Exports increased from $2.8 billion in 1995 to $3.2 billion in 2000, with the highest volume of export reached in 1996. Export revenues come mainly from agricultural production of cotton and wheat. Imports to Uzbekistan are insignificant. As a result, the trade balance for 2000 was estimated at $100 million.[15] Uzbekistan still suffers from the highest inflation rate in the region, which causes further declines in real incomes; as a result, an increasing percentage of the population is living below the poverty line.[16]

Kyrgyz Republic

On January 1, 2002, the total external debt of Kyrgyzstan was estimated at $1.4 billion, while the forecasted GDP for 2002 was about $1.824 billion (at 46.1949 sums to the dollar). In 2003, Kyrgyzstan was supposed to pay out $103.7 million for debt service to foreign creditors. This is the largest annual debt payment in the past decade, amounting to some 50 percent of state income for 2002. According to Ministry of Finance forecasts, the country will not be able to cover all of its obligatory payments; even in optimistic scenarios, the government will cover only about $62 million. The situation is aggravated by insufficient gross hard currency reserves held by the National Bank of Kyrgyzstan. The January 1, 2002 reserve estimates were $285 million, that is, $24 million more than in 2001. However, according to independent estimates at the beginning of the 2003, the reserves actually may be down by $10 to $12 million.

In the early years of independence, Kyrgyzstan pursued a market reform program of liberal policies, agreeing in 1994 to an IMF economic restructuring program. Kyrgyzstan began the first phase of privatization in 1995. The second phase—privatization of medium-sized industry—was suspended in 1997, when it was approximately 60 percent completed, amid allegations of corruption. Privatization was resumed in 1998, and Kyrgyzstan joined the World Trade Organization (WTO) in October 1998.[17] The government still retains ownership of some strategic industries, and although it moved to privatize the telecom and energy sectors in late 2002, these privatization efforts have been unsuccessful, due to domestic opposition combined with a lack of investor interest.[18] Land privatization has had some limited success.

Kyrgyzstan inherited one of the least competitive and underdeveloped economies of the former Soviet Union. This condition was aggravated by weak governance, ethnic tensions, limited access to trade routes, a heavy burden of external debt, and a weak banking sector. The current outlook for the economic situation in Kyrgyzstan is tied closely to the remote geographical location of the country, and to resource endowments—for example, a single gold mine, Kumtor, accounts for 7 percent of GDP.

Some hope relief will be provided by the IMF whose forecasts revised the 2002 GDP growth estimate for Kyrgyzstan from 4.5 to 1.5 percent. As a result, a loan will be provided through the IMF Poverty Reduction and Growth Facility (PRGF). Since December 2002, the IMF already has provided two payments amounting to $30 million, with double that amount promised.

For Kyrgyzstan, however, many economic problems remain unresolved. Positive movement is not apparent in many of the social and economic indicators, and the improvement of others is inconsistent. There are problems with production; arrears in wages, pensions, allowances and stipends; unemployment and underemployment of labor; and the repayment and installment payments for external debt of the state. Low wages, pensions, and social allowances have brought much of the population to the brink of catastrophe. Existing pensions and allowances, as well as the minimum wage, do not provide a minimum subsistence. At the present time, approximately half the population lives below the poverty line, and GDP remains 27 percent below 1991 levels in real terms.[19] Official estimates put unemployment at 12 percent, but multilateral agencies working in Kyrgyzstan estimate the level at closer to 20 percent.[20] Current account deficits have been consistently high and the debt burden heavy, making it impossible for Kyrgyzstan to invest in sectors that would contribute to long-term sustainable development. Infrastructure, education and the health sector have all deteriorated significantly since the collapse of the Soviet Union.

Conclusions

To date, the reforms that have been implemented do not give due attention to sustainable development. The economies of Kazakhstan, Uzbekistan and Kyrgyzstan, first and foremost, were formed under conditions of an inter-republican division of labor within the Soviet Union. In this respect, the national economies of the Central Asian countries are complementary to a certain degree, and self-interest should favor cooperation as a more direct path to sustainable development for all. Moreover, these countries are physically contiguous and share common transboundary economic and environmental problems, as well as common interests in the areas of the rational use of water resources, energy, and land use. Effective solutions to these problems will require close cooperation among these countries, something that has not always occurred in the past.

At the basis of global cooperation among the countries of the world is the concept of sustainable development, which captures the reality of the modern economy. This is reflected in the high degree of interdependence and interactive complexity in economic, social, political, and environmental areas. Globalization provides greater access to markets and wider opportunities for technology transfer, which promises productivity growth and increases in living standards. Globalization also brings with it more competition for locally produced goods, and threats to domestic employment. Foreign capital influences also present some dangers to each country's economy. Capital inflow with significant increases in money supply and unbalanced trade with inflow of cheap imports as well as decreases in the competitiveness of domestic exports due to low-price import expansion from neighboring countries are a concern of all these states.

One solution might be regionalization, the creation of regional economic blocs with the potential to better fit in with the "new niches" of the international economy. As an example, the Eurasian Economic Association (Russia, Belarus, Kazakhstan, Kyrgyzstan and Tajikistan) represents a market of roughly 200 million people. Its vast natural resources and remaining scientific and intellectual potential could allow these countries to develop together new technology-intensive products that could compete in the world economy.

The Shanghai Cooperation Organization (SCO), which consists of China, Russia, Kazakhstan, Kyrgyzstan, Tajikistan and Uzbekistan, has good prospects as well. In this case, internal markets account for one third of the world total. Working with its regional neighbors, as well as with other more distant countries, it is possible to see Central Asia moving along the road to sustainable development. To do this, however, the proper balance must be struck between the economic, political/social and environmental elements of sustainable development—something that has not been achieved to date.

Currently, there is a strong need for new, effective policies for businesses in the commercial sector, and regulatory policies for the public sector in Central Asia. Even in those cases where such policies have been created, the implementation has been weakened, due to Soviet style managerial tools and the lack of information regarding basic concepts of competition, market structure and business performance rooted in central planning. The most constructive mechanisms of change can occur only through a partnership among state actors, private enterprises, non-government organizations, the mass media and the public in general.

When these states realize they must act not as competitors, but as partners, they will better be able to pursue coherent and combined policies that can achieve the goal of sustainable development.

It is reasonable to hope that the Central Asian states will conclude that they have more to gain from cooperation than competition. In the face of common environmental problems (water, land degradation and desertification), economic concerns (trade regulations, unemployment, underemployment of resources, and flexibility of capital and labor movements), and disproportion in social development (poverty, harmonization of legal policies, ethnic and religion identity), common solutions that arise from cooperative action hold the key to success.

Notes

[1] Gro Harlem Brundtland, "Our Common Future," Report from the United Nations Commission, 1987.

[2] Kanat Berentayev, independent expert, Institute of Economic Research, Kazakhstan.

[3] Environment for Europe, Fifth Ministerial Conference, *Invitation to Partnership on Implementation of the Central Asian Sustainable Development Initiative*, submitted by the Governments of Kazakhstan, Kyrgyzstan, Tajikistan, Turkmenistan, and Uzbekistan through ad hoc working group of senior officials, United Nations Economic Commission for Europe, Kiev, Ukraine, May 21-23, 2003.

[4] Fitch IBCA Rating Agency, <http://www.fitchibca.com>.

[5] Kazakhstan Economic and Energy Update. January 29 - February 9, 2001, <http://www.bisnis.doc.gov/bisnis/isa/010222kzenupd.html>.

[6] Decree of the Government of the Republic of Kazakhstan of May 18th, 2001, 659, <http://www.kdb.kz>.

[7] Asian Development Bank (ADB) - Key Indicators 2003 <www.adb.org/statistics>.

[8] Integration in the framework of Eurasian Economic Commission in metallurgy area may increase sustainability of Kazakhstani economy, *Panorama*, no. 31, August 2002.

[9] "Kazakhstani society has the social stratification form of Eiffel Tower", *Panorama*, no. 21, May 2002.

[10] State Program on Poverty Reduction, August 2001, Ministry of Labor and Social Protection of the RK, <http://www.enbek.kz/publik/>.

[11] The Uzbek currency, the Sum, became fully convertible on October 15, 2003.

[12] Uzbek farmers

[13] "Uzbekistan: IMF Ready To Support Tashkent, But Keeping Its Eyes Open", by Antoine Blua, June 2002, Radio Free Europe/Radio Liberty, <http://www.rferl.org>.

[14] Joint Press Statement of the Government and Central Bank of the Republic of Uzbekistan and the Mission of the International Monetary Fund, <http://www.imf.uz/pressrelease3.html>, Tashkent, October 8, 2003.

[15] "Western sources on current condition of Uzbekistan economy", *Panorama*, no. 17, May 2002.

[16] Ibid.

[17] *Economist Intelligence Unit, Country Profile: Kyrgyzstan 2003, Economic Policy Initiatives timeline*, 25.

[18] Ibid., 27.

[19] Ibid., 27-28.

[20] Ibid.,18.

Chapter 12

Land Privatization and Conflict in Central Asia: Is Kyrgyzstan a Model?[1]

Kevin D. Jones

In the summer of 1990 one of the most violent ethnic conflicts on the territory of the former Soviet Union exploded in the southern Kyrgyz town of Uzgen and spread from there to the neighboring villages that sit astride the Kyrgyz-Uzbek border. Lasting almost six days, 171 Uzbeks, Kyrgyz, and Russians were killed, and more than 5,000 assaults, rapes and robberies were committed.[2] In March 2002, five people were killed and as many as 62 wounded when police fired on a crowd protesting outside the city of Kerben, Kyrgyzstan.[3] At first look, these discrete events 12 years apart have little in common. One involves local citizens attacking each other based on their ethnicity; the other centers on government forces responding to political protests. While each event had multiple causes, one contributing factor in both instances was the dispute over the allocation and access to land.

With the breakup of the Soviet Union and subsequent independence of the Central Asian republics, large scale civil conflict was predicted by both regional scholars and State Department officials.[4] In Kyrgyzstan, after more than 10 years of independence, significant advances have been made toward privatization of land and the development of nascent land markets, without widespread civil violence. However, as the events of 2002 demonstrate, widespread inequities exist in the distribution of land, and tensions over these inequities can erupt without warning.

One of the difficulties in identifying indicators for conflict in Central Asia is caused by the extreme fragmentation of the region. Ethnic, religious, socio-political, economic and geographical fault lines exist, yet none of these is likely to cause conflict on its own. Rather, it is the interaction of these issues combined with other influences that could result in the

259

escalation or prevention of civil conflict. For example, existing ethnic tensions combined with the discrete event of a water scarcity could result in civil conflict, or concurrently, economic stagnation followed by the liberalization of the tax policy could prevent conflict through the increase in business and personal worth. One discrete influence contributing both to the current stability and to the potential for conflict in Kyrgyzstan is the privatization of agricultural land.

Each of the five Central Asian countries developed very different paradigms for conducting economic reforms. In comparison with its neighbors, Kyrgyzstan chose to move the quickest to a market economy. The actions and consequences of these efforts provide a unique opportunity to examine the entire process of land reform, as well as the impact of land reform on civil conflict and violence, within the setting of a fractious ethnic environment, poor economic growth, and a weak central government.

In its broadest sense, land reform can be defined as "agriculture policies designed to improve productivity and profitability of small farms."[5] Often, the term land reform is used interchangeably with agrarian reform; however, land reform has a much broader context and is critical to ensuring full market reform. Two other types of reform—urban land reform and water law reform—are also necessary components of full market reform. However, for the purposes of this chapter, land reform will refer only to rural agriculture land.

This chapter provides a concise background on the benefits of land privatization for a rural society, examines the relationship between land reform and civil conflict, and presents a brief history and comparison of land reform in the Central Asian Republics. The primary goal is to examine the process of land reform in Kyrgyzstan and its relationship to civil conflict, with the purpose that lessons may be applied to other countries and regions.

In the context of this chapter, three broad analytic questions are raised:

- How has the land reform process in Kyrgyzstan affected its stability (or lack thereof)?

- What results has the land reform process had on the Kyrgyz citizens' economic and social well being?

- Is the land reform process increasing the potential for violent conflict throughout the region?

Benefits of Land Reform

Privatization of land is a vital component for the development of a functioning market economy. In classical economics, land is one of three necessary factors of production, and the only one that is naturally limited.[6] However, the value of the land is much more than simply the use gained from planting and harvesting; land has a "parallel life," that is, its value as a market asset.[7]

According to legal scholars and land experts, multiple components are necessary for a functioning land market. At a minimum, a nascent legal land market must posses: simple land tenure and ownership laws; land registration with mapping; land evaluation; and markets with open price information; and transparent legal recourse.[8] These components provide a foundation for a legal land market that allows the owner to make informed decisions regarding the use of his land. This, in turn, encourages long-range planning and commitment to development of the land, which is of general benefit to society. The more people who are able to participate in the land market, the more the market's benefits spread beyond the physical plots of land. But none of this is possible without private ownership and a legal structure capable of enforcing and recognizing this process.

Conflict and Land Reform

The history of land re-distribution and privatization throughout much of the world has been marked by extensive bloodshed and violence. In the past century, unresolved issues over land rights and ownership were important components of revolutions in Mexico, Russia, Spain and China.[9] There are almost as many different theories about the causes of conflict as there have been instances of civil unrest, but the two primary theories of conflict are the greed-rebellion and the grievance models.[10] The greed-rebellion model is based mainly on economic considerations and supported by several different studies, which have concluded that economic performance is a statistically significant variable in predicting the potential for conflict.[11] The grievance model states that ethnicity or political tensions are the underlying cause of conflict, which also may be fueled by economic inequalities.[12] These models are not mutually exclusive, and understanding the causes of land conflict can be gained by recognizing the relationship between the two.[13]

Conflicts over land in Central Asia can be motivated by either ethnic or economic causes as well as some combination of both. One way to mitigate either cause is through an efficient and fair allocation of land resources. The next sections look at the process of land reform in Kyrgyzstan and its results on mitigating or exacerbating the potential for conflict.

Land Reform in Central Asia

The history of Tsarist Russia, the Soviet Union and now the newly independent Central Asian states is one of massive upheavals and numerous failed land policies that have left millions of people dead, starving or barely surviving. From the Stoylpin Reforms of Tsarist Russia to the Bolshevik Revolution and Stalin's collectivization program, agricultural land reforms have a long and tumultuous history affecting the lives of millions of rural citizens.[14] In Central Asia, an average of 28 percent of each country's population is defined as agrarian; however, the real number of people who actually depend on agriculture for their primary livelihood is much harder to quantify. This number varies between countries; Kyrgyzstan is just below the average with 26 percent while Tajikistan has more than 33 percent.

The unique geography of Central Asia, with arid deserts in one country and 7000m mountain ranges in the next, has contributed to the unusual way in which agriculture and land policies have developed for that region. Central Asia encompasses a land area of 400 million square miles, with a population of 56 million people living within borders drawn as if the cartographer's eyes had been closed.[15] These geographical obstacles present natural difficulties which directly affect the allocation, management and economic benefit from the land.

One key indicator for measuring the economic benefit and dependence on the land is the amount of Gross Domestic Product (GDP) that is derived from agriculture. Table 12–1 shows some key economic and social indicators for all five Central Asian republics. Kyrgyzstan is distinct in having the greatest amount of agricultural production as a percentage of GDP along with the second smallest total land area and percentage of arable land. Yet in 2000, it was the only country to have surpassed its pre-1990 production levels. Another important variable for evaluating dependence on the land is the amount of agricultural production that is state owned, and the amount that is privatized. In Uzbekistan, almost all of the agriculture process is still controlled by the state, while in Kyrgyzstan the majority of all farm activity has been or is in the process of being privatized. Almost 100 percent of agriculture land in the south is in private hands.[16] The individual farmer in Kyrgyzstan has a much greater stake in obtaining the legal right to land, and in being able to use that land effectively and efficiently. Dependence on the land is cause for intense competition over the dwindling amount of land and water resources available. This increases the need to protect and defend these scarce resources. If legal means are not viable, then physical force or violence may be used.

Table 12–1. **Key Economic and Social Indicators.**

	GDP, (millions US$)	GDP growth, (annual %)	GDP deflator (annual %)	Agriculture, value added (% of GDP)[iii]	Population, ('000)	Surface area (sq km)	Agriculture Population[iii]
Kazakhstan	22,635	13%	13%	9%	14,825	2,724,900	20%
Kyrgyz Republic	1,525	5%	7%	37%	4,967	199,900	26%
Tajikistan	1,057	5%	32%	19%	6,223	143,100	34%
Turkmenistan	5,961	21%	12%	27%	5,293	488,100	33%
Uzbekistan	11,269	4%	44%	34%	25,100	447,400	28%

[i] Data from Food and Agriculture Organization of the United Nations (FAO) and World Bank Development Indicators (WDI) database.

[ii] All numbers for 2001, unless noted.

[iii] 2000 data.

Land Policy Development in Kyrgyzstan

Writing in spring of 2002, long-time regional land researcher and scholar Peter Bloch stated, "If land reform is narrowly defined as an initial distribution of land and other assets from state-owned to private entities, then land reform in Kyrgyzstan is almost complete."[17] If Bloch is right, how has this happened and what does it mean for the potential for civil conflict? Several excellent studies have been conducted which analyze the extent of land reform in the former Soviet Union and specifically Kyrgyzstan, therefore it is only necessary here to briefly summarize and comment on their findings.[18]

First Legal Conceptualization (1990-1995)

In 1990, virtually 99 percent of all Kyrgyzstan land, as well as all other factors of production, were held by the state, and the parliament had passed laws regarding land ownership. The first law was passed in February of 1991, giving authority to local councils to create peasant farms.[19] The second important law was passed two months later and created a land fund comprised of "unutilized or underutilized land."[20]

While many of the new farms were unprofitable, by the beginning of 1994 approximately 10,000 private farms existed, totaling 150,000 hectares of arable land.[21] From early 1994 through most of 1995, important events occurred in privatization and land reform. The government undertook numerous activities and passed several laws. Foreign advisors began to work directly with the government to undertake the first of many extensive field research projects, and advisors from the Land Tenure Center were invited by the government to assist in the development of land reform. This began a process of a high degree of collaboration between foreign advisors, bilateral and multilateral donors, and the government on land reform.

Passage of Modern Land Laws and Moratorium (1995-1999)

In a November 1995 presidential decree, land use rights were extended to 99 years. This decree remained in place until 1998, when in a county-wide referendum, a constitutional amendment was passed which "converted all land-use certificates into ownership documents." This was followed by the landmark new Land Code of 1999 which, while simplifying the process, contained some unusual and hotly contested provisions.[22]

One line in the 1999 Land Code stated, "Purchase and sale transactions of land are permitted, but in the case of agricultural land the right is delayed for five years."[23] This "moratorium" on land sales was an unexpected consequence of the fierce debates in the parliament over moving land privatization forward. The exact reasons for the parliament implementing this change may never be known, but the reasons why they continued to support it for several years provide an important clue to the perceived and actual relationship between land reform and conflict.

Several different stated reasons were given for concern about complete land privatization. Among these were the fear of accumulation of land in the hands of a few wealthy individuals; the desire to prevent accumulation of land in the hands of foreigners; high levels of ignorance by rural population of land rights; and the lack of an existing registration and documentation process.[24] Politics is about perception, and at its root, so is conflict. The perception within the government was that immediate land privatization would spark civil unrest, leading to general violence.[25] Regardless of whether the government was right or wrong in their estimation, the important point is that fear of conflict was one of the motivating factors for many parliamentarians and government officials in delaying the lifting of the moratorium.

Gradual Lifting of Moratorium (2000-2002)

Even with the moratorium, the process of land reform did not stagnate, but moved forward substantially with a presidential decree issued in June 2000.[26] With this presidential decree, the moratorium was not overturned, but instead partially circumvented. The idea was that pilot areas would move forward with complete registration and allow the possibility for the sale and transfer of land in discrete geographic regions. Because of the ambiguities of the law, the presidential decree provided a means for those that were pushing forward land reform.

Until this time, the public was largely ignorant of key policy decisions. On one side, the government of Kyrgyzstan had promised foreign donors and governments that they would move forward with broad land reform.[27] At the same time, many parliamentarians, administrative officials and foreign government representatives still were fearful of widespread conflict, based on the region's history and the potential for inequities in the process.[28]

In January 2001, the parliament passed a law *On Agricultural Land Regulation*, which stipulated the legal purchase and sale of land under the condition of lifting the moratorium. But the actual purchase and sale of lands did not go into effect until September 1, 2001. The new law outlined, that in addition to the state, only citizens of the Kyrgyz Republic who were at least 18 years old and had been residing in the rural area for at least two years, could own agricultural land. The law clearly delineated that no foreign citizen or foreign organization could own land. Many of the limitations on ownership were placed in the law out of fear of Uzbek or Chinese citizens buying land and driving off the local citizens.[29] Yet with the passage of the January 2001 law, it was finally accepted that barring any last minute legal maneuvering, private purchase and sale of agriculture land finally was going to become a reality.

Kazakhstan and Uzbekistan Reform

For a comparison to the success of the Kyrgyzstan land reform it is useful to briefly look at the current status of reform in the other two countries in Central Asia attempting land reform, Kazakhstan and Uzbekistan.

Kazakhstan is an anomaly, in that it has the greatest amount of land area (two times more than the combined land totals of the other four countries), with the fewest number of citizens working on farms. The Kazakh economy does not depend on agriculture or the efficient use of land. Because of this, the country has been quite slow to implement land reform policies. However, in the summer of 2003, through a series of unusual events, the Prime Minister resigned ostensibly because of land reform issues. Whatever the behind the scenes machinations, the President and the Parliament wanted to send a message that privatization of land was now a key policy objective. In his 2002 address to the nation, President Nursultan Nazarbaev made the passage of a new land code a priority. In contrast to the Kyrgyz land process, the Kazakh land reform process was less burdened by fears of ethnic and civil conflict. While there are significant policy differences on the best legal structure for the farms, the contentions are generally between large farmers and small farmers.[30] Because of a stable economic environment and the lack of historical ethnic strife, these problems likely will not result in conflict. Although the Kazakh land reform has started very quickly, one key problem is Kazakhstan's lack of institutional process for the registering, buying or selling of land. In addition, several local Non-Governmental Organizations (NGOs) and institutes opposed the law as a not very well hidden "land grab" by the ruling elite.[31]

Uzbekistan, on the other hand, has resisted efforts at privatization in any areas of production. While a few efforts have been made to break up collective farms, agricultural land reform is virtually non-existent, "with the result that the agrarian sector looks on the surface very similar today to what it looked like in 1991."[32] Accurate data is difficult to obtain on agriculture production, but through individual interviews, the conclusions are that individual workers on farms are much worse off than they were five or ten years ago, with no signs of future improvement. Anecdotal stories tell of entire farms not having received any type of payment—cash or in-kind—for several years. This severe economic decline is driving local Uzbek peasant farmers to go across the border into southern Kyrgyzstan and work illegally, exacerbating border tensions.[33]

Land Reform's Impact on Conflict

The moratorium in Kyrgyzstan on land sales was finally lifted in September 2001. The change in law was not greeted immediately with widespread panic or conflict as had been feared. Yet given the expected potential, two central questions remain from the land privatization process: Are the farmers economically better off now then before the breakup of collectives? Has the tendency toward conflict increased or decreased? Both of these questions demand empirical data that is not available at this time; unfortunately, few field studies of the entire process have been conducted. However, some excellent field work has been done on the rapid rural appraisal technique, which provides significant insights into the current trends in development.

The first trend is toward smaller and smaller farms. As Malcolm Childress, a land researcher, commented, "There is currently no efficient rationalization of resources." Individual farmers are "moving back to farming their own strip of land."[34] This does not imply that it would be better for the farmers to still work on the collectives; however, most farmers are worse off economically then eight or ten years ago. As the national economy continues to stagnate, and off-farm jobs are not available, the individual farmer believes that subsistence farming provides a better living. A very small percentage of farmers are starting to improve their individual situations, but most remain very poor. The second observation is that the majority of people, in spite of their small land plots, appear to accept the redistribution as equitable. (However, there have been some gross violations in the distribution of land). The third observation is that farmers would rather own their own land and be poor, than work on the collectives. As Renee Giovarelli points out the belief is that "there is greater security in owning your own land."[35] While some farmers may speak nostalgically of the stability and predictability of the collectives, when pressed, they admit to preferring their own plots.[36] The fourth observation is that there are few, if any, markets for farm products, so little incentive exists to increase productivity or enhance quality. Most farmers produce enough for themselves and sell any extra in small, local markets. There is little amalgamation or redistribution of produce.[37] As a result of these observations, it can be said that the individual Kyrgyz farmer is poor, getting poorer, but would rather have his own land, and views the process as relatively equitable.

From the greed model of conflict analysis, as individuals get poorer, the probability of conflict would seem to increase. But in Kyrgyzstan, this would-be trend is assuaged by the increase in personal security and independence gained from owning one's own land. At this time, it appears that the tendency towards conflict is diffused, as people focus on increasing and maintaining their small parcel of land.

The lack of significant internal conflict over land also raises the question of the impact of the grievance model or the ethnic disparity factor. It appears that while definite ethnic tensions exist, primarily between Uzbek land owners and Kyrgyz farmers, these have not yet resulted in conflict. However, these exceptions still could provide the impetus for conflict.

Unresolved Land Issues

The primary unresolved issues facing the government of Kyrgyzstan are managing the economic failure in spite of land privatization and the ethnic polarization increased by land privatization. Within the broad themes of economic and ethnic problems, five specific ones come to mind: a scarcity of land in the south; an abundance of land in the north; Uzbeks moving to available land in the north; an overall lack of irrigated land; and the inequities of the land distribution fund. The agriculture land in the south of Kyrgyzstan is almost completely in the hands of private owners. Most of the available arable land is being used, while land in the north, especially the Chi valley, has not been privatized and some available land is not being farmed or managed.[38] In addition, natural market forces cannot provide balance, since the current land law (*On Agricultural Land Regulation*, 2001) prohibits owning land which is more than 50 km from one's residence. This creates a natural tension between the north and the south: lack of resources in one region and the inefficient waste of resources in another. This dynamic is increasing since the southern farmers who want more land tend to be ethnically Uzbek, while the landowners in the north are ethnic Kyrgyz. According to Giovarelli's field studies, "some Kyrgyz say that they would rather have land sit unused then used by Uzbeks."[39] This situation grows more volatile each year as available resources decrease. Unless specific policy action is taken by the government, this is an ethnic and economic flashpoint which could lead to civil conflict.

Another resource problem is the overall lack of irrigated land. Unlike much of Central Asia, Kyrgyzstan is rich in water resources; however, the country lacks the financial resources to maintain irrigation systems. Because of poor or nonexistent management of water resources, land which could be irrigated and farmed is now unusable. The second issue with water is that irrigation lines run between borders. Due to the geographical fragmentation of the southern region, many villages receive their water from pipes which must cross portions of Uzbekistan or Tajikistan. Communities or individuals in one community divert water for their use and prevent the flow into the downstream communities. This situation exacerbates ethnic, regional and economic tensions.

The final unresolved land issue, which is a significant source of tension and potential violence, is the land distribution fund. The land distribution fund was cited by every international consultant interviewed as well as numerous local government officials as one of the most significant sources of tension and problems with current land distribution. The Land Fund consists of 20-25 percent of all arable land in the country, which is set aside to be privately leased through an auction process by the regional governments. In the south of the country, this land is the only new land available to farmers who want to expand their holdings.[40] One key problem has been that the process for allocating this land has not been consistent across regions, as each regional leader establishes their own process and the proceeds from the land sales go directly to the local government. In a time when allocations from the central government are decreasing, sales of land are often one of the few significant sources of income for a regional government.[41] Cravens commented that farmers say that "they [the government] gave us this land, so they can take it away." Because the land is only leased to the farmer and not sold, "it perpetuates the illusion that the government can seize the land, which discourages the development of land and increases waste."[42] To diffuse latent attitudes toward conflict within the regions, the central and regional governments must be perceived as equitable and legitimate.

Lessons Learned and Steps Forward

This chapter began by outlining the benefits and concurrent dangers of land reform, one of many variables which contribute to widespread civil violence and conflict. While it is a potential source of conflict, it is not the land reform per se, but the process of reform, which initiates unrest. This implies that it is both the process which has been successful in mitigating conflict, and the process which must be carefully monitored to prevent conflict in the future.

Lessons Learned

What can be learned from the process of land reform in Kyrgyzstan, and applied to other countries in the region? Four general successful accomplishments should be noted: active internal political debate; a high degree of international assistance; the early creation of the mechanisms for land privatization; and an informed populace. The active internal discussion and debate over land reform policies provided a non-violent forum for resolving many disagreements on land reform in Kyrgyzstan. This does not imply that there was always a unified, clear voice within the government, but rather that the parliament and the President were forced to deal with the issue of private land through political debate. While many of the discussions were behind closed doors and a general lack of citizen involvement was noted, the process did allow disparate views to be heard. As noted earlier, for better or worse, the moratorium was put into place by the Parliament after extensive debate and heated disagreement.

The result of all the international assistance to the privatization process is difficult to quantify. However, the support from a wide range of international organizations and diplomatic missions has provided continued political pressure and financial assistance which has tended to move the reform process forward. Overall, international assistance was critical in the design of the original legal framework for the land laws. While not always in agreement, the international community consistently provided a reference point for the local government officials while they tackled the tough issues of reform. It is unlikely that the land reform process would have succeeded without the international financial support for land registration, the legal advice for laws and amendments, and the training and funding for dispersing information.

Creating and implementing the mechanisms needed for efficient land transactions is still an ongoing process. But without starting this process in the mid-1990s, reaching the point of successful land transactions in 2003 would have been impossible. This is an issue that will affect the process in Kazakhstan. The Kazakhs want to move swiftly toward land privatization, but almost no mechanisms or safeguards are currently in place. In Kyrgyzstan the process is not complete, but it has a solid foundation of laws and practices.

Informing the populace of their rights and responsibilities with regard to land laws is also still ongoing. The information process, initiated and funded by international organizations, has now reached a critical mass, where the average citizen can obtain answers to general legal land questions through a variety of forums. Both foreign and local development workers in country have claimed that increases in information available could raise the possibility of conflict.[43] The argument is that people now know that some of their rights have not been honored. The relative dangers of increasing access to information begs a question too large for discussion here; however, it appears that the growth of legal material available has mitigated conflicts, by providing accurate, timely, and understandable land law answers.

Steps Forward

Enforcement of a fair and equitable legal process and the removal of barriers in the land law which prevent economic rationalization are needed to move forward land reform and the wider development of Kyrgyzstan. While most of the key legal statuary components of the land privatization process are completed in Kyrgyzstan, this does not mean that the process is over or that the responsibility of the government is finished. In many ways, the most difficult part remains—making the new laws a reality. Granting rights is an easy step; enforcing, protecting and honoring these rights is much more difficult. Although Bloch and other land specialists have noted the need for several specific land reform steps to be completed, such as the need for the completion of the registry and functioning secondary markets, broader governmental steps still are required.[44]

If we accept that a fully functioning legal land market is greater than its separate laws, then the greatest need is for fair, impartial enforcement of the current laws by judges and regional government officials. If the population does not believe that they will receive a fair and open hearing, then they will have no interest in pursuing a legal process for their grievances. The former director of the Legal Aid to Rural Citizens (LARC) project commented that in Kyrgyzstan, "only the people with no other alternatives use the law; people with power, money, or connections don't need the law."[45] Calculated arbitrary decisions will destroy any vestige of hope that the populace has in the legal process with the result that they will resort to other extra-legal means to present their grievances. In short, legal reform is as critical as land reform in moving the country forward. Open appointment processes, publicized decisions and accountable judges are but a few of the important steps critical for providing a legal system in which rural citizens feel that their rights are respected.

Agricultural land is being used inefficiently. The government should remove the barriers to efficient economic utilization of land including laws prohibiting certain sale transactions and the restrictions on ownership by region. One way to stimulate economic growth is to allow a broader movement by landowners and sellers to maximize their return and efficiency. Much of the responsibility now lies in the hands of the national and regional government officials. Laws have been implemented and the public's awareness of their rights is growing. Protests and marches increased in the spring of 2002 in the south of Kyrgyzstan, and while the primary concern was over broader political issues, such as support for local politicians, protesters are demanding more land and shouting that their rights have not been honored. A foreign worker living in the south stated that the current civil strife consists of "popular uprisings against years of arbitrariness."[46] The issue for Kyrgyzstan is not the speed of land reform, but the perceived equity of the process and its results.

Land reform historically and empirically has been correlated with civil conflict, and while Kyrgyzstan has been singed a few times, it has managed to avoid the fire of widespread civil conflict. This is a critical time for the government of Kyrgyzstan: They have successfully implemented wide reaching land reform and have catapulted themselves years ahead of their nearest neighbors. The population is learning about their rights and the structural reform process is moving forward. Failure to follow through with fair land allocations or judicial decisions will endanger the entire process.

In any society citizens will have grievances and will seek to express their displeasure with the government on these grievances. As long as government officials arbitrarily can affect the land tenure or security of a rural landholder while the landholder believes they have no recourse to the legal process, land reform will be incapable of mitigating conflict. Land reform can only mitigate conflict if it provides a fair and equitable process for the farmer to increase or stabilize his personal welfare. This is perhaps the greatest lesson that needs to be learned throughout Central Asia.

Notes

[1] Much of the information and data concerning events in Kyrgyzstan is based on interviews conducted by the author or from meetings and conversations where he was present. The author thanks those who agreed to be interviewed and to participate in discussions regarding these events and issues. Where possible, specific attribution is made; however, there were times when, for political or personal reasons, the individuals quoted wished to remain anonymous.

[2] Valery Tishkov, "Don't Kill Me, I'm a Kyrgyz!: An Anthropological Analysis of Violence in the Osh Ethnic Conflict," *Journal of Peace Research*, 32, no. 2, 1995, 133-149.

[3] RFE 21 March 2002, 2, no. 11. <http://www.rferl.org/centralasia/2002/03/11-210302.asp>.

[4] Strobe Talbott, "A Farewell to Flashman: American Policy in the Caucasus and Central Asia," speech delivered at the Central Asian Institute, Johns Hopkins University School of Advanced International Studies, Washington, D.C., July 21, 1997, <http://www.sais-jhu.edu/pubs/speeches/talbott. html>.

[5] John D Montgomery, "Land Reform as an International Issue." *International Dimensions of Land Reform*, John D. Montgomery, ed. (Boulder, Colorado: Westview Press, 1984), 5.

[6] Capital and labor being limited through society's influence.

[7] For a careful analysis and empirical evidence on the amount of capital that is trapped in third-world countries, *see* Hernando de Soto, *The Mystery of Capital* (New York: Basic Books, 2000).

[8] For a comprehensive analysis of legal issues in land reform, *see* Roy Prosterman and Tim Hanstad, eds., "Legal Impediments to Effective Rural Land Relations in Eastern Europe and Central Asia," World Bank Technical Paper no. 436 (Washington, D.C.: The World Bank, 1999).

[9] See Roy L. Prosterman, and Jeffery M. Riedinger, *Land Reform and Democratic Development* (Baltimore: The Johns Hopkins University Press, 1987).

[10] Paul Collier and Anke Hoeffler, "Greed and Grievance in Civil War," World Bank Report, October 21, 2001, 3.

[11] The purpose here is not to present an exhaustive analysis of causes of civil conflict. Unfortunately, the literature is quite weak in identifying key causes through robust models. For a broad overview see Daniel C. Esty, Jack A. Goldstone, Ted Robert Gurr, Pamela T. Surko, and Alan N. Unger, *State Failure Task Force Report*, Working Papers, November, 30 1995 and Paul Collier and Nicholas Sambanis, "Understanding Civil War: A New Agenda," *Journal of Conflict Resolution*, 46, no. 1, February, 2002.

[12] Donald L Horowitz, *Ethnic Groups in Conflict* (Berkeley: University of California Press, 1985).

[13] James Fearon and David Laitin, "Ethnicity, Insurgency, and War," unpublished manuscript, Stanford University, 2000, cited in Nicholas Sambanis, "Do Ethnic and Non ethnic Wars have the Same Causes?" *Journal of Conflict Resolution*, 45 no. 3, June 2001.

[14] For a brief summary of Russian land history see Stephen K. Wegren, *Agriculture and the State in Soviet and Post-Soviet Russia* (Pittsburgh: University of Pittsburgh Press, 1998) and Stephen K. Wegren and David J. O'Brien, eds., *Rural Reform in Post-Soviet Russia* (Baltimore, London: The Johns Hopkins University Press, 2002).

[15] All statistics from World Band Development Index, 2001 or Food and Agriculture Organization, 2000.

[16] In the north of the country, especially the Chi valley, large enterprise reform has not occurred.

[17] Peter Bloch, "Kyrgyzstan: Almost Done, What Next?" *Problems of Post-Communism*, 49, no. 1, January/February 2002, 61.

[18] See the Land Tenure Center at University of Wisconsin and the Rural Development Institute for additional surveys and field research on land reform in the region.

[19] "Kyrgyzstan: Almost Done, What Next?" 54.

[20] Ibid.

[21] Ibid.

[22] Ibid., 56.

[23] As quoted in Ibid., 56.

[24] In several discussions with the author between 1999 and 2000, parliamentarians and government officials privately expressed many of these concerns, but some were hesitant at the time to publicly state their reasons.

[25] Author's interviews and meetings with government officials, 1999 and 2000.

[26] *On pilot projects on land market and registration of rights for agricultural lands.*

[27] Specifically, the President had committed to both the World Bank and the International Monetary Fund.

[28] Author's interviews and meetings Spring of 2000 with U.S. and other foreign officials.

[29] Views expressed to the author immediately after the passage in January 2001 by two senior government officials.

[30] Author's interview with Timour Otobekov, USAID, CAR, EDF, July 7, 2003.

[31] Medet Ibragimov, "Kazakhstan: Land Privatization Prompts Fears," Institute for War and Peace Reporting, RCA no. 142, August 30, 2002.

[32] Peter Bloch, "Agrarian Reform in Uzbekistan and Other Central Asian Countries," Working Paper, no. 49, Land Tenure Center (Madison, Wisconsin: University of Wisconsin-Madison, 2002), 1.

[33] Author's interviews with local farmers and workers along the southern Kyrgyzstan and Uzbekistan border, July and August, 2003.

[34] Author's interview with Malcolm Childress, World Bank, August 1, 2003.

[35] Author's interview, Brian Kemple, ARD/Checchi and Renee Giovarelli, World Bank, June 27, 2003.

[36] Author's interview, Kyrgyz farmers in Osh and Batkin, July and August, 2003.

[37] Author's interview, Richard Tracy, Pragma Southern Regional Director, July 28, 2003.

[38] Kemple and Giovarelli, 2003.

[39] Giovarelli, 2003.

[40] Ibid.

[41] Childress, 2003.

[42] Author's interview with Lamar Cravens, former senior legal advisor to LARC project, July 2003.

[43] Author's interview with local lawyers and two foreign aid workers, September and October, 2002.

[44] Bloch, "Kyrgyzstan: Almost Done, What Next?", 59,61.

[45] Cravens, 2003.

[46] Author's interview with foreign aid worker, 2002.

Chapter 13

Environmental Management in Independent Central Asia

David S. McCauley

O n achieving independence from the Soviet Union, the five Central Asian Republics (CARs) faced a daunting legacy of problems derived from nearly categorical neglect of environmental management in their previously planned economies. While simultaneously coping with the creation of new nation-states and the transition to market-oriented economies, the CARs have struggled to establish new environmental management systems consistent with their economic and social development goals.

Efforts to improve environmental management in the CARs since their independence have ranged from the restructuring of national and regional institutions to enhancing environmental planning and programming at both the country and regional levels. In the initial stages of their transition, emphasis was given to stabilizing and defining a new set of environmental and resources management institutions—still primarily based on those inherited from the Soviet period. Former agencies of the five Soviet Socialist Republics were upgraded to ministries and departments within the newly formed national governments.[1] As in other spheres, balance was sought between central and local government roles in environmental management, though such determinations and adjustments are far from complete. Following the path of other economies in transition, each of the five countries developed National Environmental Action Plans (NEAPs) with international assistance, each varying significantly in their quality and practicality.[2]

Efforts also have been made to develop new ways to handle environmental and natural resources management concerns at the regional level.[3] Building on the NEAPs, a Regional Environmental Action Plan (REAP) has been produced covering high priority transboundary environmental challenges in the region as well as some problems common to several or all of the countries.[4] In 2003, the CARs also presented a common environmental and natural resources management vision for the region[5] at both the United Nations (UN) World Summit on Sustainable Development in Johannesburg and the UN Economic Commission for Europe conference on Environment for Europe held in Kiev.[6] Since the five former Soviet countries previously had been under the same governmental system and planned economy, their efforts to develop new regional mechanisms for the allocation and trade of water, energy, and other resources had a common starting point. However, such regional issues remain contentious and in need of careful analysis and resolution emphasizing mutual interests. Externally introduced institutional distortions which relate to regional versus national environmental management are also present. For convenience, regional international assistance programs often have grouped together issues that are truly regional (such as transboundary water management or air pollution) with national or even local topics that happen to be of common concern in the region.

Nevertheless, the international donor community has played a vital role in helping the CARs emerge from their isolation and come to terms with inherited environmental problems as well as new challenges. Donor programs continue to assist these countries in developing new ways to better incorporate environmental considerations into their transitions to market-based economic development. Whether at the national or regional levels, the primary target of and counterpart for this assistance has been the national environmental ministries or state committees, but institutions responsible for agriculture,[7] energy and natural disasters management also have received important support.

This chapter begins with an overview of key environmental and natural resources management issues in Central Asia. This is followed by a review of environmentally-related policy and program developments at the country and regional levels. Some brief conclusions also are offered concerning common directions observed.

Environmental Challenges Facing the Region

Geographical Characteristics and Determinants

From the days of Amir Timu, or Tamerlane, Central Asia has served as a crossroads for cultures, trade and ideas. It is emerging from the isolation of its colonial period and still holds the promise of becoming a dynamic region of growth and prosperity in the heart of Asia. Bounded by the Russian Federation to the north, the Caspian Sea and Iran to the west,

Pakistan to the southeast, and the People's Republic of China to the east, the five former Soviet countries of Central Asia span an area larger than the Indian subcontinent.

Aside from a densely populated strip across the north of Kazakhstan bordering Russia, most of Central Asia's more than 55 million people reside within the area drained by the two great rivers flowing to the Aral Sea: the Syr Darya and the Amu Darya. The upstream states of Kyrgyzstan and Tajikistan are mountainous and largely dependent upon their agricultural economies, whereas the downstream states of Kazakhstan, Turkmenistan and Uzbekistan show a greater balance between agriculture and industry. Northern Afghanistan also is hydrologically and ethnically linked to the Central Asian states.[8] The downstream countries of Central Asia possess fossil fuel resources—especially oil and gas in the Caspian Sea region of Kazakhstan and Turkmenistan, gas in Uzbekistan, and coal in Kazakhstan—that place them among the most energy rich countries in the world.[9]

The major natural resource and environmental management questions facing the region can be grouped into six areas: water resources management, urban and industrial pollution, land and natural systems degradation, mountain ecosystems management, and environmental management policies and institutions. Central Asian efforts to shape national responses to global environmental challenges also have influenced domestic policies and programs. The remainder of this section briefly reviews current developments relating to each of these topics. Additional detail on country and regional responses in the context of international assistance programs follows.

Water Resources Management

Water and environmental management problems in Central Asia first gained international notoriety in response to the ecological crisis brought on by the shrinking Aral Sea. From 1960 to 1990, the area of this inland sea was halved as inflows were diverted to support cotton, wheat and rice production in the deserts of the downstream states. The results included destruction of a vibrant fishery (including the likely loss of 24 indigenous species of fish), devastation of surrounding ecosystems, and an undermining of the livelihoods and/or health of more than three million people.

The challenge of regional water management for these semi-arid lands is no less acute today. The mountains of Kyrgyzstan, Tajikistan and Afghanistan serve as the principal sources of water for the region (see Chapter 9 by Daene McKinney for full details). If it were not for the mountain relief capturing and redistributing moisture from precipitation (mostly through snowmelt into rivers), the arid downstream states would not be able to support their current populations. The three downstream CARs receive only about 13 percent of the Aral Sea Basin's rainfall but have 86 percent of its irrigated area.

The mountains also hold tremendous hydropower potential, which Kyrgyzstan and Tajikistan are eager to develop. Attention has turned in recent years from a focus on the downstream problems in the immediate Aral Sea region to the need for a stable balance between upstream hydropower and downstream irrigation interests and to wide-ranging issues of land degradation due to water mismanagement. Nevertheless, some steps continue to be taken to address the economic and social hardships facing those living around the Aral Sea. All five CARs have a mutual stake in the establishment of a stable post-independence regional water and energy management regime, and this has become a principal interest of the International Fund to Save the Aral Sea (IFAS) and its affiliate body, the Interstate Commission for Water Coordination (ICWC). Agreements were made in 1992 and 1995 establishing the mandates of these organizations. A landmark interstate agreement on irrigation and hydropower for the Syr Darya River also was signed in 1998 (outside of IFAS), but much remains to be done if long-term stability is to be achieved in these matters. Preliminary interstate agreements also have been reached between Kazakhstan and Kyrgyzstan, covering the Chui and Talas Rivers, and between Kazakhstan and China, covering the Ili-Balkash and Irtysh Rivers.

In addition to water allocation issues, water quality concerns were reiterated as a key issue during development of the REAP. Pollution from industrial point sources as well as municipal and agricultural wastes are causing serious health problems in some locations, especially where communities face shortages of potable water.[10] The heavy silt load of the region's rivers caused by soil eroded from upstream states creates costly downstream problems through sedimentation of reservoirs and irrigation canals. There also are close and confounding interactions between water quantity and quality problems.[11] Chemical, biological and sediment pollution discharged into the Amu Darya and Syr Darya Rivers eventually finds its way to the Aral Sea—aggravating other environmental and social problems from low water flows and further threatening delta ecosystems.

Issues of river pollution crossing international boundaries are commonplace. The salinity of the Syr Darya River is significantly heightened in Uzbekistan before it passes into Kazakhstan. Industrial pollutants flow from Russia to Kazakhstan through the Ural River and from Kazakhstan to

Russia through the Irtysh River.[12] The Chui and Talas Rivers flow from Kyrgyzstan into Kazakhstan, with the former carrying effluents from a paper mill in the capital city of Bishkek and the latter having its salinity increased from agricultural drainage waters. Similarly, the Surkhandarya River is heavily polluted by the large Tursunzade Aluminum Works in Tajikistan before flowing into Uzbekistan.[13] The uranium tailings of Kyrgyzstan have raised considerable international concern because of the risks they pose to downstream river contamination in both Kyrgyzstan and Uzbekistan should poorly constructed containment structures be compromised.

Urban and Industrial Pollution

Pollution problems are not limited to waterways but also extend to the air and to solid wastes. Soviet-period environmental neglect established patterns of urban and industrial development that, even today, pay scant attention to environmental considerations. The exposure of Central Asian industry to market forces has caused many of the worst polluters to shut down, but concern remains high in many communities over urban and industrial pollution. As is often the case, the poorest segments of society generally pay the greatest price for environmental mismanagement in terms of their sacrificed health and quality of life. Industrial pollution in northern Kazakhstan and in Uzbekistan's portion of the Ferghana Valley are of particular concern.

Poorly-contained stockpiles of potentially dangerous wastes, including uranium and heavy metals, have accumulated across the region. Efforts are underway to locate toxic and hazardous waste depositories and to arrange for their safe disposition—mostly through containment, stabilization and isolation, since clean-up tends to be prohibitively expensive. Such pollution continues, especially from the mining and industrial sectors. Mining results in 25 billion tons of waste annually that often is improperly disposed. Current and previous mine tailing dumps occupy vast areas.

A considerable proportion of the region's pollution is associated with energy production and consumption. Significant negative environmental impacts from past oil and gas exploitation—and associated urban and industrial development—are found in the coastal region of the Caspian Sea within Kazakhstan, concentrated around the city of Atyrau, as well as in Turkmenistan. Pressure has been placed on oil companies operating in and around the Caspian to follow internationally accepted environmental management practices for new exploration and exploitation as well as for pipeline construction. While hydropower meets an appreciable amount of the region's peak energy needs, reliance on inefficient fossil fuel-based power plants mostly burning coal and natural gas contributes significantly to urban air pollution and drives Central Asian carbon dioxide (greenhouse gas) emissions per unit of gross domestic product (GDP) to among the highest in the world. This is threatening the region's industrial competitiveness and thus is of both local and global concern.

Land and Natural Systems Degradation

The region faces a host of pressures on the productivity and even viability of its natural systems, especially from inappropriate land management practices. Soviet-period agricultural policies sought to open so-called "virgin lands" in defiance of sustainability principles, and surrounding deserts are now encroaching on many of these areas. Marginal lands face desertification driven by wind and water erosion and exacerbated by the cultivation of inappropriate lands or overly intensive tilling practices, deforestation, overgrazing and windborne salinization especially neighboring the bed of the former Aral Sea. The pollution of otherwise productive arable lands with high concentrations of pesticides and herbicides also is a widespread problem.[14] Radioactive contaminants remain around the former nuclear test site of Semipalatinsk in Kazakhstan and there are other troubling military wastes as well, including those at former biological weapons development sites in Uzbekistan.

Decades of stresses placed on fragile natural systems—deserts, wetlands, riparian zones and mountain ecosystems—have severely damaged, ,sometimes irreversibly, their natural regenerative capacities and reduced the region's biological diversity. According to the REAP, the area of forest in Central Asia has fallen by 75 to 80 percent since the beginning of the twentieth century. Large areas of *saksaul* and riparian forests (*tugai* and juniper) have been converted to arable land. The area of this vegetation in the Amu Darya River basin has been reduced from around 150,000 hectares in 1928 to 22,000 hectares in 1993, and the trend continues. Extinction threatens a growing number and range of indigenous species, with several having been moved from "rare" to "disappearing" status due to various habitat pressures since the collapse of the Soviet Union. Linking biodiversity loss to land degradation processes will be important, as it is likely to constitute a crucial element of future efforts to generate international support for programs to address these problems.

Mountain Ecosystems Management

The sustainable management of mountain ecosystems is of such special concern in the region that it warrants separate mention and action. This is particularly so in the upstream states of Kyrgyzstan and Tajikistan—which straddle the westernmost expanse of the Tien Shan and Pamir Mountain Ranges—though Kazakhstan, Uzbekistan and Turkmenistan each have mountainous areas as well. The predominantly downstream states have a heavy stake in the wise management of mountain areas, given their dependency on these water sources.

Mountain ecosystems provide habitats for a diverse range of flora and fauna and are under a variety of threats, including: overgrazing; cultivation on steep slopes; non-sustainable fuelwood and timber harvesting; introduction of alien and sometimes invasive species; illegal wildlife poaching; and poorly planned development in the transport, tourism, housing and other sectors. The most significant physical impacts are increased erosion and sedimentation of rivers and reservoirs, deforestation, decreased pasture productivity, altered patterns of water flow and loss of biodiversity. In turn, these changes are adversely affecting the livelihoods of mountain communities, who already have the lowest incomes in the region and face a disproportionate degree of threat from natural disasters such as earthquakes, landslides, avalanches, mud flows and floods.

Environmental Management Institutions

While education levels in the region are among the highest in Asia, the environmental management institutions inherited from the Soviet period were rigid and top-heavy. Though well trained, most officials and scientists had virtually no exposure to the development of international advances and thinking in environmental fields over the crucial decades of the 1970s and 1980s when most of the analytical tools and management practices prevalent in the West were devised. Post-independence restructuring in Central Asia also has created uncertainties regarding the roles and responsibilities of various central and local government entities. This has left the region with weak human and organizational resources with which to tackle its wide array of environmental challenges.

All of the Central Asian countries have some form of national environmental management ministry or state committee represented at the cabinet level. These bodies incorporate pollution control functions, and in most cases they also include oversight of the protected areas system and broader environmental planning roles (though generally only a portion of environmental monitoring responsibilities). Except where combined with line functions controlling natural resources management, these environment agencies remain relatively weak. Powerful departments, such as those covering finance, energy, agriculture and industry, have thus far given only limited attention to environmental considerations in development activities despite environmental protection laws meant to be enforced by the environment agencies. The lack of good data and analysis translating the consequences of environmental mismanagement into economic costs also contributes to a weak appreciation for their significance. This indicates that a long road remains ahead for efforts to "mainstream" environmental considerations into economic development plans, policies and programs, and it also helps to explain why Central Asian environment ministries are so keen to assert themselves internationally and tap into newly available aid to address global issues.

A range of regional organizations have evolved to help these countries deal with environmental and natural resources issues. The principal mandate of IFAS—with membership of all five former Soviet states—should be obvious from its name.[15] IFAS recently has undertaken a wider range of environmental and social development objectives in the Basin.[16] Under IFAS, the ICWC serves an important function in managing the seasonal allocation of water for irrigation within the complex array of water management systems and uses in the Aral Sea Basin. Also technically under IFAS, the Interstate Commission for Sustainable Development (ICSD) operates as a standing committee of the finance and environment ministers, though it and IFAS itself suffer from a lack of core professional staff.[17] Partly for this reason, both European Commission (EC)-IFAS and ICSD have drawn upon the recently created Central Asia Regional Environment Center (CA-REC) for analytical and organizational functions on several occasions. However, CA-REC's primary mandate is to facilitate public participation in decision making for improved environmental management, and it is playing an increasingly proactive role in the region, despite the severe challenges posed by civil society restrictions, corruption, and legal weaknesses in most countries of the region. In the past, regional economic integration bodies, particularly the Central Asia Cooperation Organization, have played important roles in helping to broker interstate agreements on environmental and natural resources subjects—covering water and energy management, environmental information sharing and transboundary protected areas management. Today, however, none of the several regional organizations devoted to improving regional economic cooperation and security is much concerned with or able to tackle these issues.[18] The Central Asia Mountain Information Network (CAMIN) was created with much fanfare when Kyrgyzstan hosted the Global Mountain Summit as a culmination of the International Year of the Mountains

(2002). But CAMIN's post-summit goal of serving as a focal point for mountain ecosystem management in the region has yet to be realized.

Global Environmental Concerns

Many of the environmental issues facing the region are large enough in geographic or physical scale to be of concern at the global level. A good deal of attention has been paid to global environmental concerns by the countries of the region—especially their environmental authorities—due primarily to the availability of assistance from international donor agencies on these topics. Certainly the transboundary water management issues of the Aral Sea Basin have attracted strong international attention and financing. As noted, Central Asia also has some of the least energy efficient countries in the world, with associated implications for greenhouse gas emissions and corresponding global interest. The region is now waking to the long-term threats from periodic droughts, desertification, and land degradation, while both its desert and mountain ecosystems represent important repositories of often unique—and threatened—biological diversity. The aftermath of and response to Soviet-period use of ozone-depleting substances and persistent organic pollutants also are of global interest. The participation of Central Asian Republics in the major multilateral environmental agreements is summarized in Table 13-1.

Because of the scale of the water management challenges in the Aral Sea Basin, the international community has supported a wide range of grant- and loan-financed investments under the framework of the IFAS-led Aral Sea Basin Program (ASBP-1). This phase of capacity-building and planning assistance—combined with selected water and environmental management investments—has now concluded. With a mandate from the heads of state of its five member countries, IFAS has prepared a new set of program plans under the Second Aral Sea Basin Program (ASBP-2), meant to serve as a blueprint for further international support to the region's improved water and environmental management.[19] However, neither the Central Asian governments nor their international donors now speak of "saving" the Aral Sea. The new goal is its division—by means of a levee financed by the World Bank—and stabilization to protect what is left of the two delta ecosystems and some measure of fisheries restoration, at least in the northern "Little Aral Sea." Disappointments over IFAS' handling of ASBP-1 and a weak strategic framework underlying the proposals of ASBP-2 suggest that the next phase of regional water and environmental management efforts is unlikely to attract the same degree of international

Table 13–1. Central Asian Participation in Multilateral Environmental Agreements

Agreement	Kazakhstan	Kyrgyzstan	Uzbekistan	Tajikistan	Turkmenistan
Climate Change (GCC)	X	X	X	X	X
Ozone Depletion (Montreal)	X	X	X	X	X
Hazardous Wastes (Basel)		X	X		X
Bio- Diversity (CBD)	X	X	X	X	X
Endangered Species (CITES)	X		X		
Wetlands (Ramsar)		X	X		
Environmentnal Information (Aarhus)	X	X		X	X
Trans-boundary Waters (Geneva)	X				
Persistent Organic Pollutants (Stockholm)	X	X		X	
Land Degradation (CCD)	X	X	X	X	X

Source: Convention Websites

X denotes ratification and/or signature.

interest seen during the 1990s. Thus far, the REAP also has failed to galvanize the attention of international environmental aid donors.

Central Asia's part in addressing the issue of global climate change also has received considerable international notice. Table 13–2 shows that the region has some of the highest per capita CO_2 emissions levels in the world, and its economies are also among the most energy intensive. According to the Pew Center on Global Climate Change,[20]Kazakhstan is ranked second and Uzbekistan sixth in energy use per GDP. The other countries of the region are ranked only slightly better: Turkmenistan–eleventh; Tajikistan–thirteenth; and Kyrgyzstan–twenty-sixth. The energy inefficiencies of the region's economies, however, also have created opportunities for them to engage with developed countries as a global market for greenhouse gas emissions credits emerges. Kazakhstan already has completed a transacion with the Gov-

Table 13–2. **Economic, Demographic and Environmental Statistics for Central Asia**

Country	Population (millions)	Population in poverty (percent)	2001 GNP per capita (US$)	Total land area (1000 km²)	Land in protected area status (percent)	Annual CO₂ emissions per capita (MT)
Kazakhstan	14.70	34.6	1,230	2,717.3	2.7	10.9
Kyrgyzstan	4.97	55.3	300	198.5	3.6	1.3
Uzbekistan	24.78	22.0	720	447.4	2.1	4.1
Tajikistan	6.29	83.0	290	143.1	4.2	1.0
Turkmenistan	5.28	n/a	660	416.0	n/a	7.4
Total or Average	56.02	36.5	763	3,922.3	2.7	5.6

Source: ADB Developing Member Countries Statistical Summary, 2002 (based on published Government data).

ernment of Japan involving the annual creation of 62,000 tons of CO_2 reduction credits, and more deals are likely to follow. Projects for improved efficiency of district heating systems, thermal power generation, industrial production, increased use of renewable energy sources and reduced energy loss from fossil fuel extraction are but a few of those likely to seek funding through either the Clean Development Mechanism or the Joint Implementation window under the Framework Convention on Climate Change and its Kyoto Protocol (assuming it enters into force).

The arid to semi-arid region of Central Asia is defined, in part, by its two great deserts: the Karakum and Kyzlkum. Concern is increasing over the advance of these deserts brought on by periodic drought coupled with unsustainable land management practices. As noted, this process of land degradation is driven especially by mismanagement of irrigation waters, unsustainable pasture lands management, and weak protection of mountainous watersheds. In response, a regional strategic partnership has been formed to prepare and implement national and regional strategies under the UN Convention to Combat Desertification and Drought (UNCCD). This is receiving organizational support from the UNCCD Global Mechanism (GM), the Asian Development Bank (ADB), and the Canadian and German governments, while the Global Environment Facility (GEF) is expected to provide project funding at the country level in the years to come.

Biological diversity losses also are gaining increased attention in the region. The main targets of natural systems protection are mountain and desert ecosystems, the aquatic ecosystems of the Aral Sea deltas and other marshlands, as well as the flora and fauna of the Caspian Sea and its shoreline. Activities are underway with support from the World Bank and GEF to conserve the deltas of the Amu Darya and Syr Darya Rivers. Several transboundary park projects in mountainous areas also have been proposed or are underway. Further efforts of this kind certainly are warranted, particularly in the fragile mountain ecosystems of the upstream states and in Uzbekistan.

While production of ozone-depleting substances has been phased out, concern still lingers over the control of persistent organic pollutants (POPs)—particularly residual pesticides dating from the Soviet period. This topic has only recently begun to receive systematic attention under the initiative of the UN Environment Program (UNEP), and additional effort will be needed to define the POP problems facing the region and to identify and implement appropriate remedies.

Responses to Environmental Challenges

Country Level Trends and Responses

This review would not be complete without a stock-taking of current national and regional efforts to address these environmental and natural resources management problems. Environmental management at the country level is strongly influenced by and correlated with each republic's economic development strategy. There remains almost the same degree of variation in approaches to and progress with environmental governance in the region as is seen in broader political and economic spheres. The country summaries which follow begin with the two upstream states of Kyrgyzstan and Tajikistan and then move to the downstream republics— providing a snapshot of the key environmental issues as well as policy and institutional responses playing out at the national level.

Kyrgyzstan[21]

The basic environmental policies of Kyrgyzstan are embodied in the Law on Environmental Protection of 1999 (as amended in 2003), which includes environmental standards, the establishment of protected areas as well as rules regarding the management of natural resources and disasters. Interpreting the provisions of the constitution, this law emphasizes individual rights to environmental protection, provides for respecting the sustainable development principle, and establishes the structure of regulatory and economic incentives governing environmental policy and the involvement of civil society in environmental management. A list of key environmental laws as an example of how this Central Asian Republic is addressing these concerns is given in Table 13–3.

As in the other CARs, the NEAP adopted in 1995 represents the best overall statement of Kyrgyzstan's environmental policies and objectives. Taking economic growth and poverty reduction as its starting point, the Kyrgyz NEAP lays out a range of environmental management activities meant to contribute to these goals and is particularly commendable in its attempt to develop an environmental policy framework grounded on the use of market-based incentives. Although seminal in its review of

Table 13–3. **Major Environmental Legislation of the Kyrgyz Republic**

Legislation	Main Subject or Resource Protected	Year Passed (Amended)
Law on Specially Protected Areas	Parks and reserves	1994
Law on Waters	Water and floods	1994 (1995)
Law on Fisheries	Fish habitats	1997 (1998)
Law on the Subsoil	Mining rehabilitation	1997 (1999)
Law on Biosphere Territories	Biosphere reserves	1999
Law on Drinking Water	Water quality	1999 (2003)
Law on Protection of Ambient Air	Air quality	1999 (2003)
Forest Code	Forest management	1999 (2003)
Law on Radioactive Safety of the Population	Radioactive hazards	1999 (2003)
Law on Ecological Expertise	Projects and EIAs	1999 (2003)
Law on Wildlife/Fauna	Endangered species	1999 (2003)
Law on Environmental Protection	Basic protections	1999 (2003)
Land Code	Land management	1999 (2003)
Law on Chemicalization and Plant Protection	Pesticides/agrochemicals	1999 (2003)
Law on Protection of Historic & Cultural Heritage	Cultural preservation	1999
Law on Protection and Use of Flora	Biodiversity conservation	2001
Law on Tailings Ponds and Dumps	Tailings management	2001
Law on Waste Production and Consumption	Waste management	2001

Sources: UNECE, 2000 and www.law.gov.kg.

environmental management priorities and pragmatic in tone, the now-dated NEAP has served as only a very broad guidance document for environmental policy development in the country. Nevertheless, many of its overall recommendations have been implemented or otherwise have helped to shape the strong evolution of the country's environmental laws and regulations.

The Ministry of Environment and Emergency Situations (MEES) is the lead executive branch agency for the environment subject, with its minister serving as the principal environmental advocate within the cabinet. MEES is directly responsible for implementing provisions of the Law on Environmental Protection, as well as environmental standards and regulations associated with most other environmental legislation that is not specifically tied to a line ministry or delegated to the President's Office, including environmental monitoring and impact assessment. Committees on Environmental Protection at the oblast and city levels complement these national institutions, and the country continues to undergo a decentralization process that is encouraging ever greater self-governance at the regional and local levels. Several other government agencies and ministries also play crucial roles in environmental and natural resources management—most notably the Ministry of Agriculture, Water Resources, and Processing Industry and the State Forestry Service.

Both the legislative and judicial branches of government also are awakening to new roles in environmental governance in Kyrgyzstan. As demonstrated by the proliferation of new environmental laws, it is clear that these subjects are receiving a high degree of attention from the national parliament. The Parliamentary Commission on Agriculture and Environment serves as the lead body for the legislative branch. Attention to environmental subjects has been less prevalent in the judicial branch, though this too is growing. Thus far an environmental/green bench within the judiciary has had only limited development, though several successful environmental cases have been brought to court in recent years. This represents a significant institutional challenge, however, because of more generic shortcomings of the Kyrgyz legal system.

Though considerable challenges remain, the Kyrgyz Republic is the most open to civil society participation in decision making—including environmental—within Central Asia. There are many non-governmental organizations (NGOs) with environmental and/or natural resources management interests, ranging from scientific and educational groups to those exercising advocacy functions. Though there is room for even further government transparency and collaboration, environmental NGOs have participated in the debate on environmental policy since the 1995 NEAP exercise and have helped to shape the many environmental laws passed since 1998.

Depite the country's impressive array of environmental laws and regulations, weak enforcement remains a serious constraint to the protection and sound management of natural resources and protection of environmental quality. Some existing regulations and incentive structures are inherently difficult to enforce, but capacity constraints among responsible government institutions—coupled with severe funding shortages and corruption—lie at the core of this problem. Despite attempts to improve data collection and management, shortages of accurate, timely and appropriate environmental information to assist decision making continue.

While a range of programs are financed as a part of government agencies' routine activities, the most visible responses to environmental protection and management needs are those involving international cooperation. Many of these have been linked with the country's fairly active participation in global affairs associated with multilateral environmental agreements. In particular, several capacity-building activities have been funded by the Global Environment Facility (mostly through UNDP). These are meant to strengthen the institutions responsible for overseeing the country's participation in global conventions, such as those covering climate change, land degradation and biodiversity conservation. The country consistently has called for international aid to help it address the high national and regional risks associated with poorly contained uranium tailings inherited from the Soviet period, and the World Bank and the Organization for Security and Cooperation in Europe (OSCE) now are leading a coordinated donor response. Kyrgyzstan has been something of a trend-setter in the region with regard to market-oriented land reform and restructuring of water management at the local level, with World Bank and ADB projects serving as the principal vehicles for developing demonstration activities and replicating them at the oblast and national levels.

Tajikistan[22]

Though Tajikistan's policies and institutions have deviated somewhat from those of Kyrgyzstan since independence, these mountainous neighbors share many of the same environmental and natural resources management problems. Unfortunately, Tajikistan's post-independence political struggles have diverted attention and resources away from natural systems and resources management. There also has been a significant inflow of international aid coupled with better communications since the end of the civil conflict, and these have strongly affected the country's ability to respond to environmental management challenges. Civil society's participation is relatively high, and this includes involvement in both the debate over and actions to address environmental concerns.

The country still lacks a clear set of environmental policies and programs to guide government and private interventions. Though considerable analysis and dialogue has been devoted to determining environmental action priorities, little consensus has emerged. More important, the fundamental land and water resources underpinnings of the economy are only weakly recognized. The prevailing policy view seems to be that environmental management can be adequately handled by the Ministry of Nature Protection. Though this Ministry is doing its best with limited staff and funds, it has only weak influence over the more powerful interests governing urban and rural development in the country. The State Environment Program (1998-2008) deals with general principles and goals but does not offer an implementable strategy for improving environmental and natural resources management in the context of efforts to promote economic growth and alleviate poverty. While the development of a NEAP could potentially help, this ongoing exercise again has been concentrated largely within the network of the Ministry of Nature Protection and delayed by differences over its scope and structure.

The considerable international assistance rendered to the country also has not made a substantial contribution to improving the coherence of either environmental policies or programs. Though some local-level initiatives have produced promising results, these have been poorly documented and seldom replicated. National-level assistance has been highly fragmented, and much of it has centered on Tajikistan's role in addressing regional or global concerns with only weak attention to national or local priorities. This includes such topics as biodiversity conservation, land degradation, climate change and waste management.[23] Reliance on donor support for environmental analysis and programming also has undermined nascent efforts to establish routine government funding channels for environmental and natural resources management topics through line ministries or the legislature.

The key to progress in Tajikistan—as elsewhere in the region—will be incorporating an understanding of and concern for sound environmental and natural resources management into the mainstream of economic development planning, policy-making and programming. This principle is gradually coming to be understood, though it requires a departure from the traditional patterns of designing "environmental" projects and

the conduct of environmental analysis in isolation from economic planning and programming of development resources for key sectors such as
agriculture and energy. The Ministry of Nature Protection appreciates
the importance of its reaching out to the government bodies—executive
or legislative—which govern such economic interests and using its links
to civil society to advocate for expanding attention to the environmental
underpinnings of the country's development path.

Kazakhstan[24]

Kazakhstan is set apart from the other CARs on the basis of several
characteristics. Its sheer size and oil-based economic growth are perhaps
the most important distinguishing factors. Along with Kyrgyzstan, it
also has embraced open-market policies to a much greater extent than
its neighbors. Despite its geographic scope, population densities remain
low—further affecting its special circumstances.

The country's natural resource base remains degraded from unsustainable practices dating from the Soviet period. The "virgin lands" policy
opened many semi-arid steppe regions to agricultural production beyond
their long-term potential.[25] Mining wastes in the East, industrial pollution
in the Northeast, oil industry pollution in the West along the Caspian,
and land degradation in the South present a diverse and far-flung set of
environmental challenges.

Isolated rural populations cut off from Soviet-era subsidies are
struggling to survive, and agricultural production has fallen substantially
since independence. Efforts such as the World Bank/GEF-funded Drylands
Management Project are testing the environmental, social and economic
viability of shifting from currently unsustainable cereal-based agricultural
production systems back to traditional livestock-based systems.[26] Decentralized and renewable energy systems also are receiving increased attention as potential means for overcoming rural productivity losses and the
high cost of keeping distant communities linked to the national electricity
grid.

Kazakhstan enjoys by far the highest level of foreign investment
among the CARs, and—though environmental regulation of industry
remains a contentious issue—interactions with multinational firms are
leading to a gradual adoption of internationally-accepted environmental
management norms. This is most clear in the oil and gas industry located
along the Caspian Sea, though international firms are balking at being
asked to clean up pollution problems left over from Soviet times.

After a period in which the government mixed responsibilities for both resource extraction and environmental regulation under a large umbrella ministry, these functions now have been divided. Regulatory authorities under the Ministry of Environmental Protection are gradually gaining some ability to enforce compliance with environmental laws despite continuing and widespread corruption. As elsewhere in the region, environmental considerations are only weakly incorporated into—or even acknowledged by—development plans and programs of key sectors such as energy, transport or agriculture. The formation of a National Sustainable Development Council to coordinate such mainstreaming efforts holds some promise. Some indications show progress being made in some areas, since both the intensity of pollution and energy use per unit of GDP have begun to fall.

At the regional level, Kazakhstan continues a strong policy of political engagement and economic integration with its neighbors (though not limited to the CARs). Consistent with this stance, it has been perhaps the most solid member of IFAS from the start and is taking direct measures to address the ecological crisis in its territory surrounding the former boundaries of the Aral Sea, particularly with assistance from the World Bank. It also is working with neighboring China and Kyrgyzstan on bilateral river basin management issues—having concluded agreements governing the Ili-Balkash and Chui-Talas Basins, respectively. Kazakhstan also actively participates in the Caspian Environmental Program.

The country is an often vocal participant in meetings of the major multilateral environmental agreements, and, as noted in Table 13-3, is a signatory to most. This stance has attracted considerable international assistance to develop national assessments and action plans for national compliance with agreement provisions—sometimes distracting from higher priority domestic concerns.

Turkmenistan

Like Kazakhstan, Turkmenistan is well endowed with oil and especially gas resources, but continued reliance on a planned economy and rigid political and social controls have limited foreign trade and investment. The country's political and economic isolation places it at something of a disadvantage within the region with respect to its access to international expertise and assistance to improve environmental and natural resources management. While a few NGOs have begun to address environmental issues, the scope of their influence is limited by the closed attitudes of the government toward the participation of civil society in public policy debate. Government agencies—including those managing natural resources and meant to protect the environment—are often tentative in their decision making due to rigidities in the authoritative structure.

Most of the country is uninhabitable desert, and the population is largely concentrated along the courses of the Amu Darya River and the Karikkum Canal which supports the capital, Ashgabad. Turkmenistan is almost completely dependent upon water flowing from its upstream neighbors, so it has an enormous stake in efforts to improve regional water cooperation. Nevertheless, it has been a reluctant partner within IFAS and other regional mechanisms promoting regional cooperation on resources management.[27] It also inherited significant land degradation challenges from the Soviet period. These comprise waterlogging and especially salinization in agricultural areas due to over-irrigation and severe drainage problems—with half of the country's irrigated lands considered to be in an unsatisfactory state.[28] The rapidly growing urbanized population also is posing increasing challenges for adequate provision of water supply and wastewater management. The country is still prone to grand construction schemes, and the proposed creation of an enormous "Golden Lake"—as a collector of agricultural drainage water just upstream of the Aral Sea and for uncertain additional uses—has been met with skepticism in the region and beyond.

A NEAP was completed in 2002, and it has begun to shape thinking about priorities for incorporating environmental considerations into national economic development plans. An ecological information network also is expanding. Much of the NEAP centers on addressing the severe land degradation problems. Though the NEAP is an important forward step, much remains to be done if it is to receive broader ownership among key government and civil society stakeholders as a necessary basis for its implementation.

Uzbekistan

Uzbekistan is able to support the largest population in the region in large measure because of the fertility of the irrigated Ferghana Valley and, more generally, due to the abundance of water resources flowing through its predominantly arid landscape. Its territory straddles the courses of the Amu Darya and Syr Darya Rivers. Yet its ability to maintain land and water management systems is increasingly threatened by severe resource degradation—due largely to mismanagement of irrigated agriculture for cotton and wheat production—coupled with intensifying regional competition over shared water resources. The most extreme problems are in the Autonomous Region of Karakalpakstan, where the Amu Darya meets the Aral Sea. Here drought and desertification have combined with the dislocations associated with the Sea's desiccation to impoverish most of the population.[29]

Beyond the constraints on rural development imposed by land degradation, the country also faces a range of environmental problems affecting the health and productivity of urban populations. These include air pollution, industrial water pollution, deteriorating infrastructure for wastewater collection and treatment, weak systems of solid waste management, and energy-related environmental issues. Although both air and water pollution from industrial sources has declined since independence (with the fall in heavy industry's output), there remain localized pockets of air pollution that can have wide-ranging impacts when atmospheric inversions trap pollution for days on end. Likewise, some areas immediately downstream of operating industries suffer from poor water quality. Problems from industrial air pollution are exacerbated by weakly controlled and gradually expanding vehicular pollution sources. Uzbekistan's air pollution problems would be far worse were it not abundantly endowed with natural gas which is widely utilized as the principal energy source—except for vehicles—throughout the country.[30] Though Uzbekistan had one of the most developed urban water supply and wastewater collection and treatment systems in the former Soviet Union, maintenance and management have suffered in recent years with a corresponding decline in service. A similar pattern may be seen with respect to solid waste management.

The "ecological safety" of the young and rapidly growing population[31] is guaranteed by the Constitution, and environmental legislation since independence has emphasized this notion along with generally accepted principles of environmental protection and rational natural resources use. The State Committee for Nature Protection serves as the lead government body in implementing environmental laws and regulations, but it is weak relative to, for example, the powerful ministries governing agriculture/water, industry, and energy. It also shares responsibilities for monitoring and managing air and water quality with other agencies such as the hydrometeorological service—often competing for budgetary and project resources. The strong scientific base in the country has led to perhaps the most rigorous analysis of environmental problems and processes in the region. However, environmental policy-making remains fragmented and outside of the mainstream of economic planning structures, which have changed only marginally since the Soviet period. Further, the high degree of state control has limited the participation of NGOs and other elements of civil society, including the media, in environmental planning and decision making.[32]

The country has been a sometimes reluctant partner with its neighbors in addressing regional environmental and natural resources challenges. A core member of IFAS, Uzbekistan has not lent strong support to its efforts since the EC-IFAS secretariat moved from Tashkent in the late 1990s. It became a signatory to the 1998 Framework Agreement on the Syr Darya River's management, but it subsequently ceased participating in the associated energy-for-water swaps. In 2003, it hosted discussions on land degradation in the region under the auspices of the Strategic Partnership for UNCCD Implementation in Central Asia, and efforts are underway to lay the groundwork for a tougher domestic policy stance on addressing severe land and water management problems. It has taken part in discussions under the framework of the REAP, but has made little commitment to implement projects emanating from the planning exercise. A recently created regional environmental planning integration and information networking activity supported by ADB achieved buy-in from all CARs except Uzbekistan. While the country hosted the ADB-organized Second Ministerial Conference on Central Asian Regional Economic Cooperation held in late 2003, it vetoed inclusion of reference to the obvious connections between water and energy in the Ministerial Statement. More than any of its neighbors (save Turkmenistan), it has viewed regional cooperation from a position of very narrow national self-interest.

Its highly scientific approach to problem analysis can be seen in the country's responses to its obligations under the key multilateral environmental agreements to which it is party. A National Strategy and Action Plan for Biodiversity Conservation was produced in 1998. A National Action Plan for implementation of the UNCCD was finalized in 1999, and an Initial National Communication under the Framework Convention on Climate Change was completed in 2001. All three of these documents place a strong emphasis on documenting the environmental problems in technical terms and scientifically identifying the underlying ecological or bio-physical processes. Conversely, they are weak in their analysis of poverty-environment linkages and the root causes of environmental problems lying in past and current government policies. These documents—and the planning exercises that led to them—are similarly lacking in strategic thinking concerning appropriate policy and institutional responses. Such weaknesses pervade the environmental governance atmosphere and need to be directly addressed if Uzbekistan is to incorporate environmental considerations into its economic development and poverty alleviation planning—taking full advantage of its scientific skills and relatively strong information base to address the wide range of environmental and natural resources management problems it faces.

International Assistance

Improving land and water resources management in the region remains the highest priority for international environmental assistance to Central Asia. The World Bank has been perhaps the most active multilateral aid agency, having served as the lead donor for ASBP-1. In addition to the analyses under ASBP-1, the World Bank's land and water management programming has included country-level investments in the irrigation sector as well as a project to divide the remainder of the Aral Sea into two parts.[33] It also has produced an insightful review of agricultural water use and needed reform measures in the CARs.[34] The ADB is playing an active role in encouraging greater regional economic integration, and it also has provided considerable environmentally-related technical assistance to the CARs—including for improved water management.[35] The ADB sponsored Central Asia's participation in the third World Water Forum of 2003 and co-sponsored the 2003 Forum on Strategic Partnership for UNCCD Implementation in Central Asia. It remains actively engaged in various efforts to address water, land and environmental management problems at the local, national and regional levels. UNDP has made regional water management one of three focal areas in its environmental program for Central Asia—centering efforts on strengthening the institutional, programming and legal framework for water resources management by assisting EC-IFAS with completion of the ASBP-1 problem analysis and helping to formulate a coherent ASBP-2.[36] The EU[37] has begun a third phase of regional water assistance focusing on demonstrating principles of integrated water management in pilot sub-catchments.[38] The OSCE is leading an activity supporting creation of a Joint Commission for the Chu and Talas Rivers, and also is involved in an Environment and Security Initiative dealing with regional water issues.[39] The Global Water Partnership's Caucasus and Central Asia program is also building regional relations to support improved integrated water management.

Several bilateral aid agencies also are assisting at the regional level. Among others, the U.S. Agency for International Development (USAID) provided the aid that led to the initial brokering of the 1998 Syr Darya Framework Agreement as well as much of the core international environmental assistance to the region in the immediate post-independence period. USAID no longer supports environmental management programs and most of its water management activities—other than a modest regional effort on the upper Syr Darya Basin—have now shifted to field-level demonstrations of irrigation systems and hydrological monitoring. The Swiss Agency for Development Cooperation is supporting a multi-year pilot-level effort on integrated management of internationally shared canals in the Ferghana Valley, involving the Kyrgyz Republic, Uzbekistan, and Tajikistan, and the German development aid agency (GTZ) has a region-wide program to address land degradation problems dealing extensively with salinization and waterlogging. The Canadian International Development Agency also has been active, though its programs are now almost exclusively focused on alleviating poverty in Tajikistan as the poorest Central Asian country.

The Central Asian REAP represents another effort to identify and organize responses to high priority environmental problems of regional significance. The REAP was initiated in 2000 with financial and institutional support from UNEP, ADB, and UNDP. It began by identifying "regional" problems in five areas: air pollution; water pollution; land degradation; waste management; and mountain ecosystem degradation. Project concepts were developed in each of these five areas, and regional work groups were to have prepared and overseen the funding and implementation of corresponding projects or programs. A number of the project ideas generated under the REAP framework also are not necessarily "regional" in nature (requiring interstate cooperation for their solution), but rather constitute problems common to two or more countries. The lack of emphasis on truly regional environmental issues, such as those of an obvious transboundary nature, has interfered with efforts to appropriately focus institutional attentions and resources. Progress with funding and implementing these projects has lagged, while considerable attention has been expended in further discussion and planning at the national and regional levels. This is partly due to the Interstate Commission for Sustainable Development (ICSD) having been entrusted with guiding REAP implementation; during this period ICSD has been struggling to get itself fully operational. In response to the institutional constraints encountered, the focus of Central Asian REAP teams as well as the key donors (UNEP and UNDP) has shifted to establishing the enabling conditions for REAP implementation through: creating a mechanism to support regional environmental cooperation in Central Asia; developing a REAP decision support system; encouraging stronger public awareness of and participation in REAP-related activities; and building capacities for REAP implementation. Despite these constraints, a proposal has been submitted by UNEP to the GEF for the financing of further REAP organizational activities.

Mountain ecosystems management is another environmental problem area that has attracted considerable regional as well as international attention. As noted, Kyrgyzstan played host in 2002 to the Bishkek Global Mountain Summit, which capped a series of events around the world marking 2002 as the International Year of Mountains.[40] A detailed strategy and action plan for sustainable mountain areas development was developed for Kyrgyzstan that was meant to serve as a model for similar national plans covering all five CARs,[41] and several papers at the Mountain Summit outlined the threats to fragile mountain ecosystems in the region—including the proposition that the region's glaciers are receding rapidly and contributing to a troubling over-estimation of available freshwater resources in the Aral Sea Basin. Though global in scope, the Bishkek Mountain Platform that resulted from the meeting was significantly shaped by the Central Asian experience and venue of the Summit.[42] Unfortunately, meaningful follow-up has not occurred at the national or regional levels, and international attention to the subject has waned somewhat after the conclusion of the Year of Mountains. Effectual responses also have been inhibited by land tenure conflicts, security concerns and a confusing array of government jurisdictions in the region's mountainous areas.

The international community, including particularly the World Bank, EU and UNDP, already has invested heavily in regional institutions for natural resources and environmental management. EC-IFAS has received considerable support through the ASBP-1, though questions within the donor community about the likely effectiveness of the ASBP-2's strategic framework have thus far limited further substantial international support. The ICWC under IFAS has continued to function as a committee of the region's water ministers while its Scientific Information Committee (SIC-ICWC) has cobbled together assistance from a variety of sources to support ICWC decision making and the training of water professionals in the region. The network of national REAP working groups represents yet another effort to establish institutional capacity for improved environmental management at the regional level, but the REAP's progress is being constrained by continuing concerns over ICSD's ability to oversee project implementation. There are corresponding networks of national focal points covering each of the global environmental agreements to which all CARs are party (climate change, land degradation, biodiversity, and ozone depletion). Another recent innovation at the regional level has been the creation of the CA-REC in Almaty, chartered by agreement of the five states at the Aarhus Ministerial in 1998. CA-REC, working with EC-IFAS and ICSD, has conducted analyses of regional issues and helped to catalyze preparations for international environmental meetings such as the WSSD and the UNECE Environment for Europe ministerial conference. Some regional stakeholders believe this may have detracted somewhat from CA-REC's mandated responsibility to facilitate public participation in environmental decision making.

Finally, although only Kazakhstan and Turkmenistan—among the CARs—are littoral states of the Caspian Sea, their active participation in the Caspian Environmental Program (CEP) should be noted.[43] The CEP was established to coordinate the resource management actions of the five countries bordering the Caspian Sea, interact with efforts under the Ramsar Convention on the protection of wetlands and, more generally, "to halt the deterioration of environmental conditions of the Caspian Sea and to promote sustainable development in the area".[44] The CEP inter-governmental process is primarily supported by the GEF, UNDP, World Bank, UNEP and the EU, but it also includes cooperation with the private sector—particularly the oil and gas industry. CEP has developed and adopted a Strategic Action Program for the protection and rehabilitation of the Caspian environment covering high priority environmental concern areas as well as helping each littoral state develop its own National Caspian Action Plan. This has proven to be quite positive for Kazakhstan and Turkmenistan, as participation in CEP has led both nations to adopt enhanced pollution control measures in their oblasts bordering the Sea.

Conclusion

Since achieving their independence, all Central Asian countries have sought to improve their understanding of environmental and natural resources constraints on their economic development. Varying efforts also have been made to strengthen policy and institutional responses to these challenges. The need for much more effective plans, policies and programs to address land degradation and water mismanagement is an important recurring theme in the region, while environmental dimensions of urban and industrial restructuring also are receiving increased attention. The capacity of most environmental agencies has been improved, and it is becoming more widely accepted that environmental considerations must be built into all aspects of economic and social reform. Broader results will require further outreach to government agencies directly charged with resource management, such as those managing the agriculture and energy sectors.

At the regional level, institutions have been formed and initiatives undertaken to address problems of common concern to the region. Most prominent among these are efforts to address the Aral Sea crisis through IFAS. More recently the REAP process has sought to identify other transboundary or common environmental problems for action through the IFAS subsidiary ICSD. The Strategic Partnership for Implementation of the UNCCD in Central Asia is becoming an important mechanism for coordinating efforts to address land degradation in the region. Institutions such as CA-REC have much to offer as resource bodies to encourage more active dialogue between government and civil society, though the rigid political atmosphere pervasive in the region continues to inhibit a participatory approach to developing and implementing environmental policies.

After quickly joining most of the key multilateral environmental agreements, Central Asian countries have taken advantage of available funding to prepare associated national strategies. Some of this analysis—such as air pollution assessments tied to the climate change treaty—have had positive cross-over benefits of improved understanding of the domestic costs of pollution and inefficient resource management. Others have had weaker links to national environmental issues, and some even have distracted attention from higher priorities at home. Few of the efforts addressing global environmental issues have engaged those policymakers most responsible for managing the resources or allocating funds to improve their management, though more recent initiatives have sought to rectify this shortcoming.

Each of the Central Asian countries faces its own set of social, economic and environmental challenges, but they also share a common heritage and many mutual development goals. Socio-political development varies greatly among the countries, and the degree of market orientation and transparency exhibited in environmental management efforts tends to mirror broader country-level trends. This suggests that environmental management gains should result from broader governance improvements, and that environmental considerations need to be woven into the very fabric of economic development policies and programs. This must go beyond mere pronouncements, the publishing of national action plans or even legislative reform to encompass fresh political will and the accompanying resources needed to realize real change. With proper attention to the strengthening of key environmental management institutions, to using renewable natural resources only within their sustainable limits, to avoiding adverse environmental impacts from other forms of development, to reducing waste while improving economic efficiency and to encouraging public engagement in decision making regarding these matters, the page can be turned on the old story of environmental neglect and a new chapter opened to wise environmental and natural resources management forming the basis for healthy and prosperous societies in the lands that straddle the Great Silk Road.

Notes

[1] The State Committee structure was retained in Uzbekistan, and Tajikistan has recently reverted to this structure.

[2] See: <http://www.grida.no/aral/main_e.html> for both the NEAPs available and national State of the Environment Reports prepared in cooperation with UNEP in anticipation of the Johannesburg Earth Summit. The NEAP for Tajikistan is scheduled to be completed by early 2004. Environmental Performance Reviews (EPR) conducted by the UN Economic Commission for Europe (UNECE) supplement the NEAPs as do Country Environmental Analyses (CEAs) prepared by the Asian Development Bank. See: UNECE, 1999. *Environmental Performance Review: Kyrgyzstan* (United Nations: Geneva; UNECE 2000); *Environmental Performance Review: Kazakhstan* (United Nations: Geneva; and UNECE 2001), *Environmental Performance Review: Uzbekistan* (United Nations: Geneva). Also see: Asian Development Bank (ADB), 2003. *Country Environmental Assessment: Kazakhstan*, ADB: Manila; ADB. 2003; *Country Environmental Assessment: Kyrgyzstan*, ADB: Manila; and ADB. 2003; *Country Environmental Assessment: Tajikistan*, ADB: Manila (an EPR for Tajikistan and CEA for Uzbekistan are planned for 2004).

[3] Afghanistan often is excluded from such activities due to its very different relationship with the former Soviet Union and because many international assistance agencies treat it as part of "South Asia" rather than "Central Asia."

[4] UNEP 2001. *Regional Environmental Action Plan for Central Asia*. UNEP.RRA: Bangkok.

[5] Or at least concurrence with analysis and positions put forward by CA-REC.

[6] UNECE 2003. *Report of the Fifth Ministerial Conference on Environment for Europe*, UNECE Secretariat: Geneva, and UNECE 2003. *Invitation to Partnership on Implementation of the Central Asian Sustainable Development Initiative*, Fifth Ministerial Conference Environment for Europe, Kiev, May 21-23, 2003, UNECE: Geneva.

[7] Generally including the agencies responsible for water resources management.

[8] Though not covered in this review, Afghanistan lies in the upstream watershed of the Amu Darya River, and it is ethnically linked with Tajikistan, Uzbekistan and Turkmenistan with which it shares a common border. For a summary assessment of its contemporary environmental issues, see: McCauley, 2003.

[9] For further detail on environmental and natural resources conditions and issues in the region, see: ADB. 1997. *Central Asian Environments in Transition*. ADB: Manila (covering Kazakhstan, Kyrgyzstan and Uzbekistan); ADB. 2000. *Environmental Profile of Tajikistan*. ADB: Manila; McCauley, D. 2001. *Central Asia: Summary Assessment of ADB Environmental Assistance*, ADB: Manila; as well as the EPRs and CEAs footnoted above.

[10] Pollution levels were considerably higher in the CARs during the Soviet period and declined thereafter with the demise of many high-polluting industries.

[11] Mismanagement of irrigation water is resulting in widespread waterlogging of soils and salinization, both from poor drainage and through a process whereby soil salts are brought to the surface on waterlogged lands. In addition to the section of the REAP on this subject, see also: IFAS. 2002. *Water and Environmental Management Project Sub-Component A1: National and Regional Water and Salt Management Plan Phase III Report – Regional Needs and Constraints*. GEF Agency of the IFAS Aral Sea Basin Program: Tashkent.

[12] The impending diversions by the People's Republic of China of waters from the Irtysh and Ili Rivers upstream of Kazakhstan also are of concern due both to the potential impacts on the rivers' pollution flushing capacities as well to their overall water volumes.

[13] Tursunzade also is a major source of air pollution.

[14] The consequences of over-irrigation, including waterlogging and salinization, have already been mentioned, as have the unstable uranium tailings of Kyrgyzstan.

[15] IFAS's role and history are discussed at length in Daene McKinney's chapter.

[16] This is under the Aral Sea Basin Program–2 (ASBP-2) described in further detail below.

[17] ICWC is slightly better off in this regard, as it is able to draw upon its Scientific Information Committee (SIC-ICWC), which serves as an analytical secretariat. ICSC also has an SIC, though it is more weakly staffed and recognized.

[18] In addition to CACO (with Kazakhstan, Kyrgyzstan, Tajikistan and Uzbekistan as members and Turkmenistan as an observer), other leading regional groupings include: the Eurasian Economic Community (EurAsEc; with Belarus, Kazakhstan, Kyrgyzstan, Russia and Tajikistan as members); Shanghai Cooperation Organization (SCO; with China, Kazakhstan, Kyrgyzstan, Russia, Tajikistan and Uzbekistan as members); and less formal groupings such as that organized by the Asian Development Bank (CAREC; with Azerbaijan, China, Kazakhstan, Kyrgyzstan, Mongolia, Tajikistan and Uzbekistan as members and Afghanistan, Iran, Pakistan, Russia, Turkey and Turkmenistan as observers).

[19] IFAS, 2003. *Program of Concrete Actions on Improvement of the Environmental and Socio-Economic Situation in the Aral Sea Basin for the Period of 2003-2010*, EC-IFAS: Dushanbe.

[20] 1995 data, see: Eileen Claussen and Lisa McNeilly. 1998. *Equity and Global Climate Change: The Complex Elements of Global Fairness*, Annex 1. Pew Center on Global Climate Change: Washington, DC.

[21] This country is given slightly greater coverage as an introduction to national-level institutional and program trends common in the region; additional details may be found in ADB, 2003b, prepared by this author.

[22] This section draws particularly from ADB, 2003c, and further background information may be found in ADB, 1999.

[23] An initiative funded by the GEF and UNDP to coordinate and integrate national action plans in response to the Biodiversity, Land Degradation and Climate Change conventions represents a promising counter-trend. As far as I know, National Capacity Needs Self-Assessment deals with analyzing the capacity needed to implement national actions plans and strategies on biodiversity, climate change and desertification.

[24] This section draws upon ADB, 2003a, and further detail may be found therein.

[25] An indication of the remaining constraints to official perceptions in this regard may be found in the early 2004 "celebration" of the 50th Anniversary of the Virgin Lands Policy in Kazakhstan.

[26] World Bank-GEF, 2003. *Project Appraisal Document on a Proposed Global Environment Facility Grant to the Government of Kazakhstan for Drylands Management Project*, World Bank Environmentally and Socially Sustainable Development Unit, Europe and Central Asia Region: Washington, DC.

[27] The country's more active participation in the Caspian Environment Program represents something of an exception to this trend.

[28] Ministry of Nature Protection, 1999. *State of the Environment of Turkmenistan*, Ministry of Nature Protection and UNEP: Ashgabat and Saigal, S., 2003. *Issues and Approaches to Combat Desertification: Turkmenistan*, Report of ADB RETA 5941: Manila.

[29] The consequently high rate of out-migration threatens to undermine the very Karakalpakstani identity.

[30] Rising domestic and export demand for Uzbekistan's natural gas against an essentially fixed supply is expected to alter the status quo over the next decade, requiring both economic and environmental adjustments.

[31] Almost one-half are 16 years of age or younger.

[32] Uzbekistan in the only Central Asian country which has not acceded to the Aarhus convention on environmental information transparency.

[33] As noted, a levee is being constructed just south of the Syr Darya River's delta to preserve aquatic ecosystems and partially restore fisheries but also effectively splitting the Aral Sea into two separate lakes.

[34] Bucknall, et al., *Irrigation in Central Asia: Social, Economic and Environmental Considerations* (Washington: World Bank, 2003).

[35] *See* McCauley, 2002.

[36] The former analysis is co-financed by the United States State Department.

[37] European Union Technical Assistance for Commonwealth of Independent States (EU/TACIS).

[38] Covering the Chui-Talas and Vakhsh River Basins.

[39] For the work to establish the Chui-Talas Rivers Commission, OSCE is partnered with the UN Economic Commission for Europe (UNECE) and the UN Economic and Social Commission for Asia and the Pacific (ESCAP); for the Environmental Security Initiative, it is partnered with UNDP and the United Nations Environment Program (UNEP). The United Nations Educational and Scientific Cooperation Organization (UNESCO) also is supporting research on sustainable water management in the region.

[40] *See* the Summit materials given at: <http://mountains.unep.ch/mtn/home_page.html>.

[41] *See*: Kyrgyz CAMIN Working Group 2001. *National Strategy and Action Plan for Sustainable Mountain Development in the Kyrgyz Republic*, CAMIN: Bishkek.

[42] *See*: <http://mountains.unep.ch/mtn/papers/BMPlatform.doc>.

[43] The others are Iran, Russia and Azerbaijan.

[44] <www.caspianenvironment.org>.

Chapter 14

The Future of Electrical Power in the Republic of Kazakhstan

Kalkaman Suleimenov

K azakhstan is rich in all forms of energy. With current production rates, the country not only can be self-sufficient in energy for the foreseeable future, but also may be able to export substantial amounts. The Republic of Kazakhstan, which covers some 1.8 percent of the land surface of the earth, enjoys roughly one half percent of the world's proven reserves of mineral fuels, or 30 billion tons. Of this, 80 percent is coal, 13 percent is oil and gas condensates and 7 percent is natural and secondary gas.[1] These resources are distributed unevenly across the Republic, as displayed in Figure 14–1. The coal deposits, for the most part, are concentrated in Northern and Central Kazakhstan. These same regions have rich deposits of minerals, which provide raw materials for Kazakhstan's industry. Here also are located the main sources of electrical energy. Western Kazakhstan is very rich in hydrocarbon reserves, while at the same time being poor in electrical power. Southern Kazakhstan does not have sufficient primary energy sources, and those found are inaccessible or as yet unexploited. The anticipated scale of hydrocarbon extraction in Southern Kazakhstan hardly can cover the region's need for electrical energy in the future. At the same time, however, this region possesses great hydroelectric potential.

The primary goals of the electrical energy sector for power generation on the domestic market and production for export are:

- To provide the country with energy security, which includes:
  - access or access rights to energy markets;
  - quality control and an uncompromising adherence to established standards;

◆ fair pricing that helps create reserves for development while taking into consideration social factors and line losses;

◆ ecological responsibility.

■ Optimization of the fuel regimen of electrical stations, with an emphasis on gas wherever possible and economically acceptable, and the use of fossil fuel secondary gas;

■ Utilization of international experience to mitigate the ecological side effects of coal, Kazakhstan's basic energy resource;

■ Restoration of electricity production at existing electric installations, through their rehabilitation or reconstruction, whichever is the least expensive and quickest;

■ Maintaining the designed capacity of electrical stations through the timely replacement of equipment that has outlived its designed service period, with new generation equipment;

■ Construction of new electrical generation capacity to replace that going off-line, while meeting increased demand for electricity.

In 1990 Kazakhstan's electrical power plants produced 87.4 billion kilowatt hours (kWh) of electrical power. [2] Of this, thermal power plants accounted for 91 percent, hydro 8.4 percent, and nuclear 0.6 percent. In subsequent years, owing to the completion of projects that had been under construction, a number of new plants were brought on line at Ekibastuz-2 District Electrical Plant, the Karaganda-3 Thermal Power Plant, and the Aktube Thermal Power Plant (Akturbo). This has brought total electrical power generation capacity up to 95 billion kWh. [3] Thus, electrical power generation in Kazakhstan is characterized by efforts to achieve self-sufficiency in electrical power and provide the necessary infrastructure for generating capacity with appropriate increases in reserve capacity for future needs. The realization of these tasks will allow Kazakhstan to trade energy profitably with its neighbors, and ensure a competitive electricity market.

For the purpose of examining the issue of power generation, Kazakhstan can be divided into three basic regions: Southern, Northern, and Western. Each of these regions will be discussed in the following sections ,with emphasis on the amount of energy produced and the issues surrounding this production.

The Southern Region

The Southern Region consists of Almaty, Jambyl, Kzyl-Orda, the South Kazakhstan oblasts, and the City of Almaty. This region comprises roughly 38 percent of the country's population, and its growth has always been above the average for the Republic. Industry here consists primarily of the energy-intensive chemical production sector (which in 1990 accounted for more than 40 percent of electricity consumption in the region), as well as metallurgy, machine-building, light industry, and other enterprises. In addition, a significant part of the railway system has been converted to use electricity. This zone has a favorable climate with fertile arable land that has allowed the region to develop a highly productive agriculture and agricultural processing sector.

Demand for electricity in this zone in 1990 reached 26.43 billion kWh,[4] while producing only 16.27 billion kWh,[5] with the shortfall being delivered from electrical power plants of the Central Asian Unified Energy System.[6] In light of the region's deficiency in primary energy resources, electricity production is based on outside coal, imported natural gas, and, in part, on locally produced fuel oil from petrochemical processing plants. The southeastern part of the region is potentially rich in hydro-electrical resources, yet only an insignificant part is utilized. It may be exploited in the future.[7] In order to connect to the energy systems of other Central Asian countries, a power grid was built with 500 and 220 kV overhead transmission lines and a throughput capacity of more than 10 billion kWh per year.[8] Thus, a very good material base is in place for subsequent cooperation with neighboring states as well as Kazakhstan's participation in the Central Asian energy market.

At present, the largest electrical plant in the southern part of the country, the Jambyl District Electrical Plant, which has a design capacity of 230 megawatts using fuel, gas and fuel oil, is practically idle. The underutilization of this station is the result of the non-competitiveness of the electricity it produces on Kazakhstan's wholesale electrical energy market, which, in turn, is affected by increases in the price of gas and fuel oil on the international market. The stoppage of the Jambyl Plant has led to the creation of a palpable deficit in electricity, especially in the fall and winter seasons. At present, the shortfall is being covered by transferring electrical power from the Northern region of Kazakhstan (3.0 to 3.5 billion kWh per year) and importing power from other Central Asian countries. It is worth noting that in the Fall-Winter season of 2001-2002, the Government of the Republic of Kazakhstan appropriated a subsidy grant from the Republic budget to acquire fuel for the Jambyl District Electrical Plant, in an effort to make its electrical production competitive.

Domestic sufficiency and even, in the long run, export potential in this region of traditional shortfalls could be achieved, both through the reconstruction and reequipping of existing thermal power facilities, as well as through new construction. As the Southern region experiences sharp shortfalls in peak load regulating capacity, priority must be given to new construction. According to official government sources, this can be achieved through:[9]

■ Installing a second 500 kilovolt (kV) North to South Kazakhstan transmission line, for a total throughput capacity (two 500 kV and one 220 kV) of 6 to 7 billion kWh of electrical energy per year;[10]

■ Constructing the planned Mainak Hydroelectric Station on the Charyn river with a capacity of 300 megawatts (0.7 billion kWh);[11]

■ Building the Kerbulak Hydroelectric Station on the Ili River with a capacity of 50 megawatts (0.3 billion kWh);

■ Building a co-generation plant of 100 to 200 megawatts capacity, using secondary gas recovered from petroleum processing at the Kumkol fields (0.6 to 1.3 billion kWh);[12]

■ The creation of mini hydroelectric stations along mountain rivers, with an overall output of 500 to 600 megawatts (2.0 to 2.5 billion kWh);

■ Completion of wind energy projects, with a capacity of 500 to 600 megawatts (1.2 to 1.5 billion kWh).[13]

The Southern Kazakhstan zone shares borders with several other Central Asian countries. Preliminary analysis suggests significant shortfalls in electrical power will occur in this area in the future. The risk of energy surplus is less than the risk of shortfalls, as any overproduction of electricity in Southern and Northern Kazakhstan could be offered to the Central Asian energy market. Supply can be provided through the existing network of electrical 220 and 500 kV transmission lines between Kazakhstan and Uzbekistan and between Kazakhstan and Kyrgyzstan, which have an overall transmission capacity of no less than 10 billion kWh per year.

The Northern Region

The Northern Region consists of East-Kazakhstan, Pavlodar, Karaganda, Akmola, North-Kazakhstan, and the Kostanai oblasts. This region possesses ample cheap and accessible fuel resources, and has a well developed energy production sector. The country's primary coal regions are located in this area: Ekibastuz, Karaganda, Maikuben, Turgai, and others. Coal mined from these deposits is used at all the thermal power plants of the southern and northern regions of Kazakhstan, and is exported to Russia as well. Electrical power generation in the Northern Region of Kazakhstan also includes very powerful hydroelectric stations located in the East-Kazakhstan Oblast, which has very high hydro electrical potential.

In the Northern Region of Kazakhstan, it would be possible to increase the output of electrical power to meet not only local demand and transmission to the south of Kazakhstan at the necessary levels, but also for export to the Central Asian countries and Russia. Currently, the electrical power produced in the Northern Region is transmitted to the south of Kazakhstan along a 500 and a 220 kV North-South Kazakhstan overhead line. A small portion (300 to 400 megawatts) is exported to the Siberian regions of Russia.[14]

In all potential scenarios, demand in the Northern Region, including transmission to the south of Kazakhstan, as well as export to Russia and Central Asia, can be met through reconstruction as well as by re-equipping and increasing capacity at existing electrical generation facilities. With minimal investment, this would transform the zone into a net supplier of energy with a significant (10 to 15 billion kWh) surplus production.[15]

The Western Region

The Western Region of Kazakhstan, in energy terms, is comprised of three regions and energy systems: the Atyrau-Mangistau (Atyrau and Mangistau Oblasts), Aktyube Oblast, and the West-Kazakhstan Oblast. The Atyrau-Mangistau system is self-sufficient and has surplus production of more than 800 megawatts. Aktyube and West-Kazakhstan Oblasts are net consumers of energy. Demand for electricity, 1.2 and 0.5 billion kWh, respectively, is covered through import from the border regions of Russia.

Since the Caspian coastal zone is rapidly developing its oil and gas sector, including the exploitation of the Caspian Shelf, the creation of elaborate oil pipelines will increase significantly the demand for electrical power. According to growth estimates and the pace of implementation of the oil and gas production program to 2015, it will be necessary to increase energy production capacity by 2,000 to 3,000 megawatts. The fuel resources in the region make it possible to meet this demand and even create an export capacity in electric power.

Current production capacity in Atyrau-Mangistau can fully satisfy demand in Mangistau Oblast in the short to medium term, since the capacity of the electrical plants of Aktau is 1350 megawatts, while current demand does not exceed 500 megawatts. Although there is a surplus at the present time, the Mangistau utility cannot be transferred completely to the Atyrau oblast because of the limited electrical capacity of the interconnecting lines.[16]

The intense growth of the oil and gas sector in Atyrau Oblast demands the construction of new electrical power generation capacity, using steam and pipeline cogeneration technologies. By 2015 new capacity likely will be needed. It is anticipated that no less than 14 billion kilowatts per hour of electrical energy will be needed for production on the offshore oil platforms of the Caspian Sea.[17] Since the increased demand for electricity in Atyrau Oblast is tied to the growth in oil production, the growth of energy capacity can be realized by the building of electrical plants and by the oil companies developing the oil and gas deposits of the region. For example, the TengizChevroil Company, which already has a pipeline cogeneration plant with a 144- megawatt capacity, has built new gas-fired turbines for a 120-megawatt electrical station. A portion of this facility is currently operational, and full production capacity should be reached by 2005.

The energy resources of Atyrau Oblast, in the form of secondary gas from the oil industry, will not only cover local demand but will also make it possible to create a large electricity export capacity. In the medium to long term, there is a proposal to create a high voltage, high capacity electrical network to transmit Atyrau electricity to Aktyube and the West-Kazakhstan Oblasts, and on to the northern regions of Kazakhstan, as well as to Russia and other countries.

In order to make Aktyube Oblast self-sufficient, new generating capacity is needed. The planned doubling of oil production in the Oblast could increase secondary gas production by some 600 to 700 million cubic meters, which is sufficient for the construction of a cogeneration plant with a 250 to 300 megawatt capacity and production of more than 2 billion kWh per year.[18]

In the West-Kazakhstan Oblast, it would be possible to construct natural gas pipeline cogeneration plants, especially at the Kapchagai condensed gas deposits, where a cogeneration plant with a 240-megawatt capacity is already under construction.[19] In light of the planned exploitation of a group of oil and gas deposits in the immediate vicinity of Uralsk, and the corresponding release of large volumes of secondary gas, electrical power generation will increase sharply. These gas resources translate into potential electricity production of more than 80 billion kWh. This gas would suffice to cover the demand for electrical power in the region for some 30 to 40 years at current levels of demand.[20]

In addition to creating electrical connections between Atyrau, Aktyube, and Uralsk, plans are under review to construct a 500 kV overland transmission line between Aktyube (Ul'ke) and Zhitigora across the breadth of Kazakhstan. The realization of this 500 kV line project across Western Kazakhstan would make it possible to unite the energy network of this region with the Unified Energy System (UES) of Kazakhstan.

Patterns of Demand: Past and Future

Kazakhstan's primary electrical energy production relies on cheap Ekibastuz coal. It should be noted that the highest production levels of electricity in Kazakhstan were reached in 1989, when it produced 88.9 billion kWh.[21] In spite of the aging of large portions of the existing plants, Kazakhstan's electrical power plants at present have a known capacity potential which can fully cover domestic demands as well as create an export potential. Nonetheless, due to peculiarities within the network, southern and western Kazakhstan, as noted above, import electrical power.

The period between 1990 and 1999 in Kazakhstan was characterized by a drop in both demand and supply of electricity. In 1990, demand for electricity was 104.72 billion kWh and production was 87.38 billion kWh. In 1999, the numbers were 50.74 billion kWh and 47.47 billion kWh respectively, while in 2000, these numbers reached 54.38 billion kWh and 51.42 billion kWh.[22] The installed capacity of Kazakhstan's electricity plants on January 1, 2001 was 18,100 megawatts with a usable capacity of 13,416 megawatts. Table 14–1 summarizes the basic data of energy production for the decade. Tables 14–2 and 14–3 show installed capacity and electricity production.

Table 14–1. General Characteristics, 1990-2000

Item	Units	1990	1995	2000
Demand	Billion kWh	104.7	74.38	54.38
Per Capita Demand	kWh	6,236	4,480	3,664
Installed Capacity	Megawatts	17,570	18,420	18,100
Supply	Billion kWh	87.4	66.98	51.42
Balance (Imports)	Billion kWh	17.34	7.4	2.96

Table 14–2. **The Structure of Installed Capacity (Jan 1, 2001)**

Type	Megawatts	Percent
Thermal, Steam Pipeline, and Organic Fuel	15,541	85.9
Gas Pipeline	332	1.8
Hydraulic	2,228	12.3
Total	18,101	100

Table 14–3. **The Structure of Electricity Production (Jan 1, 2001)**

Type	2000		2001	
	Billion kWh	Percent	Billion kWh	Percent
Coal-Burning Thermal	37.3	72.5	40.52	73
Fuel-Oil and Gas-Burning	6.61	13	6.66	12
Hydro	7.51	14.5	8.06	15
Total	51.42	100	55.24	100

Table 14–4 provides the electricity balances (demand and production) by region and for the Republic for the past decade, and estimates to 2005 and 2010.[23] As is clear from Table 14-4, the economic crisis of the transition period in Kazakhstan led to a significant drop in electricity demand. It is assumed that the country's economic reform policies will lead to a gradual recovery from this crisis, a subsequent resurgence of demand for electricity, and eventual growth past old levels. According to the *Kazakhstan 2030* Program,[24] the 1990 level of electricity demand (104.7 billion kWh) will be reached even in the worst-case scenario by 2030, and in the best-case scenario, by 2020.[25] The pace of electricity production will depend on the development of the overall economy of Kazakhstan.

It is important to note that Kazakhstan is no longer a centralized command economy and is moving in the direction of a free market. Since 1995, significant market reforms and transformations have been carried out. During this period, privatization of the most important enterprises in different branches of the economy was begun, including in such strategic sectors as electrical power and ferrous and precious metallurgy. This transformation will have a significant effect on the energy sector's ability to meet the country's future needs.

Table 14–4. **Regional and Republican Electricity Balances to 2010 (Billions kWh)**

	1990	1992	1994	1998	2000	2001	2005	2010
Electricity Demand								
Total	104.72	96.87	79.43	53.40	54.38	56.66	59.00	72.00
North	66.42	64.01	53.73	37.04	37.92	39.11	40.00	48.00
South	26.43	21.63	16.45	9.70	9.49	10.13	11.00	14.00
West	11.87	11.23	9.25	6.66	6.97	7.42	8.00	10.00
Electricity Supply								
Total	87.38	82.86	66.40	49.59	51.42	55.24	59.00	72.00
North	63.89	61.27	52.04	37.42	40.43	44.02	41.90	49.80
South	16.27	14.77	9.20	7.40	5.82	5.60	9.10	12.20
West	7.22	6.82	5.16	4.77	5.17	5.62	8.00	10.00
Balance								
Total	(17.34)	(14.01)	(13.03)	(3.81)	(2.96)	(1.42)	0.00	0.00
North	(2.53)	(2.74)	(1.69)	0.38	2.51	4.91	1.90	1.80
South	(10.16)	(6.86)	(7.25)	(2.30)	(3.67)	(4.53)	(1.90)	(1.80)
West	(4.65)	(4.41)	(4.09)	(1.89)	(1.80)	(1.80)	0.00	0.00

Transformation of the Electricity Sector

Substantial transformation already has taken place in the electrical power sector of the country. It is important to note that the reconstruction and reorganization of the electricity sector started much later than did other sectors of the economy of Kazakhstan.[26] Yet, at this point, the level of implemented market reforms in the electricity sector of Kazakhstan is far ahead of other Commonwealth of Independent States (CIS) countries. The organizational structure of Kazakhstan's energy sector has undergone significant change since the country became independent, and this reorganization itself has gone through several stages.[27]

Stage One

Stage One was the separation of the state regulatory systems from the economic functions of the industry. In February 1992, the Ministry of Energy was reorganized into the Ministry of Energy and Fuel Resources, with responsibility for regulating these branches of the energy sector.

Operations were transferred to the newly created vertically integrated State Electrical Energy Company *KazakhstanEnergo,* which was charged with the production, transmission, distribution, and sale of electricity and heat, as well as the centralized financial management of its constituent Territorial Energy and Electrification Utilities. The company also took control of the departments of planning, construction, installation, maintenance, and repair of electrical plants, and the heating and electrical networks. The creation of this company coincided with the liberalization of prices on goods and services in the larger economy, but excluded subsidized prices on energy.

Stage Two

Stage Two started in 1995, when the sector was broken up through a decree of the Government of the Republic of Kazakhstan that created a Republican-level State-owned Enterprise called "*KazakhstanEnergo* National Energy System." This enterprise was based on existing intersystem electrical transmission lines, the Republic's largest electrical power plants (as subsidiaries), and nine "Territorial Energy Systems," which also were to be State-owned. The design, research and development (R&D), construction, installation, and repair organizations were reorganized as independent contractors.

Stage Three

Stage Three of the reorganization of the electricity sector began in 1996. The Government of the Republic of Kazakhstan issued a decree on the need to reform the state monopoly of generation and distribution of electric power, which created the prerequisites for the development of a competitive electricity market. To this end, a privatization and restructuring program was developed for the electricity sector, adopted by Government Decree Number 663 in May 1996.[28] The basic idea of this program was a fundamental change in the form of ownership of generation plants in the electricity sector.

Stage Four

Stage Four was set into motion when Decree Number 1188, adopted in September 1996, created the Kazakhstani Electricity Management Company *KEGOC,* from the transmission and distribution assets of *KazakhstanEnergo* along with the transmission lines previously belonging to the territorial energy utilities and eighteen joint-stock electrical distribution companies. As a result of this stage, the basics of a market in electrical energy and capacity emerged, based on mutual agreements between sellers and consumers of electrical energy, as well as between consumers and electricity distributors.[29] Most important, the price of electricity was determined by the market and set by the producers themselves.

Stage Five

Stage Five occurred when the Government adopted a program for the further development of the electricity market during the 1997 to 2000 period, which improved the initial model of a competitive electricity market that had been operating up to that time.[30]

In this way, the reorganization of the electrical power sector of Kazakhstan, and particularly the privatization program and sector reorganization, has:

- Separated the competitive sector of the electricity industry (production and consumption) from the naturally monopolistic sectors (transmission and distribution);

- Realized the large-scale privatization of generating capacity:

  ◆ The powerful electrical plants of "national importance" (national importance means electrical plants that are essential for the economy of the country), which are located in the immediate proximity of the main deposits of cheap coal (Ekibastuz) have been privatized;

  ◆ High-capacity hydroelectric stations, used for regulating the grid load of the Unified Energy System (UES) of Kazakhstan, have remained the property of the State, and are managed as concessions;

  ◆ Industrial electrical plants, which supply electrical energy to major industrial enterprises, have been transferred to these industrial enterprises;

  ◆ Regional-level district thermal-electric systems—a source of both heat and electrical energy—have, for the most part, been privatized along with the regional electric distribution companies. The remaining systems have been transferred to municipal ownership.

- Accomplished de-statization of the electrical network through the creation of:

◆ A joint-stock company "Kazakhstan Electricity Network Company" *(KEGOC)* on the basis of the main high-tension networks of 1150, 500, and 220 kV;

◆ Joint-stock distribution companies, on the basis of regional electrical networks of 110-135 kV and local networks of 6-10 and 0.4 kV.

Structures that are defined as "natural monopolies of the electrical sector" come under the control of the State (within the Ministry of Energy and Mineral Resources). Tariffs for electrical transmission and distribution services are regulated by the Republic of Kazakhstan Agency for Regulation of Natural Monopolies, Fair Competition, and Small Business.

Conclusion

The wholesale electricity market in Kazakhstan accounts for about 60 percent of consumption, which has allowed the decrease of tariffs on electrical power within the country.[31] At present, the Government of Kazakhstan is discussing the concept of organization of the electrical power and services retail market. The development of a retail market for electrical power is a serious step in preparation for joining the World Trade Organization. Another problem under consideration is related to the price parity between the regions and inside of each network company. Also, there are questions related to the effective organization of electrical power retail trading.

In the Government's view, it is necessary to separate the selling of goods (electricity) from services (provision of electricity) in retail trading. Thus, regional electricity companies (RECs) will purchase electricity from traders on the wholesale market, and then sell it to final consumers. The Government Anti-Monopoly Committee will regulate REC services, and the trading will be competitive. It also is suggested that selling electrical power be accomplished using electronic-commerce methods, which would offer consumers the opportunity to choose their source of power.

The sale of electrical power to large-scale customers also has been suggested. In this case, factories and plants able to purchase 500 and more kWh in one transaction time may buy directly from a producing electric company. Minor consumers can form groups and jointly participate in such trading as well. Energy experts in the country support the concept of retail market formation; however, a pilot project will be required before it is introduced to the whole economy. The retail market is scheduled to start at the end of 2004.

The successful realization of the government's program for reorganization of the electrical power sector of the economy, including State monitoring of the development of the sector and the relationship between market actors, will make it possible to ensure the energy security of Kazakhstan, the reliability of the electrical supply, the reconstruction and restarting of existing electrical plants and the construction of new sources of energy.

Editor's Note

The electricity sector in Kazakhstan is deeply intertwined with regional water issues. See Daene McKinney's chapter in this volume for a discussion of the importance of the regional electricity grid in resolving transboundary water disputes. The tendency to focus on supply-side issues in energy is quite common among energy scholars in the region. International Financial Institutions, however, have tended to focus on improving transmission and management. Future demand remains difficult to predict, since it depends on the evolution of the economy: The structure of industrial development in Kazakhstan will determine its energy needs. Predicting demand is further complicated by the fact that Kazakhstan, although it has improved collections rates dramatically, still does not recover the full price of electricity. Economists focus on "effective demand," that is, demand among those who can pay full price. In Kazakhstan, the levels of "effective demand" remain unclear.

Notes

[1] *Kazakhstan's Energy: Movement to the Market*, (Russian language) (Almaty: Galim Publishing House, 1998), 582.

[2] GoK, *Program of Development of Electric Energy to the Year 2030* confirmed by resolution of the Government of the Republic of Kazakhstan on April 9, 1999, no. 384, 2.

[3] Ibid., 3.

[4] Ibid.

[5] *Kazakhstan's Energy*, 582, table 2.6.1.

[6] The Unified Energy System was the all-Soviet system, which integrated Central Asia into a single electricity grid.

[7] K.D. Dukenbayev, E.G. Ulriks, and G.A. Papafansopulo, "Volume of the Market for Electric Energy and Demand for Investment in Energy," *Energy and Heat Resources of Kazakhstan*, 2002, no. 8, 4-12.

[8] Ibid., 5.

[9] GoK, *Program of Development of Electric Energy to the Year 2030*,

[10] K.A. Bozumbaev, "Five Years of Work of the National Company OAO 'KEGOC,'" in *Energy and Heat Resources of Kazakhstan*, 2002, no. 9, 5, 11, and 25-26.

[11] GoK, *Program of Development of Electric Energy to the Year 2030*, 5, 11, and 14.

[12] Ibid., 5, 11, and 14.

[13] Ibid., 14.

[14] V.M. Barsukov and A.A. Zeibel, "Account of Electricity Output of Kazakhstan in 2002," *Energy and Heat Resources of Kazakhstan*, 2003, no. 10, 5-19.

[15] GoK, *Program of Development of Electric Energy to the Year 2030*

[16] K.D. Dukenbayev, E.G. Ulriks, and G.A. Papafansopulo, "Volume of the Market for Electric Energy and Demand for Investment in Energy," *Energy and Heat Resources of Kazakhstan*, 2002, no. 8, 64.

[17] Ibid., 6.

[18] Ibid, 4-12.

[19] Ibid., 12.

[20] Ibid., 7.

[21] *Kazakhstan's Energy*, 99.

[22] V.M. Barsukov and A.A. Zeibel, no. 6, 10-25.

[23] Maximal scenarios in 2005 and 2010 are taken from the Ministry of Energy's *Kazakhstan 2030 Electricity Development Program*.

[24] Plan 2030 for Kazakhstan, adopted as Government policy in 1998, set out the long-term goals of development for Kazakhstan.

[25] GoK, *Program of Development of Electric Energy to the Year 2030*, 12.

[26] Depending on the process of privatization in the energy sector.

[27] *Kazakhstan's Energy*, 4.

[28] GoK, *Program of Privatization and Restructuring in Electrical Energy*, Decree of the Government of the Republic of Kazakhstan, no. 663, May 30, 1996.

[29] GoK, *Concerning Several Measures for Restructuring of the Regulatory System for Electrical Energy in Kazakhstan*, Decree of the Government of the Republic of Kazakhstan, no. 1188, September 28, 1996.

[30] GoK, *Concerning Additional Measures for Fulfillment of the Program of Privatization and Restructuring of the Electrical Energy and Long-Term Reform of the Electricity Market*, Order of the Government of the Republic of Kazakhstan, no. 1193, July 31, 1997.

[31] Tulegen Izdibaev, "Government Develops Concept for Organization of Differentiated Markets for Electrical Energy and Services," *Panorama*, October 2003, no. 39.

Part III

Security Issues

Chapter 15

Forging Relationships, Preventing Proliferation: A Decade of Cooperative Threat Reduction in Central Asia

Emily E. Daughtry

O n December 21, 1991, as leaders of eleven Soviet republics gathered in the Central Asian city of Almaty, Kazakhstan, to formally dissolve the Soviet Union,[1] the newly independent Central Asian states found themselves the unwilling hosts to some of the world's most dangerous weapons. More than 1000 nuclear warheads were in place on over 100 intercontinental ballistic missiles stored at two remote locations on the Kazakhstani steppes.[2] Covering a significant corner of northeastern Kazakhstan was the primary nuclear test site for the Soviet Union, where 456 nuclear tests were conducted.[3] Several hundred miles to the west, Soviet specialists were working at one of the largest factories ever created for the manufacture and production of anthrax. To the south, the world's only known open-air test site for biological weapons lay under a blanket of snow on an island shared by Kazakhstan and Uzbekistan in the Aral Sea.[4] West of the sea, a Soviet chemical weapons test site stretched over the Ustyurt plateau in Uzbekistan. A partially constructed chemical weapons production plant lay dormant in Northern Kazakhstan.[5] Nearly 600 kilograms of highly-enriched uranium fuel from an abandoned Soviet submarine program lay stored, forgotten, in a Kazakh metallurgy plant.[6] A fast-breeder nuclear reactor, used for desalination, was operating on the shores of the Caspian Sea, capable of producing over 100 kilograms of plutonium annually.[7] Yet these particular sites and weapons comprise only a portion of the legacy of Soviet weapons of mass destruction (WMD) bequeathed to the Central Asian states upon independence.

As of spring 2003, almost all of these threats have been, or are being, eliminated by a relatively small U.S. Government initiative known as the Cooperative Threat Reduction (CTR) program. The achievements of this program have been, in short, phenomenal, and few could have predicted such success back in 1991. For the past decade, the United States has used the CTR program to help the states of the former Soviet Union dismantle and destroy infrastructure related to WMD and put in place safeguards to prevent their proliferation. While Central Asia has not been the focus of the CTR program, developments in that region have had interesting and significant effects on the program's evolution. CTR has been critically important to Central Asia and has played a key role in the development of U.S. relationships with individual countries in this strategically vital part of the world.

History

The CTR program grew out of legislation sponsored in 1991 by Senators Sam Nunn (D-GA, now retired) and Richard Lugar (R-IN), in response to their concerns about control over the nuclear arsenal in a rapidly disintegrating Soviet Union.[8] The goal of the initial legislation was to make available a relatively modest sum of Department of Defense (DOD) money each year to work cooperatively with Russia to safeguard and dismantle the Soviet nuclear arsenal.[9] For the first two years, the legislation provided $400 million per year in transfer authority to DOD, which meant that the Department had to take $400 million from already existing projects and use it instead on cooperative dismantlement projects with the former Soviet Union.[10] Senators Nunn and Lugar did not envision CTR as a foreign aid program and made efforts to restrict the money to tangible projects.[11] Their intent was that CTR would contribute directly to U.S. national security by helping to eliminate nuclear weapons aimed at the United States, while simultaneously helping to prevent those weapons and their components from falling into the hands of rogue states and terrorist organizations.[12]

After some initial reservations, the first Bush administration supported the CTR program. However, the program did not come into its own until the change of administrations in 1993.[13] Part of the initial inspiration behind Senators Nunn and Lugar's introduction of the CTR legislation had been their exposure to work on the state of Soviet nuclear weapons done by Dr. Ashton Carter and his colleagues at the Harvard

Center for Science and International Affairs.[14] In 1993, Carter joined the Clinton administration as Assistant Secretary of Defense for International Security Policy, which gave him direct responsibility for the CTR program and propelled the program forward.[15] CTR also embodied the ideas of cooperative engagement and preventive defense, philosophies espoused by Carter and Dr. William Perry, who became Clinton's Secretary of Defense in early 1994.[16] With dual CTR supporters at the helm of DOD, the Clinton administration embraced CTR and made it a key foreign policy initiative.[17] The new team included a request for an additional $400 million for CTR in its proposed budget to Congress for fiscal year 1994, and Congress promptly approved it.[18] From that year on, CTR became a regular part of the DOD budget, and it was no longer necessary to reprogram funds from other DOD projects.

Initially, and to this day, the CTR program has been directed primarily at Russia rather than Central Asia. The vast bulk of the literature analyzing and evaluating the CTR program reflects this fact by concentrating on the program's implementation in Russia alone. Such a state of affairs is hardly surprising, as Russia is the sole legal successor to the Soviet Union's nuclear weapons arsenal and host to the overwhelming majority of nuclear, biological and chemical weapons infrastructure, materials and technologies. In addition, the program initially focused on reducing the nuclear threat, which also was understandable given that nuclear warheads were the defining weapons of the Cold War. As a result, literature on CTR's presence in Central Asia is scarce. Nonetheless, several success stories have materialized over the past decade, and these stories are worthy of our attention. This chapter will document some of the ways in which the CTR program has contributed to the security of Central Asia while deepening U.S. diplomatic relations with the region and encouraging the development of strong, independent Central Asian states.

Early expansion of CTR beyond Russia was limited to Belarus, Ukraine and Kazakhstan—the only three non-Russian Soviet successor states with nuclear weapons on their territories. The primary reason these three additional states were included in the CTR program was to provide incentives for them to voluntarily give up their inherited nuclear weapons,[19] a decision that has been widely touted as one of the most significant and concrete accomplishments of the CTR program.[20] As the program developed, however, it began to be seen as more than a narrow technical initiative designed to accomplish specific goals related to weapons dismantlement. In fact, CTR evolved into a means to engage these new states, develop relationships with their leaders, and emphasize U.S. concerns about the importance of nonproliferation policies in the region.[21] In Kazakhstan, for example, implementation of the CTR program became one of the most important aspects of the U.S.-Kazakhstan relationship, and gave the United States key insights into the largely unknown and unfamiliar Central Asian region.

In the first part of the 1990s, U.S. policy makers treated Kazakhstan as a smaller, less complicated Russia, with many of the same proliferation threats and nonproliferation opportunities. As in Russia, CTR projects focused on reducing the nuclear threat. However, in succeeding years, CTR was recognized as an important tool that could be used not only to deal with threats, but also to take advantage of opportunities unique to Central Asia. For example, U.S. and Kazakhstani officials were able to build upon their existing CTR relationships and the trust they had established to expand the program into an area where it had been almost impossible to work in Russia: biological weapons nonproliferation.[22] Once that door had been opened, it become logical to draw Uzbekistan into the program as well, and as in Kazakhstan, CTR cooperation became an important means of strengthening and deepening the U.S.-Uzbekistan relationship. DOD now plans to expand the program to include border security, an area all the more critical in the post-September 11 world.[23] Thus, the CTR program is likely to have lasting benefits for U.S. security, and indeed for the security of the world.

CTR in Kazakhstan: The Early Years

After the Soviet Union fell apart, a key U.S. foreign policy goal was to prevent the emergence of three new nuclear-armed nations, by convincing Kazakhstan, Belarus and Ukraine to relinquish their nuclear weapons.[24] On May 23, 1992, these three countries signed the Lisbon Protocol, becoming parties to the Strategic Arms Reduction Treaty (START I) between the United States and Russia, which had become the legal successor to the Soviet Union for all international treaties.[25] Under the Lisbon Protocol, all three countries pledged to join the Nuclear Non-Proliferation Treaty (NPT) as non-nuclear-weapons states, which meant relinquishing legal ownership of all nuclear weapons on their territories.[26]

It fell to the Clinton administration to ensure that these countries followed through on their pledge, and that they did so as quickly as possible. To achieve this goal, administration officials turned to the CTR program.[27] According to one insider, the promise of CTR assistance "was the most consistent and productive tool available to U.S. diplomats" in negotiations on denuclearization.[28] Senator Lugar stated this fact even more forcefully when he noted, "Without [the] Nunn-Lugar [program], Ukraine, Kazakhstan and Belarus would still have thousands of nuclear weapons."[29]

Once the Kazakh Parliament ratified the NPT in December 1993, effectively ensuring a nuclear-weapons-free Kazakhstan, the United States was obligated to fulfill its end of the bargain by providing assistance under the CTR program. Together, the two countries had to figure out what types of projects to develop using this assistance. Because Kazakhstan was inclined to see CTR assistance as a blanket reward for denuclearization, it was often difficult to reconcile what the Kazakhs wanted and felt they needed, with the restraints on the program in the CTR legislation.[30] The initial legislation was quite specific, restricting the use of CTR funds to activities that were clearly related to the nonproliferation, safeguarding, destruction or dismantlement of WMD.[31] In the face of these restrictions, the United States took the path of least resistance, simply modeling the CTR projects in Kazakhstan on existing CTR projects in Russia, which clearly fit within the scope of the legislation.

The process of providing CTR assistance involved two important legal steps: first, an umbrella agreement was negotiated between the U.S. government and the recipient country governments, providing the basic legal framework for assistance.[32] Then, for each specific CTR project area, a separate implementing agreement was negotiated and signed on the agency-to-agency level. In Kazakhstan, the umbrella agreement and the first set of implementing agreements were signed December 13, 1993, the same day that the Kazakh Parliament ratified the NPT. The implementing agreements enabled projects in the following areas: provision of emergency response equipment for use during the transport of nuclear weapons to Russia; establishment of a government-to-government communications link to facilitate data reporting for the START and INF arms control agreements; strategic offensive arms elimination for the dismantlement of SS-18 Intercontinental Ballistic Missile (ICBM) silos; nuclear warhead storage elimination; strategic bomber elimination; improvement of material control and accounting and physical protection (MPC&A) of nuclear materials; improvement of export controls; and establishment of defense and military contacts.[33]

All of these program areas paralleled CTR projects in Russia. Over the course of the previous year-and-a-half, implementing agreements also had been signed in Russia for provision of emergency response equipment, strategic offensive arms elimination, improvement of MPC&A, and establishment of defense and military contacts.[34] A defense conversion implementing agreement was signed with Russia in December 1993, and a Kazakhstani agreement on defense conversion followed just a few months later in March 1994. Additional agreements were signed with Russia for other CTR program areas, such as chemical weapons destruction and the conversion of plutonium-production reactor cores, but these were not relevant to Kazakhstan. In other words, every project area in Russia that could be copied in Kazakhstan was copied.

The projects providing emergency response equipment and a continuous government-to-government satellite communications link were quickly and easily implemented. Projects to withdraw strategic nuclear weapons from Kazakhstan and eliminate ICBM missile silos, strategic bombers, and nuclear weapons storage facilities also were straightforward and considered highly successful. U.S. and Kazakhstani specialists worked together to implement these projects on the ground. One article from early 2000 found the projects for elimination of strategic offensive arms in Kazakhstan the "most successful" of all such projects in the former Soviet Union, as they were the first to achieve the complete elimination of all strategic weapons from a country.[35] Withdrawal of all nuclear weapons and strategic bombers was completed by April 1995;[36] the few remaining strategic bombers were eliminated in 1998, and all 147 missile silos were dismantled and destroyed by 1999.[37] As a result, there are no further projects to be completed under the strategic offensive arms elimination implementing agreement in Kazakhstan.

The next two project areas—of nuclear materials MPC&A and export controls—were inherently more complicated because they are premised not on the simple destruction of hardware, but on the creation of lasting systems and institutions. MPC&A projects involved the provision of equipment and training, and were established at the four primary locations in Kazakhstan where nuclear materials were located.[38] For the most part, these projects ran more smoothly than analogous projects in Russia, due to, in the words of one analyst, "fewer nuclear facilities . . . , housing less nuclear material, with fewer bureaucratic obstacles."[39] In addition, because Kazakhstan is a non-nuclear-weapons state and its facilities are subject to International Atomic Energy Agency (IAEA) safeguards, it had fewer concerns about the protection of classified information.[40] However, these projects were not without their problems. For example, concerns have been raised regarding the long-term sustainability of the MPC&A improvements and the development of a "safeguards culture" at the various nuclear installations.[41] While it is difficult to quantify success in the development of such a "safeguards culture," there is no question that nuclear materials in Kazakhstan are more secure today than they were prior to the completion of U.S.-funded MPC&A projects there.

These projects began life as CTR projects run by DOD, but in fiscal year 1996 responsibility for them was transferred to the Department of Energy (DOE) where they took on a life of their own and became part of a larger program for the safeguarding of nuclear materials.[42] In the same year, responsibility for export control assistance programs was transferred out of the CTR program at DOD and over to the State Department.[43] The Department of Commerce and the DOE also developed export control assistance programs in Kazakhstan and some of the other Central Asian states, funded primarily through the State Department.[44] Although export control projects involved the provision of some equipment (for example, it provided Kazakhstan with patrol boats for the Kazakhstani Coast Guard on the Caspian Sea), for the most part they focused on education and training. U.S. experts assisted Kazakh officials with the drafting of a comprehensive export control law.[45] In addition, the program provided the United States with the opportunity to familiarize Kazakh officials with international export control regimes, which have been described as "a fundamental but largely unappreciated part of early Nunn-Lugar contacts."[46]

Defense conversion stands out as the major exception to the success of the initial set of CTR projects in Kazakhstan. This was to be one of the most important projects for Kazakhstan, as it had the potential to contribute to the long-term development of their economy. According to Kazakh officials, "conversion to civilian and commercial purposes of industrial enterprises devoted to military production under the Soviet system is of paramount importance to Almaty."[47] However, CTR defense conversion projects were plagued by a number of problems caused by a variety of political and economic factors, and were dealt a death blow by the U.S. Congress in 1996, when it disallowed any new CTR funding for defense conversion activities in the former Soviet Union.[48] CTR defense conversion programs were particularly susceptible to criticism, and Congressional opponents argued that such programs essentially subsidized the modernization of other areas of the post-Soviet defense establishments.[49] Other arguments against defense conversion programs were that the money would be better spent converting the U.S. defense industry, and that the programs were too small to have any meaningful effect on the conversion of the mammoth Soviet defense industry. Thus, CTR defense conversion activities in Kazakhstan slowly dwindled. A few small-scale projects continued to be funded with CTR monies from earlier years, but others failed altogether.[50]

In sum, the story thus far is one in which the United States aggressively pursued its goal of a nuclear-weapons-free Kazakhstan by first promising CTR assistance, and subsequently deciding the shape of that assistance through a series of specific projects. These projects focused primarily on nuclear weapons and nuclear materials, and were modeled after those CTR projects in Russia that were relevant to Kazakhstan. By and large these projects were successful, especially when compared with the more complicated and extensive corresponding projects in Russia.

CTR in Kazakhstan: Thinking Outside the Russian Box

If, during its early years, the CTR program helped to ensure the removal of nuclear weapons from Kazakhstan and provided concrete assistance for the dismantlement and nonproliferation-related projects discussed above, it also served another, perhaps equally important, purpose: providing the foundation for a strong, bilateral relationship between the United States and Kazakhstan. As one official explained, DOD recognized early on that a strong, strategic relationship with Central Asia was important to U.S. security and a useful counterbalance to Russia.[51] The CTR program helped establish this relationship while simultaneously communicating the importance the United States placed on the development of nonproliferation policies in the region. Indeed, an article by former Assistant Secretary of Defense Ashton Carter and Steven Miller, his colleague from the Harvard University Center for Science and International Affairs, noted that the principle purpose of the Nunn-Lugar program was "less to finance specific technical steps than to set an agenda for denuclearization and cooperation and to command attention to this agenda."[52] Former administration officials have pointed out that negotiations and discussions over the CTR program were "the first in-depth direct channel of communication" between Almaty and Washington,[53] and that the non-Russian CTR recipient states viewed CTR assistance as a "symbol of continuing U.S. commitment to their independence, national well-being, security, and a non-nuclear future."[54] An early Kazakhstani analysis of the program substantiated this position, warning that Congressional reductions in CTR funding "would reduce Kazakhstan's basic trust in the policies of the United States."[55] As it turned out, trust did develop between the two countries as the initial CTR projects were negotiated and implemented. This trust led to a second wave of CTR projects in Kazakhstan, projects not modeled on CTR in Russia, but designed to address problems unique to Kazakhstan.

The first such initiative was Project Sapphire, a secret endeavor that involved the removal and transport of a forgotten stash of highly-enriched uranium from the Ulba Metallurgy Plant in Ust-Kamenogorsk to the Oak Ridge National Laboratory in Tennessee.[56] Established in 1949, the Ulba Metallurgy Plant is a massive industrial enterprise that currently produces low-enriched fuel pellets for civilian nuclear power plants and processes strategic metals such as beryllium and tantalum. However, for a number of years during the Soviet era, the plant also produced weapons-grade, highly-enriched uranium fuel for use in naval propulsion reactors. Although production of such fuel apparently ended in the 1980s, when Kazakhstan became independent in 1991, a cache of 581 kilograms of highly-enriched uranium remained in storage at Ulba. Experts estimate this amount would have been enough to build more than 20 nuclear weapons.

Kazakh officials first informed the United States of the existence of this material in August 1993, and over the course of the next few months conveyed their concerns about the safety of the material, requesting assistance to secure it or remove it from the country altogether. This request would have been practically inconceivable without the existence of the ongoing dialogue between the United States and Kazakhstan on nonproliferation issues, begun in the context of CTR negotiations. By the time the United States confirmed the quantity and enrichment level of the material in February 1994, the CTR umbrella agreement, as well as the initial implementing agreements described above, were already in place, providing a legal framework for cooperation at Ulba. After confirming that Russia was not interested in taking the material itself (Russian officials claimed initially not to have any knowledge of the existence of the material), U.S. and Kazakh officials agreed that the safest option would be to remove the material. Although removal of the highly-enriched uranium clearly contributed to nonproliferation goals by eliminating the potential for the material to be stolen, it was a novel use of the CTR program. It also was not immediately clear that the compensation Kazakhstan sought for the fuel could be provided out of CTR funds. CTR agreements restricted assistance to in-kind support in the form of equipment, materials, technologies, and training; cash grants were not allowed. In the end, however, due to extraordinary efforts on both sides, the material was airlifted in November 1994 from Ust-Kamenogorsk. Eventually, a compensation package was agreed upon that included the provision of computer equipment, vehicles, and medical supplies, all paid for using CTR funds. The delivery of this compensation was completed in August 1997.[57] With Project Sapphire, U.S.

and Kazakhstani officials proved that CTR could be used for more than the regularly scheduled CTR activities.

Another example of a unique use of CTR tailored to regional concerns was the project to destroy the nuclear test tunnels at the Degelen Mountain and Balapan underground test facilities on the Semipalatinsk nuclear test site. Between 1949 and 1989, 456 nuclear tests were conducted at Semipalatinsk, the Soviet Union's primary nuclear test site.[58] The Degelen Mountain project involved using conventional explosives to destroy the nearly 200 remaining test tunnels, rendering them useless for future nuclear testing. Kazakhstan was eager to prove its nonproliferation commitment to the United States, and every CTR project implemented in country represented jobs for Kazakhstanis. Although this project was clearly related to WMD, it, too, was not a traditional CTR project because it did not involve dismantlement and the tunnels did not represent an immediate proliferation threat. Kazakhstan President Nursultan Nazarbaev officially closed the test site in August 1991,[59] and it was highly unlikely that the test site would ever be used again as Kazakhstan had signed the NPT as a non-nuclear-weapon state. Nonetheless, the project came to be seen as falling within the scope of the CTR legislation. One U.S. official commented that the project represented America's recognition of the importance of engaging Kazakhstan for strategic and political reasons beyond proliferation threats, noting "there was a less restrictive approach to projects [in Kazakhstan]" than in Russia.[60] A CTR implementing agreement for the project was negotiated between DOD and the Kazakhstani Ministry of Science and New Technologies, and was signed October 3, 1995.[61] A Defense Department press release hailed the agreement as "a symbol of both countries' commitment to leadership in promoting global non-proliferation policies."[62]

Probably the most significant set of second wave CTR projects in Central Asia involved former biological weapons facilities. The Soviet Union had a robust but illegal offensive biological weapons program, with numerous research and production facilities throughout Russia[63] as well as a large anthrax production factory in Northern Kazakhstan, and a handful of research institutes in Kazakhstan and Uzbekistan. These outlying facilities conducted at least some research and development work for the Soviet biological weapons program.[64] U.S. attempts to expand the CTR program into the biological weapons areas in Russia were met with complete stonewalling by Russian officials. Although President Boris Yeltsin admitted in 1992 that the Soviet Union had conducted a secret offensive biological weapons program, in violation of the Biological Weapons Convention, the program is still shrouded in secrecy. According to one U.S. official, when the United States would raise the possibility of providing CTR assistance in the area of bioweapons, the Russians simply would deny the existence of bioweapons facilities on their soil. "Where can you go from there?" this official asked.[65] In Kazakhstan, however, the situation was quite different. There, former bioweapons facilities were cut off from their former institutional structures, and there were no institutional actors in the central government in denial about the former Soviet program. The Kazakh leadership was able to show its commitment to nonproliferation by being open about the legacy of Soviet bioweapons in their country, and, at the same time, lobby for assistance from the United States to deal with that legacy.

As a direct result of the personal relationships and trust that developed between U.S. and Kazakh officials during the implementation of other CTR projects, American officials finally secured permission from the Kazakh government to visit the anthrax production facility in Stepnogorsk in June 1995.[66] Although they had known about the existence of the plant, U.S. officials were horrified by what they saw—the enormous scale of the plant, the level of decay within it, and the vulnerability of bioweapons scientists to recruitment. The plant was clearly a proliferation danger. It needed to be dismantled; and it was determined that CTR would be an appropriate tool for the job. In June 1996, one year after the first U.S. visit to Stepnogorsk, an amendment was signed to the 1995 implementing agreement governing work at Degelen Mountain.[67] This new amendment provided the legal basis for biological weapons proliferation prevention activities in Kazakhstan under the CTR program.

As of Spring 2003, all the equipment for production of biological weapons at Stepnogorsk has been destroyed, and the Defense Department is in the process of destroying the buildings themselves.[68] In addition, new projects are underway to provide effective physical protection of biological agents at two research institutes: the State Agricultural Research Institute in Otar and the Anti-Plague Institute in Almaty.[69] Finally, a new cooperative biodefense project seeks to develop cooperative research projects between Kazakhstani and U.S. scientists, to "prevent proliferation of biological weapons biotechnology, increase transparency, and enhance U.S. force protection."[70]

Thus, in the second phase of CTR, assistance again has veered from its initial path of nuclear-related, Russia-modeled projects. Building on the relationships that CTR helped develop, DOD has used the agreement as a tool to address specific nonproliferation opportunities unique to Central Asia. In recent years, additional proliferation threats have been identified, such as the partially constructed chemical weapons production plant in the city of Pavlodar in Northern Kazakhstan. The initiation of significant work in the former biological weapons sector in Kazakhstan was a breakthrough for CTR in this highly sensitive area, and now represents the greater part of CTR activity in Kazakhstan. In addition to preventing the proliferation of biological weapons-materials, these projects have the ancillary benefit of giving the U.S. important insights into the Soviet biological weapons program that Russia continues to obscure. Perhaps more important to the development of the CTR program, the biological weapons-related work in Kazakhstan has provided a road map for biological weapons-related CTR work in other countries, such as Uzbekistan, Ukraine and Georgia.

CTR in Uzbekistan and Beyond

The Defense Department's expansion of the CTR program into Uzbekistan was very different from its expansion into Kazakhstan. The Uzbek government approached the United States for assistance with a discreet problem: the demilitarization of a remote facility for the research, development and testing of chemical weapons in the city of Nukus, in western Uzbekistan.[71] Following the model for the second wave of CTR projects in Kazakhstan, the project was identified as one that fit into the CTR framework, and Uzbekistan quickly joined the CTR club without fanfare. In fact, DOD was so anxious to begin work that it started under a temporary agreement in 1997 with the Ministry of Defense while hammering out the CTR umbrella agreement over a period of several years.[72]

In addition to the Nukus project, which was completed in May 2002,[73] DOD has used the CTR program to implement a number of projects in the biological weapons-related sphere. After concluding a new implementing agreement for such work in October 2001, DOD began to demilitarize the former biological weapons test site on Vozrezhdeniye Island in the Aral Sea.[74] In addition, DOD is in the process of establishing CTR projects along the lines of those in Kazakhstan for physical protection of biological agents and for collaborative bio-defense research at three research institutes: the Institute of Veterinary Science in Samarkand, the Institute of Virology in Tashkent and the Center for Prophylaxis and Quarantine of Most Hazardous Infections in Tashkent.[75]

DOD is currently developing a new set of CTR projects that is likely to expand CTR further within Central Asia. This major new initiative, called Weapons of Mass Destruction Proliferation Prevention (WMDPP), is designed to provide border security assistance to all eligible non-Russian states of the former Soviet Union, and has already received $40 million from Congress.[76] Within Central Asia, initial WMDPP projects will occur in countries where CTR has already been established, such as Kazakhstan and Uzbekistan, but it is also likely that this initiative eventually will be expanded to Kyrgyzstan.[77] The goal of WMDPP is to provide recipient countries with "self-sustaining, multi-agency capabilities to prevent, detect, and interdict WMD and related materials,"[78] and the first priority will be to address indigenous operational capabilities at key border crossings. In testimony before the Senate Armed Services Committee in July 2002, Lisa Bronson, Deputy Under Secretary of Defense with responsibilities for the CTR program, noted that this initiative will further enhance U.S. security, not only by helping to prevent the proliferation of WMD to terrorists and "states of concern," but also by "facilitating future U.S. activities in the region and reinforcing relationships with FSU [former Soviet Union] states" and "developing relationships with foreign counterpart agencies that will be useful in times of crisis."[79] This last comment could be a subtle acknowledgement that U.S.-Uzbekistan cooperation under the auspices of the CTR program played an important role in Uzbekistan's prompt agreement to allow the United States to station troops in southern Uzbekistan during combat operations in the opening phases of the Global War on Terrorism in Afghanistan in late 2001.

Conclusion

A decade of CTR experiences in Central Asia has given the United States significant insights into this strategically important region of the world. While the CTR program has been and remains overwhelmingly focused on Russia, it is useful to note the evolution of CTR in Central Asia and the ways it has strengthened U.S. relationships there. It is clear that when the program was first introduced in Central Asia, there was not a systematic evaluation of the proliferation threats in the region nor a measured application of the program to counter those threats. Instead, a top-down approach was used, in which DOD copied Russian CTR projects to the extent that they were relevant. As the program evolved, this approach gradually gave way to a bottom-up approach where individuals on both sides identified specific proliferation threats and then used CTR as a tool to deal with those threats.

During this evolution, Central Asia has come to be understood as a region distinct from Russia, with a different set of nonproliferation problems and opportunities. Furthermore, in the context of the current war on terrorism, the future of the entire CTR program is increasingly focused on the threats posed by biological weapons proliferation, an aspect of the program that has been particularly strong in Central Asia, and on border security issues addressed by the new WMDPP initiative.[80] It is noteworthy that the CTR program has evolved to a stage at which an exclusively non-Russian initiative could be pursued.

Over the course of a decade, the CTR program has provided Kazakhstan and Uzbekistan with the resources to deal with specific problems that would have been difficult to address otherwise. It also has provided America with a concrete means of engaging with Central Asia on serious issues of mutual concern. This engagement deepened the relationships between the United States and Kazakhstan, and later between the United States and Uzbekistan. Each new project reinforces these relationships—and as new threats emerge, the countries will be better positioned to address them. By engaging with Central Asia to prevent the WMD proliferation, the CTR program has advanced U.S policies and contributed to U.S. homeland, regional and global security. CTR has proven flexible enough to address unanticipated threats, and at the same time maintained its primary focus on the dangers of proliferation. It has done so at minimal expense while yielding important side benefits. In an era obsessed with the control and elimination of WMD, CTR may prove to be an effective alternative to the more costly, more problematic resort to U.S. military force.

Notes

[1] David Remnick, "In New Commonwealth of `Equals,' Russia Remains the Dominant Force," *The Washington Post*, December 22, 1991, A39.

[2] In September 1990, there were 104 SS-18 ICBMs, each armed with 10 nuclear warheads, located at bases in Derzhavinsk and Zhangiz-Tobe in Kazakhstan. Table 1-C, *Nuclear Successor States of the Soviet Union: Status Report on Nuclear Weapons, Fissile Material, and Export Controls*, no. 5, Monterey Institute of International Studies and Carnegie Endowment for International Peace, March 1998, 10.

[3] This test site, called the Semipalatinsk Test Site, is approximately 18,000 km². *See* "Research Library: Country Information, Kazakhstan," on the website of the Nuclear Threat Initiative, material produced by the Center for Nonproliferation Studies at the Monterey Institute of International Studies, <http://www.nti.org/db/nisprofs/kazakst/weafacil/semipala.html>.

[4] The island is known as Vozrozhdeniye Island (translated as "Renaissance" or "Rebirth" Island), and the test site was officially referred to as "Aralsk-7" during the Soviet period. Gulbarshyn Bozheyeva, Yerlan Kunakbayev, and Dastan Yeleukenov, "Former Soviet Biological Weapons Facilities in Kazakhstan: Past, Present and Future," Occasional Paper no. 1, Center for Nonproliferation Studies, Monterey Institute of International Studies, June 1999.

[5] This was the Pavlodar Chemical Plant in the city of Pavlodar, Kazakhstan. Gulbarshyn Bozheyeva, "The Pavlodar Chemical Weapons Plant in Kazakhstan: History and Legacy," *The Nonproliferation Review*, Summer 2000, 136.

[6] The fuel was located at the Ulba Metallurgy Plant, located approximately 20 miles outside Ust-Kamenogorsk, Kazakhstan. William C. Potter, "Project Sapphire: U.S.-Kazakhstani Cooperation for Nonproliferation," *Dismantling the Cold War: U.S. and NIS Perspectives on the Nunn-Lugar Co-*

operative Threat Reduction Program, John M. Shields and William C. Potter, eds. (Cambridge 1997), 345-346.

[7] Jon Brook Wolfsthal, Cristina Astrid Chuen, and Emily Ewell Daughtry, eds., Table 4.6, "Mangyshlak Atomic Energy Combine," *Nuclear Status Report: Nuclear Weapons, Fissile Material and Export Controls in the Former Soviet Union*, no. 6, Monterey Institute of International Studies and Carnegie Endowment for International Peace, June 2001, 165.

[8] *See* Sam Nunn, "Changing Threats in the Post-Cold War World," *Dismantling the Cold War*, xvi, supra note 6; Richard Lugar, "Forward," *Defense by Other Means: The Politics of US-NIS Threat Reduction and Nuclear Security Cooperation*, Jason D. Ellis (Westport 2001), xii.

[9] Soviet Nuclear Threat Reduction Act of 1991, P.L. 102-228. The program is also popularly referred to as the "Nunn-Lugar program."

[10] Jason D. Ellis, 80-81; Richard Combs, "U.S. Domestic Politics and the Nunn-Lugar Program," *Dismantling the Cold War*, John M. Shields and William C. Potter, eds. (Cambridge, 1997), 44.

[11] For example, Senator Nunn has noted with frustration, "For some reason, [CTR] has come under attack as if it were a foreign aid program." Sam Nunn, "Changing Threats in the Post-Cold War World," *Dismantling the Cold War*, John M. Shields and William C. Potter, eds., xvii. Senator Lugar has written, "Nunn-Lugar is not foreign aid. It is not charity." Richard Lugar, "Forward," *Defense by Other Means*, Jason D. Ellis, xii.

[12] Congressional findings included in the first Soviet Nuclear Threat Reduction Act of 1991 stated, "It is in the national security interests of the United States (A) to facilitate on a priority basis the transportation, storage, safeguarding, and destruction of nuclear and other weapons in the Soviet Union, its republics and any successor entities, (B) to assist in the prevention of weapons proliferation." Soviet Nuclear Threat Reduction Act of 1991, P.L. 102-228, available at <http://www.thomas. loc.gov>.

[13] See, for example, Ellis, supra note 10, 112; Combs, supra note 10, 47; Rose Gottemoeller, "Presidential Priorities in Nuclear Policy," John M. Shields and William C. Potter, eds., *Dismantling the Cold War*, 65.

[14] See Nunn, supra note 11, xvi, referring to Kurt M. Campbell, Ashton B. Carter, Steven B. Miller, and Charles A. Zraket, *Soviet Nuclear Fission: Control of the Nuclear Arsenal in a Disintegrating Soviet Union*, CSIA Studies in International Security (Cambridge, MA: Center for Science and International Affairs, Harvard University, November 1991); Gottemoeller, supra note 13, 67.

[15] Ellis, supra note 10, 119.

[16] *See* Gloria Duffy, "Cooperative Threat Reduction in Perspective," *Dismantling the Cold War*, John M. Shields and William C. Potter, eds., 25. Also, *see* Ashton B. Carter and William J. Perry, *Preventive Defense: A New Security Strategy for* America (Washington, DC: Brookings Institution Press, 1999).

[17] Duffy, supra note 16, 25; Gottemoeller, supra note 13, 65, 67.

[18] Ellis, supra note 10, 82.

[19] Combs, supra note 10, 47-48; Gottemoeller, supra note 13, 65.

[20] *See, for example,* John M. Shields and William C. Potter, *Dismantling the Cold War*, 386; Ellis, supra note 10, 2, (Westport 2001); John W. R. Lepingwell and Nikolai Sokov, "Strategic Offensive Arms Elimination and Weapons Protection, Control, and Accounting," *The Nonproliferation Review*, Spring 2000, 59.

[21]*See* John M. Shields and William C Potter, *Dismantling the Cold War*, 13-15; Combs, supra note 10, 48; Duffy, supra note 16, 26-27. See also, Ellis, supra note 10, 40-41. Ellis argues that there were "two major divergent approaches" to the CTR program. The first approach was broader and open to many ideas for reducing the nuclear threat from the NIS, including "intensive long-term attention to sustaining democracy in Russia and integrating it into the international community." The second approach was more limited and short-term, focusing on specific destruction and dismantlement activities.

[22] Author's phone conversation with U.S. DOD official, October 2002.

[23] Ibid.

[24] Gottemoeller, supra note 13, 65; Ellis, supra note 10, 32 ("DOD officials ranked the denuclearization of the Non-Russian NIS Republics as the Chief Aim and `Ultimate Yardstick' of the Program's Success.")

[25] Text of Protocol to the Treaty Between the United States of America and the Union of Soviet Socialist Republics on the Reduction and Limitation of Strategic Offensive Arms ("Lisbon Protocol") signed in Lisbon, Portugal on May 23, 1992, available on the Nuclear Threat Initiative website at <http://www.nti.org/db/nisprofs/fulltext/treaties/start1/s1lis.html> and on the U.S. Department of Defense website at <http://www.defenselink.mil/acq/acic/treaties/start1/protocols/start_1p.htm#VI>.

[26] Ibid., Article V.

[27] Combs, supra note 10, 47-48.

[28] Gottemoeller, supra note 13, 65. Another former official has noted that CTR, "played an important role in the decisions of Ukraine, Belarus, and Kazakhstan to forgo nuclear weapons capabilities." Duffy, supra note 16, 25. See also, Ellis, supra note 10, 31. Ellis notes that CTR funds "provided a key incentive for Belarus, Kazakhstan, and Ukraine to forgo the nuclear option . . . .None of these three states had the financial resources or capabilities to successfully undertake strategic denuclearization."

[29] Lugar, supra note 8, xiii.

[30] See Combs, supra note 10, 48; Gottemoeller, supra note 13, 66.

[31] The initial legislation for the Nunn-Lugar program limited assistance to "cooperation among the United States, the Soviet Union, its republics, and any successor entities to 1) destroy nuclear weapons, chemical weapons, and other weapons, 2) transport, store, disable, and safeguard weapons in connection with their destruction, and 3) establish verifiable safeguards against the proliferation of such weapons." Soviet Nuclear Threat Reduction Act of 1991, P.L. 102-228, available at <http://www. loc.gov/thomas>. Although the subsequent versions of the authorizing legislation expanded the program to include prevention of "braindrain" of scientists with weapons expertise, defense conversion, and military-to-military contacts (P.L. 102-484), and later even programs for environmental restoration of military sites and the construction of housing for former military officers (P.L. 103-160), these expanded programs were quickly eliminated by subsequent Congresses. See Ellis, supra note 10, Chapter Four, 77-106.

[32] CTR umbrella agreements typically include provisions that ensure that the assistance will not be taxed, that the U.S. will have the right to audit and examine assistance provided to ensure that it is being used for the purposes for which it was provided, that ensure that U.S. personnel have diplomatic protections in accordance with the Vienna Convention on Diplomatic Relations, and others. *See* Jack M. Beard, "Recent Development: A New Legal Regime for Bilateral Assistance Programs: International Agreements Governing the `Nunn-Lugar' Demilitarization Program in the Former Soviet Union, " *Virginia Journal of International Law,* 894 (Summer 1995), 35.

[33] *See* Agreement Between the United States of America and the Republic of Kazakhstan Concerning the Destruction of Silo Launchers of Intercontinental Ballistic Missiles, Emergency Response, and the Prevention of Proliferation of Nuclear Weapons, signed December 13, 1993 (United States – Kazakhstan Umbrella Agreement); Agreement Between the Department of Defense of the United States of America and the Ministry of Defense of the Republic of Kazakhstan Concerning the Provision to the Republic of Kazakhstan of Emergency Response Equipment and Related Training in Connection with the Removal of Nuclear Weapons from the Republic of Kazakhstan for Destruction and the Removal of Intercontinental Ballistic Missiles and the Destruction of their Silo Launchers, signed December 13, 1993 (Emergency Response Implementing Agreement); Agreement Between the Department of Defense of the United States of America and the Ministry of Defense of the Republic of Kazakhstan Concerning the Provision to the Republic of Kazakhstan of Material and Services for the Establishment of a Government-to-Government Communications Link, signed December 13, 1993 (Government-to-Government Communications Link Implementing Agreement); Agreement Between the Department of Defense of the United States of America and the Ministry of Defense of the Republic of Kazakhstan Concerning the Provision of Material, Services, and Related Training to the Republic of Kazakhstan in Connection with the Destruction of Silo Launchers of Intercontinental Ballistic Missiles and Associated Equipment and Components, signed December 13, 1993 (Strategic

Offensive Arms Elimination Implementing Agreement); Agreement Between the Department of Defense of the United States of America and the Ministry of Defense of the Republic of Kazakhstan Concerning Control, Accounting and Physical Protection of Nuclear Material to Promote the Prevention of Nuclear Weapons Proliferation, signed December 13, 1993 (MPC&A Implementing Agreement); Agreement Between the Department of Defense of the United States of America and the Ministry of Defense of the Republic of Kazakhstan Concerning the Provision of Assistance to the Republic of Kazakhstan Related to the Establishment of Export Control Systems to Prevent the Proliferation of Weapons of Mass Destruction, signed December 13, 1993 (Export Control Implementing Agreement); and Memorandum of Understanding and Cooperation on Defense and Military Relations Between the Department of Defense of the United States of America and the Ministry of Defense of the Republic of Kazakhstan, signed February 14, 1994 (Defense and Military Contacts MOU).

[34] *See* Agreement Between the Department of Defense of the United States of America and the Ministry of Atomic Energy of the Russian Federation Concerning the Safe and Secure Transportation and Storage of Nuclear Weapons Through the Provision of Emergency Response Equipment and Related Training, signed June 17, 1992 (Emergency Response Implementing Agreement); Agreement Between the Department of Defense of the United States of America and the Ministry of Economics of the Russian Federation Concerning Cooperation in the Elimination of Strategic Offensive Arms, signed August 26, 1993 (Strategic Offensive Arms Elimination Implementing Agreement); Agreement Between the Department of Defense of the United States of America and the Ministry of Atomic Energy of the Russian Federation Concerning Control, Accounting and Physical Protection of Nuclear Material, signed September 2, 1993 (MPC&A Implementing Agreement); and Memorandum of Understanding and Cooperation on Defense and Military Relations Between the Department of Defense of the United States of America and the Ministry of Defense of the Russian Federation, signed September 8, 1993 (Defense and Military Contacts MOU). Unlike in Kazakhstan, there has never been an export control agreement in Russia, although it was not for lack of trying. The U.S. had hoped to provide CTR assistance for the improvement of Russian export controls, but negotiations on an agreement stalled and an agreement never materialized. Additionally, there was no need for a CTR agreement with the Russian Federation on a government-to-government communications link as Russia had inherited the Soviet Union's link.

[35] Lepingwell and Sokov, supra note 20, 60.

[36] Oumirserik T. Kasenov, Dastan Eleukenov, and Murat Laumulin, "Implementing the CTR Program in Kazakstan," in John M. Shields and William C. Potter, eds., *Dismantling the Cold War*, 194.

[37] "Cooperative Threat Reduction: Kazakhstan Programs," Defense Threat Reduction Agency website at <http://www.dtra.mil/ctr/ctr_kazakhstan.html>.

[38] The four locations are: the Institute of Nuclear Physics in Alatau, a small village outside Almaty, and the Institute of Atomic Energy in Kurchatov City on the former nuclear test site near Semipalatinsk, both of which housed a few kilograms of highly-enriched uranium fuel for use in nuclear research reactors; the Mangyshlyak Atomic Energy Combine in Aktau on the coast of the Caspian Sea, the site of a BN-350 fast-breeder reactor and approximately 300 metric tons of spent fuel containing plutonium; and the Ulba Metallurgy Combine in the eastern Kazakhstani city of Ust-Kamenogorsk. The Ulba Combine manufactures low-enriched uranium fuel pellets and various other materials that have dual uses, i.e. that can be used both in the manufacture and development of nuclear weapons and that have other non-weapons-related uses. Wolfsthal et.al., supra note 7, 160-165.

[39] Jessica Eve Stern, "Cooperative Activities to Improve Fissile Material Protection, Control and Accounting," in John M. Shields and William C. Potter, eds., *Dismantling the Cold War*, 327-328.

[40] Ibid.

[41] *See* Emily Ewell Daughtry and Fred Wehling, "Cooperative Efforts to Secure Fissile Material in the NIS," *The Nonproliferation Review*, Spring 2000, 97.

[42] MPC&A programs were transferred to DOE in accordance with Presidential Decision Directive-41, "U.S. Policy on Improving Nuclear Material Security in Russia and Other Newly Independent

States." For a discussion of some of the reasons behind this move, *see* Ellis, supra note 10, 123 and Gottemoeller, supra note 13, 69-71.

[43] Ibid.

[44] These funds, which the Department of Commerce and Energy must apply for, come out of the State Department's Nonproliferation and Disarmament Fund. *See* Scott Parrish and Tamara Robinson, "Efforts to Strengthen Export Controls and Combat Illicit Trafficking and Braindrain," *The Nonproliferation Review*, Spring 2000, 114-115.

[45] Kasenov et al., supra note 35, 197-201.

[46] Michael H. Newlin, "Export Controls and the CTR Program," in John M. Shields and William C. Potter, eds., *Dismantling the Cold War*, 305.

[47] Kasenov et al. supra note 35, 203.

[48] National Defense Authorization Act for FY 1997, P.L. 104-201.

[49] See Amy F. Woolf, "Nunn-Lugar Cooperative Threat Reduction Programs: Issues for Congress," CRS Report for Congress, Order No. 97-1027-F, updated March 6, 2002, available at < http://www.fcnl.org/pdfs/nuc_nunn_lugar.pdf>.

[50] For a discussion of CTR defense conversion activities in Kazakhstan and an in-depth analysis of the attempt to convert the former biological weapons production facility at Stepnogorsk, Kazakhstan, see Sonia Ben Ouagrham and Kathleen Vogel, "Conversion at Stepnogorsk: What the Future Holds for Former Bioweapons Facilities," Cornell University Peace Studies Program, Occasional Paper #28, February 2003, available at <http://www.ciaonet.org/wps/ous01>.

[51] Author's phone conversation with U.S. DOD official, October 2002.

[52] Ashton B. Carter and Steven E. Miller, "Cooperative Security and the Former Soviet Union: Near-Term Challenges," *Global Engagement: Cooperation and Security in the 21st Century*, Janne E. Nolan, ed. (Washington, DC: The Brookings Institution, 1994), 548.

[53] Duffy, supra note 16, 26.

[54] Gottemoeller, supra note 13, 65.

[55] Kasenov et. al., supra note 35, 194.

[56] For a detailed account of this story, *see* William C. Potter, "Project Sapphire: U.S.-Kazakhstani Cooperation for Nonproliferation," John M Shields and William C. Potter, eds., *Dismantling the Cold War*, 345-362. Factual information in this paragraph is drawn from that article.

[57] "Cooperative Threat Reduction: Project Sapphire," Defense Threat Reduction Agency website, <http://www.dtra.mil/ctr/project/projkaz/ctr_sapphire.html>.

[58] See "Research Library: Country Information, Kazakhstan," on the website of the Nuclear Threat Initiative, material produced by the Center for Nonproliferation Studies at the Monterey Institute of International Studies, http://www.nti.org/db/nisprofs/kazakst/weafacil/semipala.htm.

[59] Ibid.

[60] Author's phone conversation with U.S. DOD official, October 2002.

[61] *See* Agreement Between the Department of Defense of the United States of America and the Ministry of Energy Industry and Trade of the Republic of Kazakhstan Concerning the Elimination of Infrastructure for Weapons of Mass Destruction, signed October 3, 1995 (Weapons of Mass Destruction Implementing Agreement).

[62] "U.S.-Kazakhstan Agreement to Seal Up World's Largest Nuclear Test Tunnel Complex," DOD News Release, October 3, 1995, <available at <http://www.fas.org/news/kazakh/951004-40981 1a.html>.

[63] *See* Ken Alibek and Stephen Handelman, *Biohazard: The Chilling True Story of the Largest Cover tBiological Weapons Program In the World--Told from Inside by the Man Who Ran It* (New York :Random House, May 1999).

[64] For detailed descriptions of the Kazakhstani facilities and their former activities, *see* Gulbarshyn Bozheyeva, Yerlan Kunakbayev, and Dastan Eleukenov, "Former Soviet Biological Weapons Facilities in Kazakhstan: Past, Present and Future," Occasional Paper No. 1, Center for Nonproliferation Studies, Monterey Institute of International Studies, June 1999.

[65] Author's phone conversations with U.S. DOD official, October 2002. DOD is currently using CTR funds to pursue a limited number of biological weapons-related nonproliferation activities in Russia, but because DOD has yet to sign an implementing agreement for work in this area in Russia, it is forced to do so through the International Science and Technology Center in Moscow. From a legal perspective, this is less desirable than an implementing agreement as it does not provide the same level of protections to the United States. However, the work has been deemed important enough to U.S. policy goals that this awkward assistance mechanism continues to be used.

[66] A detailed account of this first visit is provided in Judith Miller, Stephen Engelberg, and William Broad, *Germs: Biological Weapons and America's Secret War* (New York, 2001), 165-182.

[67] Ben Ouagrham and Vogel, supra note 47, 36. The agreement is cited in supra note 59 and was initially amended to allow for work in the biological weapons nonproliferation sphere on June 10, 1996.

[68] "Cooperative Threat Reduction: BW Production Facility Dismantlement," Defense Threat Reduction Agency website, <http://www.dtra.mil/ctr/project/projkaz/bw_secure_trans.html>.

[69] "Cooperative Threat Reduction: BW Materials Security and Transparency," Defense Threat Reduction Agency website, <http://www.dtra.mil/ctr/project/projkaz/bw_prod_facil_disman.html>.

[70] "Cooperative Threat Reduction: BW Cooperative Bio Defense Projects," Defense Threat Reduction Agency website, <http://www.dtra.mil/ctr/project/projkaz/bw_coop_bio_proj.html>.

[71] Author's phone conversation with U.S. Department of Defense official, October 2002.

[72] The temporary agreement was the Agreement Between the Department of Defense of the United States of America and the Ministry of Defense of the Republic of Uzbekistan Concerning Cooperation in the Area of Dismantlement of Weapons of Mass Destruction, the Prevention of Proliferation of Weapons of Mass Destruction, and the Promotion of Defense and Military Relations, which was signed on June 27, 1997. The Umbrella Agreement is the Agreement Between the United States of America and the Republic of Uzbekistan Concerning Cooperation in the Area of the Promotion of Defense Relations and the Prevention of Proliferation of Weapons of Mass Destruction. It was not signed until June 5, 2001.

[73] "Cooperative Threat Reduction: Nukus Chemical Research Institute Demilitarization [Complete]," Defense Threat Reduction Agency website, <http://www.dtra.mil/ctr/project/projuzb/ctr_nukus.html>.

[74] Alan Sipress, "U.S. to Help Uzbekistan Clean Up Anthrax Site," October 23, 2001, A2.

[75] "Cooperative Threat Reduction: Uzbekistan Programs," Defense Threat Reduction Agency website, < http://www.dtra.mil/ctr/ctr_uzbekistan.html>.

[76] Although both the State Department and the Department of Energy currently have programs that also focus on border security, neither of these programs is as well funded as the new DOD initiative. DOD plans to coordinate its new program closely with these other agencies. Author's phone conversation with U.S. DOD official, October 2002. (Turkmenistan and Belarus are not eligible because they have not been certified by the State Department as required by the CTR legislation, due to poor human rights records.)

[77] It is unlikely, however, that it will be expanded to Tajikistan or Turkmenistan any time soon. Tajikistan is still considered too unstable for the initiation of any major CTR projects. Furthermore, the heavy presence of border guards from the Russian Federation on the Afghan-Tajik border complicates any potential U.S. border-related assistance to Tajikistan. As indicated in supra note 75, Turkmenistan is not currently eligible for CTR assistance.

[78] "Combating WMD Smuggling," Testimony of Deputy Under Secretary of Defense Lisa Bronson before the Senate Armed Services Committee, Subcommittee on Emerging Threats, July 30, 2002.

[79] Ibid.

[80] Author's phone conversation with U.S. DOD official, October 2002.

Chapter 16

Building Security in Central Asia: a Multilateral Perspective

Jennifer D.P. Moroney

O ver the past decade, many actors—including Russia, the United States, and to a lesser extent multilateral security institutions— have sought to deepen their ties to the five Central Asian states for a myriad of reasons, not least being the presence of large oil and gas reserves. Russia views this region as within its sphere of influence and interest, and as a bulwark to instability coming from the south, specifically from Afghanistan, Iran, and potentially, India and Pakistan. Russia has supported the development of closer relations with the Central Asian republics on an economic, political and military level through the Commonwealth of Independent States (CIS), by including them in the security framework, the CIS Collective Security Treaty (CST). With no shortage of bilateral and multilateral security treaties signed between them, the perception among many Western analysts in the mid 1990s was that Russia and Central Asia were clearly connected in the arena of security and defense.[1]

In the aftermath of the September 11 terrorist attacks on the United States and the subsequent war in Afghanistan, a combination of support pledged by Central Asian states to the U.S.-led coalition against terrorism and the need for such support have brought Central Asia into the international spotlight. But in deepening ties with these states, the West has become more acutely aware of the plethora of security challenges in this region, including extremely porous borders, high-level corruption, economic and energy insecurity, and the presence of groups determined to overthrow the current regimes. In short, there is a new appreciation in the West of Central Asia as a strategically crucial region at the crossroads of a variety of influences. Western states and institutions now are taking seriously the security problems of the region and concerns of Central Asia's leaders. While Western governments continue to strengthen their security cooperation with these states, Western institutions continue to assist in the building of democratic regimes operating under the rule of law, the transition to market-oriented economies and the building of reliable security and economic institutions. Though progress in instituting reforms has been slow, security assistance to these states continues to grow. To date, security assistance to Central Asia has not been conditional on progress in the transition to democracy and other Western ideals.

The lack of an overarching security institution to manage security problems is mirrored in the proliferation of security threats to the region. The West and Russia are both attempting to fill the security vacuum that appeared after the collapse of the Soviet Union. Because security concerns in this region are transnational by nature, it can be argued that transnational solutions are needed, and multilateral institutions could serve in helping these states build more effective regional ties on a number of security-related areas. However, finding multilateral solutions to regional security problems in Central Asia is no easy task. Regional cooperation is a contentious issue among these states as historic mistrust and animosity loom large, particularly between the two largest states, Uzbekistan and Kazakhstan. Multilateral programs, both military and non-military, have met with limited success due to the difficulties associated with regional cooperation in Central Asia. The danger stemming from a lack of regional military cooperation is twofold according to Martha Brill Olcott, a leading specialist on the region. First, if these states were to pursue separate military developments, the inherent distrust in the region would not be alleviated and, in fact, could be exacerbated. Second, all of these states are militarily weak, and even the two largest, Uzbekistan and Kazakhstan, cannot provide for their own security.[2]

This chapter will investigate the prospects for multilateral cooperation in Central Asia and the steps to necessary address these challenges. The multilateral institutions that are discussed and evaluated for their effectiveness in the region include the North Atlantic Treaty Organization (NATO), the European Union (EU), the CIS, the Organization for Security and Cooperation in Europe (OSCE), the Shanghai Cooperation Organization (SCO),[3] and GUAM (Georgia, Ukraine, Azerbaijan and Moldova).[4]

The key questions this discussion will address include:

- What are the most visible security threats in this region?
- What are key Western and Russian security interests in this region?

- What are the discernable benefits for the participants for their membership in multilateral or regional organizations?
- Which security issues tend to polarize the actors in the region?
- Which, if any, regional or multilateral institutions are best able to provide the types of security assistance that the Central Asian states really need?
- What are the implications for Central Asia in favoring one institution over another (e.g., NATO over the CIS)?

The challenges associated with improving security in this region will continue to capture the attention of Western states, Russia and also a growing number of regional organizations, in an attempt to improve the security situation and maximize influence in the region. There may be no quick fixes to the extreme security challenges in Central Asia. Yet it will be argued that an expanded involvement of Western multilateral security organizations can have a positive effect by facilitating regional security cooperation and helping to build mutual trust and confidence.

Security Environment Overview

In order to better understand the consequences and potential benefits of multilateral engagement in Central Asia, it is first necessary to understand the security environment in which these states are operating. It should come as no surprise that the Central Asia region, a crossroads for a myriad of influences, including Slavic, Middle Eastern and Oriental, is experiencing instability along ethnic and religious lines. Moreover, a lack of economic reforms and free trade arrangements with the West, high levels of corruption and the remnants of a command economy structure left over from Soviet times add to regional stress. Although Kazakhstan and Turkmenistan inherited vast energy reserves from the USSR, the difficulty in extracting these resources thus far has hindered the economic development of the region. Non-military or "soft security" threats, such as the cross-border transit of terrorists, narcotics, small arms and materials associated with Weapons of Mass Destruction (WMD), are among the primary security concerns for the West, Russia, China and the Central Asian republics themselves.

Because border security threats are transnational by nature, many institutions and states, as well as non-government organizations (NGOs) and the private sector (especially energy-oriented businesses), have sought to support Central Asian states in their attempts to improve the border security situation. Assistance offered varies, but is primarily focused on providing training and equipment, as well as improving regional dialogue by holding a plethora of international conferences and seminars. Uzbekistan and Krygyzstan have received the greatest attention and resources because of the threat posed by terrorist groups in the region, such as the Islamic Movement of Uzbekistan (IMU). The IMU is seen as having links with al Qaeda as well as other radical Islamic fundamentalist groups, and desires to overthrow the government of Uzbekistan and create an Islamic state. Until recently there have been few mechanisms for successfully regulating the border situation, although the United States has provided a significant amount of resources—over $82 million in FY02 for the largest program, the Export Control and Related Border Security (EXBS) assistance program, as well as several other smaller initiatives.[5]

The Central Asia Security Vacuum

For the first five years following the break-up of the Soviet Union, the Central Asian republics were not a priority for the West, primarily because these states were viewed as within Russia's sphere of influence. As a result, the United States, NATO, and the EU paid little attention to the region, even given the presence of large untapped oil and gas reserves. America provided no substantial economic aid packages to Central Asia and focused instead on assisting the western Newly Independent States (NIS) of Ukraine and Moldova. The South Caucasus states (Georgia, Azerbaijan, and Armenia) were also higher on the priority list. The Central Asian republics had no "Western card" to play to counter Russia's influence in the political, economic, energy or military spheres. Further, given objections from Russia to U.S./NATO military or political outreach to these states, NATO did not attempt to reach out to Central Asia. With no Western security option for Central Asia, they retained their relatively tight security cooperation within the CIS framework.

Russia attempted to fill the security vacuum in the Former Soviet Union (FSU) by encouraging greater cooperation among CIS members. The creation of the CIS, and subsequent attempts to deepen cooperation in a number of key sectors, was an attempt to increase dependency on Russia and to create some kind of "institutional normalcy" in the region in place of the Soviet Union. In the security sphere, the Tashkent CST of 1992 was signed by seven states including Russia, Belarus, Moldova, Uzbekistan, Kyrgyzstan, Kazakhstan and Tajikistan, and accorded Russia leverage over its less powerful neighbors. The extent of these security ties between CST affiliates has varied over time in response to political and economic leverage exercised by Russia. Moreover, the individual members have differing relations with other actors in the region and with the West, which impacts their participation in the CST collective security framework.

Importantly, Uzbekistan refused to sign the second phase of the CST when it was proposed, which took place prior to September 11. Therefore, Uzbekistan was not in Russia's official security sphere when the United States went in to try to negotiate basing rights on Uzbek territory. As a result of Uzbekistan's post September 11 role in the War on Terrorism, Uzbekistan's security ties with America have been improved in the form of a "Strategic Partnership" signed in March 2002. This agreement calls for the United States to "regard with grave concern any external threat" to Uzbekistan.[6] Kyrgyzstan, Kazakhstan, and to a lesser extent, Tajikistan and Turkmenistan also have become important U.S. coalition partners and like Uzbekistan have received a considerable increase in security assistance over the past year. Although Russia is no longer unilaterally able to dictate the foreign and security policy orientation of the Central Asian states, common interests still remain between the CIS states and Russia, and Russia remains influential in the region.

In the mid 1990s, Russia's economic trade, as well as its military cooperation with Central Asian states, began to decline. Russia's main security role centered on the sale of military supplies, a peacekeeping contingent in Tajikistan, and coordination with these states over anti-terrorist measures.[7] During this time, the Central Asian states (with the exception of Tajikistan which was heavily involved in a civil war) also sought to diversify their international relations with actors outside the confines of the CIS. New trends included deepening relations with China, Turkey and Iran, in addition to the United States and other Western countries. Zbigniew Brzezinski noticed this shift in the late 1990s and called for a change in the U.S. strategy, to "consolidate and perpetuate the prevailing geopolitical pluralism on the map in Eurasia" in response to what he saw as a shift in the international orientation of some of the Central Asian states.[8]

The United States first showed interest in playing some kind of role in the security vacuum in Central Asia in the late 1990s as U.S. policymakers grew concerned over increases in small arms, narcotics trafficking, and terrorist movement across the porous Central Asian borders. Moreover, the shift of IMU to insurgency tactics as well as the increasing effectiveness of the IMU, encouraged the Department of Defense (DOD) to conduct Special Forces exercises in the region. U.S. Special Operations forces thus began engaging in Uzbekistan and Kyrgyzstan in 2000 (more modestly in Kyrgyzstan). The widely held perception in the United States was that, left to their own devices, the Kyrgyz and Uzbek governments would adopt the same tactics as Russia in Chechnya, if they were not shown alternative methods for dealing with insurgencies.[9]

The strategic interest in Central Asia among the United States, Russia, China, Iran and Turkey in filling the security vacuum has led to a situation of free competition, which has the potential to result in a zero-sum game for Central Asia. The inherent danger is that the region will become further divided, with each state preferring to develop ties on a bilateral basis with prominent states and institutions to improve their individual security situation, without reference to each other. The inability of Western institutions to agree as to their specific roles or to identify gaps and redundancies regarding the kinds of assistance and programs offered only exacerbates this situation. Instead, what is needed is cooperative dynamics with common ground for joint solutions in the framework of multilateral groups and organizations.[10]

As will be discussed in the forthcoming sections, a variety of security arrangements are taking shape in Central Asia to fill this need. Included in these arrangements is the establishment of new bilateral and multilateral ties, focused on military and non-military security issues. The success of these new multilateral arrangements will depend upon three factors: the Central Asian states' perceived value in participating; the internal and external dynamics that both reinforce and curtail the development of such ties; and the ability of the institutions to contribute in a tangible way to regional security. The following section is an overview and analysis of the more prominent multilateral security organizations and arrangements, and an evaluation of their ability to address real-time security concerns of the Central Asian nations.

Looking West

NATO

NATO's philosophy of expanding security and stability eastward and southward in the region means that, in theory, NATO should become more intrinsically involved in the security of the states of the former Soviet Union, including Central Asia. But traditionally, NATO has placed much more emphasis on the Baltic states, Russia and Ukraine, showing less of an interest in engaging the South Caucasus and Central Asian states, the latter viewed until recently as almost entirely outside NATO's purview within the Partnership for Peace (PfP) framework.

While direct contact between NATO and the Central Asian states throughout the mid to late 1990s was modest, NATO allies did monitor and participate in U.S.-led multilateral exercises with Uzbekistan, Kazakhstan, and Kyrgyzstan conducted "in the spirit of" PfP. Multilateral exercises such as the *CENTRABAT/Regional Cooperation* series, which consisted of tabletop and field exercises in the realm of peacekeeping, were held.[11] Also, the Central Asian partners have participated for several years in the annual International Workshop on Emergency Response (IWER), also an "in the spirit of" PfP multilateral exercise aimed at improving their preparedness in consequence management and disaster relief.

Operating under an "open door" policy, NATO uses the various tools at its disposal to work with partners. These tools allow for maximum cooperation between the Alliance and individual partners, assisting along a continuum to the extent desired by the partner. Beginning with membership in PfP, countries are encouraged to deepen their relationship with NATO by participating in specific mechanisms, while setting interoperability, defense, and economic reform goals to jointly measure progress along the way. Figure 16–1 is a sketch of NATO's integration progress:

Figure 16–1. NATO Integration Progress

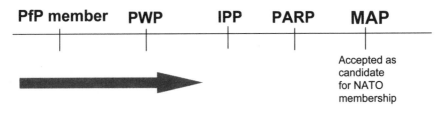

(PfP) = Partnership for Peace member
(PWP) Partnership Work Plan = Annual NATO drafted plan of activities under PfP
(IPP) Individual Partnership Plan = From the PWP, partners construct an IPP, which becomes the Forecast of Events for the year
(PARP) Planning and Review Process = Setting of specific interoperability goals
(MAP) Membership Action Plan = NATO membership candidate/Aspirant status

There is no set time for how quickly a partner should move through this process; it is up to the individual partner to determine the level and scope of cooperation with the Alliance. Geopolitical developments play a large role, and the reaction of Russia has been an important concern for all FSU states. However, because Russia and NATO have improved their relations due in part to the War on Terrorism, Russia's objections to the FSU states' ties with NATO have waned. Ukraine and Georgia officially have stated their intention to join MAP (declaring the desire to join NATO); Uzbekistan, Kyrgyzstan and Azerbaijan have joined the Planning and Review Process (PARP); and Tajikistan has recently become a PfP member.[12]

One could argue that the timing of these decisions is directly related to this new geopolitical environment, where Russia and NATO have established rapport in the NATO-Russia Council.

It is important to point out that NATO-Central Asia relations have met with some constraints, with more serious challenges along the way. Central Asian partners are, by and large, not enthusiastic PfP participants and prefer bilateral security ties with the United States and others, such as Germany. Indeed, Central Asian Ambassadors to NATO and their staffs do not actively participate in discussions at NATO Headquarters and in military planning discussions at Supreme Headquarters Allied Powers Europe (SHAPE).[13] One reason why NATO has been less successful in drawing Central Asia closer to the West is that NATO advocates a model for its engagement with partner countries in Eurasia, which is focused on improving regional cooperation. Although this model has been successful in promoting regional cooperation in Eastern Europe, and even in the Western FSU, its application to a region in which deep distrust character- ize the state of relations is a continuing challenge. However, given NATO's positive track record for spurring regional cooperation elsewhere in Eu- rope and Eurasia, hope still exists. The difficulty is finding the right 'carrot' to extend to the Central Asian partners, since the Central and Eastern Eu- rope carrot of NATO membership is not viable in the near future. NATO either has to be more encouraging and accepting of Central Asian states as partners by offering increased resources to spur defense reform and military professionalization, or it has to offer a diversification of activities within the confines of PfP to address the security needs in this region, such as improved border security.

Another challenge in bringing the Central Asian states closer to NATO and Western Europe involves providing training and equipment to improve their defense self-sufficiency. NATO is often a slow mover in terms of planning and executing security assistance programs, and does not have the money to provide extensive, capacity building assistance. The tool that NATO has at its disposal to improve interoperability, confidence building, and regional cooperation is the PARP. This process assists in both defense reform and restructuring, and is certainly noteworthy as a beneficial method of engagement. For the most part, participation in PfP has not been a political or military issue for Central Asian states, although the financial burden often stymies their involvement.[14] PARP, on the other hand, requires partners to disclose information on the state's range of de- fense and military capabilities, along with details about the force structure and the defense budgets, all of which is viewed as extremely intrusive by the Central Asian states.

Other FSU partners, such as Ukraine and Georgia, have participated in PARP, disclosing such "sensitive" information, and acknowledging the importance of improving regional cooperation, information sharing, interoperability and defense reform. As a result, they have moved closer to Western security structures. In theory, if Central Asian states follow a similar path, it is likely that they will move closer to NATO in the sense of improving interoperability and possibly, security agreements down the road. The challenge for NATO is to ensure that the mechanisms for building partnerships in Central Asia are appropriate to the needs of these countries in their threat-driven security environment. Both Uzbekistan and Kazakhstan joined PARP after September 11, which is a significant step forward, but the cooperation can still be improved.[15] Elements of PfP could include, for example, more focused exercises to improve infrastructure, military support to civilian authorities in a crisis, and regional cooperation to counter the transnational security threats. In short, NATO must ensure that the PfP activities are relevant to the security needs of all of Central Asia. Otherwise, NATO runs the risk of being an ineffective multilateral engagement tool for this region, and encouraging these states to seek bilateral security assistance from the United States and other countries. However, NATO has something unique to offer to its partners: a proven forum for increasing security cooperation among actors in a given region, as well as a tested "open door" policy. The circumstances and incentives are different for Central Asia, but the institution has many mechanisms available to assist its partners in building solid relationships with NATO and with each other.[16]

European Union

In addition to NATO, the EU also offers some positive incentives for the Central Asian states. The EU's relations with Central Asian partners have a legal basis in the Partnership and Cooperation Agreements (PCAs), which guide political and economic discussions.[17] Uzbekistan, Kazakhstan, Kyrgyzstan and Turkmenistan have concluded PCAs with the EU, though the agreement with Turkmenistan has not yet entered into force. No PCA has been concluded with Tajikistan yet, though with the civil war now ended, it is likely that negotiations could be underway soon.

The PCA was intended as a mechanism to establish a stronger political relationship in the developing network of Central Asia's connection with the EU. On the economic side, the PCA marks an important step in helping to bring these states in line with the legal framework of the single European market and the World Trade Organization (WTO). The PCAs concluded between the EU and its partners are intended to facilitate the development of free trade, and can be seen as a road map for the introduction of economic and trade-related policies in the fields of goods, services, labor, current payments, and capital movement. Although the document is in many ways evolutionary, its implementation is a precondition for the development of further trade and political relations between the parties.

Moreover, the European Commission Technical Assistance to the CIS (TACIS) program assists partner states, including Central Asia, by focusing on the promotion of cooperation in the areas of environment, networks (telecommunications, energy and transport), justice and home affairs. Their focus is on certain cross-border issues, including the activities of sub-regional cooperation bodies and initiatives.[18] In addition, the Transport Corridor Europe Caucasus Asia (TRACECA) program of 1993 aims to bring together trade and transport ministers from the original eight TRACECA countries (five Central Asian republics and three Caucasian republics). The goal is to develop a transport corridor on a west-east axis from Europe, across the Black Sea, through the Caucasus and the Caspian Sea, and onto Central Asia.[19] Uzbekistan in particular is hoping to capitalize upon its geopolitical position as the pivot in regional trade once the TRACECA program establishes a new "Silk Road," which will span from China to Western Europe. TRACECA hopes to attract investments from international financial institutions such as the European Bank for Reconstruction and Development (EBRD), which have committed U.S. $250 million, and the World Bank, which has pledged an additional U.S. $40 million towards the completion of the project.[20] TRACECA projects are deemed essential for the diversification of the traditional Moscow-centered trade and transport flows and for opening trade routes to the West.

Moreover, while there appears to be some movement in the area of EU support for police training centers and potential cooperation with the Organization for Security and Cooperation in Europe (OSCE) as well as improved border security measures in the region, in general Central Asian security issues are simply not at the forefront of the minds of bureaucrats in Brussels, and the EU does not have enough money to begin with.[21] The EU, as opposed to NATO, primarily focuses on "soft security" matters such as trade, water management, and other environmental security concerns in Central Asia. Politically, the EU relies on the PCA to guide discussions between the Central Asian partners and the EU Commission. But until a partner reaches the status of "Associate Member" (i.e., candidate for EU membership), the tangible benefits of this association are not as significant, particularly for Central Asia, which is still widely perceived by the EU as outside its immediate area of interest. Although NATO is taking a slightly more proactive role through PfP, Central Asia is still lower down on the totem pole compared to the Western CIS and the South Caucasus, particularly Georgia and Azerbaijan.

Looking Northwest

Commonwealth of Independent States

In the security and defense sphere, the CIS CST serves as the primary means for Russia to maintain leverage over the Central Asian states. The Treaty, as well as a series of initiatives to develop a CIS customs union (CIS-wide and later between Russia, Kazakhstan, Kyrgyzstan, Uzbekistan[22] and Tajikistan), was given greater impetus by a 1995 decree issued by Russian President Boris Yeltsin. The decree detailed a new direction for the CIS on closer security cooperation and embodied the belief that the CIS is the basis for Russia's reconstitution as a great power. On defense and security matters, the decree sought to "stimulate intentions of the CIS state parties to unite in a defense alliance"[23] and urged all states to conclude agreements in the military infrastructure and to encourage Russian military bases on the outward perimeter throughout CIS territory. A key goal was obtaining an obligation from the CIS member-states to refrain from participating in alliances and blocs directed against any of the other CIS members, specifically NATO.[24]

Although the CST created a formal system of collective defense, it has been activated only for the limited purpose of consultation over threats posed by Afghanistan. The important question is whether, if the CST continues to exist, it can serve any utility as a mechanism to discuss and deal with security concerns of its members, including terrorist activities, and the cross-border movement of items relating to WMD, narcotics and small arms. Uzbekistan, for one, already has determined that the CST does not have an important regional security role to play, as evidenced by its withdrawal from the arrangement, and Uzbekistan has strongly indicated its preference for developing security relationships with the West. If the Central Asian states themselves are continuing to develop security relationships with actors outside the confines of the CST and Russia is continuing to loosen the strings on the CST, then it is difficult to see how it can remain viable.

The Central Asian states have attempted to distance themselves from Russia in a number of key areas, most recently in a collective proposal to establish a nuclear weapons free zone in the region, which was recently passed. The agreement has met with controversy in Moscow. Officials maintain that the CST allows Russia the right to redeploy nuclear weapons in Central Asia in the future, which is a disputed interpretation among the Central Asian states.[25]

The lack of enthusiasm for the CST and the CIS as a whole, with the notable exception of Russia, is exemplified by the fact that its members have not attempted to implement the economic and security agreements signed within the confines of the CIS, and actively seek to deepen their participation in other regional organizations. Overall, the CIS is widely viewed as an ineffective multilateral forum for dealing with regional security concerns. The rhetoric of the CIS is similar to that of the EU, but the CIS does not display the features of the EU, such as the Common Market, the Common Foreign and Security Policy, or the movement toward a shared identity.[26]

Shanghai Cooperation Organization

The prospects for a longer-term U.S. military presence in Central Asia have raised eyebrows not only in Russia, but also in China, which borders Kyrgyzstan, Kazakhstan and Tajikistan. China has been looking to expand its influence in this region, and together with Russia has been instrumental in establishing the SCO, which includes China, Russia, Kazakhstan, Kyrgyzstan, Tajikistan and Uzbekistan.[27] The SCO originally was created to resolve ongoing border disputes in the wake of the Soviet Union's collapse. The broadening of the SCO's focus to a more institutionalized security organization was in response to the increased threat in the region from non-state actors, such as the IMU.

The states in the SCO have reached agreements on military reductions and confidence building, and the SCO has become a mechanism for consultations on trade, water and border security. Its primary goal, however, is to counter the spread of Islamic extremism and terrorism. However, it is important to note that China has not indicated a desire to offer security guarantees or provide a military presence in Central Asia. This fact reinforces the perception that Russia and the United States are the only powers that wish or intend to develop policy toward Central Asia from a more broad strategic perspective. At present, China's interests are more regionally or culturally defined, as opposed to strategic. China still perceives Central Asia as within Russia's sphere of influence, and Russia's presence in Tajikistan has dissuaded China from developing an active strategy toward this war-torn country at its border. However, if Russia's influence within Central Asia continues to weaken, China may assume a more active role in advancing its energy and economic interests.

Looking Inward

Unlike the multilateral organizations discussed above, what distinguishes those who follow is the participant's status in the organization—whether members are on an equal footing or whether there is a designated or implied leader. While members are supposed to have equal status in NATO, SCO, and CIS, this is not the case *de facto*. Russia is the dominant player in the CIS, Russia/China in the SCO, and the United States in NATO. However, in the OSCE; the Georgia, Ukraine, Uzebekistan, Azerbaijan and Moldova (GUUAM) group; and others discussed below, members are considered to have equal status. This is an important distinction to make, since Central Asian states have a long history of being dominated by a larger power and remain relatively weak in comparison with their neighbors.

Organization for Security and Cooperation in Europe

One of the main benefits of membership in the OSCE, as well as some of the other regional multilateral organizations, is that this organization is not dominated by one or two of the more powerful states. Members are officially on equal status with every other state. Thus, the OSCE is perceived as a real opportunity to gain international experience in decision-making, consensus-building and diplomacy.

The OSCE has prioritized Central Asia as a region in need of its support in the security arena.[28] The increased flow of illicit drugs, the presence of criminal groups, as well as the growing trafficking in human beings and firearms have captured the attention of the OSCE in recent years. The OSCE has established centers in Almaty, Ashgabad, Tashkent, and has sent a Mission to Tajikistan. Missions are established when more serious security concerns are perceived. These centers promote the implementation of OSCE principles and the cooperation of the participating Central Asian states within the OSCE framework. They also promote information exchange between OSCE bodies and Central Asian authorities at a multitude of levels.

The OSCE has attempted to re-focus its support to Central Asia post September 11, as evidenced in the Bishkek Conference on Security and Stability held in December 2001. This conference was co-sponsored by the

OSCE and the United Nations Office for Drug Control and Crime Prevention. Participants unanimously condemned terrorism in all its forms and expressed willingness to cooperate in improving their border security. The conference was deemed a success by participating authorities in terms of the discussions of counter-drug efforts and the establishment of new focuses, such as the transit of small arms and light weapons.[29] According to the OSCE's International Secretariat staff, some progress has been made in deepening cooperation in small arms and light weapons transfers within the OSCE forum, as well as the training of police officials in the five Central Asian states, although much remains to be done.[30] One idea is for the OSCE to focus on control of small arms and light weapons by employing an Information Technology (IT) tool to track activities and to help record proliferation hot spots.[31]

The Central Asian states pay dues into the OSCE as members, but are also recipients of OSCE financial support. According to OSCE officials, these circumstances encourage the Central Asian states to be more proactive in their discussions within OSCE fora. For example, the Tajik government recently proposed the establishment of regional training centers in Central Asia, each of which would specialize in a particular field or skill, such as border security, peacekeeping, disaster relief, or "niche capability," and provide for joint training across national lines, thus facilitating regional cooperation.[32] The argument can be made that membership in the OSCE accords a certain perception of freedom and flexibility for the Central Asian states by proposing concrete options for improving the security situation in the region.

GUAM

The Georgia, Ukraine, Azerbaijan and Moldova (GUAM) sub-grouping of pro-West, anti-CIS states is another example of a multilateral organization where the equality of members is emphasized. Uzbekistan was a member until June 2002 when it suspended its participation in the "GUUAM's" formal structures because it did not see much benefit to membership since the United States already was providing significant military and economic assistance and the other GUUAM members were relatively weak. But while the role of GUAM in promoting security in Central Asia has come into question after Uzbekistan pulled out, it is still worth considering because of the potential to promote regional dialogue and information sharing on critical security matters.

GUAM was founded in 1996 as a political, economic and strategic alliance designed to strengthen the independence and sovereignty of these former Soviet Union republics, and after much delay was formally institutionalized in 2001 with a legal charter and secretariat. GUAM has become an important structure for enhancing dialogue on regional economic cooperation through development of a Europe-Caucasus-Asia transport corridor. It has also become a forum for discussion at various levels of existing security problems, promoting conflict resolution and the elimination of other risks and threats.[33]

At a meeting of GUAM Foreign Ministers in Yalta in July 2002, the decision was made to extend observer status of the organization to interested states. A communiqué announced that third states and international organizations might participate in GUAM activities, provided that they were interested in GUAM's work and promoted its objectives. No reference was made as to participation based on geographical location.[34]

Some of the key goals which unite GUAM's members include improving the economic situation; developing an energy transport corridor from Central Asia to Western Europe; improving border security; promoting a respect for human rights; building civil society and empowered and legitimate state institutions; and most important, solidifying the independence, sovereignty and territorial integrity of GUAM members separate from Russia and the CIS.[35] The latter is particularly important for Georgia, Moldova and Azerbaijan, though less so for Ukraine, which has been more successful in developing an independent status.

GUAM's geopolitical leanings toward NATO, the EU, and the West in general has led to backing from the United States and NATO since its inception.[36] GUAM continues to receive American support (Congress and DOD, in particular) stemming from the Silk Road Act of 1999. In summer 2003, with U.S. political and economic backing, GUAM announced an initiative to refocus its efforts on the war on terrorism, particularly on border security issues, such as immigration, terrorist movements, WMD, drugs, and small arms/light weapons transfers, which could very well improve GUAM's importance for the Central Asian states. This refocus on border security, coupled with U.S. backing, may draw Uzbekistan back in to the formal structures, as well as encourage other states in the region such as Tajikistan, Kazakhstan and Kyrgyzstan, to take part. Overall, GUAM serves as a mechanism to increase security in the region, provided its membership is expanded and tangible projects result from political initiatives.

Beyond GUAM, Central Asian leaders have advanced several other multilateral frameworks that should be noted. The Central Asian European Community (CAEC), established in 1994 by Uzbekistan, Kazakhstan and Kyrgyzstan, is a consultative framework for addressing security concerns. However, though membership was expanded to include Tajikistan in 1998, the forum has proven to be unable to influence the development of the region's economies in a significant way. Kazakh President Nursultan Nazarbaev has proposed the creation of a Eurasian Union as a CIS alternative, but this proposal has not moved beyond the discussion stage. Nazarbaev also suggested the creation of an Asian variant of the OSCE—the Conference on Interaction and Confidence-Building Measures in Asia (CICA). Uzbeks and Kyrgyz officials have offered their own proposals, one of which included an initiative to create a nuclear free zone, which has subsequently been approved by all five Central Asian states. However, it is clear that the majority of the proposals advanced by the Central Asian leaders remain on paper and thus are ineffective in terms of dealing with regional security concerns at this time. Still, the fact that proposals have been offered in the first place is significant, and should be encouraged in an effort to increase regional cooperation and to find common solutions to transnational security problems.

Conclusions

The post-September 11 geopolitical environment, manifested in the U.S.-led Global War on Terrorism, has generated an unprecedented international interest in the Central Asian states from multilateral security institutions. Given the region's proximity to Afghanistan and potential for spillover of instability, each state's willingness (to varying degrees) to join the international coalition, and the potential for longer-term Western military presence in Central Asia, it is not difficult to understand the heightened interest in this region.

NATO and the OSCE arguably offer the best opportunities for the Central Asian states from a multilateral perspective. NATO has been successful in encouraging regional cooperation in eastern and southern Europe through PfP, even when significant tensions have been present. PfP exercises, for example, offer a forum through which the Central Asian states could improve their consequence management, disaster relief and other capabilities to respond to transnational threats. But the challenge for NATO is ensuring that PfP activities evolve to address the real-time security needs of the Central Asia partners, which may mean adding more border security type training activities, and perhaps expanding to include more agencies, such as the border guard, customs, ministry of interior, national guard, military police/law enforcement or other front-line security services.

The OSCE has representatives on the ground in each of the countries, which typically provides them with access to partner country officials. The OSCE tends to be more innovative in coming up with new programs for the Central Asia partners to address their security needs. The problem with the OSCE is that it does not have much money, and therefore, is dependent in part on the resources from other sources, such as the EU. But while the EU has limited money for projects in Central Asia, the EU member states are generally not that interested in this region, given its lack of geographic proximity and their own traditional focus on the Western Eurasian states. The EU, through the TACIS program, does offer a useful forum for multilateral discussions of transnational issues for the Central Asian states, but the EU tends to talk at the Central Asian partners, rather than to find common ground. Since the Central Asian states are also members of the OSCE, dialogue is generally better and on more even ground.[37]

The overall effectiveness of EU, NATO and OSCE activities in the region could be improved if these institutions collaborated to avoid duplication of effort and better identify gaps. The EU and the OSCE, in particular, tend not to coordinate their efforts very well. For example, the OSCE focuses on small/arms light weapons transfers and police training in the region, but collaboration with the EU on these matters is in its infancy. However, if these bureaucratic and resource issues can be resolved and working groups/activities established, the Central Asian partners would be well advised to take advantage of a joint OSCE/EU approach to the region. Such an approach would complement, without being in contrast to, the more capabilities-building assistance provided by the United States and NATO. Overall, the effectiveness of individual programs within multilateral institutions is hindered because of the overall lack of transparency and information sharing in the region, as well as a lack of understanding about the kind of assistance that Central Asian states truly need to address specific security threats.

In addition to Western multilateral avenues, if GUAM can come up with tangible projects for its members in the realm of border security, it would certainly be in the interest of the Central Asian states to take part. Even an informal network that facilitates the sharing of information and intelligence on border security issues would certainly be a worthwhile endeavor. The United States, NATO, OSCE and the EU are likely to take a greater interest in GUAM with a border security dimension, and may even provide the financial and political backing to move these initiatives along, thereby, attracting additional members from Central Asia and perhaps drawing back in Uzbekistan. But the original premise should come from the partners themselves in a coordinated fashion in an effort to improve their own security—it should not be jumpstarted by the United States or other, more influential multilateral institutions.

The uncertain and often volatile security environment coupled with the authoritarian nature of the regimes in power present challenges for Western institutions. Given trends over the past five years or so, it is highly likely that the Central Asian states will continue to seek external assistance, and the authoritarian leaders of these regimes will continue to play up or even exaggerate the presence of an external threat, since an outside threat is useful in garnering additional resources from Western institutions on a bilateral basis. Although there is no doubt of the region's geopolitical importance, it is not in the long term interest of the West to provide security assistance and even security guarantees to undemocratic and corrupt regimes. Therefore, while multilateral institutions continue to deepen security cooperation with these states, simultaneous emphasis should be placed on building democratic regimes, governed by the rule of law and transitioning to market-oriented economies. After progress is made in these areas, these governments will be in a better position to deal with internal and external security challenges effectively and reduce their dependency on external actors.

The internal weaknesses of these states render them extremely vulnerable to outside influences, especially from Russia. Although Russia is itself rather weak, it is far stronger than all of the states in Central Asia combined, and while its direct influence over their domestic affairs has wavered in recent years, Russia is still the dominating military, political and economic force in the region. Russia's cooperation is also required in terms of bringing stability to the region. The extent to which Western-oriented multilateral institutions will be successful in developing closer relations with Central Asia from a security standpoint will depend on Russia's reaction and on the ability of these states to realize opportunities accorded to them through multilateral cooperation. It is therefore in the interests of the Western actors and institutions to actively work with the states of Central Asia to ensure that Western methods for dealing with instabilities are adopted.

But as Roy Allison points out, it is not clear yet whether the impulse to cooperate through multilateral initiatives is stronger than the pressures among the Central Asian states for fragmentation.[38] However, the opportunity exists for the prominent Western-backed security institutions to demonstrate the benefits of multilateral cooperation as a means of improving regional security, and with this the condition of the region as a whole.

Notes

[1] Roy Allison and Lena Jonson, eds., *Central Asian Security* (Washington, DC: Brookings Institution, 2001), 1.

[2] Martha Brill Olcott, "Central Asia: Common Legacies and Conflicts" in Roy Allison and Lena Jonson, eds., 32.

[3] Formally known as "Shanghai Five," which includes Russia, China, Kyrgyzstan, Tajikistan, and Kazakhstan, changing its name after the accession of Uzbekistan in 2001.

[4] This organization previously also included Uzbekistan, at which time it was referred to as GUUAM. Uzbekistan suspended its membership in early 2002.

[5] Interview with U.S. Department of State, Europe/Eurasia Coordinator's office, August 2002.

[6] Dana Milbank, "Uzbekistan Thanked for Role in War: U.S., Tashkent Sign Cooperation Pact," *The Washington Post*, March 15, 2002.

[7] Roy Allison and Lena Jonson, eds., 19.

[8] Zbigniew Brzezinski, "A Geostrategy in Eurasia," *Foreign Affairs*, 76, no. 5, (September/October 1997), 50-64.

[9] Interviews with U.S. Central Command (CENTCOM) officials in March 2001, Tampa, Florida.

[10] Roy Allison and Lena Jonson, eds., 18.

[11] For a more detailed discussion of U.S./NATO activities in Central Asia, see Jennifer D.P. Moroney, "Western Approaches to Security Cooperation with Central Asia", in Graeme Herd and Jennifer D.P. Moroney, eds., *Security Dynamics in the Former Soviet Bloc* (London: Routledge/Curzon, 2003).

[12] Interviews conducted at NATO Headquarters with Defense Planning and Operations (DPAO) staff, Brussels, Belgium, May 14, 2002.

[13] Interviews at NATO Headquarters with US Mission to NATO, International Staff (Political Affairs), Brussels, Belgium, and U.S. Eurasia specialists at SHAPE, Mons, Belgium, May 15-16, 2002.

[14] NATO requires the partners to contribute a certain percentage to pay for the exercises.

[15] Interview with NATO official, NATO Headquarters, Brussels Belgium, May 14, 2002.

[16] Interviews conducted at NATO Headquarters with Political Affairs Division and Special Advisor's office, Brussels, Belgium, May 15, 2002.

[17] The PCA is the framework document by which progress is assessed in each of the FSU partners in bringing their economic, political, social, and legal structures in line with the *acquis communitaire* of the European Union.

[18] TACIS Strategy Paper, *Strategic Consideration 2002-2006 and Indicative Programme 2002-2003* (europa.eu.int).

[19] Interview with EU Commission officials, Brussels, Belgium, May 15, 2002.

[20] See URL <http://www.traceca.org> for further information.

[21] Interview with EU official responsible for Central Asia issues, London, October 15, 2003.

[22] Uzbekistan left the CST in 1999 to join the GUUAM regional subgroup of anti-CIS states, and subsequently withdrew from GUUAM in June 2002.

[23] As discussed in Sherman Garnett, *Keystone in the Arch* (Washington, DC: Carnegie Endowment for International Peace, 1997), 65.

[24] Ibid.

[25] Nuclear-free Zone for Central Asia, *The Washington Post*, October 5, 2002, A14.

[26] Martha Brill Olcott, Anders Åslund, and Sherman Garnett, *Getting it Wrong: Regional Cooperation and the Commonwealth of Independent States* (Washington, DC: Carnegie Endowment for International Peace), 232.

[27] Vernon Loeb, "Footprints in the Steppes of Central Asia: New BIses indicate U.S. Presence Will Be Felt After Afghan War," *The Washington Post*, February 9, 2002.

[28] Interviews with OSCE International Secretariat Staff, Vienna, Austria, May 23, 2002.

[29] Interview with UN ODCCP office, New York, July 16, 2002.

[30] Interviews with OSCE International Secretariat Staff (External Affairs), Vienna, Austria, May 23, 2002. and discussions held at a Wilton Park (UK) conference on Central Asia and the Caspian, October 2003.

[31] URL: <www.osce.org>, International Conference Held on Terrorism, Biweekly briefing, March 13, 2002.

[32] Multiple interviews with OSCE, U.S., and Danish officials, OSCE, Vienna, Austria, May 23, 2002.

[33] "The GUUAM Group: History and Principles," briefing paper, <www.guuam .org>, November 2000.

[34] See Communiqué of the Yalta GUUAM meeting, July 20-21, 2001 (www.guuam.org).

[35] <www.guuam.org>

[36] For a more detailed discussion of Western Support to GUAM, see Jennifer D.P. Moroney and Sergei Konoplyov, "Ukraine, GUUAM, and Western Support for Subregional Cooperation in Europe's Security Gray Zone," Jennifer D.P. Moroney, Taras Kuzio, and Mikhail Molchanov, eds., *Ukrainian Foreign Policy: Theoretical and Comparative Perspectives* (Westport, CT: Praeger/Greenwood, May 2002).

[37] Interviews with OSCE International Secretariat Staff (External Affairs), Vienna, Austria, May 23, 2002 and discussions held at a Wilton Park (UK) conference on Central Asia and the Caspian, October 2003.

[38] Roy Allison and Lena Jonson, eds., 254.

Chapter 17

Who's Watching the Watchdogs?: Drug Trafficking in Central Asia[1]

Nancy Lubin

A U.S. Customs Service agent won awards and accolades for seizing more than 100 tons of marijuana over four years—but was then found to have conspired with the drug traffickers themselves so that other, far more lucrative drug shipments would make it safely to the United States.[2] His story is far from unique. In early 2003, for the second time in six years, the Mexican government dismantled an elite federal anti-drug unit because the unit was found to be working closely with drug traffickers. "Virtually no Mexican anti-drug agency has remained free of infiltration by powerful drug gangs," the American press reported, largely because of "scant public oversight."[3] A recent report on National Public Radio (NPR) describes "a systemic and ongoing problem of corruption among officers" of U.S. law enforcement agencies in charge of patrolling the border with Mexico. "Easy money is an obvious factor," the report states, but blood ties among people with links on both sides of the border, as well as other factors, also play a large role.[4] And even with tough legislation, independent judiciaries, and an aggressive investigative press, many other countries have discovered that corruption in counter-drug law enforcement units can still be exceptionally high.

But not in Central Asia, this author was told last spring.[5] Or at least not until very recently. On the Tajik border of Afghanistan in May 2002, as they watched 55 kilograms of seized heroin, raw opium and hashish being incinerated in fat rubber tires, Russian military officials of the Moskovskii border guard detachment assured an onlooker that virtually none of Tajikistan's border guards had been apprehended for involvement in trafficking, at least over the past decade. Perhaps in the 1980s, the officials considered, but they couldn't remember.

Back in Dushanbe, the capital of Tajikistan, officials declared that corruption was categorically absent from the elite drug control units, and that government officials are uniformly committed to fighting this scourge. The same story was repeated by high government officials farther north in Uzbekistan and Kyrgyzstan. It was the rare exception when someone went bad—a case of a bad apple, rather than the "bad barrels" reported by NPR.

In countries with only a limited free press and no investigative journalism, where the courts and entire judicial system are heavily in the hands of the state, where living standards are low and cross border 'blood ties' extensive, and where there is no independent oversight over law enforcement, how have they done it? Or how would one know? Recently, Tajik officials say they have started a crackdown in Tajikistan, and many offenders at all levels have been arrested. Why the sudden change?[6]

These questions lie at the heart of international counter-narcotics trafficking efforts in Central Asia today. The history of Central Asian drug trafficking, and the attempts to stop it, is one of smoke and mirrors; sorting through the nature of the problem itself and how best to address it has become an often unfathomable challenge. What is the nature and scale of the drug trafficking problem through Central Asia today? Where have local and international efforts been successful in combating this problem, and where has their impact been controversial, or even counterproductive? What does this say about the challenges being faced today?

Sparked by the terrorist events of September 11, 2001, the United States has increased significantly its previously modest commitment to fight the drug trade there. In 2002 alone, the United States committed close to $100 million to counter-narcotics trafficking programs in Afghanistan and Central Asia,[7] and an army of U.S., international and local Central Asian officials and specialists have been tasked to fight this trade. But with oversight extremely weak, both from within and without these countries, the allocation of greater resources also has meant greater challenges regarding how these resources should be applied. It is critical to examine these challenges, and to examine the record of the past, if the substantial investments being made today are to address the range of drug trafficking problems in this part of the world—and to avoid inadvertently making them worse.

Background

Opium poppy used to grow wild in Central Asia. Throughout the Soviet period, Soviet authorities declared their commitment to eradicate drug cultivation on Soviet soil, but their efforts were slow in addressing this problem. However fairly or unfairly, most Central Asians believed that Soviet leaders themselves were benefiting from the drug trade. If leaders were really committed to wiping out the crop, the thought went, it would have been done much more quickly and effectively. Still, by the beginning of the 1990s, drug cultivation in Central Asia had been severely curtailed, and over the past decade, Central Asia has been relevant to the drug trade primarily as a transit point for narcotics from Afghanistan on their way to Russia, Europe and beyond. Some locals say the collapse of the Soviet Union triggered a commitment on the part of the leaders of these new states to eradicate the drug trade altogether; others more cynically suggest it triggered a commitment from those benefiting from the trade to shift their efforts to reap the profits from drug trafficking rather than cultivation. In either case, after a decade of wars in Afghanistan and Tajikistan, the collapse of the Soviet Union and subsequent political unrest, economic strains, and social upheavals, the flow of raw opium and heroin from Afghanistan grew dramatically throughout the 1990s. Opium poppy production in Afghanistan reached a peak of between 2,900 and 4,600 metric tons in 1999 and 2000.[8] The United Nations Office on Drugs and Crime (UNODC) estimated that by 2000 some three-quarters of the world's heroin supply was originating from opium cultivated in Afghanistan and smuggled through mountainous terrain that is particularly difficult to control.[9]

In early 2001, the Taliban regime began enforcing its long-stated but long-ignored ban on opium production. The sudden reversal of the Taliban, which since coming to power had drawn great profit from taxing the opium trade, led to an almost total eradication of the annual poppy crop in Afghanistan.[10] But due to huge stockpiles, the trade did not diminish dramatically. With the onset of the war in Afghanistan and the defeat of the Taliban, Afghan farmers have renewed the planting of opium, bringing the 2002 harvest almost to its 1999-2000 record levels.[11] Afghanistan is again dominating the world market for opium, and Central Asia is experiencing, in the words of the United Nations (UN), "a dramatic increase in drug trafficking across all its five countries."[12]

While there is some disagreement over the actual volume of narcotics transported through Central Asia today, the role of Central Asia as a transit point has grown significantly. Until the turn of the twenty-first century, most of the drugs grown in Afghanistan reached Western consumers through Pakistan and Iran, but a clampdown on drug trafficking in Iran, and the increasingly porous borders of Central Asia, have shifted that balance. By the turn of the century, the UN and others reported that as much as half to two thirds of all narcotics trafficked from Afghanistan passed through the Central Asian states of Tajikistan, Uzbekistan, Kyrgyzstan, Turkmenistan and Kazakhstan on their way to European and Russian markets as well as sometimes the United States and Canada.[13] Others estimate that the actual proportion is lower but maintain that Central Asia's role remains significant.[14] Most of this heroin finds its way to Russia and Western Europe, and often brings vast profits along the way. Some experts have estimated that by 2000, the opium cultivated in Afghanistan, sold in the form of heroin at retail prices, was worth roughly $100 billion. In Afghanistan, one kilogram of opium cost about $30; in Moscow, one kilogram of heroin (made from 10 kilograms of opium) cost up to $30,000; and in Western Europe, the same kilogram of heroin, sold at the retail level in gram units or smaller, cost as much as $150,000.[15]

These drug profits reportedly have been shared generously with local law enforcement and other key actors throughout Central Asia. Western observers have pointed to widespread corruption among police, border guards, customs and other government officials as one of the most important factors sustaining the large drug flow in Central Asia.[16] Customs and other law enforcement officials in all five countries customarily pay some thousands of dollars in bribes just to get an entry-level job. Even though the salary is low, it is understood that they will earn back their investment in a short amount of time. Citizens who have been detained by customs officials for possession of small amounts of narcotics independently list the same types of bribes requested for different kinds of offenses. One destitute woman, who decided to make one run as a courier to make ends meet, was detained with 200 grams of heroin. She said she was told to pay $5000 and the whole case would go away. If she had that kind of money, she lamented, she wouldn't have become involved in the first place. But clearly, she added, other people do pay.[17]

In elite forces where salaries are higher, former border guards report additional pressures to collaborate with traffickers, even for the disinclined. "Imagine a smuggler approaches," said one former border guard, describing how guards patrol in groups of two or three over sparse terrain. "He tells you that if you turn the other way for five minutes, you can be a millionaire. But if you don't, he will send your corpse to Moscow. What would you do? Two hundred dollars each month isn't enough to lose your life over."[18] A recent U.S. government interagency report on heroin trafficking concluded that "increasing heroin transit through Central Asia is contributing to endemic political and bureaucratic corruption, including in the security services and law enforcement agencies, throughout the region."[19]

Indeed, even Central Asian leaders have criticized their own law enforcement officials for being deeply involved in the drug trade in one way or another. Yet many local observers believe that corruption and drug trafficking may be directed from top leadership levels as well. Customs officials and border guards say it is not uncommon to be called by "higher-ups" and told to look the other way when particular vehicles reach the border. A previous Tajik Minister of Interior was seen to be in charge of major trafficking operations; in Kazakhstan, a Tajik Ambassador was picked up with a stash of heroin in the trunk of his diplomatic car.[20] The president of Turkmenistan is himself accused of being a major drug kingpin, perhaps explaining why the Turkmen borders are so open to trafficking in the first place.[21] The 2002 U.S. State Department report on narcotics control gives further credence to these kinds of allegations.[22] A Russian correspondent who has lived in Central Asia for many years recently shared the same skepticism towards its leaders: borders could be kept much more secure, he said in June 2002, if there were not "high level interest" in keeping them at least partially open.[23]

Yet the biggest offenders may be the Russians themselves, long-time locals lament, specifically the Russian military personnel stationed on Central Asia's border with Afghanistan who allegedly have their piece of the action, too. High-ranking Central Asian officials and low-level citizens alike—from Osh, Kyrgyzstan to Tajikistan and Kazakhstan—have long taken for granted the direct lines by which the Russian military allegedly ships heroin and other narcotics directly to Russia. At countless airports in Central Asia, locals have pointed out the Russian military helicopters that stop en route to Russia from Afghanistan: they refuel quickly and continue to Moscow; no one is allowed to check the cargo. These allegations have emerged recently into the open, prompted in part by a January 2003 article in the Russian newspaper *Trud* about the successes of Russian border guards in the fight against narcotics trafficking.[24] The article states that 90 percent of Tajikistan's border guards are Tajiks under the command of Russians, of which two percent have connections with narco-businessmen. The article's failure to address corruption among Russian border guards has sparked a firestorm of criticism, including allegations that Russian forces are more culpable of collusion with traffickers but ready to pass the blame to the Tajiks.[25]

Few of these allegations can be confirmed, but they reflect wide-spread perceptions that large profits are made both within Central Asia and outside of the region. While only a small portion of these drug profits have made their way to farmers in Afghanistan and low-level couriers throughout Central Asia, the drug trade still has benefited them in crucial ways. Opium poppy cultivation has allowed Afghan farmers to make ends meet in a way that few other crops could. For some, advances paid for their opium crop have provided their only access to credit and sometimes their only source of survival during the winter months. In Central Asia, the drug trade has enticed a sometimes overwhelmingly destitute population to risk the harsh penalties imposed for drug traf-ficking—including the death penalty—in the hope of making ends meet. These couriers not only are the rural poor and uneducated but include educated professionals as well. A former secretary at the main university in Tajikistan, for example, could not support her two chil-dren on the token salary she received (the State has not, to this day, had the budget to pay anything but token salaries). After trying her hand at business and falling deeply into debt, she decided to make one drug run to Moscow in the mid 1990s to get back on her feet. In an obvious setup, however, she found herself in prison for three years for possession of 200 grams of heroin, before being amnestied in 2001.[26] As the former Kyrgyz chairman of the Commission on Drug Control admitted in 1997, "In some regions, the only way to survive is to take part in the drug trade."[27]

The Societal Toll

The secretary's fate highlights the wide array of societal prob-lems at all levels that the drug trade has produced. The growth in the proportion of Central Asian women involved in the drug trade; the growth in drug addiction, particularly among the young; and the con-comitant growth in the spread of HIV/AIDS have led to serious social problems among rich and poor alike that may have serious political and societal ramifications in the not too distant future.

Although consistent figures are difficult to come by, all Central Asian governments have expressed serious concern about the growing involvement of women in drug trafficking, particularly as couriers, or so-called "camels." In Kyrgyzstan, for example, an estimated 30 percent of drug addicts and drug traffickers are women; in Tajikistan, the proportion of women traffickers is estimated to be even higher and rising.[28] Most of these women, and especially rural women, are enticed into the drug trade because of rampant poverty, discrimination and despair. Significantly, women have become particularly valuable to traffickers as a cover, or *shirma*, in a world where corruption and collusion between traffickers and customs officials is widespread. Customs officials allegedly are often informed in advance of whom to search so that the "bigger fish" carrying large amounts of drugs can pass through freely. The net result is that women increasingly have become the targets of law enforcement, and they comprise a growing proportion of Central Asia's prison population. They are also increasingly subject to humiliating body searches and other indignities at Central Asian borders.[29]

The impact on women is only compounded by other societal consequences of the drug trade. For example, more corrupt and stringent border control has decreased contact between family members on different sides of Central Asia borders; drug-related domestic violence is on the rise; and youth are becoming increasingly involved in trafficking. Indeed, the drug trade is now viewed as one of the key factors jeopardizing family life, traditional communities, and general social stability throughout Central Asia. This has only been further compounded by the rapid growth of HIV/AIDS associated with drug injection: Current estimates put the number of addicts with HIV/AIDS in Central Asia anywhere from about 1,500 to 10 times that amount. The rapid spread of AIDS over the past few years, however, has led adherents of even the most conservative estimates to predict a possible epidemic within the next decade.[30]

In response to these challenges, the past few years have seen increasingly strong stated commitments by Central Asian leaders to attack the drug trade and its concomitant societal problems head-on. While a strong constituency in support of the drug trade survives among those reaping huge profits—and while some argue that by addressing serious gaps in the economy that the state cannot fill, the trade has been a stabilizing force in Central Asian society—leaders say they regard the trade today as inherently destabilizing. By widening the gap between rich and poor, sharpening rivalry among criminal groups, distorting and inhibiting any serious reform of the formal economy, and creating its own system of rules and laws that challenge those of the state, the drug trade is viewed as a threat to the very domestic stability it was previously believed to preserve. These concerns have come center stage with the recognition that drug trafficking now is likely a key source of financing for terrorism—and perhaps a key source of the very disaffection that can give rise to further terrorism in its own right.

International Counter Narcotics Program

Nonetheless, the commitment of Central Asian leaders to crack down on the drug trade has been uneven. Loath to address issues of corruption beyond a rhetorical level, Central Asian officials blame their countries' traditionally weak interdiction records on the difficult border terrain and the lack of funding needed for training border guards or for purchasing specialized equipment to challenge well-financed narcotics smuggling rings. Central Asian leaders have begun to warm up to the idea of addressing the problems associated with growing drug addiction, but this has been slow in coming. Again, they cite lack of funding and expertise as major impediments. They have turned increasingly to the international community for assistance with resources to fight trafficking on Central Asia's international borders and to help address the serious side effects of the drug trade at home.

Over the past decade, and particularly since September 11, the international community has tried to support Central Asia's struggle with trafficking and addiction. The impact of these efforts to date, however, has been decidedly mixed. Beginning in the 1990s, international donors instituted crop reduction programs in Afghanistan and institution-building programs in Central Asia to limit the flow of narcotics across the Central Asian-Afghan borders. Tajikistan's Drug Control Agency (DCA), created with UN assistance, boasts an impressive seizure rate. Recently, the focus of international programs has begun to include broader societal concerns as well, including greater attention to educating the young, supporting women's groups, and instituting other demand and harm reduction programs throughout the region. Yet while these endeavors have produced impressive successes, they also have been controversial; indeed, each new success has prompted criticism that Western programs may be a double-edged sword, where success in one arena may be balanced by inadvertent harm in another.

Throughout the 1990s, for example, international donors focused their efforts in Central Asia's drug battle on institutional development. In each country, donor programs have assisted in developing a centralized counter-narcotics infrastructure and have provided training and equipment to support those efforts. In addition to creating and sustaining the DCA, donors claim success in their efforts to strengthen indigenous counter-narcotics agencies; to help draft counter-narcotics legislation, such as laws on money laundering, asset seizure, and financial crimes; and recently, to establish special courts for prosecuting crimes associated with narcotics consumption or trafficking. Today, each of the five Central Asian countries has a national drug control administrative structure, and with the help of international advisors, the Central Asian governments have set up inter-ministerial coordination bodies to centralize counter-narcotics policies and administration.

Donors also count among their successes the high number of law enforcement officials trained both domestically and abroad in counter-narcotics techniques and the large quantity of modern equipment provided to enhance interdiction and investigative capabilities among Central Asian law enforcement. Their programs have included training and equipment transfers to border guards, customs officials, and other counter-narcotic forces throughout the area, in addition to more equipment to improve forensic capacities and to store, analyze and destroy narcotic and psychotropic substances. From 1998 to 2000, for example, the U.S. State Department sponsored projects that trained some 500 Central Asian law enforcement and judicial officials per year, and these efforts are expanding. More recently, the United States has expanded its law enforcement presence on the ground in Central Asia, including the opening of an office of the Drug Enforcement Agency (DEA) in Tashkent, Uzbekistan and the placement of a regional narcotics officer in the U.S. Embassy in Kazakhstan to coordinate counter-narcotics activities throughout Central Asia.

These efforts have helped to raise interdiction rates significantly. UN and U.S. officials praise the high volume of drugs seized on the Central Asian and Afghanistan borders. According to the UN, Central Asian heroin seizures more than tripled between 1998 and 2000, rising from one to 3.2 metric tons, and continue to grow.[31]

But while some praise these efforts, others question whether quantitative indicators, such as the volume of narcotics seized, the number of people trained or the amount of equipment delivered, are useful measures to assess their full impact. Instead, some argue, they may mask serious failings that greatly impact the drug flow as well as exacerbate broader problems throughout Central Asian society.

For example, some observers question whether seizure rates on Central Asia's borders have increased significantly as a byproduct of higher trafficking rates rather than as a result of more effective law enforcement or border initiatives.[32] Critics point out that while seizures may have increased, so, too, has drug production in Afghanistan, and to this day, the amount of drugs interdicted continues to represent a very small percentage of the overall amount of drugs trafficked. Critics also argue that the focus on keeping interdiction rates high may have created detrimental side effects, such as further encouraging harassment by law enforcement officials of low-level drug traffickers, often women, in order to increase arrest totals; further eroding the fairness of interrogation and judicial proceedings in order to keep conviction rates high; and thus also contributing to growing incarceration rates in already overcrowded prisons.[33]

The net effect, they believe, is ultimately weakening the war on drugs overall as well as hindering efforts to encourage democratic reforms and establish an effective rule of law.

For example, some locals and Westerners alike fear that providing training and equipment in a corrupt environment without highly intrusive local and international oversight could be feeding the drug trade with one hand as it tries to eradicate it with the other. They express concern that international donors, like their Central Asian counterparts, are sweeping aside issues of corruption while providing significant funds and equipment to entities widely regarded as complicit in the trade itself. How does one know, they ask, if such training is helping governments to eradicate drug smuggling or simply allowing one cartel to eliminate another? How can one evaluate whether training programs are creating more honest, efficient law enforcement or are only empowering officers involved in trafficking to smuggle more effectively? Or, like the U.S. customs officer mentioned in the introduction, could training and equipment be helping well-placed officials to play both sides?

Donors argue that international organizations have attempted to identify untrustworthy individuals through a vetting process, or, in the words of one agency head, through "intuition." But donors also agree that both vetting and intuition are woefully inadequate in highly centralized and authoritarian countries where corruption is not an individual affair in the first place. Corruption in Central Asia is not a matter of corrupt individuals acting purely for personal gain; it is part of a highly organized system of economic crime that permeates all aspects of life.[34] Yet few international programs have had the capability, or the inclination, to sort through how this system works and apply that knowledge explicitly to donor programs. Limited resources and regional expertise often limit the ability of programs to assess who wins and who loses from the rampant trafficking in Central Asia—or from the Western programs introduced to combat it.

The same concerns have been expressed regarding the impact of counter-narcotics trafficking programs on human rights and other abuses.

Throughout Central Asia, the war on drugs often has been used for political ends—to repress political opposition, target particular religious and ethnic groups, limit civil liberties and tighten political control—as well as for extracting greater financial gain through bribes and extortion.

The possibility that international training and equipment may further empower authoritarian governments to crack down more forcefully on their own populations has raised new concerns. In Uzbekistan, for example, law enforcement officers are widely known to plant drugs on political opponents or religious figures and then prosecute them on trumped-up drug charges. The crackdown on the Islamic Movement of Uzbekistan (IMU) and on human rights activists has employed these tactics to increase sentences, as drug trafficking carries some of the most severe penalties, including death. Special drug courts reportedly avoid challenging police accounts or forced confessions, particularly in trials with political repercussions.[35]

How then, skeptics ask, should one evaluate the impact of training and equipment transfers when the number of human rights abuses associated with interdiction may rise along with the number of drug seizures? How useful are new laws and new courts if there are few mechanisms to ensure that they are applied fairly? And how does one prevent the courts from becoming new tools for state repression? Does the provision of more equipment to law enforcement—widely viewed as corrupt—run the risk of further strangling citizens' rights? One U.S. State Department official stated, off the record, that transferring night vision goggles to a repressive government is "abhorrent." "They might be used to fight drugs," he said, "but they're just as likely to be used to fight the opposition."[36]

These questions rarely have played a role in international law enforcement programs, which traditionally have viewed their mandate as transferring interdiction capabilities and encouraging high incarceration rates. Instead, observers and participants in these programs state that Western trainers tend to turn a blind eye to human rights abuses when they may interfere with the main goals of interdiction.[37]

Recently, international organizations have made a more concerted effort to address the range of societal problems emerging from the drug trade. The UNODC and the Organization for Security and Cooperation in Europe (OSCE)—one of the key organizations dealing with human rights as well as a range of other concerns in Central Asia—have begun efforts to coordinate more closely on the ground. They have sponsored meetings and conferences to discuss such issues as the role of the mass media in countering drug-related problems and corruption, and the root causes and economic impacts of the drug trade. The UNODC states that it recently has instituted an educational project on prevention through mass media and public events. U.S. State Department officials tasked with drug trafficking issues have spoken of the need to coordinate more closely with the State Department's human rights bureau, and U.S. aid programs have initiated seminars on promoting drug-free schools, including tips on fighting drug trafficking. The U.S. Agency for International Development (USAID) has contributed funds to needle exchange and other harm reduction programs in Central Asia conducted by the Open Society Institute and others.

Most of these efforts, however, are in their infancy and face major hurdles in the years ahead. One of the key points to emerge from media and corruption conferences, for example, is that the media is extremely reluctant to cover corruption and at times may be deeply corrupt itself. Education and public relations programs require far more funding to impact societies where, in a race against time, drugs are assuming an increasingly entrenched role. And an equally difficult hurdle is determining how to design and shape law enforcement programs themselves so that they incorporate these concerns and fit the informal economic and political realities of the Central Asian countries themselves.

Conclusion

What began as a law enforcement challenge in Central Asia, then, has unfolded into a multifaceted set of challenges—social, economic, political and security—emanating in all directions. Drug trafficking in Central Asia has been defined as a target of the war on terrorism, as a key component in the struggle for human rights, and as a part of one of the most serious health tragedies to beset our planet. It is potentially destabilizing at a time when the need for stability in this part of the world is at a premium. And it embraces such issues as widespread corruption that traditionally have been swept under the rug by all parties.

As U.S. policy makers and the international community commit to major investments to address this challenge, it is critical that strategies be refined, particularly in assessing priorities when these goals conflict. Past experience in other parts of the world demonstrate that supply reduction cannot work without a concurrent reduction in demand; but it is unclear what the balance should be between interdiction efforts on one hand, and demand and harm reduction programs on the other. Drugs and terrorism have been linked in U.S. policy as if they are part of the same battle, but they can be qualitatively different battles, where the strategies and tactics for combating one may conflict with those of the other. Which should take precedence? The same question can be asked for human rights, stability and humanitarian concerns.

At the tactical level, programs and projects demand far more attention, particularly in how they are designed, implemented, monitored and evaluated.[38] Perhaps most glaring is the need for greater local and international oversight and evaluation—particularly at a time when the trend has moved in the opposite direction. To date, mechanisms have been weak in this area, and resources for evaluations and follow-up have been limited on the part of implementing agencies. The U.S. State Department and law enforcement officials acknowledge that no formal evaluations of the counter-narcotics programs have been carried out to date in Central Asia; that they have yet to develop a standard mechanism for reporting and evaluation in the first place; and that the few evaluations that have taken place have been cursory "trip reports," focusing on numbers of people trained and equipment transferred. Other donors have conducted more formal evaluations, but the evaluation teams rarely, if ever, include any expertise on the region or local language capability, limiting their ability to conduct any kind of independent investigation.

In a region of "smoke and mirrors," programs must be closely monitored to ensure that equipment and training are applied as intended. While this should be done through both local oversight and Western personnel on the ground, ultimate responsibility for oversight and monitoring should lie with the donors who design and implement the programs.

In short, then, with record opium poppy yields and limited governmental control in Afghanistan, there is more pressure than ever before on the Moskovskii border guard detachment mentioned at the beginning of the chapter—and every detachment along the border of Afghanistan—to interdict some of the largest estimated drug flows in Central Asia's history. Donor organizations and local drug-control agencies have made important strides in Central Asia, but this should be seen as just a beginning. For these border guards and the multitude of others fighting the drug trade to succeed, much more is needed. Donor efforts must be broadened and made more nuanced and transparent, with particular attention paid to the impacts of counter-narcotics trafficking programs on corruption, as well as on human rights, gender, local economies and the like. More funding must be targeted from the international community, not only for the expansion of programs, but to support broadened oversight, transparency, and accountability on the ground. And a wider range of international and regional actors must become more involved if any "war on drugs" is to have a chance of success. Specialists in the informal workings of these societies must be encouraged to work hand-in-hand with technical experts to create programs that neither can accomplish alone; and the Central Asian public must be engaged to inject far more public oversight, both local and international, into every program. The confluence of drug money and terrorism, coupled with burgeoning societal ills in this part of the world, suggest the stakes may never have been higher.

Notes

[1] An earlier version of this chapter was published in Journal of International Affairs, Vol. 56, no. 2, Spring 2003..

[2] John Burnett, "Corruption at the Gates," Two-part Series for National Public Radio, *All Things Considered*, September 12-13, 2002.

[3] Kevin Sullivan, "Citing Corruption, Mexico Shuts Drug Unit," *The Washington Post*, January 21, 2003, A14.

[4] John Burnett.

[5] For the purposes of this article, Central Asia is comprised of Uzbekistan, Tajikistan, Kyrgyzstan, Kazakhstan and Turkmenistan.

[6] For a good review of questions concerning drug trafficking, including corruption, in these countries and Western assistance, *see* U.S. Department of State, Bureau of International Narcotics and Law Enforcement Affairs, International Narcotics Control Strategy Report, March 2003, at <www. state. ov/g/inl/rls/nrcrpt/2002/pdf>.

[7] The 2000 Congressional Supplemental allocates about $60 million to counter-narcotics and law enforcement efforts in Afghanistan, $22 million to counter-narcotics and law enforcement in Central Asia, and additional funds to the Caucasus. Coupled with prior 2002 appropriations and other agency and security funds applied to counter drug trafficking in this area, the total begins to approach $100 million--if not, some say, exceeding it.

[8] Estimates for 1999 range from 2,700 to 4,600 metric tons, and for 2000, from 3,300 to 3,700 metric tons, due to discrepancies between U.S. and UN estimates. In 1999, the U.S. estimate was 1,700 metric tons, subsequently revised upward to 2,860 metric tons, but was still only some 60 percent of the UN estimate. In 2000, however, the U.S. estimate of 3,700 metric tons exceeded the UN estimate of 3,300 metric tons. The discrepancy is due largely to different methodologies used by the different agencies.

[9] UNODC (formerly UN Office on Drug Control and Crime Prevention (ODCCP)), World Drug Report 2000, 160, at <http://www.unodc.org/odccp/world-drug-report.html>.

[10] Barbara Crossette, "Afghan Heroin Feeds Addiction in Region, UN Report Declares," *New York Times*, February 29, 2000; John Pomfret, "Drug Trade Resurgent in Afghanistan," *The Washington Post*, October 23, 2001. Although the Taliban blamed opposition forces for the high production and trafficking of opium and state its commitment to eliminate opium cultivation, the Taliban government, in fact, sanctioned the growth of opium through the late 1990s. It reportedly imposed, as on other agricultural goods, a 10 percent tax on the opium poppy and a 20 percent tax on its production and trade. Estimates of revenues the Taliban received from the opium trade range from $30 million to as high as $75 million--funds which enabled the government to finance ongoing wars against opposition forces and terrorist activities. UNODC estimates the farm-gate value of the 2000 crop of opium at roughly $91 million. See UNODC (formerly ODCCP), Afghanistan Annual Opium Poppy Survey 2000. Some argue that incursions of the Islamic Movement of Uzbekistan (IMU) in Central Asia at the end of the 1990s were not intended to found an Islamic state, but instead sought to open

new drug routes. See Scott Peterson, "Fabled Silk Road Now Paved With Narcotics," *Christian Science Monitor*, January 8, 2000.

[11] The UN reports 2002 production at 3,200 to 3,600 metric tons; other sources claim it may be as high as 4,000 tons. See UNODC (formerly ODCCP), Strategic Programme Framework: Strengthen Drug Control and Crime Prevention Activities in the Central Asian States: 2002-2005; and "Afghan Drug Crop Increasing," Radio Free Europe/Radio Liberty Crime and Corruption Watch 2, no. 8 (October 25, 2002).

[12] UNODC, Strategic Programme Framework, 6.

[13] Some experts assert that as much as 50 to 60 percent of all drugs produced in Afghanistan are traf-ficked through Central Asia. For the 50 percent estimate, *see, for example,* Prepared Testimony of Ralf Mutsche, Assistant Director, Criminal Directorate International Criminal Police Organization Interpol General Secretariat, before the House Committee on the Judiciary Subcommittee on Crime, December13, 2000; for the 60 percent estimate, see U.S. Government Accounting Office, "Southwestern Asia Heroin Production," June 21, 2000.

[14] *See, for example,* David Mansfield and Chris Martin, *Strategic Review: The Role of Central Asia as a Conduit for Illicit Drugs to Western Europe,* April 2000; Peter Reuter, RAND Corporation, private communication to author.

[15] See "As Kyrgyzstan Calculates Drug Barons' Profits," *Radio Free Europe/Radio Liberty Newsline* 4, no. 204 (October 20, 2000). The international drug trade was estimated to produce $400 billion per year for criminal syndicates.

[16] *See* survey results from Central Asian law enforcement personnel and the general population in Nancy Lubin, *Central Asians Take Stock: Reform, Corruption and Identity* (Washington, DC: U.S. Institute of Peace, 1995).

[17] Private communication to the author.

[18] Private communication to the author.

[19] Cited in Nancv Lubin, Alex Klaits and Igor Barsegian, *Narcotics Interdiction in Afghanistan and Central Asia: Challenges for International Assistance,* Open Society Institute, January, 2002. See also *International Narcotics Control Strategy Report*, March 2003.

[20] See, for example, Marat Mamadshoyev, "Tajik Drugs in Kazakh Capital: A Victory for the Special Services or for Diplomatic Intrigue?" *Eurasia Insight*, June 15, 2000, at <http://wwweurasianet.org/departments/insigt/articles/eavO6l 500.shtml>.

[21] *See, for example*, Rustem Safronov, "Turkmenistan's Niyazov Implicated in Drug Smuggling," Eurasia Insight, March 29, 2002, at <http://www.eurasianet.or departments/insight/articles/eav032902.shtml>.

[22] Regarding Tajikistan, for example, the report states: "It is impossible to determine how pervasive drug and other forms of corruption are within government circles; salaries for even top officials are extremely low and, at times, clearly inadequate to support the lifestyles many officials maintain. Even when arrests are made, the resulting cases are not always brought to a satisfactory conclusion... The lavish lifestyles of some, as noted, do give some credence to corruption allegations." *See* U.S. Department of State, International Narcotics Control Strategy Report, ix-120.

[23] Private communication to the author.

[24] Rakhim Abdukholikzoda, "Ch to skryvaet 'geroinovaia zavesa,'" (What's Behind the 'Heroin Veil?) January 28, 2003.

[25] E-mailed commentary on "Chto slcryvaet 'geroinovaia zavesa,'" ("What's Behind the 'Heroin Veil?

[26] Author's interview with courier, May 2002.

[27] "The Right Moves Aren't Working ... So the Drug Trade is Roaring," *Business Week,* June 23, 1997.

[28] Open Society Institute employee interview with Kyrgyz counter-narcotics official. For further discussion of these issues, *see* Lubin, Klaits, and Barsegian.

[29] See Erika Dailey, "Drug Searches and Human Rights Violations on the Tajikistan Border," *EurasiaNet*, February 18, 2000, at <http://www.eurasianet.org/departments/rights/articles/hrr02l800.

shtml>; *see* "Governmental and International Responses to Human Rights Abuses at Tajikistan's Border Crossing," *EurasiaNet*, May 16, 2000, at <http://www.eurasianet.orWdepartments/rights/articies/hrrO5l600.sNtml>. For an excellent discussion of women and the drug trade, see Tatiana Bozrikova, "Women and Drugs in Tajikistan," Open Society Institute Assistance Foundation, Tajikistan, February 2001. Many women view strip searches as so common they avoid cross-border travel whenever possible. The situation has contributed to further destruction of formerly strong social ties that united relatives living in different republics. Private communications to the author.

[30] The UN estimates that some 7,500 people were living with HIV/AIDS in Central Asia by 2001, most of whom were injecting drug users. Given methodological problems in assessing these totals, however, others believe that the actual number may be 10 times that amount. See, for example, Interfax-Kazakhstan News Agency, Almaty, reported in Russian, May 21, 2002 and reported by the BBC, May 21, 2002.

[31] UNODC, Strategic Program Framework, 6.

[32] Janeis Makerenko, *Intelligence Review* 12, no. 1 I (Nov 1, 2000). At the global level, this is what UNODC reports in the 2000 World Drug Report.

[33] See Lubin, Alex Klaits and Igor Barsegian, *Narcotics Interdiction in Afghanistan*.

[34] For broader description, see Lubin, "New Threats in Central Asia and the Caucasus: An Old Story with a New Twist," *Russia's Total Security Environment*, Institute for East/West Studies, 1999.

[35] For fuller discussion, see Lubin, Klaits, and Barsegian.

[36] Cited in Lubin, Klaits and Barsegian.

[37] Private communications to the authors and their first-hand experience in these programs.

[38] Previous testimony and reports by JNA Associates outline specific recommendations. See Lubin, "U.S. Policies in Central Asia," and "Aid to the Soviet Union," Congressional Testimony before the Subcommittee on Asia and the Pacific, Committee on International Relations, March 17 1999; and JNA Associates, Inc., *U.S. Assistance to the Former Soviet Union: When Less is More*, 1996.

Chapter 18

Migration Trends in Central Asia and the Case of Trafficking of Women

Saltanat Sulaimanova

After the collapse of the Soviet Union and the elimination of state regulation of population movements, migration from, to and within Central Asia has become an acute and continuous process.[1] It has substantial political, social and economic implications, negatively affecting the economies of the countries from which the migration outflow occurs. Traditionally, the Russian workforce in Central Asia tended to dominate the industrial, technical, educational and medical care sectors.[2] However, in the years since 1991, with the dramatic outflow of highly qualified professionals of Russian, German and Jewish origin, most Central Asian societies have experienced a "brain drain" and deterioration in the quality of education, medical fields, and other sectors of the economy.

Central Asian republics rightfully have been called "an astonishing ethnic mosaic."[3] Such multi-ethnicity is the result of the following factors:

- Pre-Soviet Russian Tsarist imperialistic expansion policies, which encouraged resettlement of Russians in Central Asia;[4]
- Repression and massive deportation of people to Central Asia by Stalin;
- Forced relocation of ethnic Germans, Greeks, Crimean Tatars, Koreans and Turks during World War II;[5]
- World War II and post-war reconstruction-era relocation policies, when industrial plants and factories with their entire workforce were relocated to Central Asia;
- Soviet policies of sending young graduates and professionals to work in the Central Asian republics.[6]

377

The migration of non-titular ethnic groups to the region continued to increase until the end of the 1950s. It reached its peak in 1959, when 45 percent of the region's population (over 10 million persons) were immigrants.[7] However, in the following 30 years, the number of indigenous populations in Central Asia increased threefold due to a higher birth rate, while the immigrant population grew by half.[8]

Nonetheless, by the late 1970s, migration trends began to change: some regions of Russia experienced labor deficits and became attractive areas for relocation because of the higher wages. In the 1980s, the Russian labor market became more favorable and the government actively promoted migration to Russia and Ukraine, not only by Slavs but also by the ethnic populations of non-Slavic republics.[9] During President Gorbachev's "perestroika" reforms, restrictions on travel outside the Soviet Union finally were lifted, though at first only the selective emigration of Jews, Germans and Greeks was allowed.[10] Eventually, from 1988 on, all individuals were permitted to migrate out of the country, although many republics still retained exit visa policies.

Migration within and outside Central Asia can be classified as internal, external and transit migration, as well as permanent and temporary (labor) migration. In general, ethnic minorities tend to migrate permanently out of Central Asia. Most of the migrants are ethnic Russians, who numbered more than eight million in Central Asian republics as late as 1995.[11] Table 18-1 shows the extent of this migration by country. In 1989, there were 388,000 Russians in Tajikistan, making up 7.6 percent of the population;[12] more than 100,000 Russians left the republic in 1992 alone.[13] By 1996, the Russian population in Tajikistan had decreased by a factor of two and represented 3.4 percent of the population. The civil war that broke out in 1992 and the rapidly deteriorating economy were among the reasons for the massive exodus of Russians as well as much of the Tajik population.[14] During the war years, approximately 300,000 Tajik citizens left the country, while another 692,000 were displaced to other parts of Tajikistan.

Similarly, in Uzbekistan before independence, 60 percent of the population of Tashkent, the capital, were Russians. By 1993, Russians composed only 40 percent of Tashkent's inhabitants.[15] The overall Russian population in Uzbekistan decreased from 8.3 percent in 1989 to 5.6 percent in 1996, spurred by the departure of 363,000 people.[16] Tatars also left Uzbekistan: between 1989 and 1996, their number decreased from 657,000 to 343,000.[17]

In Kazakhstan in 1989, ethnic Kazakhs were a minority in their own country, making up only 39.7 percent of the population. By 1999, the proportion of Kazakhs had increased to 53.4 percent. This increase was again partly caused by migration of ethnic people, specifically Russians who comprised 37.8 percent of the population in 1989 dropped to 30 percent in 1999. Overall, between 1989 and 1999, the "European"[18] population in Kazakhstan decreased from 44.7 to 34.7 percent.[19]

In Kyrgyzstan, out of 102,000 ethnic Germans living in the country, 80,000 left between 1991 and 1996.[20] In addition to the typical causes behind the migration of minorities from Central Asia, the main impetus for the German exodus was the program run by the German government to accept and assist German descendants from the Commonwealth of Independent States (CIS). Russians also departed in significant numbers. Where they once comprised 21.4 percent of the Kyrgyzstan population in 1989 the figure had dropped to 12.5 percent by 1999.[21]

Turkmenistan has had the lowest migration rate among the Central Asian states. The proportion of non-Russian minorities in Turkmenistan decreased only slightly, from 18.5 to 18 percent between 1989 and 1996. The Russian population decreased from 9.5 percent in 1989 to 6.6 percent in 1996. Such low rates of migration can be explained by the absence of ethnic violence in the country, the dependence of the Turkmen gas industry on Russian personnel,[22] and government policies that allowed dual citizenship with Russia. However, this policy was reversed in 2003: Turkmen citizens now have to either give up Russian citizenship or leave the country. As a result, it has been reported that emigration of non-titular citizens from Turkmenistan is on the rise.[23]

Motivating factors behind the decision of non-titular populations to migrate from Central Asia include: ethnic motives,[25] economic motives, uncertainty about the future and desire to provide a better future for children, isolation from Russia, anti-democratic regimes, social and political instability, poor ecological conditions, criminal situations, and other personal motives (family unification, health problems, desire/need for a different climate, etc).[26] In addition to the permanent external migration, people from Central Asia have begun to migrate to other countries for temporary jobs, and engage in shuttle trade and other kinds of commercial migration. A substantial number of migrants (mostly women) engage in the shuttle trade, traveling to other countries to purchase goods to be resold in their home countries. Typical destination countries include China, the United Arab Emirates, Turkey and Russia. The traveling

Table 18–1. **Population Change in Central Asia by Ethnicity, 1989-1996**[24]

	Percent		Thousands	
	1989	**1996**	**1989**	**1996**
Tajikistan				
Tajiks	62.1	68.1	3,172	4,006
Uzbeks	23.4	24.4	1,198	1,435
Russians	7.6	3.4	388	199
Other	6.9	4.1	350	244
Uzbekistan				
Uzbeks	71	76.6	14,142	17,614
Russians	8.3	5.6	1,653	1,280
Tatars	3.3	1.5	657	343
Jews	0.5	0.1	94	18
Germans	0.2	0.1	40	22
Other	16.7	16.3	3,318	3,730
Kazakhstan				
Kazakhs	39.5	47.0	6,535	7,781
Russians	37.7	33.9	6,228	5,615
Germans	5.8	2.6	957	426
Other	17	16.4	2,817	2,721
Kyrgyzstan				
Kyrgyz	52.0	59.9	2,230	2,721
Russians	21.4	15.6	917	707
Uzbeks	12.8	14.1	550	640
Ukrainians	2.5	1.6	108	73
Germans	2.4	0.5	101	21
Jews	0.1	0.0	6	2
Other	8.9	8.3	379	381
Turkmenistan				
Turkmen	72.0	75.4	2,536	3,163
Russians	9.5	6.6	334	278
Other	18.5	18.0	653	757

Population changes due to natural increase/decrease as well as emigration/immigration. Source: Tim Heleniak. The Changing Nationality Composition of the Central Asian and Transcaucasian States." Post-Soviet Geography and Economics 38, No. 6: 357-378.

conditions of such migrants are usually miserable, and they are subject to harassment from corrupt customs and law enforcement officers. They also may have to pay high "passage fees."[27]

Hundreds of thousands of Central Asians have left their homes for other CIS countries in search of better work opportunities. Many leave their families behind and send remittances back home. Russia is the most popular destination country for such labor migrants. It is estimated that over 160,000 Tajik citizens work in Russia, primarily in the construction sector and open markets where unskilled labor is in demand.[28] They tend to concentrate in Moscow, St. Petersburg, Samara, Volgograd and major cities of Western Siberia. Overall, anywhere between 200,000 to 400,000 Tajik citizens are labor migrants in other Central Asian countries and the Russian Federation.[29] Similarly, the Kyrgyz also migrate in large numbers to the Russian Federation for work. In addition, it is estimated that 6,000[30] to 50,000[31] Kyrgyz migrants are working in Kazakhstan.[32] Many of them work on tobacco plantations, often living in horrendous conditions and abused by the plantation owners. The United States is also a growing destination for emigration. Over 500 Kyrgyz citizens are estimated to be working in the New York area, as nannies, maids, care-givers to senior citizens and other low-level jobs. Typically, these migrants arrive in the United States on tourist visas and stay to work for a few years with the intention of saving their wages to take back home and support families in Kyrgyzstan.[33]

Internal migration is also an acute problem in Central Asia. The collapse of the Soviet Union resulted in the breakdown of industry, the collective farm system and the rural infrastructure of the region. Unemployment soared as land was privatized, and jobs that were traditionally available at collective farms disappeared. Salaries for teachers, doctors and others became irregular, and many schools and hospitals were forced to close. Even those institutions that remain open, experience chronic shortages of personnel. These circumstances forced rural residents to move to the cities in search of employment and educational opportunities.[34]

Internal migration includes internally displaced persons (IDPs), who have to move within the territory of their country. For example, over 100,000[35] persons were displaced during the 1980s and 1990s because of the environmental disaster in the Aral Sea region.[36] In addition, over 161,000 persons[37] were forced the leave the Semipalatinsk area, a nuclear testing site.[38] In Kyrgyzstan, at least 17,000 people had to migrate between 1992 and 1997 because of landslides, mudflows, floods and earthquakes.[39] Overall, according to the estimates of the United National High Commissioner for Refugees (UNHCR), at least 250,000 people have been forced to leave their homes in Central Asia because of ecological disasters.[40]

Another aspect of migration that affects Central Asia is transit migration of third country nationals en route to more developed countries. The lax border control that accompanied the demise of the Soviet Union opened the region, to human smuggling criminal networks and migrants from as far away as South Asia and Africa en route to Western Europe.[41] This issue presents a particular challenge to law enforcement agencies in the region, as the smuggling of migrants often involves fraudulent passports and/or visas. Central Asian republics have reported irregular migrants originating from China, Pakistan, Afghanistan, India and Iran.[42]

Refugees who had to flee their homes because of the brutal civil war in Tajikistan, the ethnic violence against Meskhetians in Uzbekistan, the continuous fighting in Chechnya, and the crimes of the Taliban regime in Afghanistan constitute another major group of people on the move in Central Asia. UNHCR estimates that 600,000 refugees were displaced within Tajikistan as a result of the civil war that killed at least 20,000 people. Over 60,000 Tajik refugees fled to Afghanistan, and another 13,000 sought refuge in Kyrgyzstan.[43] By 1996, almost all internally displaced Tajik refugees returned to their homes. Seventy five percent of Tajik refugees who fled to Afghanistan also have returned. Over 74,000 Meskhetians fled from the Ferghana valley in 1989 because of serious outbreaks of ethnic violence. Two-thirds of them found asylum in Azerbaijan, while the remaining group moved to Russia.[44]

Overall, it is likely that migration in Central Asia will continue as regional economies deteriorate. Since channels for legal labor migration are limited, irregular migration is likely to prevail. The consequences of this migration are serious for the countries concerned, as well as for labor migrants themselves. The International Organization for Migration (IOM) reports, "99 percent of labour migration in the Eurasian Economic Union formed of Tajikistan, Kyrgyzstan, Kazakhstan, the Russian Federation, and Belarus is irregular. Due to their irregular situation, most labour migrants do not benefit from the same protection rights other regular citizens enjoy and are thus more vulnerable to exploitation by underground employers."[45] The most despicable form of irregular migration is human trafficking. The trafficking of human beings for the purposes of sexual exploitation, which is becoming a salient characteristic of migration dynamics in Central Asia, is the most onerous form of migration throughout the region.

Human Trafficking: The Scope of the Problem

Trafficking in women is a modern form of slavery that exists in most countries of the world. It is a transnational global problem and one of the fastest growing criminal enterprises. Traffickers find it attractive because the profits are enormously high and the risks are low. Each year, illicit profits from trafficking in women generate an estimated seven to 12 billion dollars for organized criminal groups.[46] Trafficking in persons has increased significantly since the end of the Cold War, as borders have become more open, and more people, especially women, have become economically vulnerable. For many years, Thailand and the Philippines have been the main source of young women, but Eastern Europe and the former Soviet Union are rapidly becoming growing markets. The increase in trafficking in women is an unintended consequence and a "female underside" of globalization.[47] This chapter seeks to illustrate trafficking patterns in Central Asia through analysis of existing data, conversations with women's rights activists, Non Governmental Organizations (NGOs), international organizations in Central Asia, and personal observations in the field.

Given the complex nature of trafficking, it is not surprising that there are many debates as to its definition. The IOM, a Geneva-based intergovernmental organization, defines trafficking as occurring when: "a migrant is illicitly engaged (recruited, kidnapped, sold, etc.) and/or moved, either within national or across international borders; Intermediaries (traffickers) during any part of this process obtain economic or other profit by means of deception, coercion and/or other forms of exploitation under conditions that violate the fundamental human rights of migrants."[48] *A Protocol to Prevent, Suppress and Punish Trafficking in Persons, especially Women and Children* supplementing the UN Convention against Transnational Organized Crime of 2000, offers a more comprehensive definition of trafficking.[49]

Political, economic and social changes, which took place after the Soviet Union collapsed, resulted in poverty and unemployment, and created a pool of women from which traffickers could recruit. Thousands of women are lured into prostitution under false pretenses of high paying jobs abroad as waitresses, dancers, models and au pairs. Impoverished women of Central Asia are an easy target for traffickers, who take advantage of the high level of unemployment among women, their poverty and the lack of a stable future.

Trafficking in human beings is a multifaceted problem and it takes various forms—sweat shop labor, domestic servitude, begging, trafficking of boys to be used as camel jockeys, and sexual exploitation. Trafficking in women for the purposes of sexual exploitation is a more dangerous form of trafficking in humans compared to others because victims are exposed to serious health risks, including sexually transmitted diseases (STDs) and HIV/AIDS. Trafficking in children and men also occurs, but the majority of victims are women. In Central Asia, the trafficking of women is a new phenomenon. Prior to 1992 virtually no cases of trafficking in women were reported from this region to the West; since the break-up of the Soviet Union, the phenomenon has reached epidemic proportions.

It is difficult to determine how many women have been trafficked abroad from the former Soviet Union. The trafficking "business" keeps a low profile, victims are threatened by the traffickers to remain silent, and no official statistics are available. Estimates of how many people are trafficked worldwide vary significantly. The U.S. Government estimates that approximately 800,000 to 900,000 persons are trafficked each year.[50] Other reports state that up to four million people are trafficked around the world annually.[51] The estimates of the number of persons trafficked into the United States annually vary from 18,000[52] to 50,000.[53] Other sources estimate that up to 175,000 persons are trafficked from Central and Eastern Europe and the CIS annually.[54] In the case of Central Asia, the IOM estimates that approximately 4,000 women from Kyrgyzstan, about 5,000 from Kazakhstan,[55] and 1,000 from Tajikistan are trafficked abroad each year. There are no estimates on the scale of trafficking from the other Central Asian republics, but the U.S. Government deems Uzbekistan to have a significant number of trafficking cases.[56]

Most of the research on trafficking has been conducted in the traditional sending and receiving countries by the IOM, NGOs, and independent researchers. In light of the changes in the post-Cold War era, IOM has conducted studies in the newly independent states of the former Soviet Union (Ukraine, Moldova, the Kyrgyz Republic, Armenia, Georgia and Tajikistan) that have become a major source of trafficked women. These studies identify the scope of trafficking in human beings, trafficking routes, common destination countries, methods of recruitment, trafficking networks, profile of victims and estimates of the number of trafficked women.

Nature of the Problem

One of the first writings on sexual exploitation of women from a feminist and human rights perspective was undertaken by Kathleen Barry in the 1970s. Her *Female Sexual Slavery* was ground-breaking research on forced prostitution and trafficking in women, at a time when there was a belief that "women are not forced into prostitution; sexual violence is simply part of their work, and further, that some women are made for that."[57] Most of the prior research on prostitution looked at female motivation rather than the circumstances that got them onto the streets. Barry came up with the concept of female sexual slavery and defines it as follows:

> Female sexual slavery is present in all situations where women or girls cannot change the immediate conditions of their existence; where regardless of how they got into those conditions they cannot get out; and where they are subject to sexual violence and exploitation.[58]

Barry's definition of female sexual slavery reflects the situation in which many trafficking victims find themselves. The majority of trafficked women are kept in squalid conditions in a state of virtual house arrest and are transported only to and from work. Even when women have relative freedom of movement, their illegal immigration status, inability to speak the local language, lack of documents, and fear of being arrested, mistreated, or deported, keeps them from seeking help from local law enforcement authorities.[59]

Human trafficking is often viewed from the perspective of international migration. As Paul J. Smith points out, international migration is often explained by a basic "push" and "pull" model: "economic deprivation, high fertility, and unemployment (push factors) in lesser-developed countries work in concert with such elements as family reunification, higher wages, and increased demand for labor (pull factors) in industrialized countries, to create an influx of immigrants."[60] This model holds true for the trafficking phenomenon as well. Poverty, unemployment and lack of future perspectives are among the push factors; demand for "services" and potentially higher wages are the pull factors in receiving countries, for women taking the risk of going abroad and getting trafficked.

Bolstering the pull factors are "stories of better opportunities overseas," which are often naive and unrealistic. During a study of trafficking from the CIS, one respondent said she knew she would have to engage in prostitution, but she thought it would be similar to the film *Pretty Woman*, where one man would support her.[61] One could argue that this is an extreme level of naiveté, but considering that the former Soviet countries were totally isolated from the rest of the world for almost 70 years, these kinds of illusions are not surprising. Ideas of the lifestyle in Western countries, and especially the United States, are drawn mainly from the movies and soap operas televised on a daily basis. Women watching "Santa Barbara" and "Dallas" expect to have the kind of life they see in the movies once they get to the West. They do not anticipate being manipulated, deceived, or physically abused, and believe nothing bad could happen to them in wealthy countries.

Though limited, existing literature provides some insight into the links between human trafficking and organized criminal groups. In most cases, trafficking is carried out by organized criminal groups with extensive international links.[62] These criminal groups intimidate the trafficked women and threaten retaliation against family members at home if the women do not obey them.[63] In the same vein, Sietske Altink of the Dutch anti-trafficking NGO *STV* writes:

> As the traffickers are highly organized, most of their victims dare not speak out. Ana from the Dominican Republic said, 'They were like a mafia. I couldn't even discuss my situation with other girls. Whenever I told someone my story, the next day the traffickers knew that I had talked. The man who kept me prisoner explicitly forbade me to speak to other girls. If these criminals have the address of your parents' home, they can keep you a prisoner. They say you endanger your father and mother when you don't obey them. That's how the traffickers subdue us.[64]

Root Causes of Trafficking

In general, women get trafficked because of poverty, unemployment, the low social status of women in their home countries, lack of opportunities and prospects for the future, and in many cases, because of an idealistic view of the Western world and the wealthier countries in general. All of these rationales can be found in Central Asia. Poverty in Central Asia has reached unprecedented levels: 51 percent of the Kyrgyz population lives below the national poverty line, as do 34.6 percent of Kazakh citizens and 26.5 percent of the Uzbeks. Forty four percent of Turkmen live on less than $2 a day.[65] The population groups most affected by poverty are women, children, and the elderly. Women are the first ones to lose their jobs due to downsizing and economic shifts.[66] The National Statistics Committee of Kyrgyzstan reports that 70 percent of women in Kyrgyzstan are suffering from financial difficulties.[67] The unemployment rate is very high, and even those who are employed, make an average of $28 per month.[68] As the 2000 IOM survey of trafficking victims in Kyrgyzstan reports:

> Seventy nine percent of the respondents said that unemployment drove them to look for work abroad. The main reasons they were working as commercial sex workers abroad were said to be related to their lack of money and hopes for a better future. The lack of alternative opportunities encourages them to take risks. In focus groups discussions the women said that they want more for themselves and their families than to just earn enough money to feed themselves. They want a better life.[69]

Even when women are employed, they often face job discrimination and sexual harassment at work. In many businesses throughout the CIS, it is not uncommon for a male boss to demand that his female subordinate engage in sexual relations with him.[70] Newspaper job advertisements targeting women often mention "no hang-ups," as one of the qualifications required for the job.[71] Not surprisingly, when women are promised payment of $60,000 a year to work abroad,[72] an amount they could never dream of at home, it is not very difficult for them to be enticed by such lucrative "job offers."

The collapse of the Soviet Union resulted not only in poverty and unemployment but also in the drastic deterioration of the system of social protection. Many of the social services taken for granted under the Soviet system are no longer offered. Before the collapse of the Soviet Union, day care for children, education at all levels, and medical services were provided by the government. Now many day care centers have closed and the remaining ones are unaffordable to most parents. Health care and education systems also are closed or deteriorating, due to lack of funding.[73]

The social status of women in Central Asia has been on the decline in the last decade as well. As the economic situation continues to worsen, more and more men lose their jobs, often plunging them into a spiral of alcoholism and abuse of the family at home. Increasingly, women have become the victims of domestic violence, while local law enforcement officials refuse to take this offense seriously.[74] Domestic violence is one of the major reasons why children run away from home. Street children, in turn, are especially vulnerable to being recruited by traffickers. Further, young girls from households where domestic violence is the norm, grow up "seeing women as inferior beings that men can use and abuse as they please."[75] The mistreatment or abuse they receive in trafficking situations only confirms their worst fears.

In addition, since the collapse of the Soviet Union, the Central Asian nations have witnessed a revival of "national traditions," which often come into conflict with Soviet policies that promoted women's equality. Not long after independence, politicians began advocating a return to "traditional roles" for women, which is interpreted by many as an attempt to "drive women out of the labor force and higher education and back into the home."[76] The Parliament in Kyrgyzstan has discussed seriously legalizing polygamy, and ultimately, rejected the proposal by only a small margin.[77] Unofficially, polygamy is not uncommon in Central Asian republics.[78] The deteriorating economic situation, high unemployment among women, religious and traditional sentiments, as well as the consequences of the civil war (in Tajikistan) are cited as some of the reasons why polygamy is spreading across Central Asia;[79] traditional male chauvinism is another. This dramatic decline in women's social status has created a situation favorable for traffickers.

Recruitment of Women in the Countries of Origin

Traffickers use the following methods to recruit victims:

- Advertisements in newspapers;
- Marriage agencies or mail-order-bride agencies;
- Friends, relatives, or acquaintances;
- The "Second Wave" (trafficked women returning to recruit other women);
- False marriages (women marrying a false groom who is, in fact, a trafficker);[80]
- Kidnapping.

Advertisements in newspapers are the most popular recruitment method because traffickers can reach a wide pool of potential victims. Such advertisements usually offer young women highly paid work abroad as waitresses, dancers, or shopkeepers.[81] When a woman responds to an advertisement, the traffickers sometimes sign a "contract" with her that promises high earnings, but also stipulates that travel expenses as well as room and board will be deducted. Room and board often can eat up over half of their daily earnings. Women also are bound to pay back the travel expenses that are "calculated" at rates often exceeding the real cost of transportation by as much as three to five times. According to the Global Survival Network, an NGO based in Washington, trafficking networks in Russia and the Newly Independent States (NIS) charge women anywhere from $1,500 to $30,000 for their "services" in facilitating documentation, jobs, and transportation.[82] This leaves victims with a huge debt that takes months, if not years, to pay off. The women often are deprived of all their earnings until this "debt" is paid in full, which makes them, in fact, indentured servants.

Mail-order-bride and marriage agencies via the Internet have become increasingly popular among women who want to marry a foreigner. Their hope is to improve their economic situation and/or escape their native country, where they see no prospects for the future. Most of these women are somewhat naively searching for happiness, and often become victims of men who "order" them only to sell them to pimps.[83] The paramount problem is that mail-order-bride agencies do not conduct any screening of their male clients, some of whom may have a history of violence or criminal background. As a result, mail-order brides may become victims of abuse. In a recent case, a 20 year old mail-order-bride, Anastasia Solovieva-King from Kyrgyzstan, was murdered by her American husband, Indle King. He had been married twice before, both times through matchmaking agencies. Within a month of marrying Anastasia, the man was writing to other prospective mail-order-brides. Two years later, as his marriage to Anastasia started falling apart, he wrote to more women and began planning to marry another mail-order-bride.[84] Following the murder of Anastasia King, the U.S. Congress proposed a bill in 2003, that would allow foreign mail order brides to check the criminal background (including protective orders issued because of domestic violence allegations) of their potential grooms. If such legislation had been in place, Anastasia Soloeiva may have learned that her prospective husband's first wife had obtained a protective order against him in 1995.[85]

Some victims of trafficking have indicated that they have been recruited by friends, relatives or acquaintances. These people gained the woman's confidence, then offered them highly paid work abroad, often sharing their alleged "experience" and showing off newly purchased goods or property.[86] "Second wave" recruitment occurs when trafficked women return home to recruit other women. For some women this is the only way they can return home—a common ploy for pimps is to pose a condition that the trafficked woman find someone else to replace her. Other women become recruiters voluntarily, making a profit from other women's victimization. One woman who had been trafficked from Kyrgyzstan expressed her intention to become a trafficker: "In the future I want to become an agent myself. I think I could be very successful. I could recruit girls to send to Kazakhstan, there's money to be made there too. I can earn more working for just three months abroad, than I can earn in five years here. A pimp earns at least $5,000 from each woman he takes on."[87] The cycle can be self-perpetuating. There are also cases of women who have not been recruited being kidnapped off the streets.[88]

Transportation to Destination Countries and Involvement of Government Officials

In most cases traffickers arrange for a woman's travel documents, visas and airline tickets. Occupations typically listed on a victim's visa applications include dancer, entertainer, student or au pair. Tour firms are found to assist in the trafficking of women and girls abroad, claiming they are "shop-tourists" who buy goods abroad to resell them in their home countries.[89] Having entered the country with fake passports, women usually overstay their visas, which makes them even more vulnerable because they are viewed by the local police as illegal immigrants.

Almost every trafficking network in Central Asia has a contact who makes it possible for them to obtain genuine state issued passports at the passport issuing department of the Ministry of Internal Affairs.[90] This indicates that corrupt local law enforcement officials are an integral part of the trafficking chain. If a woman does not have a passport, or is underage, a fraudulent passport is arranged for a bribe, ranging from $100[91] to $800.[92] Corrupt law enforcement officials have a monetary motive for facilitating the trafficking of women—salaries at the government agencies are very low, and corruption is a way to supplement their income. Another reason why government officials are reluctant to intervene in human trafficking is due to fear of reprisals by organized criminal groups.[93]

It also has been reported that law enforcement officials in some receiving countries are involved in trafficking. For example, women under the age of 31 are not allowed to enter the United Arab Emirates, which is a major destination for women trafficked from Central Asia, unless accompanied by male relatives. When 15 and 16 year-old girls enter the U.A.E with passports that indicate they are over 31, traffickers bribe the immigration officials at the airport to let the girls pass through immigration control.[94] Trafficking victims interviewed by the IOM in the Kyrgyz Republic, reported that 73 percent of them were harassed by the customs and law enforcement officers upon return. As one of the women recounts, "When I got to Almaty, the customs officials took $500 cash off me, they also took my jewelry. They said, 'We know what you are. It's written all over your face.' Then the cops stopped us and said 'We know what you've been doing.'[95]

The Role of Organized Criminal Groups in Trafficking

The former Soviet republics are experiencing an organized crime epidemic. The Center for Strategic and International Studies (CSIS) estimates that some 8,000 criminal gangs operate throughout the NIS.[96] About 200 are now global conglomerates and operate in 58 countries of the world.[97] Twenty six of them have established a presence in the United States.[98] Overall, organized criminal groups from the CIS are involved in all types of criminal activities, including, but not limited to: money-laundering, drug-trafficking, gambling, prostitution, trafficking in women and children, child pornography, contract killings, racketeering, banking and insurance fraud, extortion and kidnapping for ransom.[99] The trafficking networks are controlled by criminal gangs that provide security, logistical support, liaison with brothel owners in many countries, and false documents. According to Marco Gramegna of IOM, there are large-, medium- and small-scale networks of trafficking women.[100] Large-scale networks recruit women in a seemingly legal way, as language students or au pairs, which leads to the conclusion that these networks have extensive international contacts. The medium-scale networks usually traffic women from one country, while the small-scale networks traffic a few women at a time when a brothel owner places an "order."[101] In many cases, trafficking is carried out by organized criminal groups with foreign connections.[102]

The fact that organized criminal groups in various states of the former Soviet Union have links with each other allows them to organize illegal trafficking effectively. For example, Russian and Ukrainian women are trafficked through Georgia to Turkey and the Mediterranean.[103] Tajik women are trafficked to the UAE, Russia, Turkey and other countries transiting through NIS states.[104] Women from Kyrgyzstan are trafficked to the UAE, Turkey and European countries through Kazakhstan and directly from Kyrgyzstan.[105] According to Louise Shelley, "While the links among the States have declined since the collapse of the Soviet Union, the organized criminals still manage to function effectively together. And in the Russian Far East you see links with Korean and Japanese organized crime groups that are facilitating the trafficking of women."[106]

Methods Used by Traffickers to Control Women

The Dutch NGO working against trafficking in women, *Stichting Tegen Vrouwenhandel* (STV), reports that organized criminal groups involved in trafficking are extremely violent and use every kind of threat to intimidate women. The so-called "red mafia" are said to have made a woman dig her own grave and have taken women's family members hostage in order to force them to comply or keep silent.[107] As Shelley points out, "many of the women refuse to cooperate with the authorities because there is little or no protection, and they face deportation and threats against their families if they cooperate with foreign law enforcement."[108]

Once a woman is in trafficker's hands, the latter uses any and all means to control her: violence, including sexual assault, threats to the victim's family, drugs, and threats to turn the woman over to unsympathetic local authorities. Traffickers take away women's passports immediately upon arrival in the receiving country, either by force or by claiming that they need to extend the visas. Passports then are kept hostage to control the victims. According to Human Rights Watch, the most common form of coercion is debt bondage.[109] Women are told they must work without wages until they repay their purchase price and/or travel expenses. Employers also maintain their power to "resell" indebted women into renewed levels of debt. In some cases, women find that their debts only increase and can never be fully repaid.[110] It also seems that pimps/traffickers let some women keep just enough of their earnings to take back home to attract other potential victims.

Trafficked women who do not obey the rules are treated severely. The corpses of several hundred trafficked women, strangled, shot or beaten to a pulp, are found in Europe every year.[111] Europol believes that many more bodies are never discovered. The Russian organized criminal groups are especially known for their cruelty. As Friedman puts it, "Russian mobsters, in the United States, simply don't play by the unwritten rules of the acceptable uses of gang-land violence."[112] And IOM reports that, "The organized gangs of traffickers who lure and smuggle young women into prostitution are ruthless."[113] One trafficked victim from Kyrgyzstan testified, "Russian pimps, unlike most European ones, are also hardened criminals. It's no big deal for them to kill someone. They're the greediest, cruelest people in the world. They warned me, 'If you try to go to the police, we'll kill you.' I believed them."[114]

What is Being Done to Fight Trafficking?

The U.S. Government passed the Trafficking Victims Protection Act in 2000 to combat trafficking in persons. Among other provisions, this federal law provides for punishment of traffickers, protection of trafficking victims and monitoring of other countries' efforts to fight trafficking. The law also requires the State Department to submit an annual report to Congress on the status of trafficking worldwide. This report rates countries' efforts in combating human trafficking by placing them in "tiers." Tier 1 countries are those whose governments "fully comply with the Act's minimum standards." Minimum standards for the governments include prohibiting and punishing trafficking, as well as making serious efforts to eliminate trafficking.[115] Governments of countries in Tier 2 do not fully comply with the minimum standards, but are making significant efforts to do so. Tier 3 countries do not comply with the minimum standards and are not making significant efforts to comply with those standards.

Four Central Asian countries have been reported in the State Department's 2003 trafficking report. Kyrgyzstan and Tajikistan have been placed in Tier 2, while Kazakhstan and Uzbekistan have been placed in Tier 3.[116] Governments that are not making significant efforts to combat human trafficking might be subject to sanctions from the United States, including withdrawal of certain types of U.S. aid. Uzbekistan, until recently, did not even recognize trafficking as a problem. One of the limited preventive measures taken by the government of Uzbekistan is denying exit visas to young women.[117] Despite numerous known cases of trafficking from Kazakhstan, and many reported investigations, the Kazakhs have not convicted any of the traffickers.[118] However, new anti-trafficking legislation was passed by the lower houses of the Parliament both in Kazakhstan and Tajikistan in the spring of 2003.[119] Kyrgyzstan is reported to be making "significant efforts" to combat trafficking and has introduced draft anti-trafficking legislation to the Parliament.[120] It is interesting to note that both Kyrgyzstan and Pakistan, U.S. allies in the war against terrorism, were moved up from their rankings as Tier 3 countries in 2002 to Tier 2 in 2003, raising the question of whether this was done for political reasons.

Conclusions and Recommendations

Trafficking in women is a fundamental human rights violation that needs to be combated at the national and international levels. The consequences of trafficking are grave, both to the women and the countries involved. According to Marco Gramegna of the IOM, the consequences of trafficking are a threat to legal migration and growth in clandestine immigration.[121] Both of these problems could have substantial implications for political, economic and diplomatic affairs of the sending and receiving countries. At the human level, victims of trafficking face intolerable situations, including sexual and physical abuse, and deprivation of their basic human rights and dignity.

There is a glaring need for comprehensive trafficking research in Uzbekistan, Kazakhstan and Turkmenistan. Such research is essential to thoroughly assess the scope of trafficking from these countries, identify the main destination countries, study how people are trafficked, and who the traffickers are. Based on the results of such studies, the respective governments should be able to design and implement strategies to fight trafficking.

Trafficking is driven by poverty and unemployment of women, as well as by demand in the receiving states. To solve the problem by tackling its root causes would be the optimal solution, which, unfortunately, is an enormously complex and multidimensional task. Such a solution, however, cannot wait until the local economies recover and all women are employed. The international community must confront this issue and take aggressive steps to stop the trafficking of women and children.

The following steps might be carried out in "sending" countries, including the five Central Asian states, to help alleviate the problem:

- Foster creation of job opportunities for young women;
- Improve law enforcement efforts to prevent and punish trafficking of women;
- Crack down on official complicity in trafficking of women (including stricter control over issuing passports) and combat corruption which fuels organized crime;
- Carry out information campaigns in the media and on TV about the nature, realities and risks of "lucrative" job offers;
- Provide legal, medical and psychological assistance to victims of trafficking;
- Guarantee safety to victims who testify against the traffickers through witness protection programs.

The following actions should be considered by "receiving" countries:

- Amend laws, including immigration law, to exempt victims of trafficking and/or servitude from being prosecuted for illegal status that have resulted directly from these practices. Deportation may be appropriate, but punitive measures, including detention, should be waived;
- Prosecute traffickers and enable victims to bring lawsuits against traffickers by granting temporary residence permits for the duration of the case;
- Impose tougher penalties for trafficking. The United States has already taken such measures with the adoption of the Victim Protection Act of 2000;

■ Protect safety of victims of trafficking through strong witness protection programs;

■ Ensure that victims of trafficking have access to essential social services, including shelter and medical care;

■ Distribute information brochures at the receiving countries' Embassies abroad with each visa issued to a woman, on the realities and risks of being trafficked and what to do if she finds herself trafficked and abused abroad.

Trafficking in persons is an acute problem in Central Asia and is likely to increase as the economies continue to worsen, unless the region's governments and the international community take serious measures to fight this phenomenon. Organized criminal groups in both sending and receiving countries are actively involved in trafficking. All countries involved, sending, receiving and transit, should continue their efforts to crack down on organized crime. International cooperation and coordination between law enforcement agencies is crucial for combating trafficking in women. When available, the information needed to prosecute the traffickers and protect the victims should be made available to all parties.

Trafficking occurs because women are poor and desperate, do not have any prospects for improvement in their lives at home, and possess illusions and unrealistic expectations about what awaits them abroad. Traffickers take advantage of these circumstances and exploit them. However, trafficking would not be so profitable if there was no demand in the wealthier countries. It is obvious that the government authorities in sending countries are involved in the trafficking process at various levels, but are the authorities in the receiving countries also looking away from the problem? How aggressively governments combat this problem in the next few years will determine if the international community is going to eliminate this modern form of slavery in the twenty-first century.

Notes

[1] Rafis Abazov, "Economic Migration in Post-Soviet Central Asia: The Case of Kyrgyzstan," *Post-Communist Economies* 11, no. 2 (1999), 237.

[2] Paul Kolstoe, *Russians in the Former Soviet Republics* (Bloomington, IN: Indiana University Press), 219.

[3] United Nations High Commissioner for Refugees, "Central Asia on the Move." *Refugees Magazine,* May 1, 1996; Internet available from <www.unhcr.ch>; accessed September 25, 2003.

[4] For example, 1,500,000 Russians had moved to Turkmenistan by 1917. More Russian immigrants arrived in Central Asia after 1918, seeking to escape hunger and civil war.

⁵ See Yuriy Kulchik, et al., *Central Asia After the Empire* (Chicago, IL: Pluto Press,1996), 3; Rafis Abazov, "Economic Migration in Post-Soviet Central Asia: The Case of Kyrgyzstan," *Post-Communist Economies* 11, no. 2 (1999), 240.

⁶ International Organization for Migration, 2001, "Internal Migration in the Kyrgyz Republic," 3.

⁷ Yuriy Kulchik, et al., 4.

⁸ Ibid.

⁹ Zhanna Zaionchkovskaya, "Migration Patterns in the Former Soviet Union," in the Conference Report *Cooperation and Conflict in the Former Soviet Union: Implications for Migration*, RAND, 1996, 15; Internet available from <http://www.rand.org/publications/CF/CF130/>, accessed September 19, 2003.

¹⁰ Ibid., 18.

¹¹ Galina S. Vitkovskaya, "Relocation to Russia from the States of Central Asia: Understanding the Decision to Migrate" in the Conference Report *Cooperation and Conflict in the Former Soviet Union: Implications for Migration*, RAND, 1996, 113; Internet available from <http://www.rand.org/publications/CF/CF130>/, accessed September 19, 2003.

¹² Tim Heleniak, "The Changing Nationality Composition of the Central Asian and Transcaucasian States," *Post-Soviet Geography and Economics* 38, no. 6: 373.

¹³ "The Russians Say Goodbye to All That," *The Economist* 328, no. 7827 (Sept 4, 1993), 38.

¹⁴ International Organization for Migration, 2001, "Deceived Migrants from Tajikistan: A Study of Trafficking in Women and Children," 10.

¹⁵ "The Russians Say Goodbye to All That."

¹⁶ Tim Heleniak.,no. 6: 375.

¹⁷ Ibid.

¹⁸ Russian, Ukrainian, Belarus, Polish, and German nationalities.

¹⁹ Peter Sinnott, "Population Politics in Kazakhstan," *Journal of International Affairs* 56, no. 2 (Spring 2003), 105.

²⁰ Rafis Abazov, "Economic Migration in Post-Soviet Central Asia: The Case of Kyrgyzstan," *Post-Communist Economies* 11, no. 2 (1999), 247.

²¹ International Organization for Migration. 2001. "Internal Migration in the Kyrgyz Republic," 11.

²² Tim Heleniak, no. 6: 374.

²³ "Flight From Ashgabat," Institute for War and Peace Reporting (Central Asia), no. 220, July 25, 2003.

²⁴ Population changes due to natural increase/decrease as well as emigration/immigration. Source: Tim Heleniak, no. 6: 357-378.

²⁵ "Ethnic motives" are concerns about "ethnic policy," including seizure of power by the titular ethnic group and intent to create a monoethnic state; "ethnic discrimination," including non-titular ethnic groups becoming second-class citizens and experiencing civil rights infringements, employment discrimination, unequal access to higher education, etc.; popular nationalism, including experiences with harassment, hostility; "language barrier," including lack of schooling in Russian, lack of information in Russian, unofficial status of the Russian languages, etc.; "other ethnic-based reasons for discomfort," including local cultural traditions, communication difficulties, desire to live among people of the same nationality, ethnic barriers to family creation, etc. (Source: Galina S. Vitkovskaya, "Relocation to Russia from the States of Central Asia: Understanding the Decision to Migrate" in the Conference Report *Cooperation and Conflict in the Former Soviet Union: Implications for Migration*, RAND, 1996: 126; Internet; available from http://www.rand.org/publications/CF/CF130/, accessed September 19, 2003.

²⁶ Galina S. Vitkovskaya, "Relocation to Russia from the States of Central Asia: Understanding the Decision to Migrate" in the Conference Report *Cooperation and Conflict in the Former Soviet Union: Implications for Migration*, RAND, 1996, 126; Internet available from <http://www.rand.org/publications/CF/CF130>/, accessed September 19, 2003.

[27] International Organization for Migration, 2001, "Deceived Migrants from Tajikistan: A Study of Trafficking in Women and Children," 11.

[28] Ibid.

[29] Ibid.

[30] Official estimate is 6,000-7,000.

[31] Unofficial estimate.

[32] "Poverty Fuels Labour Migration in the South. Poverty is Rife in Some Parts of Southern Kyrgyzstan." Gazeta.kg, August 15, 2003; Internet available from <http://www.gazeta.kg/view.php?i=1852>, accessed on September 30, 2003. *Also see* Labor Migration Project documents, International Organization for Migration; Internet available from <http://www.iom.elcat.kg/labourmigration.html>, accessed September 30, 2003.

[33] Personal communication with a Kyrgyz labor migrant, September 19, 2003.

[34] "Internal Migration in the Kyrgyz Republic," 4.

[35] Over 50,000 persons from this area were displaced to Uzbekistan, 30,000 to Kazakhstan and 13,000 to other CIS states.

[36] "Unable to Cope: Out-Migration from Karakalpakstan," *Medicines Sans Frontieres*: 24; Internet; available from http://www.msf.org/source/countries/asia/aralsea/2003/karakalpakstan/unable.pdf; accessed September 25, 2003. Also see United Nations High Commissioner for Refugees, "Central Asia on the Move." *Refugees Magazine*, May 1, 1996; Internet' available from www.unhcr.ch; accessed September 25, 2003.

[37] 45,000 persons relocated elsewhere in Kazakhstan, and 116,000 persons moved to other CIS countries.

[38] United Nations High Commissioner for Refugees, "Central Asia on the Move." *Refugees Magazine*, May 1, 1996; Internet' available from www.unhcr.ch; accessed September 25, 2003.

[39] "Internal Migration in the Kyrgyz Republic," 16.

[40] United Nations High Commissioner for Refugees, "Central Asia on the Move," *Refugees Magazine*, May 1, 1996; Internet available from <www.unhcr.ch>, accessed September 25, 2003.

[41] International Organization for Migration.,"Geopolitical Factors Shaping Migration in Central Asia,." Internet available from <http://www.iom.int/austria/tcc/>, accessed September 25, 2003.

[42] International Organization for Migration, "Compilation of Recent Migration Information from Eastern Europe and Central Asia"; Internet available from <http://www.iom.int/austria/tcc/>, accessed September 25, 2003.

[43] United Nations High Commissioner for Refugees, "Central Asia on the Move," *Refugees Magazine*, May 1, 1996: Internet available from <www.unhcr.ch>, accessed September 25, 2003.

[44] Ibid.

[45] "Deceived Migrants from Tajikistan: A Study of Trafficking in Women and Children," 11.

[46] Donna Hughes, "The 'Natasha' Trade—The Transnational Shadow Market of Trafficking in Women," *Journal of International Affairs* 53, no. 2 (Spring 2000), 625.

[47] Barbara Ehrenreich and Arlie R. Hochschild, eds., "Introduction," *Global Woman: Nannies, Maids, and Sex Workers in the New Economy* (New York, NY: Metropolitan Books, 2003), 3.

[48] International Organization for Migration (IOM). 1999. "Trafficking in Migrants, IOM Policy and Responses," Working Paper (March).

[49] The Protocol defines trafficking as "the recruitment, transportation, transfer, harbouring or receipt of persons, by the threat or use of force, by abduction, fraud, deception or coercion or the abuse of power or by the giving or receiving of payments or benefits to achieve the consent of a person having control over another person, for the purpose of exploitation; exploitation shall include, at a minimum, the exploitation of the prostitution or other forms of sexual exploitation, forced labour or services, slavery or practices similar to slavery, the removal of organs for illicit purposes or servitude."

[50] U.S. Department of State, 2003. *Trafficking in Persons Report,* Washington, D.C.; Internet available from <http://www.state.gov/g/tip/rls/tiprpt/2003/>, accessed September 12, 2003.

[51] Amy O'Neill Richard, "International Trafficking in Women to the United States: A Contemporary Manifestation of Slavery and Organized Crime," U.S. State Department, November 1999, 3.

[52] U.S. Department of State, 2003. *Trafficking in Persons Report.*

[53] Amy O'Neill Richard, 3.

[54] Organization for Security and Cooperation in Europe, Proposed Action Plan 2000 for Activities to Combat Trafficking in Human Beings, Office for Democratic Institutions and Human Rights, Warsaw, November 1999.

[55] International Organization for Migration, "Trafficking in Migrants," no. 23 (April 2001); Internet available from <http://www.iom.int//documents/publication/en/tm_23.pdf>, accessed September 12, 2003.

[56] U.S. Department of State. 2003, *Trafficking in Persons Report.*

[57] Kathleen Barry, *Female Sexual Slavery* (New York: Prentice Hall, 1979), vii.

[58] Ibid., xi.

[59] International Organization for Migration (IOM). 2000. "Trafficking in Women and Children from the Kyrgyz Republic."

[60] Ibid., 13.

[61] Cited in Donna Hughes, 636.

[62] Testimony of Louise Shelley at the Hearing before the Commission on Security and Cooperation in Europe on "The Sex Trade: Trafficking of Women and Children in Europe and the United States," June 28, 1999, 19.

[63] Ibid.

[64] S. Altink, *Stolen Lives: Trading Women into Sex and Slavery* (London: Scarlet Press, 1995), vii.

[65] United Nations Development Programme, *Human Development Report 2002.* Internet available from <http://hdr.undp.org/reports/global/2002/en>, accessed September 12, 2003.

[66] Gillian Caldwell, Steven Galster, and Nadia Steinzor, "Crime & Servitude: An Exposé of the Traffic in Women for Prostitution from the Newly Independent States," (Washington, D.C.: Global Survival Network, 1997), 11.

[67] International Organization for Migration (IOM) 2000, "Trafficking in Women and Children from the Kyrgyz Republic," 11.

[68] Cited in Kyrgyzstan Development Gateway <http://eng.gateway.kg>, last accessed on July 6, 2003.

[69] "Trafficking in Women and Children from the Kyrgyz Republic," 11.

[70] Ibid., 12.

[71] Donna Hughes, "Trafficking for Sexual Exploitation: The Case of the Russian Federation," International Organization for Migration (IOM), 2002.

[72] "Slaves of Chicago: International Sex Trafficking is Becoming Big Business," *These Times*, January 8, 2001.

[73] "Trafficking in Women and Children from the Kyrgyz Republic," 12.

[74] Human Rights Watch 2001, "Sacrificing Women to Save the Family? *Domestic Violence in Uzbekistan*," 3.

[75] Cited in Donna Hughes, "Trafficking for Sexual Exploitation: The Case of the Russian Federation," International Organization for Migration (IOM), 2002.

[76] "Sacrificing Women to Save the Family?," 7. Also see the UN Press Release "Since Becoming Sovereign State, Kyrgyzstan Committed to Integrating Women into National Programmes of Action, Anti-Discrimination Committee Told," Internet available from <http://www.un.org/News/Press/docs/1999/19990122.wom1081.html>, accessed July 6, 2003.

[77] "The Stolen Brides of Kyrgyzstan," *The Economist* 341, no. 7993, Nov 23, 1996.

[78] *See* "Sacrificing Women to Save the Family?" *Also see* "Central Asia: Increase in Polygamy Attributed To Economic Hardship, Return To Tradition," Radio Free Europe/Radio Liberty, October 16, 2002, available from <http://www.rferl.org/nca/features/2002/10/16102002163911.asp>, Internet accessed July 6, 2003.

[79] "Central Asia: Increase in Polygamy."

[80] "Deceived Migrants from Tajikistan: A Study of Trafficking in Women and Children," 15.

[81] International Organization for Migration (IOM). 2000. "Trafficking in Women and Children from the Kyrgyz Republic," 13.

[82] Gillian Caldwell, Steven Galster, and Nadia Steinzor, 1997. Crime & Servitude: An Exposé of the Traffic in Women for Prostitution from the Newly Independent States. Washington, D.C.: Global Survival Network, 14.

[83] Donna Hughes, "The 'Natasha' Trade—The Transnational Shadow Market of Trafficking in Women." Journal of International Affairs 53, no. 2 (Spring 2000), 635.

[84] Jim Haley, "King Case Coming to End," The Daily Herald, February 21, 2002. www.heraldnet.com.

[85] "Abuse of Mail-Order Foreign Brides Prompts Effort to Oversee Fast-Growing Industry," Associated Press, July 5, 2003.

[86] International Organization for Migration 2001, "Deceived Migrants from Tajikistan: A Study of Trafficking in Women and Children," 15.

[87] "Trafficking in Women and Children from the Kyrgyz Republic," 52.

[88] "Deceived Migrants from Tajikistan: A Study of Trafficking in Women and Children," 15; *also see* "Trafficking in Women and Children from the Kyrgyz Republic," 14-15.

[89] "Deceived Migrants from Tajikistan: A Study of Trafficking in Women and Children," 14.

[90] "Trafficking in Women and Children from the Kyrgyz Republic," 29-30.

[91] Ibid., 16.

[92] Gillian Caldwell, Steven Galster, and Nadia Steinzor, 1997, 9.

[93] Donna Hughes, "Trafficking for Sexual Exploitation: The Case of the Russian Federation., International Organization for Migration (IOM), 2002, 5.

[94] "Trafficking in Women and Children from the Kyrgyz Republic," 16.

[95] Ibid., 45-46.

[96] Global Organized Crime Project, *Russian Organized Crime* (Washington, D.C.: Center for Strategic and International Studies, 1997), 2.

[97] Global Organized Crime Project, *Russian Organized Crime and Corruption: Putin's Challenge* (Washington, D.C.: Center for Strategic and International Studies, 2000), 7.

[98] *Russian Organized Crime*, 2-3.

[99] *See Russian Organized Crime; also see* Robert I. Friedman, *Red Mafiya: How the Russian Mob Has Invaded America* (Boston: Little, Brown and Co., 2000).

[100] Cited in Andrea Bertone, "International Political Economy and the Politics of Sex," *Gender Issues*, 18, no.1 (2000), 4-22.

[101] Ibid.

[102] Testimony of Louise Shelley at the Hearing before the Commission on Security and Cooperation in Europe on "The Sex Trade: Trafficking of Women and Children in Europe and the United States," June 28, 1999.

[103] Ibid.

[104] "Deceived Migrants from Tajikistan: A Study of Trafficking in Women and Children," 18

[105] "Trafficking in Women and Children from the Kyrgyz Republic," 17.

[106] Testimony of Louise Shelley at the Hearing before the Commission on Security and Cooperation in Europe on "The Sex Trade: Trafficking of Women and Children in Europe and the United States," June 28, 1999, 18.

[107] S. Altink, 1995. *Stolen Lives: Trading Women into Sex and Slavery*. London: Scarlet Press, 125.

[108] Testimony of Louise Shelley at the Hearing before the Commission on Security and Cooperation in Europe on "The Sex Trade: Trafficking of Women and Children in Europe and the United States," June 28, 1999, 17.

[109] Human Rights Watch/Asia, *Owed Justice: Thai Women Trafficked into Debt Bondage in Japan* (New York: Human Rights Watch, 2000), 86.

[110] Ralph Regan, Testimony before the Senate Committee on Foreign Relations. "International Trafficking of Women and Children," Washington, D.C., February 22, 2000. Found online at <http://secretary.state.gov/www/picw/trafficking/tralph.html>.

[111] "In the Shadows," *The Economist*, 356, no. 8185 (August 26, 2000), 38-39.

[112] Robert I. Friedman, xvii.

[113] "Trafficking in Women and Children from the Kyrgyz Republic," 27.

[114] Ibid., 27, 47.

[115] U.S. Department of State. 2003. *Trafficking in Persons Report.* Washington, D.C, Internet available from <http://www.state.gov/g/tip/rls/tiprpt/2003/>, accessed September 12, 2003.

[116] Turkmenistan is not included in the report as no information on trafficking was available.

[117] Ibid.

[118] Ibid.

[119] Ibid.

[120] Ibid.

[121] Cited in Andrea Bertone, "International Political Economy and the Politics of Sex." *Gender Issues*, 18, no.1 (2000), 4-22.

Chapter 19

Beyond the Battle of Talas: China's Re-emergence in Central Asia[1]

Matthew Oresman

I n October 2002, China held its first military exercise in decades with another nation: the Central Asian republic of Kyrgyzstan. Aimed at training border forces on both sides to respond to a terrorist insurgency, this event highlighted the growing importance of Central Asia to China. Moreover, this exercise took place with a country that already had American and Russian forces deployed just outside of the Kyrgyz capital of Bishkek. Today U.S.-led counterterrorism coalition forces are located at Manas Airbase, and the Russian-led Collective Security Treaty Organization (CSTO) Rapid Deployment Forces (RDF) are at Kant Airbase. The presence in one Central Asian nation of Chinese, Russian, and U.S. military and security forces underscores the convergence of Great Power interests in Central Asia.

While Russia has maintained a strong presence in the region for more than a century, China and the United States are relative newcomers. Over the past 12 years, Central Asia has moved from a strategic to a vital interest of the United States, particularly given the events of September 11, 2001 and subsequent operations in the region. Since the breakup of the Soviet Union, the newly independent states of Central Asia—Kazakhstan, Kyrgyzstan, Tajikistan, Turkmenistan, and Uzbekistan—have become increasingly important on the global strategic landscape. In the wake of World Trade Center and Pentagon terrorist attacks against the United States, the countries of Central Asia have become integral allies in the war against terrorism with ongoing operations in Afghanistan and throughout Central Asia to stabilize the region and clean up the remnants of al Qaeda and other hostile groups.

While U.S. and Russian involvement in Central Asia is not surprising, one of the more intriguing developments in the region over the past decade has been China's diplomacy. China's interest in building relations with Central Asia is not startling, given the country's long history in the region dating back to the foundations of the "Silk Road." Included in this history are such revolutionary events as the Battle of Talas in 751 and the Chinese conquest of Xinjiang beginning in 1757.[2] The agility and creativity China has exercised in orchestrating its "re"-emergence has taken many by surprise though. China has moved rapidly from the difficult task of delineating and disarming its borders with Russia, Kazakhstan, Kyrgyzstan, and Tajikistan to building a multilateral organization and growing economic and security ties, all while working to alleviate traditional suspicions among Central Asian states about the true intentions of its government.

The prominence of China in Central Asia will grow over the next decade, particularly if the Russian position continues to wane and the strategic attention of the United States is drawn elsewhere. On the basis of geography and economic realities alone, China appears well placed to expand its influence in the region over the long run. Central Asian states will continue to seek robust engagement with China as their transportation infrastructure and developing economies become more intertwined. China likely will continue to exercise a light touch with its diplomacy to assure stable, productive relations along its interior frontiers, while dispelling fears that it is seeking regional hegemony.

Over the near- to medium-term, increasing activity by China in Central Asia does not present a pressing challenge to American interests in the region. Beijing appears to be attuned to U.S. sensitivities in this region in the post-September 11 environment and likely will try to avoid perceptions of a "rising China" as a regional hegemon. Instead, Beijing will seek a productive and cooperative relationship with Washington in this part of the world, as elsewhere around its periphery. At present the United States and China share similar goals in Central Asia, particularly with regard to combating terrorist activity emanating from the region. Even as the United States has moved counterterrorism forces close to China's border—a fact that has not altered Beijing's overall Central Asia policy—China has responded with restraint, seeing the current circumstances as an opportunity to improve its overall relationship with the United States. Beijing recognizes that its national priorities require benign engagement in Central Asia and will eschew balance-of-power games.

However, looking further ahead, Washington and Beijing could find themselves competing for influence in this region, as their regional priorities move beyond immediate security concerns to encompass such fundamental questions as Great Power influence, political change, and reform in Central Asia, as well as economic development and energy extraction. Moreover, China maintains a long-standing concern with "strategic encirclement" by the United States, and Washington remains wary of China's long-term rise and its implications for U.S. interests.

China's emergence in Central Asia has implications that go beyond bilateral U.S.-China relations. How the outside powers coordinate their policies in Central Asia and whether there is a common agreement as to the best method to combat regional security issues, which extend beyond terrorism to such factors as drug trafficking, political unrest, HIV/AIDS, and border security, will be a central determinant for the future of diplomatic relations between the United States, China and Russia, as well as the stability of the region. In addition, China's continued emergence in Central Asia will impact the ongoing efforts to rebuild Afghanistan; the success of Partnership for Peace (PfP) and the role of the North Atlantic Treaty Organization (NATO) in the region; the development and export of Caspian energy resources; and the future of U.S. relations with the countries of the region.

Overall, China, aided by the convergence of vital interest with Russia and the United States, has been extremely pragmatic in its approach to Central Asia. Over the next decade, it can be expected that China's influence in Central Asia will rise. This does not have to be a threat to the United States' global position, but it is critical to recognize China's interests and priorities now, in order to prepare for such an eventuality, and begin to initiate policies that will decrease future tension, before they adversely affect Sino-U.S. and Sino-Russian relations.

China's Interests and Policies in Central Asia

Understanding the immediate and long-term goals of China in Central Asia is the key to understanding its actions and intentions there, as well as how it plans to interact in the region with Russia and the United States. China has four principal sets of interests and policies in the region. First, China's strategic and diplomatic goals in Central Asia, and how they play out vis-à-vis Sino-U.S. and Sino-Russian relations, are key aspects in China's overall foreign policy. Second, and most pressing, China's interests in Central Asia revolve around issues of national security, specifically the cutting of external support for separatists in Xinjiang, and ensuring radical forces in Central Asia do not destabilize friendly governments in the region. A third key interest for China has been the demarcation, demilitarization, and stabilization of its borders with Central Asian nations, a goal that has been largely achieved, but will remain important to Beijing in the years ahead. Finally, Chinese economic and trade interests in the region, including the development of energy resources, are of growing importance.

Strategic Positioning

In its relations with Central Asia, China seeks to achieve key strategic and diplomatic interests on three fronts. First, at the broadest level, China's approach to Central Asia helps promote its overall diplomatic strategy of establishing a more peaceful and constructive external environment, while fostering an image of China as a responsible power. The Shanghai Cooperation Organization (SCO)[3] is a concrete manifestation of this overall foreign policy effort, giving substance to China's widely-touted "new security concept" and its emphasis on the Five Principles of Peaceful Coexistence.[4] The SCO also assists China in promoting other key principles of its foreign policy. For example, it provides Beijing an opportunity to demonstrate the value of a multilateral, consultative process versus unilateral or alliance-based approaches to regional security. The SCO also provides a prominent platform from which Beijing can voice, and in some cases act, on foreign policy on a range of issues, such as opposition to the "three evils" of terrorism, separatism and extremism. Moreover, in establishing and shaping the agenda for the SCO, Beijing has demonstrated its regional leadership and determination to contribute constructively to alleviating tensions and promoting mutual benefit.

Second, China's relations with Central Asia help Beijing meet broader strategic and diplomatic interests such as establishing stable and productive relationships with foreign partners and especially those on its closest periphery, so that it can focus on pressing domestic and external challenges elsewhere. The specifics of China's bilateral relations with Central Asian states will be discussed shortly; however, by and large Beijing's approach to the region has succeeded in establishing a stable and productive security environment, as well as political and economic ties that are likely to endure.

Third, China's policies in Central Asia assist Beijing in managing its bilateral relationships with the other two major powers in the region, Russia and the United States. On one hand, China seeks to use common interests in Central Asia to strengthen its relationship with Russia, the traditional "big brother" to the region, and foster a strategic environment that matches both their worldviews. On the other hand, China's bonds with Central Asia provide a certain strategic leverage in dealing with the U.S. presence in the region. As to Russia-China relations, the Shanghai Co-operation Organization represents both the cooperative and competitive nature of that relationship. The advent of the SCO demonstrated Russian self-understanding that it can no longer single-handedly maintain Central Asian stability and that China has a positive role to play in the region. It also provides Russia a mechanism by which to monitor and restrain Chinese activity in Central Asia. In addition, SCO-related security activi-ties may give China the opportunity to provide a potential alternative to the Russian dominated Collective Security Treaty Organization (CSTO), which serves as the collective defense arm for several of the Common-wealth of Independent States (CIS).[5]

China also carries out its policies in Central Asia with an eye on managing and influencing Sino-U.S. relations. Beijing's concerns over a growing American presence in Central Asia—beginning with NATO PfP initiatives in the early-1990s, the 1997 U.S.-led CENTRAZBAT military exercises in the region (which transported elements of the 82nd Airborne Division non-stop from Ft. Bragg, North Carolina to the middle of Ka-zakhstan), and the post-September 11 U.S. deployments to Central Asia, which now include a military presence in Kyrgyzstan, Tajikistan, and Uz-bekistan—underscore its longer-term interests in establishing stronger ties with its Central Asian neighbors and countering a potentially antagonistic American presence on China's western doorstep. However, in the post-September 11 environment, Beijing's tactics have changed. Throughout the late 1990s and prior to the fall of 2001, China often would beat the "anti-hegemon drum" within the SCO, without taking on the United States directly. By using the SCO to call for a "new security concept" and a more just and fair international order, Beijing held up its foreign and secu-rity policy as a preferable alternative to the U.S.-led security order. Today, however, China has toned down this rhetoric in general, and within the SCO in particular, as it seeks a "constructive and cooperative" relationship with the United States.

By and large, Beijing has been successful in leveraging its relations in Central Asia and within the SCO to achieve these three key strategic and diplomatic interests. However, Beijing's interests and policies in Central Asia still face challenges. First, to date, the SCO has been mostly a "talking shop," with few substantive mechanisms putting words into practice. That may change since the SCO has become a "full-fledged" international or-ganization in 2004, including a secretariat in Beijing, a budgetary mecha-nism, and an operating counterterrorism center in Tashkent, Uzbekistan.[6]

Second, it should be noted that China has not entirely given up all of its heavy-handed ways and has used its size, power, and economic might to gain advantage in negotiations, particularly in discussions over border demarcation and security assistance to monitor the Uyghur diaspora in Central Asia. Central Asians continue to harbor concerns as to China's long-range intentions in the region, which may ultimately limit Beijing's room to maneuver. Most important, though, is the understanding that while China may offer great potential for economic and security cooperation in Central Asia, the United States and Russia will continue to offer more in the way of concrete security and economic benefits over the near- to medium-term.

National Security

While China's broad strategic and diplomatic interests provide longer-term direction to its Central Asian policies, national security concerns present the most pressing and immediate factors shaping China's approach in the region. These challenges include what Beijing terms "the three evils" of terrorism, separatism and extremism, and involve developments within and beyond Chinese borders. These national security concerns include separatist-minded Uyghur groups in China's Xinjiang province, instability arising in Central Asian states, and elicit transborder activities, such as trafficking in drugs, guns and people. By strengthening its relationships with the Central Asian states and within the SCO, Beijing hopes to combat these pressing problems.

China's northwestern province of Xinjiang, known officially as the Xinjiang Uyghur Autonomous Region, presents a unique problem for Beijing.[7] It is a province of roughly 12 million Uyghurs, a predominantly Muslim Turkic people, who were conquered by China in the mid-eighteenth century but not brought under full Chinese dominion until the Communists came to power in 1949. Over the last 50 years, China has exercised a policy of internal colonization, manifested in a three-pronged approach. China exercises political control under the nominal title of autonomy by tightly controlling many elements of politically active or organized civil society, especially religion. It supports investment, development, and Han migration to Xinjiang in order to both serve the needs of the entire nation (particularly with its large energy reserves)[8] and strengthen the bonds between Xinjiang and the rest of China. It also exerts total control on the region by the constant presence and use of the People's Liberation Army (PLA), People's Armed Police (PAP), and the paramilitary Xinjiang Production and Construction Corp (XPCC), or Bingtuan. For their part, the

Uyghur people have not welcomed Han rule of Xinjiang and many would like to see an end to Beijing control or, at the very least, a greater measure of autonomy in their own affairs. While there is no unified Uyghur resistance movement, several small groups do exist, though coordination is poor. Still, Uyghur terrorists do, in fact, pose a legitimate security threat to the Chinese government.[9]

The central fear of Beijing regarding the Uyghur resistance is the organizing ability of Islam, and mosques in particular. This fear underscores the lengths China has gone to prevent Muslim community groups from interacting with each other and operating beyond the most local level. Islam in Xinjiang, though much less conservative than that practiced in the Middle East, is still the biggest threat for China's control of the region. China's nightmare—one actually shared by many Uyghur leaders—is that radical Islamic groups, such as those who moved from the Middle East to Central Asia throughout the 1990s, will infiltrate Xinjiang and provide aid to the Uyghurs. Thus China's primary goal in Central Asia is to cut off external support to its own internal problem.

To this end, China has sought common cause with Central Asian governments to counter Uyghur separatism and terrorist threats. The Central Asian states have large Uyghur populations of their own, the vast majority of whom are relatively peaceful and productive members of society. However, some groups maintain ties to militant Uyghurs in Xinjiang and to Pan-Turkic or Pan-Islamic radicals operating throughout Central Asia, such as the Islamic Movement of Uzbekistan (IMU) and Hizb-ut-Tahrir (HT), though the full nature of these ties is still unclear. China also is interested in ensuring these Pan-Turkic or Pan-Islamic groups do not destabilize the leadership of Central Asian states, and, in doing so, threaten Chinese interests in the region. If these nations cannot maintain their own sovereignty, the spread of Islamic fundamentalism, refugees, drugs, and terrorism would be devastating for the region.

The threat of Islamic radicals and militants is thought to be pervasive in the region, despite the widespread practice of more moderate and liberal forms of Islam throughout Central Asia. Though U.S. forces have dispersed al Qaeda and Taliban forces, many elements of these groups remain and are reconstituting. Moreover, recent reports indicate that Turkic groups, such as the IMU and HT, are gaining new strength across Central Asia. HT, an ostensibly non-violent political group that seeks to establish a theocratic caliphate across the Muslim world, has several thousand members throughout Central Asia, where it is proscribed by the ruling regimes, as well as in Russia and Europe. While there is no evidence that HT has committed any terrorist activities, it is supportive of these activities and has reportedly agreed to be a partner with the IMU if either came to power in Uzbekistan.[10] The goal of the IMU, based primarily in the Ferghana Valley, is the overthrow of the Uzbek government, though it is not as radical in its practice of Islam as HT. The IMU, which launched insurgencies against the Karimov regime in 1999 and 2000, has taken on a much stronger pan-Turkic identity, and has increased its operations in Tajikistan and Kyrgyzstan, including a bombing in Bishkek on May 24, 2003, that killed eight and injured more than 20. The IMU has also recently turned its attention against Western targets, such as U.S. government installations and travelers.[11]

Of particular significance to China have been reports that the IMU, al Qaeda, and other radical groups have ties to Uyghur separatists, including the East Turkestan Islamic Movement (ETIM). ETIM recently was placed on the U.S. Department of State Foreign Terrorist Organization list, as well as on the UN terrorist organization list. Although ETIM primarily operates in Central Asia, it appears that the IMU also has ties to some groups within Xinjiang itself. Moreover, between 300 and 700 Uyghurs were detained in Afghanistan during the U.S.-led war and occupation to oust the Taliban regime, some of whom were transported to Guantanamo Bay for further questioning.[12] This should not be seen as surprising, or as an Uyghur affinity for the politics of al Qaeda, but as the result of Chinese policies that leave little opportunity for peaceful resistance in Xinjiang, and diplomacy that has cut off support for the Uyghurs in neighboring Central Asia.

To stop cross-border cooperation between the Uyghurs in Xinjiang and those outside the country, as well as between pan-Turkic or pan-Islamic groups in Central Asia, China has developed bilateral and multilateral approaches to combating these terrorist threats, aimed to bolster both the Central Asian regimes and Beijing's rule in Xinjiang. Through the SCO, China has pushed for the establishment of a counterterrorism center in Tashkent. It is unclear whether the center will be primarily an information exchange hub such as Interpol, or if it will have some sort of rapid response mechanism. Since the 1999 Bishkek summit when first proposed, the idea of using the SCO to fight terrorism and other regional security threats has become a centerpiece of the organization, and the most salient factor in building practical cooperation and moving the SCO beyond being a discussion forum. The SCO also has announced new initiatives to address security issues beyond terrorism. Plans are underway to cooperate on emergency response activities, drug trafficking, and law enforcement.

Perhaps most significantly, the nations of the SCO, except Uzbekistan as of now, hosted a major, multi-day exercise in early August 2003 simulating responses to various counterterrorism scenarios in Kazakhstan and China. This exercise, held in eastern Kazakhstan and Xinjiang, included over 1000 troops, many of them special operations forces, and was much more prominent in scope, size, duration, and media coverage then the October 2002 exercise held between only Kyrgyzstan and China.

Much of China's bilateral aid to Central Asia consists of security assistance, particularly in the area of border control, military aid, and intelligence sharing. China recently donated 40 prefabricated border outposts to Kyrgyzstan. In addition, China is assisting Tajikistan to take over more responsibility for guarding its own border from the Russian 201st Motorized Division. In 2000, when Uzbek forces faced an IMU flare-up, China was the first to provide Uzbekistan with emergency military equipment, including flak jackets, night vision equipment, and sniper rifles. China gave 10 million Yuan (U.S. $1.2 million) worth of military-technical assistance to Kyrgyzstan in 2002, including firearms and telecom systems to combat terrorism, and, in February 2003, China donated police facilities to the Internal Affairs Ministry of Kazakhstan. In addition to this material aid, China has provided training for various Central Asian militaries. There is also intelligence sharing between the Central Asian republics and China, most of which is focused on counterterrorism.

Among the most notable developments for China-Central Asia security cooperation was the October 2002 joint border exercise held between China and Kyrgyzstan. The exercise—simulating an operation against terrorist cells within the mountainous region which forms the countries' shared border—was relatively small in size and scope: it involved about 100 soldiers from each side, operating at high elevations and using light weapons, such as anti-tank guns, helicopters, and armored personnel vehicles. The exercises took place in southern Kyrgyzstan near the Irkeshtam border crossing with China, and involved military and border troops from China's Xinjiang Military Region and the Kyrgyz military, as well as some observers from the other four SCO member states.[13] Most intriguing, this exercise marked the first peacetime joint military exercise China is known to have conducted. It signals a significant change in the way China understands the role of force, intervention, and international military cooperation in the face of transnational threats; it also marks an important advance in Chinese-Central Asian relations.

It is important to be reminded that currently Chinese aid to Central Asia in no way compares to the amount being provided by Russia and the Unites States. Russian forces have historically operated throughout the region and continue to be present in Tajikistan. The United States has become vital to Central Asia. Not only has the U.S. military campaign struck a devastating blow against many of the groups challenging regional security in Afghanistan, but material and economic assistance provided by the United States has been a huge windfall for the Central Asian states. The U.S. military maintains a presence in several Central Asian nations,[14] all of which bring these areas millions of U.S. dollars in the form of building and local spending. This is in addition to official U.S. assistance to the Central Asian states, which is substantial. Totaling almost $600 million in fiscal year (FY) 2002 (up from $230 million in FY2001), the Central Asian nations have begun to rely on this money heavily, as well as on the material support, in terms of food, medicine, security training, and more. While this overall amount will decrease in 2003 and 2004, pledged security assistance in 2004 will increase.

Finally, it is important to understand how the Uyghur diaspora living in Central Asia plays into Chinese diplomacy in the region. The diaspora is predominantly concentrated in Kyrgyzstan and Kazakhstan, with 50,000 and 180,000 Uyghurs respectively, many of whom are entrepreneurs who have achieved middle class status. Most Uyghurs in Central Asia are not politically active, but those who are make up a vocal minority, often petitioning the government to protect their rights in the face of Chinese pressures. Many also provide aid to groups operating within Xinjiang itself, with most interaction occurring along very active shuttle trade routes. The Central Asian states are loath to offend China and have been proactive in appeasing Chinese worries about the Uyghur populations living in their countries. As one analyst put it, China is having the Central Asians do its "dirty work" in the region.[15] During the lead up to the first Shanghai Five summit in 1996, the Kyrgyz Justice Ministry prohibited one Uyghur group, Ittipak (Unity), from political activism for three months for failing to curb its "separatist activities," sighting the public association provision of the constitution and the non-interference clause of its 1992 communiqué with China.[16] This has been a balancing act between domestic and international pressures though, with the Central Asian regimes not wanting to appear to be suppressing a fellow Turkic people. Uyghur gangs operating in Central Asia, particularly Kyrgyzstan, also have been involved in sensational murders and robberies of both Han Chinese and Uyghur peoples, including prominent businessmen and diplomats, keeping this issue center stage for the Chinese and Central Asian authorities.

Stability Along the Border

A third important set of goals and policies shaping China's active Central Asian diplomacy concerns the settlement of border disputes. Reaching settlements on disputed borders, which had been sources of tension during the Cold War, was important for Beijing both in order to move forward on its cooperative agenda with Central Asia and so that it could devote more attention to greater post-Cold War strategic challenges. Demarcating and demilitarizing the borders with its Central Asian neighbors (including Russia) was a priority issue for China in the early 1990s, and became the foundation on which Sino-Central Asian relations were built. In retrospect, settling border disputes and reducing military personnel along these borders has been a major accomplishment of Chinese-Central Asian diplomacy. It has given China and its Central Asian neighbors a measure of peace and security, allowing them to expend their energy on more critical and worrisome issues, such as internal development and diplomatic crises, while setting out a model for cooperative security relations among former adversaries. The Shanghai Five played a critical role in legitimizing and institutionalizing these agreements and continues to do so.

The most significant accomplishment of the group is its package of military confidence building measures, including a pullback of some troops and equipment to 100 kilometers (km) off the common borders, verification procedures along the border, and pre-notification of exercises and other military activities. These steps largely were achieved by the mid to late 1990s, as border talks eventually led to the 1996 Shanghai Five "Agreement on Confidence-Building in the Military Field Along the Border Areas" and the 1997 "Agreement on Reducing Each Other's Military Forces along the Border Regions." The 1996 agreement stipulates that: military forces in the border regions will not be used to attack one another, military exercises will not be aimed at one another and will be limited in frequency and scale, major military exercises within 100 km of the border require notification and invitation to the neighboring Shanghai Five states to send observers, and friendly military-to-military exchanges will be established. The 1997 agreement took steps to implement these measures more fully. By the July 2000 Shanghai Five summit, the five parties announced that implementation of the 1996 and 1997 agreements had "helped build for the first time, in the border belt of more than 7,000 km, a region of trust and transparency where military activities are predictable and monitorable."[17] The SCO continues to focus on border settlement issues, including a meeting as recently as April 2003 to expand border CBMs.

However, not all border differences have been settled, or settled to all parties' satisfaction. Negotiations continue on a bilateral basis between China and Kazakhstan, Kyrgyzstan, and Tajikistan. China's border negotiations with Kyrgyzstan have caused many domestic political problems for the tiny republic. In March 2002, protests erupted in the Asky region of Kyrgyzstan in response to the signing of a border treaty with China. The demonstrators, calling for the resignation of President Akaev, claimed that he had ceded too much to China and had sacrificed Kyrgyz sovereignty. In response to these protests, police tried to quash the demonstration; six persons were killed and 60 injured in the melee. This event eventually led to the resignation of the Kyrgyz Prime Minister and a government investigation.

Still, the way China has handled its border negotiations with the Central Asians has been remarkable, both for its deftness and for its efficiency. While China often has received the better bargain, due to its size and power, rarely has it been seen as heavy handed or offensive, helping to allay fears held by many Central Asian elites of China's true regional intentions. With border demarcation and demilitarization between China and its Central Asian neighbors virtually complete, remaining border security issues can be placed on the "cooperative security" column of their relationships.

Energy and Trade

China has important economic goals behind its growing interest and presence in Central Asia. During the visit by then-Premier Li Peng to Kazakhstan in 1994, he called for the construction of a new "Silk Road," connecting Central Asia with China and acting as a conduit for trade between Asia, the Middle East, and Europe. To date, this plan is still in the developmental phase. Nevertheless, many analysts see significant promise in economic and financial relations between China and Central Asia over the medium- to long-term, especially in the development of the region's enormous energy resources to fuel China's anticipated economic growth and burgeoning energy demands.

In 2015, China's projected oil needs will be 7.4 million bb/d (up from 3.4 million bb/d is 2002), 50 percent of which will be made up by imports. Natural gas, which is not yet imported, will also be a much-needed foreign produced commodity in the years ahead. In order to diversify its sources of supply and increase its energy security, China wants to establish Central Asia, particularly Kazakhstan and to some degree Turkmenistan, as guaranteed sources of oil and gas. In addition, Central Asia offers a potential market for China's export driven economy. This is particularly true as China aims to develop its vast, remote western regions, which would find a natural outlet for exports further west to Central Asia.

Chinese firms have made some investments in Central Asia. But such financial arrangements have been limited by the risky, cumbersome and, given the heavy-handed presence of gangs and mafia-like extortion rackets, even hostile investment environment in Central Asia. Current Chinese investment includes: a processing factory in Tekeli, Kazakhstan; a major stake in the Kyrgyz cloth market; an investment in the primary mine at Batken, Kyrgyzstan; a hotel in Taldy-Korgan, Kazakhstan; and cardboard box and noodle factories in Kyrgyzstan. In Kazakhstan, according to official sources, there are now more than 20 accredited Chinese companies and some 600 joint ventures.[18]

The most significant area of economic cooperation has been China's investment in the Kazakh energy sector. As mentioned above, Chinese future energy demands will be enormous. To help meet that demand, the China National Petroleum Company (CNPC) invested $4.3 billion in the Kazakh state oil company Aktyubinskneft in June 1997, entitling China to a 60 percent (now 63 percent) stake in three fields with a total estimated oil reserve of one billion barrels. Also as part of this agreement, China and Kazakhstan agreed to build a 3,000 km pipeline from the Caspian Sea area to Xinjiang. This project is expected to cost over $3 billion and, at this point, has been deemed by most experts as uneconomical. Its current status is in limbo, though construction on some segments has begun and there is strong political pressure to make this pipeline a reality, especially as it fits into other plans to build a pipeline bringing oil and gas from Xinjiang's Tarim Basin to China's East Coast (a plan whose own future is also uncertain). At the same time, China and Russia have begun forging serious energy ties, including a pipeline from Angarsk to Daqing. If these plans fully materialize, Russian oil and gas may become more important to China than its Central Asian investments.[19]

While these projects are still taking shape, Kazakhstan is exporting small amounts of oil to China. In 2002, China imported nearly 19,600 barrels a day of crude oil, representing 1.4 percent of its total imports. This oil, imported primarily by rail, underscores the importance of building more transportation links between China and Central Asia. Projects to achieve this goal include a new rail link being built between Xinjiang and Uzbekistan, which will pass through Kyrgyzstan and possibly another that will include Tajikistan. This connects with the $250 million European Bank for Reconstruction and Development (EBRD) sponsored Transport

Corridor Europe Caucasus Asia (TRACECA) project to build the new Silk Road from China to Europe. Additional infrastructure projects include the already completed Urumqi-Almaty rail line and a new 360 km road between Lake Issyk-Kul in Kyrgyzstan and Aksu in Xinjiang, to be built by China at a cost of $15 million.[20]

Overall, China's trade with Central Asia has been a boon to the region, and while the amounts are relatively low, the potential for growth is enormous. China's dynamic economy could be a powerful engine for Central Asian development, and its close proximity could provide Central Asian states with an export route to the burgeoning markets of the Pacific.

The Future of the SCO

China's future successes and failures in Central Asia will be determined, in large part, by the viability of the SCO. To date, the SCO has been little more than a discussion forum, but that appears to be changing with the formalization of the SCO as a "full-fledged" international organization in 2004. This includes an actual budgetary mechanism, a permanent secretariat to be located in Beijing (led by Zhang Deguang, the former Chinese Ambassador to Russia), and a counterterrorism center to be located in Uzbekistan. Still, many doubts remain. The member nations will have to commit even more resources, energy, and political capital to make this organization viable, a first in the history of Central Asian multilateral organizations. The political will seems to be there, but it remains to be seen if Russia and China actually will commit their scarce resources to this effort, though recent Russian actions and statements stressing the importance of the SCO and the newly reconstituted CSTO appear promising.

Three early tests will help determine the future of the SCO. The first is the formation of the Tashkent counterterrorism center. To be effective, this center will have to be able to coordinate responses to new terrorist threats, with special attention to de-conflicting the roles of China, Russia, and the United States. This center should not be expected to house a new rapid reaction force, but it has to be more than an information clearinghouse if the SCO expects to be a respected player on regional security issues. Second, the establishment of a permanent secretariat and budget mechanism will demonstrate the political and material commitment that members are willing to provide. A functioning budget and empowered bureaucracy are central to the success of any international organization, particularly one bringing together such diverse players. Finally, the SCO must prove that it can accomplish limited economic cooperation, a point stressed with unusual frequency and detail at the last SCO summit in May 2003. If the SCO can commit to a transportation pact by next year's summit, it will have proven that it is more than a "talk shop" and can assist in practical economic integration in a troubled region.

Though it is clear that the problems of Central Asia are region-wide and cannot be solved by any state alone, Central Asian states seem reluctant to embrace the promise of multilateral collaboration. The May 2003 SCO summit offered some hope that the region can pursue concrete and practical cooperative projects, an important step toward tempering interstate conflict, great power rivalries, and nationalist tendencies. In the short to medium-term the SCO represents China and Russia's cooperative nature, as well as Russia's understanding that it can no longer single-handedly maintain Central Asia stability. China also has a positive role to play in the region, particularly in funding security endeavors. However, with a new Russian push to establish the CSTO RDF to be stationed at Kant Airbase in Kyrgyzstan, tension between Russian and Chinese regional interest will become more apparent. Yet much of the future success of the SCO will be determined not by the outside powers, but by the cooperation of the Central Asian states, particularly Uzbekistan and Kazakhstan, a mighty feat that is currently nowhere near to being achieved.

Bilateral Relationships

As previously discussed, Beijing has established a coherent regional strategy in Central Asia, best illustrated by Chinese leadership in the SCO. However, each Central Asian nation has its own set of circumstances, and Chinese policy faces different challenges in dealing with each of them. Moreover, the future of Central Asia's relations with external powers will be determined in large measure by the dynamic between the various Central Asian states.

Kazakhstan

The China-Kazakh border stretches some 1,533 km, the longest frontier between China and the five Central Asian states. China's relationship with Kazakhstan is probably its strongest in the region and best represents China's most basic interests. Though Kazakhstan and Russia enjoy an extremely close relationship, Kazakh exports to China reached nearly $1 billion in 2001 (with a goal of $2 billion in 2003). With total official Central Asian exports to China equaling about $1.3 billion in 2001, Kazakh exports represented some 77 percent of that figure, further indicating the importance of China-Kazakh ties in the overall China-Central

Asia relationship. Moreover, Chinese President Hu Jintao's June 2003 trip to Kazakhstan, only his third abroad as president, after Russia and the G8 summit in France, indicates the high priority China places on its relationship with Kazakhstan. This relationship, which includes security and intelligence cooperation, as well as educational and cultural exchanges, likely will continue to grow in the coming years. Much of this growth will be fueled by increased Chinese investment in Kazakh energy and gas, as well as the long-expected construction of a pipeline between the two countries. Also, with roughly one million ethnic Kazakhs living in Xinjiang, in addition to the 180,000 Uyghurs living in Kazakhstan, Astana takes a particular interest in developments in China's west, especially as the two populations make up a large segment of the shuttle traders.

Kyrgyzstan

Hosting military and security personnel from multiple outside powers, Kyrgyzstan stands out among Central Asian countries. With the U.S.-run base at Manas and Russian-led forces at the CSTO Rapid Deployment Force base at Kant Airbase, not to mention a shared 858-km border, China has focused much of its strategic attention on Kyrgyzstan. China's first external military exercise in decades was held with Kyrgyz border forces, and China likely will post some security-related personnel to Tashkent to take part in the new SCO counterterrorism center. In addition, Kyrgyzstan is one of the main transit routes for Chinese goods and a key recipient of Chinese infrastructure investment, including new rail and road links. It is also a source of concern for China on issues including drugs, organized crime, Islamic radicalism, Uyghur sympathizers, and perhaps most-worrisome in the long-run, the presence of U.S. forces just over the border. Kyrgyzstan sees China as a potential engine for economic growth and a source of foreign aid. China was one of the few countries that would engage in barter trade with the Central Asian nations after independence, winning their early gratitude. Kyrgyzstan takes its relationship with China very seriously, and, despite some tensions over the Uyghur diaspora and border negotiations, sees China as a strong and important partner. Its Beijing embassy is equal in size to that of the United States, and Muratbek Imanaliev, Kyrgyzstan's two time former Foreign Minister and current ambassador to China, speaks fluent Chinese and is a central player in building relations between all of Central Asia and China.

Tajikistan

Having suffered through a long civil war and still relying heavily on Russian forces to help stabilize its borders, Tajikistan does not yet have the ability to forge a more balanced foreign policy. It is possible that the presence of "gas-and-go" U.S. air operations in Tajikistan signals some closer ties to Washington. However, Tajikistan is in dire need of assistance from all quarters, and accepts aid from countries such as Iran as well as China. With a 434-km shared border, China has provided Tajikistan with significant security assistance, as well as limited economic aid, including a recent $3 million aid package. According to first-hand accounts, China's defense attaché office in Dushanbe is one of the most active of its Central Asian missions. Economically, Tajikistan has little to offer China beyond a limited marketplace, but Beijing is keenly interested in making sure Tajikistan's black market—including the massive trade in drugs—does not penetrate China. And while China has a theoretically historic claim to nearly one-third of Tajikistan's territory, China has managed to negotiate its remaining border issues with Tajikistan in a constructive way. Overall, Tajikistan's vital ties to Russia dictate much of the relationship, but China still maintains active diplomacy there, with an eye on the future and its own security needs.

Uzbekistan

Among Central Asian states, Uzbekistan has charted a fairly distinctive course in its foreign policy, clearly moving away from Russia and aligning itself more closely with the United States. As the only SCO member not sharing a border with China, its relationship with China has evolved much differently from the others. With a very active embassy in Tashkent, China has enjoyed fairly good security ties with Uzbekistan, highlighted by the aid provided to Uzbekistan during the 2000 IMU flare-up. However, there have been reports that this aspect of the relationship has soured in the last years due to a Chinese sale of mortars and side arms to Uzbekistan that performed poorly, as well as the rise of significant U.S. security aid to the country. In economic terms, Uzbekistan's harshly protectionist trade policy has blocked many Chinese exports to the region and the Tashkent government has increased its complaints about shuttle traders bringing cheap Chinese goods into the country. Uzbekistan's self-appointed expectations to become the premier regional power may put it at odds with Chinese interests, particularly its obstinacy in committing more fully to the cooperative security agenda of the SCO. However, the two have succeeded in establishing a practical relationship built on individual needs and pragmatic gains.

Turkmenistan

Turkmenistan also does not share a border with China, and is even further west from China than is Uzbekistan. In addition, Turkmenistan's adherence to a policy of "positive neutrality" has kept it out of the SCO along with many other international organizations. It appears Beijing will keep Turkmenistan and its leader, Turkmenbashi, at arms length. China has invested moderately in Turkmenistan's oil and gas sector, but has limited its ties overall. Turkmenistan has little to offer China. Export routes for its oil and gas are not conducive to shipment to China and, politically and diplomatically, it is very difficult to deal with. China likely will only seek engagement with Ashkabat if it fits into its overall regional plans.

China and Other External Powers in the Region

The presence of other external powers, particularly the United States and Russia, provide China both partners and competitors for its goals in Central Asia. While China does not yet rank near the United States or Russia in terms of influence, its presence is growing. Because all three nations share the same vital interest in Central Asia—the elimination of the terrorist and radical Islamic threat—balance of power activities are limited. Still, China's fear of "strategic encirclement" by the United States persists. China can count on Russia to resist a long-term U.S. military presence in the region, although China and Russia should not be mistaken as true allies. In fact, the two countries are becoming increasingly competitive for influence in the region. Russia's deployment at Kant and its reinvigoration of the CSTO are primarily seen as countering a mounting U.S. and NATO presence in Central Asia, though it also can be viewed as solidifying Moscow's ties to Central Asia in the face of growing Chinese influence via the SCO.

China also must take other important regional players into account for their growing influence in Central Asia. These players include Europe, India, Pakistan, Turkey and Iran. Europe's presence is felt through the European Union, as well as NATO, the Organization for Security and Cooperation in Europe (OSCE), and the EBRD. European projects in Central Asia are specific and aimed at building stability. They include developing transportation infrastructure, combating drug trafficking, and making limited investments, in addition to Caspian energy operations. By and large, however, Central Asia does not "identify" with Europe. Similarly, ties with India and Pakistan are principally economic, though there is an

Islamic link to Pakistan and growing military and counterterrorism ties to India. As long as Central Asia can avoid getting entangled in the Kashmir problem, this relationship should continue to widen. Iran and Turkey share deeper cultural ties with Central Asia, but the prospects of close ties after the collapse of the Soviet Union have floundered. Turkey was unable to provide the material aid the Central Asians had hoped for, and many leaders felt that Turkey treated them as inferiors. Similarly, Iran has provided little to Central Asia, though this is also a reflection of U.S. policy towards Iran. In addition, Central Asian regimes are fearful of Iran-style Islamic fundamentalism. Turkey, Iran, and Pakistan are members along with all five Central Asian republics of the Economic Cooperation Organization (ECO), which has not developed much beyond the discussion phase. For most of the Central Asian states, relations with China probably hold out more promise than with any other external powers, excepting Russia and the United States.

In both its regional and bilateral policies in Central Asia, China is committed to steadily expanding its presence and has taken a long-range approach to its engagement in the region. Central Asians at the official level generally welcome China's involvement, though there are some lingering suspicions of China as a hegemon-in-waiting. There are also concerns, not without reason, about Chinese migration to their nations, much as their Russian neighbors have. On the other hand, all Central Asian states are too much in need of assistance to say no to such an important and growing regional power as China, and see their large neighbor as a future driver of economic growth.

Nevertheless, China's long-term interests in the region will meet with a number of obstacles in the coming years, not the least of which is competition within Central Asia itself. These regional rivalries—including unfair trade practices, harsh border regulations, sovereignty disputes, and a failure thus far to truly institutionalize cooperative action—do not bode well for any enduring external presence, let alone a Chinese one. Attempting to exercise influence through the SCO has its challenges as well: the past decade has demonstrated that multilateral organizations have achieved few concrete gains, as self-serving national interests have trumped collective endeavors. China's main regional entry point, the SCO, may very well fail, in which case China will have to continue its bilateral relationships individually with the Central Asian states or through another forum, if it hopes to achieve its regional goals.

China's relations with Central Asia, in and of themselves, are not major foreign policy priorities for Beijing. For the foreseeable future,

Beijing's Central Asian diplomacy and strategy is more of a means to other ends, including: the promotion of its "new security concept" and constructive regional and international image, management of Sino-American and Sino-Russian relations, continued domestic economic development, and dealing with security concerns in Xinjiang. By and large, China pays close attention to Central Asia so it does not become a problem. On the other side of the coin, Central Asian nations, at present, have more to gain from the United States and Russia than from China, making their ties with China a lower priority for them as well.

Taking these points together, it seems unlikely that China will be able to exert anywhere close to as much influence in the near- to medium-term as Russia or the Unites States. Beijing appears well aware of this, and is proceeding in a cautious and balanced way: on the one hand highlighting shared interests in the region with Washington and Moscow, while on the other avoiding the appearance of trying to "oust" either from Central Asia. Over the longer-term, China is likely to promote its interests and polices in Central Asia and its prominence will increase, especially as the U.S. presence diminishes and the Russians continue to focus their energies internally and toward the West. In this context, it is critical for the United States to understand and respond to China's continuing emergence in Central Asia.

Issues on the Horizon

At this early stage, Chinese leaders and strategists appear to have been quite successful in identifying and pursuing their interests in Central Asia. However, several issues on the horizon will present some difficult challenges for China in Central Asia in the years ahead, particularly HIV/AIDS, drugs and organized crime, and water.

HIV/AIDS cases are growing at an ever-increasing rate on both sides of the China-Central Asia border, especially in Xinjiang, which is China's second-most infected region. Both Central Asia and Russia also face a looming problem with HIV/AIDS that will likely affect cross-border trade, security, and stability in the coming years.

China, Russia, and Central Asia all have problems with narco-trafficking and the terrorist activities it often funds. The majority of the drug trade follows two separate routes, one from Central Asia west to Russia and Europe, and one from South East Asia up through China. There are indications of new collaboration between these groups, particularly where organized crime is involved, and reports that Chinese Triads are now operating in Kyrgyzstan.

Water is one of the scarcest resources in both Central Asia and western China and will likely be an increasing source of tension as supplies diminish and downstream demand increases, particularly from the growing industrial and agricultural centers of Uzbekistan, Kazakhstan, and Xinjiang. Currently, China has plans to siphon up to 1.5 billion cubic meters of water per year from the Ili and Irtysh Rivers for oilfield development regions in Xinjiang. Both rivers originate in China and the Ili flows through Kazakhstan and terminates in Lake Balkhash, a body of water already devastated by decreasing water levels and increasing pollution from agriculture run-off. This issue alone has the potential to sour relations between China and Central Asia.

Conclusions

China's emergence in Central Asia will continue to grow, and likely will have a more natural and longer-term fit relative to that of the United States, based on a long history of interaction and clearly defined interests. China has rediscovered its place in the region and is developing pragmatic channels to achieve its interests there. Successes are growing, particularly in the fields of security and natural resources extraction, and a future of intense interaction looks more certain. Still, China's priority in Central Asia is maintaining stability along its borders, so that it can focus on more pressing matters elsewhere. Its objective is strategic denial; act to deny the rise of elements that will challenge China's internal security, deny the use of Central Asia by the United States to contain China, and deny a Russian monopoly of influence on its border.

China will most likely give significant attention only to those problems that directly affect its vital interests, such as counterterrorism and other border security questions. Central to this will be the attention paid to the role of the Uyghurs and Xinjiang in China-Central Asia relations. It is also clear that China's goal is to foster regional cooperation only to the point that it fits into its own national interest. If China can achieve its aims bilaterally and not through the SCO, it will, though the SCO provides a very useful vehicle to address transnational threats. Moreover, continuing problems in Central Asia and the region's inability to use collective action will minimize China's region-wide reach, leaving open the likelihood that Beijing will have considerable influence in some states, such as Kyrgyzstan and Kazakhstan, but considerably less in others. China's region-wide presence will be most affected, though, by the action of the United States and Russia. The United States is the most important near-term ally of the Central Asian states and can dictate the future shape of the regional security situation to a significant degree. Russia, too, has enduring importance to the region and can undermine many of China's goals if Moscow so chooses.

In sum, China is on the rise in Central Asia and the United States will have to deal with a more comprehensive Chinese presence in the region in the years ahead. Diplomatic and strategic hedging by external powers has already begun, and Central Asia has become an important piece on the global chessboard. All sides are using it to advance their international agendas. This is not a return to the "Great Game" of the nineteenth century, however. China, Russia, and the United States are too integrated with each other to threaten a clash over what is still a second-tier priority when compared to more pressing issues like North Korea, Iraq, and the proliferation of WMD. However, given the intermingling of Great Power interests in this region, increased tension is possible. There is room for cooperation in Central Asia and no need for restrictive alliances. In the best scenarios, the United States, China and Russia will recognize their convergence of interests, and work together to shape a more secure, prosperous and stable Central Asia.

Notes

[1] This chapter is drawn from a larger monograph published in August 2003 by the Freeman Chair in China Studies at the Center for Strategic and International Studies entitled, *China's New Journey to the West: China's Emergence in Central Asia and Implications for U.S. Interests.*

[2] In the late 740s, the expansionist Tang spread its influence as far westward as Kabul and Kashmir, eventually coming into direct conflict with the Muslim people of greater Turkestan. At Talas River, in 751, a predominantly Muslim army of Arab, Tibetan and Uyghur forces defeated Chinese troops led by Kao Hsien-chih. The ramifications were significant. The Arabs were able to extend their Islamic influence throughout Central Asia and the major trading routes. Tang expansionary tendencies were halted, beginning a trend of military decline. Thus, the Battle of Talas became a demarcation line between the Muslim–Turkic and Chinese worlds and remains an important touchstone for China-Central Asia relations today. The area know as the Uyghur Kingdom of East Turkestan, created by the migration of Uyghurs from Mongolia and Central Asia during the first millennium, was invaded by the Manchus in 1757 but was not brought under the control of the Qing Emperor until 1877 when it was named Xinjiang (meaning "New Territory"). Even then, resistance against Chinese dominion continued until 1949, including the establishment of an independent Uyghur State on two occasions, most notably from 1944-1949.

[3] The Shanghai Cooperation Organization—made up of China, Kazakhstan, Kyrgyzstan, Russia, Tajikistan, and Uzbekistan—is a Chinese-initiated international forum that evolved from the border demarcation and demilitarization process, known as "the Shanghai Five" and not including Uzbekistan, begun after the collapse of the Soviet Union. The SCO became a "full-fledged" international organization in January 2004 with a secretariat in Beijing and a regional counterterrorism center in Tashkent.

[4] Mutual respect for sovereignty and territorial integrity; mutual nonaggression; mutual noninterference in their respective domestic affairs; mutual benefit; and peaceful coexistence

⁵ The CSTO was recently reformed in 2002 from the ashes of the Collective Security Treaty (CST), the near-defunct collective security apparatus of the Commonwealth of Independent States. While the CST has some enduring success in the maintenance of a region-wide extended air defense, it has largely failed to materialize as a collective-defense organization, and the overall military capabilities of the members have decreased. The CSTO is another attempt to pull together these disparate militaries, this time by focusing on practical and specific tasks, particularly counterterrorism and rapid crisis response.

⁶ This center was originally to be located in Bishkek, but it was announced in September 2003 that it would be built in Tashkent. It is reported that Uzbekistan, a relatively apathetic member of the SCO, demanded the presence of the center in exchange for continued involvement.

⁷ For a more detailed description of the Xinjiang issue, *see* the forthcoming Xinjiang Project book being published by the Central Asian-Caucasus Institute, School of Advanced International Studies, Johns Hopkins University, Fall 2003.

⁸ Encapsulated as the "Go West: campaign," Beijing has encouraged the migration of Han Chinese to Xinjiang and the development of the western economies to benefit both the development of China's interior and the continuing east coast boom. Beyond the eastern seaboard, Xinjiang represents the most developed and dynamic economy in the nation. It has become a center of trade and industry for both China's west and Central Asia. Xinjiang's greatest potential for growth lies in its natural resources. In particular, while estimates vary, nearly all experts agree that the Tarim Basin holds enormous potential as a source of energy resources. A 2000 study from the Organization for Economic Cooperation and Development (OECD) states the Tarim Basin holds at least three billion tons of oil in proven reserves and possibly 510 billion cubic meters of natural gas, all thus far untapped. Bringing Xinjiang's potential wealth east will be critical to developing China's interior and spreading the benefits of economic growth across the country.

⁹ In response to Beijing's repressive policies in Xinjiang, including several violent crackdowns that, according to some reports, left hundreds dead and thousands imprisoned, and emboldened by the independence achieved by its Central Asian neighbors in the early- to mid-1990s, the Uyghur separatist movement took a more aggressive and violent direction. On February 27, 1997, three bombs were set off in the Xinjiang capital of Urumqi, killing nine people. Two weeks later, on March 7, a bomb exploded in Beijing, the seat of Chinese authority, killing 30. In September 1997, Chinese authorities disclosed that approximately 40 small uprising occurred, with Uyghur activists occupying a half dozen government buildings across China. The forced evictions left 80 dead and 200 injured. Eight hundred Uyghurs were arrested. Fifteen bomb attacks occurred over a five-month period in 1998 and seven attacks in the first six weeks of 1999, but it is unclear if these were Uyghur actions or just another challenge to the government from some other group, possibly laid-off workers. According to Justin Rudelson, author of *Oasis Identity*, there have been more than 200 militant actions over the past decade, resulting in 162 deaths. These include attacks on police stations, communications and electric power infrastructure, the bombings of buses, movie theaters, department stores, hotels, markets, and trains, assassinations of judges, and strikes against military bases. In taking these actions, it appears elements of the Uyghur separatist movement have shifted to more blatant and violent expressions of protest and the expansion of targets from government infrastructure and instruments of their control to include innocent civilians.

¹⁰ Interviews with Central Asian security officials on background.

¹¹ "Islamists Staged Explosion, Kyrgyz Says," UPI, May 25, 2003; "Kyrgyz Republic Public Announcement," U.S. Department of State, May 6, 2003; "Uzbekistan Public Announcement," U.S. Department of State, April 5, 2003; Alexei Igushev, "Hizb ut-Tahrir Remains Active in Central Asia," *Eurasianet*, February 5, 2003.

¹² Thomas Sanderson, "China's War on Terrorism," presented at the Center for Strategic and International Studies, March 5, 2003.

¹³ Description of this exercise drawn from "China Ends War Games with Kyrgyzstan," *Associated Press*, October 11, 2002; "China, Kyrgyzstan Hold Joint Anti-terror Military eEise," *Xinhuanet*, October 12, 2002; "Joint War Games Boost Terror Fight," *South China Morning Post*, October 12, 2002.

[14] Two airbases in Uzbekistan in Khanabad and Kokaida, two "gas and go" operations in Tajikistan in Dushanbe and Kyulyab, and one major base in Kyrgyzstan at Manas outside of Bishkek, with a possible new locale at Shymkent Airport in Kazakhstan.

[15] Off the record conference.

[16] "Temporary Ban on Uyghur Society in Kyrgyzstan," *OMRI Daily Digest*, April 9, 1996.

[17] In July 1998, China and Kazakhstan reached a final agreement resolving remaining border disputes along their 1,700 km border; the first full border dispute resolution between China and one of its "Shanghai Five" partners. "China: Jiang Zemin on Nuclear Arms Race, Sino-Kazakh Border Pact," *Foreign Broadcast Information Service, Daily Report: China*, FBIS-CHI-98-187, July 6, 1998. The July 2000 quote is drawn from "Xinhua: 'Full Text' of Dushanbe Statement of 'Shanghai Five.'"

[18] "Chinese Business Interests in Central Asia: A Quest for Dominance," *Central Asian-Caucasus Analyst*, June 18, 2003; "Chinese Leader Hu Jintao Visits Astana," RFE/RL, June 07 2003; and information provided by Fred Starr, Chairman of the Central Asia-Caucasus Institute at the School for Advanced International Studies, Johns Hopkins University.

[19] Wu Kang, "China's Quest for Energy Security and the Role of Central Asia," presented at the Center for Strategic and International Studies, April 22, 2003.

[20] "Chinese President Urges SCO Economic Cooperation," *People's Daily*, Friday, May 30, 2003.

Chapter 20

Regional Security Cooperation and Foreign Policies in Central Asia: A 21st Century "Great Game"?

Robert Brannon

At least three entities are engaged in crafting and implementing security policies in Central Asia—the United States, Russia and the Central Asian states themselves—each with its own set of perceived interests and threats. The United States is engaged in the Global War on Terrorism and views the region in terms of strategic access and resources. Russia still sees its relationship with the regional states in paternal terms, including perceived inherent rights of influence. Meanwhile, the Central Asian states are anything but monolithic in terms of foreign policy. While other international entities are certainly at play in the region, including China and the European Union (EU), this chapter focuses on the complexities of the U.S./Russian/Central Asian triangle and the national security issues at stake for all three players.

During the North Atlantic Treaty Organization (NATO) summit in Prague on November 20, 2002, U.S. President George W. Bush said:

> Russia does not require a buffer zone. Instead, it needs to be surrounded by friends and neighbors. Russia is part of Europe and strong security in Europe is good for Russia. NATO enlargement does not threaten Russia because Russia has a special role in NATO, one that will strengthen the already strong ties between our two nations.[1]

Although the President was speaking about Russia and NATO enlargement, he might well have been thinking of Central Asia when he mentioned buffer zones. Russia has long seen this region as a safety zone against threats to its security both real and perceived. The United States thinks this is no longer necessary, arguing that collective security might be better achieved through closer alliances throughout the region.

What are Russia's interests in Central Asia and how does Russia view U.S. security cooperation with the Central Asian states? While President Vladimir Putin appears to have been able to marshal support within his government to tolerate a short-term American presence in Central Asia, what are the implications for a longer-term presence? What, exactly, are Russia's ultimate goals in the region? This chapter examines regional security cooperation from the standpoint of U.S. and Russian foreign policies in Central Asia. Within this context, it focuses on Russian tolerance for U.S. initiatives in the post September 11 strategic environment.

Before and After September 11

On June 28, 2000, barely six months into his term of office, President Putin issued a new foreign policy concept, asserting, "Today our foreign policy resources are relatively limited, and they must be concentrated in areas that are vital to Russia's interests."[2] Although the concept was based on work begun during President Boris Yeltsin's administration and put forth in Russia's new strategic concept and military doctrine published in 1999, the policy statements nonetheless reflected Putin's pragmatism with regard to optimizing Russia's position in world affairs, regardless of its faded superpower status. This foreign policy concept was again updated in October 2003.[3]

Described by Russia's Foreign Minister Igor Ivanov as a pragmatic effort to help the country solve its domestic problems,[4] the June 2000 document offered a restrained but critical view of NATO and the West, highlighting the importance of Russia's ties to the Group of Eight (G8) and the EU. Along with criticizing the United States for pursuing a uni-polar foreign policy instead of adopting a more stable (in Russian eyes) multi-polar view of the world, the statement also took a swipe at U.S. plans to deploy a limited national missile defense system. Yet Putin appears to recognize the complexities of international relations for Russia as well as the United States and has thus far maneuvered adeptly. He told an interviewer in January 2001 that Russia "must get rid of imperial ambitions on the one hand, and on the other clearly understand where our national interests are and fight for them."[5] Putin further put his own stamp on Russia's foreign policy for the future by declaring that Russia would be much better off "with" the West than "without."

Russian foreign policy in Central Asia is still in transition. Deeply embedded in the Russian psyche is the notion that Central Asian states are simply *"nashi,"* the Russian word for "ours." In both Tsarist and Soviet times, Moscow controlled the region by force and by altering traditional demographic boundaries almost capriciously along the way. With the break up of the Soviet Union and subsequent independence of the Central Asian states, the relationship has been slowly shifting away from a paternal one. Many in Moscow never really expected these new nations to be able to exist without considerable aid and assistance, which helped lead to the creation of spheres of influence, represented to an extent by the Commonwealth of Independent States (CIS). As the dynamics within the region change so does Russian policy, which might be best described as tolerant in varying degrees.

Thus, even now, it is difficult to think of Russia's policy toward the Central Asian states as "foreign." After the break-up of the Soviet Union, most Russian analysts insisted that close ties with Central Asia were critical to national security interests. Many believed that geographic location; shared history; common production systems, infrastructure, and institutions; and old dependences on Soviet financial subsidies and the Moscow markets would guarantee a continued interest in extensive cooperation with Russia.[6] They also believed that a shared sense of national identity, derived from a long history of cohabitation, had survived the dissolution of the Soviet Union. Unfortunately, these assumptions proved wrong.

While it was true that Central Asian leaders initially were reluctant to leave the Soviet Union, they soon realized that Russia had little role to play in their search for national identity and values. Throughout the early 1990s, Russia's often erratic behavior also served to distance the Central Asian states from Russia politically. This feeling was expressed by Kazakh President Nursultan Nazarbaev, Russia's closest ally among Central Asian leaders, who spoke out in early 1997 about his disappointment with Russian policy.[7] What had once been shared values among the Soviet republics were replaced by new or "national" identities, suspicions about Russia's intentions, and pragmatic calculations about what Russia actually could provide. Instead of a security community including Central Asian states grouped around Russia, a web of bilateral agreements developed with strongly expressed sensitivities about issues of sovereignty.

Russia watched with concern as along its southern border independently-minded states began to shift their orientation in other directions. Of the CIS members, Uzbekistan became the most outspoken critic of Russia and the most eager to enter into cooperation with the United States. Turkmenistan limited its military cooperation with Russia on the grounds of its declared policy of "permanent neutrality." As Russia saw its influence in Central Asia decline, fears arose that its position in the region might be supplanted by other external powers. The reality of the September 11 terrorist attacks caused Russia to re-evaluate its own policies and consider opportunities for exploiting new U.S. views on terrorism.

In the immediate aftermath of September 11, President Putin was the first world leader to place a telephone call to President Bush. In doing this, Putin ignored the objections of many Kremlin advisors and cemented his relationship, and personal bond, with Bush. Putin's actions in this case symbolize his policy of support for, and integration with, the West and in particular the United States. In spite of opposition from inside his own government, he made a decision to show Russia's support immediately, without waiting to build a consensus in his own government.

In the weeks that followed September 11, as it became apparent that America would court the Central Asian states for access to military facilities, rhetoric heated up in Russia as to what Russia's policy should be. In spite of President Putin's support for the United States, many of his closest advisors voiced strong concerns that America might exploit the new war on terrorism to gain a foothold in territories that had, until just 10 years before, been part of the Soviet Union. On September 18, 2001, U.S. Secretary of Defense Donald Rumsfeld announced that the United States would seek approval from several states in Central Asia and support from Russia to deploy military assets in the region to support the war on terrorism. Rumsfeld's statement seemed to imply that operations planned for Afghanistan might be launched from bases in nearby Central Asia. Russian Minister of Defense Sergei Ivanov responded by saying there was no basis for U.S. claims to a requirement for access to military bases in Central Asia.[8] Several other key government officials also issued statements denouncing U.S. initiatives in the region. Shortly thereafter, to Ivanov's apparent surprise and perhaps consternation, Putin held a press conference to declare Russian support for the U.S. request.[9]

During his remarks at Harvard's Kennedy School in February 2002, Russian Duma Deputy Grigory Yavlinsky told an anecdote about Putin's decision to side with the United States in the war on terrorism. According to Yavlinsky, out of 21 people present in a September 24 advisory meeting Putin had called, only two voted to support the United States. One person voted to support the Taliban, and 18 said Russia should remain neutral. Shortly after the meeting, Putin announced "unconditional and immediate" support for the United States, including access to military facilities in the CIS.[10] All of these statements sent confusing signals to the governments of Central Asian states. Yet despite his decision, Putin continues to operate in a political atmosphere that has not been particularly positive about cooperation with the West in general, and the United States in particular. In Russia, some wrongly believe the United States wants to see Russia fail in its foreign policy and security objectives so that it can "clean up" in the aftermath to its own advantage.

Russia's Interests in Central Asia

As Lena Johnson, Senior Research Fellow at the Swedish Institute of International Affairs and noted regional scholar, has argued:

> Russia's interests in Central Asia since the break-up of the Soviet Union are mainly related to strategic and security concerns. The strategic interests are two-fold: first to integrate Central Asian states in the CIS sphere and make them into close allies of Russia; and, second, to deny external powers strategic access to Central Asia. [11]

First and foremost, Russia regards Central Asia as a buffer zone of strategic importance to its national defense. By the end of the 1990s, events in the region had increased fears about Islamic extremism and terrorism. This atmosphere gave Putin a convenient platform from which to suggest closer cooperation in the area of military security, as well as a renewed effort to reorient the Central Asian states toward Russia. The events of September 11 changed this dynamic. Early Russian opposition to the stationing of American military forces close to its borders for operations in Afghanistan did not play well in the Central Asian states. However, as Russia changed its position and received credit for a new cooperative policy in its dealings with the United States, Central Asian attitudes changed as well. Russia's interest in the fall of the Taliban regime, and in expanding economic ties with the United States, overcame concerns about Central Asian states accepting American military bases in the region.

To allay Russian concerns, American military and civilian officials stressed the short-term nature of the American military presence in Central Asia and emphasized that troops would be withdrawn once military operations were over. However, as was sharply articulated in the press by anti-American hard liners such as General Colonel Leonid Ivashov,[12] Russia was well aware of the probability that America might try to exploit the opportunities created by the war on terrorism and remain in the region long after meeting announced military objectives.

Russia had to balance this concern against its fears that the rising tide of Islamic fundamentalism in Central Asia could evoke increased unrest in the region and cause instability that could threaten Russia directly. Many

Russians believe that their greatest security risks are associated with the country's southern flank. Related to this is the concern that Chechen separatists are being funded by the same terrorist organizations at war with the United States. Osama Bin Laden did nothing to allay this fear when he pronounced that no country that supported and aided America in their war would be safe.[13] In the wake of the horrific hostage siege at Moscow's "Nord Ost" theater during the week of October 22, 2002, Putin referred to Bin Laden's statement and concluded that there was a direct link between his decision to support America and the attack at the theater (by then attributed to Chechen terrorists).[14]

President Putin quickly became adept at interpreting the new American National Security Strategy in ways that supported Russian goals and objectives in its own "war on terrorism" in Chechnya. After the United States released its new National Security Strategy in October 2002,[15] Putin hailed it as a landmark document for its sharp focus on the threat of terrorism, not only to the United States, but also to the world. By December, Putin gave indications he would revise Russia's National Security Doctrine along similar lines.[16] Specifically, the aim was to identify terrorism more sharply as the primary threat to Russian interests. Since then, despite some acute frustration in his attempts to wield the ax of military reform against an intransigent General Staff, Putin and his Defense Minister, Sergei Ivanov, have achieved some progress in refocusing military doctrine. Recently, specific reforms have been aimed at further trimming the army's forces and implementing plans to move away from conscripts as the primary source of manpower toward an all-volunteer force similar to what is the norm in most Western countries. These positive steps might not have been possible absent the forward looking security environment that exists in the wake of September 11.

The American Point of View

The United States needs access to Central Asian infrastructure in order to more effectively and efficiently fight the Global War on Terrorism. In the immediate aftermath of the September 11 attacks against the World Trade Center and the Pentagon, America focused on striking al Qaeda at the heart of its operations in Afghanistan. Sustained support for such a military campaign required logistics bases in Central Asia and almost immediately, the United States began to work to make arrangements in the region. According to Eugene Rumer, senior fellow at the Institute for National Strategic Studies, "After 10 years of working to maintain its distance from Central Asia, the United States has landed squarely in the middle of it."[17]

Initially, the United States secured an airbase in Uzbekistan and the right to use a similar facility in Kyrgyzstan. Although Kazakhstan initially turned down a U.S. request for an airbase in that country, subsequent arrangements allowed for such use if needed. Kazakhstan did grant the U.S. over-flight and emergency landing rights, and also received support for humanitarian efforts from Turkmenistan. In return for these concessions, the U.S. budget for assistance to the five Central Asian states has more than doubled from fiscal year 2001—literally, from $230 to $595 million.[18] In response to the perceived rising threat of radical Islam in Central Asia, the United States is emphasizing security assistance and engagement with regional governments. Rumer states:

> Since September 11, the United States has emerged as the principal power in Central Asian affairs. With the troop presence in Kyrgyzstan, Tajikistan, and Uzbekistan, the defeat of the Taliban government in Afghanistan, and all signs pointing to a long-term U.S. military presence in the region, the United States has become Central Asia's security manager.[19]

Even though human rights groups have charged that Central Asian states have stepped up repression since the September 11 terrorist attacks, U.S. officials remain convinced that a positive engagement strategy can succeed in encouraging regional governments to embrace gradual liberal democratization. In an article for *The Eurasianet* in November 2002, Dr. Ariel Cohen of the Heritage Foundation cited an unnamed U.S. National Security Council official who claims that the Bush administration views the foreign policy challenge in Central Asia as a balancing act between internal reform, security, and energy: "The focus on security is overriding, but not exclusive."[20]

The upcoming years will prove critical to the United States as it further refines its policies with Central Asia. Meeting growing national security concerns must reflect a balanced view—not only for the United States but also for the Central Asian nations themselves.

Kyrgyzstan and Other Regional Deployments

When American forces were first deployed to Central Asia in October 2001, Washington stated they were there for a limited time and would be withdrawn once the mission was completed. The deployment was not welcomed by Russia, though President Putin chose not to oppose it. Since then, in Russian eyes, the U.S. build-up in the region has been out of proportion with stated intentions. More recently, leading American representatives have stated publicly that the U.S. presence in Central Asia would not only be long-term, but might even expand.[21]

Given the deteriorating relations between the United States and Russia in the aftermath of U.S. military intervention in Iraq, the situation in Central Asia has the potential to become a destabilizing factor. Late in 2002, Russian aircraft redeployed to Kant Air Base in Kyrgyzstan, ostensibly to support the war on terrorism.[22] Some observers, however, believed the return of Russian troops to Kyrgyzstan might be a sign that a new rivalry was developing between Moscow and Washington in Central Asia , with the ultimate aim of establishing political and economic control over the region. This symbolic Russian presence is apparently the vanguard of a force that might ultimately include more than 20 Russian aircraft and about 700 troops, thus becoming the most significant military deployment outside Russia's borders since the Soviet collapse. Russian aircraft will form the core of the air unit.[23] According to *RIA Novostii*, the official Russian news agency, Russia plans to deploy five SU-25 attack jets, five SU-27 fighters, two AN-26 transports, two IL-76 transports, five IL-39 training jets, and two MI-8 helicopters.

During a brief stopover in Bishkek, the Kyrgyz capital, on December 4, 2002, President Putin endorsed the recent Russian deployment of fighter jets, bombers and other aircraft in Kyrgyzstan.[24] Speaking to journalists, Putin said that Russia's new military presence was very important and brought "a new quality" to security arrangements in the region. Kyrgyz President Askar Akaev has urged Russia to become a "main strategic cornerstone of Central Asia."[25] At the same time, officials also signed a defense protocol called the Bishkek Declaration, pledging closer security and economic ties between the two countries. While some believe the move may be designed to reassert Russia's military influence in a region where the United States now has its own semi-permanent military presence, Putin reassured the press that the agreement is not directed against any third country. Both presidents emphasized that the new relationship is multi-faceted, including a deal to write off some $40 million of Kyrgyz debt to Moscow. Along with Putin, Russian Defense Minister Sergei Ivanov also visited Kyrgyzstan to inspect the new facilities. He announced that the Russian task force would provide air support for a contingent of ground forces. Known as a rapid reaction force, this group could eventually total more than 5,000 troops from Russia, Kyrgyzstan, Kazakhstan and Tajikistan, as members of an alliance of former Soviet republics known as the Collective Security Treaty Organization.[26]

The Russian deployment to Kant Air Base now means that Kyrgyzstan is host to two foreign air bases, the other being the U.S. facility at Manas, a Bishkek suburb. The U.S. base, which was established in the aftermath of September 11, is designed to provide air support for regional operations by the anti-terrorism coalition in Afghanistan. Some 2,000 American personnel now occupy Manas, and up to 5,000 coalition soldiers (including the original 2,000 U.S. troops) are expected to be based there eventually.[27] Although this force may help Kyrgyz authorities deal with terrorist threats, coalition troops are unlikely to back the government in disputes with political opposition forces, without additional security protocols. On one hand, the security deal between Moscow and Bishkek could indicate that the United States has failed to provide sufficient commitment to the Akaev administration in terms of security needs and domestic political problems. Therefore, Akaev is now turning to Russian backing in military, political and financial spheres. On the other hand, the new arrangements with Russia may be the harbinger of re-emerging Russian interests in a sphere of influence and a desire for enhanced credibility.

Russia and Kyrgyzstan have long maintained close political and military ties. Akaev has tended to support the Kremlin's policies in the region; in response, Moscow has backed Akaev's regime and warned against interference in Kyrgyz internal affairs. However, Moscow has been careful to deny that the Russian deployment in Kyrgyzstan is related in any way to the American presence. Almost tauntingly, *RIA Novostii* commented that nobody was going to push the Americans from Central Asia. The same *RIA Novostii* article added that since the United States has been unable to rid the region of terrorists despite more than two years of concerted effort, it is possible that Russian troops eventually could help defend the Americans in the event of some undefined "worst-case scenarios."[28]

Following his trip to Kyrgyzstan, Putin traveled to China and India where speculation re-surfaced about the three countries "ganging up" to form a China-India-Russia "strategic triangle," in an effort to help balance the regional dominance of the United States. Despite the rumors, Russian sources concede that such a relationship would be unlikely since Russia, China, and India all are keen to strengthen good relations with Washington, and have backed the U.S. war on terrorism.[29] Both China and India have distanced themselves from the idea of an China-India-Russia strategic axis. However, foreign ministers of the three countries later met on the sidelines of the United Nations General Assembly session in New York for informal talks, with the understanding that such meetings might be held on a regular basis. Although the "strategic triangle" concept still has some supporters in Moscow, Putin's Asian tour came in the wake of improved relations with the United States. Therefore, pursuing a strategic alliance between Russia, India and China is unlikely to become Russia's primary goal at this stage, and merely indicates that Moscow wants partners in both the East and West.

Yet, perhaps coincidentally, soon after Putin returned from his trip to China and India, Tajik President Imomali Rakhmonov met with President Bush in Washington December 9, 2002. Media reports speculated that creation of a permanent U.S. military base in Tajikistan was among the main issues discussed at this meeting. Following an interview in December 2002 with Professor Aleksei Malashenko, of Moscow's Institute for International Relations (MGIMO), journalist Zamira Eshanova claims Putin's visit to Kyrgyzstan and Rakhmonov's reception at the White House were at least indirectly connected. Malashenko apparently believes the process of the military reapportionment of Central Asia is under way, with the United States and Russia as the main players, and has said:

> I think that these visits and these cross-negotiations and cross-actions in the direction of creating military bases in Central Asia do not mean that the Russian military presence in Central Asia is simply being replaced by an American one. It means that there are attempts to adjust or provide political stability from the outside.[30]

Although the United States has given no signs that it may be preparing to court the government of Tajikistan in pursuit of any specific security related goals or objectives, there is reason to believe the Tajiks may be taken more seriously in Washington in the future.

Elsewhere in the region, Uzbekistan is already hosting some 3,000 American troops on its territory in support of operations in Afghanistan. Kazakhstan has offered an airport in the southern city of Shimkent to U.S.-led coalition forces. Thus, of the five Central Asian states, only Turkmenistan, which declared its permanent neutrality after independence, has remained apart from military developments related to the war on terrorism.

U.S. and Russian National Interests Coincide

As time passes, radical Islam has become an increasingly potent force in Central Asia. Ahmed Rashid, the Pakistan, Afghanistan and Central Asia correspondent for the *Far Eastern Economic Review* and the *Daily Tele-*

graph, London, has written extensively on the region for the last 20years and argues that the Hizb-ut-Tahrir al Islami (HT) or the Party of Islamic Liberation and the Islamic Movement of Uzbekistan (IMU) are both serious threats to the region. Followers of these movements derive inspiration from the Taliban and the extreme Wahhabi doctrine of Saudi Arabia, and were trained at militant madrassas in Pakistan. In his book *Jihad: The Rise of Militant Islam in Central Asia*, Rashid documents a September 2000 meeting to discuss future cooperation between al Qaeda leader Osama Bin Laden and representatives from the IMU, the HT, and Chechen separatists in Kabul, Afghanistan.[31] The potential for increasing linkages between terrorist organizations makes such threats transnational and sets the stage for growing international cooperation.

In Russia, President Putin appears to be exploiting anti-terrorism sentiment to his advantage and has succeeded in linking Russia's war in Chechnya with America's war on terrorism. On November 11, 2002, at a post EU meeting press conference in Brussels, Putin unleashed an especially strong invective against a reporter from the Paris newspaper *Le Monde*. Responding to a question about the potential unintended consequences of using land mines in Chechnya and specifically whether this tactic was causing too many civilian casualties, Putin cited widespread aggression against Russia as far back as 1999 in Dagestan. Putin alleged this aggression stemmed from Islamic sources and was directed at Russia because these same forces would never be willing to coexist peacefully on Russia's southern flank. He went on to point out that France must surely feel the same dangers since it, too, was an ally of the United States in the war on terrorism.[32]

Thus, despite 50 years of regional confrontation and tensions over the deployment of U.S. troops to Central Asia, the United States and Russia appear to be ready to cooperate in Central Asia in the war on terrorism. Neither side seems to be willing, or even able, to "go it alone." Each has much to gain from cooperating with the other, and each also stands to lose much if cooperation sours. Russian foreign policy under Putin has evolved over the duration of his presidency. Pragmatic and forceful, his ability to exploit opportunities for gain has steadily improved. Accordingly, Russia may be willing to tolerate, if not openly encourage, a long-term presence of U.S. security forces in Central Asia if it means the United States will assist Russia in dealing with the threat of terrorism. From the American perspective, the United States has an opportunity now to create a more positive relationship with Russia, with significant benefits for both sides. Russia's leadership wants integration with the United States, not only in the war against terrorism, but also in areas such as trade and energy. Both sides have a unique chance to exploit the current situation to craft foreign policy that will overcome old antagonisms and distrust.

The Future

Both Russia and the United States have recognized the importance of Central Asia. Their current competition for regional influence has been compared to the historical contest of Russia and Britain, referred to by Peter Hopkirk and others as "The Great Game."[33] In the current context, there is compelling evidence that the security of Central Asia has similarly high stakes for all concerned. One way to think about this is from the perspective of alternative futures. Peter Schwartz, in his research on developing a scenario planning model for business, begins with a set of visions that attempt to look 10 years into the future.[34] To frame such possibilities, it is useful to begin with two contrasting alternative futures, from among the many that are conceivable. In adapting scenario planning to international relations, especially in the context of regional security cooperation in Central Asia, alternative futures in the U.S.-Russian relationship might resemble one of the following "tales."[35] Although hypothetical, it is not difficult to imagine the plausibility of each. These narratives highlight the interconnectedness and interdependence of the participants in a regional relationship that could be described as a new great game. As each unfolds, it is useful to consider what it might take to make them real.

A Tale of Two Possible Future Worlds

First, the nightmare scenario: The year is 2011 and the United States has been at war against terrorism since September 11, 2001. Things have gone badly for the United States since it has emerged as the sole nation fighting the war. Russia has pulled out of the coalition and decided to go its own way. Mission creep has led to pursuing objectives beyond simply crushing terrorism as a threat, including nation-building throughout the Middle East and into Central and South Asia. The conflict has become global. After Russia split from the coalition and abandoned any further attempts at integration with the West, Russian military forces rallied in support of the Communist Party. This led to a more independent minded senior military leadership, less inclined to accept guidance from civilians in government. Russian military bases in Central Asia exist side by side with those of the United States, often with resultant skirmishes as each side seeks to defend its territory. Political regimes in Central Asian states generally have become even more repressive and authoritarian. The Russian economy is a shambles and corruption is deeply entrenched at every level. Proliferation of weapons of mass destruction (WMD) is widespread throughout the region. Large stockpiles of dangerous weapons continue to disappear from controlled areas and show up in various theaters of war. In sum, the world is at war and Central Asia has become an exceptionally dangerous and highly unstable powder keg.

Next, an alternative, arm-in-arm scenario: The year is 2011 and the global war on terrorism has been over for several years. The United States and its coalition allies, including Russia and all the Central Asian states, were victorious. Terrorist organizations—state-sponsored and otherwise—have been beaten back into marginal threats that are easily tracked through the advent of highly developed regional security cooperation. Russia is fully integrated with the west. NATO has changed its name to the Euro-Atlantic Security Treaty Organization and Russia is a candidate for joining the alliance as a full partner. The Russian military, firmly under civilian control, is reforming along NATO-standard lines, leaner and more efficient. Central Asian military bases are jointly occupied by Russian, American and indigenous forces. Regional economies are stable and highly productive. The post war strategic environment has led to stability for oil pipelines and export of natural resources from Central Asian reserves. Membership in the World Trade Organization, debt restructuring, and debt forgiveness have given new strength to Russia's burgeoning market capitalism. Russian leadership and influence in Central Asia are welcomed and encouraged by the United States. Corruption and proliferation of WMD are rare, as most of the reasons for black markets have been eliminated. In sum, the world is at peace and Central Asia has become model region of stability with U.S. and Russian forces cooperating side-by-side.

Getting Back to the Future

Considering the respective national interests of Russia and the United States in Central Asia, and in view of strategic security objectives that have been established by both, it is possible to see a degree of convergence in comparing these two entirely hypothetical scenarios. Regional stability, from the perspective of Russia's national interests, depends on support for authoritarian political regimes committed to maintaining the status quo. The same regional stability so critical to Russia is also important for the national interests of the United States. In order to limit threats to its own security forces in the region, America needs Russian cooperation to prevent instability and its subsequent insecurities. Therefore, close cooperation between Russia and the United States in the war on terrorism translates directly to support for current political regimes in Central Asia that seek to restrict sources of instability.

American and Russian national interests in Central Asia coincide more often than they do not. Absent close cooperation with Russia and the Central Asian states, the United States would be forced to operate at significant disadvantages in Afghanistan. Similarly, if Russia has to conduct operations against terrorists in Chechnya without cutting off support for terrorists from Central Asia, the disadvantages are legion. Even after the war on terrorism is over, the peace that follows will be influenced for all concerned by the lines of cooperation established during the war. Close cooperation in wartime will doubtless lead to closer ties in peace. These partnerships could reap benefits in areas beyond security cooperation. Although scenario planning helps to imagine the possibilities in hypothetical terms, current events also are instructive.

Putin's Real World

President Putin's initiative to make Russia's foreign policy more pro-Western has not been well received by his country's political and military elite. To some, the absence of widespread support among these groups has led to speculation about Putin's credibility, sincerity, commitment to democratization and his ability to bring his nation along with him. Opinions have been divided. The most important question is whether Putin's initiative really represents a true change in Russian foreign policy or just a political experiment. According to Dmitri Trenin of the Moscow Carnegie Center,[36] Russia's decision to support the United States in the war on terrorism was based on fundamental Russian interests. It is, however, still not clear whether other key elements of the Russian government share the President's view of precisely what those interests are.

The changes in Russia's foreign policy following September 11 are often interpreted as a personal achievement for President Putin, despite Russian public opinion.[37] His policy of supporting the United States in the fight against terrorism and Russia's active participation in the antiterrorist coalition, as well as the warming of Russia's relations with America and NATO, appears outwardly to be an extraordinary act of political courage. However, some political and social analysts[38] have observed that deeply rooted anti-Americanism (a legacy of the Cold War), and the sometimes open hostility toward the United States as a world leader, are stronger than feelings of sympathy for the victims of the terrorist acts of September 11. A sense that the Russian and American peoples are in some way united in suffering from international terrorism is also lacking.

The risks associated with those political factors driving Russian behavior in the war on terrorism center on President Putin's ability to deliver on what he promises. Despite rhetoric to the contrary, it cannot be assumed that senior military leadership simply will fall in line behind Putin's assurances to the United States about close cooperation in the war on terrorism. Retired General Leonid Ivashov, for one, is well known for his eagerness to warn Russian leaders of the perils of moving too close to the United States. Following a press conference in December 2000 at which President Putin announced that military cooperation with NATO would resume, General Ivashov emphasized the risks of closer cooperation.[39] Not yet retired at that time, Ivashov called attention to aspects of the president's policy that were of great concern to the senior officers of Russia's armed forces. Nor is this example isolated; others in the government have spoken out in similar fashion. Despite some recently positive trends, it is not yet clear whether President Putin's initiatives in support of broad integration with the United States ultimately will succeed.

Conclusion

Most Russians have accepted that they cannot dictate security terms to Central Asian states simply by fiat. The Russian government is not financially capable of providing the region with the same measure of support it can hope to garner from the United States. In view of Russian fears that without hard line governments in Central Asia, the ground might be fertile for rising Islamic fundamentalism, it is clearly in Russia's interests to support security solutions that favor the status quo, enhancing long-term stability. Toward this end, there are, and will continue to be, opportunities for Russia to supplement American initiatives in the region.

For their part, Central Asian governments remain suspicious of Russian intentions and motives. Most fear that any move to shore up relations with Russia alone might result in a loss of independence. Instead, these governments see the advantages of close ties with both Russia and the United States. If security cooperation with America is tolerated by Russia, then this is indeed the better path. Central Asia needs stability, for with stability and regional security will come improved financial and economic outlooks. Russian interests are similar, but are complicated by the war in Chechnya.

Perhaps Putin sees U.S. involvement in an even more pragmatic way than might have been suspected in the aftermath of September 11. It may be that Putin believes a U.S. presence in Central Asia will provide the necessary stability in the region, thus paving the way for increased domestic security for Russia at American expense. If this is the case, then it appears likely that Russia will tolerate U.S. military cooperation in Central Asia as long as it remains politically manageable. Russia's position could be strengthened by further deployments, such as the one to Kyrgyzstan, calling attention to Russian capabilities. Putin's 2000 presidential campaign emphasized his commitment to end the war in Chechnya. Now that he has linked international terrorism to this issue, it is even more important that he bring Russia's security policies in line with its foreign policy.

Finally, it is certainly in the best interests of the Central Asian states to embrace security cooperation with Russia and the United States to the extent that it supports (or, in some cases, even guarantees) their own political stability and national security. Valuable resources in the region are much more likely to be unlocked and converted into positive means for national wealth if there is a stable environment that encourages commercial interests. Oil extraction and marketing need strong state security guarantees in order to be safe from terrorist attacks. Even those states with limited natural resources have strategic assets, such as airfields or other defense related infrastructure, which could be useful to both Russia and the United States during the upcoming months or years in what increasingly appears to be a protracted war on terrorism. Airports may be the only marketable resource available in Kyrgyzstan, but these are important assets, on which all players seem willing to capitalize. Recent events show that Central Asia may be witnessing a new great game, with its fate in this latest round being decided not only by foreign interests, but also by its own policies. Regional security cooperation in Central Asia could be the key to success for all sides with prudently managed, security cooperation delivering enormous benefits to Russia, the United States and the Central Asian states themselves. Squandered, the negative implications are disproportionately worse. Now, more than ever, the next moves must be carefully considered. Even as one plays chess, strategic players think many moves ahead. Russians are traditionally superb at this game, and the United States should be aware of all the options and potential impacts before entering into agreements or implementing policies that might have far reaching consequences.

Notes

[1] White House press release, November 20, 2002.

[2] Igor Ivanov, *Foreign Policy of the Russian Federation*, (Moscow: Russian Ministry of Foreign Affairs, June 28, 2000).

³ Victor Litovkin, *Security is Best Achieved Through Coalition: Russia's New Military Doctrine Highlights Community of Goals with the World"* (Moscow: RIA Novosti, October 2, 2003), <www.cdi. org/russia/276-6.cfm>.

⁴ Dale R. Herspring, *Putin's Russia: Past Imperfect, Future Uncertain (Oxford, UK:* Rowman & Littlefield Publishers, Inc. 2002), 231.

⁵ Ibid.

⁶ Roy Allison and Lena Johnson, *The Changing Security Policy Challenges in Central Asia: The New International Context* (Washington, DC: The Brookings Institution Press, 2001), 96.

⁷ Interview with Nazarbayev in the Russian language newspaper *Nezavisimaya Gazeta*, January 16, 1997.

⁸ "Bush was asked about comments made by Russian Defense Minister Sergei Ivanov that there is 'no basis,' as he put it, for Central Asian states bordering Afghanistan to offer their territory to the U.S. or the North Atlantic Treaty Organization to launch strikes against Afghanistan," <http://www. cdi.org/russia/172-pr.html##5>, Washington, September 20, 2001 (RFE/RL) "Russia: Support For U.S. May Be Self-Serving."

⁹ "In an abrupt change of policy and heart, Russia's President Vladimir V. Putin said this week that the United States could use Russian airspace to carry out strikes against Afghanistan. Putin, who until then had been eager to put more and more distance between himself and Washington, also withdrew his objections to a U.S. military presence in the former Soviet republics Uzbekistan and Tajikistan,." <http://www.cdi.org/russia/173-pr.html##7>, *Baltimore Sun*, September 27, 2001 "In Russia, doubts, skepticism" (quoting from recent Russian press: Novaya Gazeta, Nezavisimaya Gazeta, Izvestiya, Komsomolskaya Pravda, Kommersant).

¹⁰ Grigory Yavlinsky, Russian State Duma Member (Yabloko Party), "Russia and the United States: New Challenges, New Strategies," Belfer Center for Science and International Affairs (BCSIA), John F. Kennedy School of Government, Harvard University, February 6, 2002.

¹¹ Roy Allison and Lena Johnson, *Central Asian Security: The New International Context* (Washington, DC: The Brookings Institution Press, 2001), 97-101.

¹² General Colonel Leonid Ivashov, recently retired from his post at the helm of International Military Cooperation for the Russian Ministry of Defense, gave an interview to Vladimir Mukhin, a journalist with *Nezavisimaya Gazeta*, appearing in *The Russia Journal* (December 17, 2001). In the interview, Ivashov said he thinks there is a lot wrong with President Putin's new policy of moving Russia toward increased cooperation with the United States. Ivashov apparently believes Russia would be well served by maintaining a healthy distance from all things western.

¹³ In an audiotape released to Arabic television station Al Jazeera on November 11, 2002, Osama Bin Laden issued his first statement in many months. In a voice that intelligence analysts agree is probably authentic, Bin Laden indicts America for unjust war against Islam and specifically threatens to engulf in its vengeance any other nation that allies itself with the United States.

¹⁴ Gregory Feifer, "Russia: Moscow's Vow to Fight Terrorism Criticized Amid Theater-Raid Fallout," RLE/RL, Moscow, Russia, October 30, 2002, <http://www.cdi.org/russia/229-2.cfm>. Using rhetoric strikingly similar to that of U.S. President George W. Bush after September 11, 2001, Putin said Russia would take the initiative in combating threats to its national security. "Russia will respond with measures appropriate to the threats wherever there are terrorists, organizations of these criminals, or their ideological or financial sponsors."

¹⁵ National Security Strategy of the United States of America, The White House, October 2002.

¹⁶ Interfax News Agency, Moscow, Russia, January 30, 2003, <http://www.cdi.org/russia/242-3.cfm>. According to the First Deputy Chairman of the Federation Council's Defense and Security Committee, Colonel General (ret) Valeriy Manilov, "A new edition of the Russian national security concept will take into consideration every threat the international community has encountered."

¹⁷ Eugene B. Rumer, "Flashman's Revenge: Central Asia after September 11," Institute for National Strategic Studies, Strategic Forum, no. 195, December 2002.

[18] Ariel Cohen, "US Officials Relying on Engagement Strategy to Promote Change in Central Asia," *Eurasianet,* November 14, 2002.

[19] Ibid.

[20] Ibid.

[21] Hooman Peimani, "Military Buildup Ends US-Russian Honeymoon," *Asia Times,* August 28, 2002, and *"US Presence in Central Asia Antagonizes Russia,"* published in the Jamestown Foundation's *CDI Russia Weekly,* Issue no. 228, Item no.11, October 23, 2002. Dr. Hooman Peimani works as an independent consultant with international organizations in Geneva and does research in International Relations. Peimani attributes the claim that U.S. military presence in Central Asia would not only likely be long-term, but might also be growing, to General Tommy Franks in his meetings with senior government officials in many Central Asian states during negotiations in the run-up to operations in Afghanistan.

[22] On December 2, 2002, two Russian SU-25 attack jets and two IL-76 military transport planes (along with 70 troops to establish air traffic control systems and provide security) arrived from neighboring Tajikistan and landed at a military airfield in Kant, about 20 kilometers east of Bishkek. Two days later, three SU-27 fighter jets arrived from the Lipetsk base in Central Russia. According to Sergei Blagov, writing for the *Asian Times* on December 5, 2002, Russian pilots had dubbed one specific aircraft the "presidential plane" because Putin had used it to fly over Chechnya in an unprecedented public relations exercise two years before (supporting the conclusion that these aircraft were front line equipment in good working order). According to Blagov, official government statements revealed that the three SU-27 fighter jets were scheduled to return to Lipetsk soon, with the two SU-25s to remain in Kyrgyzstan indefinitely.

[23] (AFP) "Russia's Putin in Kyrgyzstan to boost waning influence in Central Asia," December 5, 2002, < http://www.cdi.org/russia/234-3.cfm>.

[24]Ibid.

[25] Sanobar Shermatova, "Russia's Motives in Kyrgyzstan: Russia's intent in building an air base in Kyrgyzstan is clearly to counterbalance U.S. forces stationed in that region," *Moscow News,* December 25-31, 2002, <http://www.cdi.org/russia/237-13.cfm>.

[26] Valeriy Volkov and Nikolai Khorunzhii, "Sharing Central Asia With America: Russia Maintains its Presence in Central Asia," *Izvestia,* December 5, 2002 (from WPS Monitoring Agency, < www.wps.ru/e_index.html>).

[27] Zamira Eshanova, "Central Asia: Diplomatic Visits Highlight U.S.-Russian Cooperation," (RFE/RL) JRL, December 4, 2002, no. 18, <http://www.cdi.org/russia/johnson/6585.cfm>. Note: This figure is widely disputed but seems to have the strength of popular credibility in press reports. Because of this, it is suspected that the data may represent "circular reporting" and is thus misleading.

[28] Sergei Blagov, "U.S. and Russia Marching On Central Asia," article published in the *Asia Times,* December 5, 2002, quotes *RIA Novostii* sources, December 6, 2002. <http://www.cdi.org/russia/johnson/6591-11.cfm>.

[29] Sergei Rogov, Director of the Russian Academy of Sciences Institute of Canada and U.S.A. Studies in Moscow, speaking at the Center for Naval Analyses in Washington, DC, September 25, 2002.

[30] Zamira Eshanova.

[31] Ahmen Rashid, *Jihad: The Rise of Militant Islam in Central Asia* (New Haven: Yale University Press, 2001).

[32] According to James Schumaker, Special Assistant to U.S. Ambassador Sandy Vershbow, in a newsletter from the U.S. Embassy in Moscow November 19, 2002: Working up his anger to a still higher level, all directed at the same hapless French reporter whose bad luck seemed to catch the Russian President in the mood for a good fight, Putin challenged the fellow to come to Moscow and "be circumcised in such a way as to be irrevocably identified with this Muslim horde."

[33] Peter Hopkirk, *The Great Game: The Struggle for Empire in Central Asia* (Kodansha International, Reprint edition, April 1994).

[34] Peter Schwartz, "Appendix: Steps to Developing Scenarios," *Art of the Long View* (Doubleday, 1996), 241-248, and Kees van der Heijden, "Dealing With Uncertainty," "Scenario Development," *Scenarios: The Art of the Strategic Conversation*, John Wiley (1996), 83-106, 183-237.

[35] Robert Brannon, *U.S.-Russian Relations in the War on Terrorism*, (under commitment for publication by the Naval War College Review, Newport RI, 2004). Adapted to illustrate the application of scenario planning to regional security in Central Asia.

[36] Alexander Mineev, Opinion Editorial, Russian language newspaper *Novaya Gazeta*, January 21, 2002.

[37] William Zimmerman, *The Russian People and Foreign Policy* (Princeton, New Jersy: Princeton University Press, 2002), 89-102. Actual figures, cited on page 91 of Zimmerman's book, reveal that 62 percent of elites and 68 percent of the mass population see the United States as a threat to Russian security.

[38] Michael Kochkin, "Russia and the United States Post September 11: What do the Russians Think?" Jamestown Foundation, *Russia and Eurasia Review* 1, Issue 11 (November 5, 2002). Mr. Kochkin works for the non-governmental organization "Eurocontact" in Volgograd and is occasionally published in English language by *CDI Russia Weekly* (in this case, 230, no. 12).

[39] Annual briefing for foreign military attaches, December 2000, author's personal notes, American Embassy, Moscow, Russia.

Chapter 21

Friends Like These: Defining U.S. Interests in Central Asia [1]

Olga Oliker

It is clear the United States will stay involved in Central Asia. It is less clear to what extent and in what ways. At a time when U.S. forces are deployed to this region in comparatively large numbers, it is worth remembering that if Central Asia is new to most of the soldiers and airmen who find themselves there, it is not new to the U.S. military as a whole. Amercian forces have provided training assistance to several Central Asian states over the past 10 years, and the U.S. government has built ties with the leaderships of these countries since they first gained independence.

This is not to say, however, that the present U.S. involvement in the region is a direct outgrowth of past activities. In fact, it is not. Past U.S. efforts in Central Asia were very limited and contacts with the leaderships of these countries were best described as "stop and go," due to concerns about the reliability, human rights records, and various foreign and domestic policies of these regimes—as well as, quite simply, fairly limited perceived U.S. interests in the region.

Operation *Enduring Freedom* (OEF) created a more immediate need for U.S. military involvement, and the U.S. government did a masterful and precedential job of attaining access to several remote locations where American forces had never been before. At these sites, they set up facilities and promptly began successful operations. The extent to which prior contacts helped make this happen, as some have argued they did, is unclear. Doubtless, it was useful to know whom to talk to in Uzbekistan and Kyrgyzstan, countries where the United States had built military contacts in prior years. However, such contacts had not been built to anywhere near the same extent with, for example, Turkmenistan and Tajikistan, and both of those states also were willing to provide access to U.S. forces. If anything, prior contacts influenced U.S. decisions to ask for access more than they did regional states' willingness to grant it. This willingness had more to do with regional powers' support for the U.S. effort to defeat the Taliban in Afghanistan and the hopes that U.S. presence would translate into tangible benefits for the country and the regime.

This experience has implications both for U.S. policy on access related issues[2] and for short and long term U.S. policy towards Central Asia. Beyond OEF, U.S. interests in this region are amorphous and predominantly non-military. Caspian energy, often touted as a justification for closer U.S. ties with Central Asia's often unsavory regimes, is largely a matter of oil that will be sold on the global market (and not so much of that as to significantly affect prices and thus engender particularly strong U.S. interest), and gas that will be sold locally, thus having no particular impact on the United States. Other economic interests are minimal. America has little trade with these countries and few reasons to expect this to change in the foreseeable future. In terms of security concerns, the United States has few traditional strategic reasons to build and maintain closer ties with the five Central Asian states. Those who argue for stronger relationships say that U.S. ties could help stem Russian, Chinese, or Iranian influence in the region. Even the greatest proponents of close relations had, before OEF, tended to see Central Asia as low on U.S. priority lists, arguing that other allies, such as Turkey, could advance U.S. interests just as well. Finally, the dismal human rights records of many of these regimes continue to create difficulties in justifying with the U.S. Congress and general public the contacts that do exist.

This is not to say, however, that the United States has no interests in Central Asia. In fact, the experience of OEF has demonstrated not only that the United States can access this region, but also that the region is critical for battling a broader, more complicated set of threats. The region's porous borders and proximity to Afghanistan have made it a key transit route for the narcotics trade and other criminal activities including human, weapons and other illegal goods trafficking. These problems must now be understood as part of a larger family of transnational threats to which global terrorism and proliferation of weapons of mass destruction (WMD) belong. As the United States and others learn how to combat these threats, Central Asia may become a key battleground for it is an epicenter (unfortunately one of several) for these problems. The way to fight in this realm, however, may not be by means of military influence, but rather through a range of economic development and security assistance; not through competition with other great powers, but via cooperation with them to achieve common ends; and not by finding quick solutions, but by committing to long-term involvement and engagement. This would, of course, require a qualitatively different approach in Central Asia than the United States has taken in the past.

Background

Prior to September 11, U.S. interests in Central Asia were limited. The relatively low level of energy resources assessed by most estimates meant that although U.S. firms were involved, and the U.S. government was fairly vocal in its support of "multiple pipelines" for Caspian oil, Caspian energy was not a top priority for Washington. Strategically, the region appeared to be of little significance. Thus, U.S. interests in Central Asia were secondary economic concerns; interests derivative of the goals of others, such as concern about Russian imperialism or support for Turkish efforts to build influence in the region; and ideological goals such as democratization.

This did not mean, however, that the United States was not involved in Central Asia. As America sought to define national interests in the seemingly non-threatening global environment of the 1990s, it sought to prevent threats from emerging and to pursue ideological and humanitarian goals it felt it could afford. These included global peacemaking efforts, as well as the pursuit of democratization in a variety of regions.[3] To a lesser extent, in part because solutions were difficult to define or implement, the Unites States sought to mitigate the non-immediate but dangerous threats of WMD proliferation, terrorism and international crime.

Thus, the United States built military and political relations with the Central Asian states, seeking to influence regional governments in a variety of strategic and ideological directions. U.S. policy focused first on the elimination of nuclear weapons from Kazakhstan, which were seen as the most significant security threat in the region. It then sought to build low-level military-to-military contacts with the Central Asian states, both on a bilateral basis and through NATO's Partnership for Peace (PfP) program. It provided democratization and economic assistance and sought to support U.S. firms, particularly energy companies, that were investing in the region. These activities also were intended to limit the capacity of Russia to strong-arm the Central Asian states, without directly confronting Russia in the region, by steering clear of promising security guarantees to the local regimes.[4]

Military cooperation in the period leading up to 2001 focused particularly on Special Forces joint training with Uzbek, Kazakh and Kyrgyz armed forces, as well as providing non-lethal military equipment.[5] After Islamic Movement of Uzbekistan (IMU) incursions in 1999 and 2000, the United States provided some support to Kyrgyzstan to enable it to better respond to such threats. Assistance was also provided by Turkey, Russia, and Uzbekistan at this time.[6] The United States built a significant program of military cooperation with Kazakhstan, which began with Cooperative Threat Reduction assistance to eliminate the Soviet legacy of WMD and evolved into a more general program of cooperation with International Military Education and Training (IMET), export and border controls, and so forth.[7] Such cooperation was limited in the wake of revelations of Kazakh arms sales to North Korea.[8] Cooperation with Tajikistan was restricted significantly first by its Civil War, which lasted through much of the mid 1990s, and then by the limited capacity of the new government to support such programs. Turkmenistan in its increasing isolationism was also a difficult partner, with the result that few contacts and activities emerged.

The regional states welcomed or rejected U.S. involvement and co-operation for a variety of reasons. Tajikistan's civil war left it, in essence, a Russia protectorate and prevented much discussion of further ties with the United States. Turkmenistan rejected U.S. aid, as it did cooperation with other states. Kazakhstan, Uzbekistan and Kyrgyzstan all welcomed U.S. assistance, although for different reasons. Kazakhstan felt its interests were best served by maintaining good relations with both the United States and Russia as well as, insofar as possible, China, Iran, and others, and it had little interest in playing one off against another. U.S. support for multiple pipeline routes for its oil and gas aided Kazakhstan's goal of ensuring economic independence from Russia, but Russia's proximity and a large ethnic Russian population made complete estrangement from Moscow impossible. Kyrgyzstan, too, sought friendship and assistance from a variety of countries, although where Kazakhstan was motivated by wealth, Kyrgyzstan, being small and economically and militarily weak, could not afford to alienate any of its neighbors or other interested parties. Uzbekistan, however, took a very different tack. President Islam Karimov made it a central facet of his foreign policy to turn away from Russia and to demonstrate Uzbekistan's independence from Moscow's control. He hoped in part to do this through closer ties with the United States, an effort that was limited by U.S. concerns about Karimov's human rights record and Uzbekistan's relatively low value to Washington at the time.

The OEF Experience and Subsequent Bilateral Ties

After the September 11 attacks, Washington moved quickly to expand its options in Central Asia. It rapidly secured permission from the states of the region to overfly their territories for humanitarian missions in Afghanistan. Some also granted overflight permission for combat missions, although of the Central Asian states, only Kyrgyzstan did so openly. The United States set up substantial bases in Uzbekistan and Kyrgyzstan after looking at facilities there as well as in Kazakhstan and Tajikistan. It also set up a refueling mission in Turkmenistan. As it had in the past, Washington did not make any security commitments to these states, but it did sign an agreement with Uzbekistan that pledged Washington to "regard with grave concern any external threat" to Uzbekistan.[9]

In exchange for access, the United States promised, and delivered, a variety of assistance.[10] Uzbekistan rapidly moved to the top ranks of U.S. aid recipients, picking up both economic and military aid packages. Among the things Uzbekistan either received or expects to receive are: patrol boats to be used on the Amu Darya River, language training, radios for communications, helicopter upgrades, Non-Commissioned Officer (NCO) training support, a military modeling and simulation center, psy-op training, airport navigation system upgrades, and reportedly, joint construction of Il-114 aircraft.[11]

Kyrgyzstan, too, has received military communications equipment worth over $1.4 million and a variety of other systems, such as night vision devices. The Kyrgyz Foreign Minister has praised this aid, saying it is "extremely useful for the Army in guarding the country's borders." The cooperation program between the United States and Kyrgyzstan calls for continued military-technical cooperation and high level visits, such as that of U.S. Secretary of Defense Donald Rumsfeld in November 2002.[12] Kyrgyzstan also is receiving military medical assistance, education slots at the Marshall Center, and help in training NCOs. A joint exercise, *Balanced Knife*, had Kyrgyz forces and U.S. troops affiliated with OEF practicing mountain fighting and combat medicine in March 2003.[13] Plans in 2004 call for more joint exercises for special troops, rapid reaction forces and peacekeepers, as well as assistance with counterterrorism training and military reform.[14] Both Kyrgyzstan and Uzbekistan also have received assistance in the form of upgrades to the facilities that U.S. forces are using in those countries. Kyrgyzstan receives fees for each take off and landing by coalition aircraft at Manas. Informal joint exercises take place at Karshi-Khanabad between U.S. forces and Uzbek Air Force personnel as well.[15]

From a U.S. perspective, the experience in both of these states, which have provided the bulk of the access and basing support, has been worthwhile, although it remains frustrating and difficult to "get things done" in these post-Soviet republics. Negotiating for the use of Karshi-Khanabad was a painful process. Uzbek authorities wanted to negotiate a new Status of Forces Agreement (instead of using the one in place for Partnership for Peace activities), and wanted the U.S. base to have as low a profile as possible (hence the choice of Karshi-Khanabad, which is relatively isolated). The Uzbeks also were concerned about ensuring the security of U.S. forces, another argument in favor of the Khanabad base. The base does, indeed, appear quite secure, with multiple rings of Uzbek and U.S. security forces encircling it.[16]

With regards to the current assistance program, U.S. personnel are concerned that Uzbek officials are seeking flashier equipment and assistance, rather than more effective or needed materiel and training, and report consistent difficulties with the lack of decision authority on the part of their interlocutors in the Uzbek Defense Ministry. However, the bases continue to be useful for the OEF mission, and to a large extent, the assistance packages, which fall far short of any long-term commitment or statement of strategic alignment, are perceived as "payment" for access.[17]

The United States also has developed its military relationship with Kazakhstan in the wake of OEF. While Kazakhstan was willing to provide base access to U.S. forces, their bases were not used. The offer itself, however, set more than one precedent. The base offered, Lugovoi, was one which Kazakh officials had refused to allow U.S. personnel access to in the past. An agreement that the United States could use Kazakh facilities in an emergency never resulted in any actual activity. However, permission to overfly Kazakhstan was appreciated by OEF planners, and the willingness of Astana to support the mission was noted. The United States continues to provide assistance with border security and the relationship with Kazakhstan has to some extent been reinvigorated.[18] For example, U.S. experts have been working with the Kazakhs to develop an elite peacekeeping battalion.[19] It is worth noting that in Kazakhstan, as well, U.S. personnel report frustration with interlocutors who remain very much products of the Soviet military system. Secrecy, bureaucracy and incompetence continue to be problems in the Kazakh military.[20]

Tajikistan also offered its bases to the United States and coalition forces for use in OEF. While some members of the coalition have reportedly used Tajik facilities, U.S. forces did not conduct any major operations from that country. The OEF experience did, however, pave the way for the beginnings of a cooperation program with Dushanbe. Although less ambitious than the assistance programs underway with Kazakhstan, Kyrgyzstan or Uzbekistan, the United States is providing a variety of assistance, much of it humanitarian, to the Tajiks, and has offered to help the Tajiks and the Kyrgyz improve their permanent communications so that they can better pass on warnings. There were complaints from Kyrgyz authorities that during the 1999 and 2000 IMU incursions, Tajikistan did not provide timely and effective warning.[21]

Turkmenistan, which provided facilities but has been leery of accepting aid, has presented a different set of circumstances. Based on past experience, the United States did not initially expect much in the way of Turkmen support for OEF. It hoped overflights would be allowed, and that Turkmenistan would cooperate in the seizing of al Qaeda assets. It also was hoped that there might be some support for humanitarian assistance. In fact, Turkmenistan agreed to host U.S. forces for a refueling mission for humanitarian support purposes and President Niyazov appointed his national security advisor and intelligence chief as the primary liaison with America in regards to OEF relief operations.

However, even with this high-level support, problems remained. Turkmenistan did not want to negotiate a Status-of-Forces Agreement, arguing that this would violate its neutrality.[22] Defining contractual relationships with civil aviation personnel was another hurdle, and despite clear language defining what the United States does and does not pay for, the Turkmen authorities have tried to bill the United States for items on the "not subject to billing" list.[23]

Unlike its neighbors, Turkmenistan has expressed little interest in building on the current situation to develop closer relations or to receive assistance from the United States. Although the payments associated with refueling operations are no doubt welcome, the government has remained leery of closer ties. Over time, it has become more difficult to work with the Turkmen government. The official initially responsible for negotiating with the United States has been purged, making it far more difficult to address problems that crop up, and to ensure continued smooth functioning of the refueling effort.[24]

U.S. Interests in Context

The bases and facilities set up in Central Asia in support of OEF have proven tremendously useful to the United States, and worth the cost of additional aid and payments. They are not, however, in and of themselves a reason for continued close relations with the Central Asian states beyond the present mission. Given other U.S. commitments, the current force posture in these countries is increasingly unsustainable. Refuelings in Turkmenistan have dwindled, as have supply flights through the other countries. Moreover, the OEF experience has demonstrated that, if necessary, the United States can set up shop in this part of the world with relative speed, if not ease. Thus, the continued presence beyond the needs of the OEF mission does not seem justified by possible future missions, although some sort of relationship to ease the way for such needs is advisable.

Energy interests are also not a compelling reason for a continued U.S. military presence in Central Asia. Although in March 2003, the Kazakh foreign ministry cited the situation in the Middle East as a reason for increased U.S. interests in Kazakh energy projects, the estimates for Caspian oil vary widely.[25] Even at the high end the projections are that the region will produce perhaps one tenth of the world's oil. Low end estimates suggest that even one-third of that is optimistic. Moreover, even if the most positive assessments turn out to be accurate, it will be some time before this oil is accessed.

Beyond energy, however, the United States has very few economic interests in Central Asia. Due to the legal and bureaucratic constraints on investors in Uzbekistan, foreign businesses which thought the country presented some real opportunities in the mid-1990s have been cutting their losses and leaving. Turkmenistan never presented a friendly environment for Western investors; Kyrgyzstan and Tajikistan have had little to offer; and Kazakhstan's foreign investment is overwhelmingly tied to the energy sector. In fact, recent changes in the Kazakh government's attitude towards business, which have made it more difficult for investors to operate and have involved efforts to renegotiate some existing contracts in the oil sector, may lead investors to have second thoughts about their involvement in this country. Without massive reforms, it is unlikely much U.S. investment will occur in this part of the world, and such reforms appear increasingly unlikely, as Uzbek and Kazakh laws and practices become worse rather than better.

Despite the lack of potential economic gain, the United States has other interests in Central Asia. In the aftermath of September 11, U.S. national security agenda issues that had long been on the list of concerns, but had received little attention because they seemed insoluble rose to the top. Afghanistan presented a clear-cut illustration of the dangers of how state failure can create transnational threats, which when unchecked have the capacity to terrorize governments and populaces worldwide. Central Asia, with its combination of increasingly authoritarian regimes, limited central control, popular dissatisfaction, high levels of corruption, and criminal activity is both a waystation for and a source of these threats.

The solutions to these problems, however, are difficult to identify and implement. One thing that seems clear is that these problems cannot be solved through force alone. While security personnel and organizations have a role in controlling borders, most of the security tasks are domestic, police tasks and many of the long-term solutions must be political and economic, rather than military. Perhaps somewhat ironically, after years of debate about whether the pursuit of democratization and human rights was a worthwhile U.S. security policy goal, it now appears that such efforts are, indeed, critical to "hard" security goals—even as the task of advancing them appears even more difficult than before.

Interests, Goals and Pitfalls

It is imperative for the United States to remain involved in Central Asia. However, Washington has neither a clear-cut approach for how to do this, nor the tools in place to make an effective start. While some might argue that the U.S. military presence helps support stability and provides incentives for regional regimes to democratize, it is unclear that the existing evidence supports these assertions. Although U.S. policy statements do continue to pressure Tashkent on political and economic reforms, some in Uzbekistan report that the U.S. presence actually has made the Karimov regime feel more empowered to crack down on opposition.[26] Similarly, some have argued that Tajik President Imomali Rakhmonov has used the Global War on Terrorism as justification for limiting the activities of the Islamic Renaissance Party, the main opposition force in that country.[27]

The goals of the regional states themselves, and their own approaches to the United States, must also be considered in this context. In many ways, these have changed little from what they were prior to 2001. However, in the context of a greater U.S. interest, it is critical to understand exactly why Uzbekistan, Kyrgyzstan, Tajikistan, Turkmenistan and Kazakhstan have been willing to grant access and pursue ties, and what they hope to gain from this cooperation. It is critical as well for U.S. policy planners to be aware of how these interests differ from those of the United States, and what the expectations of regional regimes are regarding U.S. behavior.

The example of Uzbekistan is apt, and perhaps the most telling in this regard. As already noted, the Karimov regime had long hoped for closer ties with the United States as a counterweight to Russia. In addition to Tashkent's long-standing effort to distance itself from Moscow, it is important to note Uzbekistan's role in Central Asia, where it has the most capable military of the five states and is viewed as a fairly dangerous neighbor by Tajikistan, Kyrgyzstan and Kazakhstan. Indeed, as part of its campaign against the IMU, the Uzbek government has pursued suspected insurgents into neighboring states' territories and laid landmines both on their shared borders with them and on the territory of the other states.

This, combined with its refusal to provide landmine maps to Kyrgyz and Tajik officials, has contributed to the deaths of numerous civilians.

The U.S. decision to place a substantial military force in Uzbekistan was taken by many in the Uzbek government as a clear demonstration of U.S. support. The Karimov regime sought to build on this by formalizing relations with new written agreements. While it wanted a low profile for the U.S. forces in Uzbekistan itself, it also wanted its neighbors and Russia to be aware of this new "partnership." Uzbekistan also sought U.S. friendship by supporting the war in Iraq, even to the point of Uzbek experts telling television audiences that they had "ample" (if not actually presented) proof that Baghdad possessed WMD and had links to terrorism.[28] The heavily censored Uzbek press reportedly had been instructed to present the war from a "pro-U.S." perspective.[29]

Yet, it also seems likely that the Karimov regime has been disappointed in the actual benefits of the relationship with the United States to date. Although there have been real material gains in terms of defense and other assistance, America has clearly stopped short of any alliance-type commitments to Uzbekistan. Moreover, the U.S. government has been unable to deliver foreign investment while Uzbekistan continues to make the investment climate so hostile.[30]

Repercussions from Uzbek economic and social policies can be seen in a sharp increase in disaffection on the part of segments of the population. Anecdotal reports that "everyone" in Uzbekistan knows someone who has had unpleasant run-ins with the Uzbek security forces creates worrisome parallels with Stalin's Soviet Union or revolutionary Iran. With opposition political parties banned, the fastest growing unofficial movement is probably the Hizb-ut-Tahrir, which advocates the overthrow of secular regimes worldwide and the establishment of a global Caliphate. Moreover, while the Karimov regime's oppression is not new, the effects of its economic policies, which have sharply curtailed trade with neighboring states, have recently become felt. Prices have risen throughout Uzbekistan, and disaffection in cities such as Tashkent continues to grow along with them. Protests against officials at a wide range of levels, including on rural farms, are increasingly common as people find themselves trying to survive on what is left of their earnings after leaders at various levels have taken their share through punitive taxes and corruption.[31]

In a country where the potential for significant unrest is on the rise, and with few mechanisms available for peaceful resolution of conflict, it is likely that if a given situation escalates, bloodshed will result. Moreover, with an autocratic regime so centered around President Islam Karimov, his departure from the scene could well lead to potentially violent competition among those now in his inner circle, as well as those outside it, over who will take his place. Thus, with or without Karimov, Uzbekistan has a high potential for future trouble.

For its part, the United States may find itself in the difficult position of being perceived as supporting a failing and increasingly unpopular regime. This situation is exacerbated by Karimov's interest in tying the United States into such support, through public statements, assistance, and, insofar as possible, legal documents. The United States has wisely steered clear of the latter, but it must also be aware of the symbolic effects of the former two. Moreover, the potential for instability makes it particularly critical that the United States remain involved at some level and seek to find ways to improve the situation.

The other countries of the region are not in as critical a situation as Uzbekistan and are thus less worrisome in the near-term. Neither the Kyrgyz nor the Kazakh leadership seek U.S. assistance as a counterweight to other forces in the region, per se. Rather, they feel that the better their relations are with all powerful parties, the better their chances of survival and success. That said, the regimes in these two countries have become increasingly authoritarian and there is reason to believe that popular disaffection may be growing there as well. In Kyrgyzstan, in particular, the Hizb ut-Tahrir is said to be making inroads, and a series of popular protests with roots in both political activism and inter-clan conflict have occurred, resulting in a dangerous and complex situation. In Kazakhstan, increased difficulties for U.S. investors (albeit not to the extent of those in Uzbekistan) may yet lead the U.S. government to be increasingly at odds with Astana.

One point of note in Kyrgyzstan is the possible attitude of opposition forces in that country to the U.S. presence. On one hand, local complaints have surfaced about noise caused by takeoffs and landings at Manas and a traffic accident involving a U.S. servicemember, which reportedly injured two local women. On the other hand, some opposition leaders have spoken about the U.S. military presence as the solution to all of Kyrgyzstan's security problems, eliminating the need for cooperation with Russia.[32] Both sides create concerns for U.S. interests.

If Uzbekistan is seeking strategic gain and Kazakhstan and Kyrgyzstan hope for strategic parity, Tajikistan and Turkmenistan perhaps come closest to having provided the assistance for OEF purely out of support for the operation itself. Like Uzbekistan, both countries felt a significant threat was posed by the Taliban's proximity, so much so that Turkmenistan had sought a "separate peace" with the Taliban prior to September 2001.

Notwithstanding the perceived threat, Turkmenistan has largely refused U.S. offers of assistance, before and after OEF. While specific organizations, such as the airport that receives a fee for each refueling and the hotel where U.S. airmen stay, appreciate the influx of funds, there is no clear sense that the Turkmen government as a whole sees a benefit from the effort. According to U.S. personnel involved in negotiating and implementing the refueling operation, the Turkmen Ministry of Defense has gained nothing as a result of the refueling operation, while the top priority of the Ministry of Foreign Affairs is to ensure that the operation remains low-profile. The Turkmen have continued to turn down offers of military contacts, have not used the Foreign Military Financing (FMF) funds allocated them in five years, and have cut back on their participation in IMET.

Nor has Turkmenistan done anything that suggests a general warming towards the United States in other areas. In August 2003, it took steps to evict the U.S. Embassy's public affairs section from its building near the embassy grounds.[33] While President Niyazov told the new U.S. Ambassador, Tracey Ann Jacobsen, that his country would like to see more cooperation with the United States in energy and natural resources, there is no sign that the government plans to relax the rules governing business and investment so as to support such cooperation.[34]

In short, the last two years of cooperation do not appear to have effected Turkmenistan's attitudes towards the United States. Nor has the United States pushed particularly hard to affect changes, perhaps realizing its very limited leverage with this country. Thus, despite Turkmenistan's atrocious human rights record and recent moves to deny joint citizenship with Russia to long-standing citizens of Russian origin, as well as the imposition of an exit-visa requirement on Turkmen residents seeking to travel abroad, the U.S. State Department assured Turkmenistan that it would not lose its Jackson-Vanik exemption in 2003.[35]

Tajikistan, too, appears to have a fairly limited view of what cooperation with the United States can bring. The new relationship did result in a state visit by the Tajik President to the United States, and the Tajiks have been far more willing to accept aid and assistance than have the Turkmen. However, like Kazakhstan and Kyrgyzstan, Tajikistan has been careful not to allow its relationship with Washington to be perceived as a counterpoint to its close ties to Russia. This has not, however, prevented speculation to that effect in Tajikistan's more pluralistic press. Reports have repeatedly appeared in the media suggesting the United States would take over Russia's role in guarding Tajikistan's borders or that the delays in negotiating a Tajik-Russian base agreement were due to a payoff from the United States to Tajikistan to prevent that agreement from being signed.[36] Despite repeated denials from both U.S. and Tajik officials, such rumors continue. Thus, as in Kyrgyzstan, the United States faces the danger of having the bilateral relationship become a pawn of domestic politics. Moreover, because the interplay between the United States and Russia is the focus of these rumors, this domestic game has international repercussions.

The Russian perspective here is critical. Because Central Asia has long been under Russian rule, and because it remains one of few areas where Moscow retains real influence, Russia throughout the 1990s tended to perceive U.S. efforts in Central Asia and the Caucasus as hostile encroachment and an attempt to woo Russia's last natural allies away from it. Combined with increasing tension between Moscow and Washington on other issues, such as intervention in Yugoslavia and missile defense, U.S. involvement in Central Asia seemed to many in Moscow to be part of a concerted effort by the United States to lessen Russia's influence.

For the United States, the posturing of Russia and Central Asian regimes vis à vis each other has been difficult to follow, as leaders such as Uzbekistan's Karimov alternated between calling Russia a partner and berating Moscow for exaggerating the Islamic fundamentalist threat to justify Russian bases in the region. But in times of stress, even Karimov has sought Russian assistance. In part, this is because these leaders recognized that they needed some outside support to deal with the threats near and within their borders, and Russia, with its strong interests in the region, remains the most viable partner available. Russia has both offered and provided assistance, including joint training efforts, cooperative planning and border police. Russia's 201st Motor Rifle Division remains on the ground in Tajikistan as do thousands of Russian-commanded border guards deployed along the frontier with Afghanistan. Russia also views the radical Islamic threat in the same way the Central Asian governments have tended to see it—as a significant danger that justifies police crackdowns and less than liberal policies. Russia is also much less critical of human rights abuses and corrupt practices than the United States has tended to be.

At the start of OEF, it appeared to observers in Central Asia and elsewhere, that the United States could become the key security partner to the Central Asian states, with Russia's acceptance. Russian President Vladimir Putin's statement that U.S. deployments in Central Asia were "not a tragedy" was historic, and followed even more historic decisions by

Central Asian leaders to allow U.S. basing—decisions taken, in most cases, without consultations with Moscow. These events marked a sea-change in Moscow's relations with the Central Asian regimes, and with the Untied States.

From Russia's perspective, not protesting the U.S. presence had real advantages. For one thing, stopping it was all but impossible. For another, it soon became clear that the United States was solving a problem that Russia had struggled with for a decade—successfully driving the Taliban from power in Afghanistan. Certainly, such action was in Russia's interests as well as the Central Asian states'. However, Russia's feelings about the U.S. presence remain mixed, and various actors in Russian politics have very different views about what should be acceptable to Moscow. Russia is therefore watching the U.S. presence in Central Asia with a good bit of concern and making much of statements that this presence is temporary.

Increased tension between the United States and Russia over both countries' activities and interests in Central Asia have the potential to create, to paraphrase Vladimir Putin, a real "tragedy." First, the fact remains that Russia has a stronger and more immediate interest in Central Asia than does the United States. While U.S. interests in preventing instability and helping develop successful states are clear, they are no more critical than U.S. interests in doing the same elsewhere in the world. For Russia, Central Asia is the first line of defense—for the United States, it may not even be the third or fourth. Furthermore, for a wide range of reasons, which include the same transnational threats, as well as arms control and other global policy interests, the U.S.-Russian relationship is more important to the United States than are its relationships with the Central Asian regimes, together or separately.

When it comes to Central Asia, Russia and the United States are not the only interested parties. Turkey, India, China, Iran and various European states also are involved to different extents, and have a broad range of interests in the region. Many, if not all, of these states are critical to U.S. national security interests in their own right, over and above their interests in Central Asia. For these states, the primary goals are economic and focus on the energy resources of the region. For all of them, the development of economic ties with the Central Asian countries depends on stability and functioning governments. Several of these states also have other security concerns. India is concerned about extremism and the potential for Central Asian unrest to impact its ongoing conflict with Pakistan. China fears spillover to its ethnic Turkic minority, the Uighurs, in northwestern

China. Thus, all of these states share American, Russian and Central Asian interests in stability.

All are also, to varying extents, willing to let others ensure that stability if possible, even as they want to remain both involved and aware of developments. Turkey generally has been willing to take the U.S. lead, although officials complain that the United States is not sharing information about its activities and goals sufficiently to enable Ankara to coordinate its own policy with Washington's. China, while steering clear of antagonizing Russia, is seeking to build its own strategic relations with the Central Asian states, both on a bilateral basis, particularly with Kyrgyzstan, and through the multilateral Shanghai Cooperation Organization (SCO), which, despite its lack of activity to date, does have some real ambitions in regards to both counterterrorism cooperation and development of trade. India, for its part, has been developing security ties with Tajikistan since its years of support for the Northern Alliance in Afghanistan, and now has a limited military presence on Tajik soil.

For the United States, this means numerous potential partners for its efforts to promote stability and development in the region. However, as with Russia, cooperation would require a level of coordination and transparency that the United States has yet to achieve with Turkey, much less any of the other countries with an interest in Central Asia. Moreover, the interests of the surrounding countries in Central Asia, albeit quite real, pale in comparison with Russia's and are of secondary concern.

Toward an Effective Policy

In principle, cooperation between the United States, Russia and other interested parties to attain the broad range of shared goals in Central Asia should be the answer to this dilemma. Indeed, it is unlikely that much progress will be made in this part of the world without Russian participation. Its proximity, its political and economic ties to the region, and its more immediate concerns about these problems are all parts of the equation. Russia is on the receiving end of transnational threats such as narcotics trafficking, weapons smuggling, transnational crime, and potentially terrorism that come from or through Central Asia, and in some cases is the source of other such threats. Resolving these problems with Russian cooperation will be far easier and more effective than attempting to resolve them without it. Involving others who share the same goals would help spread the burden, as well as ensure a greater stake on their part in the success of the endeavor.

However, in spite of significant discussions about the need for such cooperation, it has not been forthcoming as of yet. Several reasons are behind this, most having to do with the critical bilateral relationship between the United States and Russia. The first roadblock is the continued perception on the part of some—in Russia, the United States, and Central Asia—that influence and involvement in Central Asia is, in fact, a zero-sum game. This viewpoint holds that the United States and Russia are competing for influence, and the Central Asian states are prizes to be won by one side or the other. This attitude could easily be dismissed as persisting only among those who have difficulty letting go of Cold War patterns were it not for its popularity in both governments. While in their public statements Presidents Bush and Putin appear committed to cooperation, both have advisors who feel there is no real alternative to antagonism, and who view gain by one country as a loss for the other.

In Central Asia, the perception of a zero-sum game has been more common in Uzbekistan than elsewhere, although it is also evident in statements and media reports from Kyrgyzstan and Tajikistan. A microcosm of this belief can be found in the U.S. and Russian military presence at Manas and Kant Airbases, respectively, in Kyrgyzstan. These are seen by some as reflective of U.S. and Russian efforts to exert influence, even as Kyrgyzstan tries to balance between the two great powers. In fact, the U.S. deployment was driven first and foremost by the requirements of OEF. Russia's decision to place a base so near the U.S. base can be seen both as a statement of Russia's continued interest and as a marker that regardless of what the U.S. does, Russia still has a role to play that will continue long after the United States and other coalition members have gone. For Kyrgyzstan's part, it has sought to maintain good relations with both countries, and it stands to gain, economically and in terms of security, from doing so.

If this is, in fact, Kyrgyzstan's attitude, as it also appears to be Kazakhstan's and Tajikistan's, it is a remarkably rational one. These countries stand to gain much from cooperation with the United States, Russia China, and even, potentially, each other. A good deal also may be lost by playing into the notion of competition in the region. As noted, energy interests in Central Asia are not sufficient to drive U.S. policy, and true U.S. security interests suggest that from the U.S. perspective, the Central Asian states are not a prize to be won but a problem to be managed. It is in Central Asia's interests, as well as in America's, Russia's and others', that the countries of Central Asia eventually graduate to managing their problems on their own. In the meantime, however, they will need assistance from a wide range of sources.[37]

In order for the Central Asian states to acquire this assistance and to move forward effectively, Russia and the United States also must do their part to eliminate the zero-sum game perception. From the U.S. perspective, many reasons exist to do this. It is not in the U.S. interest to be seen as a bulwark against Russia by any of these states. This will needlessly antagonize Russia and give the impression of unconditional support for increasingly unsavory regimes. Moreover, even if it wanted to, the United States does not have the resources or interests to be the primary partner to any Central Asian state. The less the perception of competition, moreover, the greater likelihood that other states will seek to become involved, without fear of being caught in the middle of a U.S.-Russian rivalry.

The experience of Afghanistan demonstrates that even limited Russian-U.S. cooperation towards common goals can be extremely fruitful. However, both countries have, to a large extent, failed to recognize that benefits can be gleaned from such cooperation. There seems to be little interest at the working levels in building better ties and little understanding of the repercussions of failing to do so. Indeed, some U.S. officials view the U.S. military presence in Central Asia as countering Russian neo-imperialism, while some Russian officials see it as critical to Russian interests to reassert not just influence, but control over Central Asia.

The keys to moving forward are cooperation, multilateralism, tangible goals and small steps. If the problems are transnational in nature, the solutions must be as well; solutions that do not involve all of the states concerned can only be partial solutions at best. Certainly, there are limits to what is possible. Turkmenistan, for example, will remain very difficult to engage as long as Niyazov is President, and possibly longer. However, insofar as Russia, the United States and all of its neighbors share an interest in reform in that country, their cooperative efforts likely would stand a better chance of success than sporadic and uncertain individual efforts.

Tangible goals are also critical. It is important to identify areas of cooperation where real benefits to all concerned can be easily achieved. Even during the Cold War, the United States and Russia were able to develop dialogues and reach cooperative decisions when it was in the interests of both nations to do so.[38] More recently, the cooperation between the U.S. Federal Emergency Management Agency (FEMA) and the Russian Emergency Ministry present another example of how effective coordination can be if it is perceived as necessary by both sides. A good first step in this case might be discussions of common use of the airspace over Kyrgyzstan, now that both an OEF coalition base and a Russian base are in place near Bishkek. This also qualifies as a small step in that its implementation would require little effort. Still, these building blocks of cooperation build trust while accomplishing mutual goals, and this is critical to moving on to the larger areas where cooperation is needed.

The other key component of success must be multilateralism. It is true that the Central Asian states themselves have been loath to cooperate too closely with one another. However, there is precedent for their doing so. The solution may be, in part, to involve a variety of other players, including the United States, Russia, India, China, European powers and others as viable. This will create strong incentives for most Central Asian states not to remain on the sidelines at the risk of missing out on the potential to build ties with a range of possible partners.[39] This approach can be effective in both economic and security settings and can serve as a stepping stone towards easing some of the tensions between the states of the region, as well as helping to facilitate solutions to the transnational threats that plague them and their neighbors. The SCO was founded in part on such principles, and the United States might consider seeking observer status in that organization, so as to demonstrate its support for the efforts of others.

U.S. interests in Central Asia all but guarantee some level of involvement in the region for the foreseeable future. But its military presence should be reduced, just as other areas of involvement should grow. The challenge for America will be to manage this in a way that leaves neither it nor the region worse off than before the United States got involved. Good relations with Russia are one component of this. Transparency and coordination with other current or prospective partners are another. No less critical, however, will be avoiding stronger than needed commitments to existing Central Asian regimes, even while maintaining cooperation with them. In the end, it will be a balancing act. But the alternative may be a very dangerous fall.

Notes

[1] The author thanks RAND, and specifically Project Air Force within RAND, for providing support for research from which this paper is drawn. She also wishes to emphasize that the views reflected here are her own and do not reflect the views, attitudes, or policies of RAND, Project Air Force or the United States Air Force.

[2] For a discussion of the access issue more broadly, see David Shlapak, et. al, *A Global Access Strategy for the U.S. Air Force* (Santa Monica: RAND, 2003).

[3] While proponents of democratization have traditionally argued that it advances strategic goals due to a postulated lower propensity among democracies to fight wars (or, according to some, fight wars with one another), the literature is, in fact, inconclusive on this. Moreover, regardless of whether democracies are more or less war-prone, democratizing states are, according to some data, more likely to face conflict. Many of the key arguments in these debates can be found in Michael E. Brown, Sean

M. Lynn-Jones, and Steven E. Miller, eds., *Debating the Democratic Peace*, (Cambridge, Massachusetts: The MIT Press, 1996). In addition to the papers in that volume, see also Carol R. Ember, Melvin Ember and Bruce Russett, "Peace Between Participatory Polities," *World Politics* (July 1992); Michael W. Doyle, "Liberalism and World Politics," *American Political Science Review* (December, 1986).

[4] *See* Oliker in *Faultlines.*

[5] "Central Asia: Fault Lines in the New Security Map."

[6] Vladimir Socor, "Cheek by Jowl in Kyrgyzstan," *The Wall Street Journal*, August 8, 2003.

[7] Similar activities were also underway with Uzbekistan and Kyrgyzstan.

[8] A deal to supply North Korea with Kazakh MiG fighter aircraft was discovered in 1999. Over twenty aircraft were delivered before the deal was discovered and deliveries halted. The Kazakh government's investigation report concluded that, although government officials were involved in the deal, they were acting independently. Defense Minister Mukhtar Altynbayev was removed from his post as a result of the deal (although he resumed it in December 2002). The United States sanctioned the firms involved and waived sanctions against the country of Kazakhstan as a whole. ("The High Price of Kazakhstan's MiG Affair," Stratfor.com, *Update Weekly Analysis*, November 18, 1999, reprinted by *Asia Times*, November 19, 1999; James P. Rubin, U.S. Department of State, Daily Press Briefing No. 142, November 22, 1999, 1:20 pm; Kazakhstan, Government and NGO Descriptions, NIS Nuclear and Missile Database, Nuclear Threat Initiative website, <www.nti.org/db/nisprofs/kazakst/govt/governme.html>, downloaded December 29, 2003.)

[9] "U.S., Uzbekistan Sign Military Cooperation Agreement," *RFE/RL Newsline*, 6, no. 14, Part I, January 23, 2002.

[10] Dana Milbank, "Uzbekistan Thanked for Role in War," *The Washington Post*, March 13, 2002, A23; "U.S., Uzbekistan Sign Military Cooperation Agreement," *RFE/RL Newsline*, 6, no. 14, Part I, January 23, 2002.

[11] Interviews with and information provided by U.S. government officials, summer 2003; "U.S. to Help Finance Uzbek Aircraft Production," *RFE/RL Newsline*, 7, no. 156, Part I, August 18, 2003.

[12] "Kyrgyzstan, U.S. Sign Military Cooperation Agreement," *RFE/RL Newsline*, Vol. 6, no. 213, Part I, November 13, 2002.

[13] This also reportedly involved a medical team from South Korea. Marina Kozlova, "Analysis: Kyrgyzstan Dances with US, China," *UPI*, October 10, 2002; "Kyrgyzstan, U.S. Sign Military Cooperation Agreement," *RFE/RL Newsline*, 6, no. 213, Part I, November 13, 2002; *FBIS* November 18, 2002; "Joint U.S.-Kyrgyz Military Exercises Held Near Bishkek," *RFE/RL Newsline*, Vol.7, no. 51, Part I, March 18, 2003; Sultan Jumagulov, "Superpowers Compete in Kyrgyzstan," *IWPR's Reporting Central Asia*, no. 200, April 28, 2003.

[14] Vladimir Socor, "Cheek by Jowl in Kyrgyzstan," *The Wall Street Journal*, August 8, 2003.

[15] Interviews with U.S. personnel at Karshi-Khanabad, May 2003.

[16] Interviews with U.S. officials, personnel, Summer and Fall 2003; visit to Karshi-Khanabad, May 2003.

[17] Interviews with U.S. officials, personnel, Summer and Fall 2003.

[18] Interviews with U.S. officials, summer 2003.

[19] "Turkey, U.S. Assist Kazakh Military," *RFE/RL Newsline*, 6, no. 204, Part I, October 29, 2002.

[20] Interviews with U.S. officials, Summer 2003.

[21] There were complaints from Kyrgyz authorities that during the 1999 and 2000 IMU incursions, Tajikistan did not provide timely and effective warning. "Official: Danger of Extremist Incursions into Kyrgyzstan Still Exists," *RFE/RL Newsline*, 7, no.50, Part I, March 17, 2003.

[22] This problem was solved with an exchange of diplomatic notes.

[23] Interviews with U.S. officials, Spring, Summer 2003.

[24] Interviews with U.S. officials, Spring, Summer 2003.

[25] "Kazakh Foreign Ministry Sees Increased U.S. Interest in Kazakh Oil," *RFE/RL Newsline*, 7, no. 60, Part I, March 28, 2003.

[26] Interviews in Uzbekistan, May 2003.

[27] Antoine Blua, "Tajikistan: Government to Vet Islamic Clerics," *RFE/RL*, August 7, 2002; International Crisis Group, "Central Asia: Islam and the State," July 10, 2003.

[28] "Five Degrees of Separation: The Central Asia States' Positions Towards War in Iraq," *RFE/RL Central Asia Report*, 3, no. 12, March 21, 2003.

[29] "Unofficial Censorship on War Reporting Instituted in Uzbekistan," *RFE/RL Newsline*, 7, no. 53, Part I, March 20, 2003.

[30] It should be noted, of course, that Uzbekistan also had a good deal to gain from the elimination of the Taliban and that it had been working, with Russia, India, Tajikistan, and Iran, in a loose coalition that supported the Northern Alliance for many years.

[31] Discussions in Uzbekistan, May 2003.

[32] "Kyrgyz Opposition Party Official Questions Russian Base," *RFE/RL Newsline*, Vol. 7, no. 72, Part I, April 15, 2003.

[33] "U.S. Embassy in Turkmenistan Protests Eviction of Public Affairs Section,'" *RFE/RL Newsline*, 7, no. 159, Part I, August 21, 2003.

[34] "Turkmen President Wants More U.S. Technology,'" *RFE/RL Newsline*, 7, no. 163, Part I, August 27, 2003.

[35] The Jackson-Vanik amendment denies unconditional normal trade relations to countries with non-market economies and restrictive emigration policies.

[36] "U.S. Will Not Help Protect Tajik Border," *RFE/RL Newsline*, 6, no. 217, Part I, November 19, 2002; Yana Amelina, "Moscow Considers Tajikistan Options," *Rosbalt*, July 23, 2003; "Defense Minister Says Tajikistan Still Wants Russian Base," *RFE/RL Newsline*, 7, no. 141, Part I, July 28, 2003.

[37] Recent Uzbek warming to Moscow, in contrast to its past antagonism, suggests that Tashkent may also be coming around to such an approach.

[38] The Incidents at Sea talks and nuclear arms control are examples.

[39] This approach may be of little appeal to Turkmenistan under its current regime, but it may be an effective way to, for example, bring Kazakhstan and Uzbekistan both to the table, a historically challenging task.

About the Contributors

Daniel L. Burghart (co-editor) is a Senior Fellow at the Center for Technology and National Security Policy at the National Defense University. A specialist in Russian, Commonwealth of Independant States (CIS) and Central European Affairs, he served for 30 years as an Army Foreign Area Officer before retiring as a Colonel in June 2003. Dr. Burghart has been a professor at the National War College, Senior National Security Policy Advisor at the Defense Threat Reduction Agency, U.S. Defense and Army Attaché to Kazakhstan, and a Mission Commander at the On Site Inspection Agency, where he led arms control inspections in the republics of the Former Soviet Union. He also has been the Senior Russian Military Analyst and Eurasian Branch Chief on the Army Staff, Professor of Russian and East European Studies at the Military Academy at West Point, and Director of Area Studies at the U. S. Army Russian Institute. In addition to a B.A. in Political Science from the University of Illinois, Dr. Burghart has a dual Masters in Political Science and Russian Area Studies from the University of Wisconsin and a Ph.D.. in Russian and International Studies from the University of Surrey. He has published articles in defense and civilian journals and is the author of the book *Red Microchip: Technology Transfer, Export Control and Economic Restructuring in the Soviet Union.*

Theresa Sabonis-Helf (co-editor) is a Professor of National Security Strategy at the National War College in Washington, DC. She was previously Energy and Environment Policy Advisor for a Harvard Institute for International Development project, based in Central Asia. She received her Ph.D.. in Political Science from Emory University, her M.P.A. in International Relations from Princeton University, and her B.A. in Literature from Emory University. She has worked as a policy analyst, and as a visiting fellow at the U.S. Agency for International Development. Dr. Sabonis-Helf is a specialist in Environment Policy; Energy Policy and Energy Security; Climate Change Policy; and International Political Economy. She has lived and worked in seven countries of the former USSR, and has published articles on post-Soviet energy and environmental issues, as well as on post-Soviet culture and contemporary history.

Sylvia Woody Babus is a Professor of Behavioral Sciences in the Department of Leadership and Information Strategy at the Industrial College of the Armed Forces at National Defense University. She is a graduate of the University of Chicago, and earned M.A. and Ph.D. degrees in International Relations and Sino-Soviet studies from Columbia University. Dr. Babus has taught political science and international relations at the University of Manitoba in Winnipeg, Canada, and at Goucher College in Towson, Maryland. During 10 years at the State Department's Foreign Service Institute, she supervised training for Foreign Service Officers in negotiation, multilateral diplomacy, executive-congressional relations, arms control, and political military issues. Her assignments at State included tours in Belgium and Kyrgyzstan, as well as two years as a Foreign Service Officer in Uzbekistan. From 1998 to 2001, she managed democracy-building assistance programs in Ukraine and Belarus as a Civil Society Advisor for the U.S. Agency for International Development Mission in Kyiv. Her publications include an undergraduate text on current affairs, as well as works on Soviet-Third World Relations, Gorbachev, Soviet ideology and foreign policy, Central Asian security issues, and training of U.S. Government officials for interagency work.

Robert Brannon has served for 30 years in the U.S. Navy. During three years in Russia as the U.S. Naval Attaché, he was present for the economic crash of August 1998, the post NATO intervention in Kosovo armed riots at the embassy, and the submarine Kursk disaster. He has an M.A. in International Relations and is a Ph.D. Canididate in World Politics at The Catholic University of America, where he is currently working on a dissertation in Post-Soviet Russian civil-military relations. Following a year at Harvard University's Kennedy School of Government as the senior national security research fellow, Captain Brannon now is an instructor in the Department of National Security Studies at the National War College, where he holds the Chief of Naval Operations Chair.

Emily Ewell Daughtry will join the Office of the Legal Advisor at the U.S. Department of State in September 2004. Previously, she worked for six years at the Center for Nonproliferation Studies (CNS) of the Monterey Institute of International Studies, where she specialized in issues concerning Central Asia, export controls, and nuclear smuggling. From 1998 to 1999, Ms. Daughtry founded and served as Co-Director of the CNS office in Almaty, Kazakhstan. She holds a J.D. from the University of California, Los Angeles and a B.A. in Russian and East European Studies from Middlebury College.

Gregory Gleason is Professor of Political Science and Public Administration at the University of New Mexico. He is the author of *Federalism and Nationalism: the Struggle for Republican Rights in the USSR* (1991), *Central Asian States: Discovering Independence* (1996), and *Markets and Politics in Central Asia* (2003) as well as scholarly articles in *Europe-Asia Studies, Problems of Post-Communism, Asian Perspective, Comparative Strategy* and other journals. Dr. Gleason has had research sponsored by the National Science Foundation, the National Council on Eurasian and East European Research, and the U.S. Institute of Peace and also has conducted research under the auspices of the Academies of Science of the USSR, the Russian Federation, Uzbekistan, Kazakhstan, and Tajikistan. In addition, he has worked as a consultant to the United States Information Service, Sandia National Laboratories and Los Alamos National Laboratory. Dr. Gleason has worked in various capacities on market and political reform projects sponsored by the U.S. Agency for International Development and the Asian Development Bank. He currently focuses on the politics of Eurasian integration.

Genevieve Grabman is a public health lawyer with expertise in Central Asia. She has a Master of Public Health from Johns Hopkins University and a Juris Doctor from Georgetown University. From 1996 to 1998, she served as a U.S. Peace Corps Volunteer in Kyrgyzstan where she worked at the United Nations Children's Fund in health and human rights programming. Following her Peace Corps service, Ms. Grabman was the Kyrgyzstan program manager for a health sector reform project supported by the United States Agency for International Development (USAID) and the World Bank. She later was a consultant with the POLICY Project, a USAID reproductive health and HIV/AIDS initiative, where she helped integrate human rights law in developing countries' health policies. Currently, Ms. Grabman is a legislative and policy associate at the Center for Health and Gender Equity.

Kevin D. Jones previously worked in Central Asia for the United States Agency for International Development (USAID) as the Private Sector Advisor, Kyrgyzstan Country Office. In this position he oversaw the implementation of the enterprise development, fiscal reform and regional energy portfolio for Kyrgyzstan. He was directly involved in the land privatization process as an advisor to the host countries policy makers, land reform development projects, and U.S. government officials. Prior to USAID, he was a Sustainable Economic Development Peace Corps Volunteer in Kyrgyzstan, providing private farmers with business and economic assistance. Jones is currently pursuing a Ph.D.. in International Economic and Security Policy from the University of Maryland,

Roger D. Kangas is a specialist on Central Asia and the Caspian Sea basin at the George C. Marshall Center in Germany. Prior to joining the Marshall Center in 1999, Dr. Kangas was Deputy Director of the Central Asian and Caucasus Institute at the Paul H. Nitze School of Advanced International Studies (SAIS) and a Fellow of the Johns Hopkins University Foreign Policy Institute in Washington, DC. Dr. Kangas also served as a Research Analyst on Central Asian Affairs for the Open Media Research Institute (OMRI), and was an Assistant Professor of Political Science at the University of Mississippi, and an Adjunct Professor at Georgetown University. Since 1992, Dr. Kangas has worked with and advised a number of U.S. government departments and agencies, as well as private-sector firms and non-governmental organizations on issues relating to Central Asia, Russia, and the Southern Caucasus. Dr. Kangas graduated from the School of Foreign Service at Georgetown University and earned his Ph.D.. in Political Science at Indiana University. Dr. Kangas has written numerous articles and book chapters on Central Asian politics and society.

Nancy Lubin is President of JNA Associates, Inc., a research/ consulting firm dealing with issues of the newly independent states (NIS), especially Central Asia and the Caucasus. She has lived, worked and traveled throughout this region for 30 years–as a Congressional staffer, university Professor, and now for JNA–and consults for international donors, the media, private foundations, the U.S. government, and corporations ranging from Fortune 500 to smaller, start up companies. She has been a Fellow at the U.S. Institute of Peace, the Woodrow Wilson Center, and elsewhere, and holds a Ph.D. from Oxford University, a B.A., Magna Cum Laude, from Harvard University, has studied at the Universities of Moscow and Leningrad, and was one of the first Westerners to conduct doctoral research for one year in Uzbekistan (1978-79). She is a member of the Council on Foreign Relations, the Board of Trustees/Advisors of the Eurasia Foundation, the Board of Advisors of the Open Society Institute, Central Eurasia Project, and other organizations.

David S. McCauley is an environmental economist and policy expert with long experience in Asia. A frequent consultant and advisor to international assistance agencies and Asian governments, he is Adjunct Senior Fellow at the East-West Center in Honolulu, Hawaii and Affiliate Graduate Faculty Member at the University of Hawaii, Department of Natural Resources and Environmental Management. His paper is based, in part, on an analysis commissioned by the Asian Development Bank, but the views and positions expressed are his own. Dr. McCauley's undergraduate training was in the environmental sciences, and he holds a Ph.D. in Resource Economics from the University of Hawaii.

Daene C. McKinney is a Professor of Environmental Engineering at the University of Texas at Austin. He received his Ph.D.. and M.S. degrees in Civil and Environmental Engineering from Cornell University, and a B.S. in Environmental Resources Engineering from Humboldt State University. Dr. McKinney concentrates on research related to transboundary water and environmental issues, especially related to U.S.-Mexico border issues in the Rio Grande basin and countries of Central Europe and the former Soviet Union. He has completed various technical assignments in Russia, Eastern Europe, Central Asia, and the Caucasus that address the natural resources management legacy of the Soviet Union and the relationship between economic restructuring and environmental protection. Dr. McKinney has served as an environmental engineer for the U.S. Environmental Protection Agency and spent a two-year leave from UT Austin in Almaty, Kazakhstan as Chief of Party for the five-country U.S. Agency for International Development Environmental Policy and Institutions for Central Asia Program.

E. Wayne Merry is a Senior Associate of the American Foreign Policy Council in Washington. He was previously Director of the Program on European Societies in Transition at the Atlantic Council of the United States. During 26 years in the United States Foreign Service, he served twice in the Political Section of the Moscow Embassy, as a specialist on domestic Soviet and Russian politics. He also served in East Berlin, Athens, New York, and Tunis, while his Washington assignments included the State Department, U.S. Marine Corps Headquarters, the Office of the

Secretary of Defense (as Regional Director for Russia, Ukraine, and Eurasia), and the U.S. Commission on Security and Cooperation in Europe. An Oklahoma native, he is a graduate of the University of Wisconsin, the Wilson School of Public and International Affairs at Princeton University, and the U.S. Army Russian Institute. Since retiring from the government in 1998, his writings have appeared in a variety of American and European publications.

Jennifer D.P. Moroney is Political Scientist at the RAND Corporation where she manages and supports projects for the U.S. Departments of Defense, Homeland Security, Energy, and the National Security Council. Prior to joining RAND, Dr. Moroney worked for DFI Government Services, where she managed security-related projects for the Department of Defense. In 2000, Dr. Moroney worked in OSD/NATO Policy where she was responsible for the NATO-Ukraine and NATO-Russia portfolios. Dr. Moroney has co-edited several books on security issues in the former Soviet Union, including *Security Dynamics in the Former Soviet Bloc* (Curzon/Routledge, 2003), *Ukrainian Foreign and Security Policy: Theoretical and Comparative Perspectives* (Praeger, 2002). She also has published several book chapters, journal articles, and policy briefs on Ukraine, Central Asia, the South Caucasus, and NATO enlargement. Dr. Moroney received her Ph.D.. in International Relations from the University of Kent at Canterbury, United Kingdom, an M.A. in European Integration from the University of Limerick, Ireland, and a B.A. from Frostburg State University, Maryland.

Michael Ochs has been a Professional Staff Advisor at the Commission on Security and Cooperation in Europe [Helsinki Commission], U.S. Congress since 1987. He also has been a member of the U.S. Delegation to various OSCE meetings. Dr. Ochs specializes in the Caucasus and Central Asia, where he has traveled extensively. He has published numerous articles on politics and human rights in these countries. He also has observed and analyzed elections in virtually all of the former Soviet republics, and in fall 1995, headed the OSCE election observation mission for parliamentary elections in Azerbaijan. Dr. Ochs has been a member of the Advisory Board of the Central Eurasia Project of the Open Society Institute of the Soros Foundation, which runs foundations in Armenia, Azerbaijan, Tajikistan, and Uzbekistan. Dr. Ochs holds a Ph.D.. in Russian History from Harvard University.

Olga Oliker is an international policy analyst at the RAND Corporation. Her research focuses primarily on security and defense issues, as they relate to U.S. interests in the states of the former Soviet Union. She also writes on U.S. foreign policy and military diplomacy, and, most recently on U.S. military operations in Afghanistan and Iraq. Before coming to RAND, Ms. Oliker worked as an independent consultant and held positions in the U.S. Departments of Defense and Energy. Her recent publications include *Faultlines of Conflict in Central Asia and South Caucasus* (RAND 2003), co-edited with Thomas S. Szayna.

Matthew Oresman is the Director of the China-Eurasia Forum and serves as Editor of the *CEF Monthly*. Previously, he was a researcher with the Freeman Chair in China Studies at the Center for Strategic and International Studies (CSIS), and coordinator for the Freeman Chair's project on China's Emergence in Central Asia. As such, He was the principal author of *China's New Journey to the West: Report on China's Emergence in Central Asia and Implications for U.S. Interests* (CSIS Press, August 2003). He received a B.A. in International Relations from the University of Pennsylvania and has studied in China at both Tsinghua and Fudan Universities.

Tiffany Petros is a Senior Analyst at DFI Government Services where her work focuses on regional security issues in Europe and Eurasia. DFI provides tailored research, analysis, and consulting services to senior decision-makers in the U.S. national security community. Prior to joining DFI, Dr. Petros served as a consultant to the World Bank on Central Asia and the Caucasus. She taught politics courses at the American University of Armenia, Yerevan and in the Czech Republic at Palacký University and the Anglo-American College. Dr. Petros is currently a Research Associate with The George Washington University's Institute for European, Russian, and Eurasian Studies. She received her Ph.D.. from Miami University, Ohio.

Alma Raissova is a Regional Deputy Development Director of the Educational Network (EdNet) project, sponsored by USAID and CARANA Corporation, Almaty, Kazakhstan. Prior to EdNet, she was an Energy and Environment Policy Specialist for a Harvard Institute of International Development project based in Central Asia. She is a Candidate of Sciences in Economy (Ukrainian Scientific and Research Institute, 1991). Her specialization is in economic aspects of Energy and Environment Policy, Microloans, and Securities Market. She has published several articles regarding Environmental, Microloan and Privatization issues.

Aliya Sartbayeva-Peleo is a lecturer in the Department of Economics of the Kazakhstan Institute of Management, Economics and Strategic Research, under the President of the Republic of Kazakhstan in Almaty, where she teaches Macroeconomics, Environmental Economics, Natural Resource Economics, and Energy Economics. She received a Master of Arts in International Development from the International University of Japan in Niigata as an Asian Development Bank scholar. Prior to that, she worked for four years in the U.S. Agency for International Development financed environmental projects in Central Asia led by CH2M Hill International, International Resources Group and the Harvard Institute for International Development. Her area of specialization is economics of development and transition in Asian and former Soviet Union countries, environmental economics and policy, as well as the issues of efficient allocation and management of natural resources in developing countries. She recently co-authored the *Country Environmental Analysis* (CEA) for Kazakhstan for the Asian Development Bank.

Saltanat Sulaimanova is a Ph.D.. candidate at American University in Washington, DC, researching human trafficking and international migration. She has worked for the International Organization for Migration, the United Nations High Commissioner for Refugees, the United Nations Development Program, and the World Bank in Kyrgyzstan, Kazakhstan, Austria and the United States. Ms. Sulaimanova is also an international consultant on human trafficking issues, working with such institutions as the Protection Project of the Johns Hopkins University and the International Research and Exchanges Board (IREX).

Kalkaman Suleimenov is Head of Section on Perspective Development, Department of Development of the Kazakh Company on Electricity Network Management. He worked previously with the Ministry of Energy and Mineral Resources of the Republic of Kazakhstan, and was Head of Department of the Kazakh Energy Research Institute (the Sh. Ch. Chokin Institute). He is a Doctor of Technical Science with a specialization in thermal energy. Dr. Suleimenov holds six patents, and has published over 50 articles and monographs. His research themes have focused on development of heating processes, and gasification of low quality fossil fuels.

Abbreviations
and Key Terms

ADB	Asian Development Bank
Agenda XXI	UN plan for sustainable development
BTC	Baku-Tbilisi-Ceyhan oil pipeline
BVOs	Basin Water Management Organizations on the Syr Darya and Amu Darya rivers (established in Soviet times, still functioning)
CACO	The Central Asian Cooperation Organization, est. 2002, under Uzbek leadership, includes Kazakhstan, Kyrgyzstan, Tajikistan, and Uzbekistan. Intended to be the successor to CAEC.
CAEC	Central Asian Economic Community (regional coordinating mechanism for economic, security and water issues)
CAMIN	Central Asian Mountain Information Network
CARs	Central Asian Republics
CBMs	confidence-building measures
CENTRASBAT	(Also Centrazbat) Central Asia Battalion (founded in 1995, regional peacekeeping unit)
CFE	Conventional Armed Forces in Europe Treaty
CICA	Conference on Interaction and Confidence-Building Measures in Asia (proposed as Asian variant of OSCE)
CIDA	Canadian International Development Agency
CIS	Commonwealth of Independent States
CNPC	China National Petroleum Company
CPC	Caspian Pipeline Consortium
CPSU	Communist Party of the Soviet Union
CRDF	Collective Rapid Deployment Force includes Kazakhstan, Kyrgyzstan, Russia and Tajikistan. Component of CSTO
CST/ CSTO	Collective Security Treaty Organization (as of 14 May 2002) formerly CST Collective Security Treaty (est. 1992, includes Russia, Belarus, Armenia, Kazakhstan, Kyrgyzstan, Tajikistan)
CTR	Cooperative Threat Reduction, US program in the region

DCA	Drug Control Agency of Tajikistan
DEA	Drug Enforcement Agency (of the United States)
DHS	Demographic and Health Survey (conducted in Kyrgyzstan, supported by U.S. assistance)
DMC	Developing Member Country of the Asian Development Bank
DOD	Department of Defense (USA)
DOTS	Directly Observed Treatment, Short Course (a swift TB detection and treatment strategy)
EBRD	European Bank for Reconstruction and Development
ETIM	East Turkestan Islamic Movement, radical group with ties to Uyghur separatists
EU	European Union
EXBS	Export Control and Related Border Security (U.S. program in Central Asia)
FEMA	Federal Emergency Management Agency (of the United States)
FGPs	Family Medicine Practice Groups (health care system established with U.S. assistance)
FMF	Foreign Military Financing (U.S. program)
FPS	Federal Border Service (Russian Program securing the Tajik border)
FSU	Former Soviet Union
G8	Group of Eight (G-7 plus Russia)
GDP	Gross Domestic Product
GEF	Global Environment Facility
GM	Global Mechanism of the UNCCD
GNI	Gross National Income (New World Bank indicator, replaces GDP)
GUAM/ GUUAM	Georgia, Ukraine, (Uzbekistan), Armenia and Moldova. Was originally established as GUUAM, as a non-aligned group, but Uzbekistan withdrew in later years. The organization is now GUAM
GWP	Global Water Partnership
HIV/AIDS	human immunodeficiency virus/ acquired immunodeficiency syndrome

HT	Hizb-ut-Tahrir, Party of Liberation (Islamist organization in Central Asia). Present in all five Central Asian states, illegal in several, but with a tendency to be non-violent.
IAEA	International Atomic Energy Agency (of the United Nations)
ICIMOD	International Center for Integrated Mountain Development
ICSD	Interstate Commission for Sustainable Development
ICWC	Interstate Commission for Water Coordination
IDPs	internationally displaced persons
IDUs	injecting drug users
IFAS	International Fund for Saving the Aral Sea
IFIs	International Financial Institutions
IMET	International Military Education and Training (U.S. program)
IMU	Islamic Movement of Uzbekistan. Banned political party, with a tendency towards violence
IOM	International Organization for Migration (Geneva-based International Organization)
IPP	Individual Partnership Plan (from within the PfP program, partners construct such a plan)
IRP	Islamic Renaissance Party
ISI	import-substituting industry
KEGOC	Kazakhstan Electricity Network Company
KGB	Committee for State Security (Soviet era)
KOGG	Commission for the Protection of the State Border (Tajikistan)
kV	Kilo-volts
kWh	kilowatt-hours
LARK	Legal Assistance to Rural Citizens in Kyrgyzstan, established with Swiss support in 2000
LoS	Law of the Sea Treaty
MAP	Membership Action Plan (for NATO membership candidate)
MAWR	Uzbek Ministry of Agriculture and Water Management

MDR-TB	multi-drug resistant tuberculosis
MEAs	multilateral environmental agreements
MGIMO	Moscow's Institute for International Relations
MHIF	mandatory health insurance fund (in Kyrgyzstan)
MOU	memorandum of understanding
MPC&A	Material control and accounting and physical protection (of nuclear materials)
NAP	National Action Program under UNCCD
NATO	North Atlantic Treaty Organization
NEAP	National Environmental Action Plans in the United Nations
NGO	non-governmental organization
NIS	Newly Independent States
NPT	Nuclear Non-Proliferation Treaty
NTB	National Bank of Tajikistan
ODS	ozone-depleting substances
OEF	"Operation Enduring Freedom," the U.S. military operations in Afghanistan
OSCE	Organization for Security and Cooperation in Europe
PAP	People's Armed Police (of China)
PARP	Planning and Review Process within PfP
PCA	Partnership and Cooperation Agreements with the European Union.
PfP	Partnership for Peace, a NATO program
PLA	People's Liberation Army (of China)
PRC	People's Republic of China
PREGA	Promotion of Renewable Energy, Energy Efficiency and Greenhouse Gas Abatement Projects, a project of ADB
POP	persistent organic pollutant
PPTA	Project Preparation Technical Assistance
PWP	Partnership Work Plan (Annual NATO drafted plan of activities under PfP)

RATC	CIS Regional Anti-Terrorist Center, first based in Bishkek in 2001, now based in Tashkent.
RCLAR	Republican Center for Land and Agrarian Reform established in Kyrgyzstan in 1995
RDF	Rapid Deployment Forces of the CSTO
REAP	Regional Environmental Action Plan
REC	Regional Environment Center
RECs	regional electricity companies in Kazakhstan
RETA	Regional Technical Assistance under ADB
SCO	Shanghai Cooperation Organization, est. 2000 (formerly "Shanghai Five," est.1996)
SES	sanitary epidemiological service (Soviet era. Also called Sanepid)
SIC	Scientific Information Center
START	Strategic Arms Reduction Treaty (START I)
STI	sexually transmitted infection
STV	Stichting Tegen Vrouwenhandel, Dutch NGO working against trafficking in women
SUB	small rural hospital (*selskaya uchaskovaya bolnitsia*)
TA	Technical Assistance
TACIS	Technical Assistance for the Commonwealth of Independent States, European Union assistance program
TB	tuberculosis
TDCA	The Tajik Drug Control Agency
TRACECA	Transport Corridor Europe-Caucasus-Asia (est. 1993, aims to bring together trade and transport ministers from the five Central Asian republics and three Caucasian republics to develop a transport corridor from Europe to Central Asia across the Black Sea.)
UES	Unified Energy System of Kazakhstan
UNCCD	United Nations Convention to Combat Desertification and Drought
UNHCR	United Nations High Commissioner for Refugees
UNODC	United Nations Office on Drugs and Crime

UNDP	United Nations Development Program
UNEP	United Nations Environment Program
UNICEF	United Nations Children's Fund
USAID	United States Agency for International Development
UTO	United Tajikistan Opposition
VAT	value-added-tax
WB	World Bank
WHO	World Health Organization
WMD	weapons of mass destruction (Chemical, Nuclear, Biological)
WTO	World Trade Organization
XPCC	Xinjiang Production and Construction Corporation, a paramilitary organization in China also known as Bingtuan